At a conference held at Yal
September 1963, more than
from all parts of the world r
the present and future uses
data in international social sc
Quantitative indicators of political and social change have become increasingly important as social scientists move from speculative theory toward formulations of propositions that can be verified empirically. The selected conference papers which comprise this volume discuss the most significant research projects that have already been completed or are under way. They represent an immensely rich and original contribution, essential to the political or social scientist concerned with sharpening the tools of his discipline. The editors and many of the authors also suggest ways to increase and improve international cooperation in collecting and quantifying data and making them available.

Among the twenty-one contributors are Eric Allardt, Philip E. Converse, Karl W. Deutsch, Carl J. Friedrich, Harold D. Lasswell, Daniel Lerner, Juan Linz, and Alexander Szalai.

Mr. Merritt is in the department of political science at the University of Illinois. Stein Rokkan is research director of the Christian Michelsen Institute in Bergen, Norway.

FROM THE REVIEWS

"Merritt and Rokkan are to be congratulated on putting together a much needed work."—*The American Political Science Review.*

This is an indispensable handbook and invaluable conspectus of the promises and pitfalls of quantitative research."—*The Australian Journal of Politics and History.*

"*Comparing Nations* gives a much needed overview of the rapidly developing field of comparative inquiry based upon national entities."—*Behavioral Science.*

"This is an important volume, in which some of its most important practitioners summarize the development of comparative empirical social studies at a particular point in time."—*Midwest Journal of Political Science.*

"This collection will certainly be invaluable in acquainting graduate students with the variety of approaches that are being utilized in furthering the comparability potential of numerous national and sub-national pools of data."—*The Journal of Politics.*

Comparing Nations

The Use of Quantitative Data in Cross-National Research

Comparing Nations

The Use of Quantitative Data in Cross-National Research

EDITED BY RICHARD L. MERRITT
AND STEIN ROKKAN

NEW HAVEN AND LONDON, YALE UNIVERSITY PRESS

Second printing, March 1968.
Designed by Sally Sullivan,
set in Modern No. One type,
and printed in the United States of America by
The Murray Printing Company,
Forge Village, Massachusetts
Distributed in Canada by McGill University Press.

Library of Congress catalog card number: 66-12509

To Anna and Elizabeth, our cross-national wives

Preface

Quantitative indicators of political and social change have become increasingly important for cross-national research. In an effort to expand their understanding of such processes of change, to predict sets of alternative outcomes, and to specify the conditions under which certain outcomes are more likely than others, social scientists are turning from speculative theory of a broad character toward the formulation of propositions that can be verified empirically (and confirmed or disconfirmed) by means of quantitative data. The Yale Political Data Program and other data banks have been developed to collect and analyze such data, after verifying their accuracy and organizing them so that they will be useful for cross-national comparisons.

Recognizing the need for international cooperation and coordination in the collection and analysis of such data, the International Social Science Council and the Yale Political Data Program organized an "International Conference on the Use of Quantitative Political, Social, and Cultural Data in Cross-National Comparison." This Conference, held at Yale University from the 10th to the 20th of September 1963, brought together more than fifty experts from all parts of the world. Those invited as participants or observers for the full conference and able to attend most of the sessions were:

Hayward R. Alker, Jr., Department of Political Science, Yale University

Arthur S. Banks, Department of Political Science, University of Indiana

René Bassoul, Centre d'Etudes Sociologiques, Paris

Richard Brody, Department of Political Science, Stanford University

Philip E. Converse, Survey Research Center, University of Michigan

Karl W. Deutsch, Department of Political Science, Yale University

Mattéi Dogan, Centre d'Etudes Sociologiques, Paris

Heinz Eulau, Department of Political Science, Stanford University

Harold Guetzkow, Department of Political Science, Northwestern University

A. H. Halsey, Nuffield College, Oxford

Chihiro Hosoya, Hitotsubashi University, Tokyo

S. V. Kogekar, Fergusson College, Poona

Harold D. Lasswell, Department of Political Science, Yale University

Paul Lazarsfeld, Department of Sociology, Columbia University

Daniel Lerner, Center for International Studies, Massachusetts Institute of Technology

Francis G. Lévy, Centre de Calcul, Maison des Sciences de l'Homme, Paris

Juan J. Linz, Department of Sociology, Columbia University

Val R. Lorwin, Department of History, University of Oregon

Roy C. Macridis, Department of Politics, Brandeis University

Richard L. Merritt, Department of Political Science, Yale University

Robert Mitchell, Survey Research Center, University of California (Berkeley)

Robert C. North, Department of Political Science, Stanford University
D. N. Pathak, University of Gujarat, India
Ithiel de Sola Pool, Center for International Studies, Massachusetts Institute of Technology
Stein Rokkan, Chr. Michelsen Institute, Bergen
Bruce M. Russett, Department of Political Science, Yale University
Erwin K. Scheuch, Institut für vergleichende Sozialforschung, University of Cologne
Alexander Szalai, Veszprém University for Chemical Industries, Budapest
Robert B. Textor, School of Education, Stanford University
Harrison C. White, Department of Social Relations, Harvard University

Three of the invited experts had sent papers but were themselves unable to attend the Conference:

Erik Allardt, Institute of Sociology, University of Helsinki
Gerhard Baumert, University of Marburg
Carl J. Friedrich, Department of Government, Harvard University

The following experts attended one or two sessions of the Conference:

Ralph L. Bisco, Inter-University Consortium for Political Research, University of Michigan
Jean Blondel, University of Essex, Colchester
William A. Glaser, Department of Sociology, Columbia University
John C. Harsanyi, Department of Economics, Wayne State University
P. C. Mahalanobis, Indian Statistical Institute, Calcutta
Donald V. McGranahan, Research and Development Branch, United Nations

Rolf Meyerson, Department of Sociology, Columbia University
S. M. Miller, Youth Development Center, Syracuse University
David L. Sills, International Encyclopaedia of the Social Sciences
Adolf Sturmthal, Institute for Labor and Industrial Relations, University of Illinois.

Julian Hochfeld and Pierre Henquet represented UNESCO at the Conference. Clemens Heller and Eric de Grolier represented the International Social Science Council. Henry Riecken, Robert Hall, and Murray Aborn of the National Science Foundation attended a few of the sessions. The Conference as a whole was financed through grants from UNESCO, the Social Science Research Council, the Asia Foundation, and the National Science Foundation.

The Yale Data Conference, chaired by Karl W. Deutsch and Stein Rokkan, was organized in four parts: (1) a series of papers on the *theoretical context* of current efforts to build up data programs for comparative research; (2) an extended exchange of views on the *availability and quality of national data* for comparisons; (3) a variety of *methodological and analytical problems of comparisons across nations,* with particular attention paid to the limitations of data programs centered on the nation as the unit of analysis; and (4) various possibilities of *concrete action* to advance quantitative comparative research.

Among other things, the Conference agreed that the Yale Political Data Program should revise and publish its compilation of quantitative data for cross-national comparisons, as well as the edited proceedings of the Conference itself. The former, the *World Handbook of Political and Social Indicators,* by Bruce M. Russett and Hayward R. Alker, Jr., Karl W. Deutsch, and Harold D. Lasswell, was published by Yale University Press in the fall of 1964. The present volume, comprising the bulk of the papers presented at the Yale Data Conference, is its companion piece. It is the *second* in a series, entitled *Tools and Methods of Comparative Research,* to be sponsored by the International Social Science Council and the International Committee for Social Sciences Documentation.

The 25 papers that make up this volume follow roughly the outline of the Yale Data Conference itself. After discussions of the theoretical framework for using quantitative data in cross-national research, there are chapters on the aggregate data basis for cross-national comparisons, the cross-national comparison of within-nation differences, and the organizational focus for national and international action to advance quantitative comparative analysis. In all cases the papers are revised versions of those presented at the Conference, and take into account the discussion that ensued after their original presentation.

The editors are indebted to several institutions and persons who assisted in one way or another in the preparation of this volume. Dr. K. Szczerba-Likiernik, Secretary General of the International Social Science Council, was instrumental in the organization of the Conference. Kay Latona assisted at all stages of the Conference. Barbara Bruns, Georgette Peterson, and Grace B. Stanley at Yale University and Hjørdis Storetvedt of the Chr. Michelsen Institute did most of the typing. It was Ann Barber whose warm encouragement and expert editorial talents kept the volume alive during its most desperate moments. The editorial abilities of Ruth Davis are largely responsible for steering the volume through the Yale University Press. Anna J. Merritt prepared the index. Financial support from the International Social Science Council and the Social Science Research Council made the book possible in the first place. In acknowledging our debt to these many friends, we nonetheless reserve to ourselves the right to be blamed for our bad judgment in including or excluding a particular paper, as well as for any errors made in our introductory sections.

R. L. M.
S. R.

Contents

PART I

Issues of Theory and Method

1. Comparative Cross-National Research: The Context of Current Efforts[1]

STEIN ROKKAN, THE MICHELSEN INSTITUTE, BERGEN

The history of international efforts in the social sciences offers a series of paradoxes. The nineteenth-century pioneers in the fields of statistics, sociology, and anthropology were almost without exception ardent advocates of the comparative method and endeavored to establish an internationally and interculturally valid body of knowledge about variations and regularities in the functioning and development of human societies. But this aim proved difficult to reconcile with their other aims: to establish strict canons of evidence and inference in the social sciences and to ensure a high level of analytical precision. The very efforts made by the early pioneers to gain academic recognition for the new disciplines tended to force their disciples to abandon universal comparisons and to focus their inquiries on the local, the concrete, the specific. The social sciences had to establish their methodological status and win recognition in the academies of each nation. In this struggle it proved more and more difficult to maintain the initial worldwide perspective. The disciplines gained their academic honors through increasing attention to methodological rigor and through deliberate

1. An early version of the first half of this contribution has been printed as part of the Introduction to a special issue of UNESCO's *International Social Science Journal* on "Data in Comparative Research," *16* (1964), 7–18.

concentration on well-delimited local and national inquiries. The very success of the new sciences discouraged cross-cultural and cross-national generalization. The disciplines gained in methodological precision but in this process lost sight of the original aim: the development of systematic knowledge of the world's societies through comparisons.[2]

The result was that the social sciences were largely unprepared for the onrush of demands for concrete comparative research in the 1950s. The many efforts of international economic and political integration, the numerous programs of aid to the poorer countries of the world, the campaigns to fight illiteracy, to improve agriculture, to introduce basic industrial skills—all these varieties of efforts increased the demand for knowledge of social, economic, and cultural conditions throughout the world and accentuated the need for systematic comparative research. But the social sciences were not ready for these tasks. The theoretical underpinnings of any effort of cross-cultural or cross-national comparison were poor and fragmentary. Very little, if anything, had been done within each discipline to develop the tools of analysis and the testing procedures required in handling data at such different levels of comparability. And, what was to prove even more important, only a few scattered beginnings had been made to ensure adequate data bases for systematic comparisons across the societies of the world.

We can roughly distinguish three categories of data for comparisons across human populations: (1) *"process-produced"* data, data generated through the very processes of

2. There is no comprehensive history of the vicissitudes of the comparative method in the social sciences. Among the most insightful contributions are F. J. Teggart, *Theory of History* (New Haven, Yale University Press, 1925); A. Köbben, "A New Way of Presenting an Old Idea: The Statistical Method in Social Anthropology," *Journal of the Royal Anthropological Institute, 82* (1952), 129–46; E. H. Ackerknecht, "On the Comparative Method in Anthropology," in R. F. Spencer, ed., *Method and Perspective in Anthropology* (Minneapolis, University of Minnesota Press, 1954), pp. 117–25; Sol Tax, "From Lafitau to Radcliffe-Brown: A Short History of the Study of Social Organization," in F. Eggan, ed., *Social Anthropology of North American Tribes* (enlarged ed. Chicago, University of Chicago Press, 1955), pp. 443–80; K. E. Bock, *The Acceptance of Histories* (Berkeley, University of California Press, 1956).

living, working, interacting in the societies to be compared —from plain material evidence through all kinds of artifacts to the varieties of symbolic representations of ideas, activities, and events, whether drawings, tales, messages, or documents; (2) the data of *observations and descriptions*, whether by native historians or lawyers, foreign travelers or missionaries, academically trained linguists, ethnographers, or political scientists; (3) data from *standardized enumerations and sample surveys* of specified attributes of units within each territorial population, be they communities, work places, households, or individual subjects.

The ethnographic museums and the historical archives of the world are replete with process-produced data. The items assembled in these repositories, however, rarely lend themselves to analyses of regularities within and across societies: most of them are stored there because of their cultural or historical uniqueness, not because of their potential use in social science comparisons. To make such repositories useful for the testing of generalizations in the social sciences, efforts would have to be made to ensure representative coverage of each category of data for each society and period and to codify the items for systematic mass analysis. Important steps in this direction have been taken through the application of standardized procedures of textual analysis to such diverse process-produced data as folk tales, children's readers, and newspaper editorials. A remarkable rapprochement has occurred between the humanistic traditions of qualitative analysis in linguistic and folklore studies and the hardheaded frequency counting pioneered in the study of political communication and mass persuasion by Harold Lasswell and his associates.[3] A particularly promising example of a

3. The basic texts are Harold D. Lasswell, Nathan Leites, et al., *Language of Politics* (New York, G. W. Stewart, 1949); Harold D. Lasswell, Daniel Lerner, and Ithiel de Sola Pool, *The Comparative Study of Symbols* (Stanford, Hoover Institute Series, 1952); and Robert North et al., *Handbook of Content Analysis* (Evanston, Northwestern University Press, 1963). The single most important volume on the trends toward a convergence of textual analysis techniques in linguistics, folklore, anthropology, and mass communications research is the one edited by Ithiel de Sola Pool on *Trends in Content Analysis* (Urbana, University of Illinois Press, 1959).

cross-national content analysis of cultural products is David McClelland's *The Achieving Society*.[4] The recent development of electronic computer facilities for content analyses of written documents [5] is bound to have a profound impact on such research, and we can in the near future expect accelerated efforts to store and codify data for such mass analyses.

Data from observations and descriptions of the institutions and peculiarities of different societies provide the basis for a rich literature of anecdotes and idiosyncratic interpretations but require detailed evaluation and codification if they are to serve the needs of comparative social science. The great pioneers in the study of primitive populations made important efforts to standardize the report taking of travelers and missionaries and to ensure the fullest possible coverage in each description. A number of attempts were made to store and codify the materials from such descriptions. Decisive progress was not achieved in this direction, however, until George Peter Murdock and his colleagues set up the Yale Cross-Cultural Survey in 1937 and later built up the Human Relations Area Files.[6] This extensive repository of coded information on a sample of the world's known societies [7] has proved an essential tool in the development of

4. David C. McClelland, *The Achieving Society* (New York, Van Nostrand, 1961). A curious example of the use of cross-cultural content analysis (jokes, cartoons) in the study of modal personality characteristics is Herbert Hendin's *Suicide and Scandinavia: A Psychoanalytic Story of Culture and Character* (London, Grune and Stratton, 1964).

5. See Philip J. Stone et al., "The General Inquirer: A Computer System of Content Analysis and Retrieval Based on the Sentence as a Unit of Information," *Behavioral Science*, 7 (1962), 484–98; and the chapters by Scheuch and Stone, and North and Holsti in the present volume.

6. George P. Murdock, "The Cross-Cultural Survey," *American Sociological Review*, 5 (1940), 361–70; cf. F. W. Moore, ed., *Readings in Cross-Cultural Methodology* (New Haven, HRAF Press, 1961).

7. The code used in classifying information is given in George P. Murdock et al., *An Outline of Cultural Materials* (4th rev. ed. New Haven, HRAF Press, 1961). An up-to-date listing of the universe and the samples of the world's societies is given in George P. Murdock, *An Outline of World Cultures* (3d ed. New Haven, HRAF Press, 1963). Robert Textor is currently assembling a basic handbook of information on a sample of 400 societies; see his forthcoming work *A Cross-Cultural Summary*. Karl Deutsch and Carl Friedrich have recently launched a collective exploration of the possibilities of using HRAF data and HRAF techniques in the comparative study of political systems.

designs and techniques for the analysis of cross-cultural variations.[8] A large number of universities and research institutions subscribe to copies of the Files and more and more scholars have in recent years tried their hand at cross-cultural comparisons of this type. The Files aim at the fullest possible coverage of a representative sample of all the world's societies and will incorporate information on societies at all levels of development, from preagricultural tribes to highly industrialized nation-states. In practice, however, it has proved very difficult to apply the traditional anthropological techniques of data gathering and codification to advanced nation-states, and most of the cross-cultural comparisons have been limited to preliterate units.[9]

The comparative study of industrializing nation-states grew out of a tradition of systematic observation by travelers, journalists, and itinerant scholars: the pioneering analyses of Montesquieu, Tocqueville, Marx, Engels, Ostrogorski, Michels, Bryce, and Weber were all heavily influenced by experiences of direct exposure to foreign manners and institutions. Weber's ambitious attempt to build up a conceptual framework for the comparative study of the growth of centralized bureaucracies and mass democracies reflected more than a century of discussion of contrasts and similarities among national developments in Europe and America and between the West and the East. The data for such ventures varied enormously in reliability, precision, and coverage: from fairly well-researched historical and legal evidence over crude official statistics to impressionistic accounts of the workings of particular institutions. Scholars following in Weber's path face a serious dilemma. If they decide to continue his effort of theory construction, they will

8. See George P. Murdock, *Social Structure* (New York, Macmillan, 1949). For a host of subsequent analyses, cf. Oscar Lewis, "Comparisons in Cultural Anthropology," in W. L. Thomas, Jr., *Current Anthropology* (Chicago, University of Chicago Press, 1956), pp. 259–92, and W. J. McEwen, "Forms and Problems of Validation in Social Anthropology," *Current Anthropology*, 4 (1963), 155–83.

9. A pioneering attempt to apply HRAF-type techniques to national polities rather than societies is Arthur S. Banks and Robert B. Textor, *A Cross-Polity Survey* (Cambridge, Mass., M.I.T. Press, 1963).

either find it impossible to establish an adequate data basis for their analyses or come under heavy and justified attacks from historians and area specialists for ignorance and distortions and for procrustean classifications of institutions and processes. If, however, they concentrate their efforts on comparative data gathering and data evaluation, they soon run into difficulties of conceptual integration and theoretical interpretation.[10] Shmuel Eisenstadt's gigantic effort of comparative analysis of *The Political Systems of Empires* [11] exemplifies one possible research strategy: he develops an elaborate model of processes of centralization, bureaucratization, and debureaucratization, and then seeks to test the consequences against evidence for five prebureaucratic societies and 27 historical bureaucratic societies. The problems encountered in such attempts are twofold: first, are the categories precise enough for effective analysis and are they meaningful across so many different areas of the world? second, does the evidence available allow some measure of consensus among experts on the categorization of concrete instances? To fit a large number of different cases, Eisenstadt's categories had to leave a considerable margin of imprecision; but this very imprecision makes many of his one-man categorizations of concrete cases, despite an extraordinary display of detailed historical erudition, highly debatable. Reinhard Bendix's recent volume on *Nation-Building and Citizenship* [12] exemplifies a more cautious approach: a

10. For discussions of the potentialities and the problems of comparative history, see especially Marc Bloch, "Pour une histoire comparée des sociétés européennes," originally published in 1928, reprinted in *Mélanges Historiques* (Paris, S.E.V.P.E.N., 1963), *i*, 16–40; Sylvia Thrupp, "The Role of Comparison in the Development of Economic History," *Journal of Economic History, 17* (1957), 554–70; Fritz Redlich, "Toward Comparative Historiography," *Kyklos, 11* (1958), 362–89; and D. Gerhard, *Alte und neue Wege in vergleichender Geschichtsbetrachtung* (Göttingen, Vandenhoeck, 1960). Sylvia Thrupp has made a pioneering effort to develop regular exchanges among historians and social scientists interested in cross-national analyses through the organization of the important international journal *Comparative Studies in Society and History.*

11. Shmuel N. Eisenstadt, *The Political Systems of Empires* (New York, Free Press, 1963).

12. Reinhard Bendix, *Nation-Building and Citizenship* (New York, Wiley, 1964)

number of theoretical distinctions first set out by Tocqueville and Weber are worked out in greater detail and then illustrated through the analysis of several concrete national developments. Seymour Martin Lipset's early work exemplified the empirical strategy: *Political Man* is essentially an outgrowth of a series of efforts to assemble prima facie comparable data on society and politics for a number of countries. His most recent contribution seeks to achieve more of a balance between theory construction and empirical analysis. *The First New Nation* [13] is essentially an attempt to bring Tocqueville's interpretation of the uniqueness of American society up to date through the development of a new analytical framework and through the collation of illustrative quantitative comparisons. Although many future "comparatists" will no doubt continue to pursue such "mixed" strategies, substantial progress in this field does not seem likely unless we reach a higher level of differentiation and specialization in research roles. To meet the demands for evidence of those social scientists who will continue to pursue theoretical refinements, we must also encourage the formation of a broad phalanx of experts on a wide range of empirical data across several countries.

To get a basis for detailed comparisons of rates of development within new as well as established nation-states, it is essential to supplement the information from historical documents and observers' reports with data from *standardized counts and other efforts of systematic social, cultural, and political map making.* Only in this way is it possible to approach reliable estimates of changes over time and of within-unit variations in the conditions and sequences of development.

The statisticians of the Western world can look back on more than a century of cooperative efforts to standardize national bookkeeping and census-taking procedures. The great Belgian pioneer Quetelet established a network of contacts throughout Europe and, in 1851, took a decisive initiative in

13. Seymour Martin Lipset, *The First New Nation: The United States in Historical and Comparative Perspective* (New York, Basic Books, 1963).

launching two International Statistical Congresses. The next generation went further and in 1887 set up the International Statistical Institute. The Institute provided a basis for continuous contact among experts and administrators of many nations and prepared the ground for the systematic efforts of comparison and standardization later taken up at the governmental level by the League of Nations, the International Labor Office, and, during the last two decades, by the United Nations and its specialized agencies.[14]

It took a long time, however, before the impact of these developments was felt throughout the social sciences. The demographers were the first to develop the tools of analysis required in mastering these vast quantities of data, the economists followed suit after the Second World War, but the sociologists have only recently faced up to the challenge of the increasing masses of cross-national data. The early fascination with comparative statistics for suicide and homicide and other items of *Moralstatistik* did not herald the advent of a comparative sociology of national development: Durkheim's work was of great methodological significance but was not followed up through broader comparative investigations of processes of change in industrializing and urbanizing nations. It is characteristic that the pioneering comparison of mobility data published by Pitirim Sorokin in 1927 [15] left hardly a ripple in the scholarly world at the time and was only discovered as a true classic of cross-national research in

14. The sheer mass of documentation produced by these efforts is overwhelming. A basic list of references to proposed standards is given in Statistical Office of the United Nations, *Directory of International Standards for Statistics* (New York, United Nations, Stat. Ser. M., No. 22, Rev. 1, 1960). This, however, gives little or no information on the concrete contents of the standards or on problems of application. UNESCO is currently attempting to remedy this lacuna through the compilation of a *Manual of International Standards of Classification in the Social Sciences* which will essentially cover the statistical indicators of cross-national differences presented in the UN *Compendium of Social Statistics, 1963*. For further details on UN statistical efforts see the chapter by Donald V. McGranahan in the present volume.

15. Pitirim A. Sorokin, *Social Mobility* (London, Harper, 1927, reprinted Glencoe, Free Press, 1959). For a general bibliography of efforts to develop comparative sociology in the 1950s, see Robert M. Marsh, "Comparative Sociology 1950–1963," *Current Sociology, 14* (1966).

the wake of the establishment of the Research Committee on Social Stratification and Mobility under the auspices of the International Sociological Association in 1951.[16] The decisive breakthrough toward quantitative comparisons in fact did not occur until the 1950s, when economists finally came seriously to grips with the possibilities of precise analyses of rates and patterns of growth, when sociologists started to become concerned with comparative measures of processes of structural change, when even students of politics ceased to be exclusively absorbed in single systems and tried to work out schemes of comparison and to devise ways of testing their hypotheses quantitatively.

Two technical developments proved crucial in accelerating these movements toward greater boldness in tackling the problems of a cross-national comparison: first, the extraordinary improvements in the machinery for the handling of huge data masses; and, second, the organization in more and more countries of sample survey organizations gathering data on broader ranges of variables than normally covered in official statistical bookkeeping operations.

The development of the electronic computer has brought about a revolution in comparative research. Tasks of calculation previously judged beyond the reach of even the largest research institute can now be carried out quickly and at moderate cost at a number of academic computer centers. The very existence of these new machines has prompted a number of research organizations to build up extensive data archives on punch cards or on tape. Several archives now cover data from large numbers of countries throughout the world. The need for such data archives has proved most urgent in comparative studies of economic growth, and an impressive number of attempts has been made in recent years

16. Erik Rinde and Stein Rokkan, eds., *First International Working Conference on Social Stratification and Social Mobility* (Oslo, International Sociological Association, 1951); Seymour M. Lipset and Reinhard Bendix, *Social Mobility in Industrial Society* (Berkeley, University of California Press, 1958); S. M. Miller, "Comparative Social Mobility," *Current Sociology, 9* (1960), 1–89; David V. Glass and René König, *Soziale Schichtung und soziale Mobilität* (Cologne, Westdeutscher Verlag, 1961).

to apply complex techniques of computation to cross-national data on a variety of indicators of resources, production, income, distribution, etc.[17] The case for similar data archives has also been effectively demonstrated in a study of world urbanization through the work of Kingsley Davis and his group at the University of California at Berkeley [18] and more recently also in the study of political modernization by Karl Deutsch and his associates at Yale University.[19]

The sociologists and political scientists developing such plans have of necessity been concerned with broader ranges of cross-national variables than the demographers and the economists. They have not only brought together data from censuses, national accounts, trade statistics, and other governmental bookkeeping operations but have also sought to accumulate the best available estimates of variations in the spread of education and culture, in the sway of religious, ideological, and political movements, and in the exposure of the population to the newer media of communication. UNESCO and such regional organizations as the OECD are doing magnificent work on the evaluation of the comparative statistics of education, a field in which sociologists and political scientists attempting to build up data programs can simply take over the country-by-country estimates produced by these organizations. The situation is less encouraging for mass media statistics. UNESCO has been making valiant efforts to accumulate information on mass media but has had very little opportunity to carry out detailed evaluations and analyses. On cultural, religious, and political variables the

17. An excellent source book on such indicators is Norton Ginsburg's *Atlas of Economic Development* (Chicago, University of Chicago Press, 1961); this also includes an example (by Brian J. L. Berry) of one type of correlational analysis now made possible on the basis of such data.

18. The International Population and Urban Research Program at Berkeley has developed a systematic file of information on all of the world's cities and metropolitan areas of 100,000 inhabitants and more; cf. International Urban Research, *The World's Metropolitan Areas* (Berkeley, University of California Press, 1959).

19. See especially Karl W. Deutsch, "Toward an Inventory of Basic Trends and Patterns in Comparative and International Politics," *American Political Science Review, 54* (1960), 34–57, and the chapters on the Yale Political Data Program in the present volume.

international organizations can deliver little or nothing; here the social scientist is pretty much on his own and will have to glean, from whatever national sources he can find, such data as seem worthy of a comparison. Data on religious memberships, electoral turnout, and party strength can be assembled from official counts for a sizable number of countries, but to evaluate and interpret such data in any comparative analysis the social scientists will require detailed knowledge of the workings of each national system, and here the literature is often deficient.[20] Data on levels of participation, whether cultural, religious, or political, can only rarely be assembled from regular statistical sources but may sometimes be gathered through private counting operations (church attendance, party membership statistics) and ad hoc sample surveys. So far very little has been done to make use of such data in computer programs for cross-national comparison, but efforts are at least under way to establish a basis for such analyses through the development of archives of raw data from sample surveys for different countries.

The practice of interviewing samples of populations can be traced to several distinct historical roots. One line of development started out from the official census: sampling procedures were developed to cut down the cost of censuses of social conditions, particularly studies of poverty and substandard housing; and sampling also made it possible to gather information in greater detail than in official data

20. This is the essential rationale for the plan now under consideration within UNESCO for a series of *International Guides to Data for Comparative Research.* The first of these, the *International Guide to Electoral Statistics,* is already far advanced; the first volume was published in 1967 by the International Committee of Social Science Documentation in cooperation with the International Social Science Council. In the United States the Social Science Research Council has supported an exploratory study by Walter D. Burnham on the possibilities of assembling a central file of historical election data by county for computer processing. The Inter-University Consortium for Political Research at Ann Arbor, Michigan, is currently following up this effort and is building up a large file of census and election data by county to facilitate ecological trend analyses. For a general discussion of the potentialities of such approaches to the comparative study of political ecology, see Stein Rokkan, "Electoral Mobilization, Party Competition and Territorial Integration," in Joseph LaPalombara and Myron Weiner, eds., *Political Parties and Political Development* (Princeton, Princeton University Press, 1966), pp. 241–66.

gathering operations. Another line of development started out from the public referendum, the plebiscite: "straw polls" and opinion soundings serving as short cuts to information on the inclinations and the preferences of the general public. Up to the middle of the 1930s there were hardly any points of contact between these two traditions of inquiry. This changed radically, however, with the emergence of large-scale organizations conducting interview studies, first under commercial auspices and later also within government departments and universities. The mass interview was found to be a flexible instrument of social inquiry and soon proved its usefulness in a wide range of contexts. In fact, it combined within one unified operation at least six hitherto distinct models of social and behavioral data gathering: the census questionnaire, the standardized observation checklist, the informal reportorial conversation, the referendum, the election, and the psychological test. This flexibility proved the great strength of the interview as a research procedure but, at least in the initial phases, caused a good deal of confusion and controversy.[21]

International networks of interview organizations grew rapidly after World War II as more and more attempts were made to develop comparable procedures of opinion soundings and market studies across several different countries at the same time.[22] Only a handful of academic social scientists took an interest in these international developments during the first decade or so, but at least a few imaginative begin-

21. The sizable body of literature generated by these developments has never been systematically analyzed. Among the hundreds of articles and chapters produced in the course of the controversy these have perhaps proved the more significant: T. Harrison, "What is Public Opinion?" *Political Quarterly, 11* (1940), 368–83; H. Blumer, "Public Opinion and Public Opinion Polling," *American Sociological Review, 13* (1948), 542–65; H. Arbuthnot, "Democracy by Snap Judgment," *Listener* (March 4, 1948), pp. 367–68; Lindsay Rogers, *The Pollsters* (New York, Knopf, 1949); Hans Speier, "The Historical Development of Public Opinion," in his *Social Order and the Risk of War* (New York, Stewart, 1952); Herbert H. Hyman, *Survey Design and Analysis* (Glencoe, Free Press, 1955), Chap. 8; Paul F. Lazarsfeld, "Public Opinion and the Classical Tradition," *Public Opinion Quarterly, 21* (1957), 39–53.

22. See the forthcoming volume by Stein Rokkan, Sidney Verba, Jean Viet, and Eric Almasy, *Comparative Survey Analysis: A Trend Report and Bibliography* (Paris, Mouton, 1968).

nings were made. A pioneer in the use of these new techniques of cross-national research was the American psychologist Hadley Cantril. He showed how this machinery of data gathering could be used to throw light on central problems in the study of international communication. His UNESCO-sponsored study, *How Nations See Each Other*,[23] was the first in a series of attempts to make systematic use of national interview organizations in theory-oriented comparative research. He also pointed to the possibilities of drawing on the rapidly increasing production of interview data for comparative secondary analysis: his impressive compilation of findings through 1946 [24] paved the way for subsequent efforts to assemble not only the press releases and reports from the many interview organizations of the world but also the raw data of their studies as recorded on punch cards or tapes.

Only a few academic social scientists have been able to command the resources required to organize comparative data-gathering operations of their own design. The number of full-scale studies following the pattern set by the UNESCO study of 1949 can still be counted on two hands.[25] The five-country study carried out in 1959–60 by Gabriel Almond and Sidney Verba [26] demonstrates the immense possibilities of this line of research, but the cost of such ventures will for years to come keep them beyond the reach of most centers of research. The vast majority of academic social scientists will have to do what they can with data produced

23. William Buchanan and Hadley Cantril, *How Nations See Each Other* (Urbana, University of Illinois Press, 1953).

24. Hadley Cantril and Mildred Strunk, eds., *Public Opinion, 1935–46* (Princeton, Princeton University Press, 1951). The *Public Opinion Quarterly* listed "poll" results from 1940 to 1951 and again from 1961, but the coverage of these listings was not very systematic. Martin Brouwer at the University of Amsterdam has collected an important archive of releases and reports from polling organizations and has launched a journal registering questions and total response distributions in 1965: *Polls* (Amsterdam, Steinmetz Institute and Keesing's, 1965).

25. A near-complete listing of such projects will be found in Stein Rokkan, Sidney Verba, et al., *Comparative Survey Analysis;* see note 22 above. A major comparative survey of the "modernization" of attitudes has recently been undertaken in six countries by Alex Inkeles of Harvard University.

26. Gabriel Almond and Sidney Verba, *The Civic Culture* (Princeton, Princeton University Press, 1963).

independently of their own interests and efforts, and seek to develop techniques for comparing such information ex post facto. To judge the comparability of such independently collected data, it is clearly essential to go beyond the simple tabulations generally given in the releases to the press or even in the reports given to sponsors and clients. This is the essential rationale for the current efforts to assemble the raw data of a variety of studies from different countries into archives for subsequent secondary analysis by qualified scholars.[27]

In the early phase of commercial polling and market research the typical report simply gave for each question the per cent of all interviewed responding one way or the other: so many X, so many Y, so many Z, so many Don't Know. The underlying model of the public was plebiscitarian and equalitarian. The "pollsters" started out from the basic premise of full suffrage democracy: "one citizen, one vote, one value." They equated votes and other expressions of opinion and gave the same numerical value to every such expression, whether actively articulated independently of any interview or elicited only in the interview situation. The sum total of such unit expressions was presented as an estimate of "public opinion" on the given issue. The aim was clearly not just elicitation, classification, and enumeration; the essential aim was to establish the "will of the people" through sample interviews instead of through elections and referenda. To such pioneers as George Gallup and Elmo Roper, the "poll" was essentially a new technique of democratic control; the interviews helped to bring out the will of the "inarticulate, unorganized majority of the people" as a countervailing power against the persuasive pressure of the many minority interests.[28]

27. The first systematic report on such possibilities was prepared in 1957 by Y. Lucci and Stein Rokkan in *A Library Center of Survey Research Data* (New York, Columbia University School of Library Service). For further developments see the articles in the special issue on "Data in Comparative Research" of the UNESCO *International Social Science Journal, 16* (1964) and Stein Rokkan, ed. *Data Archives for the Social Sciences* (Paris, Mouton, 1966).

28. The plebiscitarian assumptions of commercial polling have been analyzed with great critical skill by the German philosopher Wilhelm Hennis in *Meinungsforschung und repräsentative Demokratie* (Tübingen, Mohr, 1957).

By the late 1950s, however, there were more and more signs of change. The "one citizen, one opinion" model was gradually given up and the practices of even the most "cash-oriented" of the private pollsters began to reflect the differentiated models of opinion formation developed by social psychologists, sociologists, and political scientists. A series of academic surveys of local communities and national cross-sections had helped to establish the characteristics of the strata of opinion moulders, opinion transmitters, and opinion receivers within our contemporary mass electorates. Paul Lazarsfeld's pioneering studies of the "two-step flow of communication"[29] had a profound effect on contemporary theorizing about mass democracy. David Riesman and his associates developed this line of analysis further and emphasized the importance of the social context of the interview reaction: a lower-class response to a middle-class interviewer could not be analyzed in the same terms as an upper-class response to the same interviewer.[30] The Survey Research Center of the University of Michigan has added a number of further dimensions to this mapping of the hierarchies of "publics" within the mass electorate and provided perhaps the most telling demonstration of the deficiencies of the earlier arithmetic conceptions of aggregated national opinion. Philip Converse has recently presented a most revealing analysis of the reactions of a panel of respondents to identi-

This work is of particular interest as an attempt to bridge the gap between the political theory of representation and democracy and the current controversies about the assumptions underlying the practice of mass interviews. This theme is discussed in a broader perspective of historical sociology in Jürgen Habermas, *Strukturwandel der Öffentlichkeit* (Neuwied, Luchterhand, 1961). The position of the "pollsters" has been ably defended by G. Schmidtchen, *Die befragte Nation* (Freiburg, Rombach, 1959), and Manfred Kuhn, *Umfragen und Demokratie* (Allensbach, Verlag für Demoskopie, 1959).

29. Paul F. Lazarsfeld et al., *The People's Choice* (New York, Duell, 1944); Elihu Katz and Paul F. Lazarsfeld, *Personal Influence* (Glencoe, Free Press, 1955). For a replication in Sweden see Bo Anderson, "Opinion Influentials and Political Opinion Formation in Four Swedish Communities," *International Social Science Journal, 14* (1962), 320–36.

30. See David Riesman and Nathan Glazer, "Social Structure, Character Structure and Opinion," *International Journal of Opinion and Attitude Research, 2* (1948), 512–27, and particularly the special issue on the sociology of the interview of the *American Journal of Sociology, 62* (1956).

cal questions asked three times over a period of four years.[31] On all three occasions filtering questions were used to sift out respondents definitely unfamiliar with the issue they were to express an opinion on. Nevertheless, responses on even basic issues of policy turned out to be highly unstable over the four years. Substantial proportions of those who offered opinions had clearly not given the matter any thought but only picked an alternative to please the interviewer. Only a small proportion of the panel proved stable in their responses and appeared to base their statements on information, experiences, and arguments which meant something to them personally. These "issue publics," normally only 20 to 40 per cent of the total electorate, will vary in composition from issue to issue but the citizens in the lowest of the strata of political actors would hardly ever be part of any such group of stable respondents.

Analyses along such lines are of obvious importance for an understanding of data for any single nation. They are crucial in any attempt to compare distributions of responses across several nations. How can one possibly compare one national distribution of responses with another without knowing anything about the levels of interest in the given issue in each country, the differences in education, in exposure, in knowledge? The private networks of interview organizations in Europe and America have in recent years found an expanding market for comparative studies, and it is interesting to note how much more detailed the tabulations have become as a result. To take a recent example, Gallup International, in its study of *Public Opinion and the Europe of the Six*,[32] found that 62 per cent of the Dutch sample was strongly in

31. Philip E. Converse, "New Dimensions of Meaning for Cross-National Sample Surveys in Politics," *International Social Science Journal, 16* (1964), 19–34; and "The Nature of Belief Systems in Mass Publics," in David E. Apter, ed., *Ideology and Discontent* (New York, Free Press, 1964), pp. 206–61.

32. Gallup International, *L'opinion publique et l'Europe des Six* (Paris, IFOP, mimeo, 1963); and the special issue on these surveys of *Sondages, 25* (1963), 3–58. Another comparative survey of great interest in this connection is reported on in *Products and People: A Digest of the Marketing Survey of the European Common Market, 1963* (London, The Reader's Digest Association Ltd., 1963).

favor of unification and only 36 per cent of the Italians. This difference, however, tells us very little about the chances of strains between the two countries in the articulation of policies toward Europe. It turns out that the better educated in the two national samples think practically alike: 70 per cent of them were strongly in favor of European unification. The difference between the two countries resulted almost entirely from a contrast in levels of education and information; most of the lower educated in Italy could not articulate any opinion, and in the backward areas of the South and the Islands two thirds to three fourths of those interviewed had never heard of the European unification efforts.

Such checks by education and information exemplify only one line of comparative evaluation. There are many more, some of which may without much difficulty be explored further through secondary analysis of the interview data directly from the punch cards, or when there are doubts about the classifications of cases on such cards, even from the original protocols of the field workers.

Systematic comparisons, however, must of necessity go beyond such simple evaluation of estimates of cross-national similarities and differences. The essential aims of cross-national analysis are *"micro"* replications and the testing of *"macro"* hypotheses.[33] In replicative research the aim is to test out in other national and cultural settings a proposition already validated in one setting. Thus the social psychologist who has found for one country that working-class adults are more authoritarian than middle-class adults will want to replicate this analysis for as many countries as possible to establish the generality of his finding.[34] This would be generalization at the *micro* level: the level of individuals, households, or other component units of larger culturally and politically distinct systems. The crucial tasks of cross-

33. See the "paradigms" discussed in Stein Rokkan, "The Comparative Study of Political Participation: Notes Toward a Perspective on Current Research," in Austin Ranney, ed., *Essays on the Behavioral Study of Politics* (Urbana, University of Illinois Press, 1962), pp. 47–90.

34. A proposition discussed in some detail by Seymour M. Lipset in *Political Man* (Garden City, N.Y., Doubleday, 1960), Chap. 4.

national analysis, however, lie at the *macro* level: the exploration of the interrelations of structural elements of total systems and the testing of hypotheses about structural influences on the behavior of component units. A social psychologist might want to explore the influence of childrearing practices and childhood experiences on the development of economic entrepreneurship in a variety of cultures,[35] but he would soon find it more fruitful to go beyond the mere replication of tests designed to get such information toward the exploration of "macro" conditions in the social and political structure—differences in educational systems, in opportunities for geographical and social mobility, in the legal status of entrepreneurs, etc.—which would increase or decrease the likelihood of such results of socialization. Although the distinction between "micro" and "macro" levels of analysis is essential in all cross-national research, the logical structure of these distinctions has not yet been worked out satisfactorily.[36]

Whatever the level of analysis aimed at, however, the social scientist concerned with comparing data for his own with data for other countries will of necessity face the problem of primary versus secondary research. He cannot mobilize resources for fresh data gathering in the other countries and he will often find the data at hand in the countries difficult if not impossible to compare with his own. What can he do to get closer to some solution?

It might be useful to consider this question in abstract terms before proceeding to more concrete examples. The primary–secondary distinction touches on a basic dimension of variation in the data available for comparison: the degree of interdependence between data gathering activities in different countries and territories or on different popula-

35. See McClelland, *The Achieving Society*, and E. Hagen, *On the Theory of Social Change* (Homewood, Ill., Dorsey Press, 1962).

36. An important basis for advances in this direction has been provided in Lazarsfeld's analysis of the properties of individual vs. group variables; cf. Paul F. Lazarsfeld and Morris Rosenberg, eds., *The Language of Social Research* (Glencoe, Free Press, 1955), Section IV, and Hanan C. Selvin and W. O. Hagstrom, "The Empirical Classification of Formal Groups," *American Sociological Review, 28* (1963), 399–411.

tions. The extremes of this continuum are not hard to describe. At the one end is any data gathering undertaken in complete isolation from social scientists in other cultures or societies; at the other end is any data gathering maximally controlled by social scientists from the relevant cultures or societies to ensure comparability in all phases and on all points of importance in the research process. No actual data gathering operations are of course to be found at any of these extremes. We do not find any examples of social data gathering undertaken in complete national or cultural isolation, but neither do we find any examples of completely interdependent data gathering operations controlled at every point to ensure cross-societal comparability. What we do find are a number of steps in a ladder pointing toward some maximum of comparability.

It is impossible to talk about interdependence without talking about problems of organization. To simplify matters for purposes of discussion, we may distinguish three levels of organizational activity in comparative social research:

Level I. The systematic collection and collation of the "haphazard products of natural growth," of the data and findings of research independently conceived, designed, and executed in different societies or cultures. Examples are the cross-societal analyses of kinship structures undertaken by Murdock,[37] the cross-cultural studies of childrearing and socialization by Child and Whiting,[38] and, on a different level, Lipset's and his followers' review of significant findings from a wide variety of independent investigations in different countries of the social and economic determinants of political behavior.[39]

Level II. Organized efforts to influence ongoing institutionalized data gathering processes through regular intersocietal and intercultural interaction, directed toward the development of standard methodological features: question-

37. Murdock, *Social Structure.*

38. J. W.M. Whiting and I. L. Child, *Child Training and Personality: A Cross-Cultural Study* (New Haven, Yale University Press, 1953).

39. Lipset, *Political Man,* and *The First New Nation;* Robert Alford, *Party and Society* (Chicago, Rand McNally, 1963).

naires, codes, tabulation and analysis procedures. Much progress of this sort has already been achieved in the field of demographic and economic statistics based on total counts through the efforts of the UN, ILO, WHO, FAO, and UNESCO; and some initial efforts have been taken to encourage similar developments in the parts of the world now covered by institutionalized sample surveys.

Level III. The organization for explicit purposes of comparative analysis of specifically designed data gathering operations in different societies or cultures. Examples are the UNESCO nine-country study in 1948 of "common ideas about foreign peoples,"[40] the Columbia study of communications behavior in five countries of the Middle East,[41] the studies of childrearing practices in different countries of Asia by Whiting and others,[42] the OCSR sample surveys and group experiments in seven countries of Western Europe,[43] the Almond–Verba surveys in the United States, Great Britain, West Germany, Italy, and Mexico.[44]

The long-term program of comparative research on social mobility launched by the International Sociological Association offers an excellent example of an organized attempt to move forward at all three levels through concerted efforts. *Level I:* Systematic attempts were made to collect and collate information on the available findings country by country for changes in occupational structures and the characteristic patterns of recruitment; this has not yet resulted in any major international compilation of data but much useful information has been accumulated.[45] *Level II:* Attempts were also made to incorporate questions about occupation of father and father-in-law in regular data gathering

40. Buchanan and Cantril, *How Nations See Each Other.*

41. Daniel Lerner, *The Passing of Traditional Society* (Glencoe, Free Press, 1958).

42. J. W. M. Whiting et al., *Field Manual for the Cross-Cultural Study of Child Rearing* (New York, Social Science Research Council, 1953); Beatrice Whiting, ed., *Six Cultures* (New York, Wiley, 1963).

43. Stein Rokkan, "An Experiment in Cross-national Research Cooperation," and "Party Preferences and Opinion Patterns in Western Europe," *International Social Science Bulletin,* 7 (1955), 645–56 and 575–96.

44. Almond and Verba, *The Civic Culture.*

45. See the bibliographies in Miller, "Comparative Social Mobility," and in Rokkan, et al., *Comparative Survey Analysis* (see note 22 above).

operations to allow analyses of mobility. For censuses, this kind of arrangement has proved impossible (one exception is Theodor Geiger's use of the city census in Aarhus), but with routine sample surveys there are definite possibilities along this line; thus there is a question about father's occupation in a four-country comparative survey commissioned by UNESCO from regularly operating interview organizations.[46] *Level III:* The main focus of the program, however, was on the organization of explicitly comparative data gathering operations, some focused on the exploration of the degree of consensus on occupational prestige rankings, others designed as large-scale sample surveys allowing detailed breakdowns for purposes of mobility analysis. On this level a variety of interesting results are already forthcoming, some highly illuminating, others disturbing and pointing to new problems of comparative analysis.[47]

Similar action is under way within other research committees of the International Sociological Association and the same pattern could be followed in a variety of fields of the social sciences. The scholar concerned with advancing comparative analysis need not despair: he is not faced with an inescapable dilemma between the prohibitive costs of fresh data gathering and the exasperating incompatibilities and limitations of the national data already at hand. He can work out procedures for evaluating levels of comparability in existing data and can join with others in seeking to influence current data gathering processes in different countries. So far such action has tended to limit itself to narrow fields only. What has been lacking is machinery for encouraging cooperative arrangements across the fields to accelerate these efforts of systematic comparison.

UNESCO and its international social science organiza-

46. See the report on the planning of this study by Stein Rokkan in *International Social Science Journal, 9* (1957), 121–28. The only printed account of the findings of this survey is by E. Reigrotzki and N. Anderson, "National Stereotypes and Foreign Contacts," *Public Opinion Quarterly, 23* (1959–60), 515–28.

47. See the discussion in the chapter by Thomas Fox and S. M. Miller in the present volume and in the article by Seymour Martin Lipset, "Research Problems in the Comparative Analysis of Mobility and Development," *International Social Science Journal, 16* (1964), 35–48.

tions may be able to develop such machinery in the years to come. The Department of Social Sciences, the International Social Science Council, and the International Committee on Social Science Documentation have since 1961 made efforts to develop a program of activities designed to facilitate comparative cross-national research and have taken a great deal of interest in the current endeavors to build up networks of data centers.

A first conference on "The Uses of Sample Survey Data in Comparative Cross-National Research," held at La Napoule in France in June 1962, was attended by fifteen experts and six observers.[48] On the basis of the recommendations of this conference, UNESCO and the cooperating international bodies took steps to launch a long-term program of activities designed to improve the data bases and the general facilities for comparative cross-national research. An initial report on problems of data archives was discussed at a European meeting at the University of Cologne in June 1963.[49]

The discussion of data archives was followed up in September 1963 by a large-scale international conference at Yale University on "The Use of Quantitative Political, Social and Cultural Data in Cross-National Comparisons."[50] The Yale Data Conference, the proceedings of which are presented in revised form in this volume, concentrated on four aspects of data gathering and data analysis efforts:

first, issues of theory and method in the development of data programs for comparative research;

second, problems of availability, quality, and comparability of data for cross-cultural and cross-national research;

third, variations *within* nations, the choice of units for comparison, and the problem of joining up analyses of *within-nation* differences with analyses of differences across nations; and

48. See Stein Rokkan, "The Development of Cross-national Comparative Research: A Review of Current Problems and Possibilities," *Social Sciences Information, 1* (1962), 21–38.

49. See Stein Rokkan and Erwin Scheuch, "Conference on Data Archives in the Social Sciences," *Social Sciences Information, 2* (1963), 109–14.

50. For a summary report of the proceedings of this conference, see Stein Rokkan in collaboration with Karl Deutsch and Richard Merritt, "Summary Report," *Social Sciences Information, 2* (1963), 89–108.

finally, current plans and future opportunities for concerted international action to advance comparative research. Most of the papers, and all of the discussion at the Conference, dealt in one way or another with problems of immediate importance in the further development of one concrete center for quantitative cross-national comparisons: the Yale Political Data Program, launched by Karl Deutsch and Harold Lasswell and developed by Bruce Russett and Hayward Alker, Jr.[51]

But the La Napoule, Cologne, and Yale conferences are only first steps in current efforts to coordinate data gathering and analysis internationally. Other steps include further conferences on specific aspects of the problem and, still more important, concrete programs to establish data archives as well as measures to make data gathering truly comparable on a cross-national basis.

51. To gain a fuller understanding of the underlying issues the reader should therefore consult in some detail the first major product of this program: Bruce M. Russett, with Hayward R. Alker, Jr., Karl W. Deutsch, and Harold D. Lasswell, *World Handbook of Political and Social Indicators* (New Haven, Yale University Press, 1964).

2. The Theoretical Basis of Data Programs

KARL W. DEUTSCH, YALE UNIVERSITY

An orderly attempt to think about society as a whole, or at least to think about large parts of social development as a whole at high system levels, involves configurations or contexts with many variables rather than a few. The demand for the economy of a theory is balanced—almost overridden—by the demand for breadth, for comprehensiveness of the picture. The source of general systems theories historically has been classic European social science thought, the broad theories of society in the French, German, and Russian intellectual tradition in the nineteenth and twentieth centuries, and to some extent earlier English thought in the seventeenth and early eighteenth centuries. French thought from Comte to Durkheim, German thought from Kant and Hegel to Marx, to Max Weber and Alfred Weber, Russian thought from Struve to Lenin, and to some extent English thought from Hobbes and Locke to Sidney Webb and Arnold Toynbee, are all attempts to think very broadly, to put many variables into the picture, to get a comprehensive image of what society was about or where it might be going.

The method is philosophical, historical, and descriptive; it is to some extent literary. In this broad framework data are fitted where they can be found and where they fit the overall description. Some theories tried to use more specific quantitative data—Marx used them richly, Max Weber sparingly

—or more often would shift from quantitative data to historical examples for specific cases. Such broad theories in the classic European tradition were an aid in the recognition of some overall pattern or configuration and, at their best, in the making of predictions.

These broad social theories resembled scientific theories in the natural sciences as found in certain stages in the history of biology and in the history of meteorology. In these sciences, too, practitioners would identify a certain type of plant or animal, a certain evolutionary stage, and recognize from past observations or from observations of similar stages that this type was followed by another type, and then predict that similar shifts or changes from one evolutionary stage or one biological stage to another would follow. If the biologist felt more confident, he would even say that he could predict that this change would occur within so many days, or months, or years. The famous "ontogenetic law" of Ernst Haeckel would be an example of biological thinking at that level.

Some of these predictions turned out to be wrong; other predictions, however, turned out to be worthwhile. In meteorology, for example, a United States Air Force project during World War II compiled weather maps from many parts of the world for the last fifty years, and cut them up into small geographic sectors. A computer then fitted current weather reports as closely as possible to the most similar weather situation in the past, or to ensembles of such situations, so as to derive the most likely forecast. This was a highly imperfect method of forecasting the weather, but it did improve the performances of the Air Force beyond what random guesses or the consulting of ancient fishermen would have done.

A variant of this method is simple persistence forecasting, that is, predicting that tomorrow's weather will be much like today's. This is again better than random guesses. It might be added that conservative theories of social thought are very roughly analogous to persistence forecasting in meteorology. At best, these broad descriptive, literary, evocative, and philosophical theories could lead to the assumption of stages, to the forecasting of either persistence or future change, and even to the prediction of certain patterns of change, the quality and direction of change, and to judgments whether this change would be slow or rapid in the future. These, however, still would be highly inaccurate forecasts.

The typical weakness of all these theories, characteristic of the attempted forecasts of Marxism, is quantitative. Certain future developments which were forecast to happen within five years had not occurred fifty years later. In the meantime all the contingencies would have changed and, therefore, the pattern that was originally forecast could no longer be expected in quite that form. But the fate of other classic descriptive social scientists has not been better. Max Weber's assumption that bureaucratization would lead to rationality was followed by the spectacle of Germany, the most bureaucratic country of Europe in the 1920s and 1930s, behaving as the most irrational. Nevertheless, from Montesquieu, Marx, Hobbes, Machiavelli, and Locke to the work of Max Weber, Joseph Schumpeter, and Arnold Toynbee, this tradition has remained vigorous.

Carl J. Friedrich's recent book, *Man and His Government,* is a major contribution toward building a bridge between the best tradition of this descriptive, historical, and philosophical approach to political and social phenomena and the new efforts to develop a more specifically verifiable science of social and political behavior.[1] This more recent way of dealing with social science most often has consisted of attempts to isolate very small classes of special aspects of social life, to define them as sharply and as reproducibly as possible, so that the definition will enable any number of observers to pick out pretty much the same events, and then to generalize only about these limited classes under sharply specified contingencies. It is even possible to generalize about something much smaller, the subset where several classes meet or several contingencies meet (that is, in the technical language of set theory, the products of two or more sets). An example of

1. Carl J. Friedrich, *Man and His Government* (New York, McGraw-Hill, 1963).

this might be a generalization about the effects on political stability associated with high levels of literacy at very low income levels.

Such a procedure is analogous to the classic late eighteenth and nineteenth century method of the natural sciences. Although the source of a great deal of this work has been English social science since the eighteenth century, there are exceptions: Herbert Spencer tried to generalize in the grand manner, and some continental European theorists have tried to make very specific predictions in the hard-boiled, rigorous scientific manner. But on the whole a great deal of English as well as American work has been in this tradition, close to the natural sciences. Here social scientists have tried to define very sharply, very precisely, a subset of phenomena, but at its best such work has pointed to implications of broader significance.

An example of this approach is some of the work that Ithiel de Sola Pool has been interested in. He would ask: How many people does it take to link any two persons in the United States by a network of face-to-face acquaintances? It may turn out that it takes four people in the United States in most cases; this would compare to some other societies where it possibly takes six or eight. It might also be interesting to find out how many alternative pathways link any two people. Again there might be a difference between societies where there is only one linkage, through someone like the chieftain or the chief priest, as against societies where there are half a dozen alternative linkages among people. This kind of approach ignores about a hundred other things that social scientists have written about, to concentrate on doing a thorough job on just this one aspect in order to gain some really hard, reproducible, verifiable knowledge about a limited subject. This is, in short, the empirical, the logical, the mathematical style and method of science, using concepts and conceptual schemes, implicitly or explicitly, to lay out an experimental observational sequence.

Public opinion polling, interview techniques, survey techniques, and, for that matter, much of classic economics come out of this style of social science. For example, by studying prices, stating the law of supply and demand, one can develop limited concepts such as marginal utility, and gradually build up a system from the limited observations and the specific concepts developed. The goal is to get an image of society as a whole. But this time it is not begun from the broad, poetical, literary, historical, philosophical viewpoint; it has been built up "brick by brick," by sharply defined concepts of particular findings.

Another kind of theory is concerned with relatively large-scale theories which, nevertheless, stay below the general system level. This kind of theory involves either special theories or special techniques or both. An example is game theory, which cuts across the whole series of levels and has very broad implications, but which does not pretend at any stage to give a comprehensive picture of society. We may think in a similar way of the attempt of Richardson models to show automatic social processes, such as conflict processes, by pairs of differential equations.[2] It is clearly more than a rigorously specific theory, but it falls far short of a comprehensive picture of society. Communication theory and cybernetics also belong in these middle-range theories or models. Cybernetic models as well as information and communication theory can be applied in principle very widely, but they cannot cover comprehensively all of our knowledge of society. There are important processes in social development which are not primarily communication processes or control processes and where, therefore, cybernetic models are not helpful. Balance of power theory would be still another example of a middle-range theory in classic political thinking.

Sometimes the theories come first and the techniques come later. To some extent game theory was an intellectual conception before mathematical techniques were invented. But sometimes the technique grows first, and this forces some

2. Lewis F. Richardson, "Generalized Foreign Politics: A Study in Group Psychology," *British Journal of Psychology,* Monograph Supplement No. 23 (Cambridge University Press, 1939); also his *Arms and Insecurity* (Pittsburgh, Boxwood Press, 1960); and *Statistics of Deadly Quarrels* (Pittsburgh, Boxwood Press, 1960): Anatol Rapoport, *Fights, Games and Debates* (Ann Arbor, University of Michigan Press, 1961), Part I.

theoretical development. I suspect that simulation began as a technique, and that it is now begetting an offspring of theoretical implications that are gradually unfolding before us. All these are middle-level activities, much larger than the special ad hoc theories and yet below the system level.

There are before us an intellectual need and a desperately difficult task, a task that cannot be accomplished in itself by committees or conferences, but can only be pioneered by individuals and then developed by the criticisms, the discussions, and the cooperation of many scientists over many years. It is necessary to put together these three types of theory—the broad general perspectives, the hard specific findings, and the middle-range models and techniques—so that we will eventually get a choice of broad intellectual systems, encompassing a wide range of phenomena and permitting the recognition of rich and complex patterns, including even judgments of the probability and speed with which certain patterns may be followed by others. The continuation of the classic work of the Darwinian revolution in genetics is a good example of how the need for such very broad theories persists even in a science that has become very hard and very specific in hundreds of particular studies. In the social sciences, too, there is the persistent need for articulating broad, high-level, system theories with more specific findings and, secondly, for the sharp definitions and counting of particular aspects required as bases for specific and precise predictions. Moreover, intermediate generalizations—*principia media* or middle-level theories and techniques—will be needed to link the precise predictions of the relatively isolated small-scale subsystems and to make predictions of the behavior of such small-scale subsystems within the overall context of much larger systems.

We need to put together what economists and others have called microanalysis and macroanalysis. Such steps are beginning to be taken in economics. The work begun by Keynes, and since then carried on by at least a full generation of mathematical economists, has gone fairly far toward giving us a discipline in economics that can now make statements about price levels, employment levels, and currency levels for whole national economies and to some extent even for the international economy. This economic discipline also makes it possible to make statements about the behavior of firms or the behavior of consumers, of labor, and of others—both in the aggregate and for special subclasses. In political science, the most substantial effort that I know of putting together theories at these levels has been made by Harold Lasswell; in sociology Talcott Parsons has done much of this, as has, in a different style, Paul Lazarsfeld.

A DIALOGUE OF DATA AND THEORY

But what can data do in this ongoing process? A microlevel theory might deal with all the aspects of small group behavior, or of the actions of individuals or a firm. The theoretical notion that if either individuals or societies are extremely tense their value scale changes is a generalization which is not limited to the microlevel. It cuts across all system levels. It is nevertheless a narrow and specific generalization. If we can find a sharp way of defining tension and an equally sharp way of measuring value scales, then this is a simple, testable proposition: if A, then B. What could data do to this? Data could change the if–then pattern theory to "if amount x of a, then amount y of b," that is, if *how much* change in A, then *how much* change in B? It could begin to make the statements quantitative.

If a microtheory is true, certain quantitative data can be expected and certain other quantitative data ought to be excluded. If a special aspect theory—as, "if more tension, then change in values"—is true, again certain data are expectable and again certain other data are excluded. The same is true of middle-level theories: if governments behave to some extent similarly to game players following minimax strategies, then certain patterns of behavior are expectable, certain data ought to be found, and certain other data should not occur, or occur very rarely, in the cases inspected.

The same is true even of the great generalizations. Max Weber suggested that the spirit of Protestantism is closely linked to a sharp sense of accountability for money. If he was right, Protestant school children given unfinished stories which include a mention of money in the beginning of the story ought to account for what became of the money in significantly higher percentages than school children in Catholic countries. This turns out to be the case in the stories completed by several thousand school children in eleven cities. The final disposition of the money was accounted for in a majority of the stories gathered in the schools of predominantly Protestant communities, ranging from over 90 per cent in Birmingham, Stockholm, and Helsinki, down to 57 per cent in Protestant South German Karlsruhe; in predominantly Catholic cities, the money was accounted for only by a minority of the children, ranging from 47 per cent in Catholic South German Munich to about 34 per cent in San Juan, Puerto Rico, and Veracruz, Mexico.[3]

With data collections we can test such well-known theories as that of advocates of economic integration who believe that economic growth ought to be in some sense substantially promoted by market size, so that national income in countries with a larger market ought to grow more quickly. This was freely asserted in many of the discussions preceding the European Common Market. But a tabulation of growth rates in 22 countries in 1955–58, as reported by the United Nations, shows only a very low correlation—no more than —0.016—with market size.[4] Even if one should deflate the growth rate of Communist bloc countries, which were

3. Harold H. Anderson, and G. L. Anderson, "Cultural Reactions to Conflict: A Study of Adolescent Children in Seven Countries," in G. M. Gilbert, ed., *Psychological Approaches to Intergroup and International Understanding* (Austin, Texas, Hogg Foundation for Mental Hygiene, University of Texas, 1956), pp. 27–32; see also Harold H. Anderson and others, "Image of the Teacher by Adolescent Children in Four Countries: Germany, England, Mexico and the United States," *Journal of Social Psychology, 50* (August 1959), 47–55

4. See Karl W. Deutsch, "Towards Western European Integration: An Interim Assessment," *Journal of International Affairs, 16* (1962), 89–101, esp. pp. 94–95. Cf. also K. W. Deutsch and Alexander Eckstein, "National Industrialization and the Declining Share of the International Economic Sector, 1890–1959," *World Politics, 13* (1961), 267–99. Bruce Russett with Hayward R. Alker, Jr., Karl W. Deutsch, and Harold D. Lasswell, *World Handbook of Political and Social Indicators* (New Haven, Yale University Press, 1964), p. 276, find a .29 correlation between GNP and GNP per capita growth rate for 68 countries. This finding is significant at the 0.02 level, but

used as given by the United Nations, or if one excludes Communist countries altogether, there still seems to be no strong relationship between market size and growth rate. In other words, it is possible to approach a theory by asking whether and to what extent it is confirmed by data which are clearly beyond the noise level. Is it disconfirmed by data clearly beyond the noise level but incompatible with the theory, or must we go back to the Scottish verdict of "not proven," saying that the data at the moment cannot be pulled out of the noise level? It may then be possible later to get better data or to find the important discriminating variables.

There are certain classes of data which are not unique to one theory but rather are stressed by many theories. Machiavelli, in discussing with his Italian countrymen how they could make themselves free from foreign invasion, pointed out that it is very important to know whether only a few people are able and willing to fight or whether, like the Swiss, the whole population comprises a nation in arms. Machiavelli thus stressed the importance of the military participation ratio. Historians of the French Revolution and students of the process of revolution point out that the shift from less than one per cent of the people having weapons to more than five per cent serving in the armed forces is a revolutionary shift. Similarly, Andrzejewski, in his recent sociological study of military organization and society, makes the military participation ratio one of three key variables for his typology.[5] If we knew the level of military participation found in certain societies at certain times, and if we could

---

only accounts for less than 9 per cent of the total variance observed. While investigating the direction and strength of relationship between Gross National Product and the rate of growth of Gross National Product ($r = -.016$, as reported above) in our sample of 22 countries, we also computed Pearsonian correlation coefficients to test the direction and strength of relationship between: (1) per capita GNP and 1955–1958 rate of growth of per capita GNP ($r = -.553$); (2) GNP and per capita GNP ($r = -.407$); (3) GNP and the rate of growth of per capita GNP ($r = .173$); and (4) the rate of growth of per capita GNP and the rate of growth of GNP ($r = .790$). These results confirm the particularly weak relationship between GNP, and hence market size, and economic growth.

5. Cf. S. Andrzejewski, *Military Organization and Society* (London, Routledge and Kegan Paul, 1954).

get, therefore, a sharp rank ordering of societies the world over at one and the same time, and then eventually of one and the same society at different times in its evolution in terms of the military participation ratio, this information would be useful for the evaluation of several important theories from the past and possibly for the construction of a new one.[6]

The same would be true of per capita income. This was clearly of interest, at least implicitly, to Adam Smith when he talked of the wealth of nations. It was of interest to Karl Marx; it was of interest to Charles Beard and to Colin Clark; it was important to Kenneth Galbraith and to Gunnar Myrdal. It is by now a household concept. Aggregate national income, which therefore is per capita income times population size, is of similar importance for theorists of market size such as Hollis Chenery and many others.[7]

Literacy is a key variable, insofar as it indicates educa tional levels. This is true not only for historians of the Refor mation but also for theories of communication like those of Daniel Lerner and Lucian Pye; and it was important earlier for Jean Jacques Rousseau and for Thomas Jefferson.

We find, in other words, that both modern theorists and classical theorists explicitly or implicitly are interested in similar variables. The *World Handbook of Political and Social Indicators* by Bruce M. Russett and his associates has about seventy of these variables, each of which is to some extent involved in several theories, either classically formulated or popularly asserted, about social development. We might now specify what contingencies or correlations each theory predicts. What range of data would confirm the theory; what range of data would clearly disconfirm it? What range of data would remain within the undecided level? In the United States at this time, both Harold Lass-

6. This rank ordering is now available in Russett et al., *World Handbook*, pp. 74–78.

7. Hollis B. Chenery, "Patterns of Industrial Growth," *American Economic Review, 50* (1964), 624–54; Charles P. Kindleberger, *Foreign Trade and the National Economy* (New Haven, Yale University Press, 1962).

well and I have felt that we are theory-rich and data-poor. This is different from other periods as, for instance, in the late 1920s when economists were beginning to become embarrassingly rich in data about business cycles (indefatigably compiled by Wesley Mitchell and his associates) at a time when they were still poor in theory. The accumulation of the needed data will enable us to put engines or numbers into some of the great theoretical edifices of our time.

Let me give an example. Talcott Parsons has been accused of having produced mainly a filing system, a taxonomic system. The history of biology, however, shows that from static taxonomy to a dynamic theory of evolution there is a very clear sequence of steps, and that trying to get an efficient taxonomy is by no means an unworthy contribution to the development of a social science. But we see now the next steps and eventually we ought to be able to put numbers to every pattern variable Parsons has considered important. He pays a good deal of attention, for example, to such pattern variables as ascription versus achievement motivation or expectations in societies.[8] David McClelland's effort to use content analysis to measure the achievement motive often gives a direct opportunity for putting a number into this particular box of the Parsonian system.[9] If it turns out that any one of Parsons' pattern variables cannot be given a number, however, we ought to know why not, and then we may find out either whether anything is wrong with this aspect of the theory or whether there is any peculiarity in this particular aspect of human behavior.

Parsons also has a very basic notion of the fundamental functions of every political system, which are described as

8. Cf. Talcott Parsons, *The Social System* (Glencoe, Ill., Free Press, 1951) ; *The Structure of Social Action* (New York, McGraw-Hill, 1937) ; Parsons and Neil E. Smelser, *Economy and Society* (Glencoe, Ill., Free Press, 1956) ; and also Parsons and Edward A. Shils, eds., *Toward a General Theory of Action* (Cambridge, Harvard University Press, 1951). See also Parsons' introduction to Max Weber's *The Theory of Social and Economic Organization*, trans. A. M. Henderson and Talcott Parsons (Glencoe, Ill., Free Press, 1947).

9. David C. McClelland, *The Achieving Society* (Princeton, Van Nostrand, 1961).

pattern maintenance, adaptation, goal attainment, and integration. It might be worthwhile to try to find out whether one can define these categories in operational terms sharp enough so that, for instance, in the analysis of budgets—of families, of governments, of time, of individuals—or in the analysis of symbol flow and communications, one could say how much at a given time and place goes to each of these four basic functions, and what societies, systems, political organizations, or cultural groups shift between these functions and in what direction. Parsons does postulate interchanges between the subsystems, primarily serving in particular functions. He assumes, for example, that the economy of a society primarily represents the adaptive subsystem of a society to nature; the government in many cases represents the goal-attaining subsystem; families or households represent largely pattern-maintenance systems; and churches and educational machinery in the cultural world represent the integrative subsystem.

Between these four subsystems there are four flows of interchanges involving altogether 24 channels. It ought not to be too difficult eventually, as this system gets worked out, to make quantitative statements as to what is going on, for instance, in the interchanges between households and the political system; the interchanges between households and the economy have been quantified and studied by economists already. What begins as a verbal system thus turns out at a later stage to become a series of injunctions to get numbers. As the numbers come in, however, the verbal system will have to be restated and developed; and we may then see whether this system still survives, or whether it has to be adapted, or whether it turns out to be unworkable.

In a similar sense, we may think of what to me is a particularly useful contribution to political analysis: Harold Lasswell's success in condensing the vast and variegated collection of human values into eight broad categories of value orientation—power, enlightenment, wealth, well-being, skill, affection, respect, and rectitude or righteousness. These are broad categories, but they can be defined fairly sharply.

In content analysis, both between countries or for the same source over time (we should like to do this, for instance, from samples of the London *Times* since 1770), it might be possible to show how value orientations in a culture have changed. One can do this, of course, with much more narrow and special symbols. A preliminary survey of American party platforms traces the disappearance of the word *property* from the language of American party platforms of both major parties.[10] We find, in other words, shifts in symbol orientations; we can put numbers into these schemes, and the schemes will have evoked and begotten the numbers by calling for them.

Just as the theorists will evoke and demand numbers, the correlations and configurations of data may in turn evoke new theories. What theory, old or new, will make sense of a given constellation or configuration of data as it emerges from the evidence? Which theory can supply a context for the recognition of related matters, and for the extrapolation of a found pattern from a known range of phenomena into the unknown, the past, the unexplored part of the present, or into the future?

The actual process will most likely turn out to resemble a dialogue. I would agree with the point made by Carl Friedrich in warning against possible overemphasis on hypothesis testing.[11] Friedrich argues that it is often better to get your data with a very loosely held preliminary hypothesis of relevance, listen to them very carefully and receptively, and only then formulate your hypothesis to be tested sharply at a later stage. In the dialogue between theories and data, a premature closure, a too sharply formulated hypothesis which must be tested—and if it does not come out the whole operation is considered unsuccessful—is quite likely to mislead.

Possibly the most fruitful approach would be, first, to try to think of not one hypothesis to be tested, but immediately of that hypothesis and its reverse. It is surprising how many

10. Student research, M.I.T., 1956–58, unpublished.
11. See Chap. 3 in this volume

hypotheses will sound equally plausible in reverse. An example is Ernst Haas' theory of the "spill-overs": if two countries have merged one functional activity, they will find it necessary in the near future to merge other activities.[12] If we generalize this, we may say that if any two politically connected countries, cities, suburbs, or other political units have merged one functional service, there can be three alternative results. One would be the spill-over or reinforcement theory: if they have got tangled up in one functional tional arrangements. The second would be a disenchantment theory: if they have got tangled up in one functional merger which has been disappointing to them, they will become markedly less likely to get caught a second time. The third would be an indifference theory: previous functional arrangements will make no significant difference to the probability of future functional arrangements.

Three ranges of data correspond to these three conceivable theories. If the frequency of agreements is markedly higher among countries or cities which have already made one agreement, the spill-over hypothesis will seem confirmed; if the frequency of agreements is markedly lower, the disenchantment theory will appear to hold; if the frequency of agreements makes no difference, the indifference theory would seem to be endorsed. It turns out that among four hundred suburbs in the Philadelphia area, each of these theories holds for certain classes of agreements.[13]

Not only single hypotheses but families of hypotheses can be generated when you try to formulate all logical alternatives. By changing the assumptions you might still open an extra bin, a "thirteenth sorting bin," so to speak, where data are put that do not fit any one of the theories that were thought of in advance. And there will quite often be such

12. Ernst Haas, *The Uniting of Europe* (Stanford, Stanford University Press, 1958)

13. Philip E. Jacob and others, University of Pennsylvania Program for Studies of Social Values and Public Policy, Nos. 1–10 (Philadelphia, 1962–63). It seems that sewage mixes successfully among several municipalities but school children do not; having made a sewage agreement predisposes pairs of municipalities to make other agreements, although school agreements do not work that way.

data that do not fit. Sometimes the hypothesis which came out of data will include the scale effect, for instance. I do not think there are very many explicit advance theories of the scale effect, that is, the effect of *size* of an organization on its political behavior or on the behavior of its members. They emerge to some extent from experience. In the end we may hope to get either completely new theories or improved reformulations of older ones.

What is the nature of data that we can most hopefully expect to use for this dialogue between data and theories? Four kinds seem in the forefront at the moment. The first are *aggregative data,* the kind of data which in the first approximation one can get out of libraries and statistical offices. These are census statistics, economic and trade statistics, price statistics, budget data, and voting data. All these are public and, to some extent, the task of gathering these data has already been done by governmental or private institutions for purposes of their own. The task of the scholar then is first to find out something of the bias in the selection, the probable error margins, the inaccuracies, and the possibility of supplementing these data; but the main intellectual effort has then to be spent upon the analysis of the data which are already gathered. Many of the nineteenth century political and social theories in the grand manner were built up with the help of such data, such as Werner Sombart's hypothesis of the declining importance of foreign trade with industrial development and economic growth, a thesis which now seems to be confirmed long after Sombart's time.[14]

The second type are *sample survey data* which have given us a whole world of new evidence and, in addition, a major tool for closing the gaps in the aggregative data.[15] Sample surveys are divided into the polling techniques of

14. Werner Sombart, *Die Deutsche Volkswirtschaft im neunzehnten Jahrhundert* (3d ed. Berlin, Bondi, 1913). See also note 7 above.

15. By now, in turn, the census offices have learned the art of using the sample survey. The United States census office is using samples for certain figures, and the Indian statistical office uses a 25,000 family sample for many important points. Quite often private sample surveys can be used to ask questions that governments for political reasons do not wish to ask. The Indian government, for instance, does not ask questions about caste since officially it is already unimportant; as caste does make a difference in the

asking a very few questions of very many people, and the depth surveys where very few people are asked many questions in series of interviews which may stretch over fifteen hours.[16]

The third type of data stem from *content analysis,* as discussed above.

Finally there are the *cultural data* which cultural anthropologists or the perceptive literary scholar can uncover. The configurations of symbols, the configurations of cultures are examples, and so are the psychiatrist's evidence, the anthropologist's evidence, the evidence of the student of literature.

Several other needs are apparent. One is the need for the systematic correlation of these data. We do not even know, for instance, how well the Adorno F-scale correlates with the Minnesota Personality Inventory. We suffer from the curse of enforced originality which makes it a crime for a graduate student to replicate somebody else's experiment and forces the unhappy man to think up a new wrinkle on every experiment. I wish we could get an interuniversity agreement that we expect everybody who earns a degree to do two things: first, to replicate honestly one experiment in social science and then, if he must, invent a new one. If physicists and chemists had not replicated each other's experiments, they would still be in the age of alchemy.

Just as we do not have replication, we do not have intercorrelation among different tests. There is, for instance, very little correlation between what appears in government statistics and what is found in sample surveys, although such work is now being begun. For a sample of Turkish voters, for example, the researcher usually takes the government's statistics as a yardstick for knowing whether his sample was correctly drawn. It may be that the sample was right in the first place and the government statistics were wrong. But we

---

practice of politics, we must depend on private surveys to get this information.

16. E.g. in Robert E. Lane, *Political Ideology* (New York, Free Press, 1962).

will not know when a particular country's official statistics are inaccurate, deliberately or not, until we have sampled about 50 countries and compared these sample data with the aggregative data in the statistical yearbooks.

We need to know more than we do now about the relationship between the few questions answered on mass surveys and the many questions answered on depth interviews. For instance, we have some questions asked about anti-Semitism in Germany on mass surveys, and some attempts to make depth studies of anti-Semites; we also have similar materials for the United States. But I have not seen a systematic attempt to correlate the number or percentage of "off-the-cuff" anti-Semitic answers given on a quick survey with deep-seated anti-Semitic attitudes as revealed in a depth interview. The same, of course, is true of all ethnic and race prejudices and discrimination. It is conceivable that people who give superficially a prejudiced answer on a survey may only be conformists, and less than half of them may actually have deep-seated racial prejudices. Although the political and social implications are very large, we do not yet know very much about these processes.[17]

Similarly we do not know what the correlation is between attitudes given by opinion surveys and attitudes revealed in content analysis. If we knew for ten countries, which had both surveys and mass media, whether and to what extent a frequency of achievement aspiration symbols in samples of elite communications is correlated with achievement aspiration or achievement needs revealed in depth interviews among this elite, then we could make at least some guesses for ten other countries where we have only content analysis but no surveys.

And we do not know yet what the correlation is between a cultural pattern—for instance, of a Weberian "Protestant spirit" or an African *négritude*—and particular, measurable

17. A fascinating theory by Merton says it depends mainly on what is defined as conforming behavior at the time and place where the survey is made, but we do not know figures or have any numbers on this. See Robert K. Merton, *Social Theory and Social Structure* (Glencoe, Ill., Free Press, 1957).

traits emerging in content analyses. It may turn out, for instance, that there is no discoverable difference between the distribution of symbols in the communications of Leopold Senghor of Senegal, who is an exponent of cultural *négritude,* and those of the average educated French radical.

STATISTICAL TECHNIQUES AND DISTRIBUTIONS

One of the easiest things to be done—it can be done without machines, but must have loving care—is to get the rank order distribution of several variables. This already will begin to give us, oddly enough, a style of thought and some political implications. We may think of the 100 or more nations of the world as a fascinating multitude. If we rank order them by population, however, it turns out that more than one half of mankind lives under four governments. Eventually we shall have two tables (see Table 2.1) for each rank order profile. The first table should be for all the units for which we have data. The second table should be for a standardized ensemble of units, including, let us say, all countries in the United Nations as well as those which have been proposed seriously for membership and would be in the United Nations had not some other member nation vetoed their membership. This would bring in for statistical purposes West Germany, the East German regime, North and South Korea, mainland China, and possibly others. A universe of 133 countries with effectively operating governments would enable us to eliminate from consideration many of the small units which clutter up the statistics and distort the rank order and which, more seriously, greatly distort the median and average values of the distribution. As Table 2.1 suggests, we cut greatly the median and average values for many series by inflating the number of units from 133 to 218.

Using a standardized set of units has operational importance. If we can make world leaders and social scientists aware of the fact that, for example, half of the world's population is in four countries, then they may realize that international agreements among perhaps eight or ten of the most populous countries will go far toward adequate coverage for atomic test bans or for international economic cooperation or for getting rid of a great deal of slavery and of racial peonage or race discrimination.

Often the political, social, and educational tasks of the world become different in definition once you think of them; the same is true of intracountry variations. In the days when Britain wanted to point out that India could not be independent, it was a favorite device of language surveys to say that India had 212 languages and dialects. On closer inspection it turns out that almost 200 of these are lesser known dialects on the Tibet–Burma border, with little or no political and economic significance, and that something like 80 or 90 per cent of the Indian people are covered by fourteen languages. Fourteen languages are still a handful, but they are a good deal fewer than two hundred. Now we are getting statement after statement that an African country has

TABLE 2.1. WORLD POPULATION (1961)

		Universe of 218 Countries		Standardized List of 133 Countries	
Rank	*Country*	*Population (in millions)*	*As per cent of total*	*Population (in millions)*	*As per cent of total*
1	China (M)	694	22.7%	694	22.8%
2	India	442	14.4	442	14.5
3	U.S.S.R.	218	7.1	218	7.2
4	U.S.	184	6.0	184	6.1
			50.2%		50.6%
Remaining Countries		1521	49.8	1503	49.4
	Total	3059	100.0%	3041	100.0%
	Mean	13.9		22.9	
	Median	1.6		5.5	

Source: Bruce M. Russett et al., *World Handbook of Political and Social Indicators* (New Haven, Yale University Press, 1964), pp. 18–21; and data in the files of the Yale Political Data Program.

twenty or thirty native languages or dialects. Upon investigation of frequency distributions it usually turns out that four to six languages cover more than one half the population, and that bilingualism is often present. Considerations of this sort shed light upon such important problems as the extent to which elementary education should be offered in the mother tongue rather than an alien language.

To be more precise, we would like to know what the actual mathematical shape of such rank order curves are, or rather what mathematical model will fit which curve most closely—the Zipf distribution, for example, the Yule distribution, or others.[18] If we can find a mathematical distribution which fits a set of phenomena fairly closely, we can perhaps interpolate some rough estimates of the figures for the countries for which we have no data. Alternatively, we can check whether particular countries are genuine deviants, or whether they have unusually imaginative statisticians, or whether the figure given happened to be just a misprint.

Finally, just as we should have one record or profile for all units as well as for the standardized universe of 133 countries, we also need a cumulative summation. This could be obtained for each variable by first ranking the countries in order of the variable, but then computing for each such rank order profile how many of the world's population are at or above each point as we go down the range of that particular variable. This is essentially the same as correlating each variable with population. The same procedure could then be followed for the cumulative percentages of the total amount of the specific variable covered by that particular rank order profile. Thus, in ranking countries in order of the ratio of foreign trade to Gross National Product, one computation should show how many per cent of the world's people live in countries whose foreign trade is at least, say, 35 per cent of their GNP, and another computation should show how many

18. For a recent discussion of some other politically relevant aspects of the Zipf distribution and its close fit to certain communication data, see Richard L. Merritt, "Distance and Interaction Among Political Communities," in *General Systems Yearbook, 9* (1964), 255–63.

per cent of world exports are represented by this class of countries. A good mathematical and/or graphic method for presenting such relationships ought to be feasible and would tell us a great deal.[19]

Another way of looking at the distributions would be to get the geographic distribution of transactions both between countries and within countries. This would immediately permit us to test certain hypotheses. For instance, it is Myrdal's hypothesis that the national state is a major instrument for reducing intracountry inequalities, whereas it is the theory of Lenin that an empire is precisely the opposite, an engine for exacerbating and increasing intracountry differences between exploiting and exploited areas. It ought not to be too difficult, as we get enough data on intracountry variations, to find out whether on the whole most countries in the world now correspond more to Myrdal's model or to Lenin's model, or which model fits which countries best.

We could also find out more about the distribution of variables over time. We know, for example, that intracountry differences in most advanced countries have been declining. We suspect that, at least between 1900 and 1960, intercountry differences have been increasing. We may find out, therefore, in many different ways, what an "alien," or alienated, political relationship is—that is, a relationship where variations, on the whole, seem to follow the regularities observed in international life; and what a national and integrative political community is, a community where the distribution of variables follows more regularly the patterns observed in modern advanced national states. This would give us a statistical definition of alienated communities or of deeply or fundamentally divided communities.

We could get other distributions. For instance, Alker and Russett have done very important and helpful work comparing systematically available techniques for the measurement

19. A beginning has been made in Russett et al., *World Handbook of Political and Social Indicators*, by stating for each of 75 variables the percentage of the relevant world population covered by the table, and then presenting the quartiles of the "table population" alongside the rank order profile.

of inequality used by certain statisticians—the Gini index, the Schutz coefficient, and others.[20] It ought to be one of the services of the Yale Political Data Program to provide what might be called "translation tables" between the precise measurements of the social scientist who has to keep his value commitment in the background (or who must, though he has values, be willing to make his evidence available to anyone, including those whose value commitments are different from his own) and the language of action, the language that the legislator or the public servant might understand, for instance, about the inequality of land tenure, or the inequality of legislative and electoral apportionment between districts.

Here again we can interpolate. If we know, for instance, the income shares for nine countries and distribute these among the different deciles of income from top to bottom, we can draw a Lorenz curve for each of these countries. In a Lorenz curve we measure vertically the per cent of incomes and horizontally the per cent of population. If every per cent of population received exactly the same per cent of income, the resulting plot would be a straight line at forty-five degrees. If, in fact, the poor get a smaller share and the rich a larger one, the Lorenz curve will look more or less curved; the greater the inequality, the steeper the curvature of the resulting "boomerang." Even if we have only ten, or four, or three points—if really out of luck, only one or two—we could still fit a Lorenz curve to the few points we have, knowing that there could be a flattening in the middle indicating that the curve was wrong by a definite but moderate amount.

We could therefore arrive at estimates of inequality and, in addition, comparisons of the estimates of inequality between many different countries. In one country we will be told how much land the top one per cent of landholders own, and in the second country we will get the figure for the top five per cent; in the third country, for the top two-and-one-half per cent. By drawing Lorenz curves for all these countries we can arrive at estimated values, knowing that they carry error margins of some size; nevertheless, we can make

20. See Chap. 16 in this volume.

what previously were incomparable figures a great deal more comparable than they were before.

We can then go on from distribution functions to paired correlations. We can ask, first of all, if the overall correlations are significant or not. We can then ask for two quite different but related things which should be given in a standard manner: one number saying how *accidental* the correlation is, and a second number saying how *strong* it is. This is particularly important with small numbers. If you toss a coin twice and it comes up heads twice, the strength of the relationship, in a certain sense, is one hundred per cent; that is to say, if you assume that the coin is loaded in the direction of heads and it came up heads twice, you predict a very strong load. But since you have actually made only two tosses of the coin, the statistical significance of what you did is fairly low, and you may be dealing in fact with a perfectly true coin.

Quite often these two descriptions of correlations are confused. Some studies give the significance level of the findings but do not indicate for how many per cent of the observed variation the findings actually account. It is quite possible to have a factor which is based on so many cases that it is significant almost beyond peradventure of a doubt. Only once in a thousand times would you get such a factor by chance; nevertheless, this factor may account for no more than ten per cent—or even for only two per cent—of the observed variation in the outcome. This is quite different from another factor which is significant only at the five or ten per cent level but which, if it exists at all, would explain thirty or forty per cent of the outcome. We do not as yet have a highly satisfactory standardized system of notation for reporting such data.

We may find that the correlation between two variables is nonlinear and is different for different parts of the range of one of them. As numbers increase, the slope of the regression may change sharply. Thus, if one of the two correlated variables is income, it may be that among the poor, correlation is very weak; among the rich, it is very strong; and somewhere in the middle, it is about even. There may be many paired variables where the correlation varies over parts of the range. In fact, there may be thresholds, there may be step functions, so that eventually we will want to know a great deal about these pairs.

In the *World Handbook of Political and Social Indicators* alone, with its 75 variables, 2,775 pairs can be generated. Clearly, not all pairs will be of interest. A computer can be programmed to pick out only those pairs with statistical significance at the five or ten per cent level. We might even ask the computer to rank the correlations by statistical significance and also by the strength of relationships; we might then extract all those correlations that are high on both counts and go through them a second time, to see which correlations are predicted by what theories. We will therefore eventually match the correlations against propositional inventories such as the series proposed by Harold Lasswell. If in the near future we can prepare a punch card for every numbered proposition in *Power and Society*[21] as well as a number or card for every proposition in Paul Lazarfeld's voting studies,[22] then eventually we shall find which correlations are predictable by means of what theories, models, and data. This is possible only in the future because it will involve working out matching criteria for testing verbal predictions by quantitative data. Eventually we shall be able to build some three-way correlations as, for instance, of literacy and income with political stability. Clearly, however, we cannot grind out all possible triplets on a computer; the number becomes too high. But we shall find possibly a few dozen which are of particular interest.

So far I have spoken only of deterministic statistics; I have treated all these figures as given. We might eventually want to know something more about probability distributions. If we use the full range of variance, we begin to take in

21. Harold D. Lasswell and Abraham Kaplan, *Power and Society: A Framework for Political Inquiry* (New Haven, Yale University Press, 1950).

22. Paul F. Lazarsfeld et al., *The People's Choice: How the Voter Makes Up His Mind in a Presidential Campaign* (2d ed. New York, Columbia University Press, 1948); Bernard R. Berelson et al., *Voting: A Study of Opinion Formation in a Presidential Campaign* (Chicago, University of Chicago Press, 1954).

the deviant cases; we shall be able to make more full use of standard deviations and of extreme values that occur more rarely in the same distribution. We shall therefore find out what the distribution of phenomena is. Eventually we can induce theorists to pay more attention to the following paradox: If an outcome depends on the presence of several conditions, or on the completion of several actions or stages, or on many repeated trials, then this overall outcome may be improbable, even though every component condition, action, or stage is highly probable in and by itself. It may be dangerous, therefore, to concentrate only on the central tendencies of each statistic (assuming that the statistics include all the factors we are interested in), even if they are all distributed in well-peaked standard distributions. Thus, if it would take seven mutually independent elements to produce an outcome, and each element had a 90 per cent probability of being present at the average number, then the resulting likelihood of the outcome would be .9 to the seventh power, which is less than one half. The matter can be put conversely. If each of the component conditions or stages has a probability distribution such that it could produce a relatively rare outcome, or take an extreme value once in, say, ten, or a hundred, or a thousand times, then the likelihood that at least one of these rare outcomes will occur in at least one of the component conditions or stages will increase with the number of components, or with the number of repeated trials, in the system with which we are concerned.

Let me repeat: if many conditions or factors are needed for an outcome, even a very high probability of every component still yields a relatively low probability for the final outcome. This is, I would say, a mathematically crude statistical formulation of Carl Friedrich's suggestion to expect in politics the unexpected. More sophisticated work on "extreme values" in statistics has been done by the mathematician E. J. Gumbel.[23] With many different factors, all of which have strongly marked central tendencies, we must expect with reasonably high probability that at least one of

23. Emil J. Gumbel, *Statistics of Extremes* (New York, Columbia University Press, 1960).

the factors present in every concrete situation will have a deviant value rather than a central one.

We will need time series. Here I would suggest that we develop a standard way of describing all time series, by trying to compress every time series into at least four standard components. The first component would be the trend, which is an average trend usually over time. Second is the variance distribution around the trend, and, in the third place, there is a cyclical component. Very often there are fluctuations and it is often possible to model these fluctuations as a simple wave motion or a combination of two or more wave motions. Think, for instance, of economic growth, which is a clear trend but which is modified by regional variance as well as by a business cycle fluctation with a fairly marked periodicity in certain times of history. And finally, the fourth component is the stochastic component, which is a random process superimposed on the whole series.

If we could get a standard system of notations for these four components, it would give us a more sophisticated model than the nineteenth-century scientists had, who only tried to find either trends or cycles and felt terribly bold if they combined the two. We could then get alternative models for contingencies and for the overall output. What is the general pattern that we find at a particular time and place? What are the deviant cases to be expected? We have some such models. Keynes' model emphasized savings and investment. Anatol Rapoport tried to divide many international conflicts into fights which could be modeled on Richardsonian equations, games which could be modeled on rational decisions according to von Neumann and Morgenstern, and debates which would involve mind or attitude changes and which could be modeled on the theories of students of semantics and communication and persuasion processes.[24] In my own work, I have tried to develop simple flow models for national assimilation, differentiation, and social mobilization. These are all highly simplified models, trying to provide, nevertheless, an overall picture of some particular process with predictions of the quality, direction, and, if possible, the speed and size of some output

24. Rapoport, *Fights, Games, and Debates.*

function. When we have such models and others, we will need computer programs that can be shared for dealing with them.

One of the dangers of the sociology of social science arises at this point. As every cobbler resents the competition of factory-made shoes, so too every hand-loom weaver dislikes power looms, and almost every historian resents the idea that a social scientist should pick up his book, find a fact in it, and use it for a social science theory. The historian feels that he is being degraded to the level of an instrument. Similarly the man who has done the actual interviewing resents the coder who simplifies the subtleties of the interviews; the coders are slightly jealous of the people who write up the findings of the survey because the coders think they know much more about the details of these findings; and the person who has written the survey resents the man who is trying to compare ten surveys, because how can a man who tries to compare ten surveys understand the infinite subtleties of every one of them? By the same token, the man who runs a computer program for making rank order profiles will try every six months to change it a little. He will also try to develop the program in such a way as to fit only his unique IBM 709 Model DZ, so that it will take about three days and $700 to adapt it to the next IBM 709 with another subscript; and many of his colleagues elsewhere will do likewise. This seems to be part of the sociology and economics of intellectual work; partly it may be human playfulness; and it also seems to promise making almost every programmer indispensable.

Despite these ubiquitous tendencies toward fencing in every little plot of knowledge, we must try to make such knowledge much more freely and impersonally transferable if the computer age is to reach its full potential in the fields of social science. We need to work out nationally or internationally a certain set of minimum basic routines for people who want to use computers for matrix analysis, for simulation, for rank order profiles, for latent structure analysis, for correlations.

Eventually the day will come when computers will be used for pattern combination, for initiating new techniques of analysis in social science, so that we can use the computer not as a substitute for the scholar but as a partner—as a partner not only for the drudgery but even as a partner in the work of imagination and discovery.

To accomplish all this, perhaps we should follow the example of the United States Air Force in World War II. It waged a permanent war against the designers who would have so endlessly improved fighter planes that they would never have gone into production. The Air Force said that, after all, their pilots needed planes and not drawings; and so they froze the P-38 fighter at a certain moment saying, "Now, let's get this show on the road!" Only after a period of production did they again permit design changes. We ought to agree that every three or five years we would change the basic computer routines, but the demands of dissemination militate against the demands of constant computer improvement.

THE CONTRIBUTION OF DATA PROGRAMS TO THE STYLE OF THOUGHT

How does all this apply to the policy-maker in education, in economic development, in local self-government, to the hundred and one ways in which social science is used for the improvement of human affairs? Refinements in data collection and analysis may help him to pinpoint more sharply the information actually needed. What information is worth looking for because it makes a real difference to the expectable outcome? What information is marginal? Such refinements may tell him what to expect if we have massive amounts of data for cross-national profiles for the world, and a rich sample of intracountry variations for many different nations. The policy-maker would know much better what kind of variability to expect and how it may be correlated with other variables—income groups, age groups, skill levels, and so on. The policy-maker might then know which variables are more likely to respond to manipulation. We can then help him to raise the question of *how to preserve the capacities of his own acting system,* including its capacities for learning and for choice, which might be even more important to him than the mere question of how to manipulate one or another aspect of his environment.[21]

This, as you notice, leads to a general style of thought, a style of thought that asks how much? how soon? how likely? with what deviations? with what variance and variability? how much would it take at what time to change what aspects of reality? If we can ask these questions, then we may find that this era of data will do for social science what the development of the microscope did for medicine, or what the development of particle experimentation did for physics. I think we are on the threshold of an age of basic reorientation.

The coming of the computer has vastly increased both the demand for mathematicians and the demand for a general level of mathematical competence among broader sectors of society; that is, both the distribution of mathematical skill and its concentration in certain individuals have become more necessary to social science. The coming of data programs, like the coming of the computer, will have a similar effect in human society at large.

It is important to stress the perspective of a living dialogue between theory and data, and also between raw data and their statistical and mathematical processing and analysis. Data are not dead and buried. In the days when chemicals were kept labeled in museums we had cabinets of curiosities. When chemicals were put into laboratories and used we got chemistry. So long as data are thought of as reposing in archives, and the custodians of these archives think of themselves as librarians—and if possible as librarians of rare medieval books which can only be let out with infinite caution—we will not have much in the way of social science. As we make social science data as freely reproducible and as readily available as elementary chemicals are available to chemists, as we get the social science data into the laboratories, and as our data archives and repositories become linked with data laboratories, we shall witness, I believe, a renaissance of social science.

21. On some theoretical aspects of this problem, see Karl W. Deutsch, *The Nerves of Government* (New York, Free Press, 1963).

3. Some General Theoretical Reflections on the Problems of Political Data

CARL J. FRIEDRICH, HARVARD UNIVERSITY

It is perhaps banal to remind oneself at the outset that many data relative to politics are not quantitative data. To illustrate, the typology of forms of government, though vital, is inherently qualitative, even when combined with a quantitative dimension: when the ancients spoke of the rule of the one, the few, or the many, they raised quantitative problems, and put a quantitative proposition in the center of their typology. But when Plato insisted that asking how many was not enough (which Herodotus shows to have been conventional wisdom), and that we must also ask whether those who rule do so according to sacred tradition (*nomos*), he raised an issue of qualitative import which no quantitative inquiry could ever hope to cope with. Yet both of these inquiries are obviously decisive for the typology.

Contemporary parallels come readily to mind—what is the foreign policy of country X and how it might be improved may involve some quantitative data, but the core of the problem is not of this order. Such an account might say that countries Y and Z are friends whereas A and B are enemies, that X's manpower is less skilled and its weapons less effective than those of A, that its government is badly organized and slow to arrive at decisions, etc. But some of these propositions contain a quantitative dimension, and skillful analysis will depend upon the successful blending and balancing of qualitative and quantitative data. Someone might argue, however, that each of the seemingly qualitative data may be analyzed into quantitative components, that "friendship," for example, is a cover for certain types of acts and that these acts or behavior patterns, when identified, may be subjected to quantitative data processing. This is true enough, but it merely shifts the focal points: the acts as identified have now become the "qualitative" givens which are being counted.

In short, how quality and quantity are combined depends upon the nature of the problem. Take the role of ideology in a totalitarian system as another concretization: one speech of Stalin or some pages from Hitler's *Table Talk* may tell more about this problem than a hundred newspaper clippings or a thousand interviews. Indeed, the quantitative data may engender a false sense of certainty. The old gag about the facilities for misrepresentation which statistics provide may apply here. Yet, it would be a mistake to rule out the quantitative as irrelevant. A word count type of content analysis of Soviet newspapers may be very significant and provide highly suggestive data for a working hypothesis on the shifting emphasis and the consequent role of totalitarian ideology.

Indeed, it is rather striking how many promising paths for quantitative inquiry remain unexplored. In a recent work on general theory [1] I have pointed out quite a few of these potential roads of inquiry. Thus on the subject of rulership, after developing a comprehensive typology of "systems of rule," I pointed out that "the degree of general consent is evidently very significant for the analysis of rule." [2] (I use the term "general consent" for "consensus" due to systematic considerations.) Such a proposition obviously calls for quantitative specification, like all propositions about "degrees" of relations. Thus I wrote:

1. Carl J. Friedrich, *Man and His Government: An Empirical Theory of Politics* (New York, McGraw-Hill, 1963), pp. 145, 176, 190, 209, 362 and throughout.
2. Ibid., p. 189.

> There would appear here the need for some effective quantification. If all human energies present in a certain populace are of the magnitude E, and those energies needed for nonpolitical purposes by x, the amount available for consenting to the political order will be $E—x$. The energy of each individual in the populace being e^n, likewise his energy available for support of the system of rule would be $e^n - x^n$. Of any determinate number of individuals it can be said that a minority of them may expend so large a part of their energy on supporting the government that the sum of this energy exceeds the sum of energy expended by a majority which might be available for another type of activity.[3]

This set of interrelated hypotheses obviously calls for effective quantification in order to test its validity.

The long-range importance of quantification and of the mathematical equations which it presupposes has unfortunately been obscured by the tendency to make exaggerated claims on its behalf. Proceeding upon the mistaken belief that such quantitative data are more "scientific" than other data, some of the protagonists of the use of such methods of inquiry have even advanced the claim that the study of politics will only be truly a science when all of its propositions are cast into such quantitative form. It can be confidently predicted that, if that is true, politics never will be a science. As the introductory illustrations given above indicate, there are large ranges of problems in politics which are inaccessible to quantitative analysis. Indeed, some highly significant areas such as past human experience in politics—in short the entire historic dimension—are beyond such analysis. Should we therefore disregard it? Extreme claims on the score of the "scientific" value of quantitative data are limiting, rather than broadening, the scientific, empirical basis of politics. In many areas of inquiry they describe marginal rather than central phenomena. This is due to the need of mechanical models which quantification presupposes.

In spite of the constant use of the term "mechanism" for

3. Ibid., p. 190.

describing aspects of the political order, the mechanical features are rather limited in scope. In many political situations mechanical aspects are nonetheless present, and it is useful to study these as thoroughly as possible in quantitative terms. Many problematic situations will become more manageable once the mechanical aspects are known and can therefore be "bracketed out." If these aspects or factors can be handled by appropriate techniques, including computer techniques, the remaining nonquantitative aspects may be evaluated with a higher degree of confidence. The process is similar to that in modern medicine. The many tests, mechanical and other, which the patient is subjected to and which provide the diagnostician with objective data for his analysis, do not eliminate the need for but assist in the empirical grounding of scientific diagnosis.

In a recent paper, Bruce M. Russett subjected a general proposition of de Tocqueville to certain quantitative tests.[4] These tests, while highly interesting, led him to "conclusions" which are more uncertain and tentative than the original proposition which was to be tested by them. In that sense, they serve as a striking illustration of the limited value of such "tests." I do not believe that many critical readers will feel more certain about the generalization taken from the work of de Tocqueville in light of the data presented by Russett than they did before. What Alexis de Tocqueville had written was: "Remove the secondary causes that have produced the great convulsions of the world and you will almost always find the principle of inequality at the bottom." [5] Relating this thought to land tenure, and especially its concentration in relatively few hands, chronic political instability is said to be the result of such concentration of landed property. This proposition the author undertakes to buttress by the exploration of accessible quantitative data. But what is perhaps even more important, certain other his-

4. Bruce M. Russett, "Inequality and Instability: The Relation of Land Tenure to Politics," *World Politics, 16* (1964), 442–54.

5. Alexis de Tocqueville, *Democracy in America, 2* (New York, Vintage, 1954), 266.

torical and nonquantitative data might have done more to "prove" the proposition—in the sense of making it more probable. For "proving" in such fields as politics and medicine typically means "making more probable," and hence the logic of probability judgments is essential to scientific proof here. The author's own data only provide such probability judgments. His "conclusions" are all stated in such terms—and I believe rightly and necessarily. The correlations he develops show some degree of probability. Thus we read: "Nevertheless, even the strongest relationship found among these variables leaves over half the variance 'unexplained.'" And as for the relation of stability to a democratic regime, we hear that in spite of some support for the generalization, "There are many instances where relative equality of land tenure is not associated with stable democracy; it is no *guarantee* of democratic development. Land reform may provide the soil to nourish free institutions, but the seed must first be planted." [6]

One rather serious handicap of much quantitative work is the failure of considering counter-evidence. This handicap is by no means "in-built," but to avoid it the quantifier and data gatherer has to go beyond the evidence. In the particular case of the de Tocqueville proposition examined by Russett, the important counter-evidence is to be found in the known support of Fascism and National Socialism by small landholders.[7] This support runs counter to the expectations of Jefferson, de Tocqueville, and others who would relate the freeholder to constitutional democracy. Surely an inquiry into the why and wherefore is not a task calling for quantification. Vast amounts of correlation may not lead to the

6. Russett, p. 453. The italics are in the original.

7. Cf. Carl J. Friedrich, "The Agricultural Basis of Emotional Nationalism," *Public Opinion Quarterly, 1* (1937), 50 ff. and the supporting evidence in Rudolf Heberle, *From Democracy to Nazism* (Baton Rouge, Louisiana State University Press, 1945); *Social Movements* (New York, Appleton-Century-Crofts, 1951); and *Landbevoelkerung und Nationalsozialismus: Eine soziologische Untersuchung der politischen Willensbildung in Schleswig-Holstein 1918 bis 1932* (Stuttgart, Deutsche Verlags-Anstalt, 1963). Some interesting deviant evidence has recently been presented by Hans Beyer in "Die Agrarkrise und das Ende der Weimarer Republik," *Zeitschrift für Agrargeschichte und Agrarsoziologie, 13* (1965), 62 ff.

qualitative insight that such support of the peasantry occurred in response to the threat a revolutionary movement posed to private property, first in France and afterward in the form of communism.[8] The support of the peasantry to counterrevolutionary movements, whether Napoleonic, Fascist, or National Socialist, was rooted in values, beliefs, and convictions that are inaccessible to quantitative analysis. Yet only a quantitative analysis of election data could produce the knowledge which called for the evaluation just stated.

Further reflection upon such situations as the one just briefly described leads into a basic issue: the relation of data gathering and hypothesis construction. There exists today a widespread belief that scientific method is based upon the formulation of an hypothesis which then leads to the collection of data to test, to prove or disprove, the hypothesis. Suggested by the supposed history of classical mechanics and related subjects, it is actually not a universally valid description of scientific inquiry and discovery. I myself held this view for a long time, because undoubtedly much scientific inquiry has proceeded in this way. But as a matter of fact, there has also been a great deal of straight fact gathering, with hypotheses for the interpretation of the facts growing out of the consideration of these data as gathered. It is also unquestionably true that facts suggested by a hunch (hypothesis) produce by implication new and often quite unexpected hunches (hypotheses). In the historical sciences, the effort to "explain," to make comprehensible, a particular event about the occurrence of which there can be no doubt often leads to a series of conflicting hypotheses, all of which are supported by some of the data. The same occurs in much judicial work. Thus the murder of John F. Kennedy, as such beyond all controversy, has already given rise to a number of possible "explanations," all of them hypothetical for the time being. The same has been true of other murders of prominent historical figures, such as Henry IV, Wallenstein, Lincoln. The methods of critical historical scholarship, developed in

8. Cf. Carl J. Friedrich, "The Peasant as Evil Genius of Dictatorship," *The Yale Review, 26* (1937), 724 ff

modern time, constitute essentially scientific efforts at achieving maximum probability in connection with "explaining" what "happened," by elaborating the details of the happening itself. Typically certain pictures and testimony by eye witnesses have become part of the story, the data to be interpreted.

This predominance of the data gathering and processing is a major reason for systematizing the search for data as such. Correlation techniques may heighten their value, but, as is well known, many correlations are meaningless unless and until a suitable "interpretation" has made the coincidental data meaningful. Indeed, quite a few phenomena have turned up in the amassing of data which happened to become available. This is just as true of political as of other kinds of data. If, as has been true in many places, the relative amount of money contributed in a political campaign appears directly related to the subsequent victory and its extent, it *may* mean that the money contributed brought about the victory; but it may also mean that the greater support which brought about the victory produced the larger contributions as well. Either proposition, stated as an hypothesis, may then be subject to further quantitative inquiry or qualitative interpretation.

Many of the most important scientific discoveries, especially in unexplored ranges of data gathering, are made on the basis of surprising phenomena observed more or less at random. Sometimes such observations occur because the researcher is looking for some other data; at other times he is "just looking." Modern industrial research has systematized and institutionalized these procedures by reviewing large areas of unexplored data merely in the hope of finding something. It is well known that the startling discoveries in sulfa and later antibiotics were due to such "review." When systematically tested, unexplored data may exhibit qualities or relationships which may *lead* to an hypothesis, rather than presupposing it. Such hypotheses are constructed in order to *account* for an observed regularity of pattern or sequence, that is to say, the hypothesis provides a rational explanation for a phenomenal given.

It is apparent that this kind of procedure much more

nearly resembles the researcher's task in the historical sciences where it is usual, as mentioned above, for the facts to be at hand, but the interpretation of these facts is the difficult task to be accomplished. To give a striking example from the history of the biological sciences, Mendel did not *first* have an hypothesis and *then* grow his peas to prove it. Rather, he grew his peas to see what would happen if certain regular sequences were followed, and then formulated his celebrated "law" to account for the regularities he had observed. It would, of course, be possible to object by saying that he had a more general hypothesis to the effect that inheritance, a natural event, must exhibit some kind of regularities, and that he then proceeded to test this hypothesis. This is true enough, but the universal premise of all science that nature exhibits regularities of relations and sequences does not really qualify as a scientific premise in the specific sense, since it is not capable of ever being proved or disproved. It is an axiom, not an hypothesis, and so are subdivisions of it in terms of particular parts of nature.

By way of analogy, one might say that such research does not crossexamine nature, as Kant thought, but rather listens to it with bemused interest and perhaps eggs it on by suitable dialogue. The nature of politics is particularly suited to this kind of procedure because it constantly produces vast amounts of data which call for interpretation. Not only such startling developments as the rise of totalitarianism, the decline of colonialism, and the evolution (revolution?) of race relations in the United States, but also smaller occurrences such as the rise of de Gaulle, the transformation of the Federal Republic of Germany, and the many new political orders in developing countries are indicative of this plethora of data shoved at the political scientist for inquiry and interpretation. The kind of research carried out in industrial laboratories produces the same flood of new data. Data processing has become of such urgency precisely because of the magnitude of the data which are accumulating under contemporary conditions of political and industrial life. Others in this colloquium will be concerned with the more technical aspects of such processing,[9] but from a broadly theoretical viewpoint it is important to realize the close parallels which exist between the natural and the social sciences. More particularly we must not be misled by theories of scientific discovery which are antiquated, related to a time when ingenious hypothesis building was the necessary stimulus to successful data gathering.

An interesting lesson may be derived perhaps from von Frisch's remarkable achievement in a special field of biology, that of communication between animals and more especially insects, and more especially still, bees. For many years it was known, or at least highly probable, that bees communicated with each other. It was, for example, not possible otherwise to account for the rapidity with which other bees appeared at a source of honey, after one bee had discovered it. Rather poetic "hypotheses" had been advanced, including a suggested "language" of the kind spoken by human beings but supposedly at a range inaudible to the human ear. Von Frisch discarded all these hypotheses and did not substitute any others for them, but he did proceed to set up hives in which the activities of the bees could be observed in detail. By reverting to strict and pure *observation,* he was able to *discover* the dance of the bees. This is not the place to enter into the details of this fascinating subject, which has since been greatly expanded by fellow researchers. Rather, for my purpose here it suffices to point out that a technique of pure data gathering succeeded in identifying patterns (the dance) and causal relations (the bees' communication system) which could then be related to other observed phenomena in a group of hypotheses. These hypotheses, which have a bearing well beyond the immediate field of observation (even including human communication), have since been validated again and again; they have also contributed to a greatly broadened concept of "language" as that of "any means of communicating by signs."

It is incidentally interesting that one important aspect of the discarding of existing hypotheses in favor of pure obser-

9. See particularly Parts II and III of this volume.

vation (data gathering) was the abandonment of anthropomorphic analogies. It is well known that such anthropomorphism has been a potent source of mistaken hypotheses. The obverse is equally patent: namely mechanomorphic (to coin a corresponding term) analogies, when made the basis of hypotheses on man and applied to the interpretation of human relationships, have proved risky too. These hints at the problems of hypothesis formation are, of course, in need of careful elaboration which we cannot provide here. Two recent distinguished writers on specific methodology who are sharply at odds with each other, Polanyi and Popper, illustrate well the difficulties involved.[10] My own position is an intermediary one.

For neither induction nor deduction but a complex and multiform interaction seems to be the basis of scientific discovery. As the preceding discussion has indicated, any large-scale exploration of scientific data, whether political or any other, calls for open-mindedness as far as techniques of gathering them are concerned. The successful researcher will forever be alert to new sources and unanticipated phenomena. Bacon was not as wrong as his extravagancies on the score of induction suggest. His *Novum Organum* rightly stressed just these points, and if he was in error when he thought that interpretation springs automatically from the data it "induced" from them, he was right in thinking that only new data are likely to precipitate that innovative process which scientific discovery involves.

In his remarkable although little known and appreciated recent study on scientific discovery, Norwood R. Hanson tells us at the outset that philosophers misrepresent the problems of microphysics.[11] He thinks the reason is simple. "They have regarded," he writes, "as paradigms of physical inquiry not unsettled, dynamic research sciences like microphysics,

10. Cf. Michael Polanyi, *Personal Knowledge* (Chicago, University of Chicago Press, 1958), and Karl R. Popper, *The Logic of Scientific Discovery* (New York, Basic Books, 1959).

11. Norwood R. Hanson, *Patterns of Scientific Discovery: An Inquiry into the Conceptual Foundations of Science* (Cambridge, Cambridge University Press, 1958). Political theorists, of course, do the same.

but finished systems, planetary mechanics, optics, electromagnetism and classical thermodynamics." And he adds, I believe quite rightly, that these approaches "afford an artificial account even of the kinds of activities in which Kepler, Galileo and Newton themselves were actually engaged." [12] Observation, evidence, facts, as much as theory, hypothesis, law, causality, and principle are seen in mistaken perspective, when approached thus. Elaborating on observation, for example, he comments that "physical science is not just a systematic exposure of the senses to the world, it is also a way of thinking about the world, a way of forming conceptions. The paradigm observer is not the man who sees and reports what all normal observers see and report, but the man who sees in familiar objects what no one else has seen before." [13]

Even more to the present purpose is what Hanson has to say on hypothesis formation. He rejects both the Baconian induction "by simple enumeration" as too simple, and the hypothetico-deductive system as too abstract. "Physicists do not start from hypotheses; they start from data," he writes,[14] and then cites Newton who wrote: "The main business of natural philosophy is to argue from phenomena." [15] It is not merely a matter of adding up the data, of stating a sum of observed phenomena, but also of giving a "hypothetical" explanation of the data as observed. The theories stressing deduction and hypotheses usually overlook the way the hypotheses are come by; they do not think of them as "hunches." Hanson warns us not to overestimate the psychological aspect; the "catching" of an hypothesis is a "reasonable affair," that is to say, there is much hard work and logic to it. "It is not so often affected by intuition, insight, hunches, or other imponderables as biographers or scientists suggest." [16] Here as elsewhere, Frederick of Prussia's saying applies that "genius is industry." (It ought to go without

12. Ibid., p. 1.
13. Ibid., p. 30
14. Ibid., Chap. 4, entitled "Theories"; the quotation is on p. 70.
15. Newton, *Principia*, Preface.
16. Hanson, p. 71.

saying that this does not mean that "industry is genius.") And what Hanson claims for physics, that "the ingenuity, tenacity, imagination and conceptual boldness which has marked physics since Galileo shows itself more clearly in hypothesis-catching than in the deductive elaboration of caught hypotheses," [17] applies with equal if not with greater force to the historical sciences. This crucial fact is the basic ground for saying: "data, yes" but "theory, too."

To return, then, from this brief excursion into general methodology [18] to the political sphere, I might illustrate somewhat further the general point I am trying to develop by reference to the plentiful data which anthropologists have developed on "primitive" societies in terms of the utilization for political theory. Any broadly conceived theory of politics needs to make all possible use of the kind of data which anthropology is able to furnish. At times these data fit received opinions well; at others they present novel and perplexing problems. The vast amount of data which the Human Relations Area Files have sought to correlate in terms of general categories presents an intriguing field of inquiry. It is bedeviled, however, by precisely the problem which our previous discussion has sought to bring out: In terms of what categories are we to inspect this material? Are there universal ones applicable to all human societies, or are the conceptions in terms of which political orders are shaped completely culture-bound? The Human Relations Area Files proceeded on the first of these premises. In a series of categories (in their scheme running from 62 to 72) the political order is epitomized; they run from community (62) through territorial organization, state, government activities, political behavior, law, justice, and armed forces to war (72). It was the original purpose of the HRAF "to organize in readily accessible form the available data on a statistically representative sample of all known cultures—primitive, historical

17. Ibid., p. 72.

18. Cf. also what is said in the introductory chapter of Friedrich, *Man and His Government*, as well as the "Notes" there on "system" and "typology."

and contemporary—for the purpose of testing cross-cultural generalizations." [19]

It is evident that political theory consists of cross-cultural generalizations. The avowed goal is to state propositions that are of universal validity. Hence the purpose of HRAF appears to be, inter alia, to produce political theory. No such theory has in fact been produced; but data have been gathered which are highly relevant to theory. The notion, however, that the theoretical propositions will, so to speak, emerge from the data, and which we saw to be in error, has once more been disproved. The hypotheses or hypothetical general propositions which emerge, if they emerge at all, are an inchoate scramble of whatever general theoretical propositions the particular anthropologist who investigated and wrote up the material happened to be familiar with. The rather primitive notions of an Evans-Pritchard, working with outworn conceptions of state, for example, while not invalidating the data at all obstruct their effective utilization. Problems like succession which are as basic today as ever they were, and which might be significantly elucidated, are in fact left where the timid utilitarianism and formalist legalism of the nineteenth century had left them. It is not in the interest of scientific advance to escape from these basic problems into some kind of operational pragmatism.

To group "inherently related categories" in the same section is of little help, when we do not know whether these categories are related in any but a purely semantic way. Only an explicit facing of the substantive content of categories and propositions enables one to cope with the theoretical difficulties involved here. It will not do to retreat to "common usage" and speak of "categories in general use," contrasting them with "classificatory innovations." For

19. See 4th revised edition of their *Outline of Cultural Materials* (1961), and Carl J. Friedrich, "The Uses of Anthropological Materials in Political Theory," in *Fact and Theory in Social Science*, eds. E. W. Count and Gordon T. Bowles (Syracuse, Syracuse University Press, 1964), pp. 127 ff. Under a grant from the National Science Foundation, a group of political scientists and anthropologists is reviewing the political categories and the materials for forty selected societies collected under them in the hope of arriving at firmer conclusions concerning the issues discussed in the text.

these innovations embody, or at any rate often reflect, theoretical insights of major significance. If then such innovations are rejected the data gathering itself gets more and more arid, as the scientifically significant new directions remain unexplored. Thus reading the more recent work of the Evans-Pritchard school of British anthropologists one gathers the impression that the rapid advance in political theory in the last twenty-five years has gone completely unnoticed; the old positions are just repeated over and over. It is rather touching to read how the Human Relations Area Files found that when they tried to introduce new categories, "they were compelled," in practically every instance, "to abandon the innovation because the attempt to press the data into a new mold invariably necessitated splitting up passages in the sources and distributing the parts so widely that the context for each individual item evaporated."

This highly significant observation demonstrates, it seems to me, the complex dangers which lurk in any data gathering program that is not linked to a theoretical program in terms of which the data gathering proceeds. There must be, as the earlier discussion attempted to show, a constant interaction between the data (the phenomena, in Newton's phrase) and the hypothesis formation (including therein the categories, of course, in terms of which hypotheses are framed) which is the quintessence of theory. Such an approach avoids also a philosophical pitfall, that of "nominalism."

This is the final philosophical point to which I wish to turn with a few concluding remarks. A good deal of contemporary science, under the influence of the work of such men as Einstein and Heisenberg, inclines toward a more or less radically nominalist position. (In a sense, the use of this medieval term "nominalism" is an anachronism, since its opposite is no longer maintained.) Such a position is based upon the notion that man the observer, *homo spectator,* never knows reality, in the ultimate sense, that this reality is inaccessible, a thing-in-itself. Such a view overlooks the fact that *homo spectator* is always also *homo faber,* that man the observer is observing because he wants to make something that will solve a problem for him. Impressed with the scientifically untenable views of both medieval "realism" and modern "idealism" of Hegelian and similar persuasions, men fall into the opposite (Kantian) error of having the mind of man the observer "legislate" for the real world by constructing order (patterns, laws, and the like). In the days of the Enlightenment, this was an understandable error to fall into. It was the time when in politics everything was supposed to center in lawmaking, when the legislative power, as in Locke and many others, was supposed to be the core of the political order. And the legislative enthusiasm never found more absurdly eloquent expression than in Voltaire's famous: "Voulez-vous avoir des bonnes lois? Brûlez les vôtres, et faites-en des nouvelles." Order was necessarily law-directed order and the order of nature was imposed by the mind of man, mirroring that of God.

Ours is no longer such a hopeful outlook. Both the idealist and the realist positions are in error it would seem. "Reality" is neither fully accessible, nor is it completely inaccessible. Rather it yields to progressive "appropriation" by the observing researcher, who in a continuous process of matching data with theories (which in the very logic of this process must forever remain "hypothetical," as data remain incomplete) advances knowledge and understanding. Political Science (as well as other social sciences) is distinguished by the further complication of "creative innovation," that is to say, by the emergence of facts (data) as the result of inventive activity, rather than imaginative search for data. It has to cope with genuinely *new* data, rather than merely search for old but unknown data. Totalitarianism is actually and in reality new, whereas the nebulae and the protons are actually old, but the knowledge of them is new. Yet both the sciences which are merely looking for the old that is not yet known and those that have to cope with the new that is emerging are dealing with a reality that is there, though only partially known. Copernicus is closer to this reality than Ptolemy, Einstein closer than Newton, von Frisch closer than Maeterlinck. The social sciences (and indeed all the sciences of man) suggest this basic view of the emergent reality, the progressively appropriated reality, rather than either the "ideal" or the "real" reality; the reality with which they deal—man—imposes itself as actually there, yet inadequately known. The operative presence of this reality—men in active being—cannot but be presumed to be real, yet who will say that he knows it all, when in every generation new facets are emerging? Therefore, in political as in other social theory, the gradual approximation to the emergent reality is never going to be completed. We know more about man, not merely as phenomenally appearing, but as existentially becoming. Man would have to be dead and extinct to be fully known, and who would then be there to do the knowing?

PART II

The Aggregate Data Basis for Cross-National Comparisons

This section of the volume deals with comparisons of structural and/or aggregate characteristics for entire nation-states. At the Yale Data Conference, four distinct approaches to analyses of unit characteristics of nations were presented: the Yale Political Data Program; the Cross-Polity Survey; the Dimensionality of Nations project; and the Studies in International Conflict and Integration. The first three are similar in a number of respects.

Bruce M. Russett reported on the development of the Yale Political Data Program and reviewed the draft *World Handbook of Political and Social Indicators* (subsequently published in 1964 by Yale University Press). As in the other approaches, some of the basic independent variables are indicators of economic growth, most of which, since they are taken from standard United Nations statistical sources, are quite similar in all of the first three projects. The Yale Political Data Program has gone furthest in discussing problems of the comparability, reliability, and validity of the indicators, which include educational and mass media indicators as well as a number of quantitative political indicators such as central government revenue as a percentage of Gross National Product or average electoral participation. The Program has also explored the use of a wide variety of bivariate and multivariate techniques in analyzing these data in research on both international and comparative politics.

Arthur S. Banks and Robert B. Textor explained their technique of "pattern search" and textual presentation of findings used in *A Cross-Polity Survey* (subsequently published in late 1963 by the Massachusetts Institute of Technology Press). The survey is essentially qualitative—based on judgments made by Banks—rather than enumerative. The authors analyzed 115 "polities" in terms of such variables as "governmental stability," "political participation by the military," "freedom of the press," "racial homogeneity," and "interest articulation by associational groups," as well as such standard quantitative variables as population density and so forth. The dichotomized variables or attributes are presented in a series of computer printouts of cross-classifications of national units, mostly in terms of simple fourfold tables allowing exact calculations of the statistical significance of the association of the attributes.

Harold Guetzkow reviewed the Dimensionality of Nations project, organized jointly with Jack Sawyer and Rudolph J. Rummel, and reported some of its initial results. The Dimensionality of Nations project includes 236 quantitative and qualitative variables; its political indices are derived essentially from "event statistics" such as counts of the number of people killed in domestic violence. The relationships between the variables are studied through various factor analysis techniques.

In all three of these comparative research efforts, the units of analysis are countries: geographically and politically distinct nation-states, colonies, or similarly administered territories. In the Yale Political Data Program and the Dimensionality of Nations project, most of the analysis is correlational: matrices of product-moment correlations are established and efforts made to explore basic patterns through multiple regression or factor analysis techniques. The more qualitatively oriented Cross-Polity Survey, by contrast, relies exclusively on tables of association between dichotomized variables or attributes.

At the Yale Data Conference, much of the ensuing discussion centered on the relative merits of these approaches. There was consensus that correlational techniques made for greater economy of data handling; but for many attributes of total polities only qualitative classifications could make sense and, for these, the simpler techniques of tests of association seemed the more appropriate. The bulk of the discussion focused on the choice of units of analysis: Does the "polity" make sense as a unit? Do not these units vary too much in size? Can one really compare at the same level of analysis giant federations of states such as the United States and the Soviet Union, and tiny island-nations such as Iceland? One straightforward reply to these queries is that national polities, however much varied in other respects, have one crucial attribute in common: they collect data on themselves and define themselves as distinct statistical units.

A series of methodological issues in the use of aggregate national data for purposes of comparison was raised at the Conference. René Bassoul distinguished two types of comparison: (1) analyses of ranges of variations across units on one attribute; and (2) analyses of variations in constellations of attributes across the units. He stressed the pitfalls of comparisons of the first type. To make sure such comparisons were at all meaningful, one would have to test several alternative indicators and set up norms for variations within units (e.g. between groups within a nation) as well as across units (e.g. nations). Paul Lazarsfeld warned against excessive quantification and quite particularly against the use of correlation coefficients in the analysis of relationships between variables which are not normally distributed. There is no need to work exclusively with continuous variables: statistical techniques have been developed for qualitative attributes and for non-normal distributions. These, he suggested, might prove the most appropriate at the level of cross-national comparisons. Lazarsfeld expressed a great deal of skepticism toward the proposed analyses of partial correlations to test the influence of conditioning variables on given relationships; he much preferred a simple trichotomy of the cases along the conditioning variable and separate tests of association for each third of the range.

Lazarsfeld also brought up the possibilities of misinterpretation through exclusive concern with variations at the level of the national unit. He referred to William Robinson's warnings against the "ecological fallacy": a relationship at the level of the aggregate need not necessarily imply a relationships between the same variables for individuals. It is essential in each case to think through a model of explanation and to check the possible conditioning factors where data are available.

Two of the above projects are discussed in this volume: the Yale Political Data Program and the Dimensionality of Nations project. Chapter 4, written by Karl W. Deutsch, Harold D. Lasswell, Richard L. Merritt, and Bruce M. Russett, presents the theoretical framework of the Yale Political Data Program. In the following chapter Russett discusses the progress of the first three years of the Program, and shows how the data collected have been subjected to critical examination and used to test important issues of theory in the social sciences. Rudolph J. Rummel then elaborates upon the basic orientation of the Dimensionality of Nations project, first set up by Harold Guetzkow, Jack Sawyer, and Rummel, and outlines research currently under way.

In his chapter, Erwin K. Scheuch summarizes and discusses some of the methodological issues entailed in the interpretation of national aggregate data. He is particularly concerned about the accuracy of aggregate data, the comparability of measurements for aggregates, the representativeness of aggregate data for properties of the collective, and the types of inferences that may legitimately be drawn from correlations using aggregate data. Scheuch summarizes the dangers not only of the "ecological fallacy," but also of the "individualistic fallacy," which extrapolates all too readily from the aggregate of individual attributes or attitudes to a characterization of the territorial unit containing these individuals.

The fourth approach to the aggregate data basis for cross-national comparisons is reported by Ole R. Holsti and Robert C. North: techniques for content analysis of communications from different countries, such as messages between statesmen, speeches, newspaper statements, and so forth. The current work at Stanford University has grown out of earlier efforts by Lasswell, Lerner, and Pool at the Hoover Library, but is less concerned with the counting of joint occurrences of ideological keywords than with the measurement of changes in the level of tension and conflict between political actors. In their chapter Holsti and North focus on the documented exchanges between decision-makers in the major European states during the fateful month of July 1914, and compare their findings with external data such as the flow of gold, the prices of stocks and bonds, wheat futures, exchange rates, and interest rates. Their experience suggests great promise for the use of electronic computers in content analysis research.

4. The Yale Political Data Program

KARL W. DEUTSCH, HAROLD D. LASSWELL,
RICHARD L. MERRITT, AND BRUCE M. RUSSETT,
YALE UNIVERSITY

THE PROGRAM IN OUTLINE

What social changes are associated with the growth of political pluralism, as against the rise of a dominant single party or interest? What social and political changes accompany various stages in a nation's economic development? What conditions are associated with trends toward political centralization or decentralization, toward union or secession among the provinces of a country or the member states of an alliance? To help answer these and other questions, an international political data program has been established as part of the program of studies in international relations and comparative politics at Yale University. This program is dedicated to the gathering, analysis, and critical evaluation of quantitative data relevant to domestic political developments and to the background conditions of foreign policy in different countries.

The main focus of the program is on the social conditions conducive to political change. The central concept is the political solvency of governments; that is, the balance between the natural resources, administrative capabilities, and popular support of any particular government, on the one hand, and its formal and informal commitments, both foreign and domestic, on the other.

Social conditions may have a critical influence upon this balance. Political commitments include not only formal treaties, laws, and explicit political promises, but also the effective and articulated needs and expectations prevailing among the politically relevant parts of the population. Changes in social conditions may change these needs and expectations and thus change in effect the commitments of the governments and the conditions for their political solvency and stability.

As a result of our analysis we shall obtain some probability statements about political events, based on the frequency distribution of observed cases. How likely are governments to fall? How likely are they to prove capable or incapable of making and fulfilling future political commitments? Each such estimate of probabilities of political events or political behavior may be thought of as an "output" variable of analysis, while information about specific kinds of social, economic, cultural, or political background changes may be thought of as "input" variables. As in the input–output analysis of other interdependent systems, it should be possible to analyze political systems by ascertaining the correlation between different variables of social change and political behavior, and by finding the probabilities with which a change of given size in one variable would be followed by corresponding changes of predicted size in other variables.

This involves not only the measurement of variables and of the correlations among them, but also the testing of specific theories of political behavior. A body of comparable data will help to shed some light on questions such as these: Do certain changes in the social and economic structure of a country precede or accompany the mobilization of broader masses of its population to an active interest in nationalism and in politics? How are changes of this kind correlated with changes in the tasks and scope of governments and of administration? At what rate do such changes increase the demands made upon the capabilities of government and upon the extent and timing of political reforms? How do they affect popular responses to foreign influences, to national policies of international alliance or neutrality, to the appeals of democracy or dictatorship, of private or public enterprise, of nationalism or communism?

There are numerous hypotheses which could be tested with the help of a more general analysis connecting a larger number of variables. It would be possible to treat a number of input variables in their turn as possible output elements, if the other variables in the system were known. In short, a more general model of interdependence might be developed, which would then permit us to estimate the effect of change in any one of the major variables upon some or all of the others in the system.

THE NEED FOR DATA

To develop such an analysis of social change and political development it is essential to collect, organize, and analyze an adequate body of empirical data. Potentially relevant data include information on voting; membership in interest groups, parties, and other political organizations; survey data on political attitudes and opinions; literacy and levels of education; urbanization; audiences for mass media; industrialization; changes in the composition of the working force; shifts from subsistence to market economies; budgetary studies, including changes in the share of government expenditures as compared to national income; military vs. civilian expenditures; ratios of military personnel or of civil servants at the center of government and at field agencies to total population.

The relevance of these data to our understanding of the stability and capabilities of governments, and of the processes of political development and change, is implied in many of our current hypotheses about politics. But usually the data have not been selected, gathered, refined, analyzed, and compared sufficiently to be brought to bear productively on these hypotheses. Our ideas about politics have suggested that certain facts should be the case, or that certain social conditions should tend to be associated with certain political developments, but data have been lacking to test these notions or to suggest better ones. This long-standing deficiency has become increasingly critical in recent years, as our theories of political development, of nationalism, and of international political behavior have developed. Our program begins to provide a crucially needed resource for dealing with this problem.

Additional Uses of the Data

The data gathered and evaluated strengthen important aspects of research, now going on at Yale University and to be further developed during the next ten years, in such areas as comparative studies of political modernization and democratization, of nationalism and large-scale political integration, of political culture and socialization, of administration, of political development in non-Western countries, and of the international political system.

In all these areas such data will furnish one type of evidence, to be confronted with other evidence from case studies and from various political, historical, and cultural analyses. The study of one case usually suggests questions about its "typical" or "exceptional" character, while broad statistical comparisons will stimulate more intensive study of the representative, as well as of the deviant, cases. The opportunity for integrating the results of research on data with other types of research greatly enhances the value of having this program as part of Yale's international studies program.

Administrative Aspects

All work with quantitative data must rest upon some framework of political and intellectual judgments. The tasks of selecting potentially relevant classes of information, of deciding on priorities among different categories and countries, of judging the adequacy of available data and the extent to which they should be supplemented or refined, and the crucial tasks of analyzing and evaluating the significance of the results—all these are the responsibility of individual scholars on the faculty of the university, who have demonstrated their competence in working with such information and who are engaged in some of the substantive research for the International Relations Program. Accordingly, the Data Program is administered by a Director, under an Executive Committee appointed by the Chairman of the Department of Political Science and including members of the department whose research interests coincide with the work of the Political Data Program. The National Science Foundation has provided funds to initiate the work of the Program, and Yale University provides office facilities and administrative services. Additional funds are received from foundations, government agencies, and individuals.

THE NEED FOR A PROGRAM OF DATA COLLECTION

A very considerable supply of useful data is available from reputable sources, including the United Nations and various national governments, plus research monographs and scholarly research organizations in the United States and abroad. Most of these data, however, are scattered. The current publications of the U.N., UNESCO, the U.S. Census Bureau, and other agencies do not permit ready comparison of a wide range of refined, ordered, and politically relevant material. The data too often are neither in comparable form nor evaluated for accuracy. Not even the most elementary ratios or correlations are given. Students and scholars have to spend so much effort gathering raw information that they are short of time and resources for the basic computations and for the processing and analysis needed to develop inferences which the data are capable of yielding. This lack of adequate data handicaps both undergraduate and graduate teaching, as well as faculty research, and restricts the potential usefulness of scholarly work to the makers of public policy.

Moreover, much of the labor of data gathering, checking, and elementary processing, such as rank ordering or the calculation of percentages, is repetitive. The same items may have to be gathered to confirm a judgment on the growth or decline of nationalism in a country, the rise and fall of political participation, a change in its political culture, or the replacement of one predominant elite by another. A figure for one country often means little or nothing unless it can be compared with the corresponding figures for other countries. The significance of the magnitude and speed of a development in one country can be appraised more accurately if data are available on the size and speed of similar developments in comparable countries. Ordinarily the scholar dealing with a single country or a single aspect of international politics lacks such figures for comparison and is in no position to get them by his own efforts.

A similar situation seems to have prevailed about twenty years ago in the field of economics. Data on national income, economic development, and economic stability were often laborious to collect, and comparison figures from other countries were difficult to obtain or to refine to a point of accuracy useful for comparative analysis. In recent decades, such institutions as the National Bureau of Economic Research and the Cowles Commission have done much to remedy this condition. Economists can discuss data problems of national income, distribution or growth of unemployment, or economic stability with a substantial amount of information available for comparison of the experiences of different countries. The result of the availability of such material has not been to supersede theory. On the contrary, it has facilitated the development of theories, as well as their verification. It has helped to make economic theory more relevant and more fruitful. In political science, theories have developed to a point where further progress requires their testing against adequately large and verified bodies of data. Without such enhanced opportunities for testing, the growth of political science may be seriously retarded.

OPERATIONS

The work undertaken within the framework of this program may be considered under five headings:

1. Selection of data categories and countries in the light of research interests

2. Collection and checking of raw data.
3. Refining and processing of raw data, including the analysis of trends and distributions by computational procedures.
4. Evaluation and interpretation in terms of new or existing theory.
5. Presentation of data for teaching and further research.

1. *Some Problems of Selection*

In the long run it will be worthwhile to collect data on several hundred categories for each country to be studied, ranging from urbanization, literacy, nonagricultural employment, and voting participation to such matters as the frequency of certain political attitudes or symbols, certain cultural terms relevant to political behavior, and behavior in international politics and organization. Since not all of these figures are equally readily available and not all are equally urgently needed, first priority is given to thirty or forty categories, picking up additional items at later stages of the program.

It will be desirable to get such data for all countries significant in comparative or international politics—that is, for approximately 120 states. Here again, however, some priorities have to be imposed. First attention is given to those countries being studied in various area programs under way at Yale, such as Russia, China, and Japan, and also to countries which have to be taken into account in a wide variety of studies of international politics, such as the United States, Germany, and France. Altogether, between thirty and forty countries receive most of our attention.

Another kind of priority stems from procedures. Some data have been gathered and refined already by the original collecting agency to a point where they are useful for political analysis, while other items have been put together on the basis of such different definitions and procedures that they must be refined and adjusted before they may be considered usable for political comparisons. It is necessary, therefore, to make judgments from time to time as to how much effort to expend on the refinement of raw details already gathered, as against the gathering of further raw information for additional countries or categories. Such decisions emphasize the need for collecting only such data as appear intellectually relevant in the context of current research and theory in the fields of international relations, comparative politics, comparative administration, and comparative legal institutions and behavior.

Within the area marked out by this general criterion of relevance, priority is given to the gathering of figures that appear meaningful in terms of current research at Yale, such as the interests of Harold Lasswell in the decision process, of Robert Dahl in the conditions for the development of democracy, of Robert Lane in the relation of culture to politics, of Karl Deutsch on national and political integration, of James Fesler on problems of comparative administration, of Joseph LaPalombara on national elites, and of Frederick Barghoorn on the receptivity of different peoples to Soviet propaganda.

2. *The Collection Stage*

Sources. A very considerable body of data is available from existing sources, and many items are already given in such a way as to assure their approximate comparability. Such sources include the United Nations and its numerous agencies, the official statistical publications of national governments, various special studies like those prepared in recent years under the auspices of the United States Congress, and a considerable number of monographs and other works from nongovernmental research organizations and individual scholars. It should be remembered that, though these figures are accessible, they are not ordinarily available to scholars in any comprehensive way, since gathering them from all the scattered sources would ordinarily impose prohibitive demands upon the time and resources of a single individual.

Organization of Data. The information collected is recorded on tabulating cards, in a form for rapid analysis by large-scale computers and also for inexpensive reproduction and shipment to interested scholars elsewhere. The cards also can be listed or interpreted for easy visual examination. Together with the absolute figures, the corresponding percentages or per capita data are computed and recorded. In thus keeping available different items for the same country, or a range of different countries for the same variable, the collection goes beyond the usual handbook which rarely offers opportunities for effective comparisons.

Although the project focuses particularly on certain countries, it is often cheaper to take data for all the countries given in a certain collection. This makes it easier to prepare international profiles for the distribution of a particular variable over a larger number of countries, and it supplies a background for data collection on those countries which will be subject to a more intensive information gathering effort at a later stage. On the other hand, when key points are not readily at hand, even though they appear highly relevant in the light of some impressive political hypothesis, an intensive effort is made to get the data for those countries that are of particular research interest at the time. Additional card decks of information are sometimes obtained from such sources as the United Nations, the United States census, or public opinion services.

Information and Judgments on Quality of Data. Frequently, collecting agencies themselves publish material setting forth the different definitions and procedures by which these data were gathered for different countries or regions or in different years. Where the collecting agency itself furnishes a credible estimate of the margin of error of the figures given, appropriate notations are made on the cards without going beyond the limits of a clerical operation.

Much of the judgment, however, as to the comparability and the error margins of data supplied by various agencies is very much a matter not of clerical but of professional competence. Specialized help on some particular country or category of information may have to be invoked, or the director of the project may make a judgment on his own responsibility after having drawn upon suitable professional advice. Refined data are computed, where appropriate, by making allowances for known distortions. In any case, both the raw information and the refined data are available to scholars so that those who do not agree with the judgment of the Yale Program may still use the raw data as a basis for evaluations or adjustments of their own.

Problems of Gaps. Another professional operation is the effort to develop techniques by which missing data for particular countries or years can be interpolated or estimated or else replaced by related indices in line with the principle of the "interchangeability of indices." With the latter method, available indices known to be highly correlated with the missing ones are used as substitutes or at least as aids for estimating the missing data. Such judgments, at best delicate and hazardous, are made by the best professional judgment upon which the Program can draw. All figures obtained by such procedures are clearly differentiated from data obtained by more direct methods.

3. *Some Opportunities for Data Processing*

Processing the data includes making them more comparable, indicating their probable margins of error, and putting them into the most basic contexts of space (by country or region), time (in terms of trends, swings, or cycles), and interactions (in terms of correlations and deviant cases).

The first stage of data processing is refining raw detail in the light of existing information on the definitions and procedures by which they were originally assembled, to insure their comparability from country to country or from period to period. A part of the same operation is estimating and indicating proper margins of error inherent in certain classes of information. This is done with the help of existing surveys of data gathering methods.

A more refined step involves what might be called "calibration"—that is, developing some studies of the comparability of results obtained by different research procedures, e.g. the answers obtained by extensive as against intensive interviewing. A related problem involves a judgment of comparability of data obtained from small samples as against those obtained from larger ones. This requires decisions regarding the acceptance of levels of significance and estimates of probable error and of the propagation of error.

Another important stage of processing is the computation of rank order profiles showing the distribution of each category of data for a single year or period for the whole world or for selected regions, taking national states as units in each case. Where information is available, however, intracountry profiles may be computed, such as among the fifty states of the United States or the different states and regions of Brazil. Eventually it may be illuminating to compile rank order profiles for reporting units cutting across states, such as families, or ecological regions, such as large river valleys.

The computation of rank order profiles as well as the computation of statistical medians, modes, means, measures of skewness, standard deviations, etc., is the object of standardized computer routines that rapidly compile, print, and, with the help of some of the larger computers, even chart data and their distributions by electronic means directly from the decks of punch cards. Similarly, trends over time can be charted either for a single country or for a group of countries. Computations can then be made of the rates of change, and alternative projections can be relatively easily prepared for use in developmental constructs.

Other operations of data processing include the use of suitable index numbers for politically relevant data taken from existing sources or developed in the program as needed. With the aid of Yale's IBM 7094 computer, analyses of the interplay of several factors or conditions in a given situation are carried out by means of standard programs for factor analysis, multiple regression, and, the analysis of variance. What has been said about the measurement of the extent and distribution of particular variables within countries or regions applies in general also to measuring transaction flows among different countries, together with the measurement of changes in such transactions.

One of the simplest operations is measurement of the correlation of two or more variables—such as literacy, urbanization, income distribution—and the computation of the apparent effects upon any one of these variables by all the others. A second class of routine operations is the identification of deviant cases. If it is well known that literacy and income are generally highly related, it is possible for simple computer routines to pick out those countries that deviate from this pattern. Burma, for example, shows remarkably high literacy together with remarkably low income. This procedure singles out deviant countries for particular research attention, throwing more light upon the deviant case as well as upon the pattern itself.

Our work is made generally available in a number of ways. Data sheets, profiles, charts, graphs, and surveys of the state of research and availability of information are issued periodically. A handbook of basic political data, *World Handbook of Political and Social Indicators,* has been published by Yale University Press. Working papers, original monographs, and reprints of articles prepared by the staff for professional journals are published in the series *Yale Papers in Political Science.*

4. *Confrontations with Theory*

Another contribution of the program will be the preliminary verification of existing claims or predictions as to the growth or decline of certain countries, or as to the existence of certain trends as implied by current theories of politics or international relations. Related to this is the opportunity for the program to assist individual scholars in reformulating classic or contemporary theories of politics or international relations, to bring out their implications in terms of measurable quantities. Theories can thus be made subject to verification or revealed as nonempirical theories of that particular verbal nature which would remain unaffected by any possible measurement or evidence. Similarly, the program will assist scholars in designing future surveys, samples, and experiments and in developing new methods and instruments of research and measurement in political, legal, and administrative behavior.

5. *Training and Collaborative Services*

In addition to its service to mature scholars, the Political Data Program fulfills an important training function for graduate students through the experience of research in collaboration with senior investigators. Adequate clerical help insures that graduate students are not used as a source of cheap labor but, rather, are aided to develop their experience, skills, judgment, and initiative to the highest level. Senior faculty time is devoted to the Program not only in pursuit of their existing substantial research interests but also as an aid to this training function.

A companion research facility is the Yale Political Science Research Library. The Library's purpose is to aid study and empirical research by students and faculty in the Department of Political Science and related disciplines; its facilities are also open to scholars from other universities and research centers. The Library concentrates upon international and domestic political behavior and participation, election studies and electoral statistics, and public opinion. Among its holdings are public opinion polls from Australia, Austria, Belgium, Canada, France, Germany, Great Britain, India, Italy, Japan, Laos, the Netherlands, Norway, Okinawa, the Philippines, and Switzerland, as well as the United States. The Research Library also has the IBM punch cards and codebooks for several domestic and foreign opinion surveys including about twenty cross-national surveys. As a member of the Inter-University Consortium for Political Research and the International Survey Library Association, the Library facilitates the use of national and international survey data gathered by and stored at such institutions as the Survey Research Center of the University of Michigan and the Roper Center at Williams College.

The Political Data Program also benefits from the presence of the Yale University Economic Growth Center, which is supported by the Ford Foundation, the Agency for International Development, and other foundations and government agencies. Studies of economic development will inevitably increase the need for information about political and administrative changes in the various countries concerned, and the Political Data Program in turn will benefit from the results of the economic studies and data. The Program draws upon the resources of other centers now operating at Yale, such as the Human Relations Area Files, the Cowles Foundation for Research in Economics, the Computer Center, and in particular the programs of area studies now being carried on at Yale. Large-scale empirical research in international and comparative politics increasingly demands such a complex of facilities.

5. The Yale Political Data Program: Experience and Prospects

BRUCE M. RUSSETT, YALE UNIVERSITY

EXPERIENCE

Derek de Solla Price has indicated that the unique achievements of Western science can be traced to the confluence of Greek logic and mathematics with Babylonian skill in calculation, and of this dual stream with Greek accomplishments in mechanics and building precision instruments for measurement.[1] In another vein, David Easton has suggested that the preconditions for equilibrium analysis, so fruitful in the natural sciences, were mathematics and the quantification of measurable variables.[2] On these principles perhaps traditional political science can be roughly equated with the logical (though not the mathematical) Greek tradition. Those modern Babylonians, the computer builders, have now provided immense facilities for painless calculation. The production of measuring instruments for social science—and the collection of data with these instruments—is still on a more primitive level. It is to this last stream, and to its incorporation into the larger river of political theory, that the Yale Political Data Program is trying to contribute.

1. *Science Since Babylon* (New Haven, Yale University Press, 1962), Chaps. 2, 3.

2. "Limits of the Equilibrium Model in Social Research," in Heinz Eulau, Samuel Eldersveld, and Morris Janowitz, eds., *Political Behavior* (Glencoe, Ill., Free Press, 1956), pp. 397–404.

Collection and Evaluation

The Yale Program is concerned with the collection, evaluation, and analysis of quantitative data. To date we have gathered information on more than 600 variables, with an average of 80 political units per variable. This means a total of almost 50,000 items of data. In addition, data are usually collected for more than one year for each country, bringing the grand total to fully 100,000 pieces of information. Much of the information has been published in *World Handbook of Political and Social Indicators,* a companion volume to this book.[3]

The data gathered were selected with reference to existing theories of international and comparative politics. Each series represents an attempt to operationalize a variable which is central to several important theories of political or social change. In some cases it seems fairly clear that a given index does accurately represent a basic underlying variable of concern; in other cases the adequacy of the index is more doubtful. Where there is most doubt we have tried to include two or more alternative measures, or else we have broken down a complex concept into several simpler ones.

In addition to demands of theoretical importance, our data series were selected according to the criteria of accuracy and availability. Problems of accuracy involve two separate questions: Are the numbers *reliable,* neither exaggerations nor underestimates, and are they *comparable* even if reliable? That is, are the definitions of the relevant event the same in different countries? We have tried to estimate the probable error in the data, and to compare it with the permissible error that can still be tolerated in the inferences which are to be drawn from the data. This permissible error is in part related to the range of the series. When the value of a variable in two countries differs by 20 percentage points, an error margin of 15 points will have crippling effects; if the values should differ by 40 or 50 percentage points, an error margin

3. Bruce M. Russett, and Hayward R. Alker, Jr., Karl W. Deutsch, Harold D. Lasswell, *World Handbook of Political and Social Indicators* (New Haven, Yale University Press, 1964).

of 15 points, while damaging, may nonetheless be tolerable.

In deciding whether to collect a given series at all we had to make a preliminary judgment about the data's accuracy. We have attempted further, and this was a difficult and uncertain task given the paucity of existing information, to assess fairly precise error margins for most of the series. Few previous data collections have made more than the grossest assessments, perhaps warning the reader to use the data only with caution and due regard for incomparabilities. Obviously it is not easy to give any precise error margin either for a single datum or for a whole series. There is always the danger that such an attempt, meant to give only a very general order of magnitude, may be taken as absolute.

Nevertheless, it seemed to us that refusal to make any quantitative estimate of error when presenting series of this sort was really a kind of abdication of responsibility. Mere publication of figures with the admonition to be cautious does not tell the reader how cautious he must be, and how much confidence he may attach to the resulting calculations. He is free to draw his own conclusions, but this may be a poor sort of freedom if the information available to him is—as is usually the case—less than that available to the original compilers of the data.

In general, there is a clear tendency for the quality and availability of data to rise with the level of economic development in a country. Primarily this is simply a matter of resources. The collection and evaluation of adequate data is an expensive process requiring skilled personnel; in many countries neither the human nor the financial raw material is available. This is particularly true in small countries and with data which are normally collected by sample survey methods. When one is dealing with a population of a million or more inhabitants, the size of the sample needed for reliable data collection is not responsive to the size of the total population. The results of a sample survey of, for example, five thousand individuals are virtually as reliable for a country of two hundred million as for a country of one million. The costs of the survey are not very different in the large country than in the small one, but the relative burden on the small country may be substantial, especially if it is not wealthy. Thus sample surveys, which can form an important supplement to decennial censuses, are often not undertaken in smaller states.

Another problem stems from the lack of international agreement on the definition of certain items. The United Nations has performed a major service in attempting to establish standard definitions for census taking, accounting, and other data gathering and data analysis procedures. Yet the task is far from complete, and often in using published data one cannot in any way be sure whether standard definitions were used.

One more major difficulty is the deliberate or semi-deliberate distortion of data by national governments. Sometimes a government does not want to admit that certain data are unavailable; such an admission may seem to reflect on its own competence or the state of development of the country. In such cases "data" may be created without much empirical reference. This may even occur when one branch of a government demands data from another. A regional office, faced with a demand for data which are beyond its resources to collect, may find quite ingenious ways of reporting something. And in any case the appearance of economic strength, of rapid development, or of a literate and healthy population, may be an important asset in international politics. Where the true data do not show these things they may be modified, and it can be extraordinarily difficult for an independent researcher to determine the presence or degree of modification. As some businessmen keep two sets of books, so do some governments.

So far we have relatively little data on intracountry differences. This is a serious gap, for the importance of the distribution of values within a country can hardly be overstated. One nation may have only a moderate number of radio receivers, but they may be reasonably well spread around the countryside. Another state, with about the same overall proportion of radios to population, may have them concentrated in the urban areas while the countryside remains as inaccessible to modern ideas as it was decades ago. The results will be very different. Or a country like Venezuela may have a relatively high *average* income while the majority of the population lives in poverty. Again, the implications are quite different from those of a more egalitarian distribution. In principle one would desire to know not just the *mean* of a certain value for a country, but also the *median,* the *mode,* and the *range* of the distribution, as well as the frequency and the physical and social location of various levels of the distribution. Obviously this is a rigorous demand at the moment; even for countries where these data might possibly be available, governments may have a clear interest in suppressing them.

Analysis

Empirical social analysis can be divided broadly into two types: examination in depth of a single case or at most a very few cases, and the more general comparison of many similar though not identical cases. Too often these two approaches are treated as exclusive and incompatible. Actually each type has serious limitations, but the limitations of one are often precisely the strengths of the other. Used in tandem they can complement each other in important ways.

Attention to a single "case" may take several forms. One may look at a particular social or political unit (like a nation) or a particular event (like a war) and examine the many variables which seem to be associated with certain outcomes. But scrutiny of the single case can never be pursued exclusively. One can know where to look and what kinds of relationships to seek out only by making at least implicit comparison with other cases. It is tempting to say that what one finds after analysis is unique, relevant only to the peculiar circumstances of the particular instance. But one can *know* that only after comparing the results with what has been found for other partly similar, partly dissimilar cases. Concentration on the single case always involves the loss of important information.

To escape from this quandary may require the examination of a single variable (such as class structure) and the search for its apparent effects in many societies. This type of analysis approaches the general comparative method distinguished above, but the primary focus on a single independent variable imposes severe limits on the wide applicability and productivity of one's analysis. Social scientists have now well learned that truly valid, generalizable results can best be obtained through the study of many variables—and many units and many events. This clearly can lead to inundation by too much data, a situation where neither mind nor computer can absorb and sort out the information. Furthermore, broad comparative analysis can give rise to serious difficulties in identifying causal relationships, as contrasted merely with correlations. While some mathematical and statistical means have been developed for dealing in part with this problem,[4] the fact remains that the single case study, which loses other types of information, is often uniquely valuable in the identification of cause, at least in the particular case. In other words, we feel that each approach leads eventually to the other; the social scientist who discards one does no service either to himself or to his readers. The priorities may of course work either way. Perhaps one observes the individual case, develops a theory, and then tests it against information from many other cases. Or one may start with the large body of data and then move to the case study to better identify details and causal relationships.

This discussion suggests another possible distinction in social science, that between the use of data for testing existing theory and the use of data as an active element in theory building. The latter instance may be of the sort sometimes inelegantly referred to as "fishing," that is, going to one's data without a clearly formulated hypothesis and letting the

4. Cf. Herbert A. Simon, "Spurious Correlation: A Causal Interpretation," *Journal of the American Statistical Association, 49* (1954), 467–79; H. M. Blalock, "Four Variable Causal Models and Partial Correlations," *American Journal of Sociology, 68* (1962), 182–94; and H. M. Blalock, "Making Causal Inferences for Unmeasured Variables from Correlations Among Indicators," *American Journal of Sociology, 69* (1963), 53–62.

data themselves suggest relationships. Such activity is often disdained; at best it is a preliminary rather than a final step in theory construction because of the possibility that an apparent relationship exists only by chance, not because of any true association. Yet there is much to be said for this procedure, particularly if it takes the form of a constant dialogue between theory and data. The theorist may begin with a set of hypotheses. Examination of data bears out some to a limited extent; others are not supported. Close scrutiny of the failures as well as of the successes suggests modifications of the hypotheses, which must be tested further with new data.

For the *Handbook* an initial step in the processing of our data was the computation of simple correlations of each series with every other series. Then the data were examined in light of existing theories, and with simple and multiple, linear and curvilinear regression models. Special adjustments were required to allow for missing data in some series. The analysis involved three distinct elements:

1. Discovering the degree of correlation, or the strength of relationship, among the variables.

2. If a correlation exists, finding the amount of change in one variable which can be predicted by knowing the amount of change in another. Multiple regression can assess the separate effect of a number of independent variables.

3. In addition to knowing the amount of change over the whole range of a series, discovering the degrees of change, i.e. the "elasticities," within the different ranges of variation.

For example, we examined the degree of correlation between illiteracy and population increase. The linear correlation coefficient is only moderately high ($r = .37$). In part this means that there are a number of deviant cases which must be singled out for further examination. In some instances these apparently deviant cases seem merely to be examples of inaccurate data; in others they indicate exceptions of significant theoretical import. We then moved from a simple correlation to a multiple regression including such variables as Gross National Product per capita and GNP growth rates; these raise the correlation coefficient very substantially. We also calculated the amount of decline in one variable associated with a given decline in another, and looked for changing elasticities—whether at some point the relationship changes sharply. Plotting the regression graphically brings out the deviant cases; it also shows the value of a curvilinear model (which raises the *simple* correlation to .49) rather than a linear one. Actually one finds that *higher* rates of natural population increase are associated with higher literacy until a level of about 50 per cent literate is reached. After that the rate of natural increase *declines* sharply with further literacy. Additional refinements in analysis involved the analysis of covariance to discover the effect on the correlation between two variables when a third variable, such as region, was introduced.

We have also experimented with different measures of inequality and with techniques of interpolation for estimating Lorenz curves to make initially noncomparable distribution data comparable.[5] By computing average rates of change in the acquisition of different goods by different segments of the world population we can project estimates and measures of inequality into the future.

By making our data generally available we can facilitate the analytical work of scholars and policymakers elsewhere, but our main interest is in extracting information. The Program is primarily a laboratory, not an archive. Our data were gathered with reference to substantive questions which have particularly interested us. Some of the questions examined during the past three years with the aid of Data Program information include national and international integration,[6] the political effects of highly unequal distribution

5. Cf. Hayward R. Alker, Jr., and Bruce M. Russett, "Indices for Comparing Inequality," this volume. For a further illustration of analytical techniques being developed under the Data Program, see Hayward R. Alker, Jr., *Mathematics and Politics* (New York, Macmillan, 1965).

6. Karl W. Deutsch and William J. Foltz, eds., *Nation-Building* (New York, Atherton, 1963); Karl W. Deutsch, "Supranational Organizations in the 1960's," *Journal of Common Market Studies*, No. 2 (1963); Karl W. Deutsch and Richard L. Merritt, "Effects of Events on National and International Images," in Herbert C. Kelman, ed., *International Behavior: A*

of agricultural land,[7] and variables affecting military posture and the credibility of military threats.[8]

It is possible to use the kind of aggregate data we have collected in combination with such variables as voting alignments in the United Nations. One completed study involved a factor analysis of voting patterns and identified not one or two basic dimensions, such as East–West or rich–poor, but eight or more quite separate dimensions in each General Assembly session. We then examined the voting positions of each nation on each of these alignments to see which variables correlated highly with them, or were good "predictors" of voting position. Some explanatory variables included characteristics of the state itself (such as GNP per capita), relations with the major powers (aid received from each), and characteristics shared with other states which might help to build community relationships (racial or religious composition). The data were analyzed in terms of explicit models of change and stability in world politics.[9]

PROSPECTS

Collection and Evaluation

Data collection will be more difficult in the future. Because we have already gathered figures for many of the more

---

Social-Psychological Analysis (New York, Holt, Rinehart, Winston, 1965); Karl W. Deutsch and Bruce M. Russett, "International Trade and Political Independence," *American Behavorial Scientist, 6* (March 1963), 18–20; Richard L. Merritt, *Symbols of American Community, 1735–1775* (New Haven, Yale University Press, 1966); Richard L. Merritt, "Systems and the Disintegration of Empires," in *General Systems: Yearbook of the Society for General Systems Research, 8* (1963), 91–103; Richard L. Merritt, "Distance and Interaction Among Political Communities," *General Systems: Yearbook of the Society for General Systems Research, 9* (1964), 255–63; Bruce M. Russett, *Community and Contention: Britain and America in the Twentieth Century* (Cambridge, Mass., M.I.T. Press), 1963; and Bruce M. Russett, *Trends in World Politics* (New York, Macmillan, 1965).

7. Bruce M. Russett, "Inequality and Instability: The Relation of Land Tenure to Politics," *World Politics, 14* (1964), 442–54.

8. Bruce M. Russett, "The Calculus of Deterrence," *Journal of Conflict Resolution, 7* (1963), 97–109; and Bruce M. Russett, "Measures of Military Effort," *American Behavorial Scientist, 7* (February 1964), 26–29.

9. Hayward R. Alker, Jr., and Bruce M. Russett, *World Politics in the General Assembly* (New Haven, Yale University Press, 1965); and Hay-

accessible series, the marginal cost of future efforts will in general be higher, perhaps substantially so. Yet if data are hard to come by, it means that adequate cross-national analyses of that particular variable are rare or nonexistent. If the marginal cost of a data series is high, the marginal gains to be derived from it may also be high.

Besides adding new series, we shall want to fill in data for certain countries which are now represented by gaps in existing series. To a degree this can be done by library research in the United States. The Human Relations Area Files, for example, may provide much missing data. Obtaining the kind of reliable and comparable information we need is an extremely uncertain and laborious task but, despite the perhaps forbidding costs of extraction, an expanded data collection program should be undertaken. We hope also to establish regular contacts in other countries with trained researchers who can supply us with data.

To date our emphasis has been primarily on cross-sectional studies, that is, the examination of data for many countries at approximately the same point in time. By using countries at different stages of development one can in certain respects approximate the result of a developmental study. But this is not truly a substitute for longitudinal study—examination of the actual development of one or a few countries over a long period of time. We should like to send people, perhaps established scholars, perhaps doctoral candidates, to both developed and developing countries to gather historical data and to make a close examination of the temporal sequence of events, of cause and effect.

We also want to explore means of obtaining certain kinds of data, otherwise unavailable, through survey research. Information can be derived from past opinion surveys, some of which for Europe, Asia, and North and South America are in the collection of the Yale Political Science Research Library; others can be obtained through the Inter-University Consortium for Political Research or from the Roper Public

---

ward R. Alker, Jr., "Dimensions of Conflict in the General Assembly," *American Political Science Review, 58* (1964), 642–57.

Opinion Research Center. We collaborated with the Indian Institute of Public Opinion on its annual political survey, taken in the winter of 1963–64.[10] Our questionnaire was designed to test hypotheses about language, stratification, and social attitudes not discoverable by other methods. It was from our point of view a pilot study which we hope will be followed by arrangements for comparable studies in other countries. Even so, the use of survey data is likely to be restricted for a long time by the limited number of countries for which such information is available.

One other possibility for obtaining attitudinal data is content analysis. When done by individual readers content analysis is expensive and exhausting, but recently developed methods for content analysis by computer reduce greatly the labor formerly required.[11] Computer processing also increases both the reliability of the results and in important respects the flexibility of the analyst.

In addition to collecting data, we must evaluate what we have—we must continue to assess error margins, to refine the crude ones we now have, and to develop better criteria for the limits of permissible error. To some extent the examination of correlations and the intensive study of deviant cases will indicate what kinds and magnitudes of error are likely to occur. To a large degree it will require thorough study of existing data-gathering procedures and intensive studies of reliability. So little has been done in this area that it seems to call for a major effort.

Analysis

We shall continue with the techniques mentioned previously and with the further application of others such as the analysis of covariance and factor analysis. We must perfect com-

10. Cf. Bruce M. Russett and Coralie Bryant, "The Citizen and His Society: Indians' Attitudes Toward Government, Modernization, and Each Other," *Monthly Public Opinion Surveys of the Indian Institute of Public Opinion*, 112–113 (January–February 1965).

11. Cf. Philip J. Stone, Robert F. Bales, J. Zvi Namenwirth, and Daniel M. Ogilvie, "The General Inquirer: A Computer System for Content Analysis and Retrieval Based on the Sentence as a Unit of Information," *Behavioral Science*, 7 (1962), 484–97.

putational techniques and develop means for searching possible combinations of variables for the most promising ones. A substantial task must be experimenting with various methods for dealing with the problem of missing data.

Now that much of the necessary data-gathering has been completed we shall be able to direct primary attention to what motivates data collection—our long-term interests in theory-testing and theory-building. One of our major concerns is with the *general* process or processes of modernization; with the interrelation of political, economic, social, and cultural change. We must look both for the effects of social and cultural change on economic development, and of economic change on political participation, the demand for services from the government sector, political violence, and the complexity and stability of political structures. We cannot expect to predict specific outcomes, such as revolutions or the establishment of totalitarian regimes, but rather take a probabilistic approach, identifying high tension levels and suggesting the range of specific consequences which might be expected and the kinds of measures which would be necessary to alleviate such tensions. From the identification of general patterns we can consider the effects of deviations from these patterns, as for example an exceptionally rapid development of educational facilities.

An important tool in the examination of changes over time will be computer content analysis, applied to speeches, party statements, newspaper editorials, and other political documents. The method is suitable not only for identifying changes in the frequency with which certain symbols or goals are mentioned, but in the patterns of association between symbols. Changes in symbol usage will be correlated with social changes identified from aggregated data, enriching our understanding of both. A double effort of validation is also implied. Attitudes tentatively identified from content analysis of documents will be compared, for current or recent data, with attitude data from surveys and depth interviews, and vice-versa. The result should permit us to extend our inferences to territories not now accessible to survey research (e.g. dictatorships) and to earlier historical periods.

The use of different kinds of data to supplement each other will be a key element in further research. Another problem to which such an approach is especially appropriate is the identification of groups of states or "regions," either within a country or in the world as a whole. Regions of sociocultural homogeneity can be identified from aggregative data; regions of interdependence from trade and other transaction data; regions of similar political attitudes from data on states which vote together on different issues in bodies like the United Nations. These groupings can first be compared for the degree of congruence that emerges, and then confronted with past or present international groupings based on supranational or intergovernmental institutions such as the EEC, NATO, or the Commonwealth. Time sequences must be identified, and the analysis related to existing theoretical and empirical literature on political integration.[12] These procedures should help identify which groups of states possess some of the apparent preconditions for successful merger. Comparative politics may be enriched by a better knowledge of the differences and similarities among regions, and of the boundaries of regions as defined by different variables.

One more intriguing possibility lies in the field of simulation. Our data could be used in the computer simulation of both national and international systems. Data for most of the major variables needed for simulating political and social development, or for simulating international conflict, are either already part of the Program's collections or can be gathered within the next two or three years. The simulation itself will require careful preparation and a useful model will have to be approached by a series of approximations; nevertheless its potential seems high enough to warrant extensive research.

12. For a beginning, see Bruce M. Russett, "Delineating International Regions," in J. David Singer, ed., *Empirical Studies in International Relations: International Yearbook of Political Behavior Research, VI* (New York, Free Press, 1966).

6. The Dimensionality of Nations Project[1]

RUDOLPH J. RUMMEL, YALE UNIVERSITY

The Dimensionality of Nations Project (DON) began in July of 1962 under a National Science Foundation Grant to Harold Guetzkow of Northwestern University. Jack Sawyer, University of Chicago, has served as technical consultant to the project and collaborated with Guetzkow from the very beginning in giving concrete substance to their ideas and in drafting the first project proposal.[2] The present author helped to draft the first proposal and became project director when the grant began. In 1963, DON was transferred to Indiana University under the author's guidance when he accepted a position there. A new proposal was submitted by the author in 1964 asking for a continuation of DON to carry out a distinct but complementary research design. This phase of the project was approved, and with the author's change to Yale University was begun at Yale in July 1964. Research under the DON Project thus divides into two phases. Phase I

1. Prepared in connection with research supported under a National Science Foundation grant NSF–GS–536. This paper is a revision and updating of R. J. Rummel, "A Proposal Submitted to Division of Social Sciences, National Science Foundation, for Continued Support of Basic Research," Dimensionality of Nations Project (mimeo., January 25, 1964). Much of the material discussed in Part I, below, was presented by Harold Guetzkow to the UNESCO Conference on the Use of Quantitative Data in Cross-National Research, Yale University, 1963.

2. Discussion of some of the topics below closely parallels their presentation in this 1962 proposal.

is concerned with the dimensions of cross-national variation among nations and is almost completed. Phase II is focusing on the dimensions of variation in the interactions and "distances" between nations and is now under way. These two phases will be discussed separately.

PHASE I. THE CROSS-NATIONAL STUDY

The first goal of this phase is to identify the primary clusters—dimensions—of interrelationships among variables which index the characteristics of nations, such as their prestige, trade, stability, culture, values, political development, urbanization, and economic growth rate. Once these are determined, the second goal is to identify the basic variables which index the position (factor score) of each nation on the dimensions.

Measures for the description of nations and their relations with each other abound. Political science has contributed systems of international relations constructed around concepts of power [3] and equilibria,[4] among others. Kuznets has extensively explored one concept in international economics —variations in the industrial structure of the labor force.[5] Psychology has contributed a large number of descriptions of the "national character" of various countries, summarized by Duijiker and Frijda.[6] The Human Relations Area Files, organized by Murdock, use categories often applicable to contemporary societies as well as to the primitive societies for which they are principally employed.[7] Sociology has

3. Hans Morgenthau, *Politics among Nations: The Struggle for Power and Peace* (2d ed. New York, Alfred Knopf, 1954).

4. George Liska, *International Equilibrium* (Cambridge, Harvard University Press, 1957).

5. Simon Kuznets, "Quantitative Aspects of the Economic Growth of Nations: II. Industrial Distribution of National Product and Labor Force," *Economic Development and Cultural Change*, supplement (July 1957), pp. 1–111.

6. H. J. C. Duijker and N. H. Frijda, *National Character and National Stereotypes: A Trend Report Prepared for the International Union of Scientific Psychology* (New York, The Humanities Press, 1960).

7. George P. Murdock, et al., *Outline of Cultural Materials* (4th ed. New Haven, Yale University Press, 1961).

characterized and compared institutions existing in various societies.[8]

A measure of particular current interest is development. Although nations often are referred to as developed or underdeveloped, it is realized that development is actually a continuum rather than a dichotomy. There exist very underdeveloped countries, moderately underdeveloped countries, and highly developed countries, with many interim points. Further, development perhaps is not unitary. A nation may be moderately developed economically, but underdeveloped with respect to its educational system. What at first is thought of as a dichotomy becomes a continuum, what is one continuum becomes several continua. Add other kinds of relevant information with which nations are described—military, demographic, political—and each nation quickly becomes located on a multitude of continua. Such specification of a number of dimensions is a desirable precursor to any theoretical or empirical inquiry comparing nations and understanding their interactions.

Thus, a dilemma is posed. On the one hand, nations as extremely complex units in complex relations with each other need multivariate description. On the other hand, for reasons of both conceptual clarity and economy of description, the number of dimensions must not become indefinitely large. The appropriateness of a reasonably small number of dimensions lies in the extent to which the original measures are correlated. If, for example, GNP, energy production, telephones, vehicles, and urban population were highly intercorrelated, one of these measures would suffice to index the interrelationships, or they may be combined into a single measure.

Factor analysis, by considering all the intercorrelations among variables, determines the minimum number of dimensions represented in the original set of variables, indicates how they are related to the original variables, and provides

8. A. Rose, "The Comparative Study of Institutions," in A. Rose, ed., *The Institutions of Advanced Societies* (Minneapolis, University of Minnesota Press, 1958).

standings of each nation on each of these dimensions. Such basic measurements of national characteristics, especially those in the very fields from which the measures are derived, such as international relations, comparative institutions, national character, cross-cultural research, and international economics, may provide useful data for a number of research concerns. In the area of political science alone one may illustrate at least three kinds of uses for such information: theory construction in international relations, experimentation, and empirical studies in comparative politics.

The studies of Wright [9] and Kaplan [10] and those discussed by Knorr and Verba [11] exemplify the dependency of theories of international relations upon a definition of the basic characteristics of nations as these complex units interact with each other in world affairs. The more empirically demonstrable the basic characteristics, the more adequately grounded is the theory. Experimental studies of international relations, such as internation simulation [12] or political gaming,[13] need knowledge about the basic dimensions of nations to establish the structure of the system they are simulating. In this case, information about the correlations between the dimensions as well as the nature of the dimensions themselves is useful. Lipset, in his analysis of the relation of social structure and type of government, found it necessary to devise measures of these two concepts specifically for his study.[14] Other comparative political studies have likewise

9. Quincy Wright, *The Study of International Relations* (New York, Appleton Century Crofts, 1955), *A Study of War* (Chicago, University of Chicago Press, 1942)

10. Morton A. Kaplan, *System and Process in International Politics* (New York, John Wiley, 1957).

11. Klaus Knorr and Sidney Verba, "Introduction," *World Politics, 14* (1961), 1–6.

12. Harold Guetzkow, "A Use of Simulation in the Study of Inter-Nation Relations," *Behavioral Science, 4* (1959), 183–91. Also, H. Guetzkow, Chadwick F. Alger, Richard A. Brody, Robert C. Noel, and Richard C. Snyder, *Simulation in International Relations: Developments for Research and Teaching* (Englewood Cliffs, N.J., Prentice-Hall, 1963).

13. Herbert Goldhamer and Hans Speier, "Some Observations on Political Gaming," *World Politics, 12* (1959), 71–83. See also Oliver Benson, "A Simple Diplomatic Game," in James Rosenau, *International Politics and Foreign Policy* (New York, The Free Press, 1961), pp. 110–19.

14. Seymour M. Lipset, "Some Political Requisites of Democracy: Eco-

developed measures for various concepts.[15] Often there is a partial but incomplete overlapping between different measures which makes comparison across studies difficult.

Besides feeding into possible research concerns, DON itself fits in with and has drawn on a constellation of completed studies, many of which are related in the sense of employing a number of characteristics for a set of nations. Especially noteworthy are those of Wright, Richardson, Almond and Coleman, Deutsch, Russett, Lerner, and Lipset.[16] In his 1955 study, Wright posited twelve factors to explain relations among nations.

Three studies involve factor analysis.[17] Raymond Cattell factored 72 variables for 69 nations, identifying 12 factors

---

nomic Development and Political Legitimacy," *American Political Science Review, 53* (1959), 69–106.

15. See Daniel Lerner, *The Passing of Traditional Society* (Glencoe, Ill., The Free Press, 1958) ; Karl W. Deutsch, "Shifts in the Balance of Communication Flows: A Problem of Measurement in International Relations," *Public Opinion Quarterly, 20* (1956), 152–55, and "The Propensity to International Transactions," *Political Studies, 8* (1960), 147–55; by the same author, "Toward an Inventory of Basic Trends and Patterns in Comparative and International Politics," *American Political Science Review, 54* (1960), 34–57, and "Social Mobilization and Political Development," *American Political Science Review, 55* (1961), 493–514; Russell Fitzgibbon and Kenneth Johnson, "Measurement of Latin American Political Change," *American Political Science Review, 55* (1961), 515–26; Lyle W. Shannon, "Is Level of Development Related to Capacity for Self-Government?" *American Journal of Economics and Sociology, 17* (1958), 367–81, and "Socio-Economic Development and Political Status," *Social Problems, 7* (1959), 157–69; Phillips Cutright, "National Political Development: Measurement and Analysis," *American Sociological Review, 28* (1963), 253–64; Bruce M. Russett, *Community and Contention* (Cambridge, MIT Press, 1963).

16. See Quincy Wright, *Study of War;* also, Lewis Fry Richardson, *Arms and Insecurity* (Pittsburgh, Boxwood Press, 1960), and *Statistics of Deadly Quarrels* (Pittsburgh, Boxwood Press, 1960) ; Gabriel A. Almond and James S. Coleman, *The Politics of Developing Areas* (Princeton, Princeton University Press, 1960) ; Karl W. Deutsch et al., *Political Community and the North Atlantic Area* (Princeton, Princeton University Press, 1957) ; Deutsch, "Inventory," 34–57, and "Social Mobilization," 493–514; Lerner, *Traditional Society;* Lipset, "Requisites," 69–106; finally, Bruce M. Russett, and Hayward R. Alker, Jr., Karl W. Deutsch, and Harold D. Lasswell, *World Handbook of Political and Social Indicators* (New Haven, Yale University Press, 1964).

17. Although finished too recently to influence the substantive decisions of the first phase of DON, a fourth factor study should be mentioned: Bruce M. Russett, "Delineating International Regions," in J. David Singer, ed., *Empirical Studies in International Relations: International Yearbook of Political Behavior Research,* VI (New York, Free Press, 1966).

including size, cultural pressure, enlightened affluence, thoughtful industriousness, vigorous, self-willed order, bourgeois philistinism, Buddhism-Mongolism, cultural integration, and morale.[18] Brian Berry, using 43 economic and geographic variables for 95 countries, extracted five factors.[19] In an investigation of urbanization, Schnore factored 11 economic and demographic variables for 75 countries and found a single factor, which may be identified as an economic development factor, accounting for nearly all the common variance.[20] Findings from these studies have proved useful in extending the range of variables analyzed by DON and in interpreting the research findings.

In a recent article concerned with the analysis of stability and capabilities, Deutsch indicated the need for some 75 categories of data for the nations of the world.[21] A National Science Foundation grant is now making it possible for Professor Deutsch to accelerate his accumulation of such raw data.[22] Where the Dimensionality of Nations variables have overlapped, an exchange of data and sources has proved of mutual advantage.

Accomplishments to Date: July 1962 to June 1964

A list of about 600 variables has been compiled, providing for each variable such information as its previous use in other systematic studies, data availability, and the concept the

18. Raymond B. Cattell, "The Dimensions of Culture Patterns by Factorization of National Characters," *Journal of Abnormal and Social Psychology, 44* (1949), 443–69. See by the same author "The Principal Culture Patterns Discoverable in the Syntal Dimensions of Existing Nations," *Journal of Social Psychology, 32* (1950), 215–53; also, Raymond B. Cattell, H. Bruel, H. Parker Hartman, "An Attempt at More Refined Definition of the Cultural Dimensions of Syntality of Modern Nations," *American Sociological Review, 17* (1952), 408–21.

19. Brian J. L. Berry, "Basic Patterns of Economic Development," in Norton Ginsburg, *Atlas of Economic Development* (Chicago, University of Chicago Press, 1961), 110–19; also, Ginsburg, ed., *Essays on Geography and Economic Development* (Chicago, University of Chicago Press, 1960).

20. L. F. Schnore, "The Statistical Measurement of Urbanization and Economic Development," *Land Economics, 37* (1961), 229–45.

21. Deutsch, "Inventory," 34–57.

22. This is the Yale Political Data Program directed by Bruce Russett. The work of this program is exemplified best in Russett et al., *World Handbook.*

variable is meant to index. Over a period of several months, and in conjunction with consultants, a core of 230 approved variables was culled from this master list, according to a set of criteria: data availability, scaling properties, theoretical relevance, hypothetical relevance, previous use, and statistical independence. Data for these approved variables were collected on the total number of sovereign nations (as indicated by a foreign ministry and the exchange of ambassadors) for 1955 having a population of 750,000 or more. Because more data appeared to be available for 1955 than for any other year, it was made the base year for the project. Over one hundred statistical sources were used in the data collection and the data have been recorded in such a fashion to make them generally available for research by others.[23]

Since many of the data are from United Nations sources, the U.N. has been consulted about the reliability of their data and about various plans of the Dimensionality of Nations Project for improving its quality. As a result of research and consultation, the project has composed error scores derived from the U.N. reliability codes and qualifications, with respect to the data on 40 of the variables to be factor analyzed. Indices were also derived that measure the degree to which the data deviate from 1955 for the variables which have the least data for the base year. These error scores and indices were factor analyzed along with a separate population error score, a missing data error score, and three random variables indexing the three major types of distributions found in the data: normal, rectangular, and negative exponential. The results of the intercorrelation and factor analyses of these error scores and indices have been prepared for publication.[24]

On the basis of these analyses, the important error scores or indices which measure basic dimensions of error among the data for the variables are: (1) population error score, (2) missing data summation score, (3) GNP error score,

23. Data and codes are available through the Inter-University Consortium for Political Research, Box 1248, Ann Arbor, Michigan.

24. Rudolph J. Rummel, "Dimensions of Error in Cross-National Data in the Mid-1950s," Dimensionality of Nations Project (mimeo., 1964).

(4) a *demographic error* dimension, and (5) an *economic-welfare error* dimension. Along with a random error variable, these three error scores and two factors were included subsequently in the analysis of the 230 variables to determine the effect of error on the substantive correlations and factor dimensions found.

In order to complete the various analyses projected by DON, a number of computer programs had to be prepared. Data screening and correlation programs to handle variables when some data are missing, and factor analysis programs which accommodate more than 200 variables generally are not available. Consequently, programmers were employed to write a 236-variable intercorrelation program for the project, and to revise existing BIMD programs to manage missing data. With the help of Harry Harman, Henry Kaiser, and John Carroll, the project was able to assemble several factor routines out of which programmers have developed a 236-variable factor analysis, orthogonal and oblique factor rotation program. All programs developed by the project have been made generally available and are now part of the program libraries of Northwestern University, Indiana University, the University of Chicago, and Yale University.

With the aid of the programs, DON has completed a number of studies. The first, a pilot study, involved the factor analysis and location of 77 nations on the resulting dimensions for 22 of the 230 variables with which the project is concerned. These 22 variables are those indexing domestic and foreign conflict behavior, 1955–57. A summary of the results, "The Dimensions of Conflict Behavior Within and Between Nations," has been published.[25] In connection with the project, a replication of the above study on 1958–60 conflict behavior data for 81 nations was completed at Indiana University.[26] The results were largely the same: domestic and foreign conflict were independent; *turmoil* is a major

25. Rummel, "Dimensions of Conflict Behavior Within and Between Nations," *General Systems: Yearbook of the Society for General Systems Research*, 8 (1963), 1–50.

26. Raymond Tanter, "Dimensions of Conflict Behavior Within and Between Nations, 1958–1960" (Ph.D. dissertation, Indiana University, 1964).

dimension of domestic conflict behavior; and foreign conflict behavior takes place along *war, diplomatic,* and *belligerent* dimensions. Another analysis, but only of domestic conflict behavior data, 1946–59, for 113 countries, determined dimensions similar to those found in the above studies.[27] A discussion and comparison of these studies and of others relative to dimensions of conflict behavior has been prepared.[28]

A regression analysis substudy which had as its goal the testing of some possible predictors of 1955–57 domestic and foreign conflict behavior among nations also has been completed. To this end, nine measures of domestic conflict behavior and thirteen measures of foreign conflict behavior for 69 nations were regressed upon predictors indexing their technological and demographic levels, size, and contrasts in income and external relations, as well as the behavioral dimensions coming out of "The Dimensions of Conflict Behavior Within and Between Nations." A report and summary of this study—"Testing Some Possible Predictors of Conflict Behavior Within and Between Nations"—has been published.[29]

Among the 236 variables selected for analysis were 94 measures indexing aspects of international relations such as trade, membership in international organizations, treaties signed, aid given and received, and U.N. votes. Since these 94 measures collectively were of substantive interest in themselves, they were intercorrelated and factor analyzed to determine some of the major dimensions of international relations in the mid-1950s.[30] Several of the dimensions delineated were *cooperation, conflict, aid, ideology, international popularity, Latin American,* and *migration.*

27. Rummel, "Dimensions of Conflict Behavior Within Nations, 1946–1959," Dimensionality of Nations Project (mimeo., 1964).

28. Rummel, "Dimensions of Foreign and Domestic Conflict Behavior: A Review of Empirical Findings," in Dean Pruitt and Richard C. Snyder, *Readings on Conflict* (forthcoming).

29. Rummel, "Testing Some Possible Predictors of Conflict Behavior Within and Between Nations," *Papers, 1* (Peace Research Society, 1964), 79–111.

30. Rummel, "Some Dimensions of International Relations in the Mid-1950s," Dimensionality of Nations Project (mimeo., 1964).

The complete 236-variable (230 substantive variables plus 6 error measures) by 82-nation data matrix was factor analyzed through orthogonal rotation in the spring of 1964. Some of the major dimensions to emerge were *economic, political, power bases, Latin American, foreign conflict behavior, density, and domestic conflict.* This analysis involved approximately 17 per cent missing data. Consequently, nations and variables with the most missing data were eliminated and a reanalysis was completed on a 153-variable by 71-nation data matrix reduced to 3 per cent missing data. The results were largely the same. The findings of the 236- and 153-variable analyses are being prepared for publication.[31] Descriptive statistics on the data distributions and the intercorrelations among the 236 variables are planned for publication separately.[32]

Although the major analyses projected for DON's first phase are completed, some important tasks remain. Oblique rotations of the 236-, 153-, and 94-variable factor structures are scheduled for computation early in 1965, for comparison with the orthogonal solutions. To this end, a computer program involving the biquartimin oblimin solution of John Carroll [33] is being revised for more efficient rotation on 236 variables, and we have approached Herbert Eber about using his revision of the Maxplane program.

Once a satisfactory factor pattern has been determined for each of the analyses, it is anticipated that Euclidean distances between nations for the major dimensions will be determined.[34] These distances may then be used to group nations in terms of their similarities and as input to studies

31. Rudolph J. Rummel, Jack Sawyer, Harold Guetzkow, and Raymond Tanter, *Dimensions of Nations* (forthcoming, 1965).

32. Rummel, Sawyer, and Guetzkow, "236 Cross-National Characteristics: Sources, Descriptive Statistics, and Correlations" (forthcoming, 1965).

33. John B. Carroll, "IBM 709–7090 Program for Generalized Analytic Rotation Solution in Factor Analysis" (Harvard University, June 1961).

34. For a clarification of this concept see Brian J. L. Berry, "A Method for Deriving Multi-factor Uniform Regions," *Polish Geographical Review, 33* (1961), 263–82. For an application to cross-national data see Russett, "Delineating International Regions."

concerned with the relation of similarities and differences between nations to their behavior toward each other.

Finally, a computer program is being prepared which will allow for the systematic comparison of factor analyses from different studies, using the "transformation analysis" proposed by Yrjö Ahmavaara.[35] These comparisons should furnish better grounds for generalization about major cross-national dimensions than can be given by any one study. The completion of these comparisons should conclude Phase I of DON and permit the concentration of resources on Phase II—the dyadic study.

PHASE II. THE DYADIC STUDY

It was soon discovered after the Dimensionality of Nations Project had begun that a wide range of variables of general theoretical and experimental interest could not be included in the design originally proposed to the National Science Foundation. This design called for the intercorrelation and factor analysis of a number of variables indexing *individual* characteristics of nations (e.g. GNP, population, size) to determine the basic dimensions of variation across all nations.

A complementary design is necessary, however, if one is also concerned with dimensions of internation variation. Such variation is in terms of relational variables which indicate the structural similarities and differences between nations and the behavior they direct toward each other. These similarities and differences may lie along several dimensions. One of these might be a distance dimension, possibly indicating that between nations which are far apart there is less diplomatic intercourse, trade, and communication than between nations close together. A technological (or development) dimension might define another cluster of interrelationships, such as similarity in technological level,

35. Yrjö Ahmavaara, "On the Unified Factor Theory of Mind," *Annales Akademiae Scientiarum Fennicae*, Serial B, 160 (Helsinki, 1957).

common membership in international organizations, high trade with each other, a high level of communication, and considerable conflict. Similarity in values, common foreign policies, cooperative behavior, and similarity in population levels might characterize yet a third possible dimension. Whether such dimensions of *internation* variation or others like them exist is a question for research to decide, but a question which cannot be answered only in terms of an analysis of the *individual* character of nations.

Given the complementary individual and internation designs, the choice was made to proceed with the analysis originally envisioned and discussed in the beginning of this paper. As described below, the dimensions of variation in the characteristics of nations could then be used as input to a study of internation relations—a dyadic analysis which would constitute a second phase of the project. The analysis of individual characteristics of nations seems logically to precede an investigation of their interrelations.

Such an investigation of internation behavior will be especially relevant to the field of international relations. Although there are exceptions,[36] students in the field have been interested less in determining the dimensions of the system and of the individual units of that system than in trying to delimit internation behavior and the correlates of this behavior. Consequently, most of the hypotheses in international relations deal with individual variables which express relations between countries. For example, several propositions relating the degree of integration between two countries and their transactions, such as trade and mail, have been proposed by Karl Deutsch.[37] A. F. K. Organski has hypothesized that differences in population, economic, and technological levels and resources interrelate with the kinds of behavior two nations direct toward each other.[38] An

36. Kaplan, *System and Process.* Also, Richard N. Rosecrance, *Action and Reaction in World Politics* (Boston, Little, Brown, 1963).

37. Karl W. Deutsch, *Political Community at the International Level* (New York, Doubleday, 1954); also, "Shifts in the Balance," 152–55, and Deutsch et al., *Political Community.*

38. A. F. K. Organski, *World Politics* (New York, Alfred A. Knopf, 1960).

assumed association between military power, economic and technological levels, resources, and behavior toward other nations has served as a major theme for such students of the field as Hans Morgenthau,[39] Frederick Schuman,[40] and Quincy Wright.[41]

There have been studies attempting to deal systematically with the relations between nations. Quincy Wright has posited eight "distances" as being crucial to the behavior of nations toward each other:[42] technological distance (T), strategic distance (St), legal distance (L), intellectual distance (I), social distance (S), political distance (P), psychic distance (Ps), and war expectancy distance (E). Integrating the formula,[43] $\frac{dPs}{dt} = (4\frac{dE}{dt} - \frac{dSt}{dt}) + (3\frac{dP}{dt} - \frac{dL}{dt})$, and applying it to the August 1939 relations between the United States, Great Britain, France, Germany, Italy, Japan, and the U.S.S.R., Wright found a close fit of psychic distance (Ps) to the degree of friendliness between these six nations. Considering the same nations and period, Frank Klingberg in a 1941 study attempted to develop a method for gauging the degree of friendliness and hostility between nations from which the probability of war between them might be determined.[44] By sending schedules to students of international relations and having them rank pairs of nations in terms of hostility, he was able to arrive at indices which were predictive of the outbreak of World War II.

In a more thorough and systematic fashion than either Wright or Klingberg, the Studies in International Conflict and Integration Project at Stanford University, under the direction of Robert C. North, has been analyzing the rela-

39. Morgenthau, *Politics among Nations.*

40. Frederick L. Schuman, *International Politics* (6th ed. New York, McGraw-Hill, 1958).

41. Wright, *International Relations; Study of War, 1* and *2.*

42. Wright, *Study of War, 2,* 1240–60.

43. Ibid., p. 1282.

44. Frank L. Klingberg, "Studies in Measurement of the Relations among Sovereign States," in Rosenau, ed., *International Politics and Foreign Policy,* pp. 483–91. This article was reprinted from *Psychometrika, 6* (1941), 335–52.

tions between perceptions of hostility and threat on the part of individual nations and the outbreak of war between them.[45] Applying correlational analysis to data derived from a content analysis of the diplomatic documents of France, England, Russia, Germany, Austro-Hungary, and Serbia, North and his associates have found perception of hostility to be an "almost perfect" predictor of conflict relationships.

Also concerned with hostility, Ithiel de Sola Pool and associates have done a content analysis of the editorials of nearly a fifty-year period for the leading newspapers of the United States, Great Britain, France, Germany, and Russia.[46] One of his major findings revealed that the attitudes of these powers seem to reflect each other strongly. "There is . . . a remarkable degree of reciprocity in the attitudes of states toward each other. This reciprocity is not necessarily immediate, but in the long run if elite editorial opinion in state A is hostile to state B, then elite editorial opinion in state B will become hostile to state A to almost the same degree."[47] Another conclusion was that the more secure a nation is in its power positions vis-à-vis other nations, the less hostility it directs to other nations.

Two other studies may also be mentioned briefly. Lewis Fry Richardson in his mathematical and statistical investigation of conflict found, among other things, a relationship of conflict between nations to their rate of increase in armaments, contiguity, cultural differences, and trade.[48] Bruce M. Russett statistically investigated (in terms of transaction flows, attention, and responsiveness) the relations between Britain and the United States during the last 70

45. Robert C. North, et al., "The Integrative Functions of Conflict," *Journal of Conflict Resolution, 4* (1960), 355–74; North, "Appendix B: Propositions from the 1914 Crises," in North et al., *Content Analysis* (Evanston, Northwestern University Press, 1963). Also, Dina Zinnes, "Hostility in International Decision-Making," *Journal of Conflict Resolution, 6* (1962), 236–43; Zinnes et al., "Capability, Threat, and the Outbreak of War," in Rosenau, ed., *International Politics and Foreign Policy*, 469–82.

46. Ithiel de Sola Pool, *Symbols of Internationalism* (Stanford, Stanford University Press, 1951).

47. Ibid., p. 61.

48. Richardson, *Arms; Deadly Quarrels.*

years.[49] He found that, rather than becoming integrated with each other, these two countries are in fact growing further apart.

Several points may be noted about these studies. First, the number of interrelationships between nations considered and those variables for which they have controls is limited. Second, these studies are confined to about five of the most powerful and the most economically developed nations (although some of the relationships investigated by Richardson are exceptions). Third, some studies limit themselves further to a particular event (Wright, North, Zinnes, and Klingberg), such as World War I or World War II. Finally, few of these studies have benefited from the use of multivariate techniques and the existence of high speed computers. Although Richardson and Zinnes have used simple correlation, and continuing research under North is now beginning to use multiple correlation, analysis of variance or covariance, multiple regression, or factor analysis generally have not been employed even though they are powerful tools and one or the other is applicable to the data of most of these studies.

By using variables similar to those employed in the above studies wherever possible, the dyadic analysis is being fitted into the context of completed systematic analysis on the relations between nations. Moreover, the dyadic study is attempting to profit from a consideration of their limitations by: (1) dealing simultaneously with 50 to 100 variables covering the largest number of domains (e.g. economic, political, social) to control for the effects of unsuspected influences; (2) employing much larger samples (about 160 dyads); (3) employing a number of data screening analyses to check for the type of distributions, the existence of outliers, and for curvilinearity; (4) transforming distributions where appropriate; (5) using various devices to control for data error and bias; (6) using the most powerful multivariate techniques available appropriate to the form of the

49. Russett, *Community and Contention.*

data; (7) processing the data through a high speed computer, with advantages in scope of analysis, efficiency, and results per investment of resources that it entails.

Research Design

Figure 6.1 shows the data matrix for the 236- and 153-variable analyses of Phase I, discussed above. It is a variable by nation data matrix, where the intercorrelations are calculated between variables and across 82 nations. The data matrix for the dyadic study is shown in Figure 6.2. Here also, variables are intercorrelated, but across dyads rather than across individual nations. The variables, therefore, will be descriptive of relations between members of a dyad, such as trade and communications, or descriptive of differences between them, such as in their populations or armed forces. Whereas the factor analysis of the intercorrelations of variables in Figure 6.1 indicates dimensions of variation in the *individual* characteristics of nations, the factor analysis of the intercorrelations of the variables in Figure 6.2 will show the basic dimensions of *internation* similarities, differences, and behavior.

With the resources available, it is not possible to do the analysis across all possible dyads in the world, which for 1955 would number 3,321 dyads. Therefore, using a random number table, a *random* sample of 160 dyads was selected. To this sample were added six dyads, such as US–USSR, and US–China, which were considered of sufficient interest to warrant the slight loss in randomness caused by their inclusion. For comparison, a second *selected* sample will also be analyzed. This sample will be chosen in terms of those nations which lie at the extremes and middle of the meaningful and reliable dimensions determined by the 236-variable factor analysis of Phase I. The virtue of this approach is that information from the cross-national analyses can be applied at this later stage. That is, nations that index the primary dimensions of variation among them are sure to be chosen. Using the finding of an *economic* dimension among nations, for example, this technique of sample selection would insure that nations which were highly developed economically, markedly underdeveloped, and intermediately developed would be included in the dyads. Comparison of the results of analyzing the sample thus selected with results of the

Figure 6.1. **Cross-National 236- and 153-Variable Analyses Data Matrix**

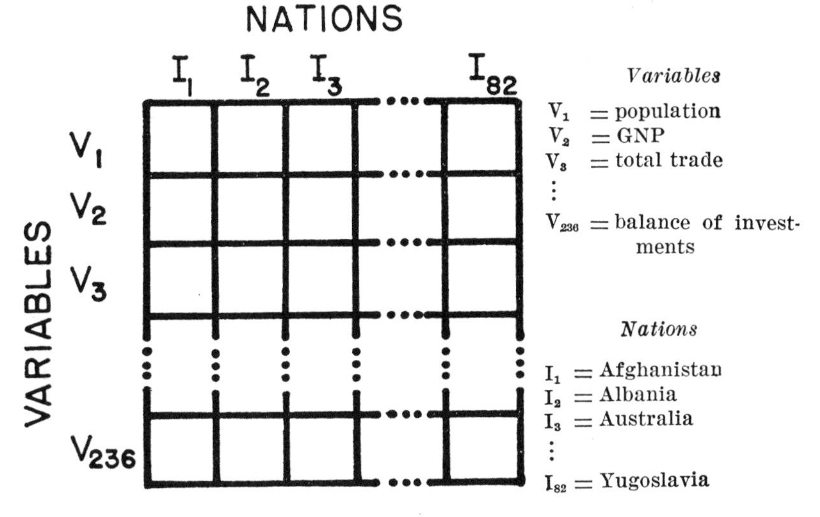

Figure 6.2. **Dyadic Analysis Data Matrix**

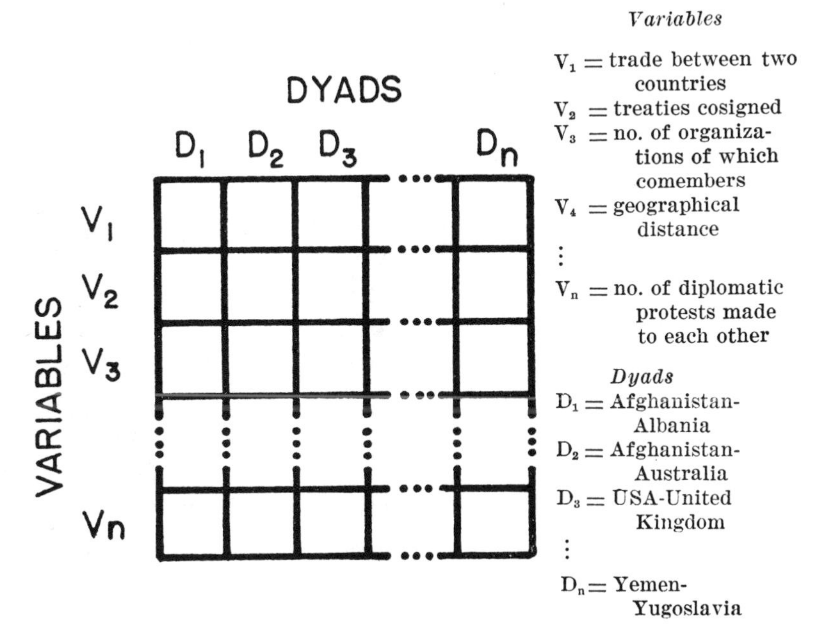

random sample should furnish grounds for generalizing about interaction between nations.[50]

The variables that may be used in the dyadic study fall into two groups: those which index the structural similarities and differences between two nations, and those which index the behavior of two nations toward each other. Since the dyadic study is still in the formative stage, the following list of variables is meant to be suggestive and not a final list. The primary criteria that will determine the final choice of variables are theoretical relevance, use by other systematically oriented studies, data availability, and scaling properties. Each variable mentioned below refers to relations between two nations.

BEHAVIORAL VARIABLES

Cooperation

1. trade
2. trade / total trade with all other countries
3. public international organizations (I.O.) of which comembers
4. public I.O. of which comembers / total public I.O. of which both are members
5. private I.O. of which comembers
6. private I.O. of which comembers / total private I.O. of which both are members
7. bilateral treaties
8. bilateral treaties / total bilateral treaties signed by both
9. multilateral treaties of which cosignatories
10. multilateral treaties of which cosignatories / total multilateral treaties signed by both

50. The factor results for the selected sample may be used in regression studies in which the concern is the regression coefficients. Using the resulting dimensions as independent variables insures that the full range of variation among nations is indexed while the regression coefficients for the selected sample are unbiased estimators of the coefficients for the universe of dyads. It should be emphasized that in the regression model the values of the independent variables may be selected to cover a range of values without losing the inferential properties of the regression coefficients.

11. military treaties of which cosignatories
12. military treaties of which cosignatories / military treaties signed by both
13. state visits of one chief of state to the other
14. state visits of one chief of state to the other / total state visits of both

Agreement–Disagreement

15–18. difference in factor scores on dimensions of votes in the UN General Assembly (one source is the factor analyses of UN votes by Hayward Alker) [51]

Attention

19. tourists
20. migrants
21. diplomatic importance in terms of: exchange of ambassadors (=2), exchange consuls only (=1), exchange no diplomatic personnel (=0)
22. mail
23. mail / total mail of both

Conflict

24. threats exchanged
25. threats exchanged / total threats
26. accusations exchanged
27. accusations exchanged / total accusations
28. diplomatic protests
29. diplomatic protests / total protests
30. existence of military action short of war
31. existence of war
32. negative sanctions exchanged
33. negative sanctions exchanged / total negative sanctions
34. troop movements directed at each other
35. mobilizations directed at each other

51. Hayward R. Alker, Jr., "Dimensions of Conflict in the General Assembly," *American Political Science Review, 58* (1964), 642–57.

Conflict

36. antiforeign demonstrations directed at each other
37. people killed in all violence between two nations
38. people killed in all violence between two nations / total for both

Structural Variables

39. geographic distance between two nations (homeland)
40. geographic distance between two nations (including territory)
41. number of countries between two nations

42–?. distance on the dimensions of variation in the characteristics *among* nations

The variables from 42 on may consist of distances or ratios on the most meaningful and reliable basic dimensions among the 236 cross-national variables. Thus the dyadic analysis is making direct use of the findings of the previous analyses of individual characteristics of nations to index the major differences and similarities among nations and to choose one of the samples of dyads to be analyzed.

The major sources of data for the dyadic analysis will be largely the same as for the 236-variable study. They will consist mainly of such statistical sources as the United Nations' *Demographic Yearbook, Statistical Yearbook, Yearbook of International Trade Statistics,* and special studies; statistical and qualitative sources such as *The Statesman's Yearbook, Worldmark Encyclopedia of Nations, Yearbook of International Organizations,* United Nations treaty series, and *Political Handbook and Atlas of the World;* and event sources such as *The New York Times, Facts on File,* and *Keesing's Contemporary Archives.*

In analyzing the data, the project will continue to use principal components factor analysis and to experiment with several kinds of rotations until a satisfactory solution is achieved. Basic variables will be selected to estimate the location of dyads on the dimensions of interactions found. Prior to the analysis, the distributions of the data on each variable will be computed and transformed to normality where possible. Extreme values of more than 3.0 standard deviations existing in the data will be eliminated. Tests will be made of the degree of curvilinearity in the relationships between the variables. If curvilinearity is sufficient to reduce considerably the linear correlations between variables, then appropriate transformations will be applied.

As with the cross-national study, 1955 will be the year for which data will be collected. As resources allow, however, data will be collected for subsequent years to permit a year-by-year replication of the findings for 1955. It is anticipated that if analyses can be completed for each of the years 1955–60, a plot of the annual changes in the movement of dyads along the major dimensions of interaction, and in their distances from each other, should furnish very useful information.

The Dimensionality of Nations Project has been concerned with determining some of the major dimensions of variation among nations on their political, social, economic, cultural, and behavioral characteristics. This goal, now largely achieved, involved the factor analysis of 94, 153, and 236 cross-national variables for, at most, 82 nations on 1955 data. Three of the primary dimensions to emerge from the 153- and the 236-variable analyses were *economic*, *political,* and *power bases.*

A second phase of the project, now in its formative stage, will factor analyze the interactions between nations to determine some of their major dimensions. Random and selected samples of pairs of nations and information from the cross-national study described above will be employed. The analysis will begin on 1955 data for 50 to 100 variables; as resources allow, the analysis will be duplicated on annual data for subsequent years to allow for a determination of the stability of the dimensions and the longitudinal changes among the dyads.

7. Cross-National Comparisons Using Aggregate Data: Some Substantive and Methodological Problems

ERWIN K. SCHEUCH, UNIVERSITY OF COLOGNE

ENTHUSIASM AND SUSPICION IN VIEWING AGGREGATE DATA

One important difference between styles of research among political scientists and sociologists in various countries is in the type of data they customarily use. There is certainly no methodological necessity for doing so, but in practice social scientists often behave as if they had to rely either on observations of individuals (now mainly through survey research) or on aggregate data (largely census data).

Working with aggregates has had a long and honorable tradition in the form of electoral statistics in several European countries, notably France.[1] In the United States aggregate data have been relatively less important for investigations of voting behavior, but in such fields as the study of delinquency and social problems in general aggregate data have been the empirical basis for "classical" studies.[2] With the development of survey research, however,

1. Cf. Austin Ranney, "The Utility and Limitations of Aggregate Data in the Study of Electoral Behavior," *Essays in the Behavorial Study of Politics*, ed. Ranney (Urbana, University of Illinois Press, 1962), pp. 91–102.

2. The following studies are cited as examples, not as a complete documentation of important investigations: William Ogburn, "Factors in the Variation of Crime Among Cities," *Journal of the American Statistical Association, 30* (1935), 12–34; Clifford Shaw, *Delinquency Areas* (Chicago, University of Chicago Press, 1929), and *Juvenile Delinquency in Urban Areas* (Chicago, University of Chicago Press, 1942); Robert C. Angell,

and with other social research techniques partly adapted from psychology, the relative importance of aggregate studies has declined even in those fields. Most of the more recent important contributions to social science knowledge have thus been based on individual measurements.

The preference for individual measurements or aggregated data is, of course, partly a consequence not of attitudes but rather of having access to either type of information. This obvious explanation, however, detracts from other reasons that are more relevant for methodology. The very availability of different types of data can in part be understood as a property of the social system, and is related to the usefulness of either type of information. The need to collect individual measurements and to develop tools for large-scale collection of such measurements—such as survey research—was not so great (or not so evident) in societies where a developed bureaucracy engaged in extensive "social bookkeeping." In the United States the growth of survey research in particular was encouraged by the lack of detailed statistical information,[3] and estimates are obtained by surveys on some population parameters that in several European countries are available from official statistical offices. Even today, U.S. electoral statistics are less reliable and less complete than in some Continental countries, and they certainly have less his-

---

"The Moral Integration of American Cities," *American Journal of Sociology, 57* (1951), 1–40; Pascal Whelpton, "Geographic and Economic Differentials in Fertility," *Annals of the American Academy of Political and Social Science, 188* (1936), 37–55; Harold Gosnell, "Analysis of the 1932 Presidential Vote in Chicago," *American Political Science Review, 24* (1935), 967–984, and *Machine Politics* (Chicago, University of Chicago Press, 1938)—the latter being an early example of large-scale use of factor analysis for aggregated data.

Demography relies so obviously on aggregate data that we choose to bypass this field in the present discussion.

3. This lack of sometimes elementary statistical information does not fit the stereotype of the U.S. as a country where everything is "counted," but it is nevertheless quite evident. As an example, there is and has been an interval of ten years between each U.S. census, while in Germany until recently the interval was five years; and yet the U.S. is a country with very high rates of change. The inadequacy of information for administrative purposes has led to the development of very important technical innovations, beginning with the invention of the punch card by the U.S. Census employee Hollerith to the quarterly sample surveys that are now also being used in other countries (e.g. Germany's *Mikrozensus*).

torical depth.[4] To forestall misunderstandings, let it be said that the earlier availability of relatively good data in many European countries has also been an impediment to methodological innovation.

Although it is obvious, it is seldom realized that a preference for either individual or aggregate measurements is related to some well-established inclinations for differing strategies in theory construction. Macrotheories are easier to connect with aggregate data, while microtheories and reductionistic explanations of systems are apparently more easily related to individual measurements. Both preference for different strategies in theory construction and the availability of either individual measurements or aggregate data often appear to be connected with the actual degree of centralization and formalization of the social systems and societies in which and with which the researcher deals. In government and political sociology, preference for macrotheories and aggregate data is specifically connected to the smaller relevance of individual citizens for political processes, and to the greater relevance of planning done and of decisions made on the level of aggregates. This characterization fits many Continental societies, just as the reverse is more characteristic of the United States as a polity. In the earlier phases of an empirical discipline, and specifically in political science, reliance on a type of theory and a kind of data which appeared isomorphic to the distinguishing characteristic of a system led to quicker success. In this way, preferences are reinforced.

From this perspective it should be understandable that the debate about the proper use of aggregates is laden with implications other than those of a purely methodological character. This should be of special relevance once a discussion of

4. During the 1962 gubernatorial elections in the Commonwealth of Massachusetts, defeated incumbent Volpe demanded a recount; and, with a margin between the defeated candidate and the victorious contender Peabody remaining around 5,000, about 50,000 votes were reassigned in the recount. In the city of Cambridge, Massachusetts (which has an unusually complicated voting system), nobody knows the real distribution of votes even for the last election, since counting is more or less abandoned once a candidate is declared elected.

aggregates versus individual measurements really begins in political science, too. In other social sciences—where preferences are perhaps less reinforced—some researchers clung to their preferences to such a degree that they declared problems "not researchable" if their particular kind of information was presently unavailable. And indeed, in discussing the use of aggregate data one was indirectly debating substantive issues in social science.

This very debate, aggregate versus individual measurement, is of course in a way quite gratuitous. With the availability of survey research and other facilities for individual measurement in developed societies, and with the improvement and extension of official statistical services, there is no need any more to behave as if one had to make a choice in principle between aggregate and individual measurements. There probably was rarely ever a real need to do so, but now it should be apparent. Using both types of data in research is as such nothing new and has been widely done, especially in community studies. The Yale Political Data Program at present relies on aggregate data, but, as Russett emphasizes, it intends also to make wider use of surveys and other individual measurements in the future.[5] If this is to be done effectively, then a clarification of the different evidential character of either type of data and a fuller awareness of the problems in working with aggregates in general will be necessary—and it will be even more necessary if the units are such large aggregates as polities or societies.[6]

5. Bruce M. Russett, "The Yale Political Data Program: Experience and Prospects," Chap. 5 in this volume.

6. Instead of the usual distinction between aggregate and individual measures (which is also used here), Lazarsfeld and Rosenberg propose a further distinction between aggregate and global properties: aggregate properties are those that are derived from information about each individual unit; global properties "deal with the product of the group without reference to any individual member's contribution." Paul F. Lazarsfeld and Morris Rosenberg, *The Language of Social Research* (Glencoe, Free Press, 1955), pp. 287–88. This distinction is based on the genesis of a datum (although this is not too clear from the definition of a "global property"), while here the emphasis is on the type of interpretation in relation to a measure's derivation. A large number of data in the CPS are global properties in the sense of Lazarsfeld and Rosenberg, in contrast to the emphasis on aggregate properties in the YPDP. We do not think this distinction to be

PROBLEM FORMULATION IN DISCUSSING THE USES OF AGGREGATE DATA FOR CROSS-CULTURAL COMPARISONS

Until very recently, in most social science disciplines except cultural anthropology, cross-national comparisons involving numbers meant using aggregate data. Since World War II, and especially during the last several years, we have observed a number of important examples of comparing large territories such as nation-states by using survey research.[7] The use of aggregate data (specifically of statistical information about nation-states) and cross-societal comparisons via survey research have proceeded simultaneously and separately without so far causing a major methodological debate.

Within the past two years we have witnessed the publication of books on the two most ambitious and voluminous cross-cultural comparisons ever on the basis of national aggregates: The Yale Political Data Program (the YPDP) initiated by Karl Deutsch and Harold Lasswell, and the Cross-Polity Survey (CPS) by Arthur Banks and Robert Textor.[8] These first true world surveys of polities attempt to

the most useful, since actually very different problems are involved in arriving at aggregate properties in the sense of Lazarsfeld and Rosenberg, while in the stage of interpretation this distinction between two types of properties may not matter at all—as should be apparent from the later discussion. Finally, in defining "global" in this way, one may run the danger of reifying an aggregate.

7. Alex Inkeles, "Industrial Man: The Relations of Status to Experience, Perception, and Value," *Society and Self*, ed. Bartlett Hicks Stoodley (Glencoe, Free Press, 1962); Seymour Martin Lipset, "Democracy and Working-Class Authoritarianism," *American Sociological Review, 24* (1959), 482–501; Gabriel A. Almond and Sidney Verba, *The Civic Culture: Political Attitudes and Democracy in Five Nations* (Princeton, Princeton University Press, 1963).

8. Arthur S. Banks and Robert B. Textor, *A Cross-Polity Survey* (Cambridge, M.I.T. Press, 1963). Both the YPDP and the CPS so far have concentrated on aggregates. However, the CPS largely works with nominal and ordinal variables derived from judgmental coding, while the YPDP preferred quantitative variables that may be treated as interval measurements. Thus, the following discussion refers to problems that are specifically relevant for the YPDP.

The YPDP and the CPS are both conceived as being applicable to individual measurements and specifically to survey data, and such application is envisaged by the authors of both data programs. The Yale Political Science Research Library has collected survey material, and this will be provide the empirical basis for generalizing propositions about polities as concrete units determined by general factors, instead of emphasizing the unique features.

In trying to implement similar programs, the two surveys follow quite different strategies in the processing of data. The differences in strategy, the scope of the comparisons, and especially the abstract way of dealing with politics are aspects of the YPDP and the CPS which call for major attention and should trigger a lively methodological debate. Hopefully, in this debate there will be some carry-over from previous methodological discussions about the use of aggregates in other social science fields which usually referred to much smaller units for aggregation than whole nation-states.

One very important example is the controversy in the early 1950s which centered around a problem referred to as the "ecological fallacy." [9] This debate cleared some important points and led to some unfortunate problem definitions, but appears to have had only a limited long-run impact.

The discussion of the "ecological fallacy" was in part just a repetition of an earlier and more generally posed controversy over the use of grouped data. And this debate again proceeded as if the character of aggregate data, the advantages of working with them, had to be discussed as a new topic.[10] Thus, the earlier heated controversy over an attempt

---

processed for the purposes of the YPDP in the same way as the aggregate statistics used so far. A central element of the CPS is the Pattern Search and Table Translation Technique, and this technique has already been applied to some survey data; plans call for its application to survey data gathered from more than one country.

The YPDP and the CPS differ fundamentally in their approaches to data; in this context it is, however, important to note one agreement: the YPDP and the CPS are not only prepared to handle individual measurement, but want to combine aggregate and individual descriptors.

9. William S. Robinson, "Ecological Correlations and the Behavior of Individuals," *American Sociological Review, 15* (1950), 351–57; Herbert Menzel, "Comment on Robinson's 'Ecological Correlations and the Behaviour of Individuals,'" *American Sociological Review, 15* (1950), 674.

10. For some earlier discussions see, e.g., G. Udney Yule and M. G. Kendall, *An Introduction to the Theory of Statistics* (14th ed. New York, Hafner, 1950), pp. 310–15; and Roy G. Francis, "On the Relations of Data to Theory," *Rural Sociology, 22* (1957), 258–66.

of the "Lausanne School of Marginal Utility" in economics to construct, e.g., aggregate demand curves from the estimation of individual preferences was ignored. In general, there has been very little carry-over between disciplines or fields of interest whenever the problem of aggregate versus individual data caught the attention of a particular group of scholars; and, characteristically, such methodological discussions proceed from a problem formulation that is peculiar to the particular situation of a discipline at a given time.

Survey research is not available throughout the world, and statistical services—not only the regular census, but also sampling by official statistical offices—have expanded in many Western countries. It will be an obvious research strategy to make use of both kinds of data, and indeed the YPDP and the CPS programs envisage just that. However, even a great number of impressive international data still means that the results are subject to the errors that triggered the methodological debates on aggregates, with the one qualification that the problems are ceteris paribus much greater when one deals with such large territorial units as nations. Combining aggregate and individual measurements creates additional problems, and some methodologists argue that it should not be done at all.

The following aspects most often cause uneasiness to those reviewing the use of aggregate data in social research, and they need to be considered when combining aggregates with individual measurements (specifically with survey research data):

1. *The accuracy of aggregate data.* There is a suspicion that on the level of aggregates the information may be more faulty than in using smaller units.
2. *The comparability of measurements for aggregates.* This question arises especially when territorial units are compared that provide information essentially by a process of self-enumeration.
3. *The representativeness of aggregate data for prop-*

erties of the collective—a problem akin to the use of summary statistics, such as averages in general (what do we know about a collective when we know its average?).

4. *Types of inference* which are permissible when using aggregate data.

In addition, we shall suggest a particular use of aggregates that, if it were more consciously employed, should contribute to the development of empirically substantiated macrotheories. This, then, is the major aim of this paper: to make suggestions for a more conscious use of aggregate data, and to attempt some clarification—rather than to continue a mistaken argument for or against using aggregates.

ON THE ACCURACY OF AGRREGATE DATA

Researchers who have dealt mostly with observations of individual units often feel uncomfortable about the accuracy of numbers reported for large aggregates—just as many researchers working with aggregates feel uneasy about the stability and generalizability of sample survey results. Aggregation obviously means being further removed from the original observations, and the greater number of cases to which a number refers (e.g. occupational distribution on the basis of a national census as against a sample survey) may indeed be purchased by sacrificing exactitude, or control over the recordings for each case. Using aggregate data for polities usually means working with complete enumerations, and it has been empirically demonstrated that these may be less accurate than samples. One of the effects of sample surveys has been to make census bureaus more conscious of the errors connected with complete enumerations, and consequently official statistical agencies now will use sampling to check on the adequacy of individual measurements prior to their aggregation.[11] These attempts to improve the quality of complete enumerations have been carried out mostly in advanced societies (with the notable exception of India) whose statistical services were already unusually developed. Thus, we know more about the problems of national statistics for those countries whose statistical services are already exceptionally well developed—at least in comparison to the majority of countries represented in the YPDP and CPS.

Some types of aggregate data that even in developed societies with strong central bureaus for statistics are subject to systematic errors and need to be interpreted with caution are (1) unemployment figures; (2) statistics for certain crimes, especially crimes against persons such as murder, assault, sex offenses, and juvenile delinquency in general; (3) statistics of traffic accidents; and (4) statistics for residential and occupational mobility. It is by no means possible in all instances to arrive at intelligent guesses (e.g. for crime statistics), and especially disturbing for time series analyses are changes in definition or policy. Thus, ethnicity in the U.S. Census has sometimes been defined as "foreign-born" and sometimes as "foreign stock." To give two examples for Germany: Rates of juvenile delinquency—especially for delinquency of well-off children—suddenly increased in Nazi Germany as a result of an order from the central government to treat as offenses acts of minors from families which, in the opinion of the prosecution, were better able to correct the child than the court would be. Traffic deaths also increased considerably in the late fifties partly as a consequence of now classifying as traffic fatalities those deaths of injured persons who died after a period of hospitalization. Even the number of households—a seemingly simple measure—is partly a function of the particular and

11. Cf. William E. Deming, *Some Theory of Sampling* (New York, John Wiley, 1950), e.g. p. 358. Samples as a means of quality control for a complete enumeration led to the discarding of a French economic statistic after World War II. The German census of 1946 was found to be highly deficient, as an example, for the attribute "occupation." Sampling also uncovered the amount of error caused by field workers for the Indian statistical office.

changing definition employed, and not just an expression of preferences in family living; thus, statements about the strength of the movement to the nuclear family have to be somewhat tempered by the recognition that "household" has become more strictly defined.

We thought it necessary to caution against a tendency, especially (though by no means exclusively) among demographers and ecologists, to consider data from complete enumerations for that very reason safe material to work with. This is clearly an unwarranted assumption—whether explicitly made or implied in one's proceedings. However, aggregate data may also be superior for the same reason that the grouping of data often results in the improvement of estimates (e.g. by reducing spuriously high degrees of dispersion).[12] This effect is most noticeable when the individual measurements are unstable, and it is questionable when the individual observations are biased. Also, different analytical operations are of varying sensitivity,[13] and too little attention is often paid to the degree to which a summary measure responds to the faultiness of data.

From these considerations follows a general caveat in treating aggregate data, but in our opinion also a simple rule of thumb: the intervals for grouped data (or when grouping them) and the threshold of sensitivity for a measure should be just greater than the possible errors in the data. Ceteris paribus, for distributions some further grouping of data would be advisable. If there is any reason to suspect error, one should sacrifice some information and settle for a rougher measure.

12. This is also often the reason for measuring a factor through some index rather than relying on one direct measurement. See in this connection the argument of Stouffer for the use of "contrived" items (combining several primary observations) rather than individual indicators. Cf. Samuel A. Stouffer, "Measurement in Sociology," *American Sociological Review, 18* (1953), 591–97. Of course, here several observations of one case are combined rather than a single observation for many cases. Although the logical problems are similar, only the latter operation is the theme of this contribution.

13. Cf. Oskar Anderson, *Probleme der statistischen Methodenlehre in den Sozialwissenschaften* (2d ed. Würzburg, Physica-Verlag, 1954), pp. 106–09 et passim. Basic to this much neglected aspect of statistics are the writings of Arthur L. Bowley.

THE COMPARABILITY OF AGGREGATE MEASUREMENTS

The quality of aggregate data needs to be even more carefully examined when the data are compared, and the dangers become greatest when the aggregates are polities. A relatively safe form is comparing aggregate measures over a period of time, that is, performing time-series analysis. Obviously, even faulty measurements may permit statements about change, provided the "faultiness" remains constant; this, however, is somewhat unlikely for longer time periods.

The same principle operates when making comparisons between collectives that commit the same kind of error—e.g. underenumerating rural areas—provided that one intends to make statements about determinants of variability between collectives. Thus, even though data on individual income in various European societies systematically underestimate the actual income (e.g. through the difficulties in accounting for nonmonetary income and for public services), this may not be too serious for a comparison between these countries; indeed, comparative measures are likely to be better than incomes for *one* society. However, if one compares income figures for Europe and the United States, the likelihood of error increases significantly through the higher monetization of the U.S. society and the relative paucity of public services. To account for the types of inaccuracy and yet prevent the bypassing of comparable information, we suggest stratifying the universe of polities into groups with presumably the same sources of error.

In spite of the efforts of the U. N. Statistical Office, statistical data for underdeveloped countries are by and large quite inaccurate. Many of the countries included in the Yale Political Data Program do not know even the size of their population. However, that by no means renders their statistical material in general valueless for the purposes of the YPDP. Apart from the possibility of comparing societies with comparable degrees of inaccuracy, this inaccuracy differs for the type of datum. While one may not know the size of one's population, the volume of newspaper circulation or of letter-writing is nearly as accurate for these countries as for developed countries.

In comparing aggregate data, the most troublesome problems arise when each of the units determines its own data collection, thus producing data essentially by a process of self-enumeration. From studies on response errors in official census work we know about the danger of this process even if a common questionnaire is supplied. Most of the data supplied by nation-states, and most of the variables represented in the YPDP, are based on self-enumeration. In the case of polities, this often means employing different definitions of the categories in counting. Efforts to standardize categories have been partly successful—as in the case of import–export statistics and postal statistics—but partly quite unsuccessful as in the case of many demographic variables.

This is partly a consequence of the real difficulties inherent in the subject matter; thus, defining a household remains a topic of controversy within the most developed countries (e.g. unit of consumption, unit in preparing meals, unit around one main provider, shared use of incomes, etc.), and differences in definition result in differences in findings which are by no means trivial. The difficulties of defining income in societies with different economic and social systems have already been referred to, and it is safe to say that differences in income between industrialized and nonindustrialized societies are probably exaggerated—if the income figures are meant to signify differences in the standard of living.

Comparisons based on monetary units are obviously affected by the meaning of exchange rates between currencies. Such exchange rates are more often than not "political prices" for a currency. This is obvious for countries which have not liberalized the exchange of currencies and sometimes have several exchange rates (as is true for some of the Communist countries with different rates of exchange for tourists, commercial transactions, and their own citizens desiring foreign currencies). Determining the meaning of monetary units, however, is also problematical for freely convertible currencies. It is luckily not our task to make statements about the determinants of the exchange rate of a currency, but we can safely state that such rates are—even for freely convertible currencies—the result of many factors: a currency may be an international medium of exchange (e.g. the U.S. dollar) and may, as such, have a (partly monetarily determined) price; a currency may be undervalued as a means of export-dumping (as in efforts to export one's unemployment to other countries) or it may be overvalued to benefit capital owners investing abroad (as in the case of the U.S.).[14] The notion that exchange rates for freely convertible currencies can be easily interpreted as parities in any other sense (and as buying power) is patently ridiculous, although by implication widely accepted by the predominantly economically naïve sociologists and political scientists.[15]

Even if the definition of categories is fairly simple and standard, their meanings may differ considerably. A prime example of this is educational statistics. Secondary education in Europe has a different meaning in terms of curriculum (i.e. content) and social significance (e.g. social prestige) than in the United States; in the U.S. the term "university" embraces institutions of world fame which are functionally equivalent to any European university as well as institutions for secondary education in the European sense. On the other hand, there are in the United States no real equivalents for certain forms of secondary education in Europe, such as the German *Berufsschule.* These difficulties

14. As an example we might refer to the many measures adopted by European countries to support the present exchange rate of the U.S. dollar. Thus, the German Federal Republic buys U.S. military equipment in part solely to support the U.S. dollar—even though some of it is considered not first rate. Even France refrains from exchanging the greater part of its holdings in U.S. paper money into U.S.-held gold. Other examples are the rescue operations in 1964 for the Italian lire and the English pound.

15. These problems associated with using variables expressed in monetary terms have been fully realized by the researchers of the YPDP. Cf. the admirable discussion in Bruce M. Russett with Hayward R. Alker, Jr., Karl W. Deutsch, and Harold D. Lasswell, *World Handbook of Political and Social Indicators* (New Haven, Yale University Press, 1964), pp. 149–51 et passim.

in comparing educational statistics and in the way these statistics are used as indicators reflect real structural differences—e.g. general education versus elitist systems.[16]

Many distortions result from a tendency to look at statistical reports as neither socially nor politically neutral. Prime examples are reports on literacy rates. Given the value structure of elites in the developing nations, literacy figures for their countries must show rapid increase as a yardstick of success in modernization efforts. In general, figures relating to standard of living (wage level, distribution of tax burden, food prices) have political and often legal implications. Thus, some Communist countries look at income figures or such a datum as rooms-per-person as information relevant to the cold war. In the France of the Fourth Republic the consumer price index for years was manipulated, deliberately and with public knowledge, in order to prevent escalator clauses in wage contracts from becoming effective. (One means of manipulation, for example, was to substitute a new item for a changing component of the index.) During the 1960 presidential election in the United States, a major political topic was the growth rate of the American economy and its insufficiency relative to the growth rates of other industrial nations. Items for defense spending are often ingeniously buried among other budget categories, and not merely for security reasons. Thus one should conclude that whenever a polity defines a statistic as relevant to its domestic or international politics, data need to be interpreted with some caution.

It is not just the categories that may present problems of comparability when using aggregate data; in terms of the usages made, the very units themselves for which properties are being aggregated may not be comparable. This is even true when the unit is a "polity." It may be acceptable to include in a data program—and assign a place in a total rank

16. Taking a "hard-headed" position, i.e. maintaining that the higher number of high school graduates in the U.S. as compared to Great Britain would mean after all a better educated general population, does not avoid the problem. Compare the results of a knowledge test in England and the U.S. as reported in the *Public Opinion Quarterly*, 27 (1963), 133–41.

ordering of cases—such diverse units as Mauritania, Luxembourg, the USSR, Singapore, Gabon, Malta and Gozo, Japan, Sarawak, the U.S.A., and Kuwait, if the variable is population. It is a bit difficult to imagine what such a rank ordering should be correlated with, if the variables are "percentage of population of working age" (first three ranks: Luxembourg, Gabon, West Germany); "percentage of population in cities over 20,000" (first five ranks: Hong Kong, Trinidad and Tobago, Surinam, New Zealand, Great Britain); "votes for socialist parties as a percentage of total vote" (first five ranks: Singapore, Burma, Australia, Jamaica, Norway); "cinema attendance per capita" (first five ranks: Hong Kong, Lebanon, Australia, Israel, USSR); or "GNP per capita" (first three ranks: Kuwait, U.S.A., Canada).[17]

No amount of checking will reduce erroneous conclusions in a cross-national comparison that result from treating as polities in a substantive sense those units which are polities only in a purely formalistic sense, and which by no stretch of the imagination refer to units that are usually meant when discussing polities. The fact that in the United Nations something is defined as a polity and has a vote in that organization does not make it necessary to treat the units as comparable in contexts other than membership or votes in the U.N. This error is, of course, not peculiar to cross-national comparison; it is, however, logically equivalent to defining as a worker anyone subject to a special form of social security, and then discussing "worker" as being a status in a social science sense.[18]

17. The examples are taken from Russett et al., *World Handbook.* The authors of the *Handbook* are aware of this problem, and, compared to earlier versions, have already eliminated a number of units that are polities in name only.

18. "Worker" in the official German statistic is someone in a special old age insurance system, the "Invalidenversicherung." In principle, the occupational categories of the German census are conceived in terms of type of income and thus, for example, include a category for all those with derived income (the "selbstständigen Berufslosen"), lumping together students, retired workers, prison inmates, and persons living on capital income only. In several investigations these categories are then treated as referring to persons with comparable occupational status. We do not want to imply that this system of categorization renders occupational statistics by the census bureau

THE REPRESENTATIVENESS OF AGGREGATE DATA

The greater the number of units that are aggregated and summarily reported for aggregates, the more likely it is ceteris paribus that the number does not meaningfully represent the property of the aggregate one intends to represent. The ceteris paribus is the degree of internal variation for the property in question. Especially affected are summary statistics such as measures of central tendency, presumably the best representation of a selected aspect of a collectivity. For example, everyone learns (or should learn) in introductory statistics the danger of using an arithmetic mean for a highly skewed distribution; computing the average income for a town with 98 farmers with an income of $6,000 each and 2 millionaires results in an average of $25,880, which represents neither the farmers nor the millionaires in any meaningful (i.e. interpretable) way.[19] While we do not doubt the work of desk calculators (or computers) leading to the report of a higher per capita income in Kuwait than in the U.S.A., we doubt that many uses can be specified where this difference would have an interpretable meaning.[20] Correlations based on averages are obviously sensitive to the internal variability of an aggregate, and for most of the measures of central tendency they are in general sensitive to the form of the distribution. The problem presents itself, however, also for the aggregation of qualitative factors. Thus, the education continuum in the U.S. is cut into

---

valueless. Theodor Geiger, *Die Klassenschichtung des deutschen Volkes* (Stuttgart, Enke, 1932), is based entirely on census material, and can be considered as a demonstration of what can be done with a critically conscious use of such figures (in this case a breaking down of larger aggregates and recombination under different criteria than those used by the census). However, the prevailing use of such terms as "nation" or "worker" in research based on aggregate data amounts to a *quaternia terminorum.*

19. A highly ingenious strategy in dealing with this problem can be found in the *World Handbook* where a new measure for expressing inequality is proposed. Cf. Hayward R. Alker, Jr., and Bruce M. Russett, "Indices for Comparing Inequality," in this volume.

20. To avoid misunderstandings, we do indeed consider the reporting of "average number of children = 2.5" useful, even though decimal children are not known to exist

"qualitative" steps in such a way that the variability of the setting tagged as "college education" is extremely great—so great as to obscure partly the effect of the factor one intends to measure.[21]

Especially important for a study of polities is the rapid change in the societies. In comparing polities this may just be the phenomenon one wants to track, but it need not be so at all. In an example from the YPDP, cinema attendance is reported for South Africa in 1950, for Italy in 1959, and for the U.S.A. in 1961; movie attendance, however, is one of the most rapidly changing behaviors. If cinema attendance were to be included in an index of communication density or an index of mobilization, the differences in time would quite materially affect the results.

And even if the time referents are identical—as in the YPDP for number of TV sets or for the Gross National Product—the problem of representativeness of a number is by no means solved except in a purely formalistic sense. Countries may differ in terms of the property represented only by a few years (as for density of TV and Gross National Product) largely due to a slightly different beginning for a growth process—but these polities may not at all represent different "stages" or different types. Thus, in 1957, the rank order in terms of GNP was United Kingdom rank #3, West Germany #4, and France #6; in 1963 the rank order was West Germany before England, and France practically identical with the United Kingdom. If, for example, rank order of GNP, based on a single observation, were correlated with turnout in national elections, the relationship one intends to measure would be obscured by many accidental factors. The following analogy may be dangerous and easily misunderstood, and is meant to illustrate just this point: One would hardly base a study of the relationship between the athletic skill of 100 schoolchildren of all different age levels with the socioeconomic status of their parents on a sin-

21. The topic of internal variation within the polities is discussed in other papers in this volume (cf. the chapters by Juan Linz and Erik Allardt); here creative use is made of these variations. Accordingly, the topic does not need to be elaborated further at this point.

gle observation in time for each case. Abstractly, one can formulate this as a warning against resting satisfied with single observations of units in a state of rapid fluctuation.

In general, and especially for such varied, unstable, and heterogeneous units as polities, we would recommend as a strategy: (1) reliance on several descriptions in addition to averages (at least a measure of dispersion); (2) in many cases averaging between repeated observations over a short period of time; (3) grouping cases into comparable classes; and (4) discarding units that are not units in terms of the inferences drawn.

THE TYPES OF INFERENCE PERMISSIBLE WHEN USING AGGREGATES

The Controversy over the Ecological Fallacy

The main controversies over the use of aggregate data center around the types of inference that appear permissible or dangerous. However, especially in sociology it is not in these terms that the issues are discussed; here the problem has been more specifically defined as the "ecological fallacy." Most influential has been an article by W. S. Robinson in 1950 which triggered one of the liveliest methodological debates in the postwar period.[22]

Robinson advised a distinction between "individual correlations" and "ecological correlations." The former he defined as a correlation in which the statistical object or thing described is indivisible, while in the latter correlation the statistical object is defined as a group of persons.[23] After surveying a number of studies, especially in the fields of delinquency and political behavior, Robinson warned against treating ecological correlations as if they were individual

22. Robinson, "Ecological Correlations and the Behavior of Individuals"; cf. also note 9. The only other recent methodological debate of comparable intensity was the discussion of the use of tests of significance, beginning with Hanan C. Selvin's "A Critique of Tests of Significance," *American Sociological Review*, 22 (1957), 519–27.

23. Robinson, p. 351.

correlations. Using data obtained for territorial units as if they were measurements of individual units was called "ecological fallacy."

The danger of this widespread practice was empirically documented when the findings of several studies were recalculated. Thus, the ecological correlation between percentage of colored population and illiteracy (based on 1930 U.S. census data) results in a Pearsonian $r = .946$ when using the large-scale area subdivision of the U.S. census for the whole country; the same correlation coefficient drops to $r = .773$ when the correlations are computed on the basis of results for 48 states. Both correlations were shown to be spuriously high, if they were intended to demonstrate a direct relationship between color and illiteracy. Using "individual data," Robinson arrived at a correlation of .203. While "ecological correlations" on the basis of large territorial units yielded a coefficient of determination of 89 per cent, "individual correlations" resulted in an $r^2 = 4$ per cent. From this Robinson concluded that ecological correlations should only be used for ecological purposes, i.e. if statements about territorial units are intended.

The great differences between correlations computed on the basis of aggregates and those computed on the basis of individual measurements are essentially a function of the increase in homogeneity between larger-scale units, resulting in a reduction of variability in the data. To use the language of Robinson, individual correlation depends on the internal frequencies of within-areas individual correlations, while ecological correlation depends upon the marginal frequencies of the within-areas correlations. Obviously it is an empirical question as to what degree marginal frequencies determine cell frequencies, but even for a fourfold table a large number of internal frequencies will fit exactly the same marginal distributions.

Working with averages or other summary statistics when relating two distributions, instead of with the individual observations that enter into the computation, quite obviously reduces variability. In the technique of computing correlation coefficients (and not least in the Pearsonian r), variability among units entering into the computation reduces the correlation coefficient. Consequently, the larger the contexts for which units are aggregated, the higher (ceteris paribus) the resulting correlation coefficient. Accordingly, in Robinson's example, we find that the larger the territories on which the data are based, the higher the correlation.[24]

The subsequent discussion was somewhat diverted from important issues by an unnecessary contention of Robinson's: "In each study which uses ecological correlations, the obvious purpose is to discover something about the behavior of individuals. Ecological correlations are used simply because correlations between the properties of individuals are not available." [25] Herbert Menzel quite correctly challenged this notion that the only reason for working with aggregated data—and specifically with census figures for territorial units—was technical, that is, substituting territorial data for individual observations, since individual measurements were not available.[26]

It is factually true that in political science and political sociology the data reported for territorial units are often used for inferences about the behavior of individuals, sometimes even for statements about their motivations. However, a factually correct statement is obviously something different from a logical necessity, such as Robinson has contended. Thus, territorial units are obviously a part of reality, and as such may be a variable in an explanation process. In Robinson's main example, identical historical circumstances and aspects of economic development probably caused certain states both (a) to import and retain large Negro populations and (b) to neglect their school systems.[27] Using territorial

24. Leo A. Goodman, "Ecological Regressions and the Behavior of Individuals," *American Sociological Review, 18* (1953), 663–64; see also Paul F. Lazarsfeld and Allen H. Barton, "Quantitative Measurement in the Social Sciences," *The Policy Sciences*, eds. Daniel Lerner and Harold D. Lasswell (Stanford, Stanford University Press, 1951), pp. 182–92.

25. Robinson, p. 352.

26. The following is based on Menzel's "Comment on Robinson's 'Ecological Correlation and the Behavior of Individuals.' "

27. Robinson, p. 352.

units to observe the correlation between the literacy rate and the percentage of Negro population is obviously justified, if one uses the territory as a contextual property in accounting for the variations in the other variables. Another example would be indicators of social disorganization computed on the basis of census tracts, where one would assume that the areas as such influence the values of the variables for social disorganization. Also, territories or other units arrived at by a process of aggregation may be elements in a social process in their own right. (I shall refer further to this at the end of the chapter.)

A number of classical investigations are guilty of committing the ecological fallacy, and their results may have to be largely discarded. This is a disturbing realization, and adding to this the vested interest in certain fields of learning in aggregate data (which for reasons that are by now obvious give one a better chance to "find" high correlations), it was to be expected that there would be strong objections and attempts to refuse the argument. Especially political scientists of the more traditional bent rejected altogether the notion that to identify the determinants of voting one should rely on individual measurements. Electoral statistics are, of course, one of the prime bodies of aggregate data in political science and will remain so. This factual condition is, however, sometimes given the status of a principle, and the following quotation is representative of the thinking of a considerable number of political scientists (even though they may be a bit more careful in their writing):[28] "It is impossible and *undesirable* [italics mine] to know how each individual votes, but it is possible to learn how voters in each precinct vote as a party; and since these citizens in these small election units have many characteristics in common, it is possible to generalize with accuracy regarding the rela-

28. E. B. Olds and D. W. Salmon, *St. Louis Voting Behavior Study* (St. Louis, 1948). Cf. also David Butler, "Voting Behavior and Its Study in Britain," *British Journal of Sociology, 6* (1955), 97 et passim; Jean Stoetzel, "Voting Behavior in France," *British Journal of Sociology, 6* (1955), 110 et passim; Ranney, "The Utility and Limitations of Aggregate Data," p. 96 et passim.

tionship between a certain way of voting and a certain kind of people." Methodologically, this type of argument of course need not be taken too seriously; it is quoted here only to show how resistant part of the audience is when important vested interests are at stake.

Determinants of the Ecological Fallacy

One cannot argue on principle against the statement that individual correlation and ecological correlation will usually not coincide—but neither can one rest with such an observation. While it may be satisfactory for discussions of the logic of inquiry to stop here, for actual empirical research it is of course more important to give an answer to the questions: What factors determine the difference between the two correlations? How important will this difference be in a concrete case? A satisfactory answer to these two questions, and preferably an answer formulated in algebraic terms, would retain the usefulness of aggregated data for research even if aggregated data are used to arrive at statements about individual behavior.

While some methodologists thought the conditions quite unusual under which ecological correlations and individual correlations would approximate each other,[29] a number of other researchers—and especially demographers—suggested general and differentiated answers. It will be recalled that the difference between individual and ecological correlations is dependent on the degree to which cell frequencies can be predicted from marginals; it will also be recalled that ceteris paribus the larger the unit, the more likely a strong difference between individual and ecological correlations. From these observations, Duncan and Davis developed an estimate of the size of error when using aggregate data in predicting individual units.[30] In principle, they employ successive subdivisions of a superordinate territorial unit; the differences in the ecological correlations that are obtained for units of

29. Cf. Goodman, p. 663.
30. Otis D. Duncan and Beverly Davis, "An Alternative to Ecological Correlation," *American Sociological Review, 18* (1953), 665–66.

varying size are used as a best estimate for the size of the ecological fallacy. "Although different systems of territorial subdivision give different results, as is the case with ecological correlation, the criterion for the choice among these results is clear. The individual correlation is approximated most closely by the least maximum and the greatest minimum amongst the results for several systems of territorial subdivision." [31]

This is in my opinion a too mechanistic formulation, since the sizes of ecological correlations obtained in a succession of subdivisions of a superordinate unit are not just a function of the size of that unit but also a function of the type of subdivision. Thus, computing correlations first for the towns of a state and then for the enumeration districts of a census may give some indication of the size of the ecological fallacy; however, if the enumeration districts of the census coincide largely with the effect of a latent third factor, influencing both the variables being correlated, the subdivision of the unit city into the smaller districts will give a quite imperfect estimate. After all, the reductions in ecological correlations which usually result from successive subdivisions of larger territorial units are a function of the increasing control over the variability of individual units. Whether this control will be effectively increased by subdividing is a question of fact, although when working with territorial units this will often be the case. In principle, some kind of weighted average for the different (not just successive) subdivisions of larger aggregates appears as the safest possible measure, and the difference between the various correlations may be taken as a rough indicator of whether such averaging should be undertaken at all.

Difficulties in Arriving at Inferences When Using Aggregate Data

The contention that ecological units are always used as a mere substitute for individual measurements, the contrary assertion that in some fields individual measurements are

31. Ibid., p. 666.

inherently inferior to aggregate data, and the technical discussion of best estimates (given the attempt to use ecological correlations as a substitute for observations of individual units)—these debates have tended to distract us from a more general problem formulation. Although the ecological fallacy is indeed especially relevant for work with such large units as polities, it is unfortunate that the issues were only discussed in terms of territorial units. Actually, the debate that I have reviewed has had little lasting impact. The ecological fallacy is still widespread, and we still come across hardly any examples where consequent use is made of Duncan's and Davis' suggestions.

What has been discussed as the ecological fallacy is, of course, only a special case of the difficulties in making inferences when working with grouped data. One of the earlier behavioral scientists to demonstrate the problems associated with the use of grouped data was E.L. Thorndike, in the course of his studies on determinants of intelligence.[32] Correlating intelligence quotients and crowded living conditions, Thorndike observed a correlation coefficient of .90 when using grouped data; the correlation between the same variables was reduced to .45 when using individual data.

In the logic of inquiry it does not make any difference whether the basis for grouping individual units is a territory or some other criterion; what is essential is the effect that this criterion has on the control over the internal variability of units. Thus, the general issue underlying the discussion of the ecological fallacy is really *the relation of the criterion, according to which units are grouped, to the types of inference intended when using the results of aggregated units.*

This more general problem formulation makes it easier to specify the conditions under which territorial units—and specifically polities—can be used with tolerable accuracy or even employed to greater advantage. A general problem formulation also makes it easier to recognize that the effect

32. E. L. Thorndike, "On the Fallacy of Imputing the Correlations Found for Groups to the Individuals or Smaller Groups Composing Them," *American Journal of Psychology, 3* (1939), 122–24.

discussed under the term "ecological fallacy" occurs in various guises. In the definition of what constitutes an ecological fallacy, let us substitute for the term "territorial" the term "grouped," and it becomes immediately apparent that the whole discussion so far applies to many fields and topics.

To give a few examples of the variety of circumstances under which the group fallacy becomes relevant:[33]

1. Let us assume that the higher the proportion of farm boys in a university, the higher the median score of that university's students on a Graduate Record Examination; and let us assume further that within any university farm boys consistently average lower on Graduate Record Examinations than other students. This seemingly contradictory information can easily be explained in terms of differential recruitment, a phenomenon which affects a wide variety of groups that one might compare by means of group data. However, when comparing polities, this will be less often a factor that one will have to consider, except in the rarer cases of highly selective and very substantial migration.

2. In a voluntary political organization, the records of every member show that he has become less active since joining. Grouping the members by length of membership, we also observe that those who have been in the organization for ten years are more active than those who have belonged for nine years; and those with nine years' membership are more active than those with fewer years. Again, there is an easy explanation for this seeming contradiction: membership turnover. While this factor is less likely to affect the comparability between polities, it does have to be taken into account when comparing smaller territorial units. The fact that a territorial unit is a constant obviously does not mean that it is a constant in the substantive sense that one uses it in the process of explanation.

3. Let us assume we are comparing the census figures for a polity from the year 1920 with those from 1960. We may observe that the proportion of men whose sons were in the same

33. I am indebted to Charles H. Tilly for these examples, although he is not responsible for the use I make of them.

occupation as they themselves was higher in 1960 than in 1920. Before concluding that occupational mobility has decreased, however, we might also note that the proportion of men in the same occupation as their fathers was lower in 1960 than in 1920. Only by taking into account both sets of results do we identify massive demographic changes in possible determinants.

4. Suppose that we want to compare the proportion of foremen to workers in industry between a capitalist and a socialist country, using this proportion as an index of direct control over the workers. Since in general the factories are larger in the socialist countries, we hold constant the size of industrial establishments. We then observe that the proportion of supervisors to workers is higher in each size class of industrial enterprises in the capitalist country than in the socialist country. Do we conclude that capitalist economies have to rely more on direct supervision? Obviously, at least one further control we would have to employ is a grouping of factories by types of products, and even then we would not be sure of accounting for structural differences as underlying factors.

This list is by no means a complete inventory of instances in which quite often the group fallacy is committed. It should also not be taken as an argument in principle against working with aggregate data. However, the list should be understood as a warning to treat grouped data just as individual observations. These cases were intended to demonstrate that—due to the more indirect relation between datum and inference—in working with grouped data the number of controls and checks against which to test an explanation has to be ceteris paribus greater than in the case of individual data.

Observations on the Use of Aggregate Data in Economics

In these discussions it is usually overlooked that economics is already one discipline where the controversy over the use of aggregate data vs. individual measurements has a long history, is of central importance, and has been related to different types of theorizing. Somewhat contrary to the present trend in the social sciences, experiences with individual measurement led for a while to such a concentration on the use of aggregates that "data" became synonymous with the use of aggregate values. And yet there has always been a strong tendency—and at repeated intervals a dominant one—to predict macroeconomic processes from the behavior of individuals.

The experience with the work of the school of marginal utility, and especially its Lausanne branch, was largely responsible for the distrust many economists now harbor against individual measurements as useful predictors. In the history of economic thought, Pareto's attempt to predict (or at least explain) movements of a total economy by simply summing up the indifference curves observed for individuals is often cited as a prime example of the doubtful value of recording individual preferences. Keynesian economics was then characterized by a nearly exclusive reliance on such grouped values as aggregate demand and aggregate supply.

At this point it is useful to distinguish between the type of data and the type of unit to which inferences refer. While economics relies heavily on aggregate data, the inferences refer to the character of the economy as an institution, to the behavior of individuals, and to some peculiar "modal character" in between. Economic man has been an ambivalent concept, sometimes used as a hypothetical construct, at other times as a "modal" individual.[34] When discussing such notions as "elasticity of demand" or "propensity to save," aggregates often turn into individuals with motivations. This dangerous personification of aggregate data is probably strongest in economics, although it is by no means completely absent in political science (e.g. in discussing voting). What the behavioral sciences especially can learn from economics is the value of working with aggregates as characterizing collectives, instead of being merely substitutes for more direct measurement.

34. See the references to Robinson Crusoe in older explanations of the "original accumulation" of capital.

THE INDIVIDUALISTIC FALLACY [35]

Today there is a strong and probably increasing tendency in the social sciences to commit what I would suggest be termed the "individualistic fallacy," and the preference for using ecological correlations merely as a substitute for inferences about the individual is closely connected with this orientation. Thus, the fallacious use of ecological correlations or of other correlations on the basis of grouped data can—ironically—be understood partly as a result of the individualistic fallacy.

The individualistic fallacy is the negation (explicitly or in one's research procedure) of the usefulness of an explanation that treats the collectivity as a collectivity, of working on a system level, and the phrasing of explanations for properties of the collectivity entirely in terms of the individual units, whose aggregated values should be the "true" value for the collectivity. Of course, this aggregation may no longer be thought of as necessarily a simple addition of individual observations but may also be based on values for the individual observations that are modified prior to their summation.

While traditionally political science may have been guilty of frequently committing the ecological fallacy, there appears to be a tendency among the newer behavioral political scientists to rely on individual measurement and in so doing to commit what we termed the individualistic fallacy. In its most naïve version, this fallacy takes the following form: In a cross-national comparative survey, samples of populations are asked whether they believe that a gifted and diligent person has a good chance of upward social mobility; the different percentages in various countries of persons agreeing that indeed there is such a chance are taken as an index of the

35. Related to this notion of an *individualistic fallacy* is the concept of "universalistic fallacy" as proposed by Hayward R. Alker, Jr. Compare for this discussion here Alker's treatment of "Regionalism versus Universalism in Comparing Nations," in Russett et al., *World Handbook*. See also, Hayward R. Alker, Jr., and Bruce M. Russett, "Correlations between Political and Social Indices," in Russett et al.

degree to which a particular society is still basically ascriptive. Another example is to count the percentage of authoritarian persons, or to ascertain the proportion of individuals who come close to a particular notion of a "democratic, civic culture" in their opinions, and take this as an index of the degree to which a society is democratic. In such studies as the international citizenship survey,[36] what is ignored is that one may have a democratic system with few "democratic" personalities, and various types of authoritarian systems with high percentages of democratic personalities. Democracy is the term for a political system, and a political system is obviously not just the aggregate of the individuals comprising it.

Peculiarly, small-group researchers—though maintaining that they are discussing groups—have often committed the individualistic fallacy too. As James S. Coleman points out, small-group research primarily works with individual measurements which are then summed up or averaged as a group measure.[37] This type of aggregation often does not lead to difficulties if one holds constant the groups to be dealt with. Obviously, when keeping the groups constant, or for the same type of group (in the sense of comparable structures), such a simple aggregation of individual measurements partly bypasses the effects of group structure. If one makes comparisons across families, friendship groups, office groups, and voluntary associations by simply adding the scores for the number of interactions as an expression of friendliness or antagonism, defining group cohesion would immediately result in problems.

If logical arguments should not be sufficiently convincing, let us turn to one of the (to our knowledge) extremely few empirical studies on the relation between aggregate and individual values.[38] Subjects of the study were committees of the

36. Almond and Verba, *The Civic Culture.*

37. James S. Coleman, "The Mathematical Study of Small Groups," *Mathematical Thinking in the Measurement of Behavior*, ed. Herbert Solomon (Glencoe, Free Press, 1960), pp. 5–149.

38. Robert L. Kahn, "Consequences of the Joint Consideration of Individual and Aggregate Data in Correlational Social Research" (unpublished doctoral dissertation, University of Michigan, 1958).

oil industry; the method was the personal interview with questions both about the respondent's own attitudes and behavior and about his report of the attitudes and behavior of other committee members. In the analysis, the individual responses were treated as predictors of other responses by the same individual; the responses for a given group were then averaged and used as predictors for responses of the individual group members. Altogether there were 430 possible comparisons of the predictive power of aggregate versus individual values. As one would expect, the individual responses were the best predictor of variables describing the behavior of individuals—but the aggregated values predicted behavior referring to group process better than the individual responses. It could further be demonstrated that the predictive power of aggregate values was a function of group cohesion, and especially of the strength of sanctions exercised in a group against deviating behavior.

A reference to economics might again help to define more clearly the problems of a common fallacy in social research. Presently, economics emphasizes the use of aggregates, and the group fallacy now constitutes a more acute problem; but there is also the continuing tradition of dealing with an economy by reference to individual observations only. This tendency was quite strong toward the end of the nineteenth century when, for instance, Bentham and Edgeworth advocated the addition of individual utilities to arrive at social welfare functions. The schools of marginal utility were based on this premise, as has already been mentioned. Post-Keynesian welfare economists (such as Bergson, O. Lange, A. P. Lerner, Samuelson, and Hicks) are continuing the discussion as to whether the summation of individual preferences is legitimate when specifying the greatest welfare of the collective—and whether in turn aggregate utility curves can be used as the basic empirical material of welfare economics.[39]

39. For details of this discussion see, e.g., Leo Goodman, "On Methods of Amalgamation," and Clyde H. Coombs, "Social Choice and Individual Preference," both in *Decision Processes*, eds. R. M. Thrall, C. H. Coombs, and R. L.

This particular discussion makes quite clear the fact that reductionism, the individual fallacy, and the group fallacy are all quite closely related. All consider the collective as a direct aggregate of individual units, and all (explicitly or implicitly) negate the relevance of the higher order units as such.

The use of indifference curves or utility functions to which I referred above should not be simply equated with the newer consumer economics. This rapidly developing branch of an empirical economics relies mainly on the prevailing field methods for data collection in social research, and is in effect just one more field of behavioral science (in the same sense as the "new" political science). For example, interviewing regularly a cross-section of the U.S. population, the Survey Research Center provided basic intelligence for the monetary policy of the Federal Reserve Board. To characterize the changes, and specifically the stages of growth of consumer markets in Western European nations, cross-national comparative surveys are increasingly used.[40] In Germany, the IFO-Institute regularly conducts a poll of executives in industry and business, and forecasts, on the basis of this information, changes in aggregate economic activity; in this prediction the technique of polling is in constant competition with both the historically descriptive and the econometric techniques of forecasting fluctuations on the level of aggregates by using aggregate data—and the poll of executives is proving worthwhile enough to have been continued for over a decade.

This kind of empirical consumer economics is uncontroversial for microeconomic purposes. It is the more successful in accounting for changes on the level of aggregate activity, the more the individual units (be they "executives" or "con-

---

Davies (New York, John Wiley, 1954), pp. 39–49; Leo Goodman and Harry Markowitz, "Social Welfare Functions Based on Individual Rankings," *American Journal of Sociology, 63* (1952), 257–62; Kenneth Arrow, *Social Choice and Individual Values* (New York, John Wiley, 1951).

40. The newest, and in my opinion especially impressive, example of such cross-national comparisons is the project "Products and People," Reader's Digest Association, London, 1963.

sumers") can be treated as comparable with regard to economic outcome, or where structural factors are relatively simple and well known (as, for example, in the case of the IFO-forecasts). Accordingly, one may now argue that the economics postulating the aggregation of individual values —such as Pareto's—was not fallacious in principle, but merely too simpleminded, always treating the various units of an economy as essentially interchangeable. Predicting in general the processes of such a complicated institution as a national economy obviously requires a high degree of information about structure.

When the use of aggregates versus individual values is discussed in economics, two issues are debated more or less simultaneously: (1) whether it is technically feasible to go from individual values to aggregates (or the reverse) in order to obtain a technically more advantageous unit to operate with; and (2) whether the collective (or economy) should be treated as a higher order unit that should not be reduced to its components.[41] I want to postpone the second question to point out how difficult it is even in a discipline that deals with a relatively restricted range of activities, with a specialized institutional sphere, and that relies on rather "hard" information, to meet the conditions for aggregating individual values in a way that fully accounts for variations in the higher order units. These problems are by no means peculiar to economics, and if anything are easier to deal with in this specialized discipline; it is also easier in economics to specify the problems, and this accounts for the usefulness of the debate there.

The first problem-area for those refusing to accept different levels of argumentation or contexts of explanation is the structure of collectives, which gives differing relevance to the individual units and provides the outlets for effective choices.

41. This argumentation may be somewhat reminiscent of the rather fruitless controversy over whether the whole is more than the sum of its parts—but it is not identical at all. By way of contrast, we would accuse those refusing to deal with higher order units as units in their own right of committing the same error as the "wholists": assigning a "higher" reality to one kind of unit in an explanation process than to another.

However, even if there were no structural arrangements among the units of a system, the preferences of the individual would only coincide with the choices made if the product choices were divisible into as many units as there are individual preferences. Instructive is an earlier discussion in economics about the consequences of the lack of a direct match between the number of preferences and the number of product choices possible; this debate was conducted under the somewhat misleading title, "The Paradox of Voting." [42]

The clearest example is perhaps political voting itself. In a multiparty system (such as that of the Fourth French Republic) individual preferences can express themselves in a considerable number of choices; but even here, the same act may result from a different combination of motives. In a two party system, where the individuals have learned that the defeated vote carries no influence, a small number of outlets (essentially three choices: vote for A, vote for B, abstain) becomes combined with strategic considerations of making the most of one's vote within the given system. As Kenneth Arrow points out: "The methods of voting and the market . . . are methods of amalgamating the tastes of many individuals in the making of a social choice." [43] Thus, for social behavior in general, there should be little argument that the same preference may result in different action, and that different actions may be based on the same preferences.

Contrary to some present tendencies in political science and sociology, polities and societies are not generally directly affected by the motives, attitudes, and opinions of their constituent parts. The referendum is an unusual provision for relating the individual preference to the system—and even here the relation may be more indirect than is implied by the writing of, for instance, Talcott Parsons.[44]

42. E. J. Nanson, "Methods of Election," *Transactions and Proceedings of the Royal Society of Victoria, 19* (1882), 197–240.

43. Kenneth Arrow, *Social Choice and Individual Values*, p. 2.

44. For a discussion of the logical problems of constructing a procedure for passing from a set of known (!) individual tasks to a pattern of social decision-making, see Arrow. Talcott Parsons in his more recent theorizing about generalized media of exchange may be close to a form of the individualistic fallacy in conceiving of a generalized medium as a means of directly

Economics can be taken as a model case for justifying working at different levels instead of claiming the superiority of one over the other. There is no general, simple way of passing from one context of explanation to another—whether by reducing a larger context to smaller components or by aggregating smaller contexts into a larger one.

Let us state again, but this time more abstractly, the logical structure of the group fallacy: *The group fallacy (and, as a special case, the ecological fallacy) results from the difference between units of observation and units of inference. The danger of committing this fallacy is always present when the unit to which the inference refers is smaller than the unit either of observation or of counting.* This abstract statement should help us to see that this fallacy is, in its formal structure, analogous to the more rarely discussed individualistic fallacy. *The danger of the individualistic fallacy is then present when the units of observation or counting are smaller than the units to which inferences are made.*

USES AND ABUSES OF AGGREGATE DATA

This short discussion of the individualistic fallacy should have made it evident that it makes no sense to argue *in general* for the superiority of either aggregate or individual measurements.[45] But it *is* important to become more aware than is now true of the many inaccuracies and ambiguities in the more commonly used aggregate data. These are widely

---

relating processes at the system level and choices of the constituent units. Of course, it would not be correct to single out Talcott Parsons in this context; he is only cited as a borderline example of how widespread the danger of the individualistic fallacy presently is. A more representative case is George Homans, who makes what we have termed the individualistic fallacy his scientific program; cf. George C. Homans, *Social Behavior in its Elementary Forms* (New York, Harcourt, Brace & World, 1961).

45. Cf. Erwin K. Scheuch and Dietrich Rüschemeyer, "Statistik und Soziologie," *Kölner Zeitschrift für Soziologie und Sozialpsychologie, 8* (1956), 272–91; Erwin K. Scheuch, "Einige Probleme statistischer Verfahrensweisen in der Sozialforschung," in *Beiträge zur Gegenwartsproblematik der angewandten Statistik* (Opladen, Westdeutscher Verlag, 1960), pp. 83–114.

overlooked because of the seeming "hardness" of aggregate measures ("hardness" = official source?) and the often (and not infrequently spurious) high correlations that they help to bring about. Therefore, this discussion began with an examination of such types of errors but then proceeded in steps to what I consider the most fruitful topic: the correct use of either type of data in the process of explanation. To achieve a bit more clarity here is especially important, due to the increased possibilities of combining for the same polity aggregate and individual measurements.

A number of methodologists have argued that such a combination is not permissible. Indeed, problems arise when one does not just report marginals (and for these a good random sample is obviously comparable to a complete enumeration) but also wants to show the distribution of values within subdivisions of a polity. For polities, the breakdowns of aggregate data have areas as an independent variable, while with individual measurements cross-tabulations refer to the joint occurrence of properties for the individual units. However, the rejection of a combination of individual and aggregate measures as wrong in principle has in my opinion never been well justified. Whether a comparison is possible obviously depends on the use made of data, and, far from rejecting such uses, we think at least one type of combination should lead to a major advancement in the social sciences.

A mix between aggregate and individual data for polities is obviously not problematic if one wants to (or has to) risk the ecological fallacy. It has already been pointed out that in many cases aggregate data are used as an indirect expression of the properties of individual units. Combining measurements obtained directly from such individual units with aggregate data as "substitutes" presents no logical problems and entails only dangers of an empirical nature.

More complicated, but much more important, is the attempt to treat the aggregate as a unit in its own right. In this case, combining individual measurements (such as survey data) with aggregate data (such as GNP, or density of population, or percentage of females in the labor force) can be used to relate an individual's reaction to a social system,[46] or a social system to differential reactions of individuals. Too often, survey research ignores the objective context in which individuals live; too often, the individual's responses are interpreted at face value. In this way social research bypasses an important chance to derive macrotheory partly from individual measurements. Relating different contexts to each other, but treating each context as nonreducible in terms of the other, obviously creates some additional difficulties. Problems of inference, and in general the analysis of this type of research, have remained largely unexplored, and, as they cannot be discussed here, we must rest with the assertion that indeed individual measurements and aggregate data should be combined.

Treating an aggregate as a system in its own right, a context in which the individuals operate, presupposes of course that an aggregate unit stands for some social system. This is by no means self-evident for aggregate data.[47] Especially in ecological work within one nation, the treatment of territorial units as systems according to the definitions of statistical offices amounts (usually by implication) to a *petitio principii.* Thus, the unit "county" is usually nothing more than a convenient administrative subdivision for purposes of enumeration.

When working with polities, except perhaps for some of the newer nations, this problem usually does not arise. However, treating polities as social systems in a general sense may be dangerous. An example is Belgium which for many spheres of behavior can be considered two societies. Whether a nation-state is really a society, and whether a society is really a general integrating context for most spheres of behavior, is sometimes open to question. Thus, for courtship patterns, one relevant territorial unit in the sense of an inte-

46. Cf. Patricia L. Kendall and Paul F. Lazarsfeld, "The Relation between Individual and Group Characteristics in the 'American Soldier,'" *The Language of Social Research: A Reader in the Methodology of Social Research,* eds. Paul F. Lazarsfeld and Morris Rosenberg (Glencoe, Free Press, 1955), pp. 290–96, especially the conclusion of that article.

47. Francis, "The Relation of Data to Theory," pp. 260 et passim; Menzel, p. 674.

grated system appears to be what Günther has called the "Alpine cultures," crosscutting the boundaries of at least five nations. However, by and large, using aggregate data for polities should lead to treating the data as properties of systems, as describing a context.

A discussion of the use of aggregate data in cross-national comparisons is at the same time a reflection about the relation of data to theory. The character of aggregate data presents some additional difficulties, and inferences on the basis of aggregate data do call for greater and not less theoretical sophistication than is true for individual observations.

8. Comparative Data from Content Analysis: Perceptions of Hostility and Economic Variables in the 1914 Crisis

OLE R. HOLSTI AND ROBERT C. NORTH,
STANFORD UNIVERSITY

Critics of content analysis have frequently pointed to the lack of studies in which inferences based on content data are tested against independent material.[1] For example, is there any significant relationship between what policy makers say and write and the actual decisions they make? If there is not, then the value of content analysis as a research methodology is placed in serious doubt. This paper reports on one attempt—from a series of systematic efforts—to correlate perceptual or affective variables, obtained by content analysis, with action variables. The focus is upon certain types of relatively "hard" data—such as the flow of gold, stock market fluctuations, and commodity futures—which can be measured in reliable, equal interval scales, and against which the results derived from the content analysis of documents can be compared. Subsequent papers will look for correlations between the same perceptual data, on the one hand, and other types of activity data such as mobilizations, troop and naval movements, and the like.[2]

1. See, for example, Bernard Berelson, *Content Analysis in Communications Research* (Glencoe, Free Press, 1952), pp. 74–75.
2. Robert C. North, Richard A. Brody, and Ole R. Holsti, "Some Empirical Data on the Conflict Spiral," *Peace Research Papers*, I (forthcoming); Ole R. Holsti, Richard A. Brody, and Robert C. North, "Violence and Hostility: The Path to World War" (paper read at American Psychiatric Association Conference, Los Angeles, 1964).

The summer of 1914 and events leading to the outbreak of World War I have provided the "laboratory" for the current study. This particular crisis period was chosen because the archives of the participating powers are relatively open, providing more decision data than are frequently available, and because the events constitute an almost classic case of an incident leading to a "localized" war, which then got out of hand and escalated into a major conflict.

The fundamental model is a mediated stimulus–response arrangement *S–r:s–R* where *S* represents an "objective" event in the environment, *r* the perceptual response of the actor, *s* the actor's asserted intent and *R* the actual or "objective" behavior of the actor. This paper will be concerned primarily with correlations between perceptions (*r*) and environmental events (*S*) and (*R*). Depending upon the perspective, gold flow and other economic fluctuations can be viewed either as (*S*) or as (*R*) phenomena.

The basic quantifiable unit for content analysis was the "perception" abstracted from the documents in terms of the following elements: *the perceiving party or actor; the perceived party or actor; the asserted action or attitude; and the target party or actor.*[3] The 1914 documents provided more than 5,000 cognitive and affective perceptions of four variables—hostility, friendship, frustration, and satisfaction —of which hostility has emerged clearly as the best predictor of state behavior. This finding is supported by a multiple regression analysis (including the variable change of status

3. For a more complete discussion of the content analysis techniques used in this paper, see Robert C. North, Ole R. Holsti, George Zaninovich, and Dina A. Zinnes, *Content Analysis: A Handbook with Application to the Study of International Crisis* (Evanston, Northwestern University Press, 1963). For other studies which have employed these data, see Dina A. Zinnes, Robert C. North, and Howard E. Koch, "Capability, Threat and the Outbreak of War," in James N. Rosenau, ed., *International Politics and Foreign Policy* (New York, Free Press, 1961) ; Dina A. Zinnes, "Expression and Perception of Hostility in International Relations" (Ph.D. dissertation, Stanford University, 1963) ; Ole R. Holsti and Robert C. North, "History as a 'Laboratory' of Conflict," in Elton B. McNeil, ed., *The Nature of Human Conflict* (Englewood Cliffs, N.J., Prentice-Hall, forthcoming) ; and Ole R. Holsti, "Perceptions of Time, Perceptions of Alternatives, and Patterns of Communication as Factors in Crisis Decision-Making" (paper read at Peace Research Conference, Chicago, 1964).

quo), which produced the following beta weights for each variable:

Hostility	9.66
Friendship	—2.11
Frustration	1.90
Satisfaction	1.39
Change of status quo	0.27

Data on the fluctuations of various economic indicators were collected from sources quite separate from the decision-making documents which had been subjected to content analysis.[4] By necessity the choice of indicators was limited to whatever had been reported on a day-to-day basis by newspapers and journals of the time. An investigation of this nature thus becomes victim, somewhat, to the conventional modes by which economic and other indicators are habitually reported. This paper does not intend to suggest causal relationships, nor does it explore whether gold flow and other fluctuations preceded or followed given perceptions. It is quite likely, of course, that both the perceptual variables and the "hard" variables were responding to some third category, that is, to the development of events during the crisis period.

The relationship between the level of affect revealed through the content analysis of documents and political decision-making may be investigated directly or indirectly. The former involves a direct correlation between the results of the content analysis and actions such as troop movements, mobilization, breaking of diplomatic relations, and the like. The indirect approach involves a correlation of the perceptual variables with an intermediate set of indices which can be shown to be sensitive to political decision-making. The economic indicators discussed below are, on the whole, of this latter type.

4. Data have been gathered from the following sources: *The Times* (London), *The Economist* (London), *The Wall Street Journal, Le Temps* (Paris), and from F. W. Hirst, *The Political Economy of War* (New York, E. P. Dutton and Co., 1915).

THE FLOW OF GOLD

Any study of the flow of gold involving the major actors in the 1914 crisis must center on London—"the financial center and the free market for gold."[5] Whereas notes could be redeemed for gold to an unlimited extent in the Bank of England, the government banks of Berlin, St. Petersburg, and Paris had been hoarding gold for a considerable period of time prior to the assassination of Francis Ferdinand.[6] As late as July 25, the influential London *Economist* opposed demands from some British bankers that England take official steps to prevent a run on gold in times of panic.[7] Thus fluctuations in the influx or outflow of gold from London took place in a market free—until July 31—of any governmental interference.

Table 8.1 shows the daily average net flow of gold in and out of London. As the crisis developed there was first a marked decrease in the influx of gold followed by a wave of withdrawals when war broke out on the Continent. Only on August 1 was there any abatement. Late in the previous day the bank rate had been raised to an almost unprecedented 8 per cent; on August 1 the rate was increased again to 10 per cent. Thus the drop in net outflow from £1,204,000 on July 31 to £60,000 was less the result of a restoration of confidence than of a consciously adopted policy on the part of the British to take remedial steps by abolishing the free market in gold.

When the movement of gold is compared to the fluctuations in the intensity of perceived hostility[8] (Figure 8.1), the configuration of the curves is quite similar. It is interest-

5. Ruth M. Jaeger, *Stabilization of the Foreign Exchange* (New York, Isaac Goldman Co., 1922).

6. Hirst, pp. 281, 290. By the law of July 3, 1913, the Bank of Germany was authorized to build up a gold–silver war reserve of 240 million marks. At the same time the French were building up a counterpart to the German fund. *The Economist*, July 25, 1914, p. 169; August 15, 1914, pp. 316, 321.

7. *The Economist*, July 25, 1914, p. 169.

8. By all perceivers (decision-makers of France, England, Russia, Germany, and Austria-Hungary).

Table 8.1. Influx (+) or Exflux (−) of Gold from London—Daily Average
(in £ thousands)

Average June 20–26	*June 27–July 2*	*July 3–16*	*July 17–20*	*July 21–25*	*July 26*	*July 27*	*July 28*	*July 29*	*July 30*	*July 31*	*Aug. 1*
+120.33	+92.0	+71.0	+9.8	+6.0	0.0	+269.0	−22.0	−911.0	−1034.0	−1204.0	−60.0
Intensity level of perceived hostility *	3.46	3.66	3.79	4.17	4.92	4.46	5.10	5.18	5.48	5.70	6.42

Correlation: Rising Hostility—Exflux of Gold

n	r	P
11	+0.850	$<.01$

* Scaled by Q-Sort; mean of all statements is 5.00.

ing to note, for example, that the marked drop in the hostility curve on Monday July 27 was matched by a sharp rise in the influx of gold. During the preceding weekend many observers and participants, including the Kaiser and Winston Churchill, had felt that the Serbian reply to the ulti-

Figure 8.1. Fluctuations in the Intensity of Perceived Hostility: Gold Flow

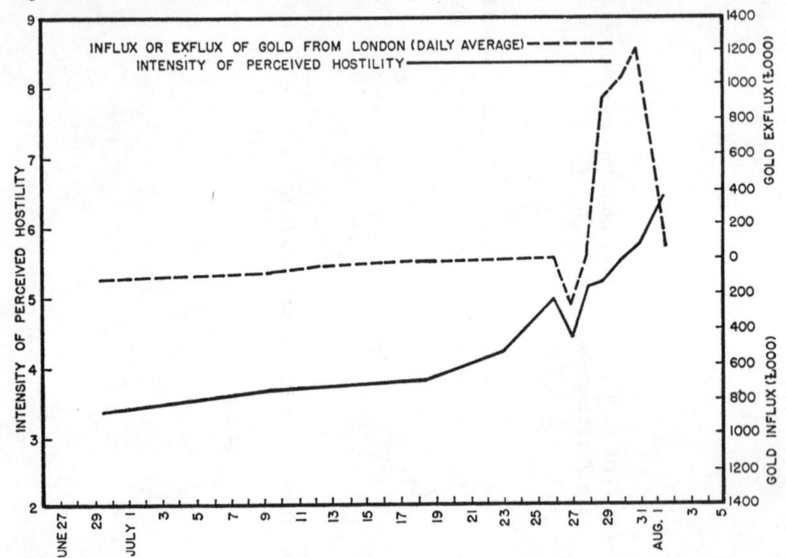

matum marked the end of the crisis.[9] Similarly the steady rise in hostility starting on July 28 corresponds to the withdrawal, in panic proportions, of gold. The Spearman rank order correlation (+0.850) between gold flow and perceived hostility is actually conservative. It includes data

9. On the text of the Serbian reply, the Kaiser wrote, "A brilliant performance for a time limit of only forty-eight hours. This is more than one could have expected! A great moral victory for Vienna; but with it every reason for war drops away, and Giesel might have remained quietly in Belgrade! On the strength of this *I* should never have ordered mobilization." Max Montgelas and Walther Schücking, eds., *Outbreak of the World War, German Documents Collected by Karl Kautsky* (New York, Oxford University Press, 1924), p. 254. Churchill wrote, "On Saturday afternoon the news came in that Serbia had accepted the ultimatum. I went to bed with a feeling things might blow over . . . we were still a long way, as it seemed, from any danger of war. Serbia had accepted the ultimatum, could Austria demand more?" Winston S. Churchill, *The World Crisis, 1911–1914* (New York, Charles Scribner's Sons, 1928), p. 208.

from August 1 when, as shown above, the outflow of gold was reduced by artificial means. If this period were not included, the correlation would be +0.878. In either case the correlation is significant at beyond the .01 level.

As stated earlier, any inferences regarding the value of content analysis data through comparisons with economic indices is greatly strengthened if evidence can be introduced to show that the latter are in fact sensitive barometers of the course of international politics. Is there any evidence that the outflow of gold was related to the European crisis? Table 8.2 reveals that the great bulk of outbound gold was in fact shipped to the Continent. The net outflow for the period was £1,440,000; included, however, are British purchases of £1,703,000 in bars and the receipt of £803,000 from various nations in South America. The net direct outflow (June 27–August 1) to continental Europe, excluding neutral Switzerland, was £3,011,000; the net outflow to the Continent from July 27 to August 1, a period encompassing the outbreak of war, was £3,018,000. Thus, gold shipments to the continent for the entire period account for 75.0 per cent of all *gross* outflow and for 211 per cent of *net* outflow. During the period of July 27–August 1, gold shipments to Europe account for 75.7 per cent of *gross* outflow and for 102 per cent of *net* gold exports. Again these figures may be conservative; the final destination of gold shipped to Switzerland, for example, might well have been one of the continental belligerents.

Finally, there is strong, although indirect, evidence that much of the gold was recalled by the governments of the major powers involved in the crisis. An examination of the weekly statements of the European national banks (Table 8.3) reveals sharp increases in gold reserves during the crisis period. While the figures in Table 8.3 undoubtedly reflect internal stockpiling of gold—the German Bank, for example, was relieved of the necessity to honor withdrawals in gold after the outbreak of war [10]—they also suggest that major

10. For some days prior to the outbreak of war German banks paid out only 20 per cent of demands in gold; on the declaration of "The State of

Table 8.2. Gold Influx (+) and Exflux (−) from London
(in £ thousands)

Source or Destination	*June 27– July 2*	*July 3–16*	*July 17–20*	*July 21–25*	*July 26*	*July 27*	*July 28*	*July 29*	*July 30*	*July 31*	*Aug. 1*	*Net*
France			− 6				−22	−380	− 971	− 143	− 16	−1538
"Continent"		− 7						−275		− 572		− 854
Belgium						− 50		− 41		− 548		− 639
Within empire				−280					− 150	− 80	−100	− 610
Egypt	+185		+45					−465	− 100			− 335
Switzerland									− 60			− 60
Germany		+ 20										+ 20
United States	+ 70											+ 70
South America	+ 77	+165		+186		+201			+ 174			+ 803
Bars purchased	+128	+815		+124		+118		+250	+ 73	+ 139	+ 56	+1703
NET	+460	+993	+39	+ 30	0	+269	−22	−911	−1034	−1204	− 60	−1440
DAILY AVERAGE	+ 92.0	+ 71.0	+ 9.8	+ 6.0	0	+269.0	−22.0	−911.0	−1034.0	−1204.0	− 60.0	——

TABLE 8.3. GOLD RESERVES OF NATIONAL BANKS *

Bank of	*Gold Reserves*	*On*	*Gold Reserves*	*On*	*Net Change*
France	£ 159,028,000	June 25	£ 165,654,000	July 30	+ £ 6,626,000
Belgium	£ 13,451,000	June 25	£ 15,980,000	August 6	+ £ 2,529,000
Germany	£ 63,712,200 **	July 2	£ 75,426,000	August 15	+ £ 11,713,800
Russia	£ 159,575,000	June 29	£ 160,204,000	August 4	+ £ 629,000

* No figures are available for the Austro–Hungarian Bank after July 23, 1914.
** 1,306.1 million Marks, converted in pounds at the rate of 20.50 M/£.

financial institutions on the continent had been in large part responsible for the run on gold in London.

THE PRICES OF STOCKS AND BONDS

The analysis of the price of securities, unlike that of gold, can be undertaken in many places. Securities exchanges operated in the capitals of the major European powers. The data analyzed here consist of 20 stocks and bonds for Serbia, Russia, France, Germany, Austria, Hungary, England, and Belgium, traded on the London, St. Petersburg, Paris, Berlin, Vienna, and Brussels exchanges. To facilitate interpreta-

Figure 8.2. **Fluctuations in the Intensity of Perceived Hostility: Security Prices**

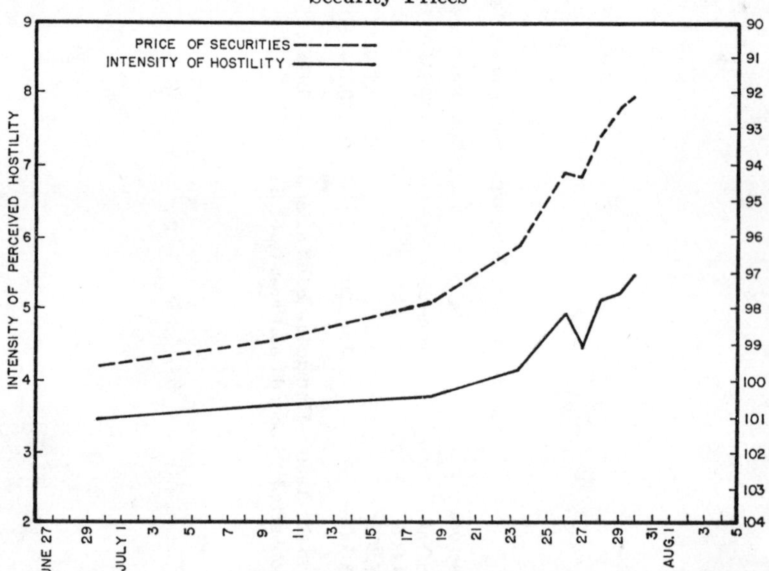

tion, the price of each security is given as a percentage of its value during the pre-crisis week (June 20–26). The index is the average value for the twenty securities. When the composite index is compared to the fluctuations in the intensity

Threatening Danger of War" (July 31) payments in gold were stopped altogether. On August 5 the Austro-Hungarian Bank Act, which required 2/5 gold backing for currency, was suspended. *The Economist*, August 1, 1914, p. 229; August 14, 1914, p. 320; December 19, 1914 (Special War Supplement), p. 13.

Table 8.4. Securities of Prospective Belligerents
(June 20–26=100)

Security	*June 27– July 2*	*July 3–16*	*July 17–20*	*July 21–25*	*July 26*	*July 27*	*July 28*	*July 29*	*July 30*
Serbia : 4% Bonds	99.0	96.2	92.0	89.8	87.2	89.7	87.6	83.5	83.5
Serbia : Monopoles	98.8	98.0	98.9	97.3	96.6	95.5	93.6	92.5	92.5
Banque Internationale	98.8	97.8	95.6	91.2	89.0	89.0	85.8		
Baku	100.2	100.1	99.0	96.0	94.4	94.4	92.0		
Moscow : Kazan	97.2	96.0	93.3	92.6	93.1	93.1	88.6		
Russian 4½% 1909	99.8	99.9	98.0	95.8	91.5	94.0			
Russia : 4% Bonds	100.1	98.3	97.5	96.5	93.8	91.5	90.2	89.1	89.1
Austria : Credit Shares	99.5	97.8	97.2	95.5	92.8	94.5	93.5	94.3	92.7
Austria : 4% Gold	99.8	99.9	99.7	99.0	98.1				
Hungary : 4% Gold	99.6	98.5	98.0	97.5	94.3				
Hungarian Bonds	101.0	97.2	97.0	94.7	91.4	90.1	89.0	89.0	89.0
Germany : 3% Imperial	99.7	99.2	98.8	97.8	96.5	95.9	95.8	94.8	94.8
3% Prussian Consols	99.7	99.2	98.8	97.7	96.4	97.0	96.9	94.7	
General Electric	99.9	99.8	98.1	94.7	91.2	92.1	91.2	88.9	86.9
France : 3% Loan	99.0	98.9	97.8	96.5	93.8	93.7	92.9	92.9	
3½% French Loan	100.0	99.9	99.7	97.0	93.6	94.4	94.4	93.1	
Bank of France	100.0	99.4	98.7	98.0	97.5	97.5	97.5	94.8	
British Consols : 2½%	99.8	101.1	101.3	100.3	98.4	96.8	95.8	94.8	93.1
Port of London B 4%	100.3	100.8	99.0	98.9	98.5	97.9	97.9	95.9	95.9
Bank of Brussels	99.9	99.5	98.5	97.6	97.0	97.0			
INDEX	99.6	98.9	97.8	96.2	94.2	94.3	93.3	92.5	92.1

of perceived hostility (Figure 8.2), the curves are strikingly similar. The drop in hostility on July 27 was matched by a slight rise in the value of securities. Some individual shares of nations most intimately involved in the Austro–Serbian dispute rose quite markedly—Serbian Bonds (2.5%), Russian Bonds (2.5%) and Austrian Credit shares (1.7%). Subsequently there was a virtual collapse in prices, corresponding to the rise in perceived hostility. The figures on the extent of the collapse in the last few days of the crisis are actually stated conservatively. In the first place, many of the quoted prices were, according to observers, nominal and thus higher than the actual price for which one could sell his securities.[11] Second, for the purpose of the index, the price of a security which was no longer traded—usually due to the closing of various exchanges[12]—is carried through July 30 at the last quoted price.

Again one might raise a question regarding the relationship between the falling price of securities and the European crisis. For purposes of comparison the price movements of the securities of traditionally neutral nations, Sweden and Switzerland, were analyzed (Table 8.5). The values of these stocks and bonds were unusually stable, falling less than one per cent during the crisis.

In contrast, the paper losses in values of the stocks and bonds of the major participants in the crisis were staggering. In the ten-day period ending with July 30, the value of 387 representative British stocks fell by £188,000,000. By July 25, the value of the securities of 23 German industrial firms had dropped from £79,000,000 to £65,900,000—and the worst was yet to come! In one sense the "cost" of the war reached catastrophic proportions even before the first shot was fired.[13] Thus the comparison with the securities of

11. *The Economist*, August 1, 1914, p. 231.

12. The closing dates of the various European exchanges are: Vienna (July 27), Budapest (July 27), Brussels (July 27), Berlin (July 29), St. Petersburg (July 30), Paris (July 30), London (July 31). The closing of the Barcelona Bourse on July 28, however, was attributed to "free fighting between members." *The Economist*, August 1, 1914, p. 220.

13. *The Economist*, August 1, 1914, p. 229; August 29, p. 383. Some contemporary accounts of the various exchanges describe something of the

TABLE 8.5. SECURITIES OF PROSPECTIVE NEUTRALS
(June 20–26=100)

Security	*June 27– July 2*	*July 3–16*	*July 17–20*	*July 21–25*	*July 26*	*July 27*	*July 28*	*July 29*	*July 30*	*July 31*
Sweden 3%	100.0	100.0	100.0	100.0	100.0	100.0	100.0	100.0	100.0	100.0
Sweden 3½%	99.7	97.9	98.4	98.5	99.2	98.3	98.0	98.0	98.0	98.2
Switzerland Chemin de Fer	100.3	99.6	99.5	99.5	99.5	99.5	99.5	99.5	99.5	99.5
INDEX	100.00	99.17	99.30	99.33	99.57	99.27	99.17	99.17	99.17	99.23

Correlations: Rising Hostility—Falling Securities Prices

	n	r	P
Securities Index (Neutrals)	10	+0.520	n.s.
Securities Index (Belligerents)	9	+1.000	$<.01$

Average Loss in Value—Securities of:

Serbia	12.0%
Hungary	8.4%
Russia	10.1%
France	6.4%
Great Britain	5.5%
Germany	7.9%
Austria	4.6%
Belgium	3.0%
Sweden	0.9%
Switzerland	0.5%

belligerents and neutrals during the crisis strongly suggests that the virtual collapse of prices during July 1914 was directly related to rising international tensions.

WHEAT FUTURES

The development of a major international crisis often brings about widespread hoarding of various commodities. Speculators, anticipating panic buying, hoarding, and diminished supplies would be expected to drive the price of commodity

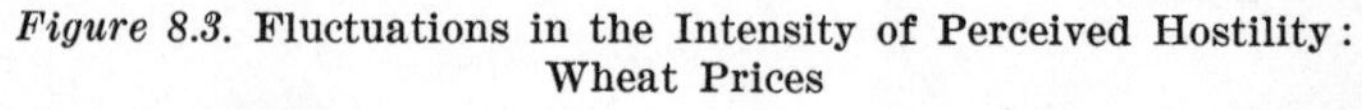

Figure 8.3. Fluctuations in the Intensity of Perceived Hostility: Wheat Prices

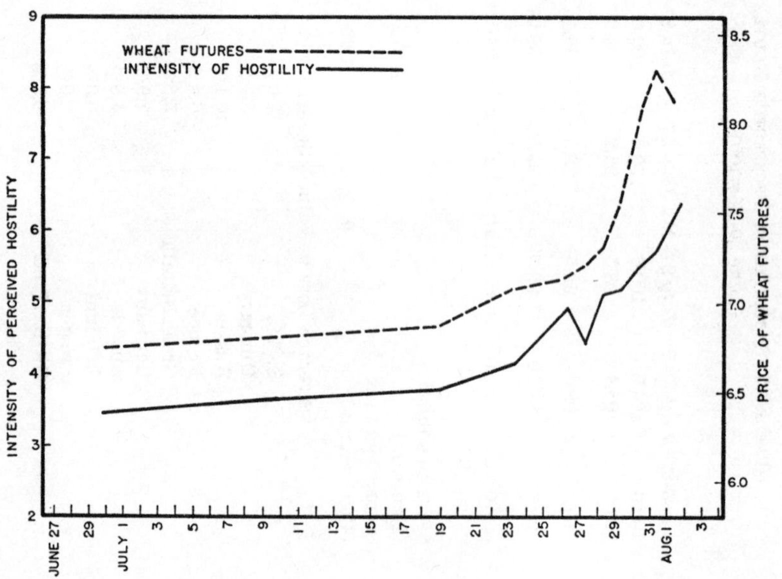

futures up as the crisis deepened. Table 8.6 reveals that during the month of July, wheat futures in London rose more than 20 per cent. Moreover, the pattern of rising prices corresponds almost exactly to the shape of the hostility curve. Similar increases in prices took place on the Conti-

atmosphere in which trading took place: Price losses "exceed anything that has happened in the past." "The Market has become completely demoralized, the chief factors being the Eastern situation." "A panic on the Bourse, on which prices fell below any recorded since 1895." *The Economist*, July 18, 1914, p. 126; July 25, 1914, p. 173; December 19, 1914, p. 13.

TABLE 8.6. DECEMBER WHEAT FUTURES IN LONDON—DAILY AVERAGE
(in shillings)

Average June 20–26	*June 27–July 2*	*July 3–16*	*July 17–20*	*July 21–25*	*July 26*	*July 27*	*July 28*	*July 29*	*July 30*	*July 31*	*Aug. 1*
6.90	6.74	6.81	6.87	7.08	7.15	7.21	7.30	7.56	8.02	8.29	8.13
Intensity level of perceived hostility	3.46	3.66	3.79	4.17	4.92	4.46	5.10	5.18	5.48	5.70	6.42

Correlation : Rising Hostility—Rising Wheat Prices

n	r	P
11	+0.983	$<.01$

nent. In Berlin, for example, the price of rye rose from 172.5 Reichsmarks per sack to 176 RM between July 27 and July 29; wheat rose from 202.25 to 207 RM and oats rose from 167.25 to 169.75 RM during the safe period.[14]

EXCHANGE RATES

The standard against which all currencies were measured in 1914 was the British pound sterling; the value of any currency fluctuated in terms of how much sterling one could buy with it. An analysis of the exchange rates of the German Mark and the Austrian Krone during the 1914 crisis reveals an unprecedented rise in the exchange rates of these currencies (and thus a drop in value) vis-à-vis the pound (Table 8.7). Figure 8.4 shows that once again the fluctuation of the economic variable correlated closely with changes in perceived hostility. Although day-to-day figures on the Russian ruble are less readily available, the trend is the same. According to one source, the ruble, which was quoted at 95.6 to the ten pound note on July 27, was quoted at 110-120 only three days later.[15]

The extent of the collapse of continental currencies is illustrated by the fact that the mark lost 1.6 per cent of its normal value; the krone fell 9.7 per cent and the ruble fell 24.5 per cent during the short span of the crisis.

INTEREST RATES

Table 8.8 shows that both official bank rates and free market money rates are also highly correlated to the fluctuations in perceived hostility during the crisis. Although official rates are usually a highly stable figure—many of the rates at the outbreak of the crisis had not been changed since 1913 or earlier—every one of the major participants for which figures are available increased rates at least once during the six-week period. Three increases in as many days brought the British figures from 3 per cent on July 29 to 10 per cent on

14. *The Economist*, pp. 230, 231.
15. Hirst, p. 283.

August 1; during a similar period the French rate rose from 3½ to 6 per cent, the Vienna rate from 4 to 8 per cent, and the Brussels rate from 4 to 7 per cent. In each case the action on interest rates was a direct outgrowth of the European crisis; a primary reason was to insure that gold would not flow out of the country.[16]

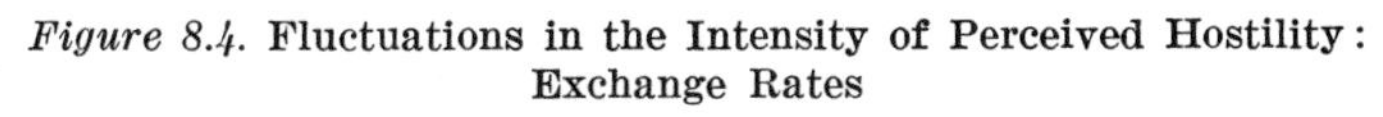

Figure 8.4. Fluctuations in the Intensity of Perceived Hostility: Exchange Rates

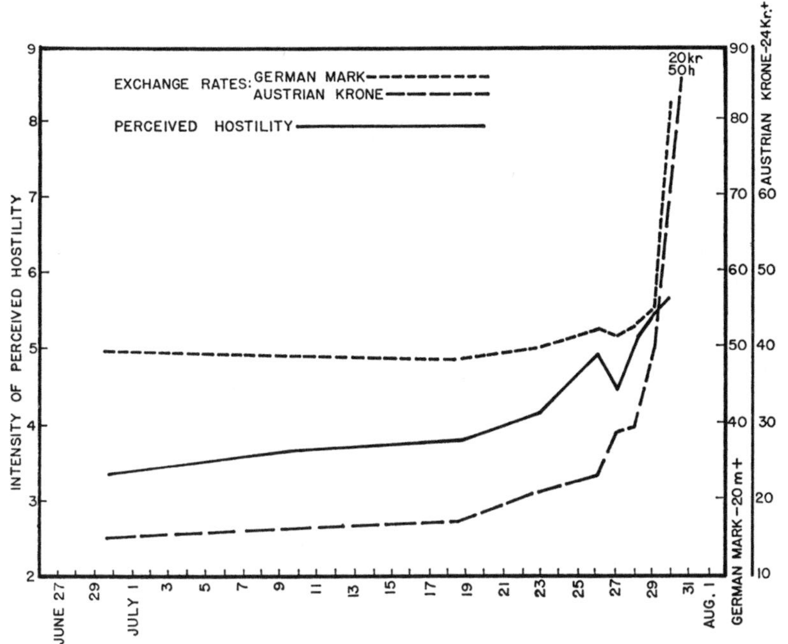

The market money rate, unlike the official rate, fluctuates from day to day much as the price of securities or exchange rates. Although figures were not quoted in Paris, London, or Berlin after July 29 the rates on that day were almost double what they had been earlier in the month. As with the official rate, the market rate fluctuated in concert with the level of hostility perceived by key decision-makers.

16. "The rise to 8 per cent (in England) marked a real panic. Almost the whole continent, from Paris to St. Petersburg, and from Amsterdam to Vienna and Rome, wants to convert paper into cash; and the great banks even in Paris and Berlin are, of course, hoarding gold against an emergency." *The Economist*, August 1, 1914, p. 219.

TABLE 8.7. EXCHANGE RATES: GERMAN MARK AND AUSTRIAN KRONE
(in relation to £ Sterling)

	June 20–26	*June 27–July 2*	*July 3–16*	*July 17–20*	*July 21–25*	*July 26*	*July 27*	*July 28*	*July 29*	*July 30*
German Mark										
Mark	20	20	20	20	20	20	20	20	20	20
Pfennig	49.6	49.7	49.3	48.9	50.1	52.5	52.0	53.0	55.0	82.0
Austrian Krone										
Krone	24	24	24	24	24	24	24	24	24	26
Heller	16.3	15.2	16.6	17.3	21.2	23.5	29.0	30.0	40.0	50.0
Level of perceived hostility		3.46	3.66	3.79	4.17	4.92	4.46	5.10	5.46	5.70

Correlations: Rising Hostility—Falling Currency Values

	n	*r*	*P*
German Mark	9	.933	<.01
Austrian Krone	9	.983	<.01

Table 8.8. Official and Market Money Rates

June 20–26	June 27–July 2	July 3–16	July 17–20	July 21–25	July 26	July 27	July 28	July 29	July 30	July 31	Aug. 1–2	Aug. 3–5
*Official money rates **												
3.92%	3.92%	3.92%	3.92%	3.92%	4.08%	4.25%	4.58%	4.58%	4.92%	5.92%	6.33%	7.17%
*Market money rates ***												
2.63%	2.48%	2.27%	2.31%	2.47%	2.71%	3.17%	4.00%	4.17%	—	—	—	—
Intensity of perceived hostility												
	3.46	3.66	3.79	4.17	4.92	4.46	5.10	5.18	5.48	5.70	6.42	6.30

Correlations: Rising Hostility—Rising Money Rates

	n	r	P
Official rate	12	+.967	<.01
Market rate	8	+.834	.01

* Average rates in London, Paris, Berlin, Vienna, St. Petersburg, and Brussels.

** Average rates in London, Paris, and Berlin.

One by-product of this analysis is a picture, albeit sketchy, of the collapse of an international economic system. That system, which Lenin had prophesied would lead to war and which many early twentieth-century liberals had predicted would make future wars impossible, was, in the words of *The Economist,* "staggering under a series of blows such as the delicate system of international credit has never before witnessed, or even imagined." [17] Hence, "In a single moment all this wonderful machinery was broken or thrown out of

Figure 8.5. **Fluctuations in the Intensity of Perceived Hostility: Bank Rates**

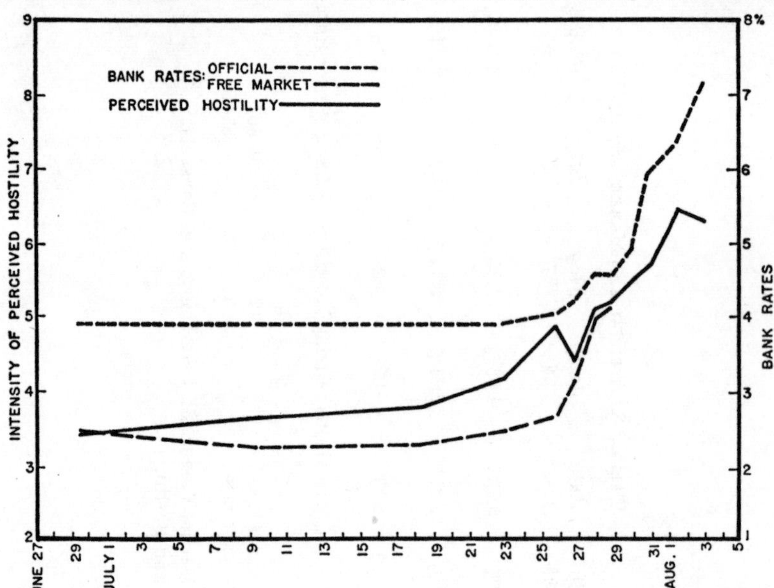

gear." [18] Gold became a weapon of war, and as a result the free movement of gold was in effect abolished as an expedient of war. Major securities exchanges were closed to prevent a more ruinous panic; not even the New York Stock Exchange escaped the effects of war in Europe. The price of commodities came to depend on the rate of merchant ship sinkings rather than the free market. Exchange rates reflected the

17. *The Economist,* August 1, 1914, p. 219.
18. *The Economist,* August 15, 1914, p. 302.

outcomes of battles rather than the finely tuned system of international credit. The effects of the crisis on the shipping insurance business were characteristic of the inability of the old system to cope with the strains that had developed. Insurance rates for the last week of the crisis and the first week of the war are given in Table 8.9. It was only the establishment of the government War Risks Office on August 7, in effect replacing the old system with a new one, which broke the virtual paralysis in the shipping insurance industry.

TABLE 8.9. SHIPPING INSURANCE RATES

Date	*Rate per £100 value*	*Rate as % of value*
July 28	5 shillings	0.25
July 31	60–80 shillings	3.0–4.0
August 4	10–15 guineas	10.5–15.8
August 6	20 guineas	21.0
August 7	10 guineas	10.5
August 9	8 guineas	8.4
August 12	4 guineas	4.2
August 14	3 guineas	3.1

Source: The Economist, August 15, 1914, p. 304.

In the final days prior to the outbreak of general war, one observer, reflecting upon the closing of the London Stock Exchange, noted the inability of the international system to cope with the situation which was developing:

> Nothing, indeed, could have given a more dramatic touch, and nothing could have testified more clearly to the impossibility of running modern civilization and war together than this closing of the London Stock Exchange owing to a collapse of prices, produced not by the actual outbreak of a small war, but by the fear of war between some of the great powers of Europe.[19]

CONCLUSION

The data presented in this paper lend substantial support to the premise that content analysis of what decision-makers

19. *The Economist*, August 1, 1914, p. 219.

say may fruitfully be used as a research tool in the study of international relations. We have analyzed a series of economic variables with the following characteristics: readily accessible data of unquestioned authenticity reported on a daily basis, measured on an equal-interval scale, and shown to be sensitive to even minor instabilities in the international system. We have then shown that the "soft" variable derived through content analysis traces a pattern almost identical with that of the "hard" variables. Thus, although we avoid the question of a direct relationship, we find that each of our measures independently describes the escalation of a local incident into a general war.

If "hard" variables such as gold flow, the stock market, and others are sensitive to crises, why bother with the content analysis data? There are two important reasons: (1) The economic indicators respond to a variety of stimuli—some economic, some political, some social. The stock market crashes of 1929 and 1962, for example, were probably related more to internal than international factors, and recent sales of gold by the Soviet Union are largely a response to agricultural difficulties. (2) The analysis of economic indicators alone may not tell us much about *why* actors are behaving the way they are.

Even by social science standards, the collection and analysis of quantifiable data in the field of international relations is at a rudimentary stage. In no field is the gap between theory formulation and theory testing so wide. Techniques such as content analysis—much of which may now be done by high speed computers [20]—appear capable of contributing to the closing of the gap.

20. Ole R. Holsti, "An Adaptation of the 'General Inquirer' for the Systematic Analysis of Political Documents," *Behavioral Science, 9* (1964), 382–88.

PART III

Cross-National Comparisons of Within-Nation Differences

Much of the discussion at the Yale Data Conference focused on the limitations of "whole-unit" approaches to cross-national comparisons: the comparison of aggregate national totals or averages used in the Yale Data Program or the comparison of global characteristics of entire nations attempted in the HRAF-type analysis developed by Banks and Textor in their *Cross-Polity Survey.* Two types of objections were particularly frequent: nation-states vary too much in size and they are too different in internal structure to allow meaningful comparisons. Russett and his associates dropped out of their *World Handbook of Political and Social Indicators* a variety of small territories but beyond that did not study the implications of variations in size for the interpretation of their analytical findings. Although the treatment of such units as the United States (population 183 million) and Iceland (population 180 thousand) as equals may be justified for some purposes, it may be highly questionable in other cases.

Several alternatives to this "one-nation, one-case" approach were brought up at the Conference. One of these, which focuses on *individuals* as units of analysis, treats nationality on a par with other attributes such as sex, age, occupation, and type of neighborhood. This is essentially the strategy of the increasingly frequent cross-national comparisons of chances for educational advancement and occupational mobility. The paper by Halsey reviews issues in the comparative study of educational statistics and the paper by Fox and Miller discusses their recent efforts to compare rates of upward or downward mobility in countries at different levels of economic growth. The interesting paper by the Hungarian philosopher and sociologist Alexander Szalai represents a new departure in this line of comparison: studies of variations in individual time budgets may not only tell us a great deal about the human meaning of industrialization and urbanization but may also, if conducted in several contrasting countries, illuminate differences in cultural orientations to work, leisure, and family life.

Another strategy centers on strains and contrasts between *competing power centers* and their dependent regions in each nation. This is essentially the approach developed in the papers by Lerner, Linz and Miguel, and Merritt.

A third strategy focuses on the analysis of variations among *local communities* within the nation. This is the technique advocated by Erik Allardt in his ecological study of Finnish Politics and by Stein Rokkan and Henry Valen in their chapter in Part IV of this volume on the organization of a Norwegian archive of data by locality.

A fourth strategy, not represented in this symposium, is the comparative analysis of *statistically defined areas within each nation.* This is the technique adopted in the extensive maps of regional variations in Europe prepared under the direction of Ludwig Neundörfer: his "regions" are all compact areas with populations of roughly 500,000 within each country.[1]

All these procedures have their advantages and their limitations. The participants at the Yale Data Conference did not opt for one method in preference to another, agreeing instead on the importance of *coordinated studies* at several levels of each system. The papers assembled in this section do not go very far in the direction of such complex research designs but they at least point the way.

A. H. Halsey concentrates upon the usefulness of literacy rates as indicators of general educational levels, particularly in the developing nations. In attempting to correlate such data with other indicators of political development, it is not enough merely to know the number of years of educational exposure per capita or the percentage of literates in the society. It is equally important, he argues, to know the cultural meaning of such educational experiences, context by context. Statistics on secondary education, for example, do not generally reveal the extent to which educational oppor-

1. Ludwig Neundörfer, *Atlas sozialökonomischer Regionen Europas* (Baden-Baden, Lutzeyer, 1965).

tunity springs from class, ethnic, religious, or other cleavages. Similarly, the biographies of many nationalist leaders in Asia and Africa suggest that exposure to the same educational experience—that is, a university education at the same Western European or American institution—does not result in a common outlook on political matters. In some cases members of the educated elite isolate themselves from or are isolated by the underlying strata of their native populations; in other cases traditions of opposition lead them to oppose existing governmental policy, whatever that policy may be. It is precisely because the character of the cultural transmission process varies from country to country, according to Halsey, that one of our most important tasks in comparative research is to establish reliable indicators of such differences.

Thomas Fox and S. M. Miller deal with a particularly thorny issue in the cross-national comparison of within-nation differences: occupational stratification and mobility. Recognizing that data gathering difficulties make any comparisons at best only approximate, they report on their effort to determine upward and downward rates of occupational mobility from one generation to another in four industrialized countries—Great Britain, Japan, the Netherlands, and the United States. Their hope is eventually to correlate these rates with levels of political stability and rates of economic growth for a larger number and greater variety of types of countries. Among their findings, one of the most striking is that, contrary to the thesis originally set forth by Lipset and Bendix,[2] advanced industrial nations have different basic patterns of mobility. This suggests the importance of cultural variations both for the definitions of occupational strata and for the openness or closedness of the channels of

2. Cf. Seymour Martin Lipset and Reinhard Bendix, *Social Mobility in Industrial Society* (Berkeley and Los Angeles, University of California Press, 1959) ; the conclusions of these analyses have subsequently been subjected to detailed scrutiny in S. M. Miller, "Comparative Social Mobility," *Current Sociology, 9* (1960), 1–5, and in Seymour Martin Lipset, "Research Problems in the Comparative Analysis of Mobility and Development," *International Social Science Journal, 16* (1964), 35–48.

recruitment and mobility. It also points to a need to pay attention to the culturally determined distances between statistical strata and the corresponding strains on family cohesion brought about through father–son mobility.

Alexander Szalai reports on research on time budgets in the Soviet Union and in Hungary. These studies have become increasingly important in socialist countries as a source of data for long-term planning: they show, for instance, marked differences in the patterns of time use between men and women in the industrial labor force, and document the heavy costs to the national economy and to leisure time culture of time-consuming household obligations (such as standing in line at markets). In Hungary detailed analyses have been undertaken of the elasticities of different categories of time demand, by comparing otherwise matched groups of industrial workers in terms of their commuting time. Szalai concludes that such studies of the "compressibility" and "expandability" of different categories of daily, weekly, and yearly activities, if carried out in a number of countries, could throw considerable light on cultural differences.

Four further papers deal with *territorial differences* within nation-states: "monocephalism" vs. "polycephalism," regional imbalances in economic growth, regional contrasts in political alignments, center–periphery differences in rates of mobilization and politicization. The unexamined use of aggregate data to characterize a country, while valuable in some respects, may in fact distort the actual distribution of values in that country. It is one thing, for instance, to note that the country's population is evenly divided between Catholics and Protestants; and quite another thing if closer examination reveals that most of the Catholics live in one distinct region and most of the Protestants live in another. The former situation might lead to a pluralist attitude toward matters of religion, whereas the latter could be an indicator of potential or actual religious strife. Moreover, it may make a difference in the stability of a given country if its political core area, rather than being a single city or narrowly circumscribed region, is split up among a number of cities or regions.

Daniel Lerner underlines the importance of such territorial strains in the formation of national politics in his discussion of Turkey (with Istanbul as the economic and cultural center, and Ankara as the political center) and Syria (with Aleppo as the economic center and Damascus as the political center). In general terms, the history of most nations can be analyzed in terms of successive phases in the policy of the centers toward their peripheries. In the first phase, the typical posture is one of disinterest: the peripheries are either exploited or ignored. In the second phase there is the acceptance of differences between the center and periphery, with neither area attempting to dominate the other. The acceptance of regional differentiation in territories where economic and political power has not been crystallized is often unstable. The third phase is one of dissidence reduction. The essential procedure is to reduce the distances in time and in space between the metropolitan and the outlying areas, possibly through the standardization of information diffusion by means of schools and mass media, and through the sharing of national experiences and symbols by means of participation in the armed forces, in political parties, and in other mass organizations. This mobilization of the periphery into the national community puts heavy burdens on the national governmental apparatus. Indeed, much of the history of the new nations could be written in terms of the decisions taken in the face of this "revolution of participation."

Juan J. Linz and Amando de Miguel focus on regional differences in the social structure of Spain and their consequences for the political integration of that country. In documenting the tensions between Madrid, Barcelona, and Bilbao, they suggest a general typology of national structures along two axes: proletarization and extent of urban middle class. Its application to Spain enables them to distinguish seven "types" of provinces—bourgeois (or "industrial"), proletarian in transition, *clases medias* in transition, Madrid, *clases medias,* gentry in transition, gentry, and proletarian—each of which is mobilizing at a different rate and each of which plays a distinctive role in the development of Spain.

Richard L. Merritt writes about the recent emergence of differential perspectives in a country long overburdened by regional differentiation. In reanalyzing public opinion data for the West German Federal Republic and for West Berlin, he introduces detailed controls to match the West Berlin sample with corresponding samples of large-city respondents in the *Bundesrepublik.* Even with such controls, a consistent pattern of differences appears not only in political alignments but in the willingness to express opinions and in perspectives on a wide range of policy issues. These differences are most likely due to the peculiar position of West Berlin, located as it is in the heart of East Germany and daily confronted by the East–West struggle. West Berliners are markedly more informed and concerned about politics and also more willing to express opinions. They are more committed politically to the West (and particularly to the United States) than are West German urban residents. On matters not related to politics, West Berlin attitudes do not differ significantly from those held by inhabitants of other West German cities.

Erik Allardt, whose factor analysis of the determinants of communist strength in Finland underscores the importance of regional differences in the process of political mobilization, demonstrates the fruitfulness of an explicitly theoretical approach to the study of such variations. He is not content merely to document the factors underlying the empirical variations among communes in the different regions but, in addition, develops an abstract model of the exchange processes at different levels of modernization which could account for the observed differences in political alignments.

The discussion at the Yale Data Conference following these various papers brought out a general agreement on the need to add to the program of aggregate cross-national comparison a series of indicators of the range and character of within-nation inequalities. In their chapter, Hayward R. Alker, Jr., and Bruce M. Russett outline and evaluate more than 20 indices of inequality. Although stressing that no single index can serve all purposes, they propose the use of Lorenz curves with Gini indices for the consideration of inequalities in income and in the size of land holdings. The possibilities for using such measures in the cross-national study of politics are great, provided that suitable data can be gathered and made generally available. And, of course, the use of such indices may itself encourage national census bureaus and independent scholars to seek out such data.

In further discussion at the Yale Data Conference, emphasis was placed on the need for guides to national sources of data on a number of basic socioeconomic, political, and cultural variables: education, occupation, property holdings, religious participation, voluntary association membership, party membership, the use of leisure time, mass media exposure, and so forth. Regarding regional within-nation differences, it was felt that one fruitful avenue for scientific exploration might be the cross-national comparison of data about subnational areas. In Western Europe, for instance, it may turn out that comparisons between the provinces of southern France and those of southern Germany would tell us more about Western European social and political behavior than would a direct comparison between France and Germany. Used in conjunction with other types of inquiries, both approaches would produce results as interesting as they are significant for cross-national research.

9. The Education of Leaders and Political Development in New Nations

A. H. HALSEY, NUFFIELD COLLEGE, OXFORD

Literacy rates are generally recognized as one of the more important indicators of political development. Karl Deutsch, for example, uses them as an indicator of social mobilization and political development, and Seymour Martin Lipset has found a positive relation between literacy and democracy.[1] This chapter will discuss some of the social processes underlying this indicator.

CHARACTERISTICS OF NEW NATIONS

Most new nations together with their governmental machinery are indeed very new; the rapidity of their emergence, usually from colonial status, is truly remarkable. Thus, of the 40 identifiable countries in the whole continent of Africa, only ten had emerged as independent states before 1960.[2] In that single year no less than 17 did so. Although the remaining 23 include the Portuguese territories (Angola, Portuguese Guinea, Mozambique) where the granting of independence is not planned by the imperial power, also included are

1. Karl W. Deutsch, "Social Mobilization and Political Development," *American Political Science Review, 55* (1961), 493–514; Seymour Martin Lipset, *Political Man* (New York, Doubleday, 1960).

2. They were Egypt, Ethiopia, Ghana, Guinea, Liberia, Libya, Morocco, Sudan, Tunisia, and the Union of South Africa.

areas which are rapidly approaching autonomy, or have subsequently attained it, such as the British territories of Kenya, Uganda, Nyasaland, and the Rhodesias. Indeed, outside the communist world there is only one area, Oceania, where the end of imperialism is not in sight.

Most new nations are highly traditional in their culture and social structure. This means that the position of an individual in society, whether as a leader or not, is *ascriptively* determined, i.e. a function of his kin membership and, in some societies, caste and linguistic grouping. These factors, together with their economic base of agrarian poverty, constrict social participation and loyalties, and tend to separate the mass of the population from the national, metropolitan elite. The pull of traditional tribal and kinship loyalties is a common obstacle to the formation of modern political parties and the operation of effective government by uncorrupted leaders; hence the development of democratic politics is impeded.

No less characteristic of the new nations is the ardent desire to become "modern" industrialized societies. The educated elite are usually the carriers of this aspiration, but there are often divisions within the elite in the value placed on traditional indigenous culture. The urge toward modernity creates new demands for skilled scientific and professional manpower, rising standards of life, and opportunities for social mobility. These demands press hard on new and inexperienced governments and thus make even more precarious the stability of democratic government.

Certain typical educational consequences flow from the characteristic conditions of new and developing countries. Among these, and at once cause and effect of ubiquitous poverty, is the intractable combination of mass illiteracy and scarce educational resources. The literacy rate is a good indicator of the general susceptibility of a population to modern political and economic life. But the characteristic situation is that higher education is either withheld altogether from the native population or is confined to a tiny wealthy and/or fortunate minority who are, through education, sharply separated from their countrymen in outlook and style of life. The consequences are exemplified by the recent history of the Congo, which at independence found itself with 17 university graduates out of a population of 13.5 million. The extent of present inequalities may be seen in the background of foreign students from underdeveloped countries at American universities. A recent small sample study by the Stanford Research Institute shows that three quarters of the students come from big cities in their countries of origin, half of them had fathers who had been educated to the level of the American bachelor's degree, and a third were financially supported by parents or relations. Their social composition is therefore highly selective from populations which are overwhelmingly rural, ill educated, and poor.

National literacy rates do not reveal the divisive forces which may be closely related to the type of political development and economic growth. Some measure of the distribution of educational opportunity between regional, ethnic, tribal, and class groups needs to be used in this connection. The basic concept here, presumably, is that of "life-chances." We used this in the form of "class-chances" to compare different strata in terms of educational opportunity in England.[3] In the present context a useful national index of inequality of educational opportunity might be the ratio of class-chances between the most advantaged 10 per cent and the least advantaged 10 per cent. But such measures cannot be derived from published statistics.

EDUCATIONAL LEVEL AND DEMOCRACY

Research surveyed and summarized by S. M. Lipset has shown that democracy is clearly related to the state of economic development. "The more well-to-do a nation," he writes, "the greater the chances that it will sustain democracy."[4] Thus, by comparing European, English-speaking, and

3. J. Floud et al., *Social Class and Educational Opportunity* (London, Heinemann, 1956).
4. Lipset, pp. 48–50.

Latin American countries in four groups, according to the degree of democracy exhibited by their recent political history, Lipset shows that indices of wealth are consistently correlated with the stability of democratic institutions. His table is extracted in Table 9.1.

TABLE 9.1. DEMOCRACY, ECONOMIC DEVELOPMENT AND EDUCATION [a]

	Per capita income (U.S. dollars)	*Percentage literate*	*Post-primary enrollment 1000 persons*
European and English-speaking stable democracies [b]	695	96%	44
European and English-speaking unstable democracies and dictatorships [c]	308	85	22
Latin American democracies and unstable dictatorships [d]	171	74	13
Latin American stable dictatorships [e]	119	46	8

a. Extracted from S. M. Lipset, *Political Man*, Table II, pp. 51 and 53.
b. A group of 13 countries including U.S., U.K., Norway, and Australia.
c. A group of 17 countries including U.S.S.R., Spain, France, Poland, and Greece.
d. A group of 7 countries including Argentina, Mexico, Brazil, and Chile.
e. A group of 13 countries including Bolivia, Ecuador, Panama, and Peru.

Education is also related to the likelihood of democratic politics. Lipset's group of more democratic European countries is almost entirely literate while his second group of less democratic countries in Europe has an average literacy rate of 85 per cent. The figure falls to 74 per cent for the group of Latin American countries classified as "less dictatorial" and further to 46 per cent for the "more dictatorial."

The significance of these comparisons may be gauged from a survey of the world's current literacy rates. Literacy is much less common in Asia and Africa (where the newly independent states are concentrated) than it is in Latin America. Usually not more than 10 to 15 per cent of the native populations of African states can read or write. The correlation is of course not perfect. India reported a literacy rate of

19 per cent in 1951;[5] but among the Indian states, Kerala, with one of the highest rates of literacy, elected a communist government in the late 1950s.[6] Nevertheless, the comparisons in Table 9.2 give us a rough geographical distribution of the viability of democracy as a political doctrine. The training of leaders committed to democratic politics (self-determination, tolerance of opposition, belief in orderly, nonviolent social change, etc.) is pointless without the essential social bases among which is a high literacy rate. As Lipset argues, "if we cannot say that a 'high' level of education is a *sufficient* condition of democracy, the available evidence suggests that it comes close to being a *necessary* one."[7]

TABLE 9.2. THE DISTRIBUTION OF LITERACY

	Total population (in millions)	*Per cent of adult literates*
Africa	198	15–20%
Asia	1376	35–40
South and Central America	162	56–60
Oceania	13	89–90
Europe	393	91–93
U.S.S.R.	186	——
North America	168	96–97
World total	2496	55–58

Source: Adapted from UNESCO, *Basic Facts and Figures 1959* (Paris, 1960), p. 25.

Moreover, in a society which is open or pluralistic to any degree, it seems that the amount of education experienced by leaders will influence their readiness to operate democratically.

> Data gathered by public opinion research agencies which have questioned people in different countries about their beliefs on tolerance for the opposition, their attitudes toward ethnic or racial minorities, and their feelings for multi-party as against one-party systems have showed that the most important single factor differentiating

5. UNESCO, *Basic Facts and Figures 1959* (Paris, 1960).
6. Deutsch, "Social Mobilization," p. 496.
7. Lipset, *Political Man*, p. 57.

> those giving democratic responses from the others has been education. The higher one's education, the more likely one is to believe in democratic values and support democratic practices. All the relevant studies indicate that education is more significant than either income or occupation.[8]

Investment in education then, regardless of its specific content and within a wide range of cultural and economic contexts, is an investment in political development toward democracy. Mass literacy is an essential prerequisite for identification with and political participation in a national culture, as opposed to a local or kinship culture. However, education in colonial territories has commonly been concentrated on the training of a small native elite for professional and administrative positions; and the political consequences of selective access to educational opportunity need to be explored by different indicators.

EDUCATIONAL TRAFFIC BETWEEN ADVANCED AND DEVELOPING COUNTRIES

Many of the connections between education and political development in the new nations suggest the usefulness of analyzing educational traffic between advanced and developing countries. It can be argued that Western educational institutions are the most important single vehicle on which Africa and Asia are traveling from colonial rule to self-government and from poverty to industrial standards of life. This journey may be said to be conceived within the value system of the West and to be mapped in detail in Western universities, political parties, and other centers of intellectual life. "Nationalism in Nigeria is as much the product of British liberalism as it is of British colonialism." [9] Modern ideas of democracy, of self-determination, and of progress have been brought to India and Africa by Western teachers

8. Ibid., p. 56.
9. James S. Coleman, *Nigeria: Background to Nationalism* (Berkeley, University of California Press, 1958), p. 414.

and students returning from study abroad. Modern science and technology are similarly dependent on Western education for transmission to the underdeveloped world. The leaders of African and Asian nationalist movements, and the scientific and professional manpower which forms the spearhead of economic advance, are almost exclusively products of Western education.

The decisive element in the lead taken by India in Asia and Ghana in Africa in the movement toward national independence may be traced to the method of colonial rule which involved the creation of an educated class among the subject peoples, combined with the declared British colonial policy of eventual self-government. In other areas, freedom of development was denied to this educated class by such factors as the presence of European and other settlers, as in East and South Africa, or the colonial policy of assimilation to the metropolitan country, as in French and Portugese territories. By contrast, in India before independence 12,000 Britons administered a country of 400 million people. This necessitated the British educational policy which was stated by Macaulay in 1835: "We must do our best to form a class who may be interpreters between us and the millions we govern, a class of persons Indian in blood and colour, but English in tastes, in opinions, in morals and intellect." [10]

Under these conditions a Western educated minority emerged in the colonial territories. They were employed as clerks and subordinates in government and business enterprises and, through their position as intermediaries, were exposed most acutely to the inequalities and frustrations of alien rule. The elite in this emergent class was composed of a small group of European or American educated professional men (lawyers, doctors, and teachers) who had become deeply imbued with Western ideas, particularly the ideas of democracy, political organization on a national scale to achieve national freedom, and the desirability and possibility through science of rapid economic development. (The attrac-

10. Quoted in J. and R. H. Useem, *The Western Educated Man in India* (New York, Dryden Press, 1955), p. 14.

tion of Soviet Russia, and more lately China, is often more as a model for economic growth through national "political" planning than as the source of a social and political philosophy.)

However, it is by no means a simple task to estimate the probability that Western ideas carried by the educated will survive in the emerging political and economic structure of the new states. Some of the educated are clearly making an enormous contribution to political and social development as politicians, administrators, and scientists, as well as sympathetic and responsible critics of those who hold the responsibilities of office. Nevertheless, the relation of some segments of the educated classes to the processes of political leadership is attended by many difficulties.[11]

First, the experience of Western education, whether in his native country or in Europe or America, inevitably separates the educated man from the uneducated in outlook and style of life. Western education introduces him to new styles of dress, speech, and behavior; teaches him the worth of Western culture; and, by implication, teaches him the worthlessness of tribal life and primitive custom. His "reference group" tends to become not the kin and region from which he sprang, but the community of the educated by whose standards he has been taught to live. Also, he is likely to be cut off from indigenous religious and intellectual traditions and to become not only critical of traditional sources of authority but also oriented to the secular industrial, urban, and international culture of the West.

Second, the burden of political and economic advance is borne almost exclusively by the educated in the underdeveloped countries under conditions of unprecedented difficulty. They work in the absence of those traditions of responsible empiricism through which craftsmen and artisans were able to make a crucial contribution to industrial and political development in the Western countries. The objective needs of

11. These are analyzed by Edward Shils in his "Political Development in the New States," *Comparative Studies in Society and History, 2* (1960), 379–411.

their poverty-stricken countrymen are immediate and the desire for higher standards of life urgent. The educated have been impressed with the high material standards enjoyed by the West and indoctrinated with the ideals of freedom and progress; at the same time, they are particularly motivated to pursue these goals after being subjected to major and minor racial indignities. The consequent temptation to seek quick methods toward large-scale solutions makes them vulnerable to the theory that democracy is an obstacle to rapid growth. Great strain is therefore put upon the precariously established framework of parliamentary democracy which the new nations inherit from colonialism.

Perhaps most serious of all, however, are the forces which tend to produce in the educated man what Edward Shils calls "traditions of oppositional politics." [12] These forces often combine with "an ambivalent relationship to his indigenous culture and preoccupation with 'abroad' " to generate a dangerous political alienation. One illustration of this is referred to by David Apter in his study, *The Gold Coast in Transition,* where "particularly those educated abroad have a sense of mission, full of enthusiasm for the benefits which they can bestow upon their people. Many have been in touch with Western radical ideas, and have had communist affiliations. Yet on their return to the Gold Coast, often after five or six years as students in England or the United States, they find to their dismay that they are rarely welcomed with open arms into the policy-making ranks of the Convention People's Party." [13]

In general, the large Congress-type national party, when fully established, tends to recruit and reward party loyalists of the "populist" sort who are more closely identified with traditional culture, and who are disesteemed by the modern "Western-oriented" intellectuals. Moreover, in countries such as India enormous prestige is attached to a university degree and yet university graduates, especially in nonvoca-

12. Ibid., p. 275.
13. David E. Apter, *The Gold Coast in Transition* (Princeton, Princeton University Press, 1955), p. 295.

tional subjects, find that their services are not readily salable to government or business. Consequently, a widespread resentment and contempt for politicians is generated, resulting in a willingness to join extremist movements which promise to sweep away an "ineffectual" and "corrupt" political order.

Both the leaders of African and Asian nationalist movements and those in the forefront of economic advance are almost exclusively the products of Western education. In the newly emerging countries, where education has become an almost automatic qualification for entry into elite positions, it has become inevitable that top leadership should be recruited from the minority with higher education. The lack of adequate indigenous provision for education at the higher levels has meant that in each country the majority of those with a higher education have probably received it outside their own country. This number has been rapidly increasing: for example, those educated in Britain increased from between 500 and 600 in 1939 to 11,000 plus in 1959–60. It is still true that in a country where the mass of the people has little or no educational experience, "the responsibilities of leadership . . . must fall to a large extent (and fall early) upon the shoulders of the relatively small number of colonial students who are gaining the advantage of higher education and specialized training in Britain." [14] From student to minister may be a matter of only a few years. This is rather similar to a point argued by Shils: in newly emerged countries the absence of the craftsmen and entrepreneurial groups which made Western development so rapid means that the only alternative leadership must come from the "educated classes." [15]

There has as yet been no comprehensive comparative study of the educational backgrounds of the men who are emerging as nationalist leaders. Some indications are, however, apparent from the limited information which is available. It is

14. Political and Economic Planning (P.E.P.), *Colonial Students in Britain* (London, 1955), p. 3.

15. Edward Shils, "Intellectuals, Public Opinion and Economic Development," *Economic Development and Cultural Change, 6* (1957), 55–62.

clear that the average academic achievement of the leaders is high—probably much higher than that of cabinet members in countries with well established democratic and educational institutions and with political elites recruited from a much broader base, such as trade unions and local politics. Particular evidence may be found in Robert C. North's analysis of cabinet members and ministers of cabinet rank in India in 1956.[16] All but two (who described themselves as privately educated) were graduates. Of the 16 cabinet members, 93.7 per cent attended institutions of higher education as compared with 76.6 per cent of British cabinet members for the period 1886–1950.[17] Just under half had degrees from a European university and, counting European and Indian universities, 15 men had two or more degrees each. Nehru himself, for example, had qualifications in the natural sciences (at Cambridge) and had been called to the English Bar. A somewhat similar pattern emerges in Africa. To take

TABLE 9.3. FOREIGN STUDENTS AS A PERCENTAGE OF THE TOTAL NUMBER OF STUDENTS ENROLLED IN INSTITUTIONS OF HIGHER EDUCATION, 1957

	Students enrolled		
Country of study	*Total*	*Foreign*	*% Foreign*
Australia	65,937	2,956	4.48
India [a]	798,174	3,643	0.46
Pakistan	107,134	141	0.13
Belgium	37,890	2,011	5.31
France [b]	180,634	17,176	9.51
Federal Republic of Germany	153,923	12,833	8.34
U.K. [c]	97,000	10,899	11.20
U.S.A. [d]	3,036,938	43,193	1.42
U.S.S.R.	2,110,900	11,300	0.54

a. Figures refer to 1956.
b. Universities only, including Algiers.
c. Estimated figures.
d. Including teacher training.

Source: Adapted from UNESCO, *Basic Facts and Figures* (Paris, UNESCO, 1959), Table II.

16. Robert C. North, "The Indian Council of Ministers: A Study of Origins," in Richard L. Park and I. Tinker, *Leadership and Political Institutions in India* (Princeton, Princeton University Press, 1959), pp. 103–14.

17. T. E. Summers and R. B. Fisher, "The British Cabinet 1886–1950," draft memorandum of the RADIR project, p. 48, cited in North, p. 110.

only a few examples, Kojo Botsio (Ghana) was a student at Oxford and at London University, Jomo Kenyatta (Kenya) had studied at the London School of Economics and worked on social anthropology at Moscow, and Kofi Busia (Ghana) held a doctorate from Oxford and was a university teacher.

The relative proportions of foreign students in various "host" countries are shown in Table 9.3. Britain continues to take the greatest proportion of foreign students. In 1959–60 between 10 and 11 per cent of total admissions to British universities were from overseas. Another 11,000 foreigners were accepted at technical colleges. Counting all full-time students who stayed for longer than six months in the session 1959–60, in universities, teachers' training colleges, nursing (which incidentally accounts for the majority of women overseas students), practical training, private colleges, etc., the total is over 47,000.

Although the intake of foreign students into United States colleges and universities has increased by 300 per cent[18] from 1930 to 1953, while enrollment of American students has increased by only slightly more than 100 per cent over the same period, the percentage of foreign student enrollment is still small—about 1.7 per cent in 1958–59. This small American percentage is, however, somewhat misleading as it is based on the total heterogeneous body of college students. Probably a reduction of the denominator to one third, raising the proportion to over 5 per cent, would make for fairer comparison. However, a comparison of the spread of foreign students by country of origin shows that recruitment to American universities and colleges is geographically much narrower than to the British universities.[19]

The reception of students from the new nations is not confined to the Western democracies. Since 1950, for example,

18. Cf. Cora DuBois, *Foreign Students and Higher Education in the United States* (Washington, American Council on Education, 1956), p. 3.

19. Cf. UNESCO, *Basic Facts and Figures 1959*. The contrast between the two countries is marked. In 1957–58, of the one hundred countries listed, only one (Cuba) sent students to the U.S. and not to the U.K. Those sending to the U.K. and not to the U.S. included Argentina, Brazil, Burma, Ceylon, Ghana, Indonesia, Iraq, Malaya, Pakistan, and the Union of South Africa.

India has been receiving foreign students in increasing numbers, while at the same time "exporting" students to Britain and the United States: 1,511 and 2,585 respectively in 1957–58. Asian students have studied in Australia since World War II. The People's Friendship University for Asian, African, and Latin American countries was formed in Moscow in 1960. From an initial intake of 500 students in 1960, an eventual maximum of 3,000 to 4,000 was envisaged.

The impact of different countries on the outlook of students from abroad is a complex and changing one. Franklin Frazier [20] has pointed out, for example, that the older elite of British West Africa (i.e. the former leaders who had generally been educated in England and had returned to Africa as barristers, civil servants, and politicians) has been submerged by a larger educated class with different foreign experience and a different outlook. Frazier maintains that in both Ghana and Nigeria the leaders in the revolutionary political changes are men who were not educated along traditional English lines, but received an important part of their education in the United States and in Negro schools. In addition, most of their informal education was acquired from observation of American political methods, as well as the relations of whites and Negroes in the U.S. Thus Kwame Nkrumah (Ghana) studied at Lincoln University and the University of Pennsylvania, in addition to a period at the London School of Economics. Dr. Nnamdi Azikiwe (Nigeria) was at Lincoln and Harvard before doing graduate work at Columbia and Pennsylvania. Hastings Banda (Nyasaland) took a degree in history before turning to medicine. Dr. Cheddi Jagan and Dr. Lachmansingh (British Guiana) were also American educated.

An understanding of the complexity of the problem involves exploration of the factors which condition the influence of educational institutions on foreign students, including the reasons for which they come, the attitudes and images which they bring with them, and the speed of their

20. "Education and the African Elite," *Transactions of the Third World Congress of Sociology, 5* (1956), 92.

adjustment. The enormous differences in race, social background, religion, and educational standards of those whom the mass of the population of the host country tends to see as a homogeneous group—foreigners—make valid generalization difficult. Although an oversimplification of a complex situation, it is possible to distinguish two main categories, both based primarily on the status of the country from which the student comes. The first (and one which was probably much more common before World War II) corresponds to the attitude based on respect and a desire to emulate the culture and values of a "mother country," and is probably directly related to the degree of Westernization to which a student has previously been exposed. More important than the content of education is the way in which assimilation to Westernization is seen as a goal, as in the case of Indians in the pre-independence era, the *évolués* of French territories, or the *assimilados* of Portuguese possessions. The student then wishes to participate in a culture which he has convinced himself is not alien to him, and to share in the prestige which that culture carries.

The second category lies at the other end of the scale—the resentment felt when the image of the dominant culture is seen as imperialist and exploiting. Then the desire is to break what is seen as the monopoly of the power-giving mystique of education held by the dominant power, and, by participating in this education, to acquire the means to rid themselves of domination. There is ambivalence in this attitude. Students of this type have a strong motive for adaptation to the social setup of the host country, as Carey says, "in so far as this serves their desire for independence, or because they see in social participation a test of their own worth." [21] This link of self-esteem with national status, which may almost amount to virtual identification in some cases, is more likely to be encountered in students from countries having achieved or approaching independence, where as DuBois

21. A. T. Carey, *Colonial Students in Britain* (London, Secker and Warburg, 1956), p. 42.

points out, national growth and personal advancement are closely meshed.[22]

Thus, in appraising the role of education in social mobilization and political development, one must look beyond the aggregate statistics. Literacy rates must be supplemented by detailed knowledge about the kinds of education available to the national population and, in particular, about the education of present and potential leaders.

22. DuBois, p. 44.

10. Occupational Stratification and Mobility[1]

THOMAS FOX AND S. M. MILLER,
SYRACUSE UNIVERSITY

THE STUDY OF SOCIAL MOBILITY

The sociological study of social mobility is almost exclusively concerned with occupational mobility. Changes in the distribution of citizenship rights or in social acceptance are not likely to be in the forefront. Within the investigation of occupational social mobility primary emphasis is on ranking occupations by prestige levels rather than by indicators of skill, income, or span of control. Occupational prestige indicators, based on surveys of attitudes of a national cross-section, are assumed to be adequate summaries of the other dimensions of job positions. The emphasis in present-day studies is still chiefly on intergenerational mobility (the relation of son's occupation to father's) rather than on intragenerational mobility (the course of job movement in one individual's career) or of stratum mobility (the movement of one stratum relative to other strata along the relevant dimensions). Thus, the definition of social mobility and the indicators employed to measure it provide only a limited slice of the phenomena commonly regarded as social mobility by other social scientists.[2]

1. This work has been supported by Project 6-25-124 of the National Science Foundation. A slightly different version of this chapter appeared as Vol. 1, No. 1 (1965) of *Studies in Comparative International Development* (St. Louis, Social Science Institute of Washington University).

2. Cf. S. M. Miller, "Comparative Social Mobility: A Trend Report," *Current Sociology, 9* (1960), 1–5.

In making comparisons among nations, a leap of courage must be made. Many of the difficulties of individual studies are compounded in comparative perspective. Some national studies are of poor technical quality; time periods differ in various studies; and occupational titles and ratings are not fully comparable. But we have no choice of substitutes if we wish to include a particular nation in a comparison. Consequently, it is important to recognize that *any comparisons are at best only approximations.*

Mobility studies usually deal with the movement of sons of manual families into nonmanual occupations.[3] The concern is with vertical mobility. Downward mobility from nonmanual strata into manual strata has been widely neglected. Cross-national studies of manual–nonmanual mobility make the heroic assumption that the manual–nonmanual divide has equal importance in all nations at all times. This assumption is obviously untrue but it is difficult to make comparisons without it. The manual–nonmanual comparison also suffers from a neglect of intrastratum mobility, e.g. the movement from unskilled to skilled; from the lower levels of the middle class to elite positions. This kind of movement can be substantial and important but is not caught when the manual–nonmanual divide is the focus of attention.

A number of technical problems intrude in international comparisons. The number of strata employed in a study affects the amount of mobility: the more strata, the more mobility. Therefore, for comparative purposes it is necessary to compress categories into a similar number of groupings. This technical need encourages the utilization of manual–nonmanual compressions. Another difficulty is that while we speak of the sons' generation and of the fathers' generation, we do not in actuality have such pure categories. There are fathers and sons in each occupational category but we treat our data as though each could be factored out.

A number of different types of comparisons are possible with the same data. Movement can be viewed from so many

3. We are interchangeably and loosely using terms like stratum, occupations, and categories.

perspectives that it is easy to become dizzy with perspectives and to overproduce results. In the standard mobility matrix the rows represent the outflow: "What is the occupational distribution of sons born of fathers in a given stratum?" This type of analysis is the usual one; we can look across the principal diagonal of the matrix and note the degree of inheritance by sons of fathers' occupations. The columns provide inflow data: "What are the social origins of individuals presently in a given occupational stratum?" Now, the same sons are involved in outflow and inflow analyses; the difference is in what base they are related to in computing rates or percentages. For example, an outflow analysis can show that of 1,000 nonmanual sons, 250 or 25 per cent move into manual strata. From the point of view of manual strata which are larger than the nonmanual strata, say 2,500 sons, the inflow is only 10 per cent. The same movement can have different implications from varying perspectives.

Despite myriad difficulties, comparative studies of social mobility have endured. Sorokin, in his classic study of *Social Mobility* in 1927, amassed a great deal of data but it was not subjected to careful, systematic analysis. Yet, his work was prescient in many ways. For almost two decades comparatively little work was done that referred to nations as a whole. David Glass and Theodor Geiger, in their own work and in the work they fostered in the Research Sub-Committee on Social Stratification and Social Mobility of the International Sociological Association, emphasized in the 1950s national studies executed with similar concerns and well developed methodologies. As a result, we now have many more studies of national rates of social mobility. Seymour Martin Lipset and his collaborators, Reinhard Bendix, Hans Zetterberg, and Natalie Rogoff Ramsoy, attempted to make sense out of the array of national mobility data by suggesting a basic similarity in the rates of advanced industrial nations. Miller, in his appraisal of the data, emphasized the neglect of downward mobility in most generalizations about mobility, the varied contours of mobility (e.g. knowledge of manual–nonmanual movement is not revealing about manual–elite movement), and the value of developing typologies of mobility. The work of Peter Blau and Otis Dudley Duncan—a careful analysis of mobility patterns in the United States based on fresh data in a comparative perspective—may have great significance. At the moment, though, there seems to be a standstill in developing international comparisons of mobility.

The present paper illustrates a few of the various ways of utilizing mobility data. It does not question the international comparability of the data but attempts to improve comparability by restricting analysis to four nations. The concern is with both outflow and inflow. Its particular contribution is that it introduces a new measure which facilitates statements comparing the degree of equality and inequality of mobility among nations.

THE MANUAL–NONMANUAL DICHOTOMY

The conventional profile of social mobility is projected by the manual–nonmanual dichotomy. Table 10.1 presents profiles for the four nations by way of passage into (inflow mobility) and away from (outflow mobility) the manual and nonmanual strata. Our analysis encompasses both upward and downward mobility in contrast to the more frequent solitary emphasis on upward mobility.[4] Manual inflow and nonmanual outflow illustrate *downward* mobility for sons of nonmanual origins from two points of view—the manual stratum and the nonmanual stratum. Conversely, manual outflow and nonmanual inflow record the *upward* mobility of sons of manual origin into the nonmanual stratum. The importance of qualifying statements about mobility rates by specifying a particular point of reference (inflow or outflow for a particular stratum) is exemplified by studying Table 10.1. Beginning with the data on outflow mobility we see that in Great Britain the rate of outflow is greater for the non-

4. Cf. Seymour M. Lipset and Reinhard Bendix, *Social Mobility in Industrial Society* (Berkeley and Los Angeles, University of California Press, 1959).

manual stratum than for the manual: downward movement is greater than upward movement. This description also applies to Japan and the Netherlands but not to the United States where upward mobility predominates.

TABLE 10.1. COMPARATIVE MANUAL AND NONMANUAL INFLOW AND OUTFLOW MOBILITY
(in percentages)

	Manual Mobility		Nonmanual Mobility	
Nation	*Inflow*	*Outflow*	*Inflow*	*Outflow*
Great Britain	24.83	24.73	42.01	42.14
Japan	12.43	23.70	48.00	29.66
Netherlands	18.73	19.77	44.84	43.20
United States	18.06	30.38	32.49	19.55

Source: Data sources for computations are D. V. Glass et al., *Social Mobility in Britain* (London, Routledge and Kegan Paul, 1954), p. 183; special tabulations of Johannes van Tulder based on the survey of the Institute for Social Research in the Netherlands; Sigeki Nisihira, "Cross-National Comparative Study on Social Stratification and Social Mobility" (Japan), *Annals of the Institute of Statistical Mathematics, 8* (1957), 187; Richard Centers, "Occupational Mobility of Urban Occupational Strata," *American Sociological Review, 13* (1948), 138 (limited to sons of urban whites). These social mobility matrices are given in the appendix of S. M. Miller, "Comparative Social Mobility," *Current Sociology, 9* (1960), 1 ff. (Note: In Centers' data for the U.S. as cited by Miller above, categories VIII—farm owners or managers—and IX—farm tenant or laborers—which appear only in the sons' generation have been omitted.)

A comparison of the nations on the outflow indicators shows that the United States has the highest rate of upward movement, i.e. manual to nonmanual. It also has the lowest rate of downward movement from the nonmanual stratum. Great Britain has the most downward movement but is second in terms of upward mobility.

Downward mobility may be more indicative of social fluidity than upward mobility. To illustrate, we are well aware that the process of industrialization has been associated with a decline in the size of the manual stratum relative to the nonmanual—a phenomenon contributing to upward intergenerational mobility. Downward movement, on the other hand, may be evidence that sons are not always entitled to their fathers' social position as heirs apparent but must be capable in their own right or suffer displacement by more able individuals from lower social strata.[5] If this argument is valid, then the social structures of Great Britain and the Netherlands are less congealed in some respects than in the United States and Japan—contrary to popular opinion.

The inflow patterns pertain to mobility into a stratum. All four nations are characterized by more heterogeneity of social origins in the nonmanual stratum than in the manual. Heterogeneity is measured by the extent to which sons born into another stratum become members of a given stratum. With Herrington C. Bryce, we have elsewhere dealt in depth with the concepts of heterogeneity–homogeneity that are used here.[6] Britain has the highest heterogeneity in the manual stratum, as we would expect from its nonmanual pattern of outflow. But the Netherlands, with a similar percentage of nonmanual outflow, has less heterogeneity in the manual stratum. Even though nonmanual outflow is high in the Netherlands, its compositional effect on Dutch manual inflow is less than in Great Britain because of the relatively larger proportion of manual sons in the Netherlands.

Japan and the United States are similar in their changing occupational patterns. Japan has a lower rate of movement out of the manual stratum than the United States but an even higher degree of nonmanual heterogeneity: almost half the nonmanual workers originated in manual families. The United States has an expanding nonmanual stratum which absorbs many from manual homes and, as the nonmanual outflow figure (19%) shows, has the highest level of inheritance of the nonmanual strata.

The data for Great Britain and the Netherlands show little change in the contours of the occupational structure between

5. But the possibility of downward mobility by choice cannot be denied. In this case the son simply prefers an occupation and way of life that differ from his "origin."

6. Herrington Bryce, S. M. Miller, and Thomas Fox, "The Heterogeneity of Social Classes in Industrial Societies: A Study in Social Mobility" (paper presented at the Spring meetings of the Eastern Sociological Associations, New York City, April 1963).

generations: a contour map which *only approximates* reality is presented in Table 10.2. In the British manual stratum (Table 10.1), about 25 per cent are of nonmanual backgrounds, "replacing" the 25 per cent born in manual families who have moved up into nonmanual occupations. The corresponding Dutch occupational interchange is about 19 per cent. The inference is that a virtual exchange of social position occurred between the manual sons moving up and an equal *absolute* number of nonmanual sons moving down.

TABLE 10.2. PERCENTAGE DISTRIBUTION OF STRATA BY FATHERS' GENERATION AND SONS' GENERATION

	Great Britain		Japan		Netherlands		United States	
	Fathers'	*Sons'*	*Fathers'*	*Sons'*	*Fathers'*	*Sons'*	*Fathers'*	*Sons'*
Non-manual	37.11	37.02	26.74	36.17	29.98	30.87	43.97	52.40
Manual	62.89	62.98	73.26	63.82	70.02	69.13	56.03	47.60
Total	100.00	100.00	100.00	99.99	100.00	100.00	100.00	100.00
Elite	7.98	7.49	11.15	11.74	7.18	11.08	8.92	16.86
Middle Class	29.13	29.53	15.59	24.45	22.80	19.79	35.04	35.54
Skilled	38.74	33.91	8.52	12.06	32.65	34.22	29.59	19.50
Semi-skilled	13.09	16.95	4.02	7.50	26.41	27.39	20.16	20.33
Unskilled	11.06	12.12	60.72	44.26	10.96	7.52	6.28	7.77
Total	100.00	100.00	100.00	100.01	100.00	100.00	99.99	100.00

Source: See Table 10.1.

As we have seen in Table 10.1, the nonmanual strata are characterized by higher rates of both inflow and outflow mobility than the manual strata in these four countries. For Japan and the United States, the relative growth of the nonmanual stratum, as seen in Table 10.2, can account for much of the observed upward mobility. But in Britain and the Netherlands, with relatively constant occupational distributions, technological or demand induced mobility fails to explain the considerable interchange among social strata.

The lower portion of Table 10.2 pictures changes in occupational structures between generations in greater detail. The elite and middle class were formerly subsumed under the nonmanual category; the skilled, semiskilled, and unskilled collectively composed the manual stratum. In Great Britain, little change is evident in the sizes of either the elite or middle-class groups—little mobility can be attributed to variations in the relative number of positions within the nonmanual stratum. However, the structure within the manual category has altered between generations. The data suggest a decrease in the level of manual skills: the relative size of the skilled substratum has diminished while the semiskilled and unskilled groups have expanded in the sons' generation.

Japan shows little change in the relative size of elites between generations, but a large increase in the middle class. The quality of the manual stratum has shifted upward; the proportion of unskilled declined while both the skilled and semiskilled proportions have increased. Use of the manual classification blankets considerable intrastratum mobility due to structural changes over time.

The compositional change within the Dutch nonmanual stratum is unusual. Here we note that the relative size of the elite increases, but it is accompanied by a shrinking middle class. (The other countries portray, at minimum, a moderate middle-class expansion.) Within the manual category, the qualitative trend parallels that in Japan; the unskilled proportion diminishes while that of the skilled and semiskilled increases.

The trend for the elite in the United States shows a large increase, but little change for the middle class. A sharp decline is evident for the skilled group. The semiskilled and unskilled substrata have moderate increments in proportions in the sons' generation. Over half the sons are in the nonmanual stratum, which, as in Japan, is characterized by a large increase in the relative number of nonmanual positions between generations.

Skilled, Semiskilled, and Unskilled Outflow into the Nonmanual Stratum

Table 10.3 breaks down the manual stratum into integral parts—skilled, semiskilled, and unskilled—for a closer look at the sources of upward mobility into the nonmanual category.

TABLE 10.3. OUTFLOW OF SONS OF SKILLED, SEMISKILLED AND UNSKILLED ORIGINS INTO THE NONMANUAL STRATUM
(in percentages)

Social Origin	*Great Britain*	*Japan*	*Netherlands*	*United States*
Skilled	29.08	30.19	26.92	38.55
Semiskilled	18.78	29.33	14.79	21.31
Unskilled	16.54	22.42	10.47	21.05

Source: See Table 10.1.

In Great Britain, the chances of sons of skilled workers entering the nonmanual stratum approach twice that of semiskilled sons. Unskilled sons have the greatest disadvantage for such movement but not strikingly less than the semiskilled. The data for the Netherlands and the United States roughly parallel those of the British case: all three nations are characterized by a large gap between the skilled and semiskilled components of the manual stratum, with a relatively smaller gap between the semiskilled and unskilled substrata. In Japan there is little difference between the skilled and semiskilled movement into nonmanual occupations although intuitively one would expect the skilled to enjoy a relative advantage over the unskilled for upward mobility; both have considerably better opportunities than the unskilled.

Great Britain, the Netherlands, and Japan have quite similar percentages of skilled sons entering the nonmanual stratum, but considerably less than in the United States. Intercountry similarities are less pronounced as we turn to the semiskilled and unskilled groups. Semiskilled outflow in Japan is greater than skilled outflow in the Netherlands and has an 8 percentage point edge on United States semiskilled outflow, which in turn is less than 3 points greater than Great Britain and almost 7 points higher than the Netherlands. Unskilled outflow is similar in Japan and the United States, followed at some distance by Great Britain, and at a much larger interval by the Netherlands.

This table demonstrates the importance of compositional effects. Despite the highest rate of overall manual movement into the nonmanual stratum, the United States ranks but second in terms of semiskilled and unskilled movement into the top stratum. The United States' highest overall manual rank is primarily attributable to considerably more skilled outflow than observed in the other nations, and to the numerical importance of the skilled component within the manual stratum.

Sources of Nonmanual Heterogeneity

Table 10.4 shows the contribution of skilled, semiskilled and unskilled mobility to the composition of the nonmanual stratum. We are now looking at the sources of heterogeneity in social origins among the nonmanual occupations.

TABLE 10.4. SOURCES OF NONMANUAL HETEROGENEITY
(in percentages)

Social Origin	*Great Britain*	*Japan*	*Netherlands*	*United States*
Skilled	30.42	7.11	28.47	21.77
Semiskilled	6.64	3.26	12.65	8.20
Unskilled	4.94	37.63	3.71	2.52
Total Nonmanual Inflow	42.00	48.00	44.83	32.49

Source: See Table 10.1.

In Great Britain, almost three quarters of the heterogeneity of the nonmanual stratum is due to the mobility of sons of skilled workers. The semiskilled contribution to nonmanual heterogeneity is slightly higher than the unskilled, but considerably less than the skilled. In the Netherlands, the entry of skilled sons accounts for somewhat less than two thirds of the nonmanual heterogeneity; the semiskilled sons are decidedly more important than the unskilled. Two thirds of United States nonmanual heterogeneity is due to the movement of skilled sons; semiskilled sons are three times as numerous in the nonmanual stratum as are unskilled. Japan is an anomaly: unskilled sons are the predominant source of nonmanual heterogeneity. This is largely, but not fully, due to the high percentage of the Japanese labor force which is classified as unskilled. Except for Japan, the skilled category is the greatest contributor to nonmanual heterogeneity. Movement of the semiskilled is greatest in the Netherlands and the United States.

Elite and Middle-Class Movement into the Manual Stratum

A breakdown of the nonmanual stratum into the elite and middle class permits a closer look at the sources of manual heterogeneity. Taking the outflow mobility dimension first, Table 10.5 gives the percentages of *downward* elite and middle-class mobility.

TABLE 10.5. OUTFLOW OF SONS OF ELITE AND MIDDLE-CLASS ORIGINS INTO THE MANUAL STRATUM
(in percentages)

Social Origin	*Great Britain*	*Japan*	*Netherlands*	*United States*
Elite	17.92	26.92	24.26	14.81
Middle Class	47.62	31.62	49.16	20.75

Source: See Table 10.1.

The United States and Great Britain have low rates of elite outflow. The low figure for the United States was anticipated from prior observations where we noted nonmanual inheritance to be high. Given the extremely high rate of nonmanual outflow in Great Britain (42.1 per cent), a much greater rate of elite outflow would be expected if this substratum is almost as congealed as in the United States. Elite inheritance is lowest in Japan and is similar to the Netherlands in terms of elite outflow.

Middle-class outflow in Great Britain and the Netherlands is similar and high, 50 per cent higher than in Japan and more than double that of the United States. The difference between elite and middle-class outflow rates into the manual stratum is greatest in Great Britain, lowest in Japan.

Table 10.6 shows the impact on manual heterogeneity by the *downwardly* mobile sons of elite and middle-class origins. For all countries the elite contribution to the composition of the manual stratum is relatively small, less than 5 per cent (less than 3 per cent if Japan is excepted). Most of the heterogeneity results from the downward movement of the workers of middle-class origins. Middle-class origins in the manual stratum account for over 20 per cent of the sons in this category in Great Britain and over 15 per cent for the other countries. The four nations each have a noticeable middle-

TABLE 10.6. SOURCES OF MANUAL HETEROGENEITY
(in percentages)

Social Origin	*Great Britain*	*Japan*	*Netherlands*	*United States*
Elite	2.27	4.70	2.52	2.78
Middle Class	22.56	15.28	16.22	15.28
Total manual inflow	24.83	19.98	18.74	18.06

Source: See Table 10.1.

class origin effect on the composition of the manual stratum but elite representation is almost nil.

INTRACOUNTRY EQUALITY OF MOBILITY OPPORTUNITY

Within each country the distribution of opportunities for sons of other social origins entering any given stratum can be studied with the aid of Feldmesser's index of equality of opportunity.[7] This index takes the proportion of sons remaining in their stratum of origin (e.g. nonmanual sons of nonmanual fathers) in each country as 100. The proportions of sons of other origins entering the given stratum are expressed as ratios to 100. If the proportions or frequencies of sons of all social origins entering any given stratum are equal, all ratios will have the value of 100. In other words, this index examines the proportional representation of all social strata in any given stratum. The farther any ratio is from 100, the less opportunity that group has for entering any given stratum than do the sons who inherit the status.

7. Robert A. Feldmesser, "Aspects of Social Mobility in the Soviet Union" (Ph.D. dissertation, Harvard University, 1955), pp. 223–25.

Table 10.7 presents the indices of intracountry equality of opportunity for the elite, middle-class, skilled, semiskilled, and unskilled strata for each of the four nations.

TABLE 10.7. INDICES OF EQUALITY OF OPPORTUNITY FOR ENTRY INTO ELITE, MIDDLE-CLASS, SKILLED, SEMISKILLED AND UNSKILLED STRATA

Elite	*Great Britain*	*Japan*	*Netherlands*	*United States*
Elite	100	100	100	100
Middle Class	19	39	22	37
Skilled	7	21	20	22
Semiskilled	3	17	6	6
Unskilled	2	18	5	9
$\overline{X}$	26.2	39.0	30.6	34.8
Middle Class				
Middle Class	100	100	100	100
Elite	88	65	57	51
Skilled	61	41	41	45
Semiskilled	39	43	29	31
Unskilled	36	29	20	27
$\overline{X}$	64.8	55.6	49.4	50.8
Skilled				
Skilled	100	100	100	100
Semiskilled	84	53	64	70
Unskilled	80	18	62	56
Middle Class	76	20	68	28
Elite	29	20	39	27
$\overline{X}$	73.8	42.2	66.6	56.2
Semiskilled				
Semiskilled	100	100	100	100
Unskilled	75	23	89	47
Skilled	54	50	46	47
Middle Class	36	29	31	21
Elite	16	25	13	8
$\overline{X}$	56.2	45.4	55.8	44.6
Unskilled				
Unskilled	100	100	100	100
Semiskilled	57	33	48	27
Skilled	48	19	28	18
Middle Class	23	24	18	6
Elite	7	18	3	5
$\overline{X}$	47.0	38.8	39.4	31.2

Equality of Opportunity in Entering the Elite and Middle-Class Strata

In Great Britain, sons of middle-class fathers enjoy a distinct advantage over sons of skilled, semiskilled, and unskilled in securing membership in the elite stratum. The middle-class sons have almost three times the opportunities of the skilled sons (19/7) of entering the elite, six times the opportunities of the semiskilled (19/3), and nine times the chances of the unskilled (19/2). But the son of an elite father has the best opportunity to become an elite himself—his chances are five times greater than for the son of a middle-class father (100/19) and fifty times that for the son of an unskilled father (100/2). Thus equality of opportunity for movement into the elite category appears extremely limited in Great Britain.

The son of a middle-class father in Japan enjoys almost twice the opportunity of a skilled son (39/21) for gaining admission to elite status, and only slightly more than twice the advantages of the semiskilled and unskilled (respectively, 39/17 and 39/18). Japanese sons of middle-class origins are more than one third of the way toward achieving elite entry equality with the sons of elite fathers (100/39).

In the Netherlands, sons of middle-class origins have very little advantage over the sons of skilled origins in securing elite status; their chances are almost equal (22/20). But skilled and middle-class sons have considerably better chances of entering the elite than the semiskilled or unskilled sons. The close proximity of the opportunities of the middle-class and skilled for elite entry suggests, as a possibility, that these groups are more closely related to each other than to the elite category.

Turning now to the United States, we find that here, as in Japan, the sons of middle-class fathers have traveled more than a third of the route leading to equality of opportunity with sons of elite fathers (100/37). Middle-class advantage over offspring of the skilled exists but is less than double the chances of the latter (37/22). The son of a skilled father has almost four times the opportunity of a semiskilled to reach the elite stratum (22/6). (Although the index for equality of opportunity for entry into the elite in the United States is greater for the unskilled than for the semiskilled, its validity may be questioned and perhaps attributed to weaknesses in the original study.)

An average value for the index is given below the last stratum for equality of opportunity of movement into the elite (and for each stratum below) but can be compared only within countries, not between them. The data in Table 10.7, then, do not say that equality of opportunity is greatest in Japan and least in Great Britain.

Equality of Opportunity in Entering the Skilled, Semiskilled, and Unskilled Strata

One of the most striking findings, with the exception of Japan, is that the averages of the indices of equality of opportunity are largest within each country for entry into the skilled stratum, not the middle class, which might have been expected. Lloyd Reynolds has recently argued (with respect to the manual stratum) that there is a tendency for the skilled category to become more of a closed group, with the opportunities of movement from unskilled and semiskilled occupations into the skilled stratum declining.[8] Although our data are not appropriate for directly questioning this hypothesis, our calculations for Great Britain, the Netherlands, and the United States show that the skilled stratum is the group in which equality of opportunity is the greatest.

Turning to the unskilled in the United States, an interesting pattern shows a relatively lower degree of equality of access to this occupational substratum than in the other nations. At this end of the occupational ladder, low access has different implications than it does at the other end. At the high end, it shows the inability of those below the elite to

8. Lloyd G. Reynolds, "Economics of Labor," p. 277 in Howard S. Ellis, ed., *A Survey of Contemporary Economics* (Philadelphia, American Economic Association, Blakiston Co., 1948), pp. 255–87.

overcome the barriers. But at the low end, it represents the pooling of the unskilled, their low ability to leave, and the relative invulnerability of the higher strata to such drastic falls in position.[9]

INTERCOUNTRY EQUALITY OF OPPORTUNITY

Feldmesser's index of equality of opportunity for each of the four nations can be made directly comparable by selecting the proportion of occupational inheritance within any given country as the base of the index for each stratum. This measure, developed by Fox, gives the intercountry equality of opportunity indices for all countries relative to the nation selected as the base. Great Britain has been used as the base nation for this paper. If the index for, say, elite inheritance is above 100 in the United States, occupational inheritance would be greater in the United States than in Great Britain with the difference between the respective index values indicating how much greater. (The values of the comparative indices for the base country, Great Britain, in Table 10.8 are the same as in Table 10.7.)

Elite Stratum Comparisons

Table 10.8 clearly shows that the ability of sons of elite fathers to inherit their fathers' socioeconomic status is greatest in the United States, 24 per cent greater than in Great Britain. The proportion of elite inheritance is second greatest in the Netherlands and least in Japan. Middle-class and skilled sons in the United States also have better chances of becoming elites than their counterparts in the other three nations. The United States has high inheritance and high accessibility. The opportunity of the Japanese middle class to gain elite membership is almost double that of the British and 30 per cent better than for the Netherlands middle class. Skilled opportunity for elite entry in the Netherlands is about three-and-one-half that of the skilled in Great Britain and one-and-one-fourth that in Japan. The Japanese semi-

9. Cf. Lipset and Bendix, pp. 57–58 and 64–68.

skilled and unskilled have the advantage over their counterparts in Great Britain, the Netherlands, and the United States in terms of their chances of becoming elites—almost the opportunities of the middle class in Great Britain.

TABLE 10.8. COMPARATIVE INDICES OF EQUALITY OF OPPORTUNITY FOR ENTRY INTO ELITE, MIDDLE-CLASS, SKILLED, SEMISKILLED AND UNSKILLED STRATA (Base=Great Britain)

Elite	*Great Britain*	*Japan*	*Netherlands*	*United States*
Elite	100	86	119	124
Middle Class	19	34	26	46
Skilled	7	18	24	27
Semiskilled	3	15	7	7
Unskilled	2	15	6	12
$\bar{X}$	26.2	33.6	36.4	43.2
Middle Class				
Middle Class	100	143	92	137
Elite	88	93	53	70
Skilled	61	59	38	62
Semiskilled	39	61	27	42
Unskilled	36	42	18	37
$\bar{X}$	64.8	79.6	45.6	69.6
Skilled				
Skilled	100	111	112	81
Semiskilled	84	59	72	56
Unskilled	80	19	69	45
Middle Class	76	22	77	22
Elite	29	22	43	23
$\bar{X}$	73.8	46.6	74.6	45.4
Semiskilled				
Semiskilled	100	81	148	144
Unskilled	75	19	132	67
Skilled	54	40	69	68
Middle Class	36	23	45	30
Elite	16	20	19	12
$\bar{X}$	56.2	36.6	82.6	64.2
Unskilled				
Unskilled	100	233	74	144
Semiskilled	57	78	35	39
Skilled	48	44	21	26
Middle Class	23	56	14	9
Elite	7	42	2	7
$\bar{X}$	47.0	90.6	29.2	45.0

Strikingly, the averages of the indices for elite entry show opportunity to be greatest in the United States (more than one-and-one-half that in Great Britain), followed at some distance by the Netherlands, then Japan and Great Britain. When we examined the intracountry equality of opportunity in Table 10.7 (within countries), Japan had the highest rate of intracountry elite equality, followed by the United States. This means that in Japan there is less difference between the proportions of various strata entering the elite and the proportion of elite inheritance. But in the United States (with its expanding elite) the *actual* proportions of the different strata entering the elite are greater than those in Japan. In other words, relatively larger proportions of non-elite and elite origin sons tend to become members of the elite stratum in the United States than in Japan.

Middle-class Comparisons

Middle-class stratum inheritance is proportionally highest in Japan, then the United States—both with a degree of middle-class inheritance at least 35 per cent greater than in Great Britain. The Netherlands has the lowest proportion of inheritance. Sons of elite fathers have the highest relative chance of falling into the middle class in Japan and England. This might be expected since elite inheritance was lowest in Japan and England; therefore, relatively more sons of elites experience downward mobility of one step to the middle class. Strikingly, although United States elite inheritance was the highest, closely followed by the Netherlands, sons of elite fathers in the United States have considerably greater relative likelihood of entering the middle class than in the Netherlands.

There is little difference between the proportion of skilled entering the middle class in the United States and Great Britain, with Japan in close proximity. But much less opportunity for skilled movement into the middle class exists in the Netherlands. Semiskilled and unskilled opportunity for middle-class movement is greatest in Japan and the United

States, then Great Britain. The opportunity for unskilled entry into the middle class in Japan is about two-and-one-half times as great as in the Netherlands.

Skilled Comparisons

When the focus of attention shifts to comparison of equality of opportunity for entry into the skilled category, the United States loses much of its former prominence, showing considerably less skilled inheritance than the base country Great Britain and the other two nations. Dutch skilled inheritance is slightly greater than Japan; both are about 10 per cent greater than in Great Britain. The proportion of semiskilled entering the skilled category is highest in Great Britain, strangely enough, with this holding also for sons of unskilled origins. In the Netherlands, the opportunity of semiskilled and unskilled movement into the skilled stratum is considerably less than in Great Britain but well above that in the United States and Japan. Japanese sons of semiskilled fathers have but a slight advantage over those in the United States. The Japanese unskilled are the most disadvantaged, having but about one half the chances of the United States unskilled to enter the skilled stratum and one third the Dutch unskilled chances. The unskilled in Great Britain have four times the proportion of sons in the skilled categories as in Japan.

Overall, averages of the indices show the chance to become a member of the skilled stratum is highest in the Netherlands and Great Britain, with both countries ranking well above Japan and the United States.

Semiskilled Comparisons

The Netherlands and the United States have considerably greater semiskilled inheritance than Great Britain; in turn, Japan has about 20 per cent less. The proportion of unskilled entering the semiskilled stratum in the Netherlands is double that in the United States, less than twice that in Great Britain. Skilled and unskilled chances for semiskilled stratum entry are about equal in the United States. The middle classes and elites are less represented in the semiskilled stratum.

Unskilled Comparisons

Unskilled socioeconomic inheritance in Japan is two-and-one-third that in Great Britain—significantly greater than in the United States, the second highest nation on unskilled inheritance. Dutch unskilled inheritance is but about one half that in the United States. Japanese unskilled inheritance of such astronomical proportions is in part explained by the tremendous size of this group in the Japanese social structure. But the most astounding index value for the unskilled stratum occurs for the elite chance in Japan of becoming a member of the unskilled. Elite entry into the unskilled in Japan is six times greater than in the United States and Great Britain, twenty times that in the Netherlands. The unskilled entry values in Japan for skilled, middle-class, and elite movement are similar within a limited range, whereas the spread between these social strata is considerably greater for the other three countries. In the case of Great Britain, we find, however, that the proportion of the skilled entering the unskilled is somewhat greater than in Japan, but about twice that in the United States and the Netherlands.

We wish that we could offer a concise and parsimonious explanation of the variations in the rates of social mobility both within and between the countries. But we cannot. The following fragmentary observations are substitutes for all-encompassing empirical generalizations or explanatory theorems.

There are a host of different ways of measuring mobility. And mobility has many varied contours. Mobility statements, as we have said elsewhere,[10] must be specific—indicative of a particular frame of reference (e.g. only manual into nonmanual, or the degree of heterogeneity of the elite sub-

10. Miller, p. 5; and Bryce, Miller, and Fox.

stratum). As a corollary, patterns of mobility seem to differ in different parts of the class structure. A statement of accessibility to elite status is inadequate for describing (let alone understanding) accessibility to the unskilled stratum. Inheritance and accessibility are different dimensions of similar phenomena.

Aware of the pitfalls inherent in mobility analysis, we still find it a fruitful area of research. We think it can be further extended, as we plan to do, attempting to see under what conditions of social mobility political stability is greatest. If political scientists and others can give us indicators of political stability, it would be helpful.

Mobility analysis is not an "open sesame" to understanding everything—studies of fertility have shown this. We think American sociologists have a dreadful predilection to explain *everything* in terms of status panic or reward, instability or stability. (This status concern may be more revealing about sociologists than about societies.) But we believe that the study of social mobility, especially if broadly conceived, gives us a picture, though not complete, of changes taking place in socio-occupational patterns. And it gives snapshots of different periods of time which, if used judiciously, should be illuminating.

11. Differential Evaluation of Time Budgets for Comparative Purposes *

ALEXANDER SZALAI, VESZPRÉM UNIVERSITY FOR CHEMICAL INDUSTRIES, BUDAPEST

PHYSICAL TIME AS A MEASURE OF SOCIAL ACTIVITIES

A day has 24, a week 168, a year nearly 8,800 hours. From day to day, week to week, year to year this amount of time falls to the share of the poor and the rich, the young and the old, men and women—to everyone on this globe of ours, irrespective of nationality, language, color, political or religious conviction, and of his position in his society. Having gone so far, we can hardly help adding the melancholy statement that it is most probably physical time and nothing else that is fairly distributed among people, the only thing from which everyone has the same lot and from which everyone can spend the same amount: 24 hours a day, neither more nor less.

The question of *how* he spends these 24 hours, how he *has to* and *may* spend them, is not so simple and not so fairly resolved. Here, there are differences between the poor and the rich, the young and the old, men and women. The individual differences are great but even greater are those between different societies and between the various classes, strata, and groups of people within them. Naturally, it holds true only for physical time that everybody has an equal share, and this only if we interpret the conception of time in the above playful manner as a "physical matter," as some commodity

* Earlier versions of this chapter appeared in *Valóság* No. 3 (Budapest, 1964), pp. 11–25; and in *The New Hungarian Quarterly, 5* (1964), 104–19.

that man can possess and consume. Actually, physical time is not matter but a measure of movement and change—*ἀριθμὸς κινήσεως*—as Aristotle has put it. Man has learned to use physical time for measuring human activity.

It is primarily his own and his fellow man's *social* activity that man quantifies and coordinates by means of time. He even carries a special measuring instrument for this purpose, a watch concealed in his pocket or strapped to his wrist. The wearing of a watch has become in our civilized life almost as indispensable as wearing clothes and, what is more, it is the only mechanical device that man suffers constantly in the close vicinity of or even on his body in this highly mechanized age of ours. It may be worthwhile to point out in this connection that we hardly ever cast a glance at this physical measuring instrument in order to fix the time and duration of our activities of a private nature. We seldom find it necessary to find out how long we have been reading, having breakfast, playing with our children, or to know the exact time when we kissed our lover. When engaged in these kinds of private activities, we only "look at the watch" if we have *some other* business to do, not in our private life any more but in the "great society" that sets the exact time and duration of our occupations by the hour and by the minute.

Those who have some experience in studies with questionnaires and interviews concerning the daily time consumption of people know fairly well the difficulties in establishing the actual time demand of daily activities falling into a person's free time, activities more or less devoid of social duties and "leisurely" spent. From a subjective point of view, the reign of physical time covers, even in our civilization, first of all the period of daily work and its accessories (commuting to and from the working place, etc.) and other parts of the waking stage, whose utilization in time and contents is regulated by the clockwork of the great society such as the busy period between the ring of the alarm and the moment of leaving for work. All that is left, if any, of the remainder of the 24 hours of the day *not* claimed by the physiological demand of sleep (and by some other physiological necessities of lesser importance) is called free time or leisure time, in the stricter sense of the word. During this time, if it is indeed undisturbed, we do not hear the ticking of the clock of physical time inside us.

That we measure human activity with the equally shared hours and minutes of uniformly passing physical time is not obvious at all. It is general knowledge that the custom is not even of long standing. It became widespread on a large scale as a consequence of manufacturing and industrial workdays or shifts of fixed durations, which have definitively separated workplace and home. Nowadays, in the age of timetables and schedules, it sounds almost funny to learn when reading Herodotus that this great traveler and well-informed man of his age never met the concept of "hour" in his world and could not even find the right word for it. In his time, and even much later, human activity served much more as a measure of time and not the other way round. The "parasang" so often read in Xenophon's *Anabasis* did certainly mean an hour's walk, but its measure was the distance covered, i.e. the fatigue the soldier felt in his legs—somehow as if light measured its own lifetime by the distance of the light-years covered. In Athens and in Rome the period between sunrise and sunset, the main period of human activity varying in length with the changing seasons, was always divided into twelve parts. The sixth hour of this period, the "sexta hora," was the time of *siesta.* Much complaint was heard about the water clocks of antiquity, the *clepsydrae,* that they did not keep time; they showed the time uniformly in summer and winter alike, whereas the length of day and night, and consequently that of hours, was constantly changing. Ctesibius, the great engineer of Alexandria, found the remedy for this trouble. He designed dials with shorter and longer spaces for the hours and, exchanging them with the changing length of daylight, he succeeded at last in adjusting the physical time of water clocks to the daily routine of social activity. Even Caesar found it quite natural to determine time by the order of camp life and not the other way round. He speaks of events at the time of the third changing of the night guards, although some possibilities of fixing the physical time had long been known even at his time.

It is not because they are unique and exotic that we have mentioned here the seemingly farfetched examples of antiquity. They have been included because this type of "flexible" handling of time—not measured in its physical context but only in its relation to human activity—appears, with certain restrictions, even today in our modern way of handling free time or leisure. This flexibility will play some part in the evaluation of our time bridges. Since the birth of the quite specific concept of free or recreation time goes back to Greco-Roman times, these examples deserve our attention.

Today, school is the place where all of us become acquainted with the duties of a life divided into hours and disciplined according to these hours. Practically, it is here that we are first told about the idea of worktime. Those who are not familiar with the historical literature of leisure may be surprised to hear that the word from which "school" derived originally had no other meaning in Greek than true free time, "leisure," to be spent according to one's liking. The theory of "scholé" (σχολή) has been elaborated with far-reaching effect and in all of its details by Aristotle in his *Politics,* and to some extent also in his *Ethics and Metaphysics.* "Scholé," for him, is the time spent in something for its own sake—in the company of friends, in the enjoyment of poetry, in listening to music, and above all in worthy thought, in contemplation. The opposite of this is, of course, "ascholia": the state of being busy in any kind of business and work, for which the best word Aristotle can find is the *negation* of the word "scholé" or "ascholia." The Latin language, too, says "negotium" (nec-otium) to express what we would call "business" today by the negation of the word "otium," that is, "leisure."

We would be taking the easy way if we interpreted this terminology simply as an ideological expression of the contempt the slaveholder felt for any kind of work and business. No doubt, it does betray such contempt but it can be interpreted as more than that. Aristotle, for example, is quite clear in saying that mere amusement and recreation serving only to restore working power *do not* comprise part of the concept "scholé." Because of this he holds the opinion that to work but for the sake of amusement and recreation is childish and silly. These are needed only for restoring the working power of man, who, after all, cannot go on working forever. If, however, man is engaged in any kind of occupation, its true object can only be to attain "scholé" in the above sense, that is, leisure, which secures higher culture and the unfolding of the personality. By its relation to education and culture and, of course, through the educational and cultural monopoly of the leading stratum of the classical slave-estate, the Greek word "scholé" has changed its original meaning of leisure to school in our language.

We cannot follow here the course of this most interesting and, in the true sense of the word, dialectical evolution of time spent in work and spent free of work which has led to a number of states today including in their constitutions the right of their citizens to both work and leisure. We cannot miss, however, pointing out one landmark of this long and winding path which is of some interest also for our case at hand.

In the early 1840s, young Karl Marx, before engaging in his studies on working conditions, happened to write his dissertation for the doctor's degree specifically on Epicurus. In the course of his work he found time to inspect closely the classic concepts of leisure. In the best part of the Appendix to his dissertation, he elucidates the epicurean ideal of ἡδονη (pleasure). It is perhaps this antecedent, completing a most thorough study of Aristotle's *Politics,* that made him analyze the question of the length and function of the workday from quite a novel approach when investigating the economic and social characteristics of the contemporary industrial workday, in the course of his ever deeper studies of the relations between worktime, wages, and the value of production. The new element in his conception was correct in terms of the functional unity of the entire time of the worker's day, even of his *entire lifetime.* As is well known, he laid great emphasis on the fact that under given conditions the daily time spent by a worker away from his job was not only too short to permit his personality to unfold or his cultural level to rise, but it was insufficient even for the recreation necessary to restore his working power.

At the same time, the young Marx—in a manuscript published for the first time as late as 1939—sketched his conception of an age to come when, with the abolition of every kind of oppression and exploitation and as a consequence of a large-scale development of the productive forces, social welfare "will be measured instead of by work time by the yardstick of free time." And this meant the free time spent by every member of society in the fulfillment of all of his abilities, in the expansion of his talent, and in satisfying his demands for intellectual activity. Marx thought that the growth of human knowledge and science resulting from the free time at the disposal of all working people, far in excess of the time needed for restoration of their working power and sufficient to be used in actual freedom for cultural productivity, would raise the scientific and technical level of productive work higher than any attained so far. This level—as he foresaw—will depend not only on the perfection of machines but to a decisive extent on the culture and knowledge of the workers operating them. Growing productivity, on its part, will put more and more free time at the disposal of man to be spent in occupations resulting, in turn, in knowledge and science of productive use. In this way, the young Marx predicted, leisure becomes productive and productive work becomes leisure.

We have given an account of this conception not because we think that such a favorable relation between work and leisure has been achieved anywhere in contemporary industry. We do, however, find it most essential to point out that Marx put something in the limelight that is often neglected in the evaluation of the data of work and leisure time studies. This neglected idea is that there are not only transitory forms between work for one's living and leisurely activities—like the "semi-loisir" mentioned by Joffre

Dumazedier—but that "work" and "leisure" form sociohistorical categories themselves. In other words, something that is considered work both by subjective and by objective judgment under given social and historical conditions may become leisure under changed conditions, and vice versa. It is by no means a natural law that productive work or work for one's living cannot offer as much inner and external freedom, as many possibilities for self-expression and relaxation, as are to be looked for and found in most cases only in leisure spent outside the working place by modern man and by the man of historical ages. And yet, we have to say that only men of special luck or importance have succeeded in turning their productive work into leisure and in making their leisure productive, at any time or in any society. (Let us remember in this connection some great productive personalities.) One can conceive of grades and forms in the progress of social and cultural development in which the number of such exceptions will grow or where the exceptional of today will be turned into the more or less ordinary.

It is essential, however, even *today,* especially in the comparison of the work and free time balance of groups of people living under greatly differing social and cultural conditions, that we should not compare, without any second thought, physical amounts of time covering duties and liberties, cultural waivers and satisfactions of quite different natures. As will be shown in the following, this does not mean that *any kind* of methodical quantitative comparison would be impossible! Unfortunately, even today, we often see that activities supposed to be "free," beyond work time, are in their real contents turned by economic obligations into the heavy burden of work, serving practically toward self-support or the preservation of the status level or living standard, although not necessarily being regarded as burdensome by those affected. (It is, of course, not moonlighting or hobbies bringing in extra money that are referred to. We have in mind, rather, some of the so-called leisure of housewives or some manifestations of the "do-it-yourself-kit.")

All that has been said and many other factors that go beyond the scope of this paper mean great difficulties and methodological problems even in the preparation of work and free time budgets. Problems and difficulties grow if we aim at a comparative estimation of data expressed in physical time units when such time studies are collected under different social and cultural conditions. We shall see, however, that when following a proper method they do not constitute an obstacle for all kinds of methodical quantitative comparison. The aim of our work is to present a possibility for such comparative evaluation of time budgets and to propose this as a basis for intercultural comparisons.

TIME BUDGET TYPES

As is generally known, time budgets used in social research give quantitative information about the amount of time spent by a specific group of people in various activities, and about the division of their time among various possible kinds of activities during the recurrent time period serving as a temporal frame of reference for the budget. Depending upon the objective of the report, the frame of reference may cover such periods as the 24 hours of a day, the daily time spent outside the job site, a weekend, or a full week. It is essential, however, that the time budget should have the character of an account: surveying the distribution of activities according to their kinds throughout the entire duration of the amount of time chosen as a temporal frame of reference. Since human activity has a great variety of forms, time budgets can generally estimate only the amount of time consumed by somewhat arbitrarily defined major classes of activity—earning a living, communication, housework, family meals, recreation in and out of one's home, studies, sleep, etc. The possibilities of evaluating the data of a time budget depend in part on the choice of the temporal frame of reference, but primarily on the structure of its system of categories.

Since time budget research was done in the past primarily

within the working population of industrial societies and for the purpose of discovering in full detail the structure of activities either at the job site or in free cultural activities, and since the investigations were often restricted only to a particular part of the day, an incorrect terminology dividing daily life into work time and free time or leisure has found general application. We know that a considerable portion of the time spent outside the job site is taken up by activities that could not be called "leisurely" by any means and that one disposes only of a fraction of the day's time "freely" (if one has daily free time at all). There are many who do not restrict their work to the "work time" only. In spite of this, a study of the literature shows that incorrect terminology is very difficult to eliminate and, what is more, it often causes a chaotic interpretation of concepts. Suggestions for the creation of a uniform and correct terminology have resulted only in an international circulation of several such uniform terminologies and in various authors using different words for the expression of the same idea, or using one and the same word with different meanings. This, of course, does not cause much trouble if an explicit definition of the terms is always added.

In order to avoid misunderstanding we shall not use the concepts of work time and free or leisure time. Instead we are going to speak about time spent at the job site and its parts used for work and of time spent outside the job site and its parts spent in various activities. An account of life activity covering a whole day will be called simply a general time budget.

In the last ten to fifteen years such general time budgets have been made for many social strata and many groups of people in various countries. The way that people divide their daily life among various activities is an important characteristic of their social existence and situation as well as of their culture in the broader sense of the word. Although the number of time budget studies published in the international literature is quite significant, comparatively few experiments have been made to evaluate the data as a basis for international or more widespread intercultural comparisons.

This can be explained partly by the fact that no uniform practice has been found for the construction of general time budgets or for the definition of the categories of data even within individual countries, not to mention a lack of coordination between various countries and a lack of adequate uniform principles, making it difficult to compare time budgets of different origin. Uniform principles of this kind, elaborated in detail and considered as a national standard, are to be found, as far as we know, only in the Soviet Union; they have been published as the findings of the 1960 Stalinsk Conference, which was convened for the discussion of research into the general time budget of the working population. On an international scale the situation would improve if cooperative research work were planned from the very beginning for purposes of comparison, such as the information gathered about the social-cultural dynamics of leisure by scientists of eleven countries within the scope of UNESCO in a recent study.[1]

The lack of uniformity in the principles underlying the various time budgets at our disposal is not the only difficulty. The classification of various activities also shows differences to a lesser or greater extent and the handling of data generally varies, too. In most cases such differences could be partly surmounted by reconciling work, by reducing the categories of data, by corrections through estimation, and similar means.

From the standpoint of an international or wider intercultural comparison of the general time budgets at our disposal, we find the following to be much greater obstacles:

1. The temporal frames of reference of most of the general time budgets are narrow, covering only the 24 hours of a day or one or two days of the weekend.

1. Since these lines were written a multinational comparative time budget research project has been initiated at the Vienna Center of the International Social Science Council. Sixteen research groups in ten countries (East and West) are participating in a pilot study begun in 1965.

2. It is very difficult to draw relevant social or cultural conclusions merely on the basis of the absolute or proportional amount of time spent in various kinds of activities within the given frame of reference.

The two problems are closely connected. The inner proportions of social time consumption—the ratios of those portions of the lifetime which are used by the members of society for various kinds of activities—give different pictures depending on the temporal frame of reference in which they are presented, be it a day, a week, or a year.

It is obvious the eight hours spent at the job site on five days of the week will figure one third of a 24-hour time budget. In the frame of reference of 168 hours in a week, the same amount of time will come out only one quarter. This is a fact so trivial that it is hardly worth mentioning. And what about the yearly time budget? Can it be constructed by mathematical methods only in the separate knowledge of the time budgets of workdays and weekends or of their summary in weekly time budgets? Not at all. The data of the *yearly* time budget will not only comprise days spent in professional occupation and in free time at the rate of 5 : 2 but will also necessarily include a considerable number of days spent on leave, on holidays other than Sundays, etc. It is just in the frame of intercultural comparisons that the most characteristic differences may be expected from the length of yearly vacation time, from the number and nature of special rest days, on the one hand, and from the ways that people spend their holidays and their rest days other than weekends, on the other. What is more, in a yearly time budget, time consumed by disability and many other things may become statistically relevant. Unfortunately, time budgets readily adaptable for intercultural comparison are still not too often found, however great would be their value in the comparative research of the stages of social and cultural progress.

The social and cultural specifying force of yearly time budgets is so great that, even with a thorough knowledge of the workday and weekend time budgets, an estimate of the major items in the yearly time budget can be undertaken only with the help of other statistical sources and by those who have a very reliable idea—possibly based on personal experience—of local conditions, and who are familiar with all factors that may be considered within the temporal frame of reference of one year. Since, however, yearly time budgets, unlike daily or weekly ones, generally cannot be based exclusively on direct observation and questioning, adequate statistical computations and "special purpose" investigations into important seasonal activities are needed for their construction.

Even if we avail ourselves of all possibilities offered for the collection of data by direct observation, a time budget covering the *entire lifetime* of a population or of a section thereof can be constructed today only with the help of special computations and statistical sources. These, however, are affected by such factors as schooling time or adult education, and the date of retiring. In this case, the temporal frame of reference can be of demographic character (e.g. the average lifetime). The multiple "length cut" that daily, weekly, yearly, and lifelong time budgets can give of the "time husbandry" of society as a whole, or of that of any of its groups, is essential also because the periodicity of one day or one week built up as the unity of one working week and a weekend has a definitive effect on the rhythm of the social and cultural life of one part of the population only. There are other social groups (also entire societies) whose time husbandry cannot be truly analyzed within daily or weekly temporal frames of reference, such as farmers or workers employed in certain types of seasonal work. In the case of intercultural comparisons also, only the *yearly* time budget can reveal differences unnoticed in the daily or weekly time budget, however characteristic they may be. This holds even more true in regard to *lifelong* time budgets.

It goes without saying that it is not always possible or reasonable to construct all kinds of time budgets for every purpose. We should like to place great emphasis on the fact that *all* time budgets of the types discussed here—serving as bases for social or cultural comparisons—can be useful *only* if they are based for the most part on the gathering of factual (observed, questioned, or described) time data of activity rather than on extrapolated or deduced data. It is most dangerous, of course, to rely on "prescribed" data, like the weekly work time set for a certain type of job in one branch of production, or the maximum number of hours permitted for overtime work. The laws regulating compulsory school time do not allow any valid conclusions to be drawn as to the number of illiterates among the population!

In lifelong time budgets not only the difficulties of their construction but also the surprising insights they reveal can best be illustrated by the widespread scientific dispute going on as to whether in advanced industrial countries (for example, in the United States or in France) the average duration of work done by man has decreased or not since 1900. Daily and weekly work times have decreased, of course, though detailed analyses have shown that de facto the decline is by no means as considerable as supposed by public opinion and "prescription." But what does the time spent in earning a living show in relation to the lifetime? Since 1900, the average span of life and average life expectation, respectively, have grown by *decades* in every advanced industrial country. This means that there are incomparably more people who reach the average of the upper age limit of participation in economic activity, who work 35, 40, or even more years in the course of their lives than before. In France, for example, Pierre Naville demonstrated in 1954 that as life expectation had risen since 1900 from 35 to 62 years the time spent by one person in productive work throughout his lifetime had grown in spite of shorter "workdays" and "working weeks." When we make comparative time budget surveys in order to judge the social and cultural progress of underdeveloped countries and of former colonies, the data of lifelong time budgets will be hard to develop and to use.

We think we have provided an approximate answer to the question why it is unfavorable to have at our disposal only time budgets of very narrow temporal frames of reference for the purposes of international or other "longer distance" comparisons. Now, we should like to demonstrate the positive advantages of having at hand the data of several kinds of time budgets constructed within various temporal references when applying adequate methods and principles.

THE DIFFERENTIAL EVALUATION OF TIME BUDGET DATA

In recent years, we have made time budget investigations covering both time spent at the work site and time spent outside it among the workers of several Hungarian plants. The investigations were part of a complex sociological survey aimed at discovering the productive, social, cultural, and other effects of shift work.

The data necessary to the construction of the time budgets were collected by means of "yesterday interviews" on a large scale. We interviewed the workers about the activities they had been engaged in during the previous 24 hours in the sequence of their daily routine, and about the time consumption (duration) of these activities. The data of each interview were put down on an adequately divided data sheet on which time consumption for the individual activity categories was summarized in the usual manner.

As we were proceeding with our work, for ecological purposes that need not be discussed here a comparatively large number of data sheets (about 1,000 of them), from a factory on the outskirts of Budapest which employed workers living at rather faraway places, were classified according to the time spent by interviewed persons in traveling to the factory and back home. The amount of time spent daily in commuting varied from a minimum of half an hour to a maximum of about five and a half hours. (The factory itself has no housing and there are no dwellings in the close vicinity where workers could take up quarters.) The data sheets were roughly divided into five classes according to the increasing measure of commuting time. Classification was refined later, but we do not wish to go into detail about it here. Then, from the totality of data sheets, the specific average daily time consumption falling in the various activity categories was calculated for the five classes and in subclasses arranged according to various group criteria (men–women; married–unmarried; qualified employees–skilled workers–helpers, etc.).

When we began to consider the extent to which the growth of commuting time compresses *all other daily activities* beyond the practically fixed period of work done in the factory (activities like household work, other jobs in and around the house, family life, recreation, study, sports, sleep, etc.), we were faced with a most interesting phenomenon that seems almost obvious in retrospect: the effect of the increasing "pressure" of the one, two, three, four, or five hours of commuting time, added to the fixed eight-and-a-half hours of work in the factory, was not a uniform shrinking of other daily activities but rather a "compressibility" of considerable variation. And what is more important from our point of view, *the relative compressibility of various activities characteristically differs according to the social and cultural criteria of the groups of persons in question.*

It was observed for instance that while the total time spent on the job site and commuting was gradually rising from about nine-and-one-half hours ($8\frac{1}{2} + 1 = 9\frac{1}{2}$) to thirteen-and-one-half hours ($8\frac{1}{2} + 5 = 13\frac{1}{2}$) sleeping time proved in general to be relatively incompressible, decreasing in most cases an insignificant degree. Not so with time spent in recreation or study, which began to shrink upon the first impact of "pressure" and sometimes even disappeared as pressure increased. Obviously, the day has but 24 hours and if the total time spent at the job site and in commuting is given, and sleep is difficult to shorten, then *all* the rest of the daily activities *must* find places in the remaining hours. The data did indicate that daily study time was considerably longer with skilled workers than with helpers, showing, perhaps, a much greater resistance to "pressure."

Perhaps this is only a more trivial side of the matter, but it is remarkable that the incompressibility of sleeping time *did* prevail to such an extent. With married women—and especially with mothers of many children—it was found that the compressibility of sleeping time increased somewhat, while

—and this is no wonder—the time spent in household work and with members of the family lost some of its compressibility.

Naturally, all these observations have been made here without the presumption that they could be generalized in content and that we could say, for instance, that sleeping time was less compressible in general than recreation time, that household work for mothers of large families was of necessity more incompressible than for single women, or that skilled workers spent more time in study and were less willing to curtail it than helpers. In quite a number or even in the majority of cases this may hold true—or it may not. It could not be conclusively decided on the basis of data gathered among the working people of a single country, anyway, not even on the basis of time budget data collected on a much larger scale than we did. We think, however, that our research experience, illustrated by the above examples and supported since then by considerably more comprehensive experimental material, may serve as a basis for some *methodological* considerations of a more general character.

To all appearances, within a given temporal frame of reference and related to one group of persons living under given conditions, a certain portion of lifetime may be considered as *fixed* in the sense that it can be spent by a member of the given group only in activities defined by physiological or social compulsions (e.g. the person must sleep a minimum of six hours a day; he must remain at his job site for 8½ hours; and he must spend two hours in commuting). Naturally, the "given conditions" are not unalterable; neither are physiological and social compulsions. The necessary minimum of sleep changes with age; it is not impossible to look for another job or job site. This, however, will shift the person over to another category as far as such investigations are concerned.

Nor can man dispose quite freely of all the time left beyond the portion defined as fixed in the above sense. He has various family, social, and moral obligations which force him to a lesser or greater extent to spend some time in activity categories which he can hardly manage in his fixed time, if at all. The time left for him after all this, or the time he is not willing to use up for such purposes, will be spent in activities to his own liking or in activities forced on him by the effect of social conventions.

It follows from the above that the general time budget will reflect the quantitative proportions of time consumption defined by physiological or social compulsion, on the one hand, and (without any sharp demarcation) the proportion of activities determined by individual instinct, taste, and social conventions, on the other hand. It is just for these decisive and affecting factors that general time budgets are analyzed and examined.

The trouble is that the volume of time consumption in the various activity categories often permits only uncertain conclusions to be drawn concerning the actual determining and contributing factors or the force which these factors have come to display. As shown by the time budget, for example, the members of a given group of people spend seventeen minutes a day in study, in self-education. Is this much or little? Do they do it because they have nothing better to do or because they are urged on by a strong passion? The "seventeen minutes" in itself is but a descriptive statistical figure whose evaluation can only be based subjectively on our own practical experience, on our own inward scale of values.

But now let us consider the observations made about the "time husbandry" of workers in the Budapest factory. We have seen that the skilled workers spent much more time on study than the helpers. And it was also pointed out that even if a certain fixed time, that is, the length of stay at the job site plus commuting time, was longer by one or two hours among the subcategory of skilled workers, the time spent in study did not shrink to such a great extent as did that of helpers under similar conditions. How may we explain this phenomenon? This is just the question put above in connection with the "seventeen minutes." Can the answer really be based solely on our general knowledge about society and man or on intuition? Or are there perhaps other possibilities which could make *controllable* such obvious suppositions as saying that skilled workers have a stronger desire for culture, that they attach greater importance to study promising higher professional training?

With the data from the subgroup of skilled workers whose fixed time is ever growing, we may see whether or not the time consumption of *the rest* of their cultural activities is shrinking at the same rate as that of their studies: whether or not there is any positive correlation between the position of these items in the budget. Should there be none or very little, then the explanation referring to a general desire for culture loses quite a lot of its probability. Or perhaps it is just that *learning* is so important to skilled workers that they give less time to other activities in order to keep up their study time or to curtail it only to a small extent. Apparently, then, if skilled workers feel like studying because of some special interest, instinct, or passion, and this urge accounts for differences in their time budgets when compared to those of helpers, then it is correct to suppose that decreasing "pressure" from time spent at the job site and in commuting will increase the time spent in study and lead to even greater differences compared with the helpers. How could we verify this supposition? For instance, on days when there is no time fixed by job site and commuting, the time ratio of studies for skilled workers should *expand* significantly more than that of helpers. Whether this happens can be (and has been) determined by a *differential* study of the daily and weekly (or yearly) time budgets of skilled workers and helpers, since the temporal frames of reference of these include Sundays and rest days as well. (Even more useful for this purpose are weekend time budgets if we have any at our disposal.)

Research so far shows that a quantitative analysis and differential comparison of time budgets of different temporal frames of reference may indicate answers to similar questions more intricate than the above very simple, paradigmatic example.

Let us stop here and sum up what the results of our

research have told us. First, it was seen that within a certain given period of activity (daily or weekly) of the population, or of a social group, the share of different activity categories in the total time can become smaller or greater. In other words, the duration of various activities can shrink or expand. It has also been demonstrated that compressibility and expandability are limited by certain conditions: the duration or the minimal duration of some kind of activity can be compulsorily fixed for physiological or social reasons (as, in general, the time spent daily at the job site or set aside for sleeping as a physiological necessity); also the expansion of one kind of activity or another has its physiological and social limitations (here again worktime and sleep offer the best examples). The most essential point is that the compressibility and expandability of different activities within a given temporal frame of reference can show greatly differing values, in many cases *characteristic* of the social group, by demonstrating the importance members attach to these types of activity, what esteem they have for them, what *demand* members of the group show for a certain way of making use of their lifetimes. This again qualifies the given group in several social and cultural respects.

The ratio between the compressibility and expandability of various activities can be quantitatively expressed by comparing the daily and weekly time budgets of the given group or by dividing them into component time budgets (time budgets of subcategories), in which the relative volume of fixed time and consequently the limitation of disposable nonfixed time (the "time pressure" exercised) can be smaller or greater.

I have written at some length about compressibility and expandability—concepts that could be summed up in the expression *elasticity*—and have mentioned finally the *demand* shown in the consumption of time for various purposes. Since the phrase "time budget" itself calls forth economic associations, one might wonder if the process of analyzing the distribution of a time fund consisting of the 24 hours of the day, the 168 hours of the week, the nearly 8,800 hours of the year, and finally of the lifetime as a whole in a budget-like manner, and of studying the dynamics of time consumption in a balance-like way, does not recall the types of economic research concerned with the elasticity of demand.

The formal models together with the mathematical technique, not mentioned here in detail, are more or less identical with those employed in economic research. It is no wonder that the difficulties and problems of this subject focus partly around similar questions. As with the demand of consumers for goods, here too the question arises as to the effect that substituting or replacing one kind of goods—or in our case, one type of activity—with another, under given circumstances, can have on the budget and its evaluation. The spheres of the single goods or activity categories, their demarcation, the definition of de luxe goods and leisure activities, respectively, present serious problems. The task of the mathematician is rendered difficult by the fact that the compressibility and expandability of time consumption often prove to be far from linear and do not even lend themselves to easy approximation by any well-known analytic function.

Since, however, concrete research into the elasticity of demand has led—in spite of all difficulties and problems—to the revelation of very important dynamic factors, and since the quantitative distribution of the demand for different categories of goods can well be used as a factor of economic and living standards, we may hope that *time budget research* into the dynamics of social and cultural time consumption will also give some insight into relations barely recognized today. Adequately evaluated daily, weekly, yearly, and lifetime time budgets of the population should supply suitable criteria for intercultural comparisons and other serious tasks facing social research.

12. Some Comments on Center–Periphery Relations

DANIEL LERNER, MASSACHUSETTS INSTITUTE OF TECHNOLOGY

One problem in discussing center–periphery issues is vocabulary. To avoid vocabulary problems, I am going to employ the literary device of alliteration.

Center–periphery problems start from the center; that is, the center (if it is a center in any meaningful way) has control over the periphery. This seems obvious, yet it is crucial in the matter. Much of what we think about as conflict in politics can be restated in terms of the ways in which the center exercises its control over the periphery.

There are only three general modes of exercising central control over the periphery—whether we are considering the center of a family, or of a nation, or of an international coalition. One, historically a very important one, is to ignore the periphery. Pay no attention to it. Pretend it does not exist and give it no particular concern. This mode of handling the periphery I call *Disinterest.* An obvious example of disinterest is Marie Antoinette's imperious "Let them eat cake!" This is a marvelous center–periphery relationship illustrating disinterest. For the French court at that time the periphery began at the court gates. Anybody who really belonged to the center had a pass and could get in; people who could not get in did not belong to the center. They were peripheral in the literal sense of "external boundary." Only, since the gates defined the external boundary, the peripheral people were on the far side of the boundary—beyond the pale. The gates did matter; and so long as they stood, the people did not matter. Historically, disinterest has been the major way in which ruptured centers have dealt with their peripheries, as, for example also, the Ottomans and their superbly symbolic *Sublime Porte.*

A second mode is generated when the human periphery refuses to be treated with disinterest—when it can, and does, tear down the gates. At that moment *people,* instead of gates, become the "external boundary" on operations at the center. A moment later, the center begins to negotiate with the periphery. This is the *Difference Promotion* mode of relationship—coexistence, if you like—between the center and its periphery. It is a style which says: "Let's each of us eat our cake or bread as we have it or can get it." This style typically does not last very long. Once people form the external boundary of the reigning center, they rapidly learn the difference between bread and cake, perceive that they don't have cake—and set out to get it. This puts the center in a really new position.

The central style, once it moves from disinterest ("ignore them") to difference promotion ("live and let live"), is obliged rapidly to culminate in a third mode, which we call *Dissidence Reduction.* When a center is playing the game of difference promotion (or at least difference toleration), one element or another outside the center is bound to get out of hand on one issue or another—most often bread and cake. Then the center has the problem of how to reduce dissidence.

Now, each of these three alliterative modes occurs within a context. I have already suggested what disinterest meant in the context of Marie Antoinette. It is the tone of voice, the style, which says: "Out there beyond the gates are people who don't matter to me, except for certain limited purposes which I can control without much trouble."

Difference promotion is a very different and more complex style, which is adopted by the center only when disinterest does not work. Difference promotion, which sounds like "pluralism," could be the most durable and important style, but it is durable only under certain conditions. These are conditions, I would say, under which *functional specification* is developed in the periphery. We have many examples in the world today, and in the historical world, of a political center which is "divided" or which shares control over some major values with its periphery, with other centers of functionally specific character. The center protects itself by delegating, or accepting, competing centers with other (nonpolitical) functions. In the U.S. today Washington and New York have this kind of relationship: New York is clearly the economic (or at least financial) center and Washington the political center. As one looks around the older world there are many examples. The ones that occur immediately are Rome and Milan; Berlin and the Ruhr; and, in my favorite area, old Damascus and Aleppo.

The general point I am making is that a political center can follow, and is well advised to follow, the policy of difference promotion as a mode of control—sharing with new centers in the periphery—so long as there is specification of function. The area of *political* control as such must not come into question. When the political control of the center is either divided or disputed, or even doubted, then the mode of difference promotion becomes unstable and disruptive. In such a case, central control cannot be successfully maintained over a long period of time.

As an example of divided political control, consider the great Greek city-states. These came, in time, to think of themselves as adversaries (as rival nations in our modern sense) owing no allegiance to anything above and beyond their parochial yet all-encompassing aspirations. Instead of division of labor and complementarity of function, each wanted to control the full scale of social values for itself and thereby *dominate* the others. This represented a clear case of divided political control. Its destabilizing, disruptive outcome is familiar. Italy took two centuries longer than other Western societies to become a modern "nation," for example.

A controversial case in American history was the Civil

War, when the Confederacy decided to try for *political* control: Washington versus Richmond. Richmond set itself up as a capital, as a center, with the aspiration of taking over control of the whole. It could have done other things; it could have had other pretensions; but this is what it did. The results are familiar a century later; one can still wonder whether certain Confederate states are parts of the U.S.A.

Consider finally, the marvelous example of Syria—Damascus and Aleppo. This case is endlessly fascinating for political scientists. It involves the phenomenon of "two cities," both clearly operating as "centers" in the sense that New York and Washington are centers. Damascus was the capital, the seat of government, with the highest authoritative control of politics. Aleppo was, if you like, a combination of New York and Detroit (if there were such a place in Syria). When there is no clear adjudication of jurisdictions, both cities compete. If you look over the past two decades of history in Syria—statistically the most unstable country, in terms of regime turnovers, anywhere in the world—you will find that the game has been to see which of these competing centers could, through a variety of complicated structural relationships, get a sufficiently predominant portion of the army on its side and, given time, make a coup that would give it total (i.e. undifferentiated political) control over its area.

In this kind of situation, difference promotion cannot occur because the center is unsure of its power, because its power is challenged somewhere in the periphery or even doubted somewhere in the periphery. The result is instability, which calls for the third kind of center-periphery relationship, dissidence reduction. The center finds itself either divided, disputed, or doubted. What can it do? The center must attempt in some way to bring the periphery under its control and try to restore one of the prior modes of relationship—disinterest ("let them eat cake") or difference promotion (coexistence). But if that effort fails, then what occurs is some version of revolution, which means a transfer of power, usually to another geographical—as well as socioeconomic—center.

Let me mention a few classic cases with which we are all familiar. The French Revolution produced the remarkable phenomenon of Paris. The Russian Revolution produced Moscow, as distinct from St. Petersburg or Leningrad. The Turkish Revolution produced Ankara. From an ecological point of view, revolutionary displacement often is a wasteful process—as the history of Paris, Moscow, and Ankara suggests. It forces the allocation of human resources to the creation of the new center. (One may argue cogently that a political center is essential—and, in psychic terms, this argument is strong. But a chronicler of non-psychic rationality could make this argument look silly.) These human resources, as hindsight shows, could be used more productively in other ways.

For example, Paris historically has drained all France of skilled human resources—the best minds, the most ambitious, the most energetic come to Paris. This results from the influence of an overly powerful center on its periphery. Ankara—forty years after becoming the capital—is tremendously concerned with the "disparities" it has created or made conspicuous. As one moves about Ankara (or Istanbul), Turkey looks like a modern, civilized world. But as one leaves these capital centers one is immediately in a different world altogether—not only a world without plumbing, but a world without interest in plumbing (and the latter is more critical). The great issue of urban–regional disparities leads Ankara to concerted efforts in community development and other methods designed to mobilize the periphery. Moscow, too, has the problem of trying to get some movement into the periphery which will mobilize human energies and resources outside of the greater Moscow area. The proclaimed, but unachieved, program of building "Science Cities" in Siberia attests to the gravity of the problem.

All of these revolutions, with their geographic transfers, bring a point where the center has to reconsider its relationship with the periphery. Once it has bullied the periphery into submission and wasted the life of perhaps several generations, it then comes to the problem formulated with great clarity by Karl Deutsch in that fine article on "The Mobilization of the Periphery." It is the nature of a center that it has limits. If you keep expanding the circumference, it becomes a periphery—so remote from the center that the radii are too elongated to function effectively.

The mobilization of the periphery into a fully participating society under central control becomes, in such cases, the critical problem of center–periphery relations. A fully participating society is one in which a maximum number of people are performing productive functions required for the maintenance of equilibrium-with-growth in that society. Mobilization must involve participation, which in turn involves the reduction of all distance relationships—physical, social, and psychological. The problem of dissidence reduction—which in its milder, gentler forms is distance reduction—raises these questions: How do you reduce the spatial kind of distance, and why is it important to do so?

It has been found that geographic distance is, in some direct way, associated with the capacity to be interested in, to understand, and to respond to information coming from the center. The farther the distance from the center, the less did people care what the center was saying. Even those who cared a little found it difficult to understand the messages. The very few who understood found it difficult to interpret the center's messages in terms of responsive action. Distance in this purely physical sense is a major problem of center–periphery relationships. This problem, all too obviously, can be "handled" by distance-reducing measures such as roads, mass media, educational facilities, and so forth. But as physical distance is reduced social distance tends to be heightened. The social distance problems are familiar. These are the problems of differential wealth, security, status relationships—or, as defined by Harold Lasswell: income, safety, deference. What is not so well understood is the tremendous human cost involved in moving from the nonentity of peripheral existence to a sense of participation in one's society.

A final aspect I would mention, therefore, is the *psychic* gap which exists between the center and the periphery. In the world today—whether you like it or not, whether it is advisable or not, whether it is good policy planning or not—tremendous developments in communication linkages between center and periphery are occurring in every country. As a result, physical space-time differences are being reduced at a very rapid rate, which, in turn, makes social wealth–status distances more conspicuous. This imposes upon millions of individuals around the world the crucial problem of how to cope with the psychic requirements of being a participant in a fast-linking center–periphery relationship.

When a periphery is being mobilized, the ideal relationship with the center is, in my judgment, *Difference Promotion.* I have no prescriptive formula to offer; I am suggesting this is the nature of the problem. Yet, it does seem to me that, if the art of thinking about these matters consists of asking relevant questions, then what I might contribute at this point is to insist on these as the critical questions:

1. If you are getting a world in which center–periphery physical distances are being eliminated, and in which the social differences are being perceptually (attitudinally) exaggerated, what kinds of psychic devices are available to form and maintain a reasonably stable ratio of center–periphery relationships?

2. How can a center mobilize the previously isolated persons of the periphery into participant relations with the public life of their society, without acute disarray of the psychic mechanisms that govern life at the periphery?

3. How can the apathetic peripheral man become the aspiring participant man without a deep sea-change in the psychic weather?

4. How can a center deal in a reasonable, humane, stable, and durable way with a mobilizing periphery which, inevitably, wants certain new satisfactions quicker than most centers in the world are prepared to deliver them?

These questions articulate the elements of a single concise and elegant question which George Bernard Shaw, socialist and observer, asked a half century ago: "How can you dare teach a man to read before you have taught him everything else?"

13. Within-Nation Differences and Comparisons: The Eight Spains*

JUAN J. LINZ, COLUMBIA UNIVERSITY, AND
AMANDO DE MIGUEL, DATA, S.A.

We are witnessing a return of comparative and evolutionary sociological concepts that are quite different from those that were abandoned in favor of more microsociological problems. Our intellectual interests and the available data will lead to a focus on comparisons between political units using aggre-

* This paper is based on research being done by the authors on Spanish social structure. In the course of our work one or the other of the authors has had support from the Social Science Research Council Committee of Comparative Politics, the Council for Research in the Social Sciences of Columbia University, the Juan March Foundation of Madrid, and the Research Center for Economic and Cultural Development of the University of Chicago. None of these institutions is responsible for our findings and interpretations. The data from the study of the Spanish businessmen come from a survey sponsored by the *Escuela de Organización Industrial* of Madrid on the initiative of its director, Fermín de la Sierra. Those from the National Youth Survey are from a quota sample survey of youth between 16 and 21 conducted in 1960 by the *Delegación Nacional de Juventudes* in which 1318 males and 421 females were interviewed. The study resulted from the initiative of the head of the organization, Jesús López Cancio, and the joint intellectual efforts of P. de Balle, J. Bujeda, J. Castillo, A. García Bernal, E. Gómez Arboleya, C. González Reguera, L. González Seara, M. Lizcano, J. M. López Cepero, L. M. Vázquez, F. Vigil, and the authors. However, the responsibility for the interpretation given to the data is exclusively ours. The data used refer only to males. The authors also want to acknowledge the use of data from the studies of Professor Francisco Murillo Ferrol and Juan González Anleo.

We also wish to thank the Center for Advanced Study in the Behavioral Sciences for its facilities and especially to acknowledge the editorial assistance of Katherine Holbrook, the typing of Helena Smith, the statistical work of Ted Cooper, and the work on graphs and map by Chris Dodds.

gate data. It has been repeatedly noted that averages for very heterogeneous units might not be the best data to use, particularly if no account is taken of measures of dispersion. Here we want to go a step further to argue that intranation differences are not solely troublesome, but can be of great value in comparative sociological research and in the study of social change. Furthermore, intranation comparisons can be combined with internation comparisons to make them more valid and relevant to specific problems. The comparison of those sectors of two societies that have a greater number of characteristics in common while differing on some crucial ones may be more fruitful than overall national comparisons. The comparison of within-nation processes of change for different countries can be of great help in understanding social change. One of the greatest problems of macrosociology has been the limited number of cases available for systematic analysis, particularly when we are interested in the effect of changing and different social contexts—structural contexts—on relatively similar institutions, behaviors and attitudes. Using the whole nation, the number of cases that can be studied tends to be limited and consequently the range of variation considered is limited; but with research designs that take into account intranation differences we can multiply the number of cases without comparable increases in the size of our studies. The methodological advantages of using a contextual approach and including a structural setting among our interpretive factors (rather than isolated variables—an approach that has been fruitful in the study of individual behavior and attitudes in groups and institutions with distinct climates of opinion, dominant or shared norms, distinctive sociometric structures of leadership and communication) [1]—can be extended to the study of individuals

1. For a general introduction into the methodological problems of this type of approach see: Patricia L. Kendall and Paul F. Lazarsfeld, "Problems of Survey Analysis," in Robert K. Merton and Paul F. Lazarsfeld, eds., *Continuities in Social Research: Studies in the Scope and Method of "The American Soldier"* (Glencoe, Free Press, 1950), pp. 187–96. The whole focus on environment—context—as a variable in the analysis of survey data started with this essay. For a development of these methodological considerations, see Paul F. Lazarsfeld and Herbert Menzel, "On the Relation be-

and institutions and their relationship to the larger social structure.

In within-nation comparisons it is always difficult to isolate the more interesting and comparable sociological variables (usually positional variables like class, education, generation, religiosity, and measures of well-being) from those more unique to a particular social system (such as its political system, recent history, legal systems, and basic common culture). In intranation comparisons the system characteristics can be held relatively constant. In intercountry comparisons, however, it is extremely difficult to explore how such system characteristics as type of government, particular historical crisis, national culture, or legal system, affect certain institutional or individual patterns (as political behavior, feelings of political efficacy, labor–management relations, religious attitudes) since they are also related to economic development, rural property systems, stratification, urbanization, and degree of industrialization.

How can we say, for example, whether differences in voluntary association membership between Spain and Italy are due to the different political system or to the difference in economic development or difference of educational levels, when we know that the overall level of modernization of Italy is higher than that of Spain and that the political systems differ? If we compare regions of similar socioeconomic and cultural characteristics in the two societies, however—e.g. comparing advanced and backward sections in each society—we can specify further whether the intercountry differences really result from the global characteristics of the national unit or the different composition of the national

tween Individual and Collective Properties," in Amitai Etzioni, ed., *Complex Organizations: a Sociological Reader* (New York, Holt, Rinehart, and Winston, 1961), pp. 422–40. Peter M. Blau, "Structural Effects," *American Sociological Review*, *25* (1960) 178–93, has continued the exploration of the methodological problems of combining the study of individual attitudes and behavior with those of the group of which he is a member and the impact structure of the group on them. The articles by David L. Sills, James A. Davis, John A. Michael, Martin L. Lewin, and James S. Coleman published in the *Public Opinion Quarterly*, *25* (1961), 571–610, under the rubric "Three 'Climate of Opinion' Studies," are another step in the same intellectual tradition.

aggregates. The greater overall underdevelopment of Spain disappears as a difficulty once we compare units of similar characteristics in both countries. Often, in fact, the relationships may be specified: the two countries differ not in their backward sectors but in their modern sectors (or the reverse). This specification should lead to new interpretations and new questions about social change. Such comparisons based on carefully selected intercountry comparisons of relevant social contexts will be very helpful in avoiding unilinear interpretations of change. The logic for such an approach is available in survey analysis, particularly since we have become aware of the importance of componential effects.[2]

TABLE 13.1. TYPES OF INTERCOUNTRY AND INTRACOUNTRY COMPARISONS

Country A	Country B
Sector a	Sector a
Sector b	Sector b
Sector c	Sector c

Internation comparisons: A vs B
Intranation comparisons: Aa vs Ab, Ba vs Bc, etc.
Internation comparisons of intranation sectors: Aa vs Ba, Ab vs Bb, Ac vs Bc
or
Internation comparisons of differences between intranation sectors: Aa-Ab vs Ba-Bb

The starting point of these considerations is the great internal heterogeneity within some societies among its constituent units and sectors, often as great if not greater than that between national aggregates. The integration, communication, and sharing of attitudes and values within some countries are relatively low, allowing for interesting com-

2. A type of analysis already implicit in Durkheim's methodology; see: Hanan C. Selvin, "Durkheim's Suicide and Problems of Empirical Research," *American Journal of Sociology, 63* (1958) 607–19; see pp. 609–10 on contextual analysis, pp. 612–13 for unit replications both "external" and "internal." His remarks about the ecological fallacy (pp. 615–18), to which Robinson called attention, are, like those of Herbert Menzel to which he refers, particularly important for our use of "internal comparisons" and the reader is referred to them.

parisons between those occupying similar positions and roles in them. Such an approach would not be useful for the study of highly integrated and homogenized societies where the difference from a national mean of different units, sections, and regions is small. We have no evidence for it but it appears that internal differences within advanced modern societies are less, in spite of their greater complexity, than those within underdeveloped or semideveloped societies. What is more, it would seem that many societies we call semideveloped on the basis of a number of national indices are really a mixture of developed and underdeveloped sectors (or regions), and that their peculiar problems result from that imbalance. It would seem that in some cases, particularly in Latin America, much of the difficulty lies in the further diffusion of modern elements from some regions to others, the modernization of some sectors while others are already highly modernized but suffer under strains created by the lag in others. Overall internation comparisons would not help much to clarify such problems. Studies not designed with intranation differences in mind but focused on overall national patterns might even altogether miss basic aspects of the problem of social change.

We can get some sense of the problems heterogeneous societies with uneven degrees of development will face in the process of change, not by extrapolating only from the experience of other relatively similar advanced societies, but from the processes of change and their outcomes that have already taken place or are taking place in them. Extrapolation from internal comparisons is somewhat less hazardous than extrapolation from internation comparisons. Further, we can make inferences about probable changes based on what happened to a comparable sector within another nation, holding constant most factors while changing others (generally system characteristics).

The transition from synchronic intranation comparisons and internation comparisons of intranation differences to diachronic comparisons of the same type would increase our understanding immensely. Suppose we concluded that the most advanced sector of the Spanish economy was similar in a great number of respects to that of Northern Italy two or three decades ago. The comparisons of those two, particularly the identification of the presence or absence today in Spain of the features that have been used to account for the present success of the Italian industrial organization, would be decisive.

While we have started with these methodological considerations, the substantive implications are equally important; the internal heterogeneity, the regional differentiation, and the imbalances in development constitute some of the essential characteristics of many societies and account for many of their problems. Their description and interpretation should be a major task for sociology. Many of the political tensions taking the forms of nationalism, separatism, and sectionalism have their origins in such differences of development that make other "differential facts" like language or ethnicity or history more salient than they otherwise would have been. Certainly the early and successful industrialization of Catalonia and the high standard of living of the Basque country gave their peculiar character and importance to the conflict with the central government and gave force to the appeals of romantic nationalism. The contrast with Galicia, whose language is as distinct as Catalan but which does not have the same level of development and social mobilization, and whose elites had closer ties with those of the central government, could not be greater. There the nationalism did not go much beyond that of the Provence under the inspiration of Mistral.[3]

INTRANATION UNITS OF COMPARATIVE ANALYSIS

In the preceding we have consciously used vague terms like units, sections, and sectors to refer to the objects of compari-

3. The impact of the imbalances in economic and social development on national integration and politics in Spain has been discussed in greater detail in Juan J. Linz, "An Authoritarian Regime: Spain," in Erik Allardt and Yrjö Littunen, eds., *Cleavages, Ideologies and Party Systems: Contributions to Comparative Political Sociology* (Helsinki, Westermarck Society, 1964), pp. 291–341.

son.[4] The specification will depend largely on the problem to be studied and the data available in each case. Some examples of units serving as contextual variables for individual or institutional behavior include: How do people of similar occupation perceive the class structure in areas of great inequality and high proletarianization? Does the number of voluntary associations vary in regions of different industrialization or within regions of similar economic development but of different cultural traditions? Do businessmen whose plants are located in developed areas differ in their opinions from those of similar characteristics located in underdeveloped areas?[5] Do those who are members of a socially integrated business community differ from the rest in their attitudes? How does the differential social structure affect the recruitment of elites? Do labor courts decide cases differently in different regions?[6] The units considered in these questions range from abstract aggregates obtained from individual attributes like occupation or variables like income or industrial production (analytical properties) to relational data like social integration as indicated by friendships between businessmen (structural properties). In some cases we deal with units that are likely to be geographically more or less discontinuous—all the provinces with a certain proportion of proletarians; in others, specific communities (provinces or regions) with a distinctive "personality," historical tradition, or institutions not derived from individual data (global properties).

For our purposes here we want to distinguish analytically two main types of units, even though in our research we might wish they would actually coincide. In one type, using

4. This section owes much to the discussion in Kendall and Lazarsfeld, "Problems of Survey Analysis," pp. 187–96. Their discussion of the correspondence between personal and unit data and of the interchangeability of such data is a pioneer and most fruitful effort and should be reread in this context.

5. This point is documented extensively in a forthcoming monograph by the authors on "The Spanish Businessman Today." In the articles published in Spanish journals (quoted below) the reader can find numerous examples.

6. See the article by the authors, "El Empresario ante los problemas laborales," *Revista de Política Social, 60* (1963), 5–105, esp. pp. 93–101.

indicators for one or preferably several variables, we select certain cutting points to characterize units as "industrialized," "religious," or, by combining such dimensions, as "developed" (i.e. areas whose industrialization, literacy, and per capita income are within certain ranges). The selection of one or another set of cutting points will lead us to include several dispersed units (provinces, cities, etc.) in a common type without regard for their geographical continuity, historical or administrative links, and, what is more interesting, without consciousness of common interests or solidarity among those composing them.

Another possibility is to take actual social units, perceived by participants and observers as having distinctive characteristics such as institutions, traditions, climate of opinion, social integration, power structure, etc., that are hard to define and for which adequate indicators may not be available. The usefulness of units of the latter type will depend on how far they help us to focus our attention on interesting differences, to explain otherwise unexplainable variations in attitude or behavior between individuals (or institutions) comparable to those in other contexts. To take one example, businessmen in Barcelona tend to be more hostile to the Spanish banking system than those of other industrialized regions and this attitude, while characteristic of family textile entrepreneurs, is found in almost all sectors of the business community.[7] Certainly the heirs of textile businesses, particularly small ones, constitute a very important element in the Barcelona business community and we must assume that they contribute to a widespread climate of opinion. If, however, we consider that Barcelona, being the largest industrial center in Spain, has not created nor does it control any of the large industrial investment banks of Spain that

7. Amando de Miguel and Juan J. Linz, "Los Empresarios Españoles y la Banca," *Moneda y Crédito, 84* (1960), 3–112, see pp. 77–78, 83–89. While in our study region appeared as a central variable in understanding the relations between business and the banks, in terms of both attitudes and behavior, George Katona with the collaboration of Albert Lauterbach and Stanley Steinkamp in *Business Looks at the Banks* (Ann Arbor, University of Michigan Press, 1957), p. 94, found no regional differences in the use of credit.

play a major role in the economic power structure, the separate analysis of the attitude toward banks of the Barcelona business community is necessary to understand the problem. In dealing with many other attitudes we could nonetheless group Barcelona entrepreneurs with those of other highly industrialized areas of the country. In many such cases the choice of units of comparison is based on previous knowledge of the researcher and the generally shared images of significant differences in the society; in others the units are discovered only in the course of research.

Ideally, the "operationally" defined units based on systematic indicators should coincide to a certain degree with actual social units perceived as "real" by the participants, with historical, administrative, and political continuity, self-consciousness, and solidarity. It is equally desirable to find "operational" indicators to characterize more precisely and systematically such "real" units—from whose "Gestalt" we may have started our description and understanding of intranation differences. Sometimes we do not have data to proceed this way; it is common knowledge that significant proportions of the population in Catalonia and the Basque provinces—mainly Guipúzcoa and parts of Biscay—share in one way or another resentments against the central administration, and consequently these regions have to be treated separately in the analysis of certain attitudes; but it would be difficult to obtain valid indicators of such sentiments. It would be a great mistake to leave such a context out of the analysis until we had more adequate quantitative indicators.

The operationally obtained types of units—abstract types like industrialized Spain, middle-class Spain, religious Spain —are likely to be of greater value for internation comparison of intranation units defined in terms of similar characteristics. Relatively similar indicators of religiosity could be obtained for Spanish and French dioceses, and the social characteristics or attitudes of people in them could then be compared to ascertain the impact of a religious milieu. Furthermore, the comparison of people of similar levels of practice in them would give us a better understanding of the

"Spanish" and "French" Catholicism. Evolutionary hypotheses about change concomitant to different levels of development are subject to testing in this way.

The historically, geographically, and socially more "real" units sensitize us to new contextual variables and serve as ad hoc explanation of differences observed when people in identical positions, playing comparable roles, differ greatly in their behavior or attitudes. The implicit assumption is that they are involved in some form of interaction or communication that would account for a certain climate of opinion, shared even by those we would not expect to be predisposed in such a direction.

The data used in definition of units for intranation comparison can be derived from a multitude of sources: from qualitative judgments to sophisticated aggregation of survey data collected for the purpose, like sociometric data that define an occupational community or the degree of social integration across class lines. However, in research in nations where little empirical sociological research has been done, much of our information will come from censuses, official statistics or records, and the units defined will be mainly ecological units. Often it will be possible to combine data collected from published sources and library and archive research with survey data. In planning research in societies with very different levels of development, types of property and tenure systems in the countryside, and political traditions, the selection of sampling points should include these considerations, if necessary stratifying the sample and even oversampling or concentrating cases to allow comparisons otherwise impossible. A study of Spanish businessmen limited initially to those in the four most industrialized provinces (with 44.6 per cent of the firms with over 50 workers and 47.4 per cent of the workers employed in them) acquired a completely different intellectual scope when we added nine much less industrialized provinces in different parts of the country. A whole series of findings about the attitudes that go with endogenous vs. exogenous industrialization would have been missed without such intranation comparisons.

Just as crosscutting group affiliations have become an important tool in sociological analysis, particularly when reference group theory is tested, multiple social contexts within a nation, rather than a single set, should be considered: relative social integration, proportion of large or small factories, land tenure systems, educational level, regional origin of immigrants, and "religious climate." For some phenomena one or another set of such characteristics of the unit may turn out to be relevant. Our study of businessmen shows that different regions of Spain were relevant to an understanding of their attitudes toward the banking system, pressure group activities, conception of their own role, labor relations, and prestige assigned to different occupations, showing that different contexts became salient in relation to different problems and that no "mechanical" a prioristic approach to such intranation comparisons can be satisfactory.

In the following pages we will explore some specific problems using data from our research in Spain, illustrating some of the points advanced above.

HETEROGENEOUS SPAIN

Spain is the 15th country in population and 46th in area in the world but ranks at 21 in Gross National Product and 47.5 in GNP per capita.[8] It shows as much internal diversity as any European country. Its early unification under a single monarch in 1515 and its strong cultural tradition have not destroyed that diversity, and late economic development seems to have made it perhaps even more acute.[9] Many authors have insisted that one cannot speak of Spain but of Spains, an exaggeration that has a kernel of truth. In 1920

8. Data from Bruce M. Russett and Hayward R. Alker, Jr., Karl W. Deutsch, Harold D. Lasswell, *World Handbook of Political and Social Indicators* (New Haven, Yale University Press, 1964), pp. 140, 152, 156 (the data for GNP per capita are for 1957 and the rank indicates a tie with Brazil).

9. Manlio Rossi-Doria, "Agriculture and Europe," *Daedalus* (Winter 1964), pp. 335–57, refers to Folke Dovring for making the same point in his *Land and Labor in Europe* (The Hague, M. Nijhoff, 1958), p. 6, and to Maurice Neufeld, for modern Italy, in *Italy: School for Awakening Countries* (Ithaca, New York State School of Industrial and Labor Relations, Cornell University, 1961), pp. 499–500.

Ortega y Gasset[10] referred to its lack of integration: "Spain is today not so much a nation as a series of water-tight compartments." The tensions between autonomous regions and the central government contributed much to the crisis of the oligarchic constitutional monarchy in the first decades of the twentieth century and the separatist tendencies under the second Republic contributed to its difficulties and exacerbated "Spanish" nationalism, particularly of the Army, and with it the crisis that led to the Civil War.[11] The uneven economic and social development of a relatively industrial and advanced Spain and a rural Spain, with problems characteristic of many underdeveloped countries, contributed to make the social conflicts of the thirties so explosive. As in some Latin American countries the successful industrial-capitalist development in some areas is threatened by the revolutionary potential of a backward rural social structure that perhaps requires basic changes politically imposed rather than the result of spontaneous economic development.

Paradoxically, in the recent history of Spain, the most developed regions have felt alienated from the nation state.[12] Having "economic power" and well-being they felt, rightly or wrongly, deprived of "political power." Most countries with sectional or regional tensions are opposite cases: the undeveloped, agrarian, and traditional areas (the American South, Quebec, Bavaria, Flanders, Slovakia, and Sicily), feeling exploited or neglected by the economically developed metropolitan centers, express their feelings in sectional or separatist movements. The Spanish case is not without interest for some underdeveloped areas where the center of economic development may well find itself in a minority position, particularly if the more rural and traditional sectors

10. José Ortega y Gasset, *España Invertebrada* (Madrid, Revista de Occidente, 1921); trans. Mildred Adams, *Invertebrate Spain* (New York, W. W. Norton and Co., 1937), p. 41.

11. It should not be forgotten that the leader of the extreme Right, José Calvo Sotelo, making a play on words in one of his speeches, said "I prefer a red (*roja*) Spain to a broken (*rota*) Spain," emphasizing the importance he and many of his followers attached to this issue. The phrase has been repeated since then in editorials and speeches.

12. Ortega, pp. 47–48, among others has called attention to this problem.

get politically mobilized and gain power. The differential location of economic, political, intellectual, and other centers of power or influence in a society, particularly if that location is associated with processes of differential recruitment of elites, is likely to create tensions that might well affect national integration and overall development policies.

The sources of heterogeneity in a society like Spain are many. It would be difficult to discuss them in detail, but it might be useful to list them broadly with some examples of the kinds of differences that we would include under different rubrics. The main groupings are:

1. *Differences in economic development:* industrialization, agricultural production, subsistence vs. market agriculture, industrial as well as agricultural productivity, importance of the commercial and service sectors.

2. *Differences in the social structure,* particularly in social stratification and urbanization: the differences in the rural social structure (in a country which in 1950 had 53 per cent of its active male population in agriculture, reduced in 1960 to 42 per cent), property and tenure patterns and their respective mixes (so important for the feelings of relative deprivation and community integration), dominance of mini- or latifundia structures, the proportion of farm laborers and rural unemployment, rural settlement patterns (i.e. the prevalence of agricultural towns); in the urban structure, the occupational structure and particularly the relative importance of the "middle class" and what we will call later "bourgeoisie" and "clases medias" as two sectors of it. These basic structural differences are obviously reflected in social processes like geographical and social mobility and the attitudinal correlates: differences in perception of the class structure, class identification, and prestige of occupations.

3. *Differences in education at various levels:* particularly when those differences are not explainable in terms of economic or even class differences.

4. *Differences in linguistic and cultural tradition:* the areas in which Catalan, Basque, Galician, and different dialects are spoken dominantly or with varying degrees of

intensity, and the attitudinal correlates of such differentiation.

5. *Differences in religious "climate":* reflected in various levels of practice and participation.

6. *Differences in social mobilization:* social participation in voluntary associations, membership in religious and political organizations, exposure to mass media, frequently of travel, and commitment to a "civic culture" that largely correlate with economic differences, but in some cases might respond to other factors, like tradition, that are difficult to specify.

7. *Different political traditions:* These, often traceable to the nineteenth century, might well be independent of present social structural determinants. In view of Allardt's work in Finland,[13] it would seem that the geographical alignments in the Civil War and the experiences that went with them for different sectors of the population might not be irrelevant for the understanding of attitudinal differences.

8. *Differential representation of those recruited from different regions (and strata) in the various elites:* as factors predisposing them to certain viewpoints, facilitating communication with different sectors of society and the development of integrated viewpoints or "particularistic" ones in the sense of the term used by Ortega y Gasset.

9. *Differences in values, norms, and basic personality:* or similar variables used by social scientists to describe constructs affecting in complex ways different areas of behavior. To mention some on which we have found interesting differences (controlling by class): belief in luck as determinant of success, particularism–universalism, or such psychological factors as those tapped by different tests and scales.

10. *Differences in family patterns:* both demographic and structural. If we were to accept Freudian approaches to culture and personality, such differences would be important for

13. Cf. for instance, Erik Allardt, "A Theory on Solidarity and Legitimacy Conflicts" and "Patterns of Class Conflict and Working Class Consciousness in Finnish Politics," in Allardt and Littunen, eds., *Cleavages Ideologies and Party Systems*, pp. 78–96, 97–131.

understanding some of the problems listed above. They are also important for understanding the rural social structure that is so deeply linked to inheritance patterns.

The list we have just presented, without being exhaustive, shows the large number of factors that can give a very different profile to different units, creating contexts whose compositional effects may be worth exploring as far as possible. Their number already suggests that an inclusion by direct indicators obtained in any particular study is neither easy nor likely. Therefore it seems even more important to include them indirectly by using the knowledge derived from different studies and data collections as contextual information on the basis of careful consideration of the "location" of those obtained directly. That is, in the absence of "individual" data, we might still make good use of "unit" data by placing the individual in the context of the community, region, or type of area for which we have obtained independent information. It is not difficult to say that if a man of low income lives in an area with a high or low per capita income, this fact is likely to affect his attitudes (and we do not need to find them out by asking him—in fact he probably could not tell us).

The crosscutting and cumulation of these different lines of cleavage raise many interesting problems that would be often dismissed if we stopped at a correlational analysis: the existence of regions, like the Basque country with strong religious traditions and high industrial development, and others, like Andalusia, with a traditional social structure and probably traditional values, limited industrialization, but where religiosity seems extremely low. One of the most striking phenomena in Spain is that the highly industrialized areas are surrounded by rural areas with a stable and conservative peasantry while dominantly middle class cities in the South are often surrounded by a proletarian and potentially radical rural area. Sometimes the crosscutting of such patterns of diversity leads to paradoxical consequences. Despite political alienation from the "Center," the tendency toward participation and affiliation in all areas of life makes the

Basque participate more in organizations linked with the regime, making them more effective than is the case in other regions likely to be more in sympathy with them but without such a predisposition toward social mobilization.

Since we have put so much emphasis on internal differentiation, it seems justified to document the point in somewhat greater detail.

Economic Differences

Within the overall semidevelopment of Spain[14] we can find areas of advanced industrialization like the Basque provinces with a per capita income (1957) of 29,315 pesetas or Catalonia with 18,791 pesetas, and vast regions with limited industrialization like Andalusia with over six million population and where the per capita income is 15,131 pesetas.[15] The three Basque provinces and the four Catalan ones—mainly Barcelona—with 16.4 per cent of the population produce 24.9 per cent of the national income, while Andalusia with 20 per cent of the population produces 12 per cent of the income.[16] The Basque country and Catalonia are the

14. The dichotomy developed–underdeveloped, while initially helpful and valid, is, like so many similar concepts (democratic–totalitarian, rural–ruban, *Gemeinschaft–Gesellschaft*), obscuring important problems. We need a distinctive intellectual approach to those Western societies—in the Mediterranean and Latin America—that share many key institutions closely associated with the modern industrial society that has emerged out of the Western culture, whose elites, particularly the intellectuals, professionals, and civil servants, are Western and in contact with the ideas that move the Western world but whose countries have failed in economic development and in accepting certain values that go with the methods of an advanced industrial society. The partial modernization may be an as great or greater obstacle for certain social changes than a traditional underdeveloped society and culture. In any case it creates special problems deserving research.

15. Data from the study by the Banco de Bilbao, *Renta Nacional de España y su distribución provincial* (1957), p. 8. This and subsequent comparisons are made between large units: regions or provinces with considerable population, large cities or aggregates of cities comprising a substantial proportion of the population. Otherwise they would be misleading since, by taking small enough units and extreme cases, even in the most homogeneous society we could find great differences on almost any dimension. The official exchange rate was 42 pts.=$1, around 50 pts. on the black market.

16. The per capita income—10,415 pts. in 1957—of the combined gentry and proletarian Spain (that is, all areas with over 35% proletarization—most of Spain south of Madrid) is 53% that of bourgeois Spain (with 19,827 pts.) This proportion is higher than the 45% estimated for the south of Italy

residence of 28.8 per cent of all the workers in plants employing more than 5 persons and 40.9 per cent of those employing over 50 persons, compared to 10.3 per cent and 9.7 per cent respectively in Andalusia. Taking provinces with more than one million inhabitants the proportions employed in plants with over 50 workers range from 16 per cent in Barcelona to 3.6 per cent in Seville.[17]

The rural world presents similar structural differences in productivity, property, and tenure systems. The production per man active in agriculture ranges from 29,460 pesetas in Badajoz to 9,494 in Orense. Provinces like Seville where 75 per cent of those active in agriculture are farm laborers and others like Corunna with 11 per cent, the first with farms of an average size of 235 acres and the second of 21 acres, exemplify the differences between lati- and mini-fundia.[18]

Table 13.2 shows the number of agricultural units and their size in the "eight Spains," with the exception of Madrid, which we will describe in the next section. These data show the very different social and economic rural structure of Southern Spain ("gentry and proletarian" in our typology), with a large number of latifundia owners and the dominance of medium sized farms in "clases medias" Spain —mainly Castile—and the absence of latifundia together

---

compared to Italy north of Rome, despite the fact that the Spanish comparison is made between more extreme cases: the most industrial and the most proletarian parts of the country. The Italian figure is quoted from Vera Lutz, *Italy: A Study in Economic Development* (New York, Oxford University Press, 1962), p. 5. The differences in economic development are also reflected in imbalances in the geographic distribution of the population, particularly between the coastal periphery and the interior, and the special position of Madrid as an isolated center, that have been studied by Román Perpina Grau in: *Corología, Teoría Estructural y Estructurante de la Problación de España (1900–1950)* (Madrid, Consejo Superior de Investigaciones Científicas, 1954) and in "Corología de la Población 1950–1960," *Boletín de Estudios Económicos de la Universidad Comercial de Deusto, 17* (1962).

17. The data on the size of plants have been calculated from the *Censo Numérico de Empresas de más de cinco trabajadores y de su personal classificados por Mutualidades Laborales y Provincias* (Madrid, Ministerio de Trabajo, Secretaria General Tecnica, May 1959).

18. The data for the average size of a farm are from G. García-Badell, "La Distribución de la Propiedad Agrícola en España," *Revista de Estudios Agro-Sociales, 30* (1960), 1–26. The source used is "Servicio de Catastro de Rústica" (Treasury Department).

TABLE 13.2. RURAL PROPERTY STRUCTURE OF THE SEVEN SPAINS (PER CENT), 1960

			Hectares				
	"Without land"	*Under 1*	*1.0 to 4.9*	*5.0 to 49.9*	*50.0 to 199.9*	*Over 200*	*Total*
Bourgeois	1.15	38.0	38.64	20.68	1.05	.45	548,063
Proletarian in transition	2.94	28.8	41.89	23.31	1.65	1.39	75,493
Clases medias in transition	2.68	24.8	35.44	34.22	2.24	.63	497,930
Clases medias	3.58	20.8	32.80	39.46	2.46	.90	618,441
Gentry in transition	7.22	29.0	31.18	28.63	3.15	.86	433,940
Gentry	8.89	24.8	33.87	28.06	3.07	1.33	706,875
Proletarian	8.31	21.3	32.92	30.10	5.20	2.13	89,169
National average (including the province of Madrid, left out of the detailed breaks)	4.95	26.7	34.95	29.98	2.49	.92	
Total agricultural units	149,916	809,290	1,029,410	908,535	75,333	27,927	3,000,411

Data from the Censo Agrario de España 1962 (provisional data), *Anuario Estadístico de España 1963* (Instituto Nacional de Estadística), pp. 530–31.

with the presence of a large number of small and medium farms in "bourgeois" Spain. The presence of an often prosperous peasantry surrounding the industrial centers of the Basque country and Catalonia is another source of differentiation, which might not be unrelated to the appeal of regionalism and even local nationalism in those sections. The contrast between the 51 per cent of the vote (1936) for the Basque nationalist party in Biscay province and the 30 per cent it obtained in the capital district is certainly not unrelated to the peasantry's susceptibility to a religiously colored nationalism.

Social Structure: Social Stratification

The social structure reflects differences in economic development in the occupational structure, the distribution of wealth, property, and income.[19] A few figures taken almost at random reflect this: the proportion of unskilled labor in city and country, out of the total labor force—what we can call the degree of proletarization—ranges from 62 per cent in the province of Seville to 16 per cent in Madrid and Barcelona, with a national average of 34 per cent (1950).[20] The urban middle sectors—all those not engaged in manual work—range from 39 per cent of the nonagricultural population in Granada to 26 or 27 per cent in the industrial provinces of Biscay, Barcelona, and Guipúzcoa (all with capital cities over 100,000). The proportion of self-employed among men active in agriculture ranges from 6 per cent in Seville to over 50 per cent in several provinces. The inequality of income measured by the Lorenz index—computed on the basis of an interval distribution and based on not overly reliable survey data—also seems to vary considerably, from an

19. This section builds on the pioneer effort of Francisco Murillo Ferrol, "Los problemas específicos de las clases medias españolas," *Actas del Congreso Internacional del Instituto de Clases Medias* (Tomo II, Informes y Comunicaciones, Madrid, 1960), pp. 131–82.

20. Proletarization as indicated by the proportion of unskilled wage earners (*jornaleros no calificados*) among the active male population, Table VI of Vol. 2 of the *Censo de la Población de España de 31 diciembre de 1950*, published by the Instituto Nacional de Estadística.

index of .385 in Catalonia to .453 in East Andalusia, with a national average of .421.[21]

With such differences in the occupational structure and in the distribution of property and income, we can assume that the stratification systems of diverse parts of Spain are likely to be very different. How can we systematize some of those differences with the available data—essentially a census using industrial and occupational classifications—without giving simultaneously income or independent vs. dependent status data? One solution has been to locate all 50 provinces on two dimensions: *proletarization*—that is, the number of unskilled workers in city and country among the occupationally active males—on one side, and the proportion of the *urban middle class* with respect to the total nonagricultural population on the other.[22] By urban middle class we really mean active males engaged in urban nonmanual occupations, that is, those in the professions (civil service, industry and commerce, professional military) irrespective of their rank in each of these spheres, from the lower white collar to the tycoon, from the sergeants to the generals, and from the lowest middle class to the upper upper class.[23] The proportion of all these groups in the active male population not devoted to agriculture, forestry, and fishing is 30 per cent, varying from a maximum of 39 per cent in the province of Granada

21. Calculations based on the income reported for their families by the youth sample in an unpublished study on social stratification in Spain by Amando de Miguel. The differences between the extremes quoted would be comparable to those between an estimate for the U.S. and one for Guatemala.

22. These two dimensions of the stratification system are independent from each other (the correlation for the 50 provinces is .06). The lack of association between the proportion of urban middle class and other variables reflects the different composition and significance of this stratum that the typology brings out. The correlations between the proportion of urban middle class, and even more between the middle stratum in cities and countryside (as used by Murillo), show the limitations of the correlational analysis without the addition of a typological or contextual approach. We are sure that within each of the Spains we could find interesting associations between variables which on the national level would show a low association.

23. The urban middle class has been defined as those active in the professions, sales and office employees, and professional military, with respect to the active males not engaged in agriculture, fishing, or hunting (Table VII, Vol. 2 of the *Censo . . . 1950*). The occupational data by province do not allow a more sophisticated breakdown of the middle class.

Figure 13.1. Types of Social Structure in Spain

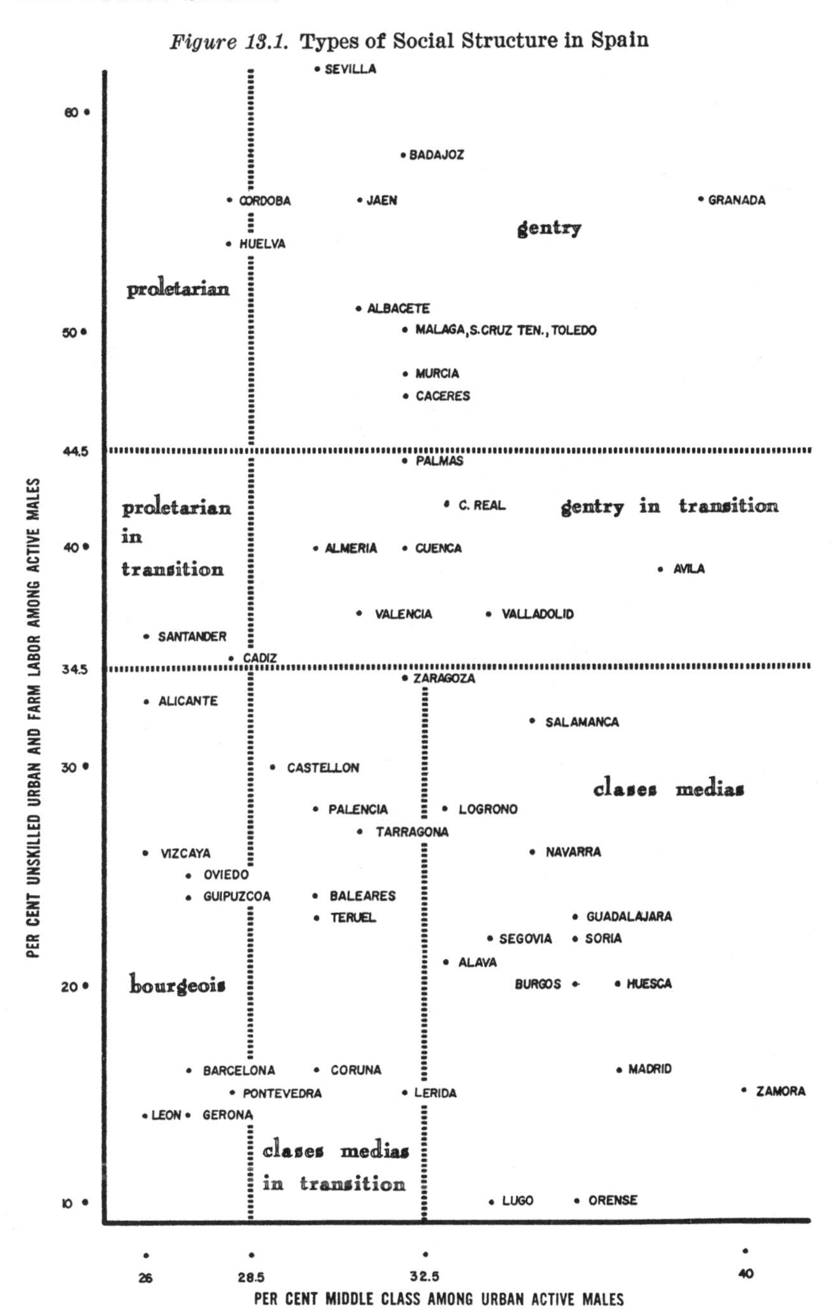

to a minimum of 20 per cent in Asturias. We will have occasion to return to the point, but it is significant that the proportion of middle class tends to be higher in the

Figure 13.2. **Types of Social Structure in Spain According to Regions**

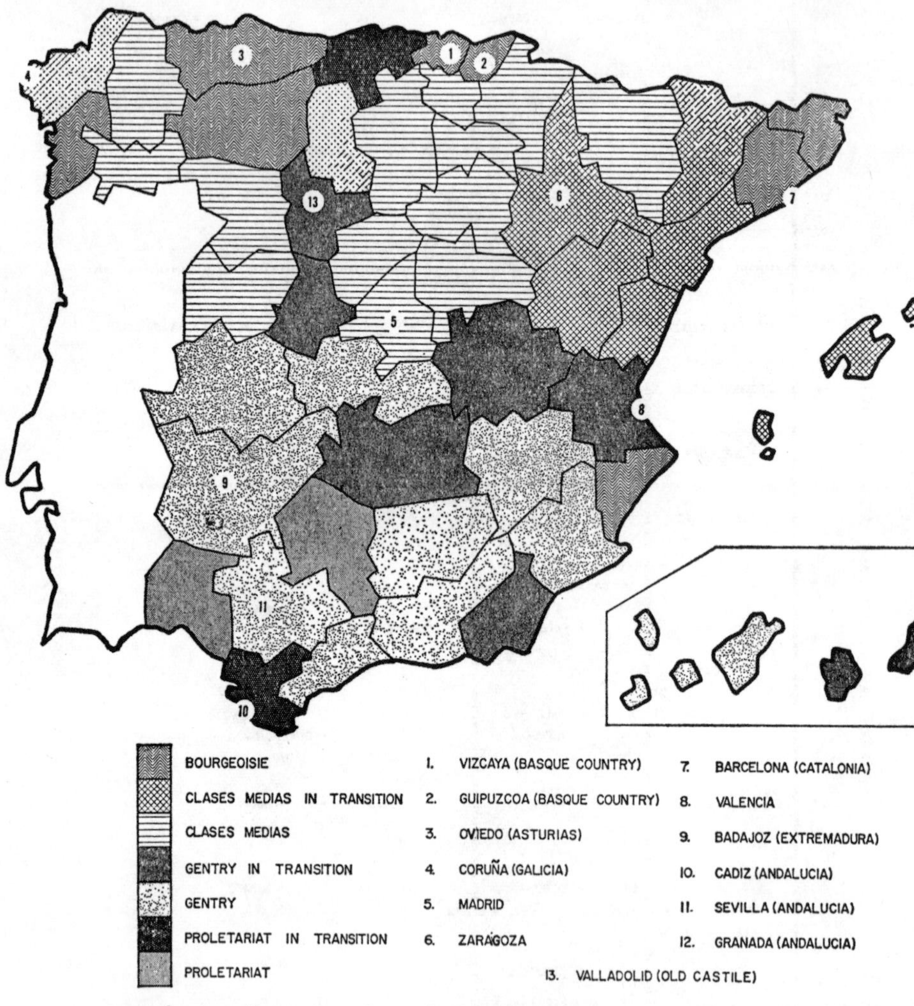

provinces that are less industrialized, suggesting that the generalization that economic development is needed to create a middle class may deserve some second thoughts.[24] Indus-

24. See John J. Johnson, *Political Change in Latin America: The Emergence of the Middle Sectors* (Stanford, Stanford University Press, 1958)

trialization more than anything else means more workers, particularly skilled and semiskilled, and this may well mean that the relative proportion of those in nonmanual occupations in the nonagricultural population might even decrease. Naturally this would not be the case if a country entered the new industrial revolution (the advanced countries are experiencing this with automation) without undergoing the more classical one of the machine age.

The combination of the two dimensions, proletarization and urban middle class, allows us to distinguish a number of types of provinces, selecting appropriate cutting points: three in the middle class dimension (less than 28 per cent, 29 to 32 per cent, and 33 per cent and over) and three in the proletarization (less than 34 per cent, 35 to 44 per cent, and 45 per cent and over). A typological reduction leads us to distinguish seven types of provinces to which we have to add Madrid (really a unique metropolitan area with no hinterland) as a distinctive unit. The seven types [25] will be labeled: bourgeois, proletarian in transition, clases medias in transition, clases medias, gentry in transition, gentry, and proletarian.

1. *Bourgeois Spain* (we could also call it "industrial") is an area characterized by a low proportion of unskilled workers—few in the countryside and not too many in the cities—but with a sufficient number of workers to reduce the proportion of those in nonmanual, that is, middle class, occupations in the cities and towns. In it businessmen, managers, technicians, salesmen, and white-collar employees constitute a significant part of the middle class. Here we find the industrial and commercial metropolis of Barcelona and its suburbs, the heavy industrial center of Bilbao, Guipúzcoa with its many small industrial towns, the coal and steel complex of Asturias, and other adjacent provinces.

---

whose analysis assumes that the growth of the middle sectors is a modern phenomenon and the basis for a more stable and hopeful political situation.

25. It is important to stress that these types are *not* derived from *economic indicators* (e.g. proportion active in different sectors or income), but *social indicators* (e.g. social position in the city and the countryside).

2. *Proletarian in transition* is a residual heterogeneous grouping of two provinces where the proportion of unskilled workers is higher than in the preceding, with a similar proportion of middle class. Both have been undergoing considerable industrialization in the past decades and one of them, Cadiz, shares with the gentry provinces a sizable proportion of farm laborers working on large estates.

3. *Clases medias in transition* is both geographically and conceptually between "bourgeois" and "clases medias" Spain, an area having no rural proletariat and a certain industrialization that has not increased much the number of unskilled workers, but whose cities are not as dominantly "middle class" due to that same factor. Here we find the less industrial provinces of Catalonia, the Balearic Islands with consumer good industries, and Saragossa, an emerging industrial center halfway between Barcelona, Bilbao, and Madrid.

4. *Clases medias* covers a wide area of interior Spain (in fact, only one province touches the sea) and its hard core is Castile, the region that unified the country. Its core is a traditional landowning or permanent leaseholding peasantry, without great economic inequalities. Its medium sized cities are little industrialized; professionals, merchants, small rentiers, civil servants, officers, and priests constitute its predominant sectors. We might say that this urban middle class is largely a "preindustrial middle class." We shall refer to it by the Spanish expression "clases medias." A not insignificant part of this "urban" population still has ties with the land, owning some land though not necessarily much, and derives some of its income from it. There are not even isolated large plants; its agriculture is largely noncommercial. In many ways it is the most traditional part of the country but one where an absence of too marked inequalities allows a maximum of social integration and a minimum of class conflict. Madrid, the national capital, with its huge official establishment, the residence of noble and non-noble absentee landowners, the professional and intellectual capital, was at one time probably close in its social structure to

this clases medias Spain,[26] with its antagonist, Barcelona, the head of bourgeois Spain.[27] On the basis of 1950 census data it would still fall into this category, but its recent industrialization and its enormous demographic weight (2.4

26. José Ortega y Gasset in his articles written in 1927, *La bedención de las provincias* (Madrid, Revista de Occidente, 1931) made this tension between Madrid and the provinces, the mutual dependency and alienation, central to the analysis of Spanish social structure and politics (see especially pp. 71–73 and 79–90).

The different social structures in nineteenth-century Madrid and Barcelona are reflected in these census data from 1860 (Murillo, p. 141):

	Madrid		Barcelona	
Clergy	1.2		1.1	
Military	7.5		6.2	
Liberal professions	3.0		1.7	
Teachers	0.4		—	
Students	2.1		0.6	
Employees	4.0		1.3	
		18.2%		10.9%
Owners	4.5		4.3	
Tenants	0.6		0.7	
		5.1		5.0
Merchants	3.2		4.3	
Entrepreneurs	10.3		7.3	
Manufacturers	0.1		0.8	
		13.6		12.4
Artisans	25.2		28.6	
Factory wage earners	0.9		17.0	
Farm wage earners	9.6		7.4	
		35.7		53.0
Servants	25.5		11.4	
		25.5		11.4
Other and poorly defined	1.9		7.3	
Total	100.0		100.0	
Total population	(281,170)		(178,625)	

Source: Jaime Vicens Vives, *Historia Social y Económica de España y América*, *4*, 53–54.

27. The different occupational structures of Barcelona and Madrid in 1950, with a comparable population size, show what we mean by "bourgeois" and "clases medias." The proportion of the middle class was respectively 35.3% and 43.1%, with the difference due to the larger number of professionals (7.5% vs. 6.4%), military and security services (5.8% vs. 2.4%), white-collar employees (19.4% vs. 16.7%), and even people in "sales" (10.3% vs. 9.8%) in Madrid. The first two groups and part of the third would be in the clases medias rather than the bourgeoisie. The difference is also reflected in the importance of personal and domestic service workers

million in 1964) as a metropolitan center lead us to refer to it separately.

5. *Gentry in transition Spain,* several provinces where the number of unskilled workers, particularly farm laborers, is already above the national average and with a significant middle class in the cities, constitutes another type. Here we find a province like Valladolid whose capital has many of the characteristics of the smaller Castilian cities, but whose larger and more productive wheat fields employ more laborers. Valencia with a highly commercial agriculture and a growing industry is almost on the cutting point between gentry in transition and clases medias in transition. Other provinces are geographically and socially on the border of the large bloc of "gentry" Spain dominating the South and Southwest. The latifundia begin to appear in the plains of Ciudad Real.

6. *Gentry Spain* is a distinctive social structure [28] where

---

(7.5% vs. 4.7%). Most of the difference is accounted for by the larger proportion of wage workers and artisans (56.0% vs. 44.3%) in Barcelona. The comparison between a large provincial city in gentry Spain like Granada and the capital of an industrial region like Oviedo, whose active male population is relatively similar (34,230 vs. 29,051), also exemplifies the importance of the middle class in economically underdeveloped cities: In Granada 47.1% can be classified as middle class, while in Oviedo it is 33.9%; the professionals constitute 7.3% of the population of the Andalusian capital and 6.1% of the Asturian capital (incidentally both are university cities); the proportions of army and police are quite comparable, but those of employees and particularly sales are completely different. The different structure is also revealed in personal and domestic service: 6.8% in Granada and 2.6% in Oviedo, to which tourism might contribute somewhat, but which also exists if we look solely at female domestic servants. The industrial and artisan sector, reflecting the very different economic development, is respectively 41.7% and 59.5%.

28. We do not want to use the term gentry in any specific and technical sense. The presence of an absentee landowning nobility living in the cities and larger towns or in Madrid and of non-noble landowners who have assimilated in the course of the nineteenth century the values and style of life that were closer to those of the nobility than to those of the commercial and industrial bourgeoisie suggested this term. Perhaps the term neoserfdom used by Dobrogeanu-Gherea in his analysis of Rumanian social structure makes reference to a similar situation, where modern elements are superimposed and mixed with traditional structures; he referred to an unfortunate hybrid, the form of liberal bourgeois institutions superimposed upon a feudal reality. *Neoiobăgia* (Bucharest, n.d.) quoted by Henry L. Roberts, *Rumania* (New Haven, Yale University Press, 1951), passim.

unskilled workers, mainly farm laborers mostly temporarily employed, are almost one half of the population. Its cities, some of them passing the 100,000 mark, have little or no industry and consequently are dominated by the middle sectors which, given the lack of modern industry, cannot be entrepreneurs, managers, technicians, or even merchants or salesmen (since the standard of living of the masses does not allow a developed commercial economy) but are largely constituted of what we have called "clases medias." A minority of that group comprises wealthy, absentee landowners, noble or more often not, who combine their rentier life with the exercise of some profession.[29] It would be interesting to know to what extent there is a "hidden unemployment" or underemployment in such middle class occupations. In the "agricultural towns" (many of 20,000 or more) of Andalusia and Extremadura we find what Díaz del Moral [30] calls "burgesía agricultora," and Macias Picavea [31] terms

29. Antonio Bermúdez Cañete, a politician and a journalist specializing in financial problems, has dealt in an impressionistic way with the social structure of gentry Spain, its urban middle class—of señoritos—based on the exploitation of a rural economy; see one of his essays of the 1930s reproduced in *Información Comercial Española* (September 1962), pp. 53–59. Data for the law students of Granada (collected by F. Murillo) show that 73% of those whose fathers were professionals (lawyers, doctors, engineers, and professors) reported ownership of land in their family; among the sons of businessmen and professionals the proportion goes down to 57%, confirming the rural ties of the occupational middle class of Andalusia on which Bermúdez Cañete comments. Among all Granada law students whose fathers were not economically active in agriculture, 59% came from families holding land.

30. J. A. Pitt-Rivers, *People of the Sierra* (New York, Criterion Books, 1954) commenting on the statement made by a Spanish social reformer that Andalusia had no middle class—similar to that made by many writers on Latin America—writes: "What [he] appears to mean . . . is that the society is composed only of rich and poor, that there is no middle class in the sense of people of intermediary economic position. This is plainly untrue, even in the areas where *latifundismo* is most accentuated. What is missing is not the category of people of medium wealth, but the ideal type of the *bourgeois* distinguished by occupation, and place of habitation and values from the landowners and the agricultural laborers. Where all live in towns the term 'bourgeoisie' (taken in its literal sense) clearly becomes meaningless. Díaz del Moral uses the term *burgesía agricultora* in order to refer to this class" (p. 181 n.).

31. Ricardo Macías Picavea, *El Problema Nacional* (Madrid, Victoriano Suárez, 1899), p. 163: "The national folklore has divided them into 'peasants of the jacket' (labradores de chaqueta) and 'peasants in tails' (de levita)

"labradores de levita" (farmers in tails), similar to the Southern Italian "gentilhuomi di campagna." In recent decades there has been some effort toward economic development but industrialization has been largely at the initiative of the central government or of bank capital rather than local enterpreneurs.[32] Certainly the group we describe as a self-conscious industrial and commercial bourgeoisie is not the dominant group in these "urbanized" (if we take the standard demographic definitions) but nonindustrialized provinces where illiteracy and poverty are outstanding.

7. *Proletarian Spain* consists of two provinces, Huelva and Cordova, surrounded by gentry provinces, that show some of their characteristics in an even more extreme form: the high proportion of proletarians is increased by a sizable proportion employed in mining; their capital cities, being close to the metropolis of Seville, have even fewer of the administrative, professional, intellectual, and commercial functions; and consequently their middle class is even weaker. In a sense, they approach the social and economic structure of some colonies—producers of raw materials, agricultural goods, and mining for absentee owners and corporations (of which some of the leading ones are partly foreign owned).

The terms "bourgeois" and "clases medias" have been used to describe two types of "middle classes" or "middle sectors" normally not distinguished by sociologists.[33] On the one side

adding to the latter the comment 'get away' (¡ Quita!). The first are the innumerable generations of ants that transmit by inheritance their agrarian instincts: the second are generally lawyers that have given up the codes."

32. See the articles by the authors: "Fundadores, Herederos y Directores en las Empresas Españolas," *Revista Internacional Sociología, 21* (1963), 5–38, esp. pp. 36–38; "Movilidad Geográfica de los Empresarios Españoles," *Estudios Geográficos, 25* (1964), 5–29. One consequence is that the industry of the underdeveloped parts of the country tends to be composed of very large and modern plants—shipyards, large chemical plants—with their social services, etc., that contrast with the surrounding poverty.

33. Jaime Vicens Vives, *Historia Social y Económica de España y América, 4, Burguesía, Industrialización, Obrerismo*, in collaboration with J. Nadal, R. Ortega, M. Hernández Sánchez-Barba (Barcelona, Teide, 1959), pp. 126–40, 151–80, has called attention to this internal differentiation of the upper and middle classes and its importance to an understanding of Spanish politics and particularly the Catalan problem.

the "bourgeois," directly related to the development of a modern industrial–commercial economy; the "clases medias" on the other, in which urban elements like professionals, civil servants, army officers, intellectuals, and rentiers, not necessarily tied to industrialization (and in fact often deriving at least part of their income from land rents), play an important role. Early sociologists like Saint Simon [34] and Comte were aware of this differentiation, but it was to be neglected under the influence of Marxian analysis and the prediction based on British industrialization and the attention devoted in the twentieth century to the emergence of the new white-collar middle class and the distinctions between owners and managers. Only Pareto's distinction between speculators and rentiers [35] touched on similar problems particularly relevant to developed societies where urbanization, cultural and political modernization, were ahead of industrialization.

Economic Differences and the Future of the "Eight Spains"

Bourgeois Spain has a per capita income 31 per cent above the national average, its population has been growing

34. The texts of Saint Simon are scattered throughout his work and the references can be found in Frank E. Manuel, *The New World of Henri Saint Simon* (Cambridge, Harvard University Press, 1957), pp. 244–45, 250–53, 264–71, particularly the interpretation of the Revolution of 1789 as one in which the industrials had called upon two "bastard classes" to represent them: the lawyers and metaphysicians. As Manuel summarizes his point: the industrials, unaware of the degree of their own maturity, allowed the Revolution to fall into the hands of classes who proceeded to organize society in their own image, in terms of metaphysical abstractions like the rights of man and lawyer's constitutions, which were more concerned with political forms and mechanisms than with the establishment of a new social order based on the real forces of society. In his final version Saint-Simon added to the lawyers and metaphysicians (we could use the term intelligentsia), the non-noble military men, landowners, and rentiers, to which he adds the "honorary professions," which constituted a stratum together with the "feudal theological classes" from which they had sprung and the "industrial scientific" classes. He sometimes uses the term bourgeois for this stratum, but we prefer to use the Spanish expression "clases medias" to contrast them with the traditional European use of bourgeois as linked with the economic changes that went with the commercial and industrial revolution.

35. Vilfredo Pareto, *The Mind and Society: A Treatise on General Sociology* (New York, Dover Publications, 1963) pp. 2231–36, 2310–28, on "speculators" (who in large part coincide with the "entrepreneurs") and "rentiers" and their different interests, political attitudes, and styles.

TABLE 13.3. DEMOGRAPHIC, ECONOMIC, AND SOCIAL DATA FOR UNITS REPRESENTING DIFFERENT TYPES OF SOCIAL STRUCTURE IN SPAIN

	Population 1957	*Population 1960*	*Production 1957*	*Income 1957*	*Per capita income 1957 in pts.*	*Per capita income compared with national average 15,131=100*	*Contribution to the Treasury (1960)*	*Per capita ordinary municipal expenditures in pesetas*	*Per capita ordinary municipal expenditures in relation to national average 420=100*	*No. of inhabitants per practicing physician (36,750 practicing physicians)*
	%	%	%	%			%			
Bourgeois	23.67	24.20	31.01	31.16	19,827	131	38.23	570 pts	135	780
Proletarian in transition	4.27	4.10	3.93	3.86	13,658	90	3.74	410	98	1023
Clases medias in transition	11.90	11.88	11.96	11.44	14,542	96	7.75	370	88	756
Madrid	7.49	7.67	11.30	12.31	24,858	164	25.57	800	190	614
Clases medias	12.19	12.67	10.77	10.53	13,065	86	6.04	250	59	940
Gentry in transition	12.48	12.56	11.69	11.61	15,582	103	7.28	360	86	854
Gentry	24.00	23.67	16.67	16.44	10,363	68	10.98	320	76	1120
Proletarian	4.00	4.04	2.88	2.81	10,638	70	1.74	320	76	1172
Total Spain	(29,934,202)	(30,739,427)	452,948 million pts.		15,131			420		836

For sources see footnotes to the text.

(largely by immigration), its share in the national production is close to one third, and its contribution to the Treasury even larger.[36] Gentry Spain with almost the same population contributes just a little over half of the production of "bourgeois" Spain and its per capita income is 32 per cent below the national average. The provinces of "clases medias" Spain have experienced a relative (and a few even an absolute) loss of population in the last 50 years. Their productivity is somewhat below their population share and their per capita income is 16 per cent below the national average. The transitional Spains are the ones closest to the average in their income and in the proportion between population and production. Madrid, with its growing share in the population, its important share in production and national income, and the high per capita income of 24,858 pesetas stands out in its uniqueness, even though it does not reach the macrocephalic position in Spanish life comparable to a Buenos Aires, Paris, or Vienna. Nevertheless its dominance in certain spheres of Spanish life and with respect to the surrounding central Spain is a conspicuous fact. On the other hand, the tension between Madrid and Barcelona as the two metropolitan centers with similar population but with very different social structure and functions has something in common with that existing between Rome and Milan, Quito and Guayaquil, and, in the past, between Lisbon and Oporto. Like Rome or Quito, Madrid is more receptive to the influence and ways of life of the agrarian regions even though in the last decades the changes have been toward increasing modernization.

The types we are discussing are fundamentally descriptive and to be used as social context. We can also consider them potentially as developing from one to another: with increased industrialization, clases medias in transition is likely to become more similar to bourgeois–industrial Spain, and the same is probably true for proletarian in transition (Santander is already far in that direction and there are

36. Ingreso del Estado, data from the *Atlas Comercial de España* (Madrid, Cámaras de Comercio, Industria y Navegación, 1963).

signs that this will be the case with Cadiz). Modernization of agriculture (reducing the agricultural proletariat) among gentry in transition provinces with some industrialization may well move some of them into the "clases medias" in transition. Gentry Spain, if its high birth rates continue, with nine out of ten provinces above the national average, if its industrialization (particularly labor-intensive production) does not speed up, and if agrarian reform does not change the property structure, is likely to remain in that category and even move toward the proletarian type. Clases medias Spain, with some important exceptions like Alava, Navarre, Guadalajara, and Burgos (due to their proximity to industrial centers that may become transitional areas), is not likely to change its social structure much. The emphasis on land consolidation in the recent Development Plan may raise its productivity, making the gap with the gentry and proletarian Spain even more marked, even though one of its goals is to reduce the regional imbalance.[37]

REGIONS AND THE RECRUITMENT OF ELITES

The different elites of a society are not recruited equally from all strata of the population. As elite studies in most societies have shown, marked inequalities of opportunity exist. There may nonetheless be considerable interchange between elite strata all over the nation or a differential recruitment into different elites in terms of social and geographical origin. It might well be that the social, cultural, and political integration of a society depends on the degree of homogeneity or differentiation of the recruitment of its elites.[38] Undoubtedly, with significant internal differences in economic and industrial development, regional differences in the

37. For a brief summary in English of the problems of regional differences in economic development see: *The Economic Development of Spain: Report of a Mission of the International Bank for Reconstruction and Development* (Baltimore, Johns Hopkins University Press, 1963), pp. 86–90, 256–59, 359–63.

38. On the importance of an integrated elite for national integration, see Karl W. Deutsch, *Nationalism and Social Communication* (Cambridge and New York, M.I.T. Press and John Wiley, 1953), pp. 18–21.

recruitment of the business elite and other elites are likely to be great, particularly where family capitalism is important. As Albert Hirschman [39] has formulated the problem on the basis of his experiences in Latin America: "The poorer sections of the country, where careers in industry and trade are not promising, often produce, for this reason, a majority of the country's successful politicians and thereby acquire influential spokesmen in the councils of the government."

Differential recruitment of the economic and political elite is accompanied by feelings of estrangement, of superiority and resentment, and lack of understanding. Hirschman's description of this process is so apt for the case of Spain—and has been viewed as such by at least one leading Spanish economist [40]—that it deserves to be quoted at length:

> The progressive sectors and regions of an underdeveloped economy are easily overimpressed with their own rate of development. At the same time, they set themselves apart from the less progressive operators by creating a picture of the latter as lazy, bungling, intriguing, and generally hopeless. There seems to be a cliquishness about progress when it first appears that recalls the same phenomenon among adolescents.
>
> Thus the successful groups and regions will widely and extravagantly proclaim their superiority over the rest of their country and their countrymen. It is interesting to note that to some extent these claims are self-enforcing. Even though the initial success of these groups may often be due to sheer luck or to environmental factors such as resource endowment, matters will not be left there. Those who have been caught by progress will always maintain

39. Albert O. Hirschman, *The Strategy of Economic Development* (New Haven, Yale University Press, 1958), pp. 185–86.

40. Fabian Estape, "La Economia Catalana y el Desequilibrio Economico Regional," *Información Comercial Española* (February 1962), pp. 43–55. The same theme is found in the work of a Catalanist politician, Carlos Pi Sunyer, *L'Aptitud Economica de Catalunya* (Barcelona, 1927), and the interpretative essay by a leading modern historian, Jaime Vicens Vives, *Noticia de Catalunya* (Barcelona, Editorial Ancora, 1960). See also the introduction to Pierre Vilar, *La Catalogne dans l'Espagne Moderne* (Paris, S.E.V.P.E.N., 1962).

> that they were the ones who did the catching; they will easily convince themselves, and attempt to convince others, that their accomplishments are primarily owed to their superior moral qualities and conduct. It is precisely this self-righteousness that will tend to produce its own evidence: once these groups have spread the word that their success was due to hard work and virtuous living, they must willy-nilly live up to their own story, or at least will make their children do so.

Hirschman also analyzes some consequences for those not sharing in the progress (in Spain this would apply to Castile) when he writes:

> Faced with the sudden improvement in the fortunes of some of their own compatriots, they will frequently retort to the claims of superiority of these *nouveaux riches* by accusing them of crass materialism, sharp practices, and disregard for the country's traditional cultural and spiritual values. While such charges are directed with particular relish at minorities, whose importance in the process of development is well recognized, purely indigenous entrepreneurial groups are by no means exempt from them. In this way these groups are, as it were, converted into minorities in their own country, often estranged from the rest of their compatriots, and ostracized by the traditional elites. Such a development is particularly likely when the first stages of commercial and industrial progress are localized in a center other than the capital city. In this case the rift between this center and the capital city may well widen cumulatively over a long period of time. The very fact that the leading families of such cities as Barcelona, São Paulo, Medellín, and Guayaquil lived far away from, and often in conflict with, the centers of politics, public administration, and education made for a dogged concentration of succeeding generations on business pursuits rather than for absorption of the most talented by other careers that carry more prestige in a traditional society.

Our data show clearly that the different Spains and, in particular, Catalonia and the Basque country contribute very unevenly to the recruitment of different elites. It must be stressed that such differential recruitment is not necessarily nor generally the result of any conscious or even latent discrimination but more often of a self-selection process resulting from different opportunities. A young law school graduate from a bourgeois Catalan family has better opportunities in business or law practice and is unlikely to be attracted by most civil service positions or into the relatively underpaid judiciary. The underrepresentation of the Catalans among the village and small town judges in their late twenties and early thirties will mean years later their underrepresentation among the members of the higher courts of Catalonia and ultimately in the prestigeful bench of the Supreme Court.[41]

The differential prestige in various parts of Spain of different activities and the alternative opportunities open to young people contribute to a myriad of unrelated individual decisions which in turn contribute to great differences in the recruitment of elites. The bureaucratic and military elites, which play such an important role in Spanish life, particularly in an authoritarian regime, are less likely to come from bourgeois Spain and the more so from Madrid and the traditional clases medias and gentry Spain. The elite groups of the civil service, like the *abogado del Estado,* are more likely to come from Madrid; those of lesser income and prestige may come from a broader basis, particularly from clases medias Spain, since the larger proportion of people with no secondary education in gentry and proletarian Spain has little chance to enter into the elite through educational channels. There are indications that this tendency is even stronger among the youngest age groups. Similarly the

41. Of the 73 judges of the *Tribunal Supremo*, the highest court in Spain, none was born in Catalonia, compared to 16 born in Old Castile, and 16 born in Andalusia. In the higher courts of Catalonia itself—*Audiencias Territoriales y Provinciales*—only 4 out of 40 indicated Catalonia as their birthplace. (Data from *Escalafones de los funcionarios* . . . ; see note to Table 13.4)

TABLE 13.4. REGIONAL DIFFERENCES IN THE RECRUITMENT OF ELITES IN THE EIGHT SPAINS

	Population in 1910	*Cabinet members of Franco regime*		*Cabinet members of the Republic*		*Judges (1958)*		*University professors (1955)*	
			*		*		*		*
Bourgeois	20.6	17.5	.85	27.8	1.34	11.9	.58	19.6	.95
Proletarian in transition	4.0	10.5	2.63	—	—	4.5	1.12	3.3	.82
Clases medias in transition	14.2	22.8	1.54	21.3	1.50	12.0	.85	18.0	1.27
Madrid	4.4	28.0	6.25	9.8	2.17	14.3	3.24	12.7	2.87
Clases medias	16.1	10.5	.65	9.8	.61	18.1	1.12	13.2	.82
Gentry in transition	13.1	1.8	.14	6.6	.50	14.1	1.08	13.1	1.00
Gentry	23.3	7.0	.30	19.8	.85	21.7	.93	17.2	.74
Proletarian	4.0	1.8	.45	4.9	1.22	3.5	.88	2.8	.70
Total Spain	(20,007,087)	(57)		(61)					

	(1959)		(1950)		1000 workers (1960)		of nobility (1957)	population	directors	and related occupations
		**		**	*	*			**	**
Bourgeois	20.3	.99	11.46	.60	46.5	2.26	13	.54	1.81	1.05
Proletarian in transition	3.1	.77	5.88	1.55	—	—	2	.50	.89	1.05
Clases medias in transition	19.6	1.38	13.73	1.02	12.3	.87	3	.25	.93	.97
Madrid	2.5	.57	2.77	.72	10.8	2.45	62	5.18	2.56	2.53
Clases medias	24.8	1.56	25.18	1.65	10.8	.67	3	.25	.80	1.32
Gentry in transition	9.0	.69	10.40	.78	6.8	.52	5	.42	.58	.79
Gentry	15.0	.65	25.51	.98	10.8	.46	12	.50	.65	.73
Proletarian	2.4	.60	4.95	1.15	1.4	.35	2	.50	.74	.81
Total Spain			(136,256)		73		(1683)		(32,928)	(363,872)

* Ratio of the proportion born in each "Spain" and the proportion of the population living there in 1910 (taken as a date close to the birth year of the elites).

** Ratio of the proportion of males born in each of the "eight Spains" engaged in each occupation to the proportion of all males born in each of them. (1950 Census Data). From this table we excluded those born abroad or in Spanish possessions.

Source: Data from the *Escalafón de Cafedráticos Numerarios de Universidad* (Madrid, Dirección General de Enseñanza Universitaria, 1955) including 687 professors. Data from the *Escalafones de los Funcionarios de la Carrera Judicial y Funcionarios de la Carrera Fiscal* (Madrid, Ministerio de Justicia, 1958) based on 1184 judges. Data from the *Guía de la Iglesia en España* (Madrid, Oficina General de Información y Estadística de la Iglesia en España, 1960), pp. 43, 772. The number of seminary students was 23,573 and the population for the diocese was 29,522,610.

Data for the proportion of professional military—including navy and air force—born in different provinces and the ratio of that proportion to that of the active male population born in them are from the *Censo de la Población en España . . ., 3* (Instituto Nacional de Estadística, 1950), table IV, pp. 182–83. Those born abroad or in Spanish possessions have not been included. The data refer to 136,256 professional military. The proportion of "gerentes o directores"—managers or directors—comes from the same source. The classification should exclude owners or (independent) entrepreneurs, a category in which the farmers (owners and tenants) are included and therefore is not useful for our purpose. The grouping, "professionals, technicians and similar activities," is very heterogeneous including those with the highest prestige to those of minimal qualification.

Data come from our survey of 13 provinces in which 81 of the 147 directors of enterprises were sampled. The total number of plants employing over 1,000 was 184, of which a considerable number are divisions of the same company. Those outside the 13 provinces sampled (37) could affect the general trend only in part since their management is often located in industrial Spain and more than half of them are only plants of enterprises already sampled.

Data from the *Guía Oficial de Grandezas y Títulos del Reino mandada a publicar por Orden dee 4 de marzo de 1960* (Ministerio de Justicia, Madrid, 1959–1960) referring to 1792; 2317 holding titles of which 1683 were living in Metropolitan Spain.

provincial university cities without much economic life, such as Granada and Saragossa before its recent industrialization, contribute disproportionately to the ranks of university professors. However, gentry Spain tends to produce fewer academics than clases medias Spain, and clases medias in transition slightly more judges.

The rural proletarian of gentry and proletarian Spain seems by all indications to be one of the most de-Christianized sectors of the society and therefore it is not surprising that the seminary student should be underrepresented in those regions and that the transitional areas and clases medias should be heavily represented. The religiosity and traditionalism of the peasantry of bourgeois industrial Spain explains why even that region is represented.

These differences in recruitment of the elites are naturally related to the prestige assigned to various occupations in different regions of the country. Secondary students attending schools controlled by the same religious order reflect the differential evaluation of industrial and preindustrial middle and upper class occupations in bourgeois and clases medias Spain.[42] Even the rankings of five elite occupations by business leaders themselves reflect the degree of industrialization and their own integration into an occupational community of businessmen.[43]

These processes of selective recruitment start at an early age. Among students of *pre-universitario* (last year of secondary education) of a relatively homogeneous background, often attending schools of the same religious order, we find that the proportion desiring, and even more expecting, to enter private or public employment varies appreciably in the eight Spains. In San Sebastian in the core of bourgeois Spain 90 per cent want to enter private activities and none want public life, while in Madrid the proportions are 68 per cent and 31 per cent respectively, and in Ciudad Real, a typi-

42. Data from a study by Juan González Anleo.

43. See the article by the authors: "El Prestigio de Profesiones en el Mundo Empresarial," *Revista de Estudios Políticos*, No. 128 (1963), pp. 23–76, and No. 129–30 (1963), pp. 5–31, for a detailed analysis of these data.

cal provincial city of gentry in transition, they are 39 per cent and 43 per cent.[44]

The effects of differential recruitment are reinforced, at least in the case of businessmen, by limited geographic mobility.[45] Among a sample of Spanish businessmen loaded toward the top of the elite in 13 of the most industrial provinces, 69 per cent own or direct companies (including some small ones between 50 and 100 workers) in the same province in which they were born. In France in six of the most industrial regions the proportion born in the same region was 50 per cent and in the five main industrial regions 57 per cent. What is more, among Barcelona businessmen 71 per cent were born there, and in Guipúzcoa up to 76 per cent. In the U.S. the largest proportion—62 per cent—of natives is found among the executives of the Central Northeast. These differences in geographic mobility are not without consequences since our data show outsiders more open to new ideas, more modern, and playing very different roles in the power structure of the business community.

Few data can show better the integral heterogeneity of Spanish elites by region than those on the education of businessmen, itself a very homogeneous and small elite. In Biscay 58 per cent of them had university or higher technical education, while in Barcelona the proportion was 36 per

44. Data from the study by Juan González Anleo. An Italian survey found a similar pattern of regional differences, with 38% of those in the North preferring private firms and 32% a public agency, compared to 21% and 55% in the South. In view of such preferences it cannot be surprising that the Italians speak of "meridionalizzazione" of the civil service. Quoted by Joseph LaPalombara, "Italy," in Lucian Pye and Sidney Verba, eds., *Political Culture and Political Development* (Princeton, Princeton University Press, 1965), p. 307. Alessandro Taradel, "La burocrazia italiana: provenienza e collazione dei direttori generali," *Tempi Moderni, 6* (1963), 12–13, quoted by LaPalombara, "Italy." The South and the Islands with 37.6% of the population contributed 62.5% of the *direttori generali* (highest official beneath the cabinet level), while the North with 36.8% contributed only 11.5%.

45. For more detail on the regional origin of business elites and their internal migration in comparative perspective see: "Movilidad geográfica de los empresarios españoles," *Estudios Geográficos, 25* (February 1964), 5–29, by the authors of this chapter. For references to the French and United States data, see ibid.

cent, in Madrid it was 63 per cent, and in Levante 28 per cent. Even comparing directors of companies with over 1,000 workers in Biscay and Barcelona the difference is still great,

Table 13.5. Number of Voluntary Associations per 100,000 Population (1959) and Membership in the Women's Section of the Falangist Party

	Per total provincial population (per 100,000)	*Per population of provincial capitals & equally important cities (per 100,000)*	*Per provincial population excluding capitals & equally important cities (per 100,000)*	*Sección Femenina of F.E.T. y de las JONS per 1,000 female population*
Bourgeois	39	60	28	10.6
Proletarian in transition	27	63	19	14.1
Clases medias in transition	29	52	20	15.4
Madrid	56	*	*	15.2
Clases medias	22	57	15	16.5
Gentry in transition	22	39	16	12.7
Gentry	15	29	11	13.2
Proletarian	17	34	13	15.7
National average	27	46	19	13.4
Total associations or members	8,239	4,275	3,964	212,282

* Since the population of Madrid province compared to Madrid city is very small, these distinctions are not made.

with many of the former having more than one degree and almost all one, while in Barcelona the proportion of those holding a degree is 65 per cent.[46]

46. Amando de Miguel and Juan J. Linz, "Nivel de estudios del empresariado español," *Arbor* (March 1964), pp. 33–65. In the same article the reader will find the references to comparable data for other countries. The data of Nicole Delefortrie-Soubeyroux for the French business elite show that the maximum regional difference is between the East and Aquitania—23 percentage points—(compared to 35 between Madrid and Levante), and the next largest is between Paris and Provence—5 percentage points. In the U.S. the largest difference in the proportion with college educations was between the North and the Midwest, 1 percentage point, according to W. L. Warner and J. C. Abegglen.

Differences in Social Mobilization: Voluntary Association Membership

The differences in economic development, education, and cultural values are reflected in differences in the rate of social mobilization—e.g. involvement in organized activities, exposure to mass media—and this in turn affects the feelings of social and political effectiveness.[47] Sociologists since de Tocqueville have been aware of the importance of the myriad of nonpolitical voluntary associations for social integration and the viability of democratic vs. radical politics. We were able to obtain data on 8,329 associations registered with the Spanish Ministry of Interior (in 1959), ranging from social clubs and bullfighters' fan groups to professional or business interest groups.[48] The number of such associations per 100,000 population (for want of information on membership) gives us an idea of their importance in different regions. The data furthermore allow us to distinguish the provincial capitals and comparably larger cities from the rest of the province and to control for the different weight of the rural population, considerably lower in associativity.

If we compare the rates for the eight Spains, bourgeois Spain is highest, followed by clases medias in transition—indicating the relation to economic development—while gentry and proletarian Spain are far below. For obvious reasons Madrid, the national capital, stands out. Clases medias is in between as is gentry in transition. Limiting our attention to the provincial capitals, the pattern is not changed much, except that clases medias (the provincial cities of Castile with their middle class and more integrated social structure) stand out beyond what we could expect if the only factor were economic development, compared to gentry Spain and even gentry in transition. Within the nonurban population

47. The concept of social mobilization was formulated by Deutsch, pp. 100–04, and subsequently in his article "Social Mobilization and Political Development," *American Political Science Review, 55* (1961), 493–514.

48. We are indebted to Manuel Chacón Secos, *Director General de Política Interior*, and D. Miguel Angel Pérez de la Canal for facilitating access to these data.

associativity also diminishes from bourgeois to gentry Spain.

The index is particularly high in Catalonia (43.8), the Balearic Islands (42.6)—in the same culture area as Catalonia—Navarre (42.1), and the Basque provinces (38.4). The high rate in the less industrialized provinces in the Catalan and Basque culture area (like Navarre) and in the countryside of those provinces, indicates that we are dealing with a culture trait and not only with a correlate of economic development. However, economic development reinforces the tendency; so Guipúzcoa, with its industrial development down into the small towns, has the highest index in Spain for provinces (54 per 100,000) and its capital, San Sebastian, the second highest for cities (75 per 100,000). In fact, the correlation with per capita income is +.79, the highest we have found between two not obviously related indicators.

It is interesting to explore the "compositional effect" that this tendency to join voluntary associations has when it comes to joining the *Sección Femenina* (the women's organization of the Falange)[49] in the Basque country or regions with autonomist sentiments, a large working class, and strong Catholic loyalties which favor Women's Catholic Action over the party organization. The national average affiliation rate to the S.F. is 13 per 1,000, and the Basque country rate is only slightly lower (10 per 1,000), still as high as in regions like Andalusia (10 per 1,000) where one of the nuclei of the party existed in the Republic. It is in the Balearic Islands and the Levante, however, where the tendency to join *any* association is strong—together with Old Castile where the party had some of its earliest strongholds—that the membership rate is highest.

Among businessmen we find those of Guipúzcoa, where family businesses predominate, together with those of Barcelona, more likely to express a favorable opinion about the interest groups representing their interests than businessmen of other provinces. This favorable opinion is not limited to the more or less autonomous and locally created groups, but

49. Data obtained from the statistical service of the Sección Femenina by courtesy of Ana García Bernal.

extends to the officially created corporate structure (*Sindicatos*); even though in this province it is the least esteemed organization it is still esteemed more than in all other provinces studied.

The youth study included this item: "There are people who argue that to get somewhere in this world it is necessary to be a member of associations. Do you think it is important to be a member of associations? Or do you think that it is preferable to act individually?" The lowest preference for association appears in proletarian Spain (33 per cent) followed by gentry (41 per cent) while in bourgeois Spain it is 49 per cent (unexpectedly, proletarian in transition was very high even though we knew that Santander was high in associativity). The explicit preference for individual action is most frequent in gentry Spain, where the number of those reporting that their father is a member of some association is also lowest. This also is the case in gentry and proletarian Spain for the official party, with only 3 per cent in gentry reporting that their father is affiliated with it.

POLITICS AND ELECTIONS

The last national election in which multiple and ideologically distinct parties competed was in February 1936.[50] Since then there have taken place only an institutional referendum in 1947 and partial municipal elections. The 1936 election preceded by a few months the Civil War and its returns have been the object of disagreement of Left and

50. The data on the seats gained by different parties in 1936 are from the official list of members of the parliament: Cortes de 1936, *Lista de Señores Diputados, Junio 1936*, pp. 113–31, listing party factions, and the preceding pages listing deputies by districts. The electoral data are from José Venegas, *Las Elecciones del Frente Popular* (Buenos Aires, Publicaciones del Patronato Hispano-Argentino de Cultura, n.d.) with some adjustments made for disputed elections (Cuenca and Granada) to the best of our ability. The disagreements and partisan arguments and the absence of really official data make the analysis of the 1936 election virtually impossible. The Nationalist case is stated in Estado Español, Ministerio de la Gobernación, *Apendice I al Dictamen de la Comisión sobre Ilegitimidad de los Poderes Actuantes en 18 de Julio de 1936* (n.p., Editora Nacional, 1939), pp. 29–129. Due to the electoral law a disagreement about the count of a few votes affects considerably the assignment of seats to one or the other of the two coalitions.

Right. This and the electoral law that led to the formation of the two blocs—the Popular Front and the Right coalition—in which the different parties submerged their identity, plus the fact that the province (except for the largest cities) was the electoral unit, create great difficulties for sociological analysis. However, there can be no question that the two poles of leftist support were bourgeois-industrial Spain and proletarian and gentry Spain, with the two transitional areas close to the national average and the clases medias the backbone of the Right.

If we take the two main parties, the PSOE (Socialists) and the CEDA (a conservative Christian Democratic party), we can specify the relationship between politics and social structure further. Unfortunately, in the absence of a separate vote by party, we have to use the data on the number of seats allocated to each within the electoral blocs. Gentry and, even more, proletarian Spain elected a large proportion of PSOE deputies, showing how important the agrarian working class was for the party (a factor that helps to explain the radicalization in the thirties of this essentially reformist trade-union based party). In comparison, bourgeois-industrial Spain gave only limited support to the PSOE, competing there with the Izquierda Republicana (Azaña's anticlerical and antimilitary middle-class party, with its probable appeal to the intelligentsia, the lower middle class and the white-collar employees), and in Catalonia and the Basque country with the regionalist parties, particularly the leftist Catalan Esquerre. That party benefited from the anarchist vote, which, while breaking with the antiparliamentarism of their organizations, preferred the nonsocialist Popular Front candidates. In 1933 when the PSOE fought the election alone this pattern was even more visible. The Izquierda Republicana in 1936 was the third party and its strength was in the transitional areas and in clases medias rather than in the bourgeois areas where the regional parties gained the votes it could have obtained in their absence. In gentry and proletarian Spain the lines of class conflict were more clearly drawn: the Socialists on the left and the more

TABLE 13.6. POLITICAL ALIGNMENTS IN THE "EIGHT SPAINS"

	% of seats gained in 1933 by the PSOE	*% of seats gained in 1936* [a]			*% of the popular vote for parties of the Right in 1936*	*% voting yes in the Institutional Referendum 1947*
		PSOE 1936	*IR 1936*	*CEDA 1936*		
Bourgeois	8	20	14	9	44	76
Proletarian in transition	7	19	19	19	47	84
Clases medias in transition	2	12	22	24	49	83
Madrid	60	40	24	24	45	75
Clases medias	1.5	5	17	28	60	86
Gentry in transition	5	24	22	31	50	89
Gentry	17	35	15	14	50	85
Proletarian	35	45	11	6	43	84
National average	12	21	18	19	49 [b]	82 (17,178,812) [c]

a. The total number of deputies in the 1936 Republican *Cortes* was 473.
b. 4,277,029 votes of a total of 8,722,069.
c. Total eligible voters, *Anuario Estadístico de 1948*.

conservative parties on the right. The CEDA, with its main strength in the gentry in transition and clases medias Spain, was probably competing for the more clerical sector of the urban middle class and the traditional peasantry, groups which when secularized would give some support to Azaña. The weakness of the IR and the CEDA in gentry and particularly proletarian Spain indicates how these two parties, which, with very divergent programs, could have been the core of a democratic republic with wide appeal, could not prosper in the absence of numerically strong clases medias and a stable peasantry. Their weakness in bourgeois–industrial Spain, due to the regional issue (in part an outgrowth of the tension between bourgeoisie and clases medias), which forced them to work respectively with not always reliable allies like the *Esquerra* and the *Lliga* (the conservative Catalanist party), helped to complicate the political process and added to the instability of the Republic.

The map of the February elections has much in common with the alignment of forces immediately after the uprising in July 1936 as well as with the emergence of practically autonomous regional or local political units.[51] All clases medias supported the rising army while only two borderline provinces of bourgeois Spain did so. In the remaining six the organized working class got control of the situation. The fate of clases medias in transition provinces was decided by their geographic location: those close to Barcelona went Republican and those close to the core of clases medias were controlled by the Nationalists. The farm laborers of gentry and proletarian Spain (where they were reinforced by miners) could control initially much of the countryside and some of the cities with a small middle class. The military and middle class, however, soon controlled key regional capitals like Seville, Cadiz, Granada, and Cordova; from there, with the help of the troops brought over from Morocco, they gained

51. These units, reflecting the class and ideological alignments in the population of the Republican territory after the uprising had completely shaken the official authority structure, until its reconsolidation, are well described by Carlos M. Rama, *La Crisis Española del Siglo XX* (México, Fondo de Cultura Económica, 1960), pp. 294–316.

control of the area and linked it with the northern core of clases medias Spain. The capacity to resist of the radicalized but not well organized farm laborers could not be compared with that of the urban workers of industrial Spain.

The 1947 referendum that combined a plebiscite in favor of Franco with a referendum on the future "basic law" showed that it was still bourgeois–industrial Spain where the opposition could manifest itself most effectively by *not voting,* voting *void,* or explicitly *no,* while the clases medias and gentry in transition gave the regime its strongest support.[52]

In recent years the affinity between democratic attitudes, economic development, and social modernization has been the object of discussion. The authoritarianism of the underprivileged classes, even when they identify with democratic parties, has been noted. Our data were based on answers to the following question:[53] "In other countries it has often been asked if it was preferable: (1) that each and all of us should take an interest in the politics of the country and should consider ourselves responsible for them; or (2) that an outstanding man should have all the authority and decide for us. Toward which of these alternatives are you more inclined?" The ratio in favor of one man vs. all of us is highest in proletarian and gentry Spain and lowest in Madrid, the two transitional areas, and bourgeois Spain. This ratio, which we might call "submissiveness potential," tends to be higher among the rural population but, even limiting ourselves to students and occupationally active youth, it is lowest in Madrid, Basque country, Catalonia, and Old Castile, while it is highest in Andalusia and latifundia Spain. It is important to note that clases medias Spain, and specifically Old Castile—economically underdeveloped, traditional in many respects, with above average religiosity, the core of Franco's support—showed itself favorable to the participa-

52. Referendum para la Ley de sucesion a la Jefatura del Estado, July 6, 1947. See *Anuario Estadístico de España 1948.*

53. The question is a slightly modified version of one used by EMNID, Institut für Meinungsforschung, in their study: *Jugend zwischen 15 und 24: Zweite Untersuchung zur Situation der deutschen Jugend im Bundesgebiet* (Bielefeld, 1955), pp. 238–40.

tive alternative. Further internal comparisons of responses to such questions in a country like Spain suggest that cultural rather than structural–economic factors (like social integration) should be considered.[54]

RELIGION AND VALUES

Various indicators confirm the impression that the religious climate in different regions and sections of the country is very different. Data like responses to a national survey, membership in Catholic Action organizations, and number of candidates for the priesthood point in the same direction (even when a more detailed analysis might show interesting differences, like those due to cultural tendencies to associativity). Among youth of all classes the proportion who openly admit to be not practicing is lowest in clases medias Spain and highest in Madrid, proletarian, and gentry in transition, and slightly less in bourgeois–industrial Spain. However, to speak of bourgeois Spain in this context as a unit is certainly misleading. Although relatively homogeneous for certain purposes, when we come to religiosity it has to be broken down into distinct culture areas: Catalonia and the Basque country could not be more different in their religiosity. The data on religious vocations,[55] membership in Catholic Action, and the survey data on religious practice and the birth rates[56] all point in the same direction. The

54. The cross-national comparison of such findings by class and socioeconomic development in the context of a quite different political system can also be fruitful in the exploration of hypotheses like those advanced by Lipset on working class authoritarianism. Certainly the more educated, more privileged groups in Spain, when they express this opinion, are not reflecting a civic textbook culture of democratic values, as we could suspect of their American peers, but they still reflect some of the same values, giving added strength to the importance attributed to structural factors rather than those of ideological indoctrination.

55. The monograph by Severino Aznar, *La Revolución Española y las Vocaciones Eclesiásticas* (Madrid, Instituto de Estudios Políticos, 1949), documents in great detail the differences in religiosity, as reflected by the number of aspirants to the priesthood by region and class, and the changes produced by the anticlerical tensions of the mid-thirties.

56. The different religiosity of the Basque country and Catalonia, the two most industrialized regions, probably helps to account for the very different birth rates (Barcelona, 19.08, Biscay, 24.43, and Guipúzcoa, 24.27); that is

Table 13.7. Religiosity and Attitudes among Male Youth 16–20 in the "Eight Spains"

	% of youth answering that they do not practice Catholic religion	*% not receiving communion or receiving it less than once a year*	*% perceiving a two-class structure*	*"Submissive vs. participation ratio"* [a]	*% who don't expect equal treatment by the police*	*"Ratio favoring European vs. Latin-American integration"* [b]	*Sample size*
Bourgeois	9	15	16	.82	16	1.31	(253)
Proletarian in transition	3	7	15	1.43	18	2.12	(60)
Clases medias in transition	4	17	20	.86	19	1.24	(141)
Madrid	13	22	14	.42	16	1.88	(97)
Clases medias	2	13	20	.73	19	.78	(127)
Gentry in transition	13	19	19	.48	17	.72	(174)
Gentry	5	18	39	1.13	23	.87	(379)
Proletarian	13	44	45	2.78	25	.56	(87)
National average	7	20	25	.88	19	1.01	(1318)

a. Ratio between those saying "an outstanding man should have all the authority and decide for us" and those opting for "each and all of us should take an interest in the politics of the country and should consider ourselves responsible for them."

b. Ratio between those who favor the entry of Spain into a European union and those who favor the entry of Spain into a Latin American union of nations.

membership rate for male Catholic Action in the Basque provinces is 13.9 per 1,000 and 7.4 in Catalonia, when the national average is 5.5; while the female organization rates are respectively 32, 13, and 16 per thousand. The low membership ratios in economically underdeveloped areas like Andalusia, Extremadura, and Galicia and the differences between two highly industrialized areas suggest that industrialization does not account for de-Christianization in Spain. The picture is rounded by adding to the a-religious those not complying with the minimum requirement set by the Church of receiving communion at least once a year. The proportion in that case is highest in the proletarian provinces, followed by Madrid and the two sections of gentry Spain. In contrast, bourgeois, clases medias in transition (two fairly developed areas), and above all clases medias Spain show less non-practice.[57]

The contextual analysis shows that such differences are not only due to the different class composition of the population of different regions. Certainly the peasants of industrial Spain contribute to its religiosity, but in the Basque country the religiosity extends to all classes, including the working class, and the same is probably true for some parts of clases medias; while the difference between classes in Andalusia is probably more marked than in other regions.

EXCURSUS ON "SOCIAL MOBILIZATION" AND "SOCIAL COMMUNICATION"

The data we have just presented on differences in the recruitment of elites, voluntary association membership, and religious participation suggest a problem in the study of intranation differentiation: How can such differences be

---

true even for the capital cities (Barcelona, 20.03, Bilbao, 25.94, and San Sebastian—a less industrial city than the surrounding area—37.84). Barcelona province ranks 34th among the 50 provinces and Biscay 6th, the respective capitals 48th and 37th. (Data for 1962 from *Anuario Estadístico, 1963*, p. 468). The differences between the industrial provinces of Barcelona and Biscay are comparable to those between Finland (19.9) and Portugal (23.6).

57. Data from the National Youth Study.

made compatible with national integration? The problem arises if we consider that such data suggest very different rates of social mobilization, which should facilitate or be an obstacle for political mobilization, self-consciousness, awareness of real or potential or imaginary interests, etc. The idea of a pluralistic society assumes that out of such conflicting interests some compromise will emerge, but that assumption may well require that all major sectors should be minimally aware of their interests and mobilized, not sporadically, but with some continuity. If the mobilization is limited to some sectors and particularly if those sectors think or feel that they do not share in key power structures, considerable tensions are likely to arise.

Perhaps we need to add to social mobilization another dimension, that we call "social communication" within a society. This lack of communication was called "particularism" by Ortega y Gasset in his *Invertebrate Spain*.[58] He described this phenomenon in the following terms:

> It is neither important nor necessary that the component parts of a society coincide in their ideas and their desires; the important, the essential thing is that each should know, and to a certain extent incorporate in his own life, the ideas and desires of others.
>
> Each group lives hermetically sealed within itself. It feels not the slightest curiosity about what happens to its fellow groups. They all revolve about each other like stellar worlds which mutually ignore each other's existence. Polarized around their own professional affairs, they know nothing of those that rule the lives of neighboring groups. Ideas, emotions, values created within one professional nucleus or one class do not, in the least degree, transcend it and pass to the others. The gigantic force which is exercised against one point of the social sphere is never transmitted to another. It dies where it is born.
>
> It is hard to imagine a society less elastic than ours;

58. Cf. note 10, supra.

> that is to say, hard to imagine a human agglomeration which is less a society (pp. 44–45).

And a few pages earlier he applied this conception to the problem of social integration:

> "The essence of particularism is that each group ceases to feel itself part of a whole, and therefore ceases to share the feelings of the rest." The hopes and needs of the others mean nothing to it, and it does nothing to help them win their hearts' desires . . . hypersensitiveness to one's own ailments is a characteristic of this social state. Disagreements or difficulties which are easily borne during periods of cohesion come to be intolerable when the spirit of a national life in common has disintegrated.

And in a footnote he referred to the regional problem (at that time an object of heated discussion):

> There are few things so indicative of the present state of affairs as the contention of Basques and Catalans that they are peoples "oppressed" by the rest of Spain. The privileged place which they enjoy is so evident as to make this complaint seem grotesque. But anyone more interested in understanding men than in judging them will do well to note that this feeling is sincere. It is all a matter of relativity. A man condemned to live with a woman he does not love will find her caresses as irritating as the rub of chains (pp. 36–37).

We are aware of some of the indicators of social mobilization but our knowledge about the processes of "social communication" that make differences in development compatible with national and social integration is so limited that we have not even started to look for indicators. Certainly the interlocking of elites, in terms of family origins, intermarriage, and overlap in position, should be analyzed from this perspective, rather than being totally critical or viewing these overlapping groups as conspiratorial, as it is usually done in much of the literature. Cross-national and cross-regional studies of the interlocking and communication among elites (starting with such simple indicators as mutual acquaintance, frequency and type of interaction, number and type of contacts with national leaders, etc.) would be one way to start looking into this problem area.

14. West Berlin—Center or Periphery? *

RICHARD L. MERRITT, YALE UNIVERSITY

Regional within-nation differences have long been an outstanding feature of the German scene. Political aspects of this phenomenon, such as the question of regional representation in a national government, have plagued generations of politicians, constitutional lawyers, and political analysts alike. On few issues in recent political theory, perhaps, has so much ink been spent as on the *Staatenbund–Bundesstaat* dispute. Its practical implications made themselves felt in the constitutions of the Bismarckian empire, the Weimar Republic, and the Bonn Republic. The theoretical implications of German regionalism and its effects upon the political integration of the country as a whole have occupied scholars on both sides of the Atlantic.[1]

* I would like to thank the Social Science Research Council and the Carnegie Corporation for their generous support of this project.

1. For a general summary of this point, see Carl J. Friedrich, *Constitutional Government and Democracy: Theory and Practice in Europe and America* (rev. ed. Boston, Ginn, 1950), pp. 189–221. On the question of regional differentiation and party factionalism, see Arnold Brecht, *Federalism and Regionalism in Germany: The Division of Prussia* (New York, Oxford, 1945), and Rudolf Heberle, *From Democracy to Nazism* (Baton Rouge, Louisiana State University Press, 1945). On the geographical side, see Robert E. Dickinson, *Germany: A General and Regional Geography* (New York, Dutton, 1953). Three current studies—by Erwin K. Scheuch and Rudolf Wildenmann; Kurt Shell and Otto Stammer; and Klaus Liepelt —are integrating survey data with census, electoral, and content analysis

In any regionally differentiated political community, the center–periphery issue is crucial. The political integration of the community often rests upon the emergence of a predominant and popularly accepted national core area, or upon the creation of a satisfactory balance among regional centers. The Swiss found unity in the context of regional diversity. The French virtually reduced the rest of their country to a periphery for the Parisian center. Eighteenth- and nineteenth-century Americans, streaming westward to form new urban centers in newly opened regions, continued to look to the eastern seaboard as their source of government and political guidance. The German solution to the center–periphery problem, however, has been neither so successful nor so permanent as the Swiss, French, and American examples.

Traditionally, and not entirely in a jocular vein, Berliners have considered their city to be the hub of the world. A review of recent history would lend support to this notion in many respects. For three quarters of a century, from the country's unification in 1871 under Bismarck until its division into four occupation zones in 1945, Berlin was capital of all Germany. This is not to say that loyalties to regional population centers did not exist—nor even that all segments of the German people were equally willing to accept the preeminence of Berlin. Indeed, Berlin was the symbol of Prussian militarism to many, of cosmopolitan decadence to others, of rampant socialism to still others. Regardless of the cries of dissidents or the claims of other cities, however, Berlin was Germany's center, and the rest of Germany was Berlin's periphery.

The years of unity found Berlin more than just the administrative center of the Wilhelminian Reich, the Weimar Republic, and Hitler's "Third Reich." The city was Germany's financial capital, its commercial capital, and its political capital. Berlin was the main node of the communi-

---

data in an effort to learn about the effects of regionalism, among other things. Cf. Kurt. L. Shell, *Bedrohung und Bewährung: Führung und Bevölkerung in der Berlin-Krise* (Cologne and Opladen, Westdeutscher Verlag, 1965).

cation and transportation net that covered Germany. Newspapers from Berlin were daily reading matter in the provinces. Its café society set tastes and fashions for all Germany. The artistic movements that the city generated spread not only throughout Germany, but throughout the entire world as well. The theater of Hauptmann, Reinhardt, and Brecht, for instance, was known and appreciated in dramatic circles everywhere. In short, by the end of the Weimar era Berlin had become *a* if not *the* leading metropolis of Europe. And after Hitler's rise to power in 1933 the city became the source of decisions that exasperated, startled, and eventually shattered the traditional international system with its traditional ways of looking at and doing things.

In the world that emerged after the ultimate defeat of Hitler in its bomb-gutted bunkers, Berlin again became a focal point of attention and tension. This time, however, the city was not the scene of the traditional German struggle between Potsdam and Weimar, between the militaristic spirit of Prussianism and the liberal, humanitarian spirit of Goethe and Beethoven. Rather, it became the scene of battle between two ideologically oriented world powers, the Soviet Union and the United States.

As Berlin was assuming a new and different role in the political system of the world, so too its function for Germany as a whole changed. By dividing Germany into four zones of occupation and decentralizing its economic and political structures, the victorious Allies specifically denied to Berlin many of the functions that it had traditionally performed. The city's banks, for instance, could no longer operate in Saxony or in Bavaria; nor could political organizations be formed that crossed zonal boundaries. And even after these institutions were merged in the three western zones in 1947 and 1948 no great effort was made to locate their central offices in the old capital city. The Allies also divided Berlin itself into four occupation sectors and isolated the entire city from its geographic environment. The Soviet sector eventually became the capital of the communist German Democratic Republic—although it did not attain many of the attributes of a capital city until after August 1961 when the East Germans forcibly separated their part of Berlin from the West by building a wall of brick and barbed wire.

The status of West Berlin, however, remained clouded and anomalous. Technically it continued to be governed by the three Western occupying powers. The Western Allies resisted the efforts of West German constitution writers to include West Berlin as a state in the West German federal system. Despite this, the Allies, no less than the governments of West Berlin and the German Federal Republic, have done much in the years since 1949 to tie West Berlin to West Germany: constitutional measures enabling representatives of the city to participate in federal decision-making processes and providing for the semiautomatic adoption of federal laws in West Berlin; economic measures such as tax preferences and subsidies to encourage commercial and industrial firms to remain in the city or to move at least some of their offices or factories to West Berlin; and provisions permitting many of the city's social organizations, including political parties, labor unions, and sport clubs, to be an integral part of the West German social fabric.

Institutional arrangements, however, often tell us little about the political processes that are important, such as the human links of communication between West Berliners and their fellow citizens in the Federal Republic. How have the events of the past two decades affected these ties of community? What differences in perspectives have emerged? Has Berlin remained Germany's center? Or, more properly, has West Berlin become the center—politically, economically, socially, and, most important, psychologically—of the West German Federal Republic or, alternatively, is the island-city only peripheral to the new German state?

One approach to answering such questions lies in large-scale public opinion surveying. Unfortunately, few studies of public opinion have specifically tried to contrast the attitudes and perceptions of West Berliners with those held by their West German contemporaries. From an examination of a variety of sources of data, however, it is possible to piece together the essential relationships into a consistent pattern. Wherever possible this chapter will deal with three sets of data: views and attitudes held by West Berliners, by the West German population at large, and by West German respondents living in cities with 100,000 or more inhabitants. In most cases the attitudes of West Berliners and of West German urbanites stem from sample surveys of the entire West German population. Thus, in a survey in which the total number of respondents is about 2,000, the number of those residing in West Berlin may be close to 100, and those in other major West German cities close to 500. It is imperative, therefore, that these data not be overinterpreted. But even with this caveat in mind, it is remarkable how consistent a picture of differences between West Berliners and West Germans these small sample sizes present.

West Berliners do not seem to differ significantly from West German urbanites on nonpolitical topics. To take a simple example, in four separate surveys from October 1952 to July 1960 Germans were asked whether or not they would like a life without work. As may be seen in Table 14.1, the re-

TABLE 14.1. WEST BERLIN AND WEST GERMAN PREFERENCES FOR A LIFE WITHOUT WORK

Question: "Do you believe that it would be nicest to live without having to work?"

	West Berliners (N=379)	*West German Urbanites * (N=2131)*	*Other West Germans (N=c.5643)*
Yes	16%	16%	13%
No	77	79	82
Undecided	7	6	6
Total	100%	101%	101%

* In cities with populations of more than 100,000 (excluding West Berlin).

Source: Institut für Demoskopie, Allensbach-am-Bodensee; cumulated data from surveys of October 1952, March 1955 (in which total N is estimated), June 1958, and July 1960.

sponses of West Berliners did not differ to any important degree from those of West German urbanites, although it would appear that the West German population not living in cities was slightly more disinclined than the metropolitans to prefer a life without work. Similarly, it is a maxim among West German market researchers that the residents of Berlin are not very different from the residents of other large cities regarding their tastes in clothes, automobiles, household utensils, and other consumer goods. Periodically, for instance, the Institut für Demoskopie presents a picture of four living rooms decorated in different styles, asking respondents to state which style they would prefer for their own living rooms. Again it turns out that West Berlin respondents are closer in their preferences to inhabitants of other large West German cities than either group is to the rest of the West German population (Table 14.2). The four surveys shown in composite form in Table 14.2 also indicate that shifts over time from May 1955 to March 1962 were roughly similar for all three groups.

TABLE 14.2. WEST BERLIN AND WEST GERMAN PREFERENCES FOR STYLES OF LIVING-ROOM FURNITURE

	West Berliners (N=391)	*West German Urbanites * (N=2174)*	*Other West Germans (N=5321)*
Style 1 (Danish modern)	34%	36%	32%
Style 2 (Middle-class standard)	38	38	46
Style 3 (Wilhelminian Imperial)	3	3	3
Style 4 (Futuristic)	20	20	16
Undecided	5	4	3
Total	100%	101%	100%

* In cities with populations of more than 100,000 (excluding West Berlin).

Source: Institut für Demoskopie, Allensbach-am-Bodensee; cumulated data from surveys of May 1955, June 1958, September 1960, and March 1962.

If we turn from nonpolitical to political topics, we get an entirely different picture of the similarities and variations between West Berlin and West German attitudes. One fairly consistent pattern is that West Berliners are more informed about events and are more likely to have opinions about them than is the case with West Germans. Surveys performed by

American occupation authorities as well as by local German research agencies from 1946–64 indicate that the percentage of respondents with no opinion or who answer "don't know" to questions on political issues is between 5 and 20 percentage points higher in West Germany than in West Berlin. Consider, for example, a survey performed in the spring of 1959 by the Deutsches Institut für Volksumfragen (DIVO) on a topic about which there was a generally high level of awareness (Table 14.3). The average level of awareness about NATO among West Berliners was 5 percentage points

TABLE 14.3. WEST BERLIN AND WEST GERMAN AWARENESS OF NATO

	West Berliners (N=320)	*West German Urbanites * (N=260)*	*Other West Germans (N=546)*
Had heard or read of North Atlantic Treaty Organization	95%	92%	86%
Aware that the United States is a NATO member	88	82	73
Aware that West Germany is a NATO member	86	85	79
Aware that the Soviet Union is not a NATO member	91	81	74
Average level of awareness about NATO	90%	85%	78%

* In cities with populations of more than 100,000 (excluding West Berlin).

Source: Research Staff, United States Information Service, American Embassy, Germany, *Reports*, Series No. 3, Report No. C-25 (6 July 1959); the survey was performed by DIVO G.m.b.H., Frankfurt/Main.

above that of metropolitans in West Germany and 12 percentage points above that of the rest of the West German population. Moreover, besides being more knowledgeable, available survey data reveal that West Berliners take a more active interest in political topics. In response to the question, "Approximately how often do you discuss political questions?" 64 per cent of a sample of 1,395 West Berlin young people said either "daily" or "several times during the week," as against only 29 per cent of a sample of 167 young people from the West German city of Hamburg who made similar responses.[2] This greater awareness of and interest in politics on the part of West Berliners will also be apparent in the remaining surveys reviewed in this chapter. (The characteristic that West Berliners have opinions more frequently than other Germans will not, by the way, greatly surprise the reader familiar with the Berliner's reputation

TABLE 14.4. WEST BERLIN AND WEST GERMAN ATTITUDES TOWARD NAZISM

	US Sector of Berlin (N=199)	*US Zone of Germany * (N=993)*
1. Percentage who believe that Nazi regime began and must bear responsibility for World War II	59%	56%
2. Percentage who think that the individual should *not* always obey the orders of the State without question	65	53
3. Percentage who think National Socialism was a bad idea (not a good idea badly carried out)	51	37
4. Percentage professing they never had any faith in Hitler or didn't believe in Hitler	51	35
5. Percentage *not* agreeing that parts of Europe with considerable German minorities, e.g. Sudetenland, should be legally reincorporated into Germany	51	38
6. Percentage *not* agreeing that international Jewry profited from World War II	92	73
7. Percentage *not* agreeing that the Nordic race is superior to all other races in the world	77	70
Average percentage of "anti-Nazi" responses	64%	52%

* Includes Bavaria, Hesse, and Wuerttemberg-Baden.

Source: Surveys Branch, Office of the Director of Information Control, OMGUS (Rear), *Reports*, Series No. 1, Report No. 22 (25 September 1946).

for his "grosse Schnauze" or, in good Brooklynese, "big lip.")

On specific aspects of the political process, such as preferred form of government and views of recent German history, West Berliners seem somewhat more "liberal" than West Germans. Looking backward, first of all, West Berliners see themselves as having been more opposed to the Nazi

2. Institut für angewandte Sozialwissenschaft, *Berliner Jugend 1962* (Bad Godesburg, 1962), p. 36.

regime than do inhabitants of southern Germany. (Electoral data from the early 1930s would substantiate this perception.) The average percentage of persons giving "anti-Nazi" responses to the seven questions listed in Table 14.4, for instance, was 64 per cent in West Berlin and only 52 per cent in Bavaria, Hesse, and Baden–Wuerttemberg. One and a half decades later West Berlin youth expressed a much more intense desire to learn about the Nazi past than did a sample of young people in Hamburg: Asked about the extent to which the Third Reich should be discussed in classroom in-

TABLE 14.5. WEST BERLIN AND WEST GERMAN PREFERENCES FOR A ONE-PARTY VS. A MULTIPARTY SYSTEM

Question: "Do you believe that it is better for a country to have one party so that the greatest possible unity obtains, or more than one party so that different opinions can be freely represented?"

	West Berliners (N=555)	*West German Urbanites* * *(N=3433)*	*Other West Germans (N=c.8532)*
One party	10%	16%	19%
More than one party	81	73	65
No parties at all	2	2	3
No opinion	8	9	13
Total	101%	100%	100%

* In cities with populations of more than 100,000 (excluding West Berlin).

Source: Institut für Demoskopie, Allensbach-am-Bodensee; cumulated data from surveys of September 1950, April 1953, May 1954, May 1955, May 1959, and June 1961 (in which total N is estimated).

struction, 79 per cent of West Berlin youth responded "as completely as possible" and 12 per cent "as briefly as possible"; comparable figures for Hamburg youth were 60 per cent and 24 per cent respectively.[3] Regarding their present form of government, West Berliners are somewhat more inclined than are West Germans to favor traditional democratic institutions. Six times from September 1950 to June 1961 the Institut für Demoskopie asked national samples about their preferences for a single-party as opposed to a multiparty system (Table 14.5). Over the entire eleven years,

3. Ibid., p. 122.

81 per cent of West Berliners indicated a preference for a multiparty system, whereas only 73 per cent of West German metropolitans and 65 per cent of the remaining portion of the West German population did so. Earlier, during the months when the West Germans were setting up their Federal Republic, surveys conducted for the American occupation authorities revealed that greater percentages of West Berliners than West Germans felt it was possible for individuals to influence political parties, had attended a political meeting since the end of the war, considered it desirable that political meetings be held, understood what the term "democracy" meant, favored a democratic form of government for Germany, and understood their civil rights.[4] In the international sphere, too, West Berliners appear to be more "liberal" than West Germans: Buchanan and Cantril, for instance, found that in 1948 only 46 per cent of a random sample of West Germans in the British occupation zone favored the idea of a world government as against 58 per cent (66 per cent in 1949) in West Berlin.[5]

Differences between West Berliners and West Germans are even more marked in their views of and attitudes toward the international situation. Generally speaking, West Berliners are much more inclined to favor a pro-Western or even pro-American policy than are their countrymen in the Bonn Republic. The DIVO survey cited in Table 14.6 reveals that more than twice as many West Berliners as West German urbanites favor a strengthened German commitment to NATO. Buchanan and Cantril, in their cross-national survey of the late 1940s, found that, when asked to specify which of a list of words applied to Americans and to Russians, West Germans in the British Zone ascribed 8.6 positive characteristics to Americans for every negative characteristic, while identifying the Russians with only .4 positive characteristics for every negative one; the ratio of positive to negative terms

4. Surveys Branch, Office of the Director of Information Control, OMGUS (Rear), *Reports*, Series No. 1, Reports No. 167 (25 April 1949) and No. 191 (9 December 1949); Series No. 2, Report No. 15 (24 April 1950).

5. William Buchanan and Hadley Cantril et al., *How Nations See Each Other: A Study in Public Opinion* (Urbana, University of Illinois Press, 1953), pp. 155, 163.

for Americans among West Berliners was 12.9 to 1 in 1948 and 18.2 to 1 in 1949, and .3 positive terms to each negative term for Russians in both years.[6] Other surveys conducted in the postwar era demonstrate that West Berliners also are less hostile (and indeed are friendly) toward Allied occupation troops, more receptive to American cultural products, more favorably disposed to take a firm course of action against the Soviet Union, and more likely to view American foreign policy with favor.

Not only are West Berliners more pro-Western than their counterparts in the Federal Republic, they are more confident about Western defense measures as well (Table 14.6). They attribute to NATO a greater part of the credit for maintaining peace in Europe during the decade from 1949 to 1959; they have greater confidence in its effectiveness as a defense organization for Western Europe; and they are more inclined to feel that NATO will be of great assistance in maintaining German security in the future. Moreover, they tend to view the future of international politics with glasses that are rosier than those of West Germans. Asked to estimate whether America or Russia would be the more powerful 50 years in the future, the ratio of those in West Berlin responding "America" to those answering "Russia" (3.6 to 1) is well over three times as great as the ratios among the West German urban and nonurban populations (both with ratios of 1.1 to 1).[7]

The question arises at this point: Why do the perspectives and attitudes of West Berliners differ so from those of other West Germans? One possible explanation lies in the peculiar social structure of the city—the fact, for instance, that the median age of its population is considerably higher, or that the income per capita is lower than in other West German cities, or that the following of the Social Democratic Party is larger in West Berlin than elsewhere. To examine the ap-

6. Ibid., pp. 46, 169.

7. Institut für Demoskopie, Allensbach-am-Bodensee, surveys of August 1953, October–November 1955, November 1957, October 1959, and March 1962.

TABLE 14.6. WEST BERLIN AND WEST GERMAN VIEWS OF NATO EFFECTIVENESS

	West Berliners (N=320)	*West German Urbanites* (N=260)*	*Other West Germans (N=546)*
1. *Question:* "In the light of all you have heard up to the present time, how much confidence do you have in the effectiveness of NATO as a defense organization for Western Europe? Great deal, some, not very much, or none at all?"			
Great deal/Some	80%	67%	64%
Not very much/None at all	13	20	14
Don't know/Not aware of NATO	7	13	22
Total	100%	100%	100%
2. *Question:* "In the ten years since the establishment of NATO there has been no aggression in Europe. Do you feel that this has been exclusively due to NATO, largely due to the existence of NATO, or did NATO make only a minor contribution to peace or none at all?"			
Exclusively/Largely due to NATO	68%	49%	49%
Minor contribution/None at all	26	35	28
Don't know/Not aware of NATO	6	16	23
Total	100%	100%	100%
3. *Question:* "Of how much help will NATO be to us in maintaining our security in the future? A great deal, some, not very much, or none at all?"			
A great deal/Some	80%	68%	62%
Not very much/None at all	13	18	16
Don't know/Not aware of NATO	7	14	22
Total	100%	100%	100%
4. *Question:* "In view of present circumstances and what you have heard concerning NATO, do you think that we should withdraw from NATO, strengthen our contribution, or keep it about the same as it is now?"			
Withdraw	3%	8%	6%
Strengthen our contribution	36	16	19
Keep the same	55	63	57
Don't know	6	13	17
Total	100%	100%	99%

* In cities with populations of more than 100,000 (excluding West Berlin).

Source: Research Staff, United States Information Service, American Embassy, Germany, *Reports*, Series No. 3, Report No. C-25 (6 July 1959); the survey was performed by DIVO G.m.b.H., Frankfurt/Main.

propriateness of this explanation, the Institut für Demoskopie performed a detailed multivariate analysis of responses to three political and nonpolitical questions.[8] The technique was to construct a model "city" weighted as if West Berlin had the same social structure (in terms of sex, age, income, education, party preference, and religion distributions) as all other West German cities of more than 500,000 population. A comparison of the responses from the "real" West Berlin with those from the "model" West Berlin indicates that any difference in opinions between West Berliners and other *Bundesbürger* is not due to differences in social structure. This in turn suggests that differential attitudes stem from the peculiar environment of West Berlin, an environment quite different from that of any other West German metropolis.[9]

The years of separation and crisis that have confronted West Berliners have left their mark in the form of diverging political images and attitudes. What the data summarized above do not tell us is the nature of the interaction between the diverging populations. The three most plausible alternatives are that West Berlin could have remained Germany's center; that the political center of that part of Germany that did not fall into Soviet hands could have shifted from the banks of the Spree to some point in West Germany; and that a bicephalous political community could have emerged along the lines suggested by Daniel Lerner elsewhere in this volume, with West Berlin and Bonn playing roles comparable to New York and Washington in the United States, to Milan and Rome in Italy, to Aleppo and Damascus in Syria.

None of these possibilities did result. That West Berlin with its unique atmosphere and outlook could have remained Germany's center, dictating policies and fashions no less than it had before the war, would clearly have been the path

8. I am indebted to Mr. K.-H. Hinz for performing these computations.

9. Another explanation is that the differences in perceptions and attitudes derive from differences in the modal personality structures of West Berliners and West Germans. Disregarding the argument that such differences are inherited, this explanation points to environmental factors (e.g. family, political socialization, etc.) that existed before the postwar period.

chosen by most West Berliners had they been asked. Perhaps the most nagging fear of any cosmopolite is to be labeled provincial; and West Berliners have been extremely sensitive to any depreciation in the status of their city. In fact, however, West Berlin did not reemerge as Germany's center after the western Allies reversed their decentralizing policies. Governmental agencies could not, and industrial, commercial, and financial firms did not, relocate in the former capital. Nor did the city regain the type of population that it had before the war. There were to be sure many who stayed in or moved to Berlin for sentimental reasons, to live in an atmosphere charged with international tension, to pursue particular career objectives, or just to enjoy the famous Berlin climate. But in general aspiring civil servants, businessmen, industrialists, bankers, and even actors looked elsewhere than to Berlin as a source of jobs and other rewards; professors turned to the older and more established universities in the West rather than to the new, unproved, but occasionally exciting Free University of Berlin; politicians (with occasionally spectacular exceptions, such as West Berlin's present Lord Mayor, Willy Brandt) followed parties whose main offices were on the Rhine rather than on the Spree, parties catering to an electoral clientele in the West German states, not to West Berliners who may not vote in federal elections. Even Berlin newspapers, once read throughout Germany, gained the reputation of provincial sheets read primarily by West Berliners. But, then, if it is true that West Berlin was unable to reestablish itself as postwar Germany's political, economic, social, and psychological center, it is equally true that this role did not pass from Berlin to some city in the West, nor did any genuine center emerge in West Germany to compete coequally with West Berlin.

No single West German city has been able to assume all the functions performed by Berlin before the war. Indeed, structures performing significant economic and political functions are more dispersed in West Germany than in perhaps any other modern state, whether in Europe or elsewhere. In some instances entire branches of Germany's political and economic life have centered themselves in individual cities: the federal government in Bonn, high finance in Frankfurt, and so forth. In still other instances cities formerly thought of primarily as provincial capitals have modernized, industrialized, and diversified their activities and interests to such an extent that they are now of national and even international importance. The megalopolis extending from Bonn to Düsseldorf may have gained an ascendant position in West Germany, but it is as primus inter pares rather than as Berlin's successor. In a very real sense modern West Germany has become a multicephalous political community.

Despite this development, Berlin has not passed totally to the periphery of West German life. If a modern state may be imagined to have a conscience, it is this function that West Berlin performs for West Germany. The voices of the city's leaders persistently warn the West to guard against complacency and smugness and against any tendency to ignore long-range political values in the pursuit of such short-range material goals as a higher standard of living. They have taken advantage of adverse circumstances to turn their city into a symbol of German unity—a symbol so important to West Germans that they are prepared to spend billions of Marks every year to keep it alive. Moreover, these voices are a constant reminder of West Germany's commitment to the Western alliance. "We in Berlin," they seem to say, "know the Russians and the dangers of communism at first hand, and know full well that Germany cannot afford the luxury of 'neutral' attitudes." In this respect it is striking that the political attitudes of West Berliners cited earlier are more nearly reflected in official Bonn policy than are those images and opinions of the rest of the West German population.

West Berlin's function as a conscience also goes far beyond German borders. Time and again its leaders have reasserted the proposition that the city is a symbol of America's determination to protect its allies from communism. If West Berlin is given up or lost, they argue, then no longer will any nation be willing to entrust its fate to an American-backed defense system. It was this obligation that President Kennedy acknowledged in his trip in June 1963 to West Berlin where, from the steps of the city hall, he delivered his now famous "Ich bin ein Berliner" speech.

The central role of West Berlin in the consciousness of West Germans is in marked contrast to its peripheral role in the day-to-day life of West Germany. This paradoxical situation stems essentially from a high level of international tension, the tension of the East–West struggle for Europe and the repeated "Berlin crises." Were this tension to disappear—relieved, perhaps, by a Soviet–American détente, or by a system of treaties stabilizing and guaranteeing the status quo in central Europe—West Berlin would doubtless become a peripheral island, no more the center of postwar West Germany than Danzig was of prewar Germany. Alternatively, the reunification of Germany would in all likelihood be followed by the relocation of the capital to Berlin, thus restoring the city to its central position in German politics if not (at least not immediately) in other aspects of German life.

The prospects, however, are for neither a stabilization of the status quo in central Europe nor the reunification of Germany. As long as international tension continues, West Berlin's center–periphery relationship with West Germany will fluctuate with the level of that tension. The ability of West Berlin to command a central position in the multicephalous political community that is West Germany depends upon the continuation of a fairly high level of friction between East and West. It is the recognition of this fact that has led many West Berliners to seek a new function—as an educational and cultural center—that will render their city more impervious to the vagaries of international politics. Until it attains such a goal, as one Berlin politician expressed it privately, the city's main export is tension. Without it, West Berlin runs the risk of becoming peripheral to the core of West German life.

15. Implications of Within-Nation Variations and Regional Imbalances for Cross-National Research

ERIK ALLARDT, UNIVERSITY OF HELSINKI

Regional imbalances refer to marked economic, social, and political variations within the same country. Studies of regional imbalances are important for cross-national research partly because the methodological problems are similar to those of cross-national studies, and partly because the countries with regional imbalances constitute exceptionally difficult cases in cross-national analyses. Among the difficulties, the following may be mentioned:

1. When great intracountry variations exist, it is important in cross-national analyses to include variables measuring dispersion or variance. Most cross-national comparisons rely on national averages only, probably because data about dispersion are harder to obtain and often presuppose some kind of regional division within each compared country.

2. Regional imbalances may lead to situations where variation in the same aspect of political behavior, such as the amount of radicalism or the degree of mobilization, is explained by different social and economic factors in different parts of the same country. Moreover, the same political behavior may be positively correlated with particular economic and social factors in some areas of the country, but negatively correlated in other areas, making the total national correlation come close to zero.

3. Variables which have different correlates in different parts of the country, or variables which show positive correlations in some parts and negative correlations in other parts of the country, tend to have low validity as national measures. For example, strong religious interest in backward areas is an indicator of traditionalism but in developed areas it may indicate nonconformity.

The implications of these problems can be more precisely discussed in terms of a concrete example of a country with regional imbalance. The case discussed here is Finland.

VARIABLES

The Institute of Sociology at the University of Helsinki has a file of ecological variables for the 550 Finnish communes, the smallest administrative units in the country. The file was originally established in order to have available quantitative data which would be relevant for describing and explaining voting patterns in Finland in the 1950s. The nature of the approximately 80 variables can be described with the help of the following distinctions:

1. Variables denoting (a) averages or percentages, such as the disposable income per capita in 1950 or the voting turnout in the parliamentary election in 1951, and (b) dispersion or variance, such as the variance in farm size in 1950.

2. Variables describing (a) traditions or occurrences in the past, such as the number of "Reds" who were killed or died in prison camps during the Civil War in 1918, and (b) the present situation, such as the proportion of Conservative voters in the election of 1954.

3. Variables describing (a) developmental patterns, such as the increase in per capita income, 1950 to 1956, or the change in the Communist vote from 1948 to 1958, and (b) the situation at one specific point in time, such as the proportion of individuals employed in agriculture in 1950.

4. Variables related to different institutional realms: (a) political, such as the proportion of Communist voters

in 1954 or the proportion of Social Democratic voters in 1916; (b) economic, as for example, the frequency of individuals on social relief in 1950; (c) religious, such as the frequency of church attendance, 1953 to 1956; (d) educational, such as the proportion of children who in 1950 were continuing their schooling after the compulsory age; and finally (e) legal, such as the frequency of homicides or frequency of thefts from 1951 to 1953.

5. Variables describing different aspects of the social structure: (a) social stratification, such as the variance in per capita income in 1950; (b) geographical mobility–immobility, such as the measures of migration into and out of the communes in 1953; (c) modernization, such as the proportion of electrified households in 1950; (d) indicators of security–insecurity, such as the proportion of unemployed in the labor force in 1931–32 or the proportion of crowded dwellings in 1950; and (e) geographical, such as population density or the proportion of individuals working in retail trade in 1950 (often regarded as a measure of geographic centrality).

All the above-mentioned variables have been fitted to the normal curve and have been coded into seven categories based on a normal curve. There are both assets and liabilities in this procedure. Some statistical techniques require the variables to be normally distributed. There is, however, a loss of information when bimodally distributed variables such as population density are fitted to a normal curve.

DATA UNITS AND ANALYTICAL UNITS

As mentioned above, the collected data refer to communes; every commune has a numerical value with regard to each variable. The selection of the commune as a data unit is based on the fact that communes are areas with which people identify themselves. Other ecological divisions could also have been used. Political behavior data can be obtained for the following geographical units, ordered here according to size, starting from the largest: provinces, electoral districts, communes, and precincts. The provinces and electoral districts are too large, and accordingly also too few, to be suitable units. Precincts are purely administrative units, important only in elections. If causal interpretations are attempted on the basis of ecological data, it seems important to use data units which really correspond to areas that people are aware of and with which they identify themselves and others.

The associations between the variables describing the communes can of course be analyzed by many different techniques, including multiple correlation analysis or factor analysis. However, if such analyses are done for the country as a whole, the results are bound to be theoretically less interesting than if applied to several areas. This is true whatever statistical technique is applied. Unless the associations found between variables are replicated and specified the results are hardly of theoretical interest.[1] A multiple correlation analysis based on the country as a whole may of course indicate how the variation in some political behavior variables can be explained by other variables, but unless this result can be replicated it is almost impossible to assess its theoretical fruitfulness. This is even more true for factor analysis. All that may be gained by a single factor analysis of the variables describing the communes would be a conceptual system which can of course be useful in descriptions. In order to provide theoretically important results, however, several factor analyses must be compared. Such a comparison allows for replication and specification. In fact, the Finnish study compared several factor analyses, separately performed for specific areas of the country.

It is customary to distinguish between external and internal replications. In external replications, the associations between variables are tested independently in another study. In the Finnish study there are no possibilities for external replications. There are, however, possibilities for internal replications, that is, reanalysis of findings for smaller groups

1. See, for example, Hanan A. Selvin, "Durkheim's Suicide and Problems of Empirical Research," *American Journal of Sociology, 63* (1958), 607–19.

within the original set of cases (communes). The country has been divided into five areas, within each of which a separate correlational and factor analysis has been done, to allow for replication and specification.

The aims of the procedure indicated above can also be characterized in another way. Instead of studying just the correlations between variables in a particular setting, ecological patterns in different settings have been compared. In ecological studies we need not only data units, but also what could be labeled analytical units, areas within which definite ecological patterns are observed. These ecological patterns can then be compared. Here, the communes are the data units, and the five areas into which the country is divided are the analytical units.

METHODS OF ANALYSIS

Due to the large number of variables, factor analysis has, up to this date, been the main technique used in the Finnish study. Many variables were dropped before the factor analysis was performed. There were two main reasons for dropping variables: (1) When variables are technically correlated, the variable which can be assumed to give less information has been dropped. In some cases two variables, which for theoretical reasons are assumed to be technically correlated, but which nevertheless have an empirical correlation close to zero, were both included. This is the case for "per capita income" and "variance in per capita income," because it was assumed that both variables contain very important information. (2) Another reason for dropping a variable was its low correlations with other variables. Such variables can be assumed to have both low informative value and a low degree of validity.

The correlation matrices have been factorized and the factor structures rotated by different procedures. The first method of factoring that was used was Thurstone's centroid factor method, and the centroid structures were rotated by what is known as Varimax orthogonal solution. Second,

Hotelling's method of principal components was used, and the results of the principal component analysis were then rotated by the so-called cosine solution, an analytical oblique rotation method invented by the Finnish psychometrician Yrjö Ahmavaara.[2] Since both the orthogonal and the oblique solutions provided very similar results, arguments over the fruitfulness of different factor analytical models would be rather futile.[3]

As indicated above, hypotheses and patterns have been tested by comparing the results of the factor analyses for the five areas. This comparison has been mainly done by more or less intuitive interpretation of the factors and factor loadings in the five different areas. A more exact technique for comparing the results of the factor analyses has been applied without much success. This method—Yrjö Ahmavaara's transformation analysis[4]—transforms the factors in one group into the factor space of another group so that a more exact comparison is possible. In addition, the factor scores for each commune on each factor have been computed, but the factor scores have not yet been used in actual analysis.

The factor analysis has not been described in detail since the main methodological point here refers to the general principles of multivariate survey analysis. When the results of the factor analyses are compared, the comparisons provide sociologically meaningful results. A single factor analysis gives mainly a system of theoretical concepts and dimensions. The comparisons, however, make it possible to test hypotheses and to establish types which are sociologically interesting.

2. T. Vahervuo and Yrjö Ahmavaara, *Johdatus faktorianalyysiin* (Introduction to Factor Analysis) (Helsinki-Porvoo, 1958), pp. 90–100.

3. Results of the orthogonal solution have been presented in Erik Allardt, "Institutionalized versus Diffuse Support for Radical Political Movements," *Transactions of the Fifth World Congress in Sociology, 4* (1964), 369–80. Results based on the oblique rotations have been presented in E. Allardt, "Social Sources of Finnish Communism: Traditional and Emerging Radicalism," *International Journal of Comparative Sociology, 5* (1964), 49–72.

4. Yrjö Ahmavaara and Touko Markkanen, *The Unified Factor Model* (Helsinki, 1958), pp. 80–88.

AN EXAMPLE OF REGIONAL IMBALANCE

Regional imbalance can be said to prevail in Finland. The areas in the western and southern parts of the country are industrialized and economically developed, whereas the areas in the eastern and northern parts are predominantly rural and economically backward. This gap is, of course, rapidly diminishing as economic development increases in the rural and backward areas.

Up until now the Finnish data file has been used mainly for studying the correlates of political radicalism, measured primarily by the proportion of Communist voters in national elections. A point of departure is the fact that the strength of Communist support varies considerably both in developed and backward areas. In other words, both types of areas contain communes in which the Communist vote is very heavy and communes where it is very light.

The crucial point, however, is that the variation in Communist strength in these two types of areas is associated with very different kinds of variables. Regional imbalances exist not only in the distribution of important variables but also in ecological patterns or the associations between variables. The factor analyses reveal this by the fact that Communist strength in the two types of areas is explained by, or is heavily loaded in, very different kinds of factors. The results can be summarized in the following way:

1. Communism is strong in those industrialized and developed areas where very strong political traditions constitute barriers for interaction between individuals from different groups. These areas are furthermore characterized by a rigid class structure, good social conditions, the absence of factors causing insecurity, and slight in- and out-migration.

2. Communism finds its strength in those rural and undeveloped areas where political traditions are weak, insecurity is great, development is rapid, and migration considerable.

In summary, then, Communism tends to be strong in developed areas which are characterized by rigidity, few cross-pressures, and strong community ties. Communism in backward areas, on the contrary, is strong where social conditions tend to uproot and alienate the individual.

These results are supported by a comparison of existing Communist strength and the increase in Communist strength. Although the increase has been mainly concentrated in the rural and economically backward northern and eastern areas, a clear variation also exists in the amount of increase in more developed areas. The growth in Communist strength in the developed areas is explained by the same factors that account for existing Communist strength in backward areas, that is, conditions of alienation and uprooting. We may therefore say that *traditional* and *emerging* Communism tend to occur under very different conditions. Traditional Communism exists in developed areas where there are strong and uniform pressures on the individual, whereas emerging Communism exists in backward areas where there are no clear norms and rules for the individual to follow. The results may be formulated in two propositions:

1. The more economically developed the areas and the stronger the pressure toward uniformity, the stronger the political radicalism.
2. The more backward the areas and the weaker the pressure toward uniformity, the stronger the political radicalism.

In other words, regional imbalances not only reveal themselves as differing greatly on single variables but also in very different ecological patterns or associations between variables. These results could hardly be specified without internal comparisons within the original set of communes.

THE NECESSITY FOR CONTEXTUAL OPERATIONAL DEFINITIONS

It should be made clear that some theoretical concepts must have entirely different operational definitions for different areas. Lazarsfeld has spoken about the interchangeability of indices in sociology,[5] and Deutsch has referred to the same phenomenon in comparative research.[6] This interchangeability means that if one indicator (operational definition) should be missing, it could be replaced in many cases by the remaining ones, or other and new indicators could be chosen. In comparative research, however, one also encounters a situation where, in fact, the same operational definition or indicator for the same theoretical concept would lead to erroneous results when applied within different subgroups or different areas. In such a case there is no interchangeability of indicators; in fact, they have to be different for different areas.

An example from the Finnish study can illustrate this point. Conditions under which individuals tend to feel insecure have been mentioned above. But conditions reflecting insecurity are defined very differently on an operational level in rural backward areas than in urban industrialized areas. Finland's unemployment problem is, to a large extent, a question of agrarian underemployment. In backward rural areas, unemployment is the phenomenon which is apt to arouse the strongest feelings of insecurity, not only among the unemployed but in the population in general. Unemployment is perhaps the best indicator of insecurity, as far as ecological data are concerned. However, this does not hold true for cities and industrial areas. Variations in unemployment figures exist in urban areas also, but the proportion of unemployed is small and technical matters of registration affect the figures heavily. In cities and industrialized areas the best indicators of conditions reflecting insecurity are related to housing. Variables such as the proportion of crowded dwellings and the rate of new housing construction are good indicators. They would not be very useful in the countryside, however, where regional traditions in housing are very different.

5. Paul F. Lazarsfeld, "Problems in Methodology," in Robert K. Merton, Leonard Brown, and Leonard S. Cottrell, Jr., *Sociology Today* (New York, Basic Books, 1959), p. 63.

6. Karl W. Deutsch, "Social Mobilization and Political Development," *American Political Science Review, 55* (1961), 495.

One additional methodological point may be made. Without comparisons within subgroups, it is highly unlikely that defective operational definitions will be found. Assessment of the fruitfulness of operational definitions is possible only if ecological patterns or associations between variables in different contexts are compared.

IMPLICATIONS FOR CROSS-NATIONAL RESEARCH

It has been said that the theoretically most fruitful comparisons are those in which whole patterns, or associations among several variables, are replicated or specified. One of the most interesting international comparisons to date is Alex Inkeles' study of the "Industrial Man." [7] His study is based on survey data, but the general principles also apply here. He is not comparing single responses but response patterns. He is not, for example, comparing national differences in the proportion of people who laugh or cry often, but whether differences in crying or laughing between various occupational categories remain the same when one moves from country to country. By making response patterns the main focus of his analysis, he is also able to test and formulate theoretical propositions.

In order to make it possible to test propositions and also fulfill the requirements for multivariate analysis, cross-national studies can be developed in two directions. The easier method is to establish subgroups within the original set of nations, and test whether the patterns prevailing in a subgroup of nations remain the same when one moves from one subgroup to another. For example, with computer programs for regression analysis available, these subgroups can be detected at the same time the regression analysis is performed. However, this necessarily leads to very crude results. The other, and in most cases the more fruitful, alternative is to measure not only single variables for each nation but also correlations, and then actually compare correlations. This would require in most cases that compared coun-

7. Alex Inkeles, "Industrial Man: The Relation of Status to Experience, Perception and Value," *American Journal of Sociology, 66* (1961), 1–31.

tries be divided into subareas. It may be hard to match subareas for different countries, but with the computer facilities available today this is by no means an impossible task.

The importance of establishing analytical units that are different from the data units, so that ecological patterns instead of single variables can be compared for replication and specification in comparative ecological research, has been stressed principally on the ground that it leads to theoretically more important results. Another type of rationale can also be given. A common argument against comparative studies is that phenomena measured in the same way may nevertheless have a different social significance in different countries. This is the same as saying that it is impossible to obtain valid indicators in comparative research. This is of course true if propositions, obtained or formulated from data from one country or for a group of countries, cannot be replicated. Without replications there are no means for assessing the validity of the indicators. As soon as replications can be performed, however, the situation is entirely different. The validity of indicators or operational definitions for theoretical concepts must be evaluated at the same time as propositions or theories are empirically tested. There are always three main paths open in scientific research for handling negative instances. One can regard the negative cases as rejections of the advanced hypotheses; one can redefine the concepts in such a way that the negative cases no longer belong to the realm of the hypotheses; or one can question the validity of the indicators for the theoretical concepts. In fact, there is no other way to assess the validity of indicators than to determine their fruitfulness in testing hypotheses. Usually the hypothesis advanced is related to other hypotheses, and in the last analysis the validity of indicators depends on their fruitfulness for entire theories or fragments of theories.[8] This is also why theory is badly needed in comparative research.

8. See Bo Anderson, "Some Notes on Operationalism and the Concept of Validity," *Acta Sociologica*, 2 (1957), 202–13.

The case for theory in comparative research can be even more strongly formulated. Theory is more important in cross-national research than in any other field. When doing national studies or studies of narrow subjects, the researcher may have hunches about the validity of his indicators or operational definitions. He is able to assess the face validity of his indicators. In comparative research, in which many and greatly varying environments are compared, it is not humanly possible to have hunches about the face validity of all the indicators. Unless the researcher in cross-national research has a theory or some system of hypotheses which guide him, he will almost assuredly encounter a situation in which he regards as similar phenomena which are actually different and which measure different things.

16. Indices for Comparing Inequality *

HAYWARD R. ALKER, JR., AND BRUCE M. RUSSETT,
YALE UNIVERSITY

Inequality and concentration have long been central concepts in social science. As is so often the case, however, there have been serious failures of communication among those concerned with such problems. Economists study inequalities in the distribution of wealth, income, productive capacity, or goods such as land. Sociologists may be concerned with social mobility—inequality of opportunity, or with inequalities in living conditions—the degree to which minority groups are concentrated in particular residential areas. A political scientist may be interested in any of these.[1] In addition, the student of politics must be concerned with *political* inequality, that is, with concentrated, unequally distributed power.

* This article stems from the research of the Yale Political Data Program. We are grateful to James D. Barber, Karl W. Deutsch, and Clark W. Reynolds for comments. A slightly different version of this chapter appeared in *Behavioral Science, 9* (1964), 207–18.

1. One political scientist has defined politics as "the study of changes in the shape and composition of value distributions in a society": Harold D. Lasswell, *World Politics and Personal Insecurity* (New York, McGraw-Hill, 1935), p. 3. Another, to distinguish political inquiry from other social science, describes it as the study of "authoritative allocation of values": David Easton, *The Political System* (New York, Knopf, 1953), pp. 129–31. Yet another asks rhetorically, "Should democracy be thought of as a purely political concept, or does it necessarily include social and economic factors?": Austin Ranney, *The Doctrine of Responsible Party Government* (Urbana, University of Illinois Press, 1962), p. 159. Although these statements reflect different approaches to political analysis, they all imply concern with describing and comparing value distributions.

He may, for instance, need a measure of legislative malapportionment. States may be compared with each other, or with some generally accepted norm like perfect equality, or the degree of inequality present in the electoral college—the minimal criterion of constitutionality as adopted by some courts.[2] Or successive redistrictings of any one state may be compared.

Though the variables in question may be different, the basic question in each case is the same: What is the degree to which wealth, or good living conditions, or power, are concentrated in a society? Since the questions are conceptually similar, it is reasonable to expect that the problems of quantification would be similar, that the tools of measurement developed in one social science might be applicable to studies in another field. Yet there has in fact been little interchange, and scholars in each field persist in using techniques which are in some respects inferior to those available in the literature of other fields. In this chapter we shall examine about twenty proposed measures in order to evaluate their strengths and weaknesses and to compare the results given by some of them when applied to sets of data on representation in state legislatures and land distribution.

To describe inequality one needs a measure, or measures, to make initially noncomparable distributions comparable. To do this any index must bear some standard relation to the distribution itself, rather than to the value in question. For example, many nations summarize their patterns of land distribution by listing the number of farms over 10 hectares in size, and those over 25, 50, and 100 hectares. In this raw form the data are useless for most purposes of comparison. The great majority of farms in Costa Rica are smaller than 10 hectares, while the typical farm in the United States is nearly 50 hectares in size. If one is interested in knowing whether the total amount of agricultural land is distributed more evenly in the United States than in Costa Rica, one must know what *proportion* of the total farm land is part of what *proportion* of the farms in each country. Most of the

2. *Sanders v. Gray*, 203 F. Supp. 158, N. D. Ga., 1962.

indices that have been suggested do in fact use proportions or percentages. A choice among these indices involves at least three kinds of criteria.

First, there is the problem of summarizing adequately the different parts or aspects of a value distribution. *How much of the available information does an index use?* Is the measure sensitive to the various possible differences in such distributions? For instance, if one uses some simple measure like the smallest proportion of the electorate that could theoretically elect a majority of the legislature,[3] one is only describing a part of the situation at hand. It may be that 20 per cent of the voters, in the smallest voting districts, could elect half the legislators, but that the rest of the districts are distributed evenly; that is, it would take 47 per cent of the voters to elect two thirds of the legislators. Or it may be that two thirds of the representatives could be chosen by a mere 27 per cent, a much more unequal situation. In principle, an index that combined measures at various points on the distribution would be preferable to one that examined only a single point.

Secondly, one wants a measure *distorted as little as possible by incompleteness or inaccuracy of the data at hand.* A related problem is how best to deal with data that are complete but grouped in an arbitrary or misleading way. There is no sense in carefully selecting a measure which describes the whole distribution when the published data one has to work with often only indicate the income of the top 5, 10, and 15 per cent of the population. Even if we can subtract to find the population receiving the rest of the income, we know little about its actual distribution among the remaining 84 per cent of the population.[4]

Third, but very important, are several *theoretical considerations.* Taking either an empirical or an ethical viewpoint,

3. Manning J. Dauer and Robert G. Kelsay, "Unrepresentative States," *National Municipal Review, 44* (1955), 571–87.

4. Our first and second points parallel the criteria of "sensitivity to differences between income distributions" and "stability under different groupings of class intervals for data from a given distribution." D. Yntema, "Measures of the Inequality in the Personal Distribution of Wealth or Income," *Journal of the American Statistical Association, 28* (1933), 423–33.

it is important to ask from which norm we want to consider deviations. Is it important for the success of democracy that there be no great extremes of wealth and poverty, or only that these extremes still allow a large middle class to exist? Do we, on normative or empirical grounds, want older people to have a greater share of power or wealth? In a study of industrial concentration, at what point do a few dominant firms begin to extract profits that may be called excessive? Does profit-making power increase sharply beyond a certain, perhaps desirable, degree of concentration? One's choice of indices for comparison will depend upon one's assumptions about the uses of inequality.[5]

In the development of empirical social theory one also wants to choose indices of inequality that relate usefully to other interesting phenomena. Like a lawyer selecting precedents, however, the proponent of a particular point of view may choose the index, with its implicit norms, which best seems to support his argument. The skeptical reader, and the careful scholar seeking insight rather than advocacy, must be aware of the peculiarities of each index and know how appropriate it is to the question at hand.

We may group measures of inequality into three classes: (1) measures of extremeness; (2) measures of average tendencies in frequency distributions; and (3) measures that compare cumulative distributions with theoretically determined norms.

MEASURES OF EXTREMENESS

Largest / smallest. Because of its ease of calculation and its dramatic possibilities, the ratio of the largest district's population to that of the smallest legislative district is per-

5. Three relevant discussions of various possible empirical or ethical distribution norms are presented by G. Garvey, "Inequality of Income: Causes and Measurement," in National Bureau of Economic Research, *Studies in Income and Wealth, 15* (New York, National Bureau of Economic Research, 1952), 25–47; Simon Kuznets, "National Income," in American Economic Association, *Readings in the Theory of Income Distribution* (Philadelphia, Blakiston, 1949); and W. von Leyden, "On Justifying Inequality," *Political Studies, 11* (1963), 56–70.

haps the most frequently cited measure of malapportionment.[6] The most obvious drawback of this measure is that it does not indicate how many districts are to be found at either extreme.

Ratios of advantage. A district's power may be established by comparing it to a measure of central or average tendency within a distribution. For example, one may make a ratio of a district's population to the average population of all districts.[7] Inversely, in his *Preface to Democratic Theory,* Robert A. Dahl computes an Index of Advantage for each state in the United States Senate by inverting this ratio:

$$\text{Index of Advantage} = \frac{\text{actual representation}}{\text{proportionate representation}} = \frac{\text{average state electorate}}{\text{actual state electorate}}$$

Thus, for example, in 1952 Iowa, with an index of 1.05, most nearly approximated the "ideal" of proportionate representation; Nevada and New York, with indices of 14.80 and 0.17 respectively, were at the extremes.[8]

Percentage of value held by a given top percentage of units. Perhaps the simplest kind of an extreme measure of distribution is to take the percentage of seats held by the most overrepresented 1, 5, or 10 representative units. In economics the well-known "concentration ratio" is determined by dividing total sales (or other dimensions of size) of

6. This standard seems to be often used by the courts; see A. J. Goldberg, "The Statistics of Malapportionment," *Yale Law Journal, 72* (1962), 1.

7. R. Silva, "Apportionment of the New York State Legislature," *American Political Science Review, 55* (1961), 870–81.

8. Robert A. Dahl in *A Preface to Democratic Theory* (Chicago, University of Chicago Press, 1956), p. 114, defined each state's electorate as equal to the number of *votes* cast in Congressional elections, and applied his index to the Senate. On the other hand, seats in the House of Representatives are allocated in a way (the method of equal proportions) that minimizes differences in ratios of advantage between states. After each state has received its Constitutional minimum of one Representative, assignment priorities are calculated for each state by dividing its *population* (not its active electorate) by the geometric mean of the number of seats already assigned and the number of Representatives it would have if a new one were added. The geometric mean is the square root of the product of two numbers. See L. F. Schmeckbier, "The Method of Equal Proportions," *Law and Contemporary Problems, 17* (1952), 302–13.

the largest four firms by the total sales of a whole group of firms.[9] Oligopoly may be said to exist if the largest four firms account for more than 50 per cent of sales, although there is nothing magical about that figure. In political analysis one might want to test varying percentage cutoffs of values (like sales) to see when sizable "monopoly" effects (such as "excess profiteering") actually are likely to take place.

The Pareto coefficient. Perhaps because of the incompleteness of available data before the introduction of the sample survey, or perhaps for ideological reasons, Vilfredo Pareto introduced in 1897 the technique of plotting, on double-logarithmic paper, the size of an individual's income against the number of income receivers having that income or larger, and considering the slope of the nearly straight line thus obtained as a measure of income inequality. Because of the logarithmic contraction, the lowest 90 per cent of value holders count no more than the 90th through the 99th percentiles in making a visual estimate of this slope. Qualitatively, extremely high incomes are much more important in estimating Pareto's coefficient.[10]

MEASURES OF AVERAGE TENDENCIES IN A FREQUENCY DISTRIBUTION

The commonest assumption about a population characteristic is that it is normally distributed. Thus the well-known normal or "bell-shaped" frequency distribution suggests that

9. M. A. Adelman, "The Measurement of Industrial Concentration," *Review of Economics and Statistics, 33* (1951), 269–96.

10. Cf. the discussion and graphs in M. J. Bowman, "A Graphical Analysis of Personal Income Distribution in the United States," *American Economic Review, 35* (1945), 607–28.

Pareto's experience nicely illustrates the earlier point about theoretical considerations. He assumed that the degree of income inequality at the very top of the scale was most relevant politically; it may be no coincidence that in comparing European nations he chose an index which emphasized the richest individuals. On this basis he decided that the degree of inequality was everywhere about the same. But had he chosen an index which placed equal emphasis on low and middle-income earners he would have found substantial differences among nations. Yntema, "Measures of Inequality," condemned Pareto's famous coefficient as both insensitive to differences in distributions and very much affected by the way the data were grouped. Of the measures he studied, the mean deviation best passed these tests.

the most frequent occurrence of the characteristic is the average one, and that extreme deviations from this mean are rare and about as infrequent on either side of it. To plot an actual frequency distribution, data must be grouped into different intervals of a more or less equal width, and then the number or frequency of individuals having values within these ranges are plotted on a vertical scale.

The mean deviation. A simple way to get a measure of the inequality present in a frequency distribution would be to average the deviations from the mean.[11] If one has a set of ratios for legislative districts, like Dahl's Index of Advantage, there is no point in averaging them all, for the mean Index of Advantage is unity. But one can average such ratios over identifiable subgroupings of a population, such as urban, suburban, and rural counties, and so have a valuable summary of the inequality of representation for citizens in each of these groupings.[12] If one ignored the plus and minus signs, however, the average would be not zero but the measure known as the *mean deviation.* Dahl suggests as a definition of "polyarchy" the situation within an organization where every individual's vote is weighted equally in reaching decisions. He then offers as an operational definition of this condition a formula centered around the concept of a mean deviation.[13]

In any complex organization, such as a state with repre-

11. Even simpler measures like the interquartile range and other indices based upon the range of a value are sometimes convenient to use, "but the omission of the influence of the items that fall outside of the selected range is a serious disadvantage for the study of . . . distributions." I. Kravis, *The Structure of Income* (Philadelphia, University of Pennsylvania Press, 1962), p. 178.

12. As thus used by Paul T. David and Ralph Eisenberg in *Devaluation of the Urban and Suburban Vote* (Charlottesville, University of Virginia Press, 1961), the "right to vote" is the ratio of a county's share of voting strength in the legislature divided by the county's fraction of the state's population. They multiply the ratio of these two fractions by 100, so that an equitably represented county has a right to vote of 100. Dahl's Index of Advantage in *A Preface to Democratic Theory* is essentially the same, except that it is normed to 1.0 as the equitable advantage, and it counts only actual voters rather than the total population of the voting unit. It should be noted that such calculations could also be done for many of the regional or urban–rural cleavages that exist in the United States and other countries.

13. Letting V_i be the value of a particular vote, f_i be the frequency of

sentative institutions, Dahl's condition is rarely approached; the problem is to estimate how close the actual situation is to the "ideal" one. Given any real data in an already summarized form, there are serious problems in knowing how to estimate the actual weighed votes of each individual. Nonetheless Dahl's measure is an attractive one. It allows for comparability among distributions using differing measuring units because it has been "normalized" or "standardized" by the total number of "votes" held by individuals in all population subgroupings.

The standard deviation. A common measure of dispersion, or inequality, is the standard deviation.[14] As Dahl did with the mean deviation, it also may be standardized. Dividing it by the mean of the variable being studied reduces its dependence on the measurement units being used, giving what is called the coefficient of variation.

Despite their several attractive statistical properties, these two measures suffer from two difficulties not found in alter-

---

individuals with this vote, and $\overline{V}$ the average vote value, the polyarchy index, *P*, is defined as

$$P = 1 - \frac{\sum_{i=1}^{k} f_i \mid V_i - \overline{V} \mid}{\sum_{i=1}^{k} f_i V_i} \qquad \text{(Dahl, pp. 84–86)}$$

The summations are over the *k* different voting classes; thus the sum of the deviations is divided by the total number of *votes* ($\Sigma f_i V_i$) rather than the total number of *voters* ($\Sigma f_i = N$), as is the case with the mean deviation. (In this notation, it becomes clear that the denominator on the right side of the minus sign is just *N* times $\overline{V}$, the average vote.) As a measure of inequality, i.e. the absence of polyarchy, *1 — P*, or the mean deviation, might be more appropriate.

14. Using notation similar to that in the previous footnote, the standard deviation (σ) for grouped data may be approximated (see Kravis, *The Structure of Income*) by

$$\sigma = \sqrt{\frac{\Sigma f_i (V_i - \overline{V}^2)}{\Sigma f_i}}$$

where summations are over the data subclasses. When the data are not so grouped, the formula is exactly correct, with all the $f_i = 1$. Then the standard deviation may be thought of as the square root of the average squared deviation.

native measures of inequality (such as the mean deviation, or the Gini index of concentration, to be discussed below). First, average *squared* deviations from a mean are not easily understood by the nonstatistician. This is especially the case when a normal frequency distribution cannot be assumed. Second, such measures are unusually sensitive to the way in which the more extreme data points are grouped.[15]

The skewness of a distribution. When the median of a distribution has a lower value than the mean, as is often the case with social phenomena, we say that a distribution is not normal but "skewed" to the right. Thus the average family in the United States has an income of over $7,000, while the median income is more than a thousand dollars lower. This fact suggests that there are more very poor people than there are very rich people. Moreover, the number of extremely rich individuals may not be much smaller than the number of those moderately well off. In 1917 Allyn Young, an economist, argued for skewness as a measure of the inequality of income distribution:

> The amount of concentration, the amount of departure from a condition of uniform incomes, does not matter so much as does the particular form of the income distribution underlying the concentration. . . .
>
> The worst thing in the present situation is undoubtedly the extreme skewness of the income frequency curve. . . . The most serious aspect of the distribution of property and incomes in this and other countries is not the presence of a larger or smaller degree of "concentration," but the general distortion of the whole income scheme, reflecting as it undoubtedly does the presence of a high degree of inequality in the distribution of opportunity.[16]

15. Kravis; Yntema, "Measures of Inequality."

16. Quoted by Bowman, p. 627. S. Lebergott in "The Shape of the Income Distribution," *American Economic Review, 49* (1959), 328–47, has suggested, however, that the apparent skewness is due largely to the inadequacy of data on the poorest segment of the population, especially part-time workers. He shows that the income of males aged 25–64 is distributed in an almost "normal" pattern. Logarithms of income are also more nearly "normally" distributed. If the utility of income is assumed to be logarithmically related to its absolute size (see Kravis), and percentage differences rather than

Certainly one is tempted to say that high positive skewness represents high inequality of some sort. Although we shall not pursue it further here, the plausibility of a standardized measure of skewness does suggest the complexity of the different aspects of dispersion or inequality in a distribution.[17]

MEASURES INVOLVING CUMULATIVE VALUE DISTRIBUTIONS AND EXPLICIT THEORETICAL NORMS

A basic alternative to studying the properties of normal or non-normal frequency distributions is the analysis of cumulative value distributions. Such distributions may be obtained by plotting total values held by increasingly better-off portions of a population. To an economist, "even when plotted on a semi-logarithmic graph, a non-cumulative distri-

---

absolute differences are deemed relevant, assessments of inequality (skewness) would be considerably different.

17. In a manner similar to ours, Stuart Carter Dodd in "Historic Ideas Operationally Defined," *Public Opinion Quarterly, 15* (1951), 547–56, has demonstrated that many of these measures can be derived from the various moments of a frequency distribution. For ungrouped data, the *j*th moment, m^j, may be defined as

$$m^j = \sum_{i=1}^{N} V_i^j/N$$

One averages over the N members of a population the *j*th power of the observed variable *V*. The *O*th moment, where $\overline{V} = 1$ if a value is present (and otherwise = O), gives the percentage of a population enjoying the value. When *V* is allowed to vary on an interval range and $j = 1$, the first moment is just the average value of a variable, for instance, a mean deviation. Taking *V* *around* its mean with $j = 2$, we have the variance of a distribution, whose square root, of course, is the standard deviation discussed above.

Defining voting scores as the percentage of possible times an individual has voted, Dodd measures voting "equality" by dividing the standard deviation of these scores by its maximum possible value. His measure of "security" is based on the desirability of a *negatively* skewed distribution (the opposite of the household income example given above). Then skewness can be measured by the third moment of a valued variable taken around its mean, divided by its cubed standard deviation. Finally, Dodd suggests that the absence of "unity" (bipolarized inequality) can be measured using the fourth moment of a frequency distribution (often called its "kurtosis") which is maximized by a bimodal distribution.

A recent study using three such moments is Glendon Schubert and Charles Press, "Measuring Malapportionment," *American Political Science Review, 58* (1964), 302–27.

bution is a less useful device than . . . cumulative distributions . . . ; this point hardly requires argument at the present date."[18] Basically, cumulative measures are more useful and more comprehensive than noncumulative ones.[19]

Minimal majority. Among currently used measures of legislative apportionment, the "minimal majority" measure of representativeness alone uses the notion of a cumulative distribution function. It may be defined as the theoretical minimum percentage of a political unit's population that can elect a majority to its legislature. For democratic theory the majority vote is certainly crucial, but in most legislatures, where a two-thirds majority is required to exercise a veto or override one, it is also important to know what percentage of the population could perform such an action. In addition, the entire cumulative distribution curve would be of interest because hypothetical bare majorities rarely vote together. If we take the magic 50.1 per cent out of politics for the moment, identifying and cumulating the distribution of power or wealth reflects a major descriptive goal for political research.

The Lorenz curve. An especially attractive feature of the Lorenz curve (see Figure 16.1) as a means of depicting a cumulative value distribution is the clarity with which it displays the size of minimal majorities or veto groups. The 45° line in Figure 16.1 represents the condition of perfect equality, wherein each percentile of the population would contribute equally to the cumulated total of Senate seats. Thus under complete equality, each 10 per cent of the population would have 10 per cent of the seats; the first two thirds of a population would have two thirds of the seats. How far in fact the actual cumulated distribution of representation or wealth falls short of the "line of equality" gives us an accurate visual measure of the inequality involved. From a

18. Bowman, p. 627.

19. Knowing that an extremely disproportionate value pattern exists, for instance, does not answer the question of how much of the total desired object, be it land, income, or power, is held by any given extreme portion of the population. In addition, like logarithms, cumulative distributions are naturally based on *percentage* value differences rather than *absolute* ones, facilitating comparisons between data in different units of measurement.

Lorenz curve, then, one can easily determine the minimal grouping of individuals required to achieve any percentage of a value, such as a legislative majority.

Figure 16.1. Lorenz Curve for Representation in the United States Senate (1960)

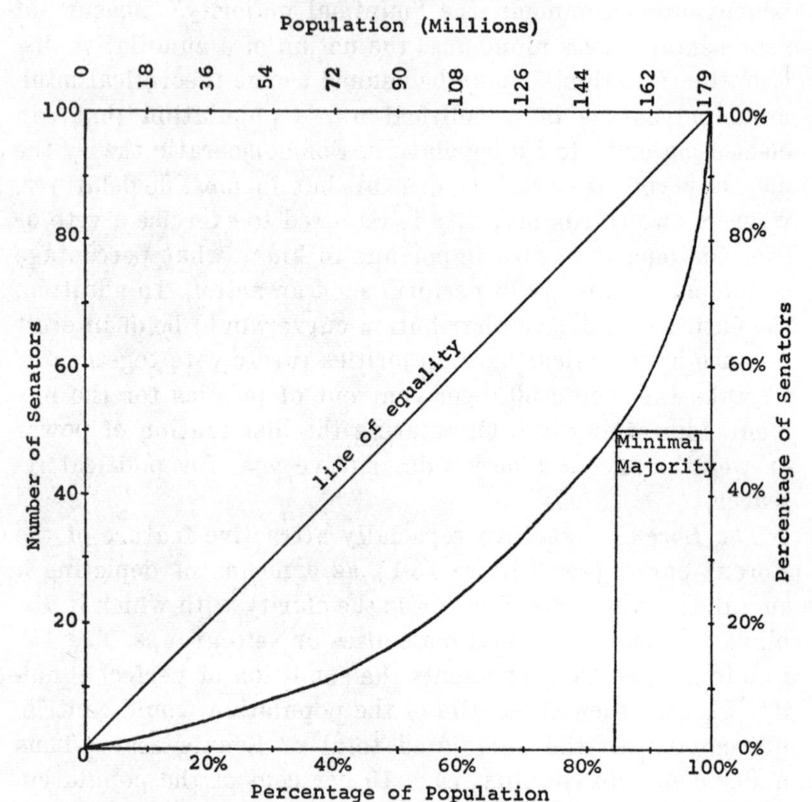

If we were to print the names of each of the states below the appropriate portions of the cumulated population along the base of Figure 16.1, the *increase* of the Lorenz curve above such a segment would represent its percentage voting strength. The slope, or *rate of increase,* of the curve at that point corresponds to a particular ratio of advantage, a state's "right to vote." [20] As with a tabular array we can see that when the slope is steeper than a 45° line the state is overrepresented, and vice versa. Thus we can identify not

20. David and Eisenberg.

only the overall pattern of inequality, but the particular beneficiaries and victims of that pattern. For these reasons it is often useful to begin an analysis by plotting Lorenz curves before further calculations are undertaken. The ease with which one can present and compare simultaneously several distributions of this sort is an additional attraction of the visual Lorenz presentation.

Nevertheless, since only a limited number of curves can conveniently be compared at the same time, some further refinement is required. Using estimates, interpolated if necessary, of the percentage of goods held by the same fraction of the population[21] (such as the top 1 or top 10 per cent) for all the cumulative distributions to be compared might solve this problem. In light of our earlier discussion, however, it would be more useful to have some means of comparison not limited to any particular point on the distribution curve.

The Gini index of concentration. The Gini index cumulates for a population the difference between a theoretical cumulative distribution of values and the actual one. In geometric terms, the *area* between a Lorenz curve and the line of equality is divided by the maximum possible area of inequality.[22] The greater this area, the more highly possession of the value is concentrated, or unequal.

It should be clear that the norm of equality from which differences are measured is an analytic one, with ethical and possibly empirical implications. Unlike indices based on logarithmic data transformations (e.g. Pareto's coefficient), the

21. It may often be convenient to use the Lorenz curve as a tool for interpolation in this way. If, for instance, data are available only for population quartiles, other points of the distribution can be estimated from the smoothest or best fitting curve. Ways to approximate Lorenz curves are discussed by Kuznets, Adelman, and Kravis, p. 179. For extremes of cumulative distributions, more complicated estimation methods based on logarithmic data displays (see Bowman) might be more appropriate.

22. An approximate formula is given in note 27 below; convenient computing procedures for grouped data are given in Julius Jahn, Calvin F. Schmid, and Clarence Schrag, "The Measurement of Ecological Segregation," *American Sociological Review, 12* (1947), 293–303. Cumulating population districts by their percentage of the total Negro population in a city and plotting a Lorenz curve of this distribution, these authors suggest the Gini index (divided by its highest possible value, given the size of Negro population involved) as a measure of social segregation.

Gini index of concentration and related measures to be discussed below assume that "equal importance may be attached to equal absolute differences in income [or some other value] even though one of the differences is taken between two low [value positions] and the other between two high [ones]."[23]

Figure 16.2. Lorenz Curve for Upper Houses, Mississippi and Texas

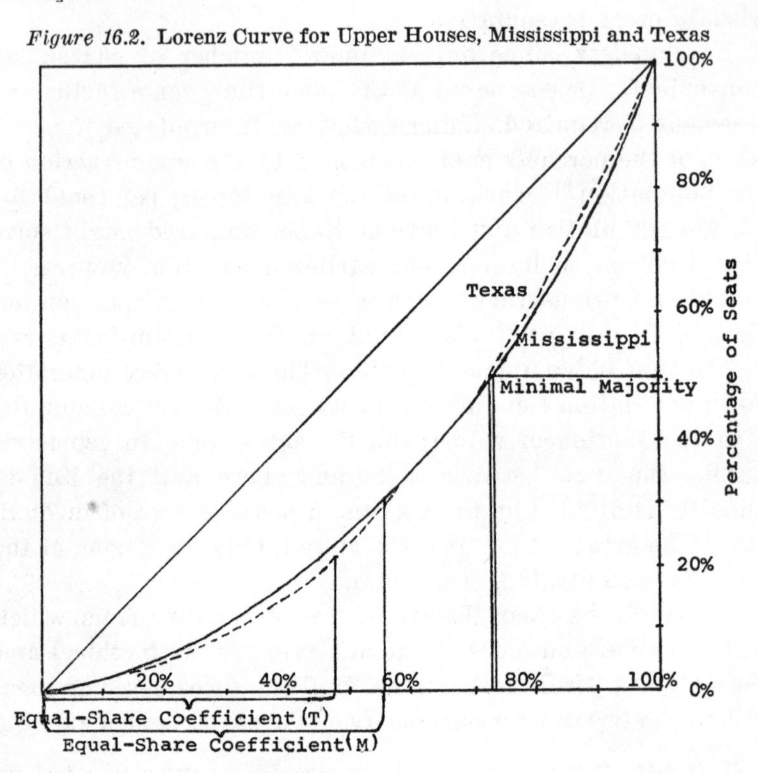

A different problem with the minimal majority measure, as well as with its natural generalization, the Gini index, is illustrated by Figure 16.2. Both cumulative distribution curves, C and C′, represent virtually the same population as having half the value concerned. Therefore their minimal majority measures would be the same. In light of the different shape of the cumulative curves, a more serious problem is

23. Kravis, p. 179.

that the Gini numbers, which take into account the degree of underrepresentation all along the distribution, are also virtually identical. Why the two Gini numbers are so similar is clear. The cumulated value distribution for Texas represents a distribution penalizing the lowest value holders more heavily than it does the moderately well-off value holders; the distribution for Mississippi does just the opposite. In other words, the cumulative curve for Texas comes much more quickly to the point where the next added population percentile gets a full one per cent of the value than is the case for Mississippi.

The equal-share point. We shall call the point where the slope of a Lorenz curve equals one the equal-share point. As its name implies, the equal-share point is the point where the cumulative distribution has the same slope as, and starts to get closer to, the 45° "line of equality."[24] The distance from the origin to the point on the horizontal axis directly below the equal-share point may be called an equal-share coefficient. *It measures the size of the population receiving less than the average share of the value concerned.* This concept is designed to distinguish among distributions, like those in Figure 16.2, which may be quite different but still yield the same Gini index or minimal majority.[25]

24. From the equal-share point the *perpendicular* distance to the line of equality is greatest. This distance, divided by its theoretical maximum under conditions of complete inequality, could be used as another measure of inequality. Similarly, Otis Dudley Duncan and Beverly Duncan, "A Methodological Analysis of Segregation Indexes," *American Sociological Review, 20* (1955), 210–17, have defined a "Nonwhite Section Index" as the maximum *vertical* distance between the diagonal and the curve. While both suggestions are of some value, with perhaps the Duncans' index an easier one to conceptualize, the Gini number and the Schutz coefficient discussed below make more complete use of the information in the Lorenz curve presentation. By suggesting an important division in the population sharing a value, the equal-share point appears more interesting as a measure of a single distance.

25. This simple concept is extraordinarily suggestive. If we call the equal-share coefficient X_{ES}, its percentage complement ($100 - .X_{ES}$) may be used to describe the size of a population receiving more than an equal share of a given value, e.g. land, income, or power. One might operationally (and visibly on a Lorenz curve) define the size of the upper and middle classes in just this fashion and attempt to correlate size and political stability. Similarly, an elite could be operationally defined as those individuals re-

The Schutz coefficient. When there are extreme cases of inequality above or below the equal-share point, we want to know how many there are, with what cumulative impact. To answer this question, Robert Schutz [26] suggested cumulating in either direction from what we call the equal-share point the difference between the slope of the cumulative distribution and that of the "line of equality." [27] Above the equal-share point (where the data are usually better), for example, this difference amounts to how much more than average an individual receives.

In terms of discrete political data, the Schutz coefficient can be interpreted as another attempt to measure the overall inequality of the "right to vote." It sums ratios of advantage on either side of a natural division point, the equal-share point. It avoids summing to zero in essentially the same manner as does the mean deviation or Dahl's index of polyarchy.[28] Of course, other population subgroupings might

---

ceiving more than, say, five or ten times as much of something as an average individual.

Finally, in a very natural way, the equal-share point may be used in assessing the degree of skewness in a cumulative distribution. The percentage of a population coming between the mean individual and the median one is just the difference between the equal-share coefficient and the 50th population percentile ($X_{ES} - 50$). The difference in goods received can be similarly measured.

26. R. R. Schutz, "On the Measurement of Income Inequality," *American Economic Review, 41* (1951), 107–22.

27. The relevant formula for grouped data is, therefore:

$$\text{Schutz Coefficient} = \sum_{0}^{X_{ES}} \left(1 - \frac{\Delta y}{\Delta x}\right) \Delta x = \sum_{X_{ES}}^{100} \left(\frac{\Delta y}{\Delta x} - 1\right) \Delta x$$

When x and y are Lorenz curve coordinates, and Δx and Δy are corresponding increments passing through these coordinates, then approximately,

$$\text{Gini index} = \frac{2}{10{,}000} \sum_{0}^{100} (x - y)\Delta x \qquad \text{(Schutz)}$$

In each case the summations are taken as many times as there are Δx increments between the stated limits.

Schutz also plots curves of slopes for his data ($\Delta y / \Delta x$ *vs.* x) in an illuminating way and generalizes the Lorenz curve presentational form to allow intergroup comparisons from the same curve. Similarly, one could plot higher derivatives of cumulative distributions and note their parameters in refining the aspects of inequality involved; see Adelman.

28. A significant by-product of this study is the large number of measures of inequality that can be generated from either frequency or (especially)

also be meaningful to use in summing the "right to vote."[29]

The Gini number and the Schutz coefficient represent two different aspects of inequality. For their respective populations, the first cumulates the "distance" between the cumulative curve and the "line of equality," while the other cumulates the difference between the slopes or rates of change of these curves. Since the slope of the Lorenz curve must increase as the curve rises, we should expect some correlation when both measures are applied.

APPLICATIONS

To illustrate the uses and limitations of some of these measures derived from cumulative distributions, we shall first apply several—the Gini index, the equal-share point, the Schutz coefficient, the minimal majority measure, and the per cent of goods held by the most favored one per cent of value holders—to a selection of 27 American state senates (upper houses) for which detailed data were readily available. All five indices were calculated for each of the 27 legislative bodies. The cumulative distributions of population and representation by district were compiled within each state. Table 16.1 presents these computed indices, and Table 16.2

---

cumulative distributions, e.g. notes 17 and 25 above. The complement of Dahl's polyarchy index, *P*, a standardized mean deviation (see note 13), is essentially equal to one-fiftieth of Schutz's coefficient. Continuing the approximate definitions for grouped data we have been using, it is easy to show that

$$1 - P = 2 \sum_{V_i > V} \frac{f_i}{N} \frac{(V_i - 1)}{V},$$

at least when (the typical case in an unequal situation) no voter has exactly the mean vote value ($\overline{V}$) as his own V_i. Considering Δy and Δx in the cumulative distribution to be for voting classes, then, in percentages,

$$\Delta x = \frac{f_i}{N} \cdot 100 \text{ and } \Delta y = \frac{f_i V_i}{\Sigma f_i V_i} \cdot 100 \quad \text{(see note 13)}$$

Substitution of these expressions in the above equation gives

$$1 - P = \frac{2}{100} \sum_{V_i > V} (\Delta y - \Delta x),$$

where the last summation equals the right hand side of the first equation in note 27.

29. See David and Eisenberg.

TABLE 16.1. TWENTY-SEVEN STATE SENATES RATED ON FIVE INDICES OF INEQUALITY *

State	*Minimal Majority*	*Gini (x 100)*	*Equal-Share*	*Schutz*	*% Seats held by most overrepresented 1%*
Georgia (1962)	46.5	05.0	51.7	03.5	08.7
Wisconsin (1953)	45.9	05.7	55.6	04.1	08.7
Ohio (1960)	43.0	10.6	34.4	07.8	09.9
West Virginia (1951)	40.9	13.3	53.1	09.2	10.2
Vermont (1960)	39.8	14.2	60.3	10.3	10.1
New York (1950)	39.3	13.1	48.7	10.8	10.8
South Dakota (1960)	36.8	21.0	46.4	14.8	11.7
Oregon (1960)	36.6	17.5	66.9	13.4	12.8
North Carolina (1960)	35.0	22.6	42.6	16.5	12.3
Maine (1960)	34.9	19.6	62.3	15.2	13.3
Pennsylvania (1950)	34.0	23.5	51.1	17.1	13.0
Indiana (1960)	33.6	23.4	57.2	16.9	12.6
Washington (1960)	33.5	23.9	57.9	17.0	13.2
Michigan (1950)	30.1	28.2	54.9	22.3	14.3
Iowa (1960)	29.8	30.8	49.7	21.7	14.8
Connecticut (1960)	29.7	29.9	52.8	22.2	14.4
Texas (1960)	28.5	33.6	48.2	25.6	14.3
Mississippi (1960)	27.2	34.0	56.0	24.9	15.4
Tennessee (1960)	25.9	33.4	60.1	26.9	17.1
Wyoming (1960)	25.6	35.3	57.3	27.7	16.7
South Carolina (1960)	22.0	43.3	60.9	32.6	18.8
Utah (1960)	18.7	39.0	74.8	32.3	24.3
New Jersey (1960)	17.8	44.6	72.3	33.9	21.9
Montana (1960)	15.4	54.1	57.1	40.1	23.8
New Mexico (1960)	13.1	56.1	80.0	42.0	23.2
Florida (1960)	11.4	58.2	74.4	45.1	27.7
Nevada (1960)	07.2	71.7	76.5	59.7	26.4
Electoral College (1961)	43.1	09.9	82.6	07.3	09.8

* In this table the equal-share coefficient marks the percentage of the population which is underrepresented. A program for computing these indices on the IBM 709/7090 is available from the Yale Political Data Program.

indicates the degree to which each measure correlates with every other measure when applied to the entire sample. Low values of the minimal majority index indicate great inequality; with all other indices a high value means great inequality. In Table 16.2 the value in each cell is the squared product moment correlation coefficient, r^2, which can be interpreted as the proportion of the total variation in one index that can be linearly explained by another.

TABLE 16.2. SQUARED CORRELATION COEFFICIENTS OF FIVE MEASURES OF INEQUALITY AS APPLIED TO SEATS AND POPULATION IN 27 STATE SENATES

	Gini	*Equal-Share*	*Schutz*	*Minimal Majority*	*% Seats held by most overrepresented 1%*
Gini	X	.44	.99	.98	.90
Equal-Share	.44	X	.47	.51	.57
Schutz	.99	.47	X	.97	.91
Minimal Majority	.98	.51	.97	X	.95
% Seats held by most overrepresented 1% of population	.90	.57	.91	.95	X

The Gini, Schutz, minimal majority, and top one per cent indices are all highly correlated with each other. That is, it makes very little difference which is used in trying to compare the degree of inequality in one senate with that in another. All give approximately the same judgment about how unequal a particular distribution is as compared with some other distribution. Each of these measures, for example, shows representation in 25 of the 27 state legislatures to be more unequally distributed than in the electoral college. Thus if these indices were used, virtually all states in our sample would have to reapportion to meet the stringent test proposed by the Federal District Court in *Sanders v. Gray*.[30]

The remaining measure, however, the equal-share coeffi-

30. *Sanders v. Gray*. A test of the political relevance of these measures is provided by a Constitutional amendment which has been proposed to deprive the federal courts of any control over state districting. For this group of state senates we find point-biserial correlations of .51 between inequality (minimal majority) and passage of resolutions favoring the amendment, and .50 between inequality (Gini) and approval of such resolutions.

cient, shows a strikingly low correlation with the others. In its concern with the proportion of the population which has less (or more) than its "equal share" of representatives, or less than average representation, it measures a different aspect of the distribution. By contrast with the situation suggested by the other indices, *all* of the 27 states in our sample show a lower equal-share coefficient (that is, greater "equality") than the electoral college. Most Americans have less, but only slightly less, than average representation in the electoral college; the 17 per cent who live in the 25 states smaller than Connecticut gain rather substantially.[31]

As a second illustration of these indices of inequality, we applied them to data for 47 countries on the number of farms of various sizes, and the number of hectares held by all farms in each size class.[32] Table 16.3 indicates the r^2 for each pair

TABLE 16.3. SQUARED CORRELATION COEFFICIENTS OF FIVE MEASURES OF INEQUALITY AS APPLIED TO 47 LAND TENURE DISTRIBUTIONS

	Gini	*Equal-Share*	*Schutz*	*Minimal Majority*	*% Land held by largest 1% landholders* *
Gini	X	.80	.96	.88	.17
Equal-Share	.80	X	.77	.76	.09
Schutz	.96	.77	X	.82	.17
Minimal Majority	.88	.76	.82	X	.13
% Land held by largest 1% landholders	.17	.09	.17	.13	X

* The 1% coefficient was calculated from a curvilinear approximation to the Lorenz curve.

of indices. Here again the Gini, Schutz, and minimal majority indices are highly correlated, and each is more closely correlated with the equal-share coefficient than was the case with the representation data. But the measure of extremes,

31. A promising computer procedure for equitable districting is presented by James Weaver and Sidney Hess, "A Procedure for Non-Partisan Districting: Development of Computer Techniques," *Yale Law Journal, 72* (1963), 288–309.

32. The actual data have been presented elsewhere in B. Russett, "Inequality and Instability: The Relation of Land Tenure to Politics," *World Politics, 16* (1964), 442–54.

the per cent of land belonging to the one per cent of land-holders with the largest farms, shows virtually no relationship to the others.

IMPLICATIONS

This chapter has confined itself to describing, not explaining, inequalities in distributions of valued goods. The applications of several such measures suggest some general conclusions about the information conveyed, the comprehensiveness, and the theoretical usefulness of these and similar measures. First, *measures which concentrate only on a single standard point near the extreme of the distribution are likely to be misleading.* The low correlation of the "top one per cent" on the land data illustrates this nicely. Unless one has sound theoretical reasons for an interest in only a small segment of the distribution, this type of measure is unsatisfactory. If such a measure is used it must not be treated as in any way a summary of the whole distribution. Use of an index like the ratio of the population in the largest district to that in the smallest is *not* an admissible summary of the overall pattern of representation.

Nevertheless, the "top one per cent" correlated highly with other measures in the set of data on legislative apportionment, and we must suggest some explanation. In part the reason lies in the quality of the data available. For the legislatures we were able to identify almost exactly in each case the number of seats held by the most overrepresented one per cent of the population; the equivalent data in the land series were estimated from a curvilinear approximation to the Lorenz curve based on nearby points. Unequal grouping of data alone accounts for much of the lower correlation in the land series.

In addition, the nature of legislative apportionment militates against particularly great overrepresentaton of a very small fraction of the population. Any apportionment scheme must be approved by many legislators; thus the agreement of others can be obtained only by permitting them to be overrepresented also. As a result, those in the top one per cent are not likely to be much more heavily overrepresented than others in the top 10 per cent, though all may be much more overrepresented than the remaining legislative districts. No such restriction seems to apply with landholdings, however. In one country most of the land may be concentrated in the hands of a very few great estates, in another there may be a fairly substantial number of rather large farms, while in both cases the great mass of farmers may have to be content with approximately the same fraction of total land. Indices concentrating on the central part of the distribution, or which even measure the whole distribution, may not identify much difference, while an index measuring extremeness will. But the analyst must be quite certain that it is extremeness in which he is interested.

Second, *certain measures concentrating on a single standard point near the middle of the distribution are likely to be more generally useful.* The minimal majority index shows a relatively high correlation with most of the other indices in both sets of data (especially in the legislature set) and thus can perhaps be taken as a reasonably adequate measure of the whole distribution, at least in these cases. It may be attractive to some researchers because it is easy to compute and directly relevant to some interesting hypotheses. Nevertheless, it should be used only with great caution, for we have no assurance that it would correlate highly with other indices when applied to value distributions other than the two sets examined above. With some distributions—for example, the degree of residential concentration of Negroes—it does not even have any very obvious meaning.

Third, *the equal-share index, showing a fairly low correlation with the other indices, measures a different aspect of the distributions.* There may often be sound theoretical reasons for retaining it in analysis, along with an index like minimal majority or the Schutz coefficient.[33]

Fourth, *both the Gini index and the Schutz coefficient provide attractive ways of summarizing important aspects of*

33. See note 25 above.

an accurate cumulative distribution. Besides allowing easy visual interpretation, they are sensitive to inequalities present in all parts of a value distribution.[34] Their high correlation with the more representative of the other indices corroborates their use, in detailed analysis, as summary measures.

Finally, *much of the reason for correlations appreciably lower than unity stems from incomplete and differently grouped data.* The data for state senates were available in such a form that points could be established all along the cumulative distribution, and be quite accurate at the same points for each legislature (that is, for 10, 20, . . . 90, 95, and 99 per cent of the population). But the land tenure data were sometimes not complete—the first point identifiable on the cumulative distribution curve might be for 40 per cent of the landowners—and data were seldom available for the same points in many different countries. Now it is for just this reason, the desire to make seemingly noncomparable data comparable, that we resort to summary indices. But however useful they are, in making approximations these measures do lose some precision.

Hence, before deciding to use a summary index of the whole distribution, one should carefully examine the raw data to be sure that in each case they cover the whole distribution fairly adequately—or at least that they are equally incomplete in each case.[35] If inadequacies are found and the use of a summary index is still desirable, it is perhaps best to use the one which is least distorted by inadequacies in the cumulative curve. In our land distribution analysis the

34. These indices provide excellent measures for comparing inequality *between* larger political units (e.g. states), and the cumulated percentages on which they are based provide the data for comparison *within* the units (e.g. counties). The latter criterion is emphasized by Alan L. Clem in "Measuring Legislative Malapportionment: In Search of a Better Yardstick," *Midwest Journal of Political Science, 7* (1963), 124–44, but for the former he suggests (p. 138) a measure which is essentially a mean deviation.

35. When the data *are* incomplete (rather than reported incompletely), as with sample survey results, estimation procedures exist for most measures derived from frequency distributions. P. C. Mahalanobis, "A Method of Fractile Graphical Analysis," *Sankhya: The Indian Journal of Statistics, 23* (1961), 41–64, has recently done important work in suggesting sampling and estimation procedures for coefficients derived from cumulative distributions.

Schutz coefficient, based on the slope of the cumulative curve, was least distorted by incomplete data. If, for example, the first point on a cumulative distribution is for holdings of the "poorest" half of the population, the Gini index measuring the area between the curve and the 45° line will indicate greater equality than actually exists. But the Schutz coefficient, which depends on the average slope below (or above) the equal-share point, will not be as distorted.[36]

We have examined more than twenty possible indices of inequality. Since equality and departures from it may be theoretically defined in different ways, there is no all-purpose index of inequality. Different measures may or may not give similar results with different sets of data. In every analysis one must therefore be aware of the range of indices available and adopt the one, or several, most appropriate to the data and hypotheses in question.

36. Because of the equivalence between the Schutz measure and Dahl's polyarchy index (a standardized mean deviation), this result reinforces Yntema's earlier findings about the merits of the mean deviation. See notes 10 and 28.

PART IV

The Organizational Focus: National and International Action to Advance Quantitative Comparative Analysis

Current trends in cross-national research bear some important implications for the context of such efforts. The first of these is organizational. To take a simple example, it is virtually impossible for a solitary researcher to conduct his own sample survey of a national population. For this he must rely upon some organizational base that can assist him in the formulation of questionnaires and in drawing an appropriate sample of the population, provide him with a staff of trained interviewers who can seek out the individual respondents, compile his data and code them on punch cards, and analyze his data in at least a preliminary fashion (e.g. through the preparation of cross-classification tables). It is for this reason that more and more scholars are turning to the Survey Research Center of the University of Michigan, the National Opinion Research Center in Chicago, the Bureau of Applied Social Research at Columbia University, and similar agencies. Still less can the individual researcher conduct a sample survey in five different countries, where five or more languages may be spoken, without using the services of survey organizations in these countries. The same type of problem faces a data gathering and analyzing project, such as the Yale Political Data Program, which requires more hardware (and, particularly, electronic computers) than the individual scholar garreted in his study normally has at his disposal. It is precisely this need for organizational bases in the social sciences that now makes it imperative to survey the current and anticipated requirements of social scientists and to work out a coordinated program to facilitate their realization in the coming years.

The second implication, not unrelated to the first, is psychological. While few would deny the importance of the individual scholar in the process of empirical research, there is a growing recognition of the usefulness of pooling intellectual resources through cooperative research. At one level, as the number of toilers in the vineyards of social science increases, the most efficient utilization of resources requires that we minimize duplication of efforts and overlapping projects. At a second and more important level, quite often cooperative research, particularly if it is of an interdisciplinary variety, can yield fruitful results.

Third is the problem of increasing the flow of *relevant* information. This is a twofold problem. On the one hand, the wide dispersion of scholars pursuing empirical research in the social sciences requires effective communication across national (and linguistic) boundaries, to promote the interchange of ideas and data as well as to avoid duplicating efforts. But, on the other hand, since the sheer volume of information seems to be increasing exponentially, some means of selecting out and communicating the most vital information is needed. This may call for specialized communication channels, whether through mimeographed newsletters or through more international meetings among scholars whose interests are similar or compatible, or for a serious effort to create a genuinely adequate abstracting service.

Fourth, data collected must be stored and made easily available. Despite surface similarities, data archives face problems quite dissimilar from those confronting other types of libraries. Not the least of these is retrievability. Data that cannot be located and retrieved rapidly are, for all practical purposes, lost data. Retrievability requires access to certain types of electronic data processing equipment as well as the development of appropriate programming skills. Equally serious are problems of method of storage (e.g. punch cards vs. magnetic tape or data drive cells), format comparability, the collection and storage of codebooks and other ancillary material, providing access to outside users (whose data processing equipment may differ from that of the archive), and so forth.

Fifth is the question of financing. Clearly, all of the above operations require considerably more financial outlay than has been needed or available in the past. And, as more scholars enter the field or begin to use electronic computers, the competition for funds will increase. In this regard the task currently facing social scientists has two ramifications: we must utilize resources on hand as efficiently as possible; and we must seek ways to make more funds available. Above all, in the distribution of research capital, the needs of ancillary services—archiving, abstracting, retrieving—must not be forgotten. If this happens the progress of empirical research will be dangerously hampered.

Finally, implicit in all that has gone before is the need for greater international cooperation—not only in the conduct of research itself, but in the creation of archives, the perfection of data retrieval processes, the facilitation of interchanges of ideas and data, and the provision of adequate financing as well. It is neither possible, necessary, nor desirable that a single country be called upon to bear the brunt of empirical social science research. And yet, at the same time, it may be that no international agency is in a position to take over a substantial portion of this burden. It is nonetheless clear that only international action can prevent the edifice of social science from becoming a modern-day Tower of Babel.

This section of the book deals with some of these organizational problems and poses some alternative solutions. Richard L. Merritt, for instance, focuses upon the organization and promotion of political research in the United States. After documenting the growth of cooperative research and outlining the types of organizational bases for research that have emerged, he points to some of the problems that will beset the American research community if present trends continue. In particular he discusses the need for syntheses of research in progress, replicate studies that can test propositions developed in previous projects (both for accuracy and for differences over time), for an adequate international abstracting service, for a data retrieval system. Although he concentrates upon the American context, the problems he examines are faced by scholars everywhere. European universities were, to be sure, slower to recover from the ravages of World War II than were most American institutions; moreover, some of them suffered under dictatorships that hindered the development of social science research and drove some of their best scholars into exile. Even so, the trends that American social scientists have witnessed in the past two decades are now well under way in Europe. The prospects for social scientists are bright. But it is equally clear that intelligent organizational efforts at this time can pave the way for more fruitful research and international cooperation than has been hitherto possible.

Stein Rokkan and Henry Valen outline the organizational means to fill an important gap: archives for statistical studies of within-nation differences. To date most data banks have concentrated upon information at the level of the individual actor or the nation-state, with little attention being paid to the archiving of information at the intermediary level of the locality. Using the commune as their basic unit of analysis, Rokkan and Valen have set up an archive for ecological data on Norway. Their goal is a delineation of the "macro-characteristics" of each locality: its ecological position within the provincial network of communication and economic exchange, its geographic structure, its economic, educational, organizational, and political institutions, and the consequent constellations of openings and opportunities for the individual inhabitants. The creation of a European archive for the statistical study of within-nation differences is proceeding apace.

Philip E. Converse surveys the current effort to build up archives for secondary analysis of sample survey data in the United States through cooperative arrangements between producers and users. The largest of these is the Roper Public Opinion Center at Williams College in Massachusetts. Other, more recently developed archives include the Inter-University Consortium for Political Research at the University of Michigan, the Survey Research Center of the University of California at Berkeley, and the Yale Political Science Research Library. With the help and encouragement of the National Science Foundation, American social scientists have recently created the framework for a national archival system that will permit widespread access to available data, and at least a preliminary attack upon such persistent problems as the standardization of format, the reporting of error, and card editing.

The next two chapters are more specifically geared to problems of data retrieval. Erwin K. Scheuch and Philip J. Stone discuss the usefulness of the General Inquirer content analysis system for classifying and retrieving questions asked in surveys and stored in archives. Initial tests reveal that it is quite possible to program an electronic computer to code questions in terms of a set concept language and to retrieve questions effectively in that way. It also seems possible to develop the system so that, in processing data in many different languages, there would be no need for human translators, since each natural language sentence in the survey questionnaires could be "tagged" to the same basic set of theoretical concepts. Francis G. Lévy outlines the SYNTOL (*Synt*agmatic *O*rganization *L*anguage) procedure for information storage and retrieval. By way of a brief definition of the differences between the General Inquirer system and SYNTOL, the former uses (and "tags") natural language statements as the basis of programs for retrieval, whereas SYNTOL seeks to develop a quasi language for the expression of content based upon the use of descriptors. Thus each has its use and limitations.

Harold D. Lasswell sets out a scheme of basic variables for cross-national comparisons and demonstrates how many of the relationships between such variables and their changes over time could be given graphic expression in charts and maps of different types. Policy makers and students of international and comparative politics, meeting in chart rooms where such graphic data could be on permanent display, would have a constant reminder of the world context in which they are working. He strongly recommends these visual techniques in the teaching of comparative politics; and suggests that efforts be made to develop appropriate modes of graphic representation of results of cross-national analyses, such as those envisaged by the Yale Political Data Program.

Donald V. McGranahan surveys the resources for social research in the United Nations. In the League of Nations years the domain of intergovernmental organizations was restricted largely to matters of border transactions: trade, communications, migration, war. Since the early 1950s, however, the United Nations has taken on a new task: poverty and underdevelopment are no longer matters exclusively for domestic action, but are of international concern. The United Nations has sought to collect information on world poverty for use in decisions on action aimed toward increased production, greater equality, better social conditions. In fact, the staff of the Economic and Social Council is now very much larger than the staff of the Security Council. But the United Nations has not concerned itself exclusively with practical measures to fight poverty. There is a patent need for fundamental research on the processes of development. Academic social scientists can play an important role in the elaboration and testing of the theories needed for practical action: the social science pioneers of the nineteenth century were generally concerned with processes of evolution and change; in the first half of the twentieth century the dominant emphasis has been on the static analysis of structures and functions. This is changing, but much more needs to be done to ensure cooperation between academic social scientists and the practical data gatherers and data analysts in the United Nations and its specialized agencies. Perhaps the most interesting work currently under way centers on the development of the comparability of national statistics, as discussed in the *Compendium of Social Statistics, 1963* (a supplement to the United Nations' *Report on the World Social Situation* in 1963). To get around many of the difficulties of data gathering in developing countries, proposals for extending sample survey facilities in different regions of the world are currently under consideration. If better data can be assembled, or at least if better ways can be found for establishing comparative estimates on the basis of current data, substantial advances may be expected in the analysis of patterns of growth and in the techniques for initiating growth. In this field it is expected that the United Nations will make considerable headway through the newly established Research Institute for Social Development in Geneva. This institute will evaluate field experiments in the initiation of change, as well as work on methodology for the type of social prognostication required in establishing long-term development plans.

Stein Rokkan, in his review of the UNESCO program in the social sciences, urges that agency to broaden the international basis for cross-national research. Its role is not to supplant but rather to supplement work carried on by national research programs; and, where possible, to seek a measure of coordination to advance knowledge in strategic areas and to reduce duplication of efforts. More specifically, UNESCO could play an active part in documentation and clearing-house activities; the advancement of the methodology of cross-national comparison; the confrontation of data and findings for different countries; the promotion of training in cross-national comparative analysis; and the planning and execution of joint international inquiries. By its very nature, UNESCO is better situated than any other international agency to carry out such tasks, providing that social scientists as well as member governments cooperate fully.

By way of a conclusion to this volume, nothing seemed more fitting than the recommendations of the Yale Data Conference itself. After outlining some of the specific problems of archival organization and interarchival cooperation, and suggesting some guidelines for resolving them, the recommendations go on to propose a program for action to promote cross-national comparative research. It is heartening that, as this volume goes to press, some of the recommendations have already been implemented and others are in the stage of concrete planning. For example, a meeting of experts in Paris in September 1964 got under way a European data archival system. During the winter of 1964–65, American scholars made considerable progress in securing agreement on technical problems (such as punch card formats, exchange of computer programs, standards for minimal "cleaning" and storage operations), as well as an interarchival program of cooperation and coordination in the United States. Despite these hopeful trends, much remains to be done. And it is clear that, for some time to come, organization for cross-national research must remain a focus of our attention.

17. The Organization and Promotion of Political Research in the United States

RICHARD L. MERRITT, YALE UNIVERSITY

However you look at it, the American political science profession has grown mightily in recent decades. While the number of colleges and universities in the United States doubled from 1910 to 1960 (Table 17.1), the number of such institutions with separate departments of political science increased fourfold by the most conservative estimate. During the same half century membership in the American Political Science Association increased by a factor of eight, the circulation of the *American Political Science Review* by a factor of seven, the number of doctorates in political science from about 10 per annum to well over 200 yearly, and the number of American scholarly journals dealing with political science and international relations doubled every 21 years. In 1958, the last year for which we have complete data, American colleges and universities granted a total of 8,633 degrees in political science, international relations, and public administration—7,287 bachelor's degrees, 1,131 master's degrees, and 215 doctorates.[1]

The political science profession has also been characterized by a number of qualitative changes. The changing subject matter of political science and its increasing specializa-

1. U. S. Office of Education, *Statistics of Higher Education 1957–58, Faculty, Students, and Degrees*, Chapter 4, Section 1 (Washington, U. S. Government Printing Office, 1962), p. 85.

TABLE 17.1. GROWTH IN HIGHER EDUCATION AND POLITICAL SCIENCE, 1910–1960
SOME BASIC DATA

	1910	*1920*	*1930*	*1940*	*1950*	*1960*
No. of universities and colleges [a]	951	1,041	1,409	1,708	1,851	2,008
Total enrollment (in 1000) [a]	355	598	1,101	1,494	2,659	3,216
No. of faculty members [a]	36,480	48,615	82,386	146,929	248,749	380,554
Univ. w/separate Pol. Sci. depts. [b]	120					466
No. of doctorates granted [c]	443	615	2,299	3,290	6,633	9,829
Political Science doctorates [d]	10	14	52	81	158	222
Membership in APSA [e]	1,098	1,309	1,819	2,857	5,126	8,500
Circulation of APSR [f]	1,300	1,500	1,300	2,635	5,295	7,020
No. of pol. sci. journals [g]	6	6	9	15	20	28
No. of research institutes [h]	1	10	16	31	74	136

a. U. S. Bureau of the Census, *Historical Statistics of the United States, Colonial Times to 1957* (Washington, D. C., U. S. Government Printing Office, 1960), pp. 210–11; U. S. Bureau of the Census, *Statistical Abstract of the United States: 1962* (83d ed. Washington, D. C., U. S. Government Printing Office, 1962), p. 134.

b. 1910 figure from data estimated in William Anderson, "Political Science Enters the Twentieth Century," in Anna Haddow, *Political Science in American Colleges and Universities, 1636–1900* (New York, Appleton-Century, 1939), p. 263; 1960 estimate from Committee on Standards of Instruction of the APSA, "Political Science as a Discipline," *American Political Science Review, 56* (1962), 418.

c. U. S. Bureau of the Census, *Historical Statistics*, pp. 210–11; and U. S. Bureau of the Census, *Statistical Abstract, 1962*, p. 134.

d. National Academy of Sciences–National Research Council, *Doctorate Production in United States Universities, 1936–1956* (Washington, D. C., U. S. Government Printing Office, 1958), p. 7 (includes public administration and international relations); figures for 1910–30 and 1960 estimated from data for 1936–56. These are not inconsistent with Anderson's data.

e. From minutes of annual meetings, in *American Political Science Review* (1910 figure is for December 1909).

f. *N. W. Ayer & Son's Directory, Newspapers and Periodicals* (Philadelphia, N. W. Ayer & Son, 1910–63).

g. Eileen C. Graves, ed., *Ulrich's Periodical Directory* (10th ed. New York, Bowker, 1963), pp. 295–98 ("International Relations") and 485–96 ("Political Science").

h. Gale Research Company, *Directory of University Research Bureaus and Institutes* (1st ed. Detroit, Gale Research Company, 1960); including "Government Affairs" and some from the "Social Science" sections.

tion have been topics of frequent comment.[2] Similarly, approaches to the same topic have shifted, often dramatically. In the field of international relations, for instance, preoccupation with diplomatic history gave way to a concern for the institutions of peace; the "realist" reaction to this trend seems to be yielding in turn to the behavioral approach to the study of relations among states. No less important has been a changing attitude among political scientists toward the problems of research.

COOPERATIVE RESEARCH: MYTH OR REALITY?

Perhaps no shibboleth has been nearer and dearer to the hearts of social scientists than the crying need for cooperative research, yes, even interdisciplinary research. In 1927, J. Franklin Jameson cast a longing glance at the physical sciences:

> Research in the physical sciences is perhaps more certain to be directed toward useful ends than research in humanistic fields, because the former is most commonly carried on in organized laboratories, where consultation is almost inevitable and a consensus of opinion as to what is worth while is easily formed, and has its effect on the investigator, whereas in most humanistic subjects the researcher can work in comparative isolation.[3]

More recently, in his stimulating book *The Future of Political Science,* Harold D. Lasswell envisioned "centers for advanced political science," where physical and biological scientists, specialists in history, prehistory, social anthropology, economics, and linguistics, communication engineers, sociologists and, above all, political scientists "recruited from the several fields within the profession" could come together on a

2. For a recent statement, see the report of the Committee on Standards of Instruction of the American Political Science Association, "Political Science as a Discipline," *American Political Science Review, 56* (1962), 417–21.

3. *American Historical Review, 32* (1927), 435 n.; cited in Frederic Austin Ogg, *Research in the Humanistic and Social Sciences* (New York, Century, 1928), p. 17 n.

more or less permanent basis "to consolidate and improve the advances that have been made in integrating frames of reference among scholars and scientists and between them and the responsible decision-makers of government and other social institutions." [4]

There is much to be said for cooperative research. Cooperative research—and let it be clear at the outset that I am talking about successful efforts in this direction—enables a more satisfactory division of labor among participants in a project than would be possible were there but one scholar trying to deal with all aspects of the topic. Sometimes it does not require two—a political scientist and an economist, possibly joined by a sociologist and a social psychologist—to dance the particular tango of a research project on, let us say, American aid to developing countries; but such cooperation is often more satisfactory in terms of results as well as more economical in terms of research time and funds. An ever more important factor favoring cooperative research is the cost of acquiring and maintaining the plant and equipment necessary for many forms of political analysis. This problem is especially acute for the growing number of political scientists who are using punch card equipment and large computers in their research. Cooperative research may also produce intellectual stimulation and cross-fertilization that is often a welcome relief "to the individual scholar working by himself, sometimes in too lonely grandeur in his own ivory tower." [5] Then, too, participation in cooperative projects gives the fledgling researcher a chance to soar the heights of knowledge with his older and more experienced colleagues. At the very least he may learn something of the discipline required to carry out joint or individual research projects.

To date, political science has not made the transition "from atomistic effort to collective, organized, cooperative or

4. Harold D. Lasswell, *The Future of Political Science* (New York, Atherton, 1963), pp. 233–34; cf., generally, pp. 208–38.

5. Harold W. Dodds, address at Princeton University, September 20, 1953, reprinted in part as "The Dangers of Project Research," *Social Problems, 1* (January 1954), p. 91.

administered activity."[6] In spite of the force of argument and the sincerity of the advocates of cooperative and interdisciplinary research, and in spite of some of the spectacular results that have emerged from such joint projects, what may be termed a vestigial element of anarchy has prevented the social scientist from subjecting his own research interests entirely to those of a research group. Perhaps rightly so. The scholar who escapes from his freedom too wholeheartedly subjects himself to the (possibly fatal) disease of "projectitis": "an unhappy addiction to limited objectives, perhaps at the very moment at which the individual should be broadening his own comprehension and deepening his knowledge of his discipline, with freedom for roving speculation in an atmosphere unencumbered by the pressures of problem-solving commitments to external agencies."[7] The other problems of cooperative and particularly interdisciplinary research are well known—problems of communication (which are not limited merely to practitioners of different arts), of paperwork and administration, and of interpersonal relationships.[8]

Cooperative research in political affairs is nonetheless gaining headway, if often slowly and painfully. From 1933 to 1937, 3 per cent of the articles and 16 per cent of the books reviewed in *The American Political Science Review* were the result of joint effort; by the period from 1958 to 1962 these percentages had risen to 11 and 24 respectively (Table 17.2). In some of the newer American quarterlies geared toward empirical political research, the percentage of multiple-authored articles is still higher: 22 per cent of the main articles in *The Public Opinion Quarterly* from 1958 to 1963 had joint authorship (as opposed to 9 per cent in the six years from 1937 to 1942); and roughly one-third of the main

6. Over eighteen years ago the Research Committee of the American Political Science Association saw this trend as well-nigh inevitable; cf. its report in *American Political Science Review, 39* (1945), 148–66.

7. Dodds, "The Dangers of Project Research," pp. 91–92.

8. Cf. Warren G. Bennis, "Some Barriers to Teamwork in Social Research," *Social Problems, 3* (1956), 223–35; and, more generally, Margaret B. Luszki, *Interdisciplinary Team Research: Methods and Problems* (New York, New York University Press, 1958).

Table 17.2. Multiauthored Articles in Some Political Science Journals, 1933–1962
Percentage of Major Articles Written Jointly by Two or More Authors, by Five-Year Periods[a]

Journal (and first year of publication)	*1933–37*	*1938–42*	*1943–47*	*1948–52*	*1953–57*	*1958–62*	*1933–1962 Number of articles*	*Total % multi-authored*
American Political Science Review (1906)	3%	7%	6%	8%	9%	11%	1405	7%
(Books reviewed in "Book Review" section)	(16)	(21)	(19)	(19)	(27)	(24)	(3064)	(20)
Journal of Conflict Resolution (1957)					10[b]	15	137	15
Journal of Politics (1939)		5[d]	4	6	4	7	578	5
Midwest Journal of Political Science (1957)					5[b]	9	109	8
Political Science Quarterly (1886)	7	6	2	1	3	7	686	4
Public Administration Review (1940)		15[c]	9	9	16	10	567	11
Public Opinion Quarterly (1937)	1[b]	11	19	29	24	22	1181	19
Review of Politics (1939)		3[d]	2	0	0	3	558	1
Western Political Quarterly (1948)				5	6	5	770	5
World Politics (1948)				5	4	6	316	5
Total number of articles	454	872	950	1241	1223	1567	6307	
Percentage multiauthored	4%	8%	8%	10%	9%	10%		9%

a. Excluding notes, comments, reviews, obituaries, unsigned editorials (and, in *Public Opinion Quarterly*, "Living Research" section).

b. Data for 1 year only. c. Data for 2 years only. d. Data for 4 years only.

articles appearing in *Behavioral Science* since its inception were written cooperatively.

Somewhat more remarkable, however, is the development of formal organizations to facilitate cooperative research on political topics. Since 1913, when only four university bureaus and institutes in the entire United States concentrated upon political research, the number of such organizations has doubled approximately every nine years. By 1959, the last year for which comprehensive statistics are available, their number had grown to 136.[9]

THE ORGANIZATION OF POLITICAL RESEARCH

In the course of the last half century four different organizational approaches to political research have emerged. For ease of communication I shall label these organizations—perhaps we should term them "ideal types" in the Weberian sense—the All-Purpose Research Institute, the Interdisciplinary Research Institute, the Basic Data and Research Institute, and the Independent Research Institute. The first of these is by far the most prevalent in the American political science profession.

The All-Purpose Research Institute

The All-Purpose Research Institute is dedicated to the anarchic principle of the sovereign scholar and, paradoxically enough, to the principle of equity in scholarship. At its center stands the individual scholar with his specific research interests. While collaborative or cooperative research may be a result, it is often the by-product of the institute's allocation of funds rather than any sort of precondition. Wilson Gee's excellent survey of social science research organizations, by now three decades old, discusses in some detail 35 such insti-

9. Cf. Table 17.1. It should be noted that these figures take into account only those research organizations that have continued in existence since the date of their inception, ignoring those that died a-borning or of old age. Precise data are to be found in Gale Research Co., *Directory of University Research Bureaus and Institutes*, (1st ed. Detroit, Gale Research Co., 1960), section 5 ("Government Affairs"), pp. 55–65, and those listed in section 2 ("Social Sciences"), pp. 17–29, that deal with political research.

tutes with interests in political research.[10] Of these, all of which sponsor individual research projects to a greater or lesser extent, only five—the Social Science Research Council of Michigan, the Social Science Research Committee of the University of Minnesota, the Social Science Research Council of the University of Washington, the Social Science Research Council of the University of Wisconsin, and the Institute of Human Relations at Yale University—indicate an interest in cooperative research. At the time of Gee's writing, only the first three of these had actually formulated such projects but in no case, doubtless due to the general shortage of research funds during the depression years, were sufficient funds available to move beyond the planning stage.

In its most primitive form the All-Purpose Research Institute may exist as no more than a departmental committee, charged with the responsibilities to review research projects proposed by individual members of the department and to make necessary arrangements for the allocation of teaching and research time. With the passage of time the committee, by now distinguished by the use of its own letterhead, may set up an office with typists, mimeograph machines, and other equipment and comforts. Not only do such accoutrements provide the scholar with a home, but they also enable him to point to existing research facilities as a cost-cutting attraction for research grants.

At a later stage the faculty committee may transform itself into a research bureau empowered to seek out and facilitate the flow of research funds to individuals in the department. It may even draw upon the credit that particularly prominent members of the department have built up for themselves in the academic world to secure financing for projects undertaken by staff members of lesser experience or fame. To the extent that the board of directors of the research bureau is successful in securing grants that are not earmarked for specific individuals or specific projects, it

10. Wilson Gee, *Social Science Research Organization in American Universities and Colleges* (New York, Appleton-Century, 1934), pp. 70–254; he also discusses eleven others without such interests.

gains a measure of control over the general allocation of research funds among its members. The research bureau may eventually reach the stage of organizational sophistication where it terminates its brokerage function altogether and acts only to disburse its funds to worthy applicants. It may even hire a permanent research staff or solicit applications from scholars at other universities.

The variant forms of the All-Purpose Research Institute are numerous. One of the more prominent of these is the research organization with specific fields of interest. The importance of the specialist in political science is of course obvious. The study of the particular, besides being intrinsically interesting, provides both a means to test theories about the general as well as a basis upon which more adequate general studies and theories may be built. As it usually turns out, empirical studies of the particular generate their own theories about the behavior of the particular; and the cycle takes another turn.

The emergence of research institutes with specific interests may take place in a variety of ways. One person in a department may be performing work in his specialty that is significant enough to attract funds enabling him to branch off from the departmental research committee or bureau. Given time and continuing financial support, he may build up an entire institute devoted to his own field of specialization. Alternatively, a single topic or range of topics may be sufficiently interesting and important to justify the creation of a specialized research institute to concentrate upon such topics in all their ramifications. In either event the trend seems to be in the direction of ever greater resources being focused upon ever narrower topics for research. A Bureau of Government, for example, was established at the University of Michigan in 1914 to concentrate upon research in state and local government. By 1947 the problems of municipal government were important enough to warrant the institution of a Metropolitan Research Project. And, five years later, the focus was narrowed to a single metropolis when a "Detroit Area Study" was set up.

A second variant of the All-Purpose Research Institute is the multidisciplinary institute. Prior to the end of World War II, such institutes were most often marriages of convenience—sometimes merely collective security agencies designed to divert research funds normally destined for the more highly organized physical and natural sciences—rather than genuine attempts to merge diverse disciplines in a common research effort. Consider, for example, Gee's description of the formation of Stanford University's Social Science Research Council: "A group of the faculty in the social sciences at Stanford University was called into conference on June 4, 1926, by President Ray Lyman Wilbur to consider measures for promoting research in that field and for securing funds for this purpose."[11] That political scientists, historians, sociologists, and other social scientists have produced a veritable wealth of scholarly studies under the aegis of such multidisciplinary institutes does not alter their basic character. Until the post-World War II years these institutes, with one notable exception, remained essentially large financial umbrellas for sovereign scholars in autonomous disciplines.

The notable exception in the 1920s and 1930s was the Social Science Research Committee at the University of Chicago. Under the tutelage of Charles E. Merriam, an entire generation of American political scientists learned to mind, as Harold D. Lasswell has pointed out, their "*p*'s and *q*'s—the emphases on psychology and quantity."[12] Merriam's students balanced their study of political theory and governmental institutions with training in psychology, sociology, communications theory, and statistics. The books that they wrote, in large part under the auspices of the University of Chicago's Social Science Research Committee, were interdisciplinary in scope and method to a degree hitherto unknown in American political science. It was the "Chicago Approach," I would suggest, that was both the inspiration and the model for the interdisciplinary research institutes that began to flourish in the late 1940s.

11. Ibid., p. 196.
12. Lasswell, *The Future of Political Science*, p. 158.

A third variant of the All-Purpose Research Institute turns toward public service, acting as a consultant for state and local governmental agencies. Thus the Commonwealth Service Council of the University of Oregon had as its functions "surveying the research possibilities of the public service type, stimulating interest among the faculty in this sort of investigation, and promoting the University's research program as it related to the life of the State."[13] One of its subunits, the Municipal Reference Bureau, concentrated upon financing, franchises, the codification of ordinances, and other special problems facing Oregon's municipalities.

The true All-Purpose Research Institute seeks to fill all of these roles—supporting monographs, providing a multidisciplinary framework for research, serving the public interest —and perhaps several others. Research organizations, such as the Social Science Research Council of the University of Wisconsin, the Institute for Research in Social Science at the University of North Carolina and the Bureau of Public Administration at the University of Virginia, have served multiple purposes and, if we may judge from the quantity and quality of the monographs and other publications emerging from such institutes, served them well.

More recently, emphasis has been placed on the interdisciplinary as opposed to the multidisciplinary or specialist character of political research. This has been accompanied by a trend toward the creation of institutional frameworks specifically organized to encourage scholars from different disciplines to pool their knowledge and techniques in the common pursuit of research problems.

The Interdisciplinary Research Institute

Truly interdisciplinary research centers may be an outgrowth of the All-Purpose Research Institutes or—and I would suggest that this is the more common origin—arise from the realization of specialists in different fields of study that they have many interests in common. The student of po-

13. Gee, *Social Science Research Organization*, p. 189.

litical organizations, for example, may notice that the problems and principles that intrigue him are closely related to aspects of industrial firms, street-corner gangs and, somewhat more generally, physical organisms (such as the Portuguese man-of-war), the human nervous system, and the human brain. The creation of a formal research institute to house experts in such diverse topics may bring to fruition research on important ideas that are not easily pigeonholed into one or another of the separate academic disciplines. Such Interdisciplinary Research Institutes have flourished in the years since the close of World War II.

One of the more important of these interdisciplinary research centers is the Institute for Social Research, established at the University of Michigan in 1946. Originally the Institute comprised solely the Survey Research Center (SRC), an outgrowth of the Division of Program Surveys of the United States Department of Agriculture created by Rensis Likert seven years earlier to conduct opinion surveys for the Agriculture Department. The Research Center for Group Dynamics (RCGD) joined the Institute in 1948. Kurt Lewin had organized the RCGD at the Massachusetts Institute of Technology in 1945 and directed it until his death two years later. During the following year the Center, now led by Dorwin Cartwright, moved to Ann Arbor and became an integral part of the Institute for Social Research. The aim of the Institute, its directors wrote:

> is to increase our understanding of social behavior through the utilization of scientific methods. Underlying this aim is the faith that scientific methods—in particular the use of quantitative measurement linked with developing theory—can make a major contribution to knowledge about social relationships and human behavior. Diverse problems have been studied. All were chosen because of their basic theoretical significance or immediate social implications. In general, they have been sufficiently broad to require group research, and since human problems overlap traditional academic bound-

> aries, the research teams usually have included persons from more than one scientific discipline.[14]

During its first fifteen years, the Institute's staff grew in number from the original group of 12 to more than 450 individuals, including about 60 senior research scientists, and produced close to 2,000 publications.

The activities of the Institute for Social Research are diverse. The Survey Research Center, on the one hand, applies sample survey methods to such psychological, sociological, economic, and political problems as leadership and organizational behavior, organizational change, economic behavior, public communication and influence, student development, and mental health. Some of the monographs that SRC staff members have written—American voting behavior by a social psychologist, a sociologist, and two political scientists; American attitudes toward the United Nations by a social psychologist and a psychologist—stand as landmarks in the history of empirical political research.[15] As a by-product of its research, the SRC has also made advances in the methodology of sample surveys.[16] The Research Center for Group Dynamics, on the other hand, concerns itself with the practice as well as the theory of group behavior. Among its areas of specialization are the study of communication among group members, the analysis of social power, the effects of group membership, group performance, and the role of theory and method in planned change. Together the SRC and the RCGD participate in intercenter research programs dealing with such topics as children, youth, family life, and mental health in industry.

Another such research center, also at the University of Michigan, is the Mental Health Research Institute (MHRI), founded in 1955. Although an integral part of the Psychiatry

14. Ten-year progress report, entitled "Institute for Social Research, 1946–1956" (Ann Arbor, no date), p. 9.

15. Angus Campbell, Philip E. Converse, Warren E. Miller, and Donald E. Stokes, *The American Voter* (New York, Wiley, 1960); William A. Scott and Stephen B. Withey, *The United States and the United Nations: The Public View* (New York, Manhattan, 1958).

16. Cf. Robert L. Kahn and Charles F. Cannell, *The Dynamics of Interviewing: Theory, Techniques and Cases* (New York, Wiley, 1957).

Department and under the direction of a psychiatrist, James G. Miller, the full-time staff of the MHRI includes biochemists, psychologists, historians, mathematicians, industrial engineers, physicists, neurophysiologists, social psychologists, chemists, psycho-biologists, mathematical biologists, and political scientists. The interests of the Institute are clearly in the field of mental health. The field is broad enough, however, to include a number of subjects that political scientists consider important in their own work, including general systems analysis, mathematical models in the social sciences, deterrence and arms control, and conflict resolution. Other Interdisciplinary Research Institutes are the Survey Research Center at the University of California, the Institute of Communications Research at the University of Illinois, the Center for International Studies at the Massachusetts Institute of Technology, the Institute for Social Research at the University of North Carolina, and the Stanford University Studies in International Conflict and Integration.

Along with the rise of organizations infusing ideas and methods from other disciplines into political research came the development of more refined ancillary services—specialized libraries, bibliographies, and collections of data—to aid the political researcher in his work. The convenience of having a collection of relevant books and documents in a central location has led many a political science department to found its own library, either within or apart from the main university libraries. In many instances it is necessary to have up-to-date collections of IBM punch cards or other types of research material and equipment that the budgets or policies of university libraries do not cover. Such departmental research libraries may also serve as training grounds to familiarize graduate students with the techniques of modern empirical research. Similarly, a glance at changes in the book review and bibliographic services supplied by the *American Political Science Review* during the course of the last three decades demonstrates the widespread extent to which the profession perceives a need for specialized bibliographies.

A more recent development is the creation of political data banks that not only serve as a new type of library but also as research institutes.

The Institute for Basic Research and Data

The idea underlying the political data bank is certainly not new. As any father of a small child knows, man's urge to collect anything small enough to be moved emerges almost simultaneously with his curiosity about his environment. With the invention of alphabets and tools for writing came the beginnings of libraries to store the accumulated knowledge about the past and ideas about the present and future. The political data bank concentrates upon the acquisition of information about man's political environment and behavior. This entails not the amassing of a general or eclectic collection of books and other documents, but the systematic collection of specific bits of information that are then put into a form rendering them immediately useful for analysis. Such is the function of the Human Relations Area Files at Yale University. In 1937 George Peter Murdock and a group of social scientists at the Institute of Human Relations began the systematic collection of data on all aspects of human behavior and social life in primitive cultures throughout the world, as well as such historical cultures as Imperial Rome and such modern cultures as twentieth-century Japan and Connecticut. "The present system of files," according to its directors, "includes approximately 180 different societies and cultures. The file on each society consists of pages from both published and unpublished sources which are photographed, reduced to a standard size, coded for topical content by trained analysts, printed in multiple copies, and cross-filed under topical categories." [17] These files, available in printed form at eighteen American universities and in microfilm form at as many again, may well serve the political sci-

17. "A Laboratory for the Study of Man," *Human Relations Area Files Report, 1949–1959* (New Haven, n.d.), p. 4; cf. John Dollard, "Yale's Institute of Human Relations: What Was It," *Ventures, 3* (Winter 1964), 32–40.

entist interested in crosscultural patterns of social stratification, government activities, political behavior, war, justice, and other topics. Still another Institute for Basic Research and Data that has grown out of the Yale community is the Yale Political Data Program (YPDP) which seeks to collect and analyze basic data relevant to political, economic, and social trends in international relations and comparative politics.[18] Other such institutes, discussed at greater length elsewhere in this volume, include the Roper Public Opinion Research Center at Williams College and the International Data Library and Reference Service at the University of California (Berkeley).

For all such basic data and research centers,[19] however, the problem of making data accessible to scholars at other institutions is of prime importance. The Human Relations Area Files has sought to solve this problem by placing printed or microfilmed sets of data at a number of universities. The approach adopted by the Inter-University Consortium for Political Research (ICPR), and discussed in a later chapter of this volume, is particularly important for students of the political process.[20]

A notable characteristic of such basic research and data centers as the Yale Political Data Program and the Inter-University Consortium for Political Research is the fact that their facilities are open to the entire academic community. This represents a significant shift from the era when a scholar's collection of data and ideas was held to be at least as inviolable as his wife and daughters. This is not to say that all duplication of effort in political research has been eliminated, or even that we shall realize this particular vision of utopia in the foreseeable future. By fostering a communal attitude toward research data, however, and by expanding the links of communication both within the political science

18. See Chaps. 4 and 5 in this volume for a more complete description.

19. For other data collections not mentioned, see the report of the Behavioral Sciences Subpanel of the President's Science Advisory Committee, dated March 21, 1962; published as a government document and reprinted as "Strengthening the Behavioral Sciences," in *Behavioral Science*, 7 (1962), 275–88.

20. See Chap. 19 in this volume for a more complete description.

profession and between it and other disciplines, we may be reducing the probability of such wasteful duplication.

An equally prominent trend is the emergence of men and women who direct their energies solely toward political research instead of trying to fulfill the traditional multifunctional role of the academic scholar. In some cases the normal academic situation imposes restrictions upon research—faculty and staff meetings, undergraduate courses, the need to counsel students and to fill out their recommendation forms, and, sometimes, the latent or active hostility of the university's administration to departures from the job of providing a liberal arts education to a body of undergraduates—that, although stimulating to some scholars, may prove burdensome to others. Possibly more frequent is the case where scholars of like interest at different institutions want to spend more time working together in their field of specialization, even if this means terminating their university affiliation. In either event the result may be a decision to found a research institute outside the academic environs.

The Independent Research Institute

Extramural research has an honorable history. In an earlier age scholarship was often the profession of gentlemen who were not forced to rely upon institutional support to finance their work. Indeed, some of the finest scientific and humanistic research stemmed from these gentlemen-scholars. More recently we have seen the proliferation of independent research institutes in the natural and physical sciences, composed of men who were scientific entrepreneurs or who sought government contracts to sustain their operations. The development of nonacademic research institutes (other than government operated agencies) in the field of political science is still newer.

In their early stages such independent centers for political research often resemble the "Invisible College" of seventeenth-century England, that band of scientists and artisans who met frequently to discuss their joint interests and who eventually, in 1662, formed the Royal Society of London. Of modern invisible colleges in the sciences, Derek de Solla Price has written:

> Starting originally as a reaction to the communication difficulty brought about by the flood of literature, and flourishing mightily under the teamwork conditions induced by World War II, their whole *raison d'être* was to substitute personal contact for formal communication among those who were really getting on with the job, making serious advances in their fields. In many of these fields, it is now hardly worth while embarking upon serious work unless you happen to be within the group, accepted and invited to the annual and informal conferences, commuting between the two Cambridges, and vacationing in one of the residential conference and work centers that are part of the international chain.[21]

In the Center for Advanced Study in the Behavioral Sciences at Stanford, California, and in the numerous conferences on such topics as arms control and general systems analysis that tend to be self-regenerative, the political scientist may recognize his own profession's invisible colleges.

The Center for Advanced Study in the Behavioral Sciences is a particularly interesting development in empirical research. Each year the Center invites approximately fifty political scientists and other scholars to sojourn in the rolling foothills of California, away from their academic duties, working on research projects of their own choice or merely deepening their knowledge of their own and other disciplines. The Center does not organize an extensive program to occupy the Fellows' time, nor does it seek to exert supervisory controls over their activities during the year. In accepting their invitations, however, the Fellows tacitly agree that they will spend at least some of their time working on systematic research or theory-building cutting across traditional disciplinary boundaries. The Center carefully nurtures a suitable collegial atmosphere, often by inviting a number

21. Derek de Solla Price, *Science Since Babylon* (New Haven, Yale University Press, 1961), p. 99, n. 2; cf. the same author's *Little Science, Big Science* (New York, Columbia University Press, 1963), pp. 62–91.

of scholars from different disciplines who are working on the same or related projects to be Fellows during the same year. By now, although only a dozen sets of scholars have "graduated" from the Center, the fellowship has come to be regarded as a badge of distinction for political scientists interested in empirical research.

Far more formal and project-oriented than the invisible colleges or the Center are the independent research institutes organized to conduct research on a contract basis on such topics as national security and arms control. Perhaps the best known of these is the RAND Corporation, founded in Santa Monica, California, in 1946 to work on broad military problems for the United States Air Force. Although its chief customer has remained the Air Force, the RAND Corporation also conducts research for the Atomic Energy Commission, the United States Congress, and, in a very real sense, the entire academic community. During the first fifteen years of its existence, according to its vice-president, RAND "distributed 500,000 copies of some 5,500 reports, research memoranda, papers, and the like." [22] Some of the works written by members of its Social Science Department are among the most important in any political scientist's library.[23]

Two other independent research centers concentrating upon problems of war and peace are the Institute for Defense Analyses (IDA), founded in 1956, and the Hudson Institute, dating from 1961. The IDA, a nonprofit corporation comprising eight member universities, was conceived by the Department of Defense as a means by which academic experts could be enlisted in the service of America's national defense policy. As is the case with the RAND Corporation,

22. J. R. Goldstein, "RAND: The History, Operations, and Goals of A Nonprofit Corporation," Research Paper P-2236-1 (Santa Monica, 1961), p. 18. Volume 1 of the *Index of Selected Publications of The RAND Corporation* (Santa Monica, 1962), covering the years from 1946 to 1961, lists 441 titles under "Social and Political Science."

23. Among these are Bernard Brodie, *Strategy in the Missile Age* (Princeton, Princeton University Press, 1959); W. Phillips Davison, *The Berlin Blockade* (Princeton, Princeton University Press, 1958); Nathan C. Leites, *A Study of Bolshevism* (Glencoe, Free Press, 1953); and Bruce L. Smith and Chitra M. Smith, *International Communication and Political Opinion: A Guide to the Literature* (Princeton, Princeton University Press, 1956).

the IDA is supported by such private organizations as the Ford Foundation as well as by federal agencies. Similarly, the newly organized Hudson Institute, located in Harmon-on-Hudson near New York City, will secure government and private contracts to study problems of national security and international order.

The Center for the Study of Democratic Institutions at Santa Barbara, California, has a broader scope of interest—the free society. In contrast to the usual research situation, in which a group of scholars search for funds to pursue their research interests, the Center arose out of the desire of a foundation to put its funds to good use. An offspring of the Fund for the Republic, founded in 1952 with a grant from the Ford Foundation, it is a part of the Fund's continuing effort to clarify and publicize the basic issues of civil liberties and civil rights. Among its other activities during the first years of its existence, the Fund for the Republic sponsored a series of scholarly studies on such problems as integration, academic freedom, censorship, and blacklisting in the entertainment industry. By 1959 the Fund had resolved to create a residential research center, under the direction of Robert M. Hutchins, to facilitate the conduct of research along these lines. The Center not only has its own staff but also invites consultants to spend time in residence to perform politically relevant research.

Clearly the Independent Research Institute, no less than the All-Purpose Research Institute, the Interdisciplinary Research Institute, and the Institute for Basic Research and Data, has established itself as a permanent feature in the landscape of organizations devoted to empirical research. At this point in our survey, then, we might pause to ask the questions: Where are we heading? What are we going to do about it?

POLITICAL RESEARCH: PROSPECTS AND PROBLEMS

On the one hand, the prospects for the future of political research are rosy indeed. If present trends continue (and I see no reason why they should not do so), by the middle of the

1980s there will be some 3,000 American universities and colleges, about 1,000 university research bureaus and institutes devoted at least in part to the study of politics, 30,000 members of the American Political Science Association, more than 700 new Ph.D.s in political science, international relations, and public administration yearly, and approximately 60 major American quarterlies (containing between 1,500 and 2,500 articles per year) devoted primarily or exclusively to the scholarly study of political science and international relations.[24] If qualitative developments keep pace with quantitative trends, we are truly approaching a golden age of political research.

On the other hand, however, sheer quantitative growth will serve only to enhance some problems that are already very much with us. One of these is the problem to which political scientists from Plato to Harold Lasswell have devoted so much of their attention—that of clarifying the goals of political science. The proliferation of research institutes and journals together with the rapid growth of the number of scholars hardly seem calculated to produce a unified approach to the discipline and its purposes. We can only hope that, in the absence of a consensus, the continuing debate will prove to be more fruitful than debilitating.

A second problem is one of guidance for our research. In one sense, of course, the value of any piece of competent research depends upon the extent to which it fulfills the goals that the scholar sets for himself. But in another sense there are certain societal criteria of value, often determined by people who base decisions upon their own perception of societal or professional goals. This is particularly true—and will become increasingly more so in the future—in the case of the scholar dependent upon foundation or government support for his research projects. In the Social Science Research Council and the American Political Science Asso-

24. These figures assume that the trends now under way do not reach their natural limits before this time. That such trends cannot continue indefinitely has been made clear by Derek de Solla Price: "To go beyond the bounds of absurdity, another couple of centuries of 'normal' growth of science would give us dozens of scientists per man, woman, child, and dog of the world population." *Science Since Babylon*, p. 113.

ciation, especially in the last decade, political scientists have found mentors with vision, organizations willing to support, promote, and even initiate empirical research on man's political behavior. The Social Science Research Council's Committee on Political Behavior, chaired at first by V. O. Key and then by David B. Truman, deserves special mention for its sponsorship of conferences for scholars working on similar topics and for its encouragement of cooperative and interdisciplinary research. More recently the federal government has begun to play a major role in financing political research, particularly basic research.

Among other perennial problems facing the political science profession there is a need for improved training facilities for graduate students, for better means to educate the larger public in political affairs, for organizational developments, both in the universities and in the private foundations and government sources of financing, to accommodate the changing nature and emphases of political research. Above all there is a growing need for competent political scientists—teachers and researchers—since the demand for full-time teachers of political science is outstripping the annual production of doctorates in the field. There is, moreover, a subtler aspect to the manpower shortage in our profession. Of the natural and physical sciences Derek de Solla Price writes:

> If the cumulative expansion of science rapidly outpaces all efforts we can make to feed it with manpower, it means that more and more things will arise naturally in the life of science and require attention that cannot be given. There will be too many discoveries chasing too few workers. At the highest level we must come to a situation at which there are too many breakthroughs per square head.[25]

It does not take much foresight to see that political science, too, is fast approaching this point.

25. Ibid., pp. 117–18.

In our concern with perennial problems, we sometimes forget that the phenomenal growth of political research has brought a newer set of problems to the fore—those of documentation. It is to these problems, the result of the ever mounting "information explosion" that characterizes political and social life in the twentieth century, that the political scientist must address himself in the here and now. The problems will not resolve themselves if we bide our time.

The need for more efficient systems of *data retrieval* is becoming increasingly apparent. Although we cannot agree with it entirely, there is a ring of truth in Robert Oppenheimer's remark, "We need new knowledge like we need a hole in the head." [26] If we could organize and comprehend fully the information that we already have we could make great strides forward in our political research. We must know what that information is, however, before we can organize it. And, given the growing number of relevant publications, research centers collecting quantitative data of one sort or another, and commercial firms as well as academic organizations sampling public opinion, the tasks of knowing what we already know and knowing how to locate it are becoming more difficult all the time.

We need not give up hope at this stage. Man apparently has a unique capacity to invent solutions just before he is inundated by the problems he is seeking to solve. In the case of data retrieval, the best prospect seems to lie in the area of electronic information systems, an area currently being explored by numerous private and governmental agencies.[27] In recent years, political scientists, notably those at some of the institutes for basic research, have begun to direct their attention to such retrieval systems. But the road is long. The realization of that utopia in which every political scientist,

26. Cited in ibid., p. 121.

27. Cf. United States Senate, Committee on Government Operations, *Documentation, Indexing, and Retrieval of Scientific Information* (Washington, D. C., U. S. Government Printing Office, 1960) ; and National Science Foundation, *Nonconventional Technical Information Systems in Current Use*, No. 3 (Washington, D.C., U.S. Government Printing Office, 1962). Cf. also Chaps. 20 and 21 in this volume.

through electronic equipment, has fingertip control over the precise information that he needs in his research is yet to come.

Two other needs, not quite so dramatic perhaps, are nonetheless of increasing importance. The first of these is for competent *syntheses of research in progress.* With an increase in the number of "invisible colleges" and separate research institutes, the load on the communications system within the discipline of political science has become well-nigh intolerable. The scholar who immerses himself in the study of legislative behavior, for example, often does not have time to keep abreast of developments in the area of general systems analysis. And yet, knowledge of the latter subject will aid him immensely in the pursuit of his specialty. The second need is for carefully organized *replicate studies of past empirical research.* In any empirical science a check on research results serves a useful purpose. At best such checks can add depth to our knowledge about the subject analyzed; at worst they may expose shoddy craftsmanship.

Unfortunately, syntheses and replicate studies are often of low prestige value for their authors. The latter type of work, particularly, is often left to graduate students for their term paper assignments. However justified the reason may be, professional recognition and advancement seem to accrue to chiefs rather than to braves; research funds seem to go to the innovator rather than to the synthesizer or the replicator. These commonly recognized facts of academic life sometimes force scholars to absurd extremes. For example, of the dozens of "authoritarianism" scale-tests that have appeared in scholarly journals during the past 15 years only a few are comparable in any real sense. In most cases, each time with good cause, the author felt constrained to devise his own variation of scales used by previous writers.[28]

The clear need for syntheses and replicate studies and the

28. A light in this particular jungle appears in Robert E. Lane's proposal to catalogue in handbook form the usage and results of a wide variety of social–political attitude tests.

profession's clear preference for original research and theory building pose a dilemma for which there seems no solution at the present time. Unlike our problem of data retrieval, which appears to be essentially technical in nature, this dilemma hinges on our attitudes toward the proper role of the political scientist. Man may well be endowed with a capacity to prevent his technical inundation, but this genius does not always cover problems stemming from differing attitudes.

The need for an adequate *abstracting journal* for political scientists is also becoming increasingly pressing. As I noted earlier (Table 17.1), in 1960 there were 28 scholarly journals in the United States devoted exclusively or primarily to political science and international relations. An average of 315 articles appeared in the ten most general of these publications during each of the five years from 1958 to 1962 (Table 17.2)—one article for each day of the year excluding Sundays. The political scientist with specialized interests, however, must read or at least scan more than just these 10 to 28 journals. By way of a concrete example, I search more than 450 American and foreign journals in the preparation of quarterly bibliographies of articles on international relations and comparative politics for the *American Political Science Review* (having pangs of conscience all the while since Yale University's library does not have all the journals that I should include). I would estimate that there are at least 1,500 journals in the world today that touch directly upon aspects of the political process. If present trends continue, these figures will have doubled by the mid-1980s.

The modern political scientist, however conscientious he may be, simply does not have the time to keep on top of this "information explosion." True, he gets some assistance in the form of bibliographies that some journals and research institutes publish. But tracking down titles listed in bibliographies is often not the best use of research time; even if the journal in which a particular title appears is available, it may turn out that the title is misleading as far as the content of the article itself is concerned. True, there are some annotated bibliographies and abstracting journals available to the political scientist. Among the most notable of these are the *International Political Science Abstracts* and the bibliographic sections of such journals as *Behavioral Science* and *The American Behavioral Scientist.* Such publications are far from comprehensive—even the former searches only 124 journals—and, moreover, often include overlapping citations.

With respect to abstracting journals, the field of political science comprises a vast underdeveloped area. Derek de Solla Price has noted that the first abstracting journal in the natural and physical sciences came in 1930, when the world's scientists were publishing about 300 journals. In the years since then the growth of abstracting journals has kept pace with the growth of scientific journals at the steady ratio of about 1 to 300. In 1950 there were about 90,000 scientific journals and close to 300 abstracting journals.[29] The field of political science, judging by these standards, should have at least 5 abstracting journals. In fact we do not have a single comprehensive abstracting journal, although the *International Political Science Abstracts* is certainly a start in the right direction.

In considering the possibility of a political science abstracting journal, we might do well to look to our sister discipline, sociology. Today, twelve years after its birth, *Sociological Abstracts* annually catalogues and cross-references about 3,600 abstracts of articles from close to 450 journals.[30] Eventually, after the abstracts are catalogued on IBM punch cards, the sociologist will be able to search the entire information system in a matter of seconds, extracting those titles that are relevant to his specific interests. This is the sort of

29. Price adds: "Thus, by about 1950 we reached the point at which the size of the population of abstract journals had attained the critical magnitude of about three hundred. This is, of course, the reason why during the last decade scientists have been concerned about the need for abstracts of abstracts, calling this an 'information problem' which seems to require some process of electronic sorting of abstracts as a means of coping with the rising flood of literature." *Science Since Babylon*, p. 98; cf., more generally, ibid., pp. 92–124, and Price's *Little Science, Big Science*, pp. 62–91.

30. I am indebted to its editor, Leo P. Chall, for taking time to discuss some of these matters with me.

experience upon which political scientists could draw in developing their own abstracting journal.[31]

The future of empirical political research does not rest upon past developments alone. We have reached the stage—actually we have been in its midst for roughly five years now and it will probably continue for another five years before burying us in the growing mass of information—where we must make some decisions that will be crucial in determining the character of this future. Data retrieval systems, syntheses and replicate studies, abstracting journals, in short, the whole range of documentation needs, rank high in the list of decisions that must be made if we are to prevent a further deterioration of channels for the flow of information within the political science profession.

31. There are, to be sure, a number of problems to be faced in considering such a task. Not the least of these is the matter of cost. The total annual cost of *Sociological Abstracts* is roughly $90,000, of which more than one half is spent on salaries and about one fifth on printing and distribution expenses. Given the potential usefulness of a political science abstracting journal, this is not an exorbitant price to pay, although it might necessitate considerable foundation support at the outset. Other problems include establishing criteria of what constitutes an abstract, procuring journals and abstracts, and creating indices and categories for the abstracts. It is particularly important that any system adopted by political scientists be compatible with other abstracting journals in the social sciences, most notably *Sociological Abstracts* and to a lesser extent *Psychological Abstracts*. Again, however, these problems are solvable and deserve to be solved.

18. Archives for Statistical Studies of Within-Nation Differences *

STEIN ROKKAN, THE MICHELSEN INSTITUTE, BERGEN, AND HENRY VALEN, THE INSTITUTE FOR SOCIAL RESEARCH, OSLO

Data for comparative research can be generated at a number of levels of the polity: (1) at the level of the *individual actor;* (2) at the level of the immediate territorial community, the *locality;* (3) at the level of the *province* and the *region;* and (4) at the level of the *total national aggregate.* The current efforts to build up data banks for rapid retrieval have concentrated on the two extreme levels: the individual and the nation. The archives and repositories set up for the storage, classification, and retrieval of materials from sample surveys focus on the individual as the basic unit of variation.[1] The Data Program set up by Karl Deutsch and his associates at Yale University focuses on variations at the national level.[2] In this paper arguments will be advanced for the development of data banks at the intermediary level of the locality. We shall explain the background for the establishment of one such "ecological" archive and will say a few words about the range of analyses possible on the basis of information collected at this level of the system.

* A slightly different version of this chapter appears in *Social Sciences Information, 4* (September 1965).

1. See the various articles on archives in the special issue on "Data in Comparative Research" of the *International Social Science Journal, 16* (1964).

2. See Bruce M. Russett, and Hayward R. Alker, Jr., Karl W. Deutsch, and Harold D. Lasswell, *World Handbook of Political and Social Indicators* (New Haven, Yale University Press, 1964).

Our Norwegian punch card archive grew out of a long-term program of research on elections and electoral behavior.[3] Our original concern was not with local variations as such: we built up our file of ecological data in an effort to analyze and to explain the individual behavioral patterns behind the aggregated results of each election. We assembled the basic statistics for each unit of electoral administration not because we were interested in variations in local political structures but because we needed to know as much as possible about the geography of the vote before proceeding to the formulation and testing of hypotheses about the sources of individual behavior. Our purposes in assembling our first decks of punch cards by locality were indeed very straightforward: we wanted to simplify the procedures for the rank ordering of units in making political maps in the style of the French *géographie électorale* and we needed a basic set of parameters in designing and evaluating a master sample of the Norwegian electorate. We were not interested in electoral mapmaking per se; we considered it essentially an expository device, possibly also a heuristic procedure in developing plausible hypotheses about sources of variation in individual behavior. Our primary concern was with such "micro"-variations and the only direct method of hypothesis testing at this level was the sample survey. To draw a workable sample of our national electorate we needed information about the ranges of variation among the smallest territorial units, and to evaluate the precision of any sample drawn on this basis we again needed information locality by locality. This in turn made it essential to establish a file of basic ecological information for the country as a whole.

It was not long, however, before we realized that the archive of local data we had begun to build up could serve a

3. For an account of this program, see Stein Rokkan and Henry Valen, "Parties, Elections and Political Behavior in the Northern Countries," in Otto Stammer, ed., *Politische Forschung* (Cologne, Westdeutscher Verlag, 1960); and Stein Rokkan, "Electoral Mobilization, Party Competition and National Integration," in Joseph LaPalombara and Myron Weiner, eds., *Political Parties and Political Development* (Princeton, Princeton University Press, 1966).

much broader purpose in our program. It has not only proved a useful tool in making maps and in the design and control of sample surveys but has offered an important basis for new lines of research into statistical geography and political ecology. We have, it is true, continued to cross-check our survey findings against ecological data but we have also taken measures to push our archive a number of steps beyond the reach of standard survey techniques.

First of all, we decided to extend the archive in *time depth.* No detailed political survey had been undertaken in Norway before 1949,[4] and before ours of 1957 none had been designed for an analysis of variations in local and regional political culture. Although, of course, it is possible to stretch the time span of current survey analyses through judicious use of generational cuts and of recall data for parents' status and politics,[5] any attempt to map differences in rates of political change between regions and between types of localities since the early beginnings of party competition must of necessity be based on ecological data culled from official statistics and from administrative and organizational records. So far we have been able to incorporate data from censuses, counts, and elections since World War II only. Our effective time span is therefore only the 20 years from 1945 to 1965. But we have already demonstrated, through a variety of time series analyses for earlier data,[6] the need for an extension of our file back to the earliest partisan elections of 1879 and 1882, and students working within our program are currently assembling sizable bodies of data for the communes of the

4. Allen H. Barton, *Sociological and Psychological Problems of Economic Planning in Norway* (Ph.D. dissertation, Columbia University, New York, 1954).

5. This procedure has been used to trace changes in class polarization in Stein Rokkan, "Geography, Relation and Social Class: Cross-Cutting Cleavages in Norwegian Politics," in Seymour Martin Lipset and Stein Rokkan, eds., *Party Systems and Voter Alignments* (New York, Free Press, 1967).

6. Stein Rokkan and Henry Valen, "The Mobilization of the Periphery," in Stein Rokkan, ed., *Approaches to the Study of Political Participation* (Bergen, The Michelsen Institute, 1962); Stein Rokkan and Henry Valen, "Regional Contrasts in Norwegian Politics," in Erik Allardt and Yrjö Littunen, eds., *Cleavages, Ideologies and Party Systems* (Helsinki, Westermarck Society, 1964); and Rokkan, "Geography, Religion and Social Class."

West and the North since the first full-suffrage elections.[7]

Of even greater importance, however, was our decision to give increasing priority to data on the *"macro"-characteristics* of each locality: its ecological position within the provincial network of communication and economic exchange, its geographical structure, its economic, educational, organizational, and political establishments and the consequent constellations of openings and opportunities for the individual inhabitants. Information on such macro-characteristics might of course to some extent be derived from aggregated census and election statistics, but in many cases we had to add information from maps and other records to establish our indices of structural properties. In this way we were gradually able to add new dimensions to our analysis. We could use our archive to study sequences of structural change and we could test hypotheses about the impact of structural conditions on the behavior of individuals. We could also, with the information in our archive, attempt to "typologize" the primary sampling units within which the interviews for our nationwide surveys had been taken. This opened up possibilities for direct tests of "macro"–"micro" hypotheses.[8] In one case it even proved possible to use the ecological archive as the basis for an officially sponsored investigation of structural conditions for variations in individual behavior. In this study—an inquiry into local differences in turnout levels among the youngest of the enfranchised residents—a sample of communes was drawn on the basis of information in the ecological archive and data on each individual collected from the standardized official records.[9]

For all these reasons we have found the archiving of data by territorial units an essential prerequisite in the develop-

7. T. Hjellum, *Partiene i lokalpolitkken* (Oslo, Gyldendal, 1967) presents a detailed study of the process of local politicization in the rural communes of the West of Norway since 1913. Another study focuses on the elections immediately after the introduction of manhood suffrage in 1898.

8. Henry Valen and Stein Rokkan, "Local Politicization and Party Commitment" (paper for session on Electoral Research, Sixth World Congress, International Political Science Association, Geneva, September 1964).

9. Stein Rokkan, *Valgdeltagelsen blant de yngste* (Bergen, Michelsen Institute, 1964).

ment of a comprehensive program of political research in our country. Ecological archives will never make fresh data gathering operations superfluous, but they will help to place any new data we can gather in a broader historical and geographical perspective and make it possible to add further depth to the analysis.

The difficulties of ecological analysis are well known and we shall not go into technicalities in this context. The most vexing problems in any effort of ecological data gathering relate to the choice and delimitation of territorial units. Our approach has been pragmatic and straightforward: we have used the units for which we could find the broadest range of comparable data, and we have not tried to create continuous time series for standard units if this involved complex and uncertain recomputations.

The best territorial unit for our purpose was the *commune:* the Norwegian terms are *herreder* for rural communes, *ladesteder* for the smaller market towns, and *kjøpsteder* for the chartered cities. The basic reasons for choosing units at this level were political: no uniform information on election results is available for smaller units, and the commune constitutes the smallest territorial unit of local self-government and external representation in the system. If we had been exclusively concerned with demographic and social variations, we might have chosen the census tract (*tellingskrets*) as our unit. Data at this level, however, are more difficult to secure. The Central Bureau of Statistics publishes its census reports by commune; and to get details on the demography and the socioeconomic structure of each tract within the commune, we would have had to engage in a great deal of digging in the archives of the Bureau, at least for the censuses before 1960.

Changes in the boundaries of local administrative units always create headaches in ecological research. The period from 1945 to 1957 was one of very stable local boundaries in Norway, allowing us to build up tolerably uniform time series for the elections during that period. Since then our system has gone through a series of complex mergers and splits, which makes it difficult to know yet whether we can meaningfully complete new time series for the resulting units. What we are more likely to do once this period of boundary adjustment is over is to start up another section of the archive based on the new units and to carry out the same types of analyses for the new section as for the old. This will not allow us to correlate time series directly but will at least make it possible to check the stability of a variety of relationships in the system and to trace the sources of change.[10]

Our main concern at the moment, however, is with improvements in the techniques of ecological analysis. So far we have largely published straightforward descriptive tables based on cross-classifications and simple calculations of differences in central tendencies and distribution characteristics.[11] We have also undertaken some exploratory multiple regression analyses on a large-scale computer, but the results reached to date will need to be checked in detail through alternative procedures.[12] We are currently trying to work out designs for new types of analyses based on models of the sources of aggregate political results for each community. This work is largely inspired by such recent analyses as those by Janson and Carlsson in Sweden[13] and by Klatzmann, Desabie, Vangrevelinghe, and Boudon in France.[14] Since

10. Our archive for the period 1947–57 comprises some 80 IBM punch cards for each of 744 communes (*herreder*, *ladesteder*, and *kjøpsteder*). After the extensive boundary changes of the years 1958–64, our 1965 archive is confined to recomputed census and election data for 466 communes only. In drawing up a new sample of primary sampling units for a nationwide survey of the electorate before and after the 1965 election, we found it impossible to work with these consolidated communes and instead decided to work with 1521 sampling units designated by the Bureau of Statistics. For these units, however, we have access only to census distributions, not to electoral data.

11. Rokkan and Valen, "The Mobilization of the Periphery."

12. Rokkan and Valen, "Regional Contrasts."

13. Carl-Gunnar Janson, *Mandattilldelning och Regional Röstfördelning* (Stockholm, Idun, 1961); Gösta Carlsson, "Partiforskjutningar som Tillväkstprocesser." *Statsvetenskaplig Tidskrift, 66* (1963), 172–213. The historian Jörgen Weibull is currently completing a statistical analysis of the occupational bases of party strength for the elections from 1911 to 1920 using the "source model" procedure.

14. See Joseph Klatzmann's chapter in Jacques Fauvet and Henri Mendras, *Les Paysans et la Politique dans la France Contemporaine* (Paris, Colin, 1958); Jacques Desabie, "Le référendum: Essai d'étude statistique,"

we hope to be able to profit from international exchanges of data and techniques in this field, we are anxious to organize regular encounters with research workers engaged in similar analyses.

Our archive grew out of a long-term program of political analysis. Given the provisions for the secrecy of the individual vote,[15] the ecological method is the only serious alternative to the systematic sample survey in the study of mass behavior in elections and referenda. But, once established, archives such as ours can clearly be used in a great variety of other social science analyses. It is enough, perhaps, to cite the importance of ecological data in the study of economic growth and patterns of industrialization and urbanization, in inquiries into cultural and educational mobilization, in research on mass communications and media exposure. It is our hope that our archive will gradually prove its usefulness to a wide range of social scientists and become a general research facility rather than a private collection.

With the advent of large-scale computers, more and more attention will of necessity be directed to the data basis for mass analyses of processes of change within each nation. The crucial advantage of ecological archives of the type we have set up is not that they facilitate machine processing of data already available in other formats (e.g. in printed statistical publications), but rather that they *open up new possibilities of analysis through the collation of data for the same units from a wide variety of organizationally distinct sources.* The collation of census and election statistics is only one example of the possibilities resulting from such mergers of data banks: data from fiscal, agricultural, industrial, and educa-

---

Journal de la Société de Statistique de Paris, 100 (1959), 166–80; Gabriel Vangrevelinghe, "Etude statistique comparée des resultats des référendums de 1958 et 1961," *Journal de la Société de Statistiques de Paris*, 102 (1961), 279–94; and R. Boudon, "Propriétés individuelles et propriétés collectives: un problème d'analyse ecologique," *Revue Française de Sociologie, 4* (1963), 275–99.

15. On the importance of the secrecy provisions for the development of political statistics, see Stein Rokkan, "Mass Suffrage, Secret Voting and Political Participation," *Archives Européennes de Sociologie, 2* (1961), 132–52.

tional enumerations can easily be added, as, after appropriate adjustments for the units used, can figures from circulation statistics,[16] membership files,[17] attendance counts,[18] and so on. In the long run, however, perhaps the most important use of ecological archives will arise out of the possibilities of developing *multivariate typologies of ecological settings for human behavior*. Only through systematic work on such typologies can we hope to break down the barriers between the "macro" and the "micro" approaches and to develop joint designs for the simultaneous utilization of aggregate data, structural information, and individual responses.[19]

16. For an example of the use of newspaper circulation statistics in ecological research, see Jörgen Westerståhl and Carl-Gunnar Janson, *Politisk Press* (Göteborg, Institute of Political Science, 1958); and Stein Rokkan and P. Torsvik, "Der Wähler, der Leser und die Parteipresse," *Kölner Zeitschrift für Soziologie, 12* (1960), 278–301.

17. Local party membership data have been analyzed in some detail in Rokkan and Valen, "The Mobilization of the Periphery." Local data for membership in teetotal organizations have been discussed in Rokkan and Valen, "Regional Contrasts in Norwegian Politics."

18. Data from a privately organized church attendance count were analyzed in Rokkan and Valen, "Regional Contrasts in Norwegian Politics."

19. A most interesting example of the construction of a typology through factor analysis of aggregate data is given in C. A. Moser and Wolf Scott, *British Towns* (Edinburgh and London, Oliver and Boyd, 1961).

19. The Availability and Quality of Sample Survey Data in Archives within the United States

PHILIP E. CONVERSE, SURVEY RESEARCH CENTER,
THE UNIVERSITY OF MICHIGAN

While questions of data quality have always been with us, the large-scale accumulation by more centralized repositories of materials from motley sources seems to pose new issues of quality control. This is true not only for the archive director who must determine institutional policy, but also for the investigator engaged in secondary analysis. These issues become particularly acute where the substance of the investigation has to do with modernization or societal development, and where the data have been generated from sample surveys.

U. S. SURVEY DATA ARCHIVES, CURRENT AND PROJECTED

Let us begin, then, with a review of the more prominent facilities that have been established in the past six years in the United States to expand the secondary use of survey research data.[1]

The Roper Public Opinion Research Center

The Roper Public Opinion Research Center, formally established at Williams College in Williamstown, Massachusetts, is both the oldest and largest repository of punch card sam-

1. For more detailed coverage, see Chap. 20 in this volume.

ple survey data in the world. Well over a dozen American survey research organizations, including virtually all of the major commercial and academic agencies, have consented to send data to this archive for storage and public use. Domestic materials are included most notably from the Roper Organization (which was instrumental in the founding of the Center) along with materials from the Fortune Survey, the Gallup Organization, the United States Information Agency, the National Opinion Research Center, and the Bureau of Applied Social Research. In recent years the Roper Center has begun to establish relationships with sources of sample survey data gathered abroad, including again the USIA as well as various Gallup affiliates and other indigenous agencies.

By early 1965, the Roper Center had received data from over 4,000 survey studies involving many million punch cards. More than one third of the data related to populations outside the United States, with 40 countries represented. While at that time three major members of the British Commonwealth (England, Canada, and Australia), along with Denmark, accounted for nearly half of the foreign studies, emphasis was shifting to a broadening of the supply of data from foreign sources, and the scope of the foreign collection was expected to increase rapidly. The Roper Center holdings are restricted to data from sample surveys. Beyond this single limitation, however, the materials are extemely varied in subject matter, for the policy of the Center is to accept all studies that are offered to it. Hence the substance of the materials extends to whatever topics contributing agencies have elected to study. While the collection includes not only national data but also some of the more important regional and community-level studies from academic sources, a fair part of the holdings are made up of the routine consumer preference materials of commercial market research.

In addition to the basic decks of cards for each study, the Center collects information on study specifications, the questionnaire itself, the code materials used to reduce the results to punch card form, and various reports or public releases which have been made from the data. The user who wishes to find detailed information typically does so through a card index file of questions. The precise wording of each item is typed on a file card, along with the designation of the survey carrying the question, the population to which the question was applied, and the date of the study. The cards are filed under the major and minor classification topics deemed most appropriate for each. Illustrative of the major headings are such categories as "Atomic Energy," "Minorities and Ethnocentrism," or "Morals and Mores." Subheads under the latter would include such items as "Annoyances," "Beauty Standards," "Clothing," "Extra-Marital Relations," and "Personal Values." Specific question items are not located in more than one place in the file, although cross-referencing suggestions are attached to various of the minor classifications.

Regulations surrounding access to the Roper Center holdings vary somewhat according to the type of data desired and the relationship of the prospective user to the Center. The Center has recently begun to offer a form of associate membership to university, government, and other nonprofit research groups or institutions. Such a membership in the International Survey Library Association of the Roper Center involves a payment of an annual fee of $500 to the Center ($1,000 in the initial membership year) which helps to underwrite the extensive costs incurred in maintaining a data retrieval and processing facility. In return, access to the Center holdings is aided in several ways. The Center makes available to each Associate a duplicate of its item index, and provides annual supplements to keep this information up to date. Furthermore, the Associate can purchase at cost duplicates of most studies that might be desired, and retain such studies for permanent "home use" provided they are not in turn reduplicated and made available to non-Associates. Such purchase rights are not offered with respect to one category of data within the Roper Center holdings that consists of material from commercial sources wishing to retain control against exploitation of the data for more than disinterested research. These more restricted data represent, however, a minority of the Center holdings, are catalogued in the index made available to Associates, and can be obtained by the Associates on a loan basis for a period of time fitting the specific research need.

Individuals or research groups not affiliated as Center Associates are also encouraged to use Center materials for scholarly inquiry. Listings of major and minor item index headings are made available on request. If the user discovers headings he thinks are relevant to his research problem, Center personnel will conduct a more detailed search for him in the index files at cost. The Center will also prepare duplicate copies of interview schedules, lists of individual questions, and relevant tabulations which have already been run. Also at cost, the Center will prepare new tabulations for him. Alternatively, it will rent to him a duplicate of the materials for any specified and appropriate research use. Scholars are also encouraged to go to Williamstown for direct exploitation of the archives, and such visitors may use data processing equipment at the Center free of charge.[2]

The International Data Library and Reference Service, University of California (Berkeley)

In 1958, the Survey Research Center at Berkeley, in collaboration with the Institute of International Studies at the same institution, established an International Data Library and Reference Service. This facility, originally operating largely to assist local social scientists in obtaining, processing, and analyzing existing foreign and domestic survey materials, has for the past two or three years been offering services to the national social science research community.

From very nearly the outset, the Berkeley repository has placed great emphasis on the collection of foreign materials, although its holdings include a number of the classic American studies as well. Unlike the Roper Center, the archive at Berkeley has developed a policy of considerable selectivity in

2. See also Philip K. Hastings, "The Roper Public Opinion Research Center: An International Archive of Social Science Survey Data," *The American Behavioral Scientist*, 7 (November 1963), 9–11.

its data acquisition, not accepting all materials made available to it. Studies are chosen on the grounds of true theoretical merit, particularly for comparative research, and methodological adequacy of the materials is taken into account. Furthermore, the Library is interested in acquiring worthwhile punch card information not only from commercial survey research organizations, but also that compiled by individual investigators, government research agencies, and other types of academic research centers. To date, several hundred studies have been collected.

Of particular interest to students of societal development is the fact that the Berkeley repository has recently been expanding its holdings of significant studies from the developing nations. While materials are being sought from all such nations, the initial emphasis has been placed on acquiring a broad range of information from relatively few nations in each of the major developing areas, selected both on the basis of theoretical interest and the existence of unusual amounts of known data.[3] Another feature of the Berkeley Center is the maintenance of cooperative contacts with other cross-cultural research centers and area study groups at the University to the point where expert resources may be drawn upon for evaluation of possible materials and for their further interpretation, once acquired.

At the time of this writing, the cataloguing of materials at the Berkeley repository at the item level (as opposed to general information on the studies held) is much less complete than at the Roper Center. However, research and development activities are going forward in the interest of more speedy and effective handling of information retrieval in the future through use of IBM 1620 and 7090 computers.

There are few if any restrictive policies surrounding data use. Reasonable searches for information are conducted for remote users, not only within the survey data archives but also in other types of documentation accumulated by related

3. For a more detailed discussion of these aims, see Philip E. Converse, "A Network of Data Archives for the Behavioral Sciences," *Public Opinion Quarterly*, *28* (1964), 273–286.

research units, at no cost. Also, clients who desire the shipping of materials are charged only the direct costs of duplication and shipping. The user is free to retain and duplicate at will the materials which he has acquired from the Library.

Among other ancillary activities which the Berkeley Library is engaged in or is contemplating, the most interesting from the standpoint of comparative research is the International Reference Service. This Service not only helps in the more far-flung searches for old data, but also is prepared to assist the scholar in the launching of new data collections. It maintains a list of survey research organizations throughout the world, as well as crucial information with respect to their resources and peculiar capabilities. It will also act as agent for the interested scholar with sufficient research funds, by supervising research agencies performing local field operations.

The Yale University Political Science Research Library

Since a more detailed description of the Yale Political Data Program is included in this volume, we shall give but brief recognition here to its sister facility, the Yale University Political Science Research Library and its growing collection of data from sample survey studies.

As was the case with Berkeley, the Yale Library was initially developed to meet research needs of the local graduate faculty and students. From the outset, however, it has followed a policy of sharing information as broadly as possible with any interested outside parties. There has been no attempt to gather any great volume of studies, and materials have typically been acquired only in response to some specific research use, not infrequently in connection with the Political Data Program. Indeed, the juxtaposition of the survey research holdings of the Library with the other aggregative data assembled by the Data Program appropriately suggests the character of the ongoing graduate research program in which the Library is imbedded. As of early 1965, the Library had acquired about 60 survey studies, including a number of the classic American studies and some foreign materials, principally from Europe. In terms of subject matter, the holdings are somewhat less catholic than those at Berkeley and Williamstown, focusing primarily on studies of clear relevance to political behavior.

Archives of the Survey Research Center, The University of Michigan

After some years of attempting to meet outside requests for data from its own portfolio of studies on an ad hoc, straight-cost basis, the growth of demand for such material at the Survey Research Center has forced an increasing institutionalization of such services. Up to now, this institutionalization has occurred principally at the program level within the Center. In 1960, for example, the Economic Behavior Program with the aid of a Ford Foundation grant published descriptions of all of its continuing program of studies of consumer attitudes, finances, and behavior and established a staff to service outside data requests.

In 1962, the establishment of the Inter-University Consortium for Political Research stimulated an evolution of repository functions performed by the Political Behavior Program of the Center toward a much more general data archive with a permanent staff. The Consortium itself consists of a formal collaborative arrangement between a large number of major graduate social science departments and the Political Behavior Program. At the moment there are 50 such full-member schools, and in response to demands from colleges without graduate faculties, as well as from universities abroad, a definition of a more limited "associate membership" is now being worked out.

Full members are assessed an annual fee of $2,500. These resources are pooled toward three interrelated ends: (1) the facilitation of access to archival resources, both of data collected by the Survey Research Center and other data being organized; (2) the expansion of specialized training both in survey research methods and broader questions of research design and behavioral data analysis; and (3) hopefully, for the future, generation of large-scale collaborative research. Here we shall occupy ourselves with the archival aspects of the Consortium only.

The Consortium Data Repository, with its policies guided by a Council elected from representatives of member schools, is less interested in volume of holdings than in methodological excellence of materials and in meeting research demands emanating from the membership. The sample survey materials in the collection, beyond the studies conducted by the Survey Research Center itself, include a limited set of the more prominent and large-scale survey studies of the past two decades, typically of academic origin. While the bulk of the materials are American at the moment, a few of the more important studies abroad, such as the Almond–Verba Five Nations Study, have been acquired. It is unlikely, in part due to difficulties in certifying methodological adequacy, that the repository will ever include much data of purely commercial origin.

In addition, the repository is organizing a variety of basic materials of a non-survey nature. These will include punch card materials on legislative roll calls, judicial decisions, and public voting statistics in increasing historical depth. Accompanying these acquisitions will be relevant census materials, organized to facilitate cross-analyses both with sample surveys for the modern period and with the aggregate records of the past.

While this repository activity is geared primarily to demands of member schools, data are available on a straight-cost basis to any investigator having ties to no member institution. Scholars from member schools are, however, accorded further access advantages. Thus, for example, copies of detailed codes, including all marginal or univariate distributions, for all repository materials are reproduced in bulk and distributed free of further charge to member schools. Hence the remote user can browse through detailed information at his leisure. Similarly, a portion of the membership fee is returned directly to the subscribing school in the form of a full range of consulting, tabulating, or data-reproducing services which, within reasonable limits, are supplied free of any charge at all. Thus the impecunious graduate student at a member school can command a fair number of data retrieval and tabulation services for the price of a postage stamp. As with the Berkeley and Yale repositories, the Consortium repository provides actual data decks with no special strings attached.

Other Archival Resources

The above sketch is not to be considered an exhaustive account of extant archival resources in the United States, although it is fair coverage of the major facilities which are investing most heavily in sample survey data per se, which have some fair topical breadth, and which attempt to make their presence known to clients on a broad geographical base.

With respect to some of the other resources, the National Opinion Research Center at the University of Chicago, as the oldest academic survey facility in the country, has a broad portfolio of past national studies with unusual time depth. While the N.O.R.C. has always attempted to fill requests for its past data at cost, it has only recently come to envision the establishment of a data archive organized to serve the research community. Current plans suggest that such an archive might focus on materials relevant to race relations and education.

Similarly, there are other narrower repository resources. Thus Columbia University's School of Journalism has launched a library of basic data referring to the New York metropolitan area. The International Population and Urban Research Program at the University of California has developed a systematic file of information on all of the world's cities and metropolitan areas of 100,000 inhabitants or more. Indeed, it is likely that small libraries of punch card data in narrower topical areas are beginning to be institutionalized within many graduate social science departments across the country, under much the same local pressures which prompted the Berkeley and Yale developments.

Interarchival Cooperation

With archival resources beginning to proliferate, questions of coordination and the ready interchange of data between archives come to the fore. In the fall of 1962 the Council of the Inter-University Consortium invited representatives of repositories interested in mutual collaboration, along with several parties from other universities interested in the repository problem, to join in some informal discussions concerning ways and means of repository coordination. This ad hoc committee found rapid consensus on the values of a more rational division of labor and increased coordination among the several nascent data repositories. A division of labor would reduce wasteful duplication of effort at the several repositories and would provide more numerous and specialized "eyes and ears" for monitoring the output of various data gathering agencies around the world. More intensive coordination while the several repositories are still in their formative stages would permit them to develop mutually compatible data-storage languages and routines, so that data could be rapidly and efficiently shuttled from one repository site to another. Perhaps most important, a pooling of resources might permit a serious assault on the problem of harnessing the most sophisticated current computer technology and information retrieval methods, in order to move beyond the already obsolete library-card system of information storage and search.

A grant from the National Science Foundation to the Survey Research Center of the University of California has permitted the above group to establish a more formal National Council on Social Science Data Archives. All of the major sample survey data archives, along with several in prospect, are represented on the Council. The Council at the time of this writing is exploring some of the differences in philosophy and practice which have grown up between the operating archives, with an eye to bridging these differences and establishing acceptable modes of data interchange. A part of the original grant also permits meetings between technical experts from each archive to consider problems of information retrieval, data format, and the like. The development of such a Council, and its interest in maintaining contact with comparable efforts in Europe, holds hope that in the long run data holdings of increasing temporal, geographic, and substantive scope will be readily available to the research community.

ERROR MARGINS AND THE PROBLEM OF QUALITY CONTROL IN ARCHIVES OF SAMPLE SURVEY DATA

There is little need to point out that sample survey estimates, by virtue of being drawn from less than complete enumerations, have a sampling error of known or unknown magnitude, depending on the nature of the sample design. With a good design, this error is nonsystematic and is, through the machinery of probability theory and statistical inference, of calculable degree. It may be more important to remind ourselves that the ultimate punch card data yielded up by sample surveys are the end product of a complex and lengthy sequence of human operations. This being so, it is inevitable that further error of some magnitude, both systematic and nonsystematic, is propagated in the data at every step.

For the purposes of this discussion, we are glad to accept the philosophy of error which Professor Karl Deutsch can expound much more eloquently than we. That is to say, we need not on the one hand ignore the possibility of error. Nor, once we have learned that error in these affairs is inevitable, need we decide that we would do better to give it all up and write poetry instead. Rather, what is important is to know the likely margins of error in any estimate, to know further whether this error is comfortably random or may be systematic, and to lay this information against the precision of the conclusions which we had hoped to draw from the data.

This view of error is impeccable. However, its very statement underscores some of the new problems which arise in the construction and use of survey data archives. It is self-evident that such a view of error presumes a very remarkable amount of information. This is true even where sampling error alone is concerned, despite the common assumption that the size of an N permits us to deduce all we need to know about likely error. For 99 per cent of the survey data in our archives this assumption is false, a fact which we shall develop a bit later. And certainly once one recognizes that there are myriad sources of error beyond sampling error, this question of sufficient information becomes much more pressing. Indeed, it is likely that the information we are presupposing typically outruns that which we possess, even when it is we ourselves who have conducted the survey study and are intimate with many of its wrinkles and frailties. Naturally, when we lack such intimacy (as is necessarily the case in wholesale use of data archives) we have no vestige of this kind of information. These are the new problems of error for the user of the archives.

There are new problems of a complementary nature on the side of the archive administrator. What are his responsibilities to his clients in terms of quality control? Let us recognize at the outset that any policy of paying even moderate attention to the quality of acquired data represents a decision of major time-cost proportions. It is in this light that we must understand one possible policy reaction, which is for the administrator to wash his hands of the problem, saying in effect, "What was good enough for the original users is good enough for any future user," and on this basis storing data from any source with no further questions asked. From the point of view of the archive and the user this is *caveat emptor,* in the strict sense of the clause. Given the difficult economics of archive maintenance, such a posture is quite a plausible one. We should like to consider a few facets of the problem of error and methodological adequacy in this light.

Card-Editing

Let us start with one of the most primitive and simple of these error problems, yet one which can be seen as a prototype of most of the others. It is rare that decks or tapes of data arrive on the doorstep of the archive or the secondary user without some discovery, usually rather rapid, that the information is in some degree (to use a picturesque term of the trade) "dirty." At the grossest level this may mean that the number of cards discovered in a deck fails to match the number promised in the descriptive material, or that out of a parallel file of eight decks, six have the same N and the other two depart from this figure. Less grossly, but with still greater frequency, "wild" punches can readily be discovered in the cards. That is, there are punches or configurations of multiple punches which match no code category, or there are combinations of punches across items of information which are logically impossible.

Anyone who has worked closely with these types of data knows how dreadfully time consuming any effort at correction of such discrepancies can be. One could blithely go on running out large quantities of substantive information in the time it takes to return to the raw materials, discover the source of the error, and make an appropriate correction. If one is working with a large study in which the error may have been propagated through many decks of analysis cards, the prospective effort may be awesome, running literally into man-days for corrections on a single item. This is sufficient to give the original investigator pause, and properly so. The difficulty is compounded for the recipient archive or the secondary user, for often the ancillary information necessary to make a correction is not at hand.

Furthermore, the weight of these discrepancies is relatively slight, running certainly to less than two per cent in most specific instances where respectable bodies of data are concerned. Hence from the point of view of our philosophy of error, a correction effort, in view of its expense, is irrational —irrational, that is, from the viewpoint of any single user taken alone. This is not, however, a proper description of the role of an archive as a reproducer and distributor, when the criteria of efficiency and economy can change rather dramatically. Even discrepancies small enough for the investigator to ignore cause stoppages in the comfortable flow of data analysis. When the investigator decides that relative to his specific analysis the discrepancy cannot be overlooked, the time and effort involved in doing something about it may actually outweigh the time necessary to complete the particular analysis. From the point of view of the distributing archive, then, the time-cost loss occasioned by leaving known discrepancies in the data must be multiplied by the number of users, or at least by the number of alert users. If we suppose that rates of use are going up exponentially, and that archives will endure for long periods of time, then the time loss caused by discrepancies to *all* users will often add up to a figure which outweighs the original cost of correction to the archives.

Thus, taking into account the total distribution–use system, serious attention to the discovery and removal of discrepancies at the source is a somewhat more rational activity economically than it might appear for the single investigator taken alone. And for discrepancies of a certain grossness, within data enjoying a certain popularity of use, it is likely that in the long run the archive itself will profit from corrections made at the outset, simply by preventing an endless dribble of plaintive inquiries from the field as to why the data fail to jibe at this or that point. There are enough such inquiries from discrepancies which the user has unwittingly built into the data through his own manipulation of them that it is of great value to remove any gross general discrepancies at the source.

There are obvious limits to such correction activity. Even when such editing is pushed irrationally far by the archive, discrepancies will remain, will be discovered, and will occasion at least analysis stoppage in the field if not the effort of formal inquiry. But it can be argued most strongly that it is a basic responsibility of any archive which anticipates some longevity and volume or dispersion of use to expend substantial effort in an initial attempt to scan for and track down sources of discrepancy in newly acquired data.[4] In short, a total posture of laissez faire by the archive itself seems untenable.

4. It has happened more than once that an apparently small discrepancy is the sole surface symptom of some crucial wrinkle in the study or item design which the contributor has simply forgotten to point out in making his donation.

Broader Questions of Methodological Adequacy

The foregoing discussion of card-editing covers only a small and relatively inconsequential sector of the error picture. It deals typically with mechanical errors of assignment, or at least those easy to detect, which have arisen in the very late stages of the data generation process. The broader question of overall methodological adequacy of given studies across the total sequence of research places a heavy burden of intangible judgments on any archive concerned with quality control.

Where survey studies are concerned, most questions of methodological adequacy beyond sampling design can be reduced to questions of the degree of control exercised over each of the various steps in the data gathering and data preparation processes. "Control" here means formal steps taken in the direction of surveillance and cross-checking of the individual efforts contributing to each phase of the operation. Questions must be pretested for comprehension; control must be exercised in the form of training to ensure that lay interviewers understand their role in the interviewing process so that they can avoid the more obvious forms of interviewer-induced bias; surveillance must be maintained on the interviewing process so that interviewers do not decide to make up the interviews at home or, if they do, to insure that their efforts are revealed and discounted; the coding process must be governed by a rigorous process of check-coding, not only to provide the analyst with necessary information as to coding error margins for various types of items, but also to spot dangerous declines in coder reliability and to take steps at correction; and so on, through a long list of other control processes, all of which have been shown to be necessary in a now ancient body of methodological research.

Sad to say, any one of these control efforts absorbs time and personnel, and thereby represents cost. Furthermore, controls can be lopped off here and there at considerable saving without the difference being detectable to the client or the outside observer either in the general study description or in the tabulations which represent the study product. These things being so, commercial agencies, whose prime attention must be focused on matters of cost and profit, are under strong pressures to cut corners on control procedures. After all, it would be the unusual commercial client who knew enough about the trade even to ask penetrating questions on such issues. Furthermore, unlike the piece of machinery which may break down and damage the quality control reputation of the manufacturing firm, it is rare that there is any real external check on the accuracy of these types of materials. In the eventuality that a competitor might study the same questions with the same tools six months later, most gross differences in results could be attributed to "real" change.

From a number of glimpses into the inner workings of some relatively prestigeful commercial houses on both sides of the Atlantic, I have come to doubt severely that there is more than a tiny handful of agencies that consistently run a well controlled survey operation. I suspect further that a significant proportion of the commercial agencies currently contributing their past data to social science research not only run virtually uncontrolled operations, but would not know how to do a well controlled operation if they were asked. Finally, it is my impression that most of the better commercial houses can and will run quite well controlled studies when the situation requires (e.g. as when the study is commissioned by a source knowledgeable about the requirements of good survey research, and particularly when such a source makes clear that he is likely to oversee the ongoing operation rather closely), but that when it is unnecessary to demonstrate the presence of such controls, most are quickly relaxed. It is this latter pattern which is most disturbing to the archive administrator for whom a good "house reputation" would be a great economy in making judgments of methodological adequacy.

Without a tremendous outlay of investigative time, it is almost impossible for the archivist to reconstruct just what kind of job was done in any given case. It is not, of course, in the interest of the commercial house to advertise its sins of omission, but this does occasionally occur. For example, we have been told by the director of one highly prestigeful commercial agency that "this, this, and this control procedures are not really necessary, and we never bother with them." Furthermore, some of the more naïve agencies may provide a description of operations which, out of sheer ignorance, make clear to the academic some blatant methodological weaknesses. Most typically, however, a proprietary cloak is drawn about the crucial information which the archivist needs to check out adequacy in methods.

Frequently, too, definitions are blurred in such a way as to misrepresent procedures. Take the simple but prestigeful phrase, "national probability sample." I wonder if even a majority of the commercial studies that enter our current archives bearing such a label are indeed what the academic would call a national probability sample. It is rare that one gets a glimpse of actual ungilded sampling procedures in these affairs. However, in three or four instances I have happened on inside information concerning procedures actually used in the preparation of what had been labeled a "probability sample." In none of these cases were the studies actually probability samples, at least as the sampling statistician understands the term. It appears that in the world of commercial surveys any sample can be called a "probability sample" if there are any probability elements at all in one or another stage of selection, even though elements are sampled purposively along the lines dictated by time–cost considerations elsewhere.

Similarly, the word "national" in this context appears to have been stretched for commercial convenience in a number of directions. At one time, "national probability sample" described a sample in which all inhabitants of a nation had a known probability of selection, and I hope this is still the academic understanding of the phrase. However, one discovers that in many settings the term "nation" in commercial survey descriptions means merely that the survey was not conducted in a single city of the nation, such as the capital, but rather in several major cities dispersed over the domain. One way of detecting such instances is to notice whether or not the population size of the place of respondent residence is included in the explicit data. Even if it is present, however, and even if the number of rural respondents matches external census criteria, one still cannot be at all confident that he is dealing with a truly national probability sample. Often where there are external census criteria, of course, the filling of these categories to a proper level is ensured by quota. Thus even when the commercial sample bears its proper proportions of rural residents, it will not be at all surprising to discover (if closer examination is permitted) that the only rural residents in the nation who had a chance of being interviewed were those just outside the major cities, or at best those residing along the major transportation arteries between cities. There is no need to point out to the student of intranational center–periphery differences that these inhabitants are scarcely representative of the true national hinterlands.

For this reason, along with several correlated reasons, I have come to the sour conclusion that for much commercial survey research not closely supervised by academic or other knowledgeable clients, there is a general tendency for the reliability of data to deteriorate progressively from the center to the periphery of the national population studied. This means in turn that where the pedigree of survey data can be held in any question at all, the most dangerous type of analysis to be undertaken on it is that which systematically compares attributes, behaviors, and attitudes of the periphery with those of the center. In other words, the student of such center–periphery differences must demand a standard of data quality in his archives much higher than may be necessary in other contexts.

I do not mean to be totally discouraging about the use of such data, and certainly there will be many instances in which valid, worthwhile, and previously unknown information may shine through the results of even a very poorly controlled survey operation. Nor am I entirely alarmed at what

I believe to be the great amount of extremely poor survey data being generated, for, as our philosophy of error suggests, the fact of error, while annoying, is not in itself the supreme consideration. What is important is a knowledge of the degree and contours of likely error, so that we can see what we may learn over and above the limits of probable error. And therefore, what does alarm me are not the poorly controlled practices in themselves, but rather the systematic concealment or misrepresentation of information necessary to gauge likely error which one finds so often in commercial survey work. It is this problem as much as any other which makes decisions concerning the methodological adequacy of survey materials extremely difficult for the archive administrator.

Sampling Error

In some ways we emerge here from the tangle of unknown errors and biases into the refreshingly clean and beautiful problem of sampling error. A single, simple index from our data (the N) is all the information we appear to need in order to apply error theory to our estimates and arrive at statements of error margins. This is true, however, of only an infinitesimal portion of the survey data building up in our archives since, strictly speaking, such sampling theory even in modified form applies only to true probability samples and hence to only a small proportion of studies in most of our archives.

More important still, few if any investigators have ever been irrational enough to attempt a sample survey over an extended geographic area without developing what is now the standard multistage, geographically clustered sampling procedure. It is economically prohibitive to do otherwise. However, the recognition seems to be diffusing only slowly that in these cases the sampling error margins calculated from textbook formulas assuming simple random samples, rather than clustered ones, inevitably understate the breadth of likely error. Geographic clustering cannot narrow these margins; it can only increase them in varying degree. Of course it becomes important to know what this degree is in any special case, and here we fall into quite a morass. For while this degree can hypothetically be calculated for any special case, the error is specific not only to the N or Ns involved, but also to the relationship between the lines of geographic maldistribution of the variables being used and the lines of clustering followed in the particular sample design. The computation is therefore almost impossibly tedious, requiring a comparison of distributions of the variables at stake within all clusters of the sample.[5]

For an attribute such as sex, which is quite homogeneously distributed over geographic areas in our societies, the increase in error margins over those suggested by the common textbook formulas may be quite slight. Many social attitudes and attributes covered by our sample surveys are, however, much more heterogeneously distributed. Here the probable error margins for cluster samples become notably larger than in the simple random sample of the same size. Since the degree of increase to be expected is vitally affected not only by the empirical distribution of the attributes in question, but also by the degree of clustering in the specific sampling design, there can be no very useful rules of thumb. However, with a sample design such as that of the University of Michigan Survey Research Center, it is not at all radical to suggest a 30 per cent increase in size of error margins relative to simple random sample calculations for the same N. This is not a trivial correction.

I trust the general point here is of sufficient familiarity that I may move directly to a corollary which seems to be consistently overlooked, even by those who understand the basic differences between simple random sample error and cluster sample error.

If we ask ourselves what attributes of people are most likely to entail the greatest increases in error margins, we would naturally turn to those attributes which are least homogeneously distributed across geographic space. And of

5. For a detailed discussion of this problem, see Leslie Kish, "Confidence Intervals for Clustered Samples," *American Sociological Review, 22* (1957), 154–65.

course no attributes are more heterogeneously distributed in this sense than the geographic attributes of persons, such as their places of residence: region, subregion, province, cities of varying size classes, and the like. Precisely what happens to error margins when survey sample data are subdivided along such geographic lines depends once again upon the exact specifications of the sample design, the way in which sample clusters intersect with the analyst's geographical subdivisions and with the empirical clustering of other attributes. Thus, for example, with the standard Survey Research Center sample the design deliberately ensures that there is no special increase in error margins beyond the customary cluster sample toll if we restrict our analyses to four gross regional subdivisions. However, once we begin to subdivide these regions according to finer geographic distinctions, the increase in expected error margins is dramatic. Computations we have made for a few common analyses with such subdivisions suggest that we can expect error margins to increase by a factor running anywhere from four to seven or higher. Thus for a given N, a simple random sample formula might place confidence intervals of + 6 per cent around an estimated proportion, while the corrected figure might be + 36 per cent with a fine geographic subdivision as one variable. At this level of error, it is clear that few interesting statements are likely to be made.

In other words, sample surveys, like telescopes, have a certain resolving power. An index of this resolving power for simple random samples is the N of the sample or subsample in question. Good cluster samples have a determinable resolving power as well, but it is not fixed. Unlike telescopes, the resolving power of any given cluster sample can vary quite dramatically according to the objects (variables) being examined. For certain objects—geographically defined ones—under certain conditions of sample design, even an otherwise good sample may have next to no resolving power at all.

This matter seems appropriate to mention here in part because people who would like to use sample survey data for studies of intranational variation in modernization are very apt to want to subdivide these survey materials in a variety of geographical ways. They deserve to be warned about these matters before rather than after they have labored at their analyses. Indeed, no single gross misuse or misinterpretation of our sample survey data is more persistent than this failure to understand the way in which sampling error can rocket upward when geographical subdivisions are applied in unfortunate ways to clustered samples. We have in our files some very painstaking graphs of what we see as 95 per cent random perturbation, worked out by people in the throes of excitement at finding such wide, if rather complex, empirical variation. More depressing still are the dozens of elegant pages of prose in which the author analyzes this maze of variation—obviously far too great to be written off as sampling error, as he understands the matter—and attempts to reduce it to a limited set of underlying theoretical principles. Such episodes are a tragic waste of time and talent. If the newly developing archives are to take any responsibility at all in matters of data quality and error, they might well include in their jurisdiction problems such as these.

Indeed, as we see it, the development of data archives puts us very much at a crossroads. The way marked "laissez-faire" or "caveat emptor" will scarcely improve the quality of research, for an increasing distance between analyst and the underlying frailties of the specific data collection only deadens his sensitivity to them. While we grant that the data archive—especially the poorly financed one—is ill equipped to carry the burden, it is likely to be better equipped than the majority of the individual clients. If this be so, then ways must be found to accept the responsibility.

20. Retrieval Systems for Data Archives: The General Inquirer[1]

ERWIN K. SCHEUCH, UNIVERSITY OF COLOGNE, AND
PHILIP J. STONE, HARVARD UNIVERSITY

INFORMATION RETRIEVAL AS A CENTRAL PROBLEM FOR DATA ARCHIVES

In the natural sciences, the efficient use of data already existing is increasingly understood to be as much a problem as the addition of new findings. Extensive studies are now under way both in the Soviet Union and the United States to solve the problem of locating information with the help of advanced technical equipment, particularly by using high speed computers with large "memory" capacities.[2] Among social scientists, the prevailing attitude is that such problems do not yet merit our attention, since our disciplines are not producing sufficient quantities of data. This is untrue, and that

1. The decision to use the General Inquirer System grew out of discussions with Professor Robert Bales of Harvard University. The actual work on which this report is based was supported partly by funds from the Laboratory of Social Relations at Harvard and by a grant from the National Science Foundation for the development of the General Inquirer. Funds from the latter source are also used to continue our work. The preparation of the report was supported by the International Social Science Council.

2. A survey of these developments in the USA and in the USSR can be found in the hearings before a Congressional committee on a legislative proposal to establish a National Data Processing Center in the U. S.; "Hearings Before the Ad Hoc Subcommittee on a National Research Data Processing and Information Retrieval Center (Bill H.R. 1946)," *1*, Parts 1, 2, and 3, and Appendices 1, 2, and 3 (Washington, U. S. Government Printing Office, 1963).

such a view can prevail is partly due to the lack of visibility of data. It is simply not sufficiently realized how many data are collected in various special fields outside a particular social scientist's area of concentration. Even more widespread is the lack of awareness that there is a considerable volume of data collection in most industrialized countries.

The activities of the International Social Science Council, the International Committee on Social Science Documentation, and UNESCO are beginning to have a significant impact, not only in encouraging interchanges and cooperation among various fields of specialization and among the generators of empirical work in different countries, but also in increasing awareness that even in the social sciences we are no longer "data poor." Once this latter fact is realized, we may expect an important change in the prevailing styles of research, and especially a sudden expansion of cross-cultural comparisons.

Probably the most important single data producing activity of sociology, of branches of economics, and of political science is survey research, and it is here that the disparity between the accumulation and the utilization of data is especially great. The establishment of archives for survey research data increased our consciousness of the extent of this disparity, of the facts (1) that the social sciences had been losing considerable data, and (2) that, literally, many thousands of studies were being conducted each year which are of potential interest. The loss of data is now declining—though it is by no means sufficiently checked—as the producers are increasingly willing to turn over their material after its initial analysis to these new repositories. This results in a massive volume of data with which these institutions have to cope, a volume undoubtedly many times larger than foreseen when such centers were founded. The Roper Center, for example, has already accumulated IBM cards for nearly seven million interviews.

While originally the primary problem facing data archives was locating and subsequently storing such studies, an additional problem of rapidly increasing importance is the retrieval of the information. Without proper retrieval systems, such data archives obviously would turn into giant morgues for IBM cards. Once an archive exceeds a minimum size—let us say, before the first 200 studies have been inventoried—it is less the quality of the collection of studies that decides the usefulness of a repository and more the efficiency of its retrieval system. The retrieval tasks in all these archives are quite similar, since all have adopted the same basic procedure: they attempt to provide users with the questions that serve their interests. If these questions are found useful, the original decks are made accessible (in one form or the other) for secondary analysis. Consequently, the units in both the storage and the retrieval operations are the individual question or group of questions from survey schedules.

Problems of acquisition and retrieval become accentuated when data archives are used as tools for international comparative research. To help in the establishment of rational arrangements, a series of meetings sponsored by UNESCO and ISSC since 1962 worked out detailed recommendations that included many references to retrieval systems.[3] To implement these agreements, work was begun first at Harvard and subsequently at other institutions to develop a system that would effectively unlock the holdings of archives to the greatest possible variety of uses. While attempts are being pursued to adapt retrieval systems from other fields or to develop new systems for the use of data repositories, archives already in operation continue to develop their older systems based on procedures existing prior to the advent of modern electronic equipment.

We will attempt to characterize retrieval systems in use, to utilize the experiences of currently operational archives in deriving the standards that an ideal system should meet, and to present one attempt to develop such a system.

THE TASKS OF A RETRIEVAL SYSTEM FOR DATA ARCHIVES

The unit of information with which retrieval systems for data archives have to deal is somewhat peculiar for a "library." The unit to be stored and to be retrieved is the indi-

3. See Chap. 24 in this volume.

vidual question or sometimes a group of related questions appearing in the survey research questionnaire. Occasionally, one may also want to store the response categories as part of the actual questions, especially for multiple choice questions. These are the units with which the users of archives perform their secondary analyses. All of the more general archives for source material have found it insufficient to classify just the general topic of studies since this would entail the loss of a vast amount of information in view of the heterogeneity of questionnaires in empirical social research.

Particular problems result from the language of questionnaires. This language is highly ritualized and unspecific in its terminology, so that a classification often calls for many inferences. Difficult problems arise from the fact that there is usually more than one way to look at a question. Such a question as "Do you intend to vote in the coming election?" may be treated as permitting a prediction of future behavior or as being an index of current involvement in politics. These two ways of using the very same question are still very close to its commonsense meaning. However, it is equally legitimate to look upon this question as one of many indicators that characterize the degree to which the respondent structures the future (*Fristigkeit des Denkens*).

We refer to the commonsense meaning of a question as its "manifest meaning"; an interpretation which deviates from this commonsense meaning we call "latent meaning." These terms have been chosen in analogy to the distinction between latent and manifest function by Robert K. Merton.[4] As a minimum, a data archive should retrieve the manifest meaning of questions. A data repository would become all the more useful if one could locate a question also according to its various latent meanings. This is especially needed in view of the new direction in survey research methodology, in

4. The use of "latent" and "manifest" is not absolutely identical to that of Merton. However, in practice it should be, since for most surveys the common sense meaning is usually identical with the meaning that the original data producing agent had in mind. Cf. Robert K. Merton, *Social Theory and Social Structure* (rev. ed. Glencoe, Ill., Free Press, 1957), pp. 19–84, esp. p. 51.

which indicators are conceived of as having only a probability relation to an underlying meaning.

Problems of Library-Style Retrieval Systems

Differences among Library-Style Systems. Although all of the retrieval systems presently used for data archives are of the library type, there is considerable difference among them. Specifically, these systems differ in the type of relations among categories and in the way they handle multiple storage of the same information.

The Roper Center employs essentially a dictionary-type retrieval system. One advantage of this system is that the coder can rely on his common sense. One of the disadvantages is that it is hard both for the coder and the subsequent user to identify the one category among the many he is looking for. The Cologne *Zentralarchiv* relies in principle on a linear type of classification system, where the categories used for actual storage are the final points of a hierarchy of classes. In this way it becomes somewhat easier to locate a category, but this system makes higher demands on both the coder and the user with regard to the understanding of concepts. If one is looking for material to substantiate a conceptual orientation, the system adopted at Cologne appears to be somewhat easier to work with; if one is interested in finding material relating to a concrete topic of current interest, the system used at the Roper Center is probably more efficient.

Of possibly greater consequence for the operation of archives is the way the problem of multiple storage of the same bit of information is handled. The *Zentralarchiv* employs the principle of multiple classification of the same question under different categories. In Williamstown, the same task is mainly handled by the system of cross-references among categories. Multiple classification is more efficient from the viewpoint of the user, but it also drastically increases the amount of work necessary to process a question.

Some Common Problem Areas of Library-Style Classification Systems. With a library-style classification system it is considerably more difficult to store questions than book titles. One may look upon such a system as reducing an extended verbal communication to one point. The longer the verbal communication, the less explicit its meaning; and the more complex its structure, the more difficult this reduction becomes. Traditionally, libraries for publications have looked upon the title of the book as sufficiently representing its content; once this reduction is found acceptable, further reductions of the title to a "point" probably entail only minor losses of information.[5] For such a complex communication as a question, we are sure that treating questions like book titles implies a much more drastic reduction of information, and even if one saw no alternative to this library procedure the process is considerably more difficult. This has important consequences for three problem areas that are common to all of the cataloguing systems of the traditional type employed in archives: the amount of work, the reliability, and the attempts to avoid loss of information.

A data archive must recognize that a person can code a smaller number of units per hour than is true of a conventional library. This also applies to the dictionary variety of codes, even though they require lower degrees of abstraction than linear codes. In estimating the time required for classification procedures, one also has to consider that its units, that is, questions, are not discrete but planned as a sequence, their meaning being partly determined by the preceding units; this implies some demands upon the memory of coders.

Reliability is obviously a function of the category system employed. However, it should be a safe generalization to state that variations in the judgment between coders and lack of constancy for each coder will be one of the major problems of data archives once codes exceed the size of about 500 classes—which occurs fairly quickly as holdings increase even beyond 100 studies. Thus, the Cologne *Zentralarchiv* has already had to expand its catalogue to cover 600 positions. The larger the holdings become, the greater the

5. Actually, scholars in the field of library science are no longer satisfied with this reduction procedure for titles, and various procedures able to deal with the whole communication are beginning to be used.

problem—and from studies of the reliability of content analysis by hand methods we know that there is an over-proportional increase in error with increasing number of categories. None of the archives has as yet performed a study on the reliability of its procedures, so that no number values can be assigned to these statements. In addition, we do not have the impression that reliability is as yet seen by archives as a major problem in developing and administering their classification system. The fact that users are not apt to notice a possible lack of reliability is probably connected with this orientation.

Using a dictionary type of cataloguing system implies losing a considerable amount of information. For technical reasons—the amount of work involved being the main one—it is hardly possible to store even the manifest meanings. Storing latent meanings is practically out of the question. During the initial phase of establishing the Cologne archive, coding the latent meaning of questions by hand was tried. This was found to be a type of work that requires a fully trained Ph.D. While such highly qualified persons may be available for the development of a cataloguing system, they will not be available for its continuous application. Since in the day-to-day operations one would have to assume the level of skill of an ordinary clerical worker, or at best a person with a B.A., coding latent meaning by hand was abandoned after a few trials.

An Alternative Principle of Classification. The principle involved in using a library-style operation for storing questions was characterized as the reduction of an extended communication to one point or at most a few points. In discussing alternative ways of improving the present classification procedures of data repositories, *it appeared that a type of content analysis not relying on this reduction, but storing a number of points per unit coded, might constitute an alternative.* In order to be practical, and not just to multiply the problems of applying any category system, such a content analysis should not have to rely on coding by hand. A system of content analysis by means of computers that had been developed at the Laboratory of Social Relations (Harvard), the "General Inquirer," was considered as a tool to make this practicable.

THE GENERAL INQUIRER SYSTEM

The General Inquirer was developed during the spring of 1961 as a computer program for the IBM 7090.[6] (Although the same program will also work with an IBM 709 or even an IBM 704, it would be too time-consuming to be very practicable.) The system grew out of the interests of Robert F. Bales, Philip J. Stone, J. Zvi Namenwirth, and others at Harvard in having a tool for analyzing the content of small group discussions. The actual system was conceived and written by Philip Stone, using a high order computer language, COMIT.[7] It was soon found that the system has a much wider range of applications than was originally envisaged.

The General Inquirer is in principle an adaptation of language translation programming facilities that originated with the Mechanical Translation Group of the Massachusetts Institute of Technology. However, instead of translating one "natural language" (i.e. the language of social intercourse) into another natural language, the General Inquirer translates a natural language into a concept language. This is done by specifying for words of the natural language the concepts to which they might refer, i.e. by constructing a dictionary. The entries in this dictionary are words and idioms of the natural language that the researcher determines as being related to concepts. This dictionary is stored by the computer, and subsequently applied automatically whenever a new text is fed into the machine. Obviously, the system is only as good as the "dictionary," but with a computerized dictionary problems

6. For a general description of the system, see Philip J. Stone, Robert F. Bales, J. Zvi Namenwirth, and Daniel Ogilvie, "The General Inquirer: A Computer System for Content Analysis and Retrieval Based on the Sentence as a Unit of Information," *Behavioral Science*, 7 (1962), 484–501. An updated description of the system by Dexter C. Dunphy, Philip J. Stone, and Marshall S. Smith, in *Behavioral Science*, *10* (1965).

7. In the fall of 1963, the accounting and retrieving sections of the General Inquirer were rewritten in autocoder for use on the IBM 1401 by Aram Grayson and Robert McCarthy, The IBM 7090 programs have since been rewritten in BALGOL by Horace Enea at Stanford and in MAD by Eric Steiner at Yale.

of reliability in content analysis disappear, as do all other restrictions which are imposed on content analysis routines due to the limited capacities of the human mind for storage, instantaneous retrieval, and simultaneous perception of a large number of information relationships.

Stone and Hunt summarized the practical operations in processing a text as follows: Written text enters the machine and is separated by the computer into words and sentences. The computer then removes regular word endings, looks each word up in a dictionary, and tags words with labels indicating each word's membership in one or more categories specified by the investigator.

> The sentences, together with their tags, are then stored on binary tape for repeated use in inquiry procedures. . . . If the keypunched text is marked with a simplified form of syntactic coding, the investigator can make inquiries not only about the co-occurrence of certain text words and/or tags, but also can specify the syntactic relationships that must appear between them.[8]

At present, some fourteen different dictionaries have been developed for various content analysis projects. The Harvard Third Psychosociological Dictionary, for example, consists of the 3,000 words most frequently used in English (Thorndike and Lorge count), plus several hundred words of special interest to behavioral scientists. The computer is instructed to print as a separate list (leftovers) all words in the text studied that do not appear as dictionary entries; from an inspection of these leftovers the entry list is empirically expanded for later applications.

The tagging of concepts to entries is nothing else but making one's theoretical interests and decisions highly explicit and constant. If one's theoretical notions change, entries need to be "re-tagged"—a procedure that involves considerably less work than the construction of an entire new dictionary.

The Harvard psychosociological dictionary presently used

8. Philip J. Stone and Earl B. Hunt, "A Computer Approach to Content Analysis: Studies Using the General Inquirer System," *Spring Joint Computer Conference* (1963), p. 242.

is already in its third revision, due to changes in orientation and the accumulation of experience. Various bodies of theory are represented in the concept system of the dictionary, since this system is intended for a wide range of applications. The most frequently used bodies of theory are: Kurt Lewin's field theory, action theory as used by Parsons and Bales, psychoanalytic theory of psychosexual symbolism, Osgood's dimensions of semantic space, and Leary's categories of interpersonal relations. In the list of concepts or tags, 83 variables are represented.

The increased order through a reduction of more than 3,000 words to 83 tags is not accompanied by such a loss of information as this relation between the two figures might suggest at first sight. The General Inquirer works partially with multiple tagging, so that an entry word may be characterized by a more specific combination of concepts. The dictionary differentiates between so-called first and second order tags: first order tags represent the estimate of the usual and explicit meaning of the word in standard usage, and no multiple tagging is permitted here; second order tags are meant to represent the significant connotative and implicit meanings, and an entry is tagged this way as often as appears necessary to represent its various meanings. Examples of first order tags are: self, other, job role, male role, natural object, social place, or action norm. Examples of second order tags are: overstate, sign-strong, male-theme, danger-theme, peer-status, recreational.

Here are some examples of the dictionary itself:

	Tag: *Male role* (first order tag)	Tag: *Male-theme* (second order tag)
Entries:	actor	arm
	boy	muscles
	brother	trouser
	fellow	handsome
	lover	tower
	master	pipe
	prince	staff
	son	sword
	wizard	

This form of the dictionary is used to identify the words and idioms that comprise each concept category. Another representation of the dictionary is organized by entry word. The following examples also demonstrate the process of multiple tagging:

actor	= artistic/male role
interpret	= academic/thought form
lover	= sex-theme/peer-status/male role
patient	= lower status/medical/neuter role
trouser	= male-theme/clothing
victor	= ascend theme/higher status/military/neuter role
commitment	= legal/sign-accept/action norm
president	= ascend theme/higher status/political/job role
shoot	= death theme/sign-reject/military/attack
relaxation	= recreational/pleasure
worthiness	= authority theme/religious/ideal value

Although the dictionary may grow into a considerable volume, this does not yet affect its applicability: the computer processes and tags 10,000 text words per minute. In retrieval, a number of separate inquiries can be handled simultaneously.

The Adaptation of the General Inquirer System as a Retrieval System for Archives

Trials in Adapting the General Inquirer. When describing what we understand to be the specifications of an optimal retrieval system for data archives, some colleagues at Harvard suggested that the General Inquirer might handle both the latent and the manifest meaning of communications. Whether this also meant that the Inquirer could actually be employed with survey repositories would, however, have to be checked empirically.

After the decision to approach the problem inductively we secured from the Survey Research Center of the University of Michigan five sample requests from clients as well as the answers given to these requests, in order to permit a check as to whether the computer system would be able to simulate the present work of archives. The requests were of very different degrees of specificity, and dealt with a variety of topics. The questionnaire items that were supplied in answer to these requests were:

1. a study of candidates for the 1958 Congressional elections
2. the 1958 general population election survey
3. the omnibus survey of Fall 1959
4. the 1962 survey of consumer finances

To these studies we added a questionnaire from a current study supported by the Laboratory of Social Relations dealing with aspects of social stratification. These studies supplied the empirical material for our various trial runs.

We began storing questions taken directly from the questionnaires and requests in the way they were phrased by their authors. Soon we realized, however, that such a procedure would be unsuccessful. At a minimum, we would have to rephrase the requests into a specific conceptual language; also, in the questionnaires certain ambiguous phrases and redundancies had to be eliminated since this verbal material would not be useful in distinguishing between questions. Even after this we did not immediately see that we could now use the General Inquirer system.

The actual problems seemed to be caused mainly by the peculiar way in which questions are used in poll type interviews. As is well known, one of the basic skills in formulating questions for surveys is to translate specific terms into a composite of everyday words. Thus one avoids suggestiveness and prevents the respondent from being exposed to unfamiliar terms. The fact that it is often the composite of words that stands for a meaning proved to be a problem for the General Inquirer. This is an example of the way that the concept "isolationalism" is translated into questionnaire language: "This country would be better off if we just stayed home and did not concern ourselves with problems in other parts of the world. Would you say you have an opinion on this or not?"

On the other hand, each question contains—so to speak—a number of words merely by implication. Another of the skills in questionnaire wording is to make use of sequence, specifying the meaning of a subsequent question by the context in which it is asked. (In a way, this is not dissimilar to the use of language in everyday discourse, where the meaning of words exchanged rely on the shared definition of the context in which they are spoken.) Consequently, it is necessary to "translate" the context back into the individual question (the question being the unit of retrieval). This was a decision crucial for what we consider our later success in performing editorial work on questions prior to submitting them to the General Inquirer.

The Successful Adaptations. During these trials we gained information both about the peculiarities of questionnaire language and about some properties of the General Inquirer. We were now ready to formulate the requirements for a revised dictionary and for the operations preceding the use of the computer.

The principle of first editing a question before processing was retained as absolutely necessary in view of the character of questionnaire language and the present stage of development of machine processing of verbal material. The main functions of the editing of questions prior to their input into the computer are:

1. specifying the context and referent of the question
2. rephrasing into a straightforward, self-contained format
3. elimination of redundancies and nonspecific embellishments

The translation is restricted to just those functions, and it is not a translation geared to a concept language. We decided against limiting the translation to a concept language for the following reasons:

1. Aside from storing the so-called manifest meaning, we wanted to make sure that the greatest number of "latent meanings" could still be retrieved.
2. In the printout of the computer, the questions should still have a recognizable identity, so that a user would be able to reach a preliminary decision about the applicability of a question without having to inspect in each case the actual questionnaire.
3. The translation task should not be beyond the skills of an advanced student or qualified clerical help.

This last point we consider another strategic decision: the decision to require only low skills for the storage routine and, consequently, to demand a high level of skills only for the processing of the inquiries to the repository. The implications for the staffing of such a retrieval center are obvious.

A precondition for the success of our storage policy was the development of a set of rules for the input operations. Samples of questions, the input rules, and the reformulation of questions according to those rules, are given in the Appendix to this chapter.[9] Of course, these are only samples of all the questions we worked with, and they have been selected to demonstrate a variety of problems.

A problem in writing the questions for retrieval operations is the striking of a balance between the two dangers of being supplied with large masses of irrelevant material and of missing information. In principle, we write inquiries (insofar as they are directed toward the concept system; pure identifications of a term do not cause any problems) as a logical product of concepts. Ceteris paribus, the more terms such a product has, the more questions are excluded as not meeting the joint occurrence of these identifiers. Thus it is up to the writer of an inquiry to decide anew in each case the proper balance between the danger of an oversupply of spurious retrievals or a loss of potentially relevant information.

Further Work and Promise. After having worked with this latest version of an adaptation of the General Inquirer, we

9. These rules have been further simplified since this chapter was written, keeping the rephrased questions closer to the original text of the question.

felt that further implementation of our program would best be handled by some outside organization accepting development work and by data archives themselves. However, since no institution was in the position to begin actual work, we decided to develop the system further as a cooperative venture between the Laboratory of Social Relations of Harvard University and the Department of Sociology at the University of Cologne.

In such developmental work, the following tasks are being performed:

1. Develop a list of entry words and idioms by indexing a sample of questionnaires, using "key-word-in-context" computer indexing programs.
2. Develop a new system of tags by checking the present concept vocabulary against registers of representative texts from the fields of marketing, political science, sociology, and behavioristic psychology.
3. Specify the rules for inquiry, and run a series of simulated requests employing different sets of rules. The purpose here is to establish optimum points of a balance between over- and under-retrieval of questions.
4. Develop foreign language equivalents of the English General Inquirer system.
5. Test how far the same vocabulary can be combined with different concept lists to serve special interests better.
6. Determine costs of using the system, assuming different volumes of input and storage.

These development tasks will be performed by processing a wide variety of public affairs studies from several countries. We selected this topic both because of our interest in this area of research and because the variety of terms used in such interviews seemed especially appropriate for the development of a complete vocabulary. The work is expected to continue until the summer of 1966. At the same time we shall maintain our efforts to have other institutions also engage in development work, and prospects are good that we will be successful in this attempt.

We think we are already in a position to specify how the

General Inquirer or a similar system should be fitted into the work of data archives. In expanding such facilities, in planning for additional archives, and in establishing a network of cooperating repositories, the following mode of operation might be considered in planning.

One or several retrieval centers with "time-shared" computer facilities will be established as clearinghouse institutions. This does not at all imply storage of the IBM cards at the same location. In view of the development of information transmission technology (e.g. data phones), the location of physical holdings is no longer a very crucial problem insofar as the retrieval center is concerned. In effect these retrieval centers are offices for processing questionnaire material and writing inquiries. Input material would be accumulated, as would inquiries, to be handled compactly. Once relevant questions are located, the same time-shared computer would be used to retrieve data files containing the responses of the subjects and perform further statistical analyses. Such procedures are currently being employed by Ithiel de Sola Pool and his associates at the Massachusetts Institute of Technology.

We are by now reasonably certain that the adaptation of the General Inquirer or similar computer system accomplishes the following tasks:

1. Large masses of data can be processed by personnel the majority of whom possess only limited skills. In this way we can expect that storage will be able to cope with a continuous flow of a large number of questionnaires.

2. By providing a concept language, the holdings of IBM cards become much more useful for scholarly purposes. Questions can be retrieved by considering either their manifest or their latent meaning.

3. In addition to asking for the material relating to specific concepts, the system handles requests for the identification of specific words and idioms in the text. This makes the system especially useful for those interested in current affairs.

4. The system can be adapted to the changing vocabulary

(as identified by occurrences in the leftover list) or changing concepts (by tagging words in the entry lists with an added concept) with a limited amount of work, a large part of which can be handled by machines—instead of having periodically to hand reclassify one's holdings or make the system inflexible.

5. The system appears especially well geared to international or cross-national work. Once lists of entries have been prepared for any "natural" language, questionnaire material can be stored in this language and can be retrieved in any other language. Thus, the laborious and uncertain task of translating every questionnaire in the holdings of an archive that has ambitions to store international data is bypassed; translation is only necessary once a question has been retrieved as relevant for a user.

APPENDIX

Data Bank Project: Questionnaire Rephrasing for Machine Retrieval

A. Principles:

1. Retrieval is to be based on the individual question as the basic unit.
2. In addition to storing the "manifest meaning," the systems should also make it possible to store most of the "latent meanings."
3. When printed out the question should still be readable, i.e. have a recognizable identity.
4. The rephrasing task should not be beyond the skills of advanced students or qualified clerical help.
5. The language is designed for use of advanced computers.

B. Procedures:

1. The questionnaires are rephrased into a series of declarative sentences. Each statement describes the actual and contextual material contained in a particular questionnaire item.

2. A code identifying the questionnaire is punched on the left side of each IBM card. The question number code is also punched before the beginning of the statement. A blank column separates the two codes.

3. Usually, a question asks about the respondent's opinion or feelings regarding a topic. If the question asks for empirical information, the statement is preceded by the word "info—."

4. Often a question is preceded with a statement of information, such as "MANY PEOPLE USE TIME PAYMENTS TO . . ." or "CUBA RECEIVES SUPPLIES IN THE FORM OF. . . ." Such information, whether preceding the question or actually embedded within it, is given the status of a separate statement. The separate statement is preceded by the word "prologue—." The statement then representing the actual question is marked "item—." If the user retrieves a statement marked "item—," he thus knows it was preceded by a prologue specific to that question.

5. If a question refers to a comparison, or asks for a choice between alternatives, these choices are separated by a diagonal. Examples: "PREFER DEMOCRAT / REPUBLICAN WINS NEXT ELECTION." Note that a space appears on each side of the diagonal.

6. If the respondent is asked to state the viewpoint of another person (as he perceives it), this is called an "attributive reference." Words involved in describing the attributive references are preceded by a star. Example: " *MOTHER *HOPES DEMOCRATS / REPUBLICANS WIN NEXT ELECTION."

7. Questions involving the supposition of some future state of affairs or requiring the assumption of a hypothetical situation are marked with the word "suppose."

8. If the respondent is asked in a question follow-up for an explanation or reasons, the term "reasons" is inserted at the end of the statement. Similarly, if he is asked to quantify his response, the term "amount" or "number" is added.

9. Time reference is made explicit by reference to "in future," "in past," "ago," "present-time."

10. Quite often the respondent is asked to identify a referent that represents his viewpoint. This relationship is noted by the single word (usually as attributive) "represent–respondent."

11. All statements end with a period. New statements may begin on the same card. Several special words may appear in front of the statement (in any order). Statements may continue from one card to another. Only the questionnaire identification appears regularly on the left of each card.

12. Since questionnaire writing is a relatively standardized procedure, it is possible to reduce ambiguity problems by the use of specific reference words.

a. Nonambiguous words can be substituted for words and idioms that are other wise ambiguous. What word is substituted depends on the context. Examples: "country" becomes "nation" or "countryside"; "value" becomes "price" or remains "value"; "charge" becomes "fee" or "accusation."

b. The rephrasing procedure becomes simplified by using a series of relatively standard reference words. Examples: brand, consumer-goods, guarantee, dwelling, well-being, duplicate, etc.

C. Examples:

1. Inter-University Consortium for Political Research, 1958, Survey Research Center, University of Michigan.

Original	*Rephrased*
9. Do you happen to know which party had the most Congressmen in Washington before the election this last month? Yes No (If Yes) 9a. Which one?	CPR58 9 INFO—WHICH POLITICAL-PARTY HAD MOST CONGRESSMEN BEFORE 1958 ELECTION?
10. Do you happen to know which party elected the most Congressmen in the elections this month? Yes No (If Yes) 10a. Which one?	CPR58 10 INFO—WHICH POLITICAL-PARTY HAS MOST CONGRESSMAN AFTER 1958 ELECTION?
11a. "The government should leave things like electric power and housing for private businessmen to handle." Do you have an opinion on this or not? (Likert scale follows)	CPR58 11A GOVERNMENT / PRIVATE BUSINESS SHOULD HANDLE ELECTRICITY AND HOUSING.
11b. How do you think the parties stand on this? Are the Democrats or Republicans closer to what you want on this question, or isn't there any difference? (Likert scale follows)	CPR58 11B *REPUBLICANS / *DEMOCRATS *REPRESENT-RESPONDENT ON GOVERNMENT / PRIVATE BUSINESS SHOULD HANDLE ELECTRICITY AND HOUSING.
13a. "This country would be better off if we just stayed home and did not concern ourselves with	CPR58 13A ISOLATIONISM.

Original	Rephrased
problems in other parts of the world." Would you say you have an opinion on this or not? (Likert scale follows)	
13b. Are the Democrats or the Republicans closer to what you want, or isn't there any difference between them on this?	CPR58 13B *REPUBLICANS / *DEMOCRATS *REPRESENT-RESPONDENT ON ISOLATIONISM.

2. Fall Omnibus Survey. Survey Research Center, University of Michigan, October, 1959.

Original	*Rephrased*
13. Speaking now of the automobile market, do you think the next 12 months or so will be a good time or a bad time to buy a car? Good Pro-Con Bad Uncertain 13a. Why do you say so?________	FOS59 13 CAR PRICE IN NEXT FUTURE YEAR GOOD / BAD / UNCERTAIN, REASONS.
14. Now about auto prices, what do you expect they will do in the next 12 months or so?________	FOS59 14 EXPECT AUTO PRICES IN NEXT YEAR FUTURE INCREASE / DECREASE / STAY SAME.
15. Do you or anyone else in the family own an automobile? Yes No (If Yes)	FOS59 15 INFO—FAMILY OWN CAR.
15a. Does your family have more than one car? Owns: Only one Two Three or more	FOS59 15A INFO—FAMILY OWNS DUPLICATE CAR, NUMBER.

C. Examples (*continued*)

Original	Rephrased
16. *For each car* — *Main car* / *2nd car*	
16a. Did you buy it new or used? — New Used / New Used	FOS59 16A INFO—CURRENT FAMILY CAR NEW / USED.
16b. When did you buy it?	FOS59 16B INFO—YEAR PURCHASED CURRENT FAMILY CAR.
16c. What year and model is it?	FOS59 16C INFO—BRAND AND YEAR OF CURRENT FAMILY CAR.
I have a few more questions about buying a car on time. We may already have discussed some of them. . .	FOS59 19 PROLOGUE—MORE QUESTIONS ABOUT BUYING ON CREDIT.
19. Is there a difference in cost if one makes the arrangements for financing with the car dealer or with a bank?________	FOS59 19 INFO—DIFFERENCE EXISTS IN CREDIT COST BETWEEN CAR DEALER / BANK.
19a. Which one is higher?________	FOS59 19A INFO—CREDIT COST HIGHER WITH BANK / CAR DEALER.
113. (As you said) car dealers make arrangements to finance a car with finance companies and sometimes with banks; would you say that the car buyer should be concerned with whom the dealer makes the arrangement?________	FOS59 113 PROLOGUE—DEALERS OBTAIN CAR CREDIT WITH MONEY FROM FINANCE-COMPANY AND BANKS. 113 ITEM—FINANCE-COMPANY / BANK AS ULTIMATE CREDIT SOURCE IS IMPORTANT DIFFERENCE.
113a. Do you have a preference?________ 113b. Why do you say so?________	FOS59 *RESPONDENT *PREFERS CAR DEALER OBTAIN CREDIT FROM FINANCE-COMPANY / BANK, REASONS.

3. Examples from 1958 Congressional Candidate Study, University of Michigan Survey Research Center

Original	*Rephrased*
12. First, on the foreign economic aid program, would you generally favor expanding the program, reducing it, or maintaining it about the way it is?	CCS58 12 SHOULD EXPAND / REDUCE / MAINTAIN FOREIGN ECONOMIC AID.
13. How about the foreign military aid program? Should this be expanded, reduced, or maintained about as it is?	CCS58 13 SHOULD EXPAND / REDUCE / MAINTAIN FOREIGN MILITARY AID.
14. What do you feel about aid for underdeveloped countries that take a neutral position between the United States and the Soviet Union? Do you think we should give them aid only if they support the West?	CCS58 14 PROLOGUE——SOME NON-DEVELOPED FOREIGN NATIONS HAVE NEUTRAL POLITICAL POSITION BETWEEN UNITED-STATES AND SOVIET-UNION. 14 ITEM—ECONOMIC AID SHOULD BE CONDITIONAL ON SUPPORT OF WESTERN ALLIANCE POSITION.
15. Speaking very generally, do you think that in the years ahead the United States should maintain or reduce its commitments around the world?	CCS58 15 UNITED-STATES SHOULD MAINTAIN / REDUCE INTERNATIONAL COMMITMENTS IN FUTURE YEARS.
16. I know that a member of the House sometimes isn't able to vote on things that really reflect his own position. How well have House roll calls dealing with foreign policy allowed you to express your basic position on foreign affairs?	CCS58 16 PROLOGUE—CONGRESSMEN IN MEETING SOMETIMES VOTE DIFFERENTLY FROM OWN OPINION. 16 ITEM—EXTENT FOREIGN POLICY VOTING OF RESPONDENT IN CONGRESS HAS REFLECTED OPINION OF RESPONDENT.
17. Has your position on foreign policy changed in recent years as a result of changing events?	CCS58 17 INFO—RESPONDENT CHANGE OPINION IN RECENT YEARS ON FOREIGN POLICY.

21. An Outline of Two Systems: SYNTOL and the General Inquirer *

FRANCIS G. LÉVY, CENTRE DE CALCUL DE LA MAISON DES SCIENCES DE L'HOMME, PARIS

With the development of comparative studies and the increasing volume of data in the field of social science, interest has grown in systems designed to store and retrieve information, especially if they include mechanized processes to perform some or all of the tasks involved. None of these automatic or semiautomatic systems is presently operational for survey research material.

Two projects will be considered here which have either been used for content analysis of documents or tested for retrieval of information in the behavioral sciences. The authors of both SYNTOL and the General Inquirer present "systems" that with minor modifications are applicable to data archives. The present study will describe these two information retrieval systems, so that a comparison can be made of their applicability to social science data, especially questionnaires. After we have outlined some fundamental requirements of retrieval systems,[1] enumerated some of the operations involved, and drawn the limits of the comparison, we shall describe each of the systems. In a following section, problems raised by the application of these systems to questionnaires will be considered.

* A slightly different version of this chapter is to appear in the *International Social Science Journal.*

1. By retrieval system is meant both the storage and retrieval of information.

A retrieval system is supposed to provide information out of a collection of documents relevant to a particular request. It is meant to be economical and reliable, i.e. to imply on one hand no costly transformation of original data, and on the other to conform to the user's judgment as to what is "relevant." On top of being a specialist's substitute reader, such formal transformations, translations, etc., as are specified by the scientist should be performed. A series of operations are thus necessary to transform a given mass of data, as yet undifferentiated (except by its physical limits), into meaningful—to a given individual, for a given purpose—units of information. These series of operations we shall outline without reference to any machine procedure.

Two types of operations can be distinguished: one bears on the content of documents, the other on their format:

1. The basic requirement of information retrieval systems is that they *recognize* content, and evaluate it "according to some relevance criterion. Evaluation in turn implies comparison of elements in terms of this relevance criterion; such a comparison then presupposes some orderly classification. . . . The ordering system used for the storage of this information can be called *indexing,* since it is comparable in purpose—though not necessarily in structure or efficiency—to the index of a file or library." [2] Indexing is thus defined as that operation of content processing (as opposed to content analysis) which imposes an order upon a set of documents to conform with the explicit or implicit criteria contained in requests. The following scheme illustrates the storage and retrieval sequence:

TABLE 21.1

Natural language documents	→	Indexed versions of data	←	Natural language requests
STORAGE		INDEXING		RETRIEVAL

Two options are possible: either indexing is performed at the storage level and untransformed requests are matched

2. Paul Garvin, "A Linguist's View of Language-Data Processing," *Natural Language and the Computer* (New York, McGraw-Hill, 1963).

against the set of preordered documents; or natural language documents are selected thanks to proper transformations applied to requests. Or, as an intermediate solution, some indexing can be performed on both documents and requests. A possible sequence can be shown in this way:

TABLE 21.2

Natural language documents ⟶ Indexing ⟶ RETRIEVAL ⟵ Indexing ⟵ Natural language requests

The significant difference manifested in this respect by SYNTOL and the General Inquirer will be discussed in the following sections.

2. The other category of operations involved in retrieval systems relates to format specifications either imposed by the economy of the system or expressly desired by the users. No system, whether manual or mechanical, has been envisaged which could simultaneously process full-length natural language texts and provide the relevant selection of full-text natural language documents to the requester. For evident reasons—to save indexing time, storage space—and also because requesters' needs differ widely, format transformations are usually performed at the input of the system (indexing of titles alone, abstracting), and/or at the output (retrieval of titles only, reference numbers, abstracts, etc.). The series of options that must present themselves to any designer of retrieval systems are:

TABLE 21.3

Input	*Storage*	*Retrieval*	*Output*
Collected data ——— Natural language requests	Format Processing and Indexing	Compilation of relevant documents and Format Processing	Bibliographies, references to relevant documents, lists of titles, etc.

The procedures are inherent in any retrieval system; but, as will be shown in the case of SYNTOL and the General Inquirer, different assumptions have led to a different "timing" —i.e. performance at different stages in the procedural sequence—thus modifying the economy of the system.

The preceding considerations were intended to provide a simple frame of reference for future description and comparison. Among many other factors that should be included to facilitate an assessment, two categories can be distinguished.

Ideally, retrieval systems should be judged as to their *operational* efficiency: quality of retrieval should be related to costs and time expenditure. Such a goal cannot be attained if no controlled experiment, based upon comparable sets of data and requests, has been designed. Without such a test, description and assessment must rely upon the theoretical, or mostly commonsense, justifications underlying the choice of particular solutions in each system. This precludes any consideration of the operational capacities of either SYNTOL or the General Inquirer, i.e. of the respective efficiency of machine programs, the value of technological solutions, and their relative costs. Since the systems include necessarily linguistic "equipment" to deal with the recognized problem of content processing, however, a reasoned evaluation of their *linguistic adequacy* is possible. The main question then is whether or not the linguistic assumptions are adequate for the services to be performed.

SYNTOL

Research directed by J.-C. Gardin on the development of a general procedure for information storage and retrieval was started in 1960 under a two year contract from EURATOM and subsequently supported jointly by the Centre National de la Recherche Scientifique and the Ecole Pratique des Hautes Etudes (VIe Section). In an experiment completed in 1963, designed to test the linguistic assumptions of the system without regard to costs of processing or program efficiency, about 3,000 documents in the fields of psycho-physiology, psychology, and cultural anthropology were processed.

Differently condensed versions of articles or books were stored and retrieved with the help of an IBM 7090 computer.[3]

A second experiment has since been started to deal with so-called "true" conditions of information processing. About 5,000 abstracts provided by the Centre d'Analyse Documentaire pour l'Afrique Noire (Paris), which deals with cultural anthropology in Africa south of the Sahara, will be stored and retrieved mechanically according to requesters' specifications, whether bearing on content or format. The operational machine program and an evaluation of costs will be completed in 1965.

The project was defined as a *general procedure* of information storage and retrieval. Such a concept of "generality"[4] applies in particular to: (1) the nature of the fields or disciplines, since there should be no inherent restriction in the SYNTOL rules or program for their application to other disciplines than the behavioral sciences;[5] (2) the output of the system, since it was felt that specialists' needs in documentation differ widely, and the retrieval system was designed to provide all the "products" traditional documenta-

3. Details of the experiment may be found in R.-C. Cros, J.-C. Gardin, and F. Lévy, *L'automatisation des Recherches Documentaires* (Paris, Gauthier Villars, 1964), Chap. 5. For a more complete discussion of SYNTOL, cf. the mimeographed reports to Euratom (1962) under the general title, *Le SYNTOL (Syntagmatic Organization Language):* 1. J.-C. Gardin, *Aspects Théoriques*, a set of logico-linguistic rules for the expression and automatic manipulation of scientific information; 2. R.-C. Cros, *Problèmes de Programmation*, an experimental program for automatic retrieval with the IBM 7090; 3. *Exemples de Lexiques*, list of descriptors used for an experiment of the system on the IBM 7090: (A) F. Lévy, "Introduction et Champ Commun"; (B) N. Gardin and R. Zygouris, "Physiologie"; (C) F. Lévy, "Psychologie"; and (D) F. Izard, F. Lévy et al., "Sociologie, Ethnologie" (issued independently from the Euratom series in 1964); 4. M. Coyaud, *Analyse Automatique*, automatic indexing of scientific abstracts in physiology, from French into SYNTOL. Mimeographed English translations of volumes 1 and 2 were prepared and distributed by the National Science Foundation in 1963. A printed version of volumes 1 through 4 (except 3-D) will appear under the following title: *Le SYNTOL, Etude d'un Système Général de Documentation Automatique* (Brussels, Presses Académiques Européennes, forthcoming). J.-C. Gardin, SYNTOL (Rutgers Seminars on Systems for the Intellectual Organization of Information; New Brunswick, N.J., Rutgers University Press, 1965).

4. Gardin, "An Outline of SYNTOL."

5. See below, p. 472, for limitations bearing on input information.

tion affords and to allow any format or content transformation deemed useful; and (3) the mechanical aid, since some applications may require the use of computers and there should be no further restriction as to the types of machine other than a "local" adaptation (interpretation programs).

Storage and Retrieval Operations Performed by SYNTOL

Ideally a retrieval system should perform mechanically all the operations listed in Table 21.3. However, for practical reasons, objectives were limited at the start, and the relation between mechanical or nonmechanical procedures included in the system is as follows:

TABLE 21.4

Input	*Nonmechanized Procedures*		*Mechanized Procedures*	
Data	**Indexing**	**Key-punching**	**Storage**	
→	→		→	
Requests	**Indexing**	**Key-punching**	**Retrieval**	**Output Format Processing**

Indexing. While a set of rules for indexing documents has been included in SYNTOL (cf. p. 476), it was not conceived as machine indexing but is carried on exclusively with the help of human analysts. This group of specialists provides the "content recognition criteria," according to different rules.[6] It follows that a group of analysts is a prerequisite of the system. And, of course, in the absence of automatic reading machines, a keypunch operator is necessary.

Storage and retrieval. Both processes have often been described in a simplified form. And of course they are central to any mechanical system. However, retrieval, if it is to show any efficiency, involves sets of logico-linguistic operations which, even if "they can be reduced to elementary boolean algebra," [7] necessitate appropriate machine formulations.[8]

6. Justifications of a "balance" between indexing applied to documents and/or requests appear below, pp. 486–88.
7. Gardin, "An Outline of SYNTOL," p. 10.
8. For further elaboration of this point, see below, pp. 473–75.

Format processing. Current criticisms leveled at retrieval systems using computers are: (a) the restrictions imposed on output format, and (b) the poor presentation of the machine-produced bibliographical tools—use of one type only, imperfect or nonexistent typesetting, etc. The SYNTOL programs carry instructions so that average quality output is attained, with flexible format specifications. Such traditional products as bibliographies, indexes, card files, and title lists can be obtained automatically from one stored corpus of data.

Basic Linguistic Equipment

To perform all the tasks mentioned above, SYNTOL provides a set of rules applicable to the content of documents so that a correct "representation" is stored. Other linguistic characteristics of the program allow control over the retrieval process.

Indexing. As previously defined, indexing is only a device —the nature of which has not been made precise—to enable content processing of data. It is assumed here that original data are not amenable, without transformations, to efficient retrieval.[9]

Among devices commonly used for indexing is the assignment of symbols to units of content considered meaningful —words, sentences, distinctive traits of objects, etc.—and variously called descriptors, index terms, tags. SYNTOL is essentially, in this respect, *a set of rules for the manipulation and machine processing of such descriptors.* SYNTOL input then consists of documents the content of which (i.e. the subject matter) is symbolized by a set of index terms. Descriptors can be borrowed from any predetermined dictionary or classification, whatever their structure.[10] Two questions arise at this point: Is representation of a document by a set of *isolated* descriptors, index terms that are not explicitly related to express the content of a document, precise enough to allow efficient retrieval? Does the corpus, through

9. For further discussions of this point, see below and pp. 484–88.
10. Structural constraints exist, however; see below, p. 474.

sheer number of items, linguistic complexity of data, etc., necessitate the insertion of artificial syntactic devices to reduce the number of ambiguous representations?

If the first solution is found to be satisfactory, no constraint is imposed by SYNTOL at the indexing stage. If not, SYNTOL provides rules for "syntactic" formulations, flexible enough to adapt the representation to the desired level of linguistic complexity. Among the great variety of solutions proposed for syntactical relations—"roles," "links," etc.—flexibility implies that representations be made up of distinct units, or components, on both the operational and meaningful levels.

To the set of descriptors, easily manageable, would be added expressions manifesting the syntactic relations that obtain *between* descriptors, in an unambiguous way and with a descriptor-like format. If index terms (a) and (b) represent some of the content of a document, unitary expression (a R b) will manifest relation R between (a) and (b). It was found, most generally,[11] that the relational network of a representation could be economically and unambiguously transcribed by reducing the network into a binary format, taking the form of dyadic relations. A representation consists of index terms and expressions, called *syntagmas,*[12] which are pairs of descriptors linked by a syntactical relation. The effect is a representation with freely separable and comparable elements, so a unique program could process indexed documents of any representational complexity. System users, according to their field of application and needs, are free to index documents without syntax.

But the resulting data should remain comparable to other representations in the same domain that include syntactic notations. For the sake of uniformity in the system, one should be sure that the type of information carried by index terms in the first application is not supported by syntagmas

11. For justifications, see Cros et al.

12. As an analogy to F. de Saussure's definition in *Cours de Linguistique Générale* (5th ed. Paris, Payot, 1960), pp. 170–75. It is "*in praesentia* relation drawn from an effective combination of words in a given utterance." This feature helped give SYNTOL its name of Syntagmatic Organization Language.

in the second. To ensure this two rather different aspects of content may be distinguished: one, of a *logical* nature, concerns the existence of a relation which may or may not be classified in terms of broad categories (causal, spatial, comparative, etc.); and the other, a *semantic* interpretation of the first, specifies the very precise nature of that relationship (e.g. "inhibiting," "between," "identical to").[13] Admittedly relative to a domain, this distinction has consequences for the nature of syntactic relations and the type of lexical organization (dictionary or classification) admitted by the system.

Retrieval. Apart from the possible usefulness of systematic subject indexes or classifications to clarify definitions of their entries, the main value rests with retrieval operations. The object is "to create a network of index terms which brings together, by a series of consecutive entries or cross-references, those terms which are used together or in a formal relationship in the literature, so that when one term is chosen as the key with which the searcher enters the index, all other relevant terms will be recalled automatically."[14]

There is no need to enlarge upon this function. The advantages of structured lists of index terms, with other than simple alphabetical arrangement, are obvious. Two problems remain, however, the first lexicographic and the second related to retrieval operations:

1. What is the most convenient index term organization? Following the principle of "generality" one is not concerned here with local semantic interpretation but with the desired structural properties of index term lists. The only means by which requests can proceed in a reasoned way, from one entry to another relevant one, is by explicitly stated relationships in the vocabulary. For automatic processing, such lexical organizations[15] have to be stored in the machine. The more numerous the connections between index terms, and the better specified the relationships, the better are the

13. Gardin, p. 31.
14. D. J. Foskett, *Classification and Indexing in the Social Sciences* (London, Butterworth, 1963), p. 39.
15. Such is the meaning of the O in SYNTOL: Syntagmatic *Organization* Language.

chances of efficient retrieval. Such structured dictionaries, examples of which have been constructed,[16] must only satisfy the above mentioned (p. 472) constraint: that logical connectives [17] be excluded from the lexical or index term entries. Up to now SYNTOL vocabularies have included single hierarchical structures, but the 1965 retrieval experiment will deal with locally multiple hierarchies.

2. The second retrieval problem is how to make the best use of both the characteristics of representations and those, related to the first through the use of index terms, of the stored lexical organization. Starting from a given request in natural language the first step is to translate it into processable idiom, i.e. index terms and syntagmas.

Requests, however, imply some ignorance. What is actually searched is a not too well defined area of knowledge; if one formulation fails to provide references, another might succeed. Any request therefore must include a list of interchangeable index terms and syntagmas which are used to express correctly its content, and if necessary to expand its meaning so that all "relevant" data are retrieved. To build up such lists SYNTOL provides a set of automatic transformations, conventionally called *modulations,* through which requests can be properly and easily formulated: as symbolic program instructions they build up automatically lists of interchangeable terms. Modulations either make use of the lexical organization (allowing, for instance, automatic matching of one index term with all that are included in the same class), or alternatively they apply to syntagmas and permit the substitution of one syntactic relation by another; others again suppress index terms and syntagmas. All function automatically under freely defined conditions.[18] In short, as will be shown on p. 488, modulations provide the elements of a *search strategy,* which can be understood as a method by which decisions are taken to allow the most effi-

16. See note 3 above.

17. A tentative definition would be: those elements of meaning which could, without de facto limitations due to the meaning of connected terms, link *all* index terms in the vocabulary.

18. The most evident conditional specification is numerical: to set down a desired number of answers to a request and automatically enlarge or expand the request until that number is met.

cient retrieval when faced with a given corpus of data and a given request.

Finally SYNTOL makes possible a distinction between what can be called two levels of "document discourse." When propositions are represented by chains or networks of syntagmatically connected index terms, some of these terms are found to carry a greater "information load" when they express the central theme of the study. It is a common device[19] to weigh the focal point of the representation differently, as is done in SYNTOL. But it was found that such a procedure, already indicative of the unequal importance of index terms in a document, was not distinctive enough as regards another useful level of discourse.

It appeared empirically that certain categories of index terms were to be frequently linked, through syntactic relations, *to all* other descriptors in the representation. In Gardin's terms, "those focal points show that they usually correspond to standard 'parameters' in the field to which documents belong—e.g. the object or being under study . . . , a quality, aspect, property of that object . . . or the observational or experimental environment."[20] In SYNTOL such categories, unwieldy because of the sheer number of syntagmas they impose on the representation, are displaced from the representational format and located in a separate register. There one would find, for instance, in the social sciences, the space and time coordinates, nature of groups—professions or races—that have been studied, etc. Relevant categories of information may be discovered empirically. Exploitation of such index terms in the register conventionally called Thematics is economically performed in SYNTOL through a facet-like organization, where each descriptor is implicitly carrying its own syntactic function.

Format Processing

Is indexed representation a conceptual notation fully equivalent to the entire content of a document, or does it imply a condensation of the original data? To the question of

19. As in the former ASTIA "thesaurus," for instance.
20. Gardin, p. 38.

SYNTOL processing capacities with respect to full text vs. abstracts should be added that of the output possibilities of the system.

As will be mentioned in the next section, indexing is by nature a normalization procedure. It follows that different formulations are reduced, to a varying degree, to less diversified expressions and that, although experiments have only been conducted upon abstracts, no limitation is imposed on the form of input. The stored data necessarily comprise a condensed version of documents.

Regarding output, four categories of "products" have been envisaged, all edited automatically (including typesetting and composition): title lists, abstract journals, catalogue cards, and bibliographical journals, in which references are grouped into any number of predetermined subject headings according to a standard classification. All these products are derived from a unique punch-tape, and distinct programs produce whatever formats are desired. As processing involves a connection between a computer and a typewriter which is used both for input and for output, types are as diversified as those present on sophisticated typewriter keyboards.

Summary

SYNTOL comprises a set of logico-linguistic rules for the expression of document and request content on one hand, and sets of programs for computer processing of data on the other.

a. Logico-linguistic rules:

1. A set of rules provides a framework for unambiguous concept notation of documents (document indexing).

2. Directives help establish organized index term lists (variously called dictionaries, classifications, or lexicons) which, properly stored, will be used for retrieval.

3. The distinction between such levels of linguistic complexity as are required by the nature of data and/or the

desired bibliographical products is the subject of particular rules and is formalized.

b. SYNTOL programs:

1. A program retrieves references according to the content of documents.

2. Program-controlled symbolic expressions help in selecting the most efficient level of concept notation—whether no syntax, a simplified, or a complex one is needed.

3. Program-controlled symbolic expressions help formulate searches so as to maximize efficient retrieval.

4. Distinct programs provide, from a unique file of stored data, diversified formats and a good quality presentation of bibliographical products.

THE GENERAL INQUIRER

The General Inquirer was developed in 1961 by Philip J. Stone and Robert F. Bales to perform content analysis of verbal data in the behavioral sciences.[21] As a language processing system it benefited from the linguistic studies carried on in particular by Yngve of the Massachusetts Institute of Technology. The General Inquirer was expanded in 1963 with the purpose of serving as a retrieval system for data

21. Philip J. Stone, Robert F. Bales, J. Zvi Namenwirth, and Daniel M. Ogilvie, "The General Inquirer: A Computer System for Content Analysis and Retrieval Based on the Sentence as a Unit of Information," *Behavioral Science*, 7 (1962), 484–98. Cf. also the chapter by Erwin K. Scheuch and Philip J. Stone on "Retrieval Systems for Data Archives" in this volume; Erwin K. Scheuch and Philip J. Stone, "The General Inquirer Approach to an International Retrieval System for Survey Archives," *American Behavioral Scientist*, 7 (June 1964), 23–28; W. R. McPherson, D. C. Dunphy, Robert F. Bales, Philip J. Stone, and Daniel M. Ogilvie, "A Revised Psychological and Sociological Dictionary for the General Inquirer: Preface to the Third General Inquirer Dictionary" (Harvard University, Laboratory of Social Relations, mimeo., December 1962); Philip J. Stone and Marshall S. Smith, "A Computer System for Finding Recurrent Patterns Within a List of Events," mimeo.; Philip J. Stone and Earl B. Hunt, "The General Inquirer Extended: Automatic Theme Analysis Using Tree Building," *IFIP Proceedings* (Munich, 1962); Daniel M. Ogilvie, D. C. Dunphy, C. Smith, Philip J. Stone et al., "Some Characteristics of Genuine vs. Simulated Suicide Notes as Analyzed by a Computer System Called the General Inquirer" (Harvard University, Laboratory of Social Relations, mimeo., 1962); and Margaret A. Boden, "On Discrimination Trees: Examples Using Three Speeches from the 1962 Cuban Crisis" (Harvard University, Laboratory of Social Relations, mimeo., 1964).

archives. It would be employed to locate relevant studies by searching for all survey questions either relevant to a specific concept or containing a specific word.[22] As the present paper is not especially concerned with problems of content analysis per se,[23] only applications and projects in the field of information storage and retrieval will be mentioned.

In the beginning of 1963 a retrieval experiment was conducted using survey research material (questionnaires) and requests provided by the Survey Research Center of the University of Michigan. Since then detailed proposals have been set forth [24] for a research program leading to an operational definition of the system as a storage and retrieval tool, and an evaluation of costs and organizational problems posed by an actual exploitation. Steps suggested to attain these goals include the tentative selection of a field of inquiry (e.g. elite studies) and the establishment of appropriate lexical tools, including a variety of dictionaries for different fields. Simultaneously an international dictionary will be built up, the first effort being a German version of the existing Harvard Dictionary.

Storage and Retrieval Operations Performed by the General Inquirer

The sharp distinction between mechanized vs. nonmechanized operations applies with some difficulty to the General Inquirer procedure. However, the authors' terminology has been kept here with respect to one operation, called "editing," of which more will be said later.

The balance between automatic and manual procedures can be illustrated as follows:

TABLE 21.5

Input	*Mechanized Procedures*		*Nonmechanized Procedures*	
Data (questionnaires) Requests	Indexing	Storage and Retrieval	"Editing"	Input format Processing

22. Scheuch and Stone, "Retrieval Systems for Data Archives."
23. See note 21 for references to applications as content analysis.
24. Scheuch and Stone, "Retrieval Systems for Data Archives."

Mechanized procedures. A notable feature is simultaneous indexing and retrieval in one machine pass.

1. Indexing: In the field of "content processing" different criteria can be considered, depending upon the meaning of "relevance." A request implying solely that the physical characteristics of data—such as number of signs, co-occurrence of specified sequences of signs, etc.—be recognized will make determination of "recognition criteria"[25] a relatively easy task. In the search for such "objective" characteristics in a given corpus and the recognition of formally unknown "units of information," different types of "meaningful" properties can be observed. That fact is exemplified by the multiple "indexing levels" of the General Inquirer.

a. "Occurrence-recognition": Words or groups of words can be recognized and counted; "all sentences containing a particular text word . . . can be retrieved." The General Inquirer thus embodies a concordance-like program, which deals in a standard way with natural language sets of signs, and in which the simplest kind of "indexing"—counting—is performed.

b. Syntactical recognition: With the help of an appropriate dictionary, words, groups of words, or idioms can be recognized and categorized in terms of "grammatical" categories. Rules can be applied so that different sign sequences—e.g. words showing different endings—may be assimilated to one sequence only; i.e. one "root" becomes a substitute to all such "roots" differently suffixed. The program automatically chops off "s," "e," "ed," and similar endings that are not needed to retain a "meaningful, basic sequence of letters." This type of indexing is a transformation of signs physically present in the data; no complete replacement of one word by another is possible. The consequences of such a limitation will be mentioned below (p. 492). To date around 10,000 natural language words are recognized. Excluding proper names, the present Harvard Dictionary is repeatedly able to find between 92 and 98 per cent of the text words.[26]

25. See above, pp. 466–67.
26. Scheuch and Stone, "The General Inquirer Approach," p. 24.

c. "First and second order tagging": As a procedure distinct from the one just mentioned, "tagging" is an automatic assignment of index terms to words or groups of words. For series of different expressions are substituted symbolic expressions, conventionally called *tags*. Insofar as they are meant to convey a meaning, i.e. as they implicitly or explicitly are symbols for *definitions,* tags are formally equivalent to descriptors. Definitions, and tags or descriptors, may apply to a whole area of discourse or to the conceptual schema of specific theories. In the first case, tags are labeled "first-order" and are supposed to "represent an estimate of the usual and explicit meaning of the word in standard usage." In the second case, "second-order tags" "represent an estimate of the significant connotative and implicit meanings which the word will evoke in certain theoretical contexts."[27] The distinction between two types of tags, it must be added, does not seem to be a permanent feature of the system.

To these three, or four, indexing levels the retrieval experiment has imposed another, called "editing," mentioned below.

2. Storage and retrieval: Output of the automatic retrieval procedure in questionnaires is the question which contains the expressions of the requests or their indexed substitutes. However, additional routines must be specified for the retrieval of contextual information along with questions. By this contextual information Scheuch and Stone mean the properties of the studies reported in the computer printout, together with the question identified as relevant.

Nonmechanized procedures. These include editing, format-processing, and indexing.

1. "Editing": This term covers, in the General Inquirer, a series of manual procedures which results in an "adaptation" of data prior to automatic storage and processing. The nature of such an "adaptation" is worth considering in some detail.[28] Three types of operations are included in the

27. Scheuch and Stone, "Retrieval Systems for Data Archives," p. 450.
28. A kind of protocol is given in the appendix to ibid.

editing procedures, of which we shall describe only those related to content processing (as regards "format interpretation," see below). All are expressed by machine recognizable symbolic instructions.

a. "Modal" interpretations: A set of rules calls for interpretation of the form of discourse of questions as found in questionnaires, without reference to the actual topics mentioned. Seven such discourse categorizations can be enumerated for manual coding:

–Informative or factual question, asking for empirical information. The question is preceded by the word "Info-."

–Declarative for "questions preceded with a statement of information." Such information, whether preceding or actually imbedded within it, is given the status of a separate statement. The separate statement is preceded by the word "prologue." The actual question is marked "item."

–Comparative, if a question refers to a comparison or asks for a choice. Alternatives are then separated by a diagonal.

–Attributive, "if the respondent is asked to state the viewpoint of another person." Such words are preceded by a star.

–Hypothetical, for questions involving a supposition or hypothesis which are then marked with the word "suppose."

–Causative, "if the respondent is asked in a question follow-up an explanation or reasons . . ." The term "reasons" is then inserted at the end of the statement.

–Illustrative, if the respondent is asked to identify a referent that represents this viewpoint. This relationship is noted "represent-respondent."

b. Content interpretation: apart from categorizing the style or form of discourse in questions, editing requires an interpretation and coding of certain elements of information, such as:

–Time references are made explicit by the insertion of

index terms "in future," "in past," "ago," "present time."
–Combinations of words—idioms—are to be reduced to a single form by hyphenating (examples are "interest-rate," "white-paper," etc.). But such single equivalence could be machine programmed.
–Ambiguities are to be reduced, and limited to single words. Thus, depending upon the context, for the word "country" will be substituted the word "nation" or "countryside," for "charge" the word "fee" or "accusation."
–Specialized references such as proper names are to be translated into more general terms.

2. Format processing: Selection of the most efficient discourse unit to be stored and processed remains a manual task. As will be observed later (pp. 485 ff.), it is conceivable that groups of questions or, conversely, isolated sentences can be stored and retrieved. The General Inquirer allows presently for coding and addressing questionnaires and questions in questionnaires so that both can be referred to at retrieval time.

3. Indexing of requests: Adequate transformation of natural language requests into index terms for future matching with stored data is left to the users themselves. Either ready-made dictionaries—lists of index terms—are available and the users select whatever assignments they feel to be "productive," or they build up their own dictionaries to fit in with their particular theoretical frameworks.

Basic Linguistic Equipment of the General Inquirer

A distinction should be made here, as in the case of SYNTOL, between formal linguistic tools of the system and particular semantic content. Formal properties of a classification, whether it shows a consistent structure or whether it is a mere collection of definitions, must not be confused with the domain it covers and the quality or pertinence of its entries for a given application. Linguistic equipment will thus be described, regardless of the field concerned, only in a formal sense.

Natural language dictionary. Any procedure of automatic indexing must be adapted to actual data, i.e. natural language texts. Those sequences of signs that are to be transformed must be recognized, after being compiled and stored in the computer. The unit or sequence recognized by the General Inquirer dictionary is the word, or eventually sets of words, compatible with the type of syntactic recognition procedure mentioned above (p. 479). It thus excludes recognition procedures based upon the sentence as a unit, or the still larger units of discourse analysis, when they implicitly convey meanings which could be equivalent to words (a standard example is the replacement of a word by its definition). Possible consequences of this limitation will be mentioned below (pp. 492 ff.).

Lists of descriptors. When recognized, words can be assigned index terms with the help of a stored list of equivalences. Descriptors, called tags in the General Inquirer terminology, belong to two groups allowing two "indexing levels" as mentioned previously. First-order tags representing the authors' "estimate of the usual and explicit meaning of the word in standard usage" are called independent variables, i.e. "only one may be used in categorizing a particular dictionary entry."[29] Along with this assumed fixity of standard usage definitions, dependent variables or second-order tags may be assigned to words. These words are selected for their affinity to particular theories in the field and multiple assignment is possible. No information is stored about possible implicit relations that descriptors can manifest: hence, no use can be made, by the computer, of an assumed order imposed upon descriptors.

Such ordering of index terms as seems useful is information external to the system: groups of descriptors, entitled, for instance, Status-connotations[30] or Psychological Themes, are provided to the requester to help manual indexing of requests.

"Editing rules." Although not formalized, the "editing

29. McPherson et al., "A Revised Psychological and Sociological Dictionary for the General Inquirer."

30. Ibid.

rules" are not the least important aspects of the General Inquirer's linguistic apparel. Their description (pp. 480 ff.) has shown how they bear either upon the form of expression in questions or upon content. A machine interpretable "code" evolved to make retrieval of units of information possible can be assimilated to another list of descriptors. Editing rules are then nothing but definitions. Some of the reasons why they have not been included in the automatic indexing procedure will be given below (p. 494).

Summary

The General Inquirer attempts to adapt a computer-oriented language, designed for content analysis, to the tasks of storage and retrieval. Although mechanical procedures are stressed, the system is nonetheless intended to be flexible enough for application to any particular field; provision is made for the insertion of any specific dictionary specialists want to build up. With respect to storage and retrieval requirements, the system can be considered as semiautomatic mechanization stopping short of a certain level of linguistic "sophistication":

1. *Automatic indexing* means either a process of quantifying data elements, or a set of strict equivalences between words and notions. It requires the creation of specialized dictionaries for every language. Use is made of lists of descriptors upon which no order is imposed. The consequences are twofold, upon format processing and request formulation.

2. Format processing: Indexing performed on natural language data *implies that full texts be the input of the system.*

3. No use can be made of the structural properties of descriptor lists *at the retrieval stage;* therefore no formal expressions other than simple encoding words can help formulate requests.

SOME PROBLEMS OF QUESTIONNAIRE PROCESSING

In the preceding section no special attention was given to specific data such as questionnaires in the field of social sciences; SYNTOL, in particular, was not primarily designed to process them. Before attempting to assess possible qualities or shortcomings of both retrieval systems, the characteristics of data that are liable to affect the "economy" of SYNTOL or the General Inquirer should be mentioned.

Characteristics of Data

Two categories of questionnaires and, within questionnaires, two types of questions may be distinguished. The first observation relates to the field of inquiry: Do questionnaires refer to census or statistical data for economics, or are they part of sociology as such? In the first instance, they probably embody what can be called *closed categories.*

Closed categories and facets: In questionnaires made of closed categories, the coupled question/answer allows only one reasonable interpretation. To the questions, for instance, "What is the age of respondent?" and "How many dollars does the respondent have in his wallet?" the same answer—34—is in no way ambiguous. Such a clear cut semantic partition is not evident if the questions "Whom do you fear most?" and "Whom do you envy most?" are answered by "bankers."

Closed categories, in questionnaires, imply a relatively coherent field of inquiry in which the *logic* of the domain—causal relationships, time and space "parameters," etc.—provides a framework for the *semantic grouping* of terms in the domain. This property is evident in very specific fields which are especially amenable to "faceted classifications or languages," where "index terms are primarily arranged on the basis of their function with respect to a common field of reference."[31] Similarly, it shows in the parts of diversified fields—in the behavioral or social sciences—that deal with "facts." And "there are obviously many statements in social science that are universally believed to be true, just as there are in science: historical and statistical statements, for example."[32]

But, equally clearly, most statements in social science may

31. Gardin, p. 41.
32. Foskett, p. 25.

involve multiple interpretations. This applies to the content of questionnaires, whether of questions or of answers, as well. It nonetheless remains true that parts of social science manifest sufficiently stable meanings to allow adoption of a proved linguistic tool for storage and retrieval, i.e. faceted classifications.

"Open questionnaires": What is the value of answers to multiple choice questions? Assuming that a retrieval system must provide a maximum of information to the requesters, it is worth considering what can be the relative informative content of elements in the questionnaire. In other words, what can be the importance, with respect to storage and retrieval, of respondents' answers? Yes or no answers can be excluded; their inclusion in the system would involve research itself and not information *about* research. At the other extreme, free statements answering multiple choice or open-ended questions may be of interest to the retrieval system user. Actually the "meanings" of a question, the motivation behind it, are not always readily apparent, either because the social scientist wants to relate explicit statments to theoretical assumptions formulated differently, or because the formulation of questions is adapted to presumed psychological or cultural traits in the respondents. It follows that, for retrieval system users working with different theoretical assumptions, the desired information may reside *in sets of answers and not in questions.* This observation is only meant to stress the fact that retrieval systems should be flexible as to the unit of information they can process: descriptors, propositions, questionnaires, or sets of questionnaires.

"Information Languages": Indexing and Retrieval

Thus social science data require a very close inspection of their content to provide criteria for efficient retrieval. Here a compromise must be found between the necessary *normalization* of natural language statements, and *fidelity* in their transcription.[33] Quite evidently, once some sort of transformation (such as a normalization of diverse formulations to

33. That normalization is a necessary step in any retrieval system is usually recognized. When and how remain under discussion.

fit with assumed content analogies) is imposed upon data, the level of fidelity comes to rest upon the procedures used for that transformation.

Alternative solutions can be considered. Normalization (which, in one way or another, will consist in symbolizing content-elements or notions present in statements) is performed by the system once for all, and indexed representations of documents are supposed to be close enough to the original texts to provide all the necessary ulterior interpretations. Or, conversely, data are to be indexed differently every time new criteria are needed for their retrieval. The adoption of one or the other solution has consequences for the nature of the "indexing tools" of the systems—i.e. the classifications, index terms lists, etc.—and their operational characteristics.

In the first instance a *unique* classification or list of index terms is used for indexing. As *fidelity* is stressed it will tend to include numerous content symbols (descriptors, terms, etc.). Consequently, a relatively great number of terms will be needed to index every document—excluding, however, the simple paraphrase which would defeat the purpose of indexing. Furthermore, to allow for the possibility of multiple interpretations, terms should be defined in the most stable and commonly recognized manner; only relatively invariant and "essential" elements of definitions should be included in the list. The term "information language" [34] is often used to express this kind of collection of symbols which attempts to describe as accurately as possible the content of documents, up to the inclusion of logical relationships that obtain in texts.

The second solution leads to the establishment of *multiple,* and separate, lists of index terms, supposedly adapted to categories of requests. (It is assumed that theories and viewpoints provide, in a given field, such a grouping of related requests.) [35] It follows that the number of terms needed to

34. "The word language is here taken in a rather inappropriate sense." Gardin, p. 4.

35. Upon "the assumption that there may exist for each language a system of content. . ." (Garvin, p. 124). Based upon "intuitive observation," as Garvin says, it will be used for linguistic retrieval devices; see below.

represent a document will be relatively smaller than the number needed for the first solution, and that definitions will tend to be restrictively related to those conceptual frameworks in the field that are explicit in every classification or list.

According to the solution chosen, retrieval procedures must differ somewhat. In the first case indexing will transcribe only the explicit level of document content. As requests relate notions in a systematic way, involving so-called latent meanings, some sort of order—or equivalences—must be imposed at the retrieval stage to "collocate" all relevant data. One such order, evidently insufficient to account for all types of requests, may characterize the information language, and thus become a classification. Others have to be simulated, and linguistic devices (such as SYNTOL modulations) may be inserted in request formulations to transcribe the desired relationships between descriptors. In this sense a search strategy can be defined as those rules applied to the formulation of requests which make retrieval efficient. If ad hoc indexing is performed when "latent meanings" are expressed—the second solution—retrieval will become a fixed procedure: a good match will occur when requests coincide with a priori viewpoints or theories.

To sum up, several options are theoretically possible for information processing of social science data. It remains to be seen whether or not practical limitations affect their applicability. This will be exemplified with the General Inquirer.

TENTATIVE ASSESSMENT

After a brief delineation of the characteristics of SYNTOL and the General Inquirer regarding storage and retrieval in general, we shall attempt to describe their main differences. Different linguistic and operational assumptions underlie each procedure, and each produces its particular consequences.

Linguistic Assumptions

The nature of respective "information languages." The fact that retrieval supposes some sort of transformation of natural language texts into sets of notions or "concepts" is recognized by both systems: to translate a natural language into a concept language is precisely the main task in processing survey material for data archives.[36] It leads to the establishment of descriptor schemes or lists (the "lexicons" in SYNTOL and the "tag lists" of the General Inquirer) called information languages and defined as "any set of terms, and such artificial syntactic devices as are used to represent the content of documents, designed to help store and retrieve information."[37] In SYNTOL, however, justifications are emphasized for the use of such "languages":[38] they not only help standardize the formulations of scientific texts but they are needed to *condense* them. This goal is not explicitly stated in the General Inquirer where at its most simplified level, the least "meaningful," the indexed representation implies a minimum amount of condensation.

The structural properties of both information languages differ widely. SYNTOL lexicons are meant to be adaptable, through near automatic transformations, to any level of linguistic complexity deemed useful for retrieval. Formal characteristics of artificial syntactic devices are enumerated, to be inserted at will in the lexicons; machine programmed instructions make processing a simple task. Furthermore, other instructions allow exploitation of the structural properties, such as hierarchies or contiguity grouping of terms, most often apparent in classifications. On the other hand, tag lists of the General Inquirer are unordered groups of terms. Separate sets of tags based on semantic differentiations make for a rough categorization of terms, but no machine exploitation of these properties is mentioned.

36. Scheuch and Stone, "Retrieval Systems for Data Archives," p. 448.

37. Cros et al., p. 26.

38. Even their necessity has been disputed by some authors; see, for instance, Don R. Swanson, "Searching Natural Language Text by Computers," *Science, 132* (October 21, 1960), 1099–1104.

The "literary warrant." The authors of SYNTOL, which is concerned solely with information storage and retrieval, have applied literally the "literary warrant" principle of D. J. Foskett.[39] The effect has been noticeable upon the lexicons established as examples, and their ensuing exploitation. For the "literary warrant" principle leads to a multiplication of index entries—terms or descriptions—until such arrangements of terms will fit any particular viewpoint or theory. The SYNTOL program accounts for the insertion and processing of up to 5,000 descriptors per lexicon in a given field. Assuming that indexing is a translation into a "concept" language, all notions that are considered useful for any request must be used to represent the content of documents. Only then will one arrangement (the actually organized lexicon) or multiple arrangements (such ordering as imposed by request formulation) of terms provide the "fit" to particular viewpoints.

The General Inquirer, by way of contrast, retains some of the characteristic properties of the content analysis system from which it evolved. Berelson's definition of content analysis as a "research technique for the objective, systematic, and quantitative description of the manifest content of communication" [40] does not point to any particular goal. Actually, such descriptive techniques may find their application in two types of domains: content analysis and content processing.

The first is an attempt to relate linguistic to nonlinguistic phenomena systematically. The aim is to correlate "objective" [41] characteristics in verbal statements to categories of psychological or sociological phenomena. This is exemplified by the numerous studies conducted with the help of the General Inquirer. In this sense, content analysis is a technique

39. Foskett, p. 30.

40. Bernard Berelson, *Content Analysis in Communication Research* (Glencoe, Free Press, 1952), p. 18.

41. "Objectivity" is one of the reasons why Berelson stresses the "manifest" aspect of content and emphasizes quantification: manifest because texts are to be taken at their "face value" and must be interpreted in terms of a particular viewpoint; quantification because it is seemingly a criterion of objectivity. For an example of nonquantitative, objective content analysis, see C. Piault, "Recherche en Analyse de Contenu," report to the C.N.R.S. (Paris, mimeo., 1962).

to relate two levels of conceptualization: one in the field of linguistics, i.e. forms and properties of statements, and the other being nonlinguistic psychological or sociological variables.

Content processing can be defined as techniques for the objective and systematic comparison of the content of communication. It follows that: (a) there is no necessary insertion of a quantitative criterion, and that indexing can be performed empirically; and (b) elements of communication —documents or corpora of documents—are to be related to each other. Thus the whole process, implying of course some sort of description of content, *remains nevertheless in the linguistic realm.* In this sense, content processing is a limited application of content analysis. And there should be no confusion between procedures used for the first application and those necessary to perform the second.

When linguistic and nonlinguistic variables are to be related, only selected sets of relevant variables are retained: on the one hand, strictly limited corpora of texts; on the other, only those categories which are relevant for a psychological or sociological viewpoint. Such a procedure is justified by the desire for flexibility in the General Inquirer; to allow insertion of any ad hoc list of tags or descriptors, and the attempt to "index" documents mechanically on various levels of complexity. But the counterpart is an implicit rejection of the "literary warrant" principle: a comparatively small number of tags or descriptors can be assigned to documents,[42] but they cannot account for the variety of interpretations wanted for retrieval. Furthermore it has led the authors of the General Inquirer and SYNTOL to differ on the subject of indexing.

Indexing, defined as a transformation of actual formulations of documents into conceptual expressions while retaining as much content as is required by retrieval, is a means to achieve content processing. The authors of SYNTOL assume that, at this time, a mechanical translation into a concept-language is not feasible. We are thus left with the problem

42. Up to now a maximum of 164 tags has been considered, to be reduced later to 83; see McPherson et al.

of finding out *how* the General Inquirer performs this task. Are the results compatible with the characteristics defined above? If not, what is actually done?

In machine indexing by the General Inquirer, *words* are recognized with the help of a dictionary. To these words may be assigned, as simple equivalences, tags (descriptors). Since strict occurrences of words may manifest differences in spelling, or syntactical forms, without supporting any different meanings, a program may normalize such words and substitute one form—assign one tag—to syntactically differentiated forms of words. Thus the most sophisticated level of machine indexing attained by the General Inquirer is an equivalence between a notion and syntactically defined groups of words. There are, however, such theoretical and practical limitations to the resolution of semantic ambiguities by syntactic analysis that one of the most sophisticated programs to date results "in the appearance of parallel outputs for only about one third of the material of an average text. While this would still represent considerably more ambiguity than would be present in a good human translation, it would hopefully not be too difficult for the reader to resolve through the use of semantic clues." [43]

Quite evidently, then, what is called a descriptor in SYNTOL cannot be an exact equivalent of the tags in the General Inquirer. We need to return to the distinction between content analysis and content processing. Indexing is conceived of as retaining all possibly useful meanings for retrieval while achieving maximal normalization. In other words, it seeks to present to a user under one rubric the maximum number of interchangeable expressions for a given one—in different contexts, different languages even. To achieve this goal, one must remain as close to the explicit meanings of texts as possible. Assuming that semantics is part of linguistics, the sets of appropriate substitutions are some sort of definition; and that is why a collection of descriptors and the substitutions they imply can be compared

43. W. J. Plath, "Multiple-path Syntactic Analysis of Russian" (Harvard University, Report NSF–12, mimeo., June 1963), pp. 4–146.

to a conventional dictionary, and why its creation is a lexicographic task.

It is this close and nearly circular relationship with natural language which is not manifested by the General Inquirer form of indexing, i.e. tagging. Tags belong in fact to "universes of discourse"—psychology, sociology—far removed from the "universe" of documents taken at their face value. The establishment of systematic linking between linguistic phenomena and nonlinguistic variables is part of the scientific process itself, and as such is hardly applicable to documentation.[44] Indexing, as performed by the General Inquirer, can more easily point to further research than provide a retrieval tool.

Operational Assumptions

With SYNTOL storage and retrieval are considered as specific and distinctive tasks. Formalization of storage and retrieval procedures is both possible and convenient; therefore it is possible to devise

> if not a unique program, at least a unified language, or metalanguage, to which other systems could be formally related. This language could then be used as a basis for developing a more general program in the field of automatic documentation. The word language is here taken with the two following meanings: (a) either a restricted natural language . . . devised for indexing purposes; (b) or a symbolic language, for the manipulation of expressions belonging to the former indexing language.[45]

On this assumption is based the *general applicability* of SYNTOL. Its counterpart is complex definitions of indexing and retrieval.

44. A good example is provided by Charles E. Osgood's semantic differential; discussion of its lexicographic value has led Osgood to conclude that "the semantic differential was not designed as a linguistic tool but as a psychological one." Charles E. Osgood, "Semantic Space Revisited: A Reply to Uriel Weinreich's Review of *The Measurement of Meaning*," *Word, 15* (1959), 192.

45. Gardin, p. 3.

In considering machine indexing and retrieval, and assuming that indexing is the necessary task defined above, it is apparent that to date neither theoretical knowledge nor technological developments allow automatic indexing. All that can be done at the present stage of research *is to index documents manually.* This runs directly counter to the General Inquirer procedure, which asserts a "decision to require only low skills for the storage routine and, consequently, to demand a high level of skills only for the processing of the inquiries to the repository." [46]

But several points should be stressed here. Indexing as a recognition procedure, being a necessary step in storage and retrieval, need not in theory be performed at any specific moment in the process; whether data are normalized at the input stage or request formulations expanded at the inquiry phase makes no difference. But operationally there are clear differences: if indexing is performed at the input stage, it will hold, when properly stored, for all subsequent operations, particularly for requests. Conversely, "recognition criteria" that are to be inserted for every request mean that specialists are needed *every time* data must be retrieved. "Recurrent" indexing of this kind can hardly be as reliable, or objectively defined, as one single and controlled input procedure; furthermore costs increase considerably.[47]

In any case, the need for "specialists" is not doubted. Here, too, SYNTOL and the General Inquirer show implicit differences in their definitions of the personnel required.

As a language processing system and set of rules, SYNTOL requires only that indexers be able to understand the "explicit" meanings of data. Specialization is needed insofar as the terminology of a domain must be mastered without considering local or temporary deviations from current usage definitions, and only then may the "literary warrant" principle be followed. As "translators," personnel must

46. Scheuch and Stone, "Retrieval Systems for Data Archives," p. 454.

47. That indexing should be left entirely to the inquiry phase is not, in practice, strictly applicable; its difficulty was so evident that "editing"—i.e. indexing—had to be introduced in the General Inquirer at the input stage.

be versed in the linguistic aspects of data more than in the details of research actually conducted.

As a system for content analysis, the General Inquirer is meant to be handled directly by researchers. However, apart from the clerical help needed to "edit" texts, users must, on the one hand, be familiar with the coded formulations to express requests and, on the other, acquire some knowledge of the nature of stored data, their volume and characteristics.

If a "correct" formulation of requests is the only means to ensure efficient retrieval, this formulation itself must embody all operational factors—input characteristics, rates of increase of corpus, etc.—which in one way or another will affect retrieval. None of those factors has yet been properly formalized and as an element of search strategy their observation is only empirical. A practical application of the General Inquirer to storage and retrieval should show whether such complex activity can be left to researchers, or whether a body of specialists is needed to interpret requests.

Another operational consequence of the selection of the indexing of requests (expanding their formulation) versus the indexing of input data (normalization) bears upon data format: *full texts* must be stored, if only temporarily, and compared mechanically to indexed formulations of requests. We mean here that stored data will necessarily include non-informative elements, redundancies, and "embellishments" which will or must play no part in the retrieval process.[48] Even granting possible developments in computer technology, the amount of space required in the memory and the resulting time it takes to retrieve selected elements of information are relatively important.[49]

48. Assuming of course that, as mentioned, machine indexing is not feasible today, and that we consider a "pure" system in which "editing" of input data will not be equivalent to indexing.

49. One computer pass is sufficient to tag texts, according to the General Inquirer procedure; entries, or tags, are small in number, however, and their assignment is a simplified process.

CONCLUSIONS

The basic differences in outlook of SYNTOL and the General Inquirer lead to different methods and conceivable developments. Research in the two systems seems to have started at opposite ends of the storage and retrieval process. But if the whole continuum is to be explored, and machine procedures found to realize the expression "automatic documentation," research in both cases should find common ground in this continuum. In other words, where SYNTOL has been concerned with defining a target, i.e. an appropriate quasi language for the expression of content to make retrieval possible, the General Inquirer considered the source, i.e. natural language statements, to define possible machine transformations that could eventually lead to efficient retrieval.

Such strategies point to the respective areas for development:

1. Of the two nonmechanical procedures of SYNTOL—indexing and definition of a search strategy—the first has been the object of recent studies by the Section d'Automatique Documentaire (C.N.R.S.).[50] Let us say only that indexing is there defined explicitly as a translation toward a descriptor system of expressions. The target is sets of quasi propositions in which index terms are linked by SYNTOL artificial syntax to provide nonambiguous, relatively normalized formulations. Faced with such a complex task, research has centered mainly on "feasibility" studies, i.e. to explore the possibilities of this type of translation, building up appropriate "tools" for this purpose: descriptor schemes, specific dictionaries (natural language statements in a given field corresponding to information language output), logical analysis of the corpus of texts, etc.

2. As opposed to this research, in which machine processing of natural language is purposely left in the background,[51] the General Inquirer attempts machine recogni-

50. Coyaud, *Analyse Automatique.*

51. Programs are actually developed to analyze texts to test linguistic hypotheses; natural language processing is admittedly fragmentary.

tion of texts as such. However, the target (elements of content properly symbolized, descriptors, and the types of relations they may obtain in a useful way for retrieval purposes) is better defined in terms of content analysis than with respect to "content processing." It is quite probable that a more sophisticated approach to describing or analyzing statements will be needed, while not discarding information already provided by the General Inquirer dictionaries. It seems that some amount of syntactic recognition of words in statements is an unavoidable step toward more semantic discrimination.

A common feature of SYNTOL and the General Inquirer, apart from concern with the general applicability of both systems, is the fact that both are nearly *operational*. Programs are either written or in the process of being written so that experimental applications should be relatively easy and economical in the near future.[52] As such a project has already been propounded for the General Inquirer,[53] which defines the type of material to be processed, a simultaneous SYNTOL application could be envisaged. Any program of this kind, however, apart from a close study of costs, personnel required, etc., should take into account the fact that other storage and retrieval systems may fill the social scientist's needs just as efficiently.[54]

52. The complete set of SYNTOL programs should be available by mid-1965.

53. Scheuch and Stone, "Retrieval Systems for Data Archives." See above, pp. 451 ff.

54. For instance, systems using faceted classifications may be just as suitable for computer exploitation.

22. Decision Seminars: The Contextual Use of Audiovisual Means in Teaching, Research, and Consultation

HAROLD D. LASSWELL, YALE UNIVERSITY LAW SCHOOL

The present discussion is held in a seminar room whose walls are lined with charts and maps arranged to emphasize three points: explicit considerations of method; the shaping and sharing of values (preferred social outcomes); the phases of the decision process. There is nothing novel about using audiovisual devices in teaching, research, and consultation; or in having a permanent seminar room. The point is to show how a contextual policy solving approach to government, law, and the social process at large can be furthered by the systematic employment of audiovisual means.[1]

The charts about method are reminders of the contextual approach. Whatever problems are under consideration five intellectual tasks are invariably although not always explicitly performed. Goals are clarified; trends are described; conditioning factors are analyzed; future developments are projected; policy alternatives are invented, evaluated, and selected.

To clarify goals is to specify and ground (justify) the

1. For the basic approach, see H. D. Lasswell and A. Kaplan, *Power and Society* (New Haven, Yale University Press, and London, Routledge and Co., 1950), and H. D. Lasswell, *The Future of Political Science* (New York, Atherton Press, 1963). The chart and map room is being developed with colleagues in the Yale Law School and in the Graduate School, especially Myres S. McDougal and Mary Ellen Caldwell. Miss Caldwell has the principal responsibility for technical problems.

events sought. To describe trend is to discover the sequence and distribution of historical and contemporary events which approximate the goals. To analyze conditioning factors is to identify the factor combinations which have determined the magnitude of trends. To project future developments is to assess the probable course of events in the light of available knowledge of trends and conditions. To invent, evaluate, and select policy is to deal with options according to their contribution to the maximization (optimalization) of preferred events.

Contextual methods lay stress upon the interrelations between any detail and the whole of which it is part. Hence the examination of any objective requires the making of continual reference to an image of the whole, a selective and composite image of the social process. A systematically organized chart and map room presents such an image. The cues provided by the audiovisual aids serve as storage and recall auxiliaries to the individual brain. Since each item is introduced to a seminar group in a discussion which calls attention to its limitations as well as its relevance, the continued presence of the chart or map serves as a future reminder of the discussion.

PEOPLE AND RESOURCES

In broadest terms the "social process" is characterized as "man" seeking to maximize valued outcomes ("values") through "institutions" and use of "resources." The celebrated "explosion curve" of world population presents one version of historic trends of man (Figure 22.1); the U.N. chart of estimated world population 1950–2000 provides a choice of projections (Figure 22.2). Charts on the correlation of food and population summarize some relevant research on conditioning factors. The results of policies of population control (in Japan, for instance) are of obvious relevance to the evaluation of alternatives.

"Man's Space Environment" indicates a succession of spheres designed to assist us toward orientation in the

Figure 22.1. Estimated World Population, 8000 B.C.–1963 A.D.

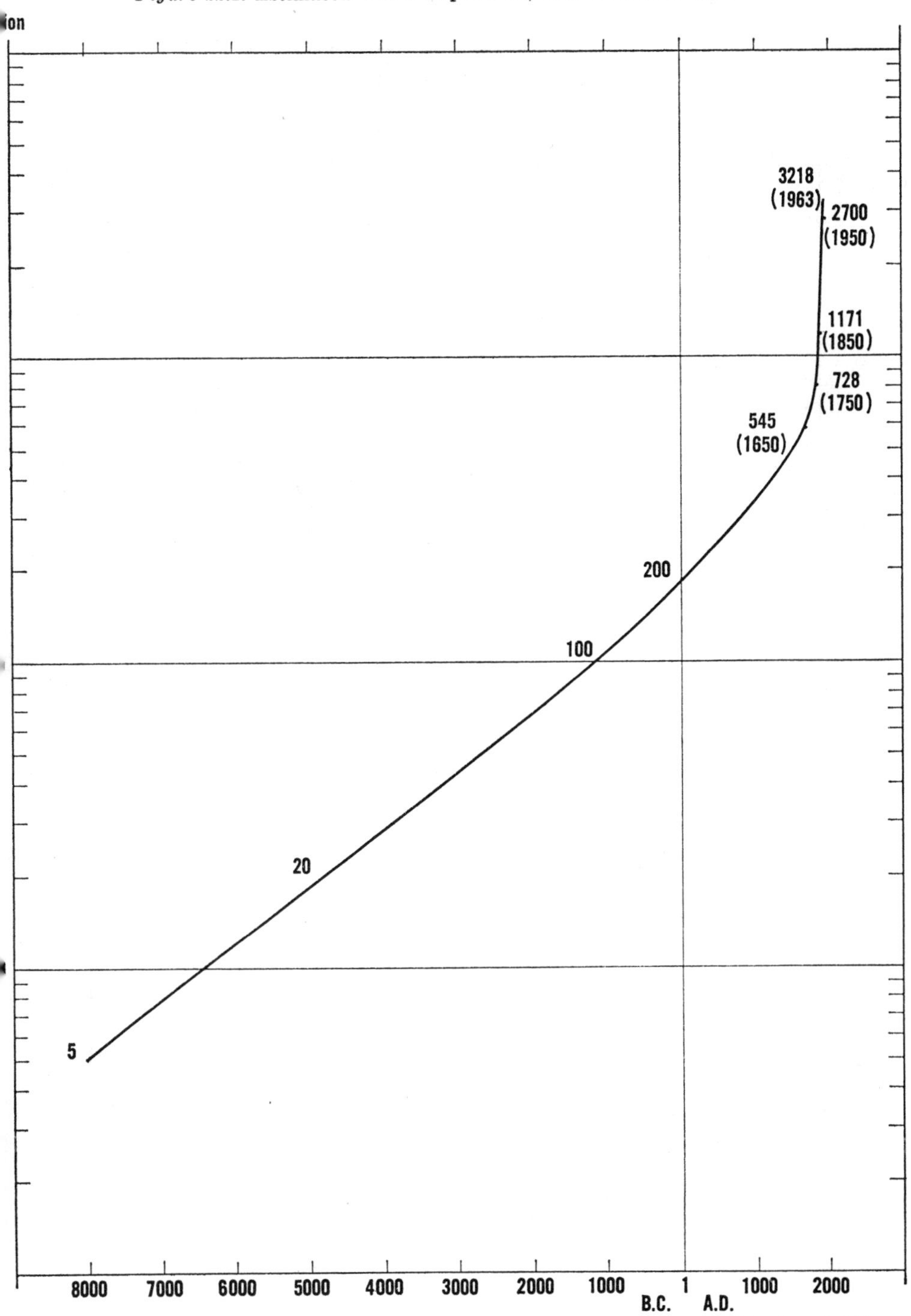

Source: Population estimates from J. Boyd Orr, *The White Man's Dilemma* (London, 1953), p. 53; and United Nations, *Statistical Yearbook, 1963.*

Figure 22.2. **World Population, 1950–2000: Three Estimates**

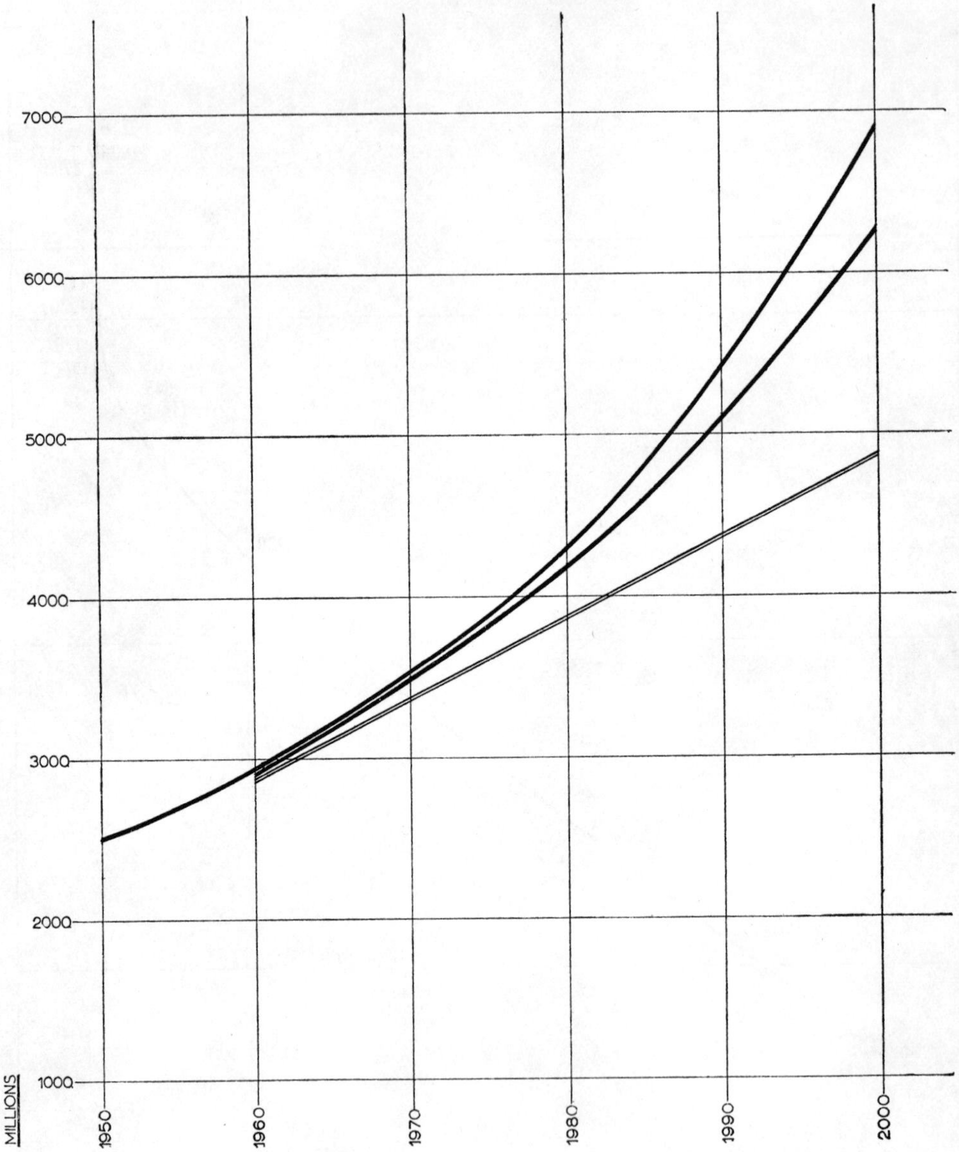

7000
6000
5000
4000
3000
2000
1000
MILLIONS
1950
1960
1970
1980
1990
2000

Source: U.N. Population Studies, No. 20 (1958).

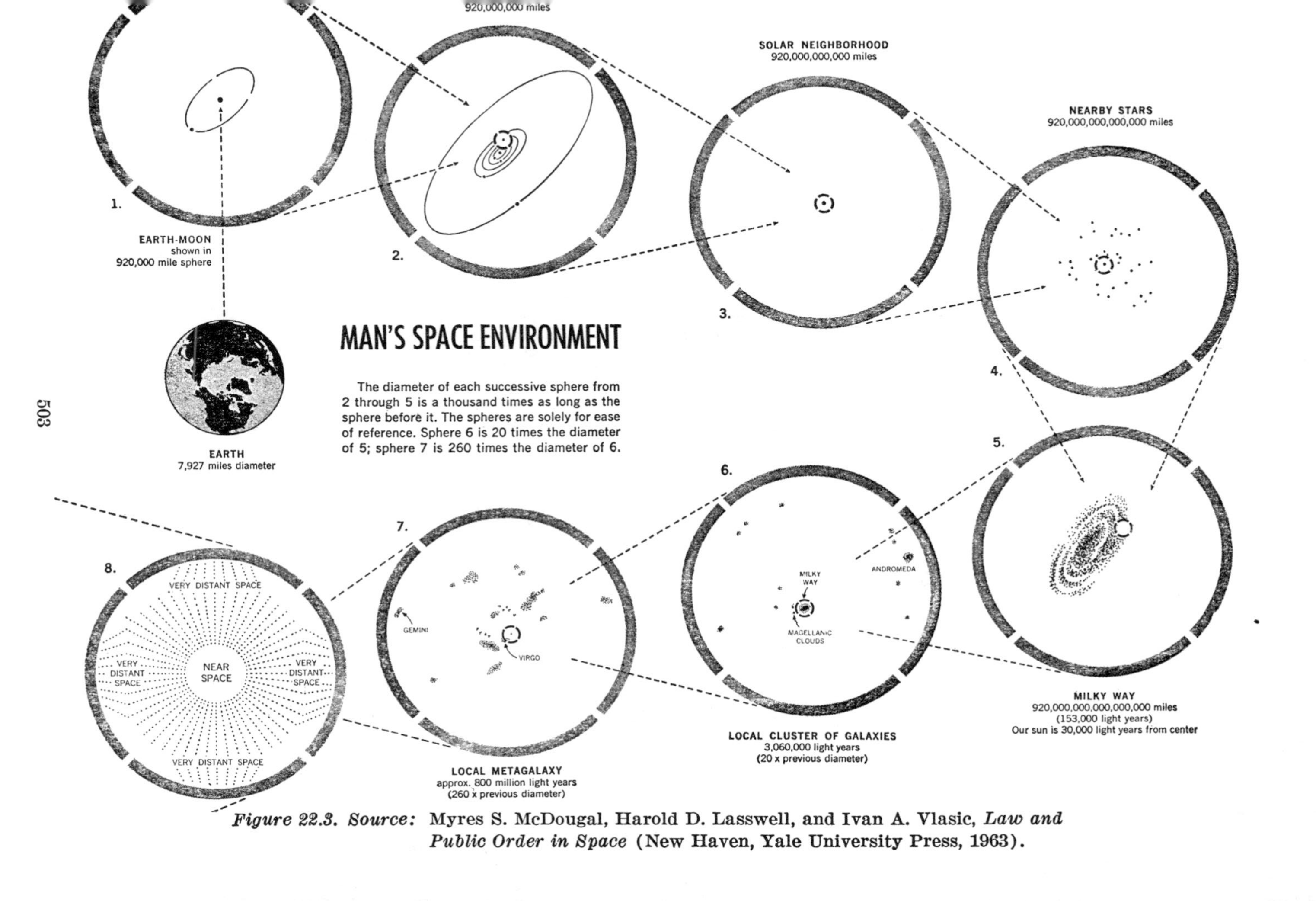

Figure 22.3. Source: Myres S. McDougal, Harold D. Lasswell, and Ivan A. Vlasic, *Law and Public Order in Space* (New Haven, Yale University Press, 1963).

resource setting of the Space Age (Figure 22.3). The diameter of each successive sphere from 2 through 5 is a thousand times as long as the sphere before it. The spheres are solely for ease of reference. Sphere 6 is 20 times the diameter of 5; sphere 7 is 260 times the diameter of 6.

VALUES AND INSTITUTIONS: OUTCOMES

The charts and maps appearing on some walls are devoted to the eight categories of value-institution processes which we use in describing any social context (national, transnational, subnational). We call attention first to typical "outcome" events for each value. Outcomes are the events regarded by scientific observers as culminating interactions in the endless flow of social process.[2] "Elections" and "victories or defeats in war," for example, are *power* (Figure 22.4. "United Nations Voting Alignments"). The giving and receiving of information are *enlightenment* (Figure 22.5. "Newspaper Content in Selected Countries"). The giving and receiving of claims to services are economic transactions or *wealth* (Figure 22.6. "World Industrial Production per Capita"). Health, safety, and comfort, are *well-being* (Figure 22.7. "Life Expectancy at Birth"). Expressions of talent are *skill* (cf. "World Speed Records"). The giving or receiving of intimacy and loyalty is *affection* (cf. "Divorce Rates: Selected Countries"—a measure of deprivation rather than indulgence). The interchange of recognition is *respect* (cf. "Areas from Which Nobel Prizewinners Are Chosen"). *Rectitude* is the formulation and application of religious and ethical norms (cf. "Canonization").

The preceding references are to social processes which are "specialized" to a value outcome. We also characterize patterns which are inclusive and "non-specialized," such as "cultures," or comprehensive patterns which are transmissi-

2. For reasons of space a limited number of charts and maps are reproduced. Titles are nevertheless cited since they provide concrete examples of each category. No attempt is made to provide the latest information in the charts. They are, however, convenient bench marks, sometimes registering the situation at a crisis period (end of war, for example) or an intercrisis year.

Figure 22.4. U.N. Voting Alignments *

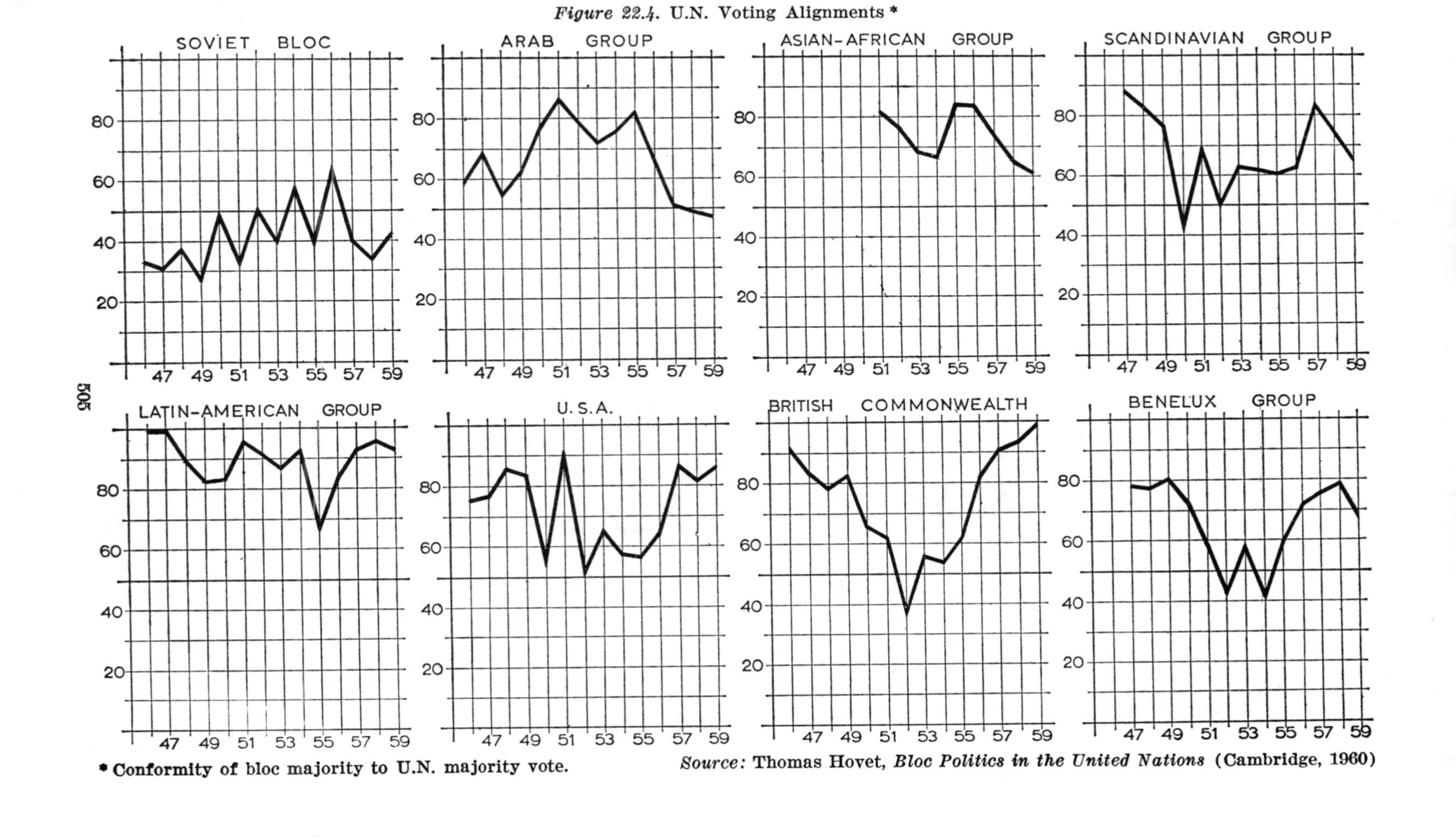

* **Conformity of bloc majority to U.N. majority vote.**

Source: **Thomas Hovet, *Bloc Politics in the United Nations* (Cambridge, 1960)**

Figure 22.5. Newspaper Content, Selected Countries, 1951

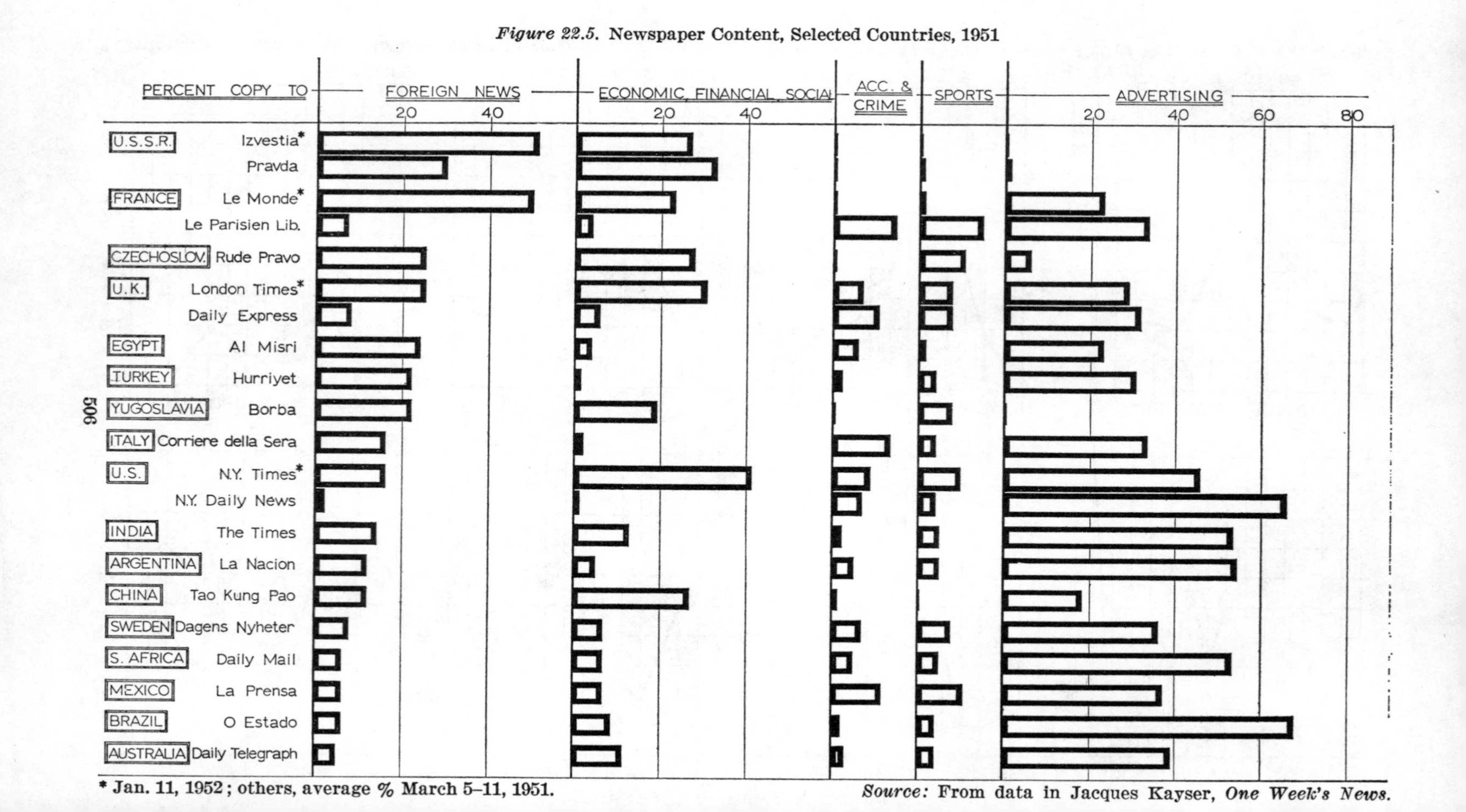

* Jan. 11, 1952; others, average % March 5–11, 1951.

Source: From data in Jacques Kayser, *One Week's News.*

Figure 22.6. World Industrial Production, 1870–1952

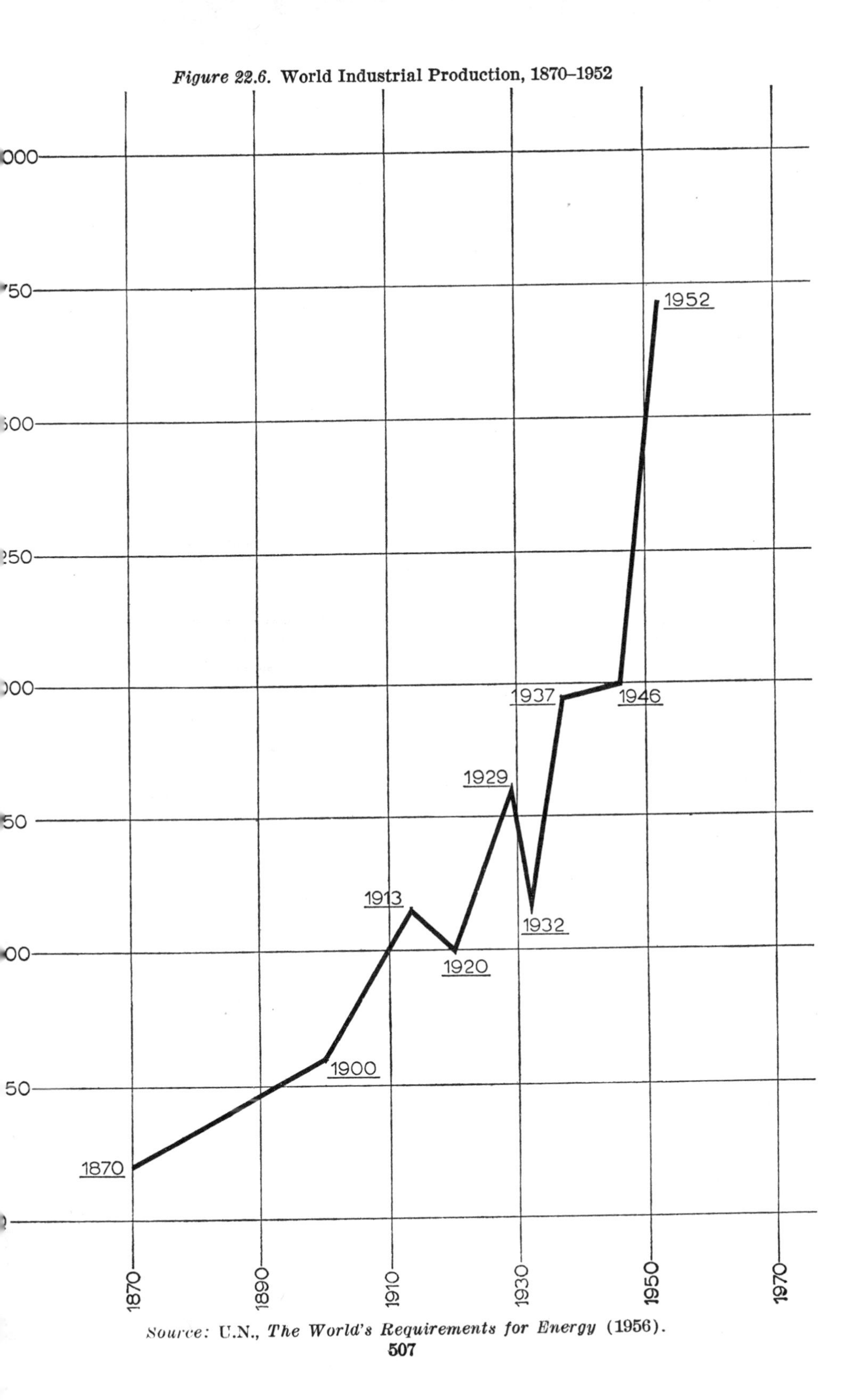

Source: U.N., *The World's Requirements for Energy* (1956).

Figure 22.7. **Well-Being Indicators: Life Expectation at Birth**

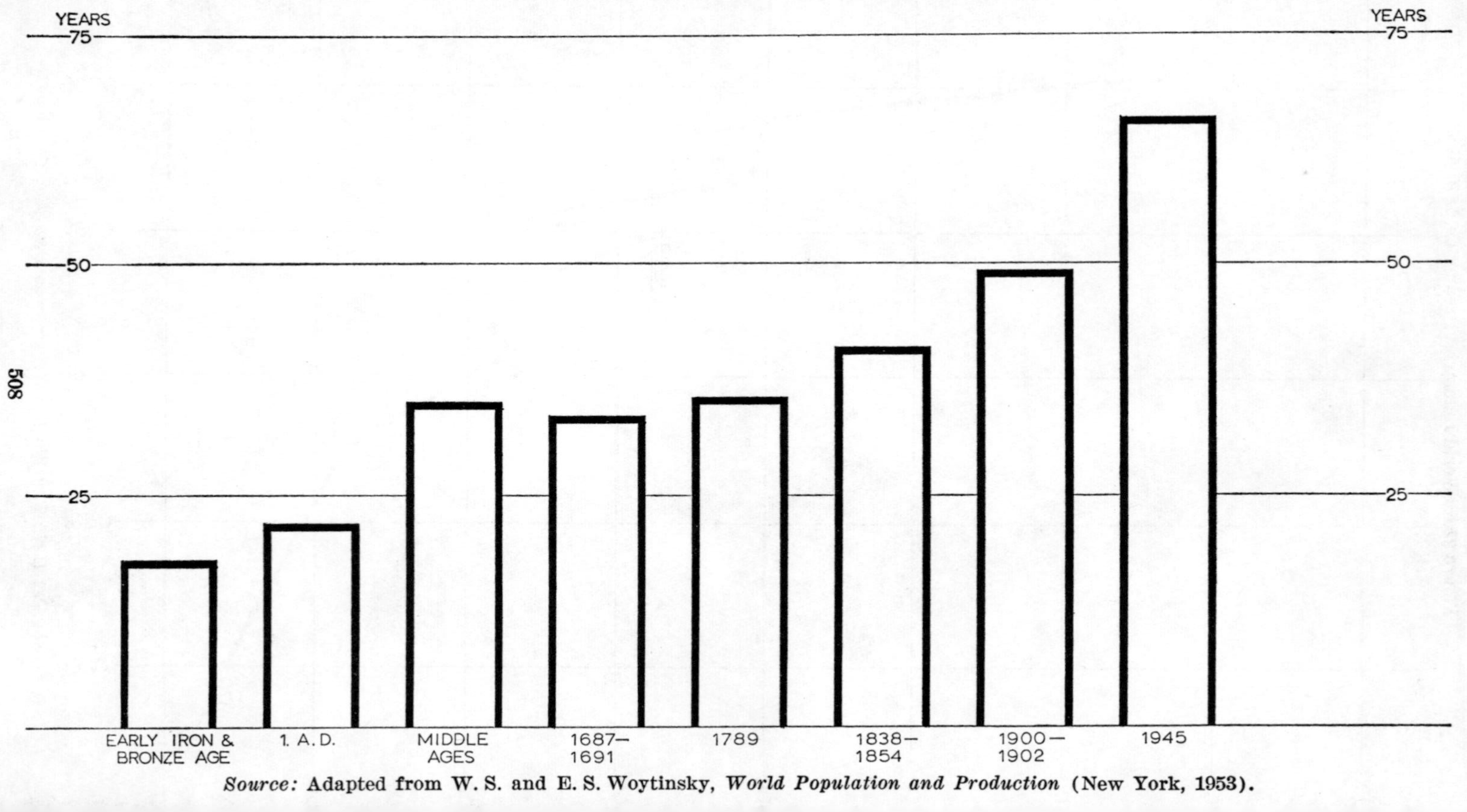

Source: Adapted from W. S. and E. S. Woytinsky, *World Population and Production* (New York, 1953).

ble to successors. The term is conveniently reserved to configurations which are relatively distinctive in the context of history and prehistory (others are "subcultures") (cf. map, "Distribution of Peoples with English Culture, Including Language," an example of "ethnic" culture; and the map summarizing V. Gordon Childe's version of the emergence of civilizations from folk societies [a "society" is a community with culture]).

The various categories of outcome events are put in pre-outcome and post-outcome context by describing participants, perspectives, base values, strategies, outcomes, effects (post-outcomes).

Participants. To some extent everyone is a shaper and sharer of every value. In describing those who specialize in shaping political activities we identify, for instance, "Political Elites of Major Powers." The specialized shapers of enlightenment include "Members of Scientific Societies." The producers of wealth are "Percent of Population Economically Active." Some specialists on well-being are mapped, e.g. "Distribution of Physicians and Surgeons." Skill acquisition is reflected in a map of "World School Enrollment." Participation in affection is suggested by Figure 22.8, "Size of U.S. Families since 1790." Low respect participation is referred to in "The Untouchables" of various countries. Rectitude participation is sketched in "Areas of Origin of New Members of Religious Organizations."

Perspectives. Any system of belief, faith, and loyalty is a "myth" (with no pejorative implications). Each myth, in turn, includes "doctrine," indicated in the map depicting "Communist and Non-Communist Powers"; "formula," shown in "World Legal Systems"; and "miranda," represented by "World Heroes." In addition to power, all value-institutions can be described according to doctrine, formula, and miranda; we cannot, however, go into further detail here. An example of enlightenment perspectives is "Articulated Values of Scientists"; wealth perspectives, "Ideology of Business Men"; well-being, "Social Attitudes of Physicians"; skill, "The Outlook of Semiskilled Groups"; affec-

Figure 22.8. **Size of U.S. Private Families**

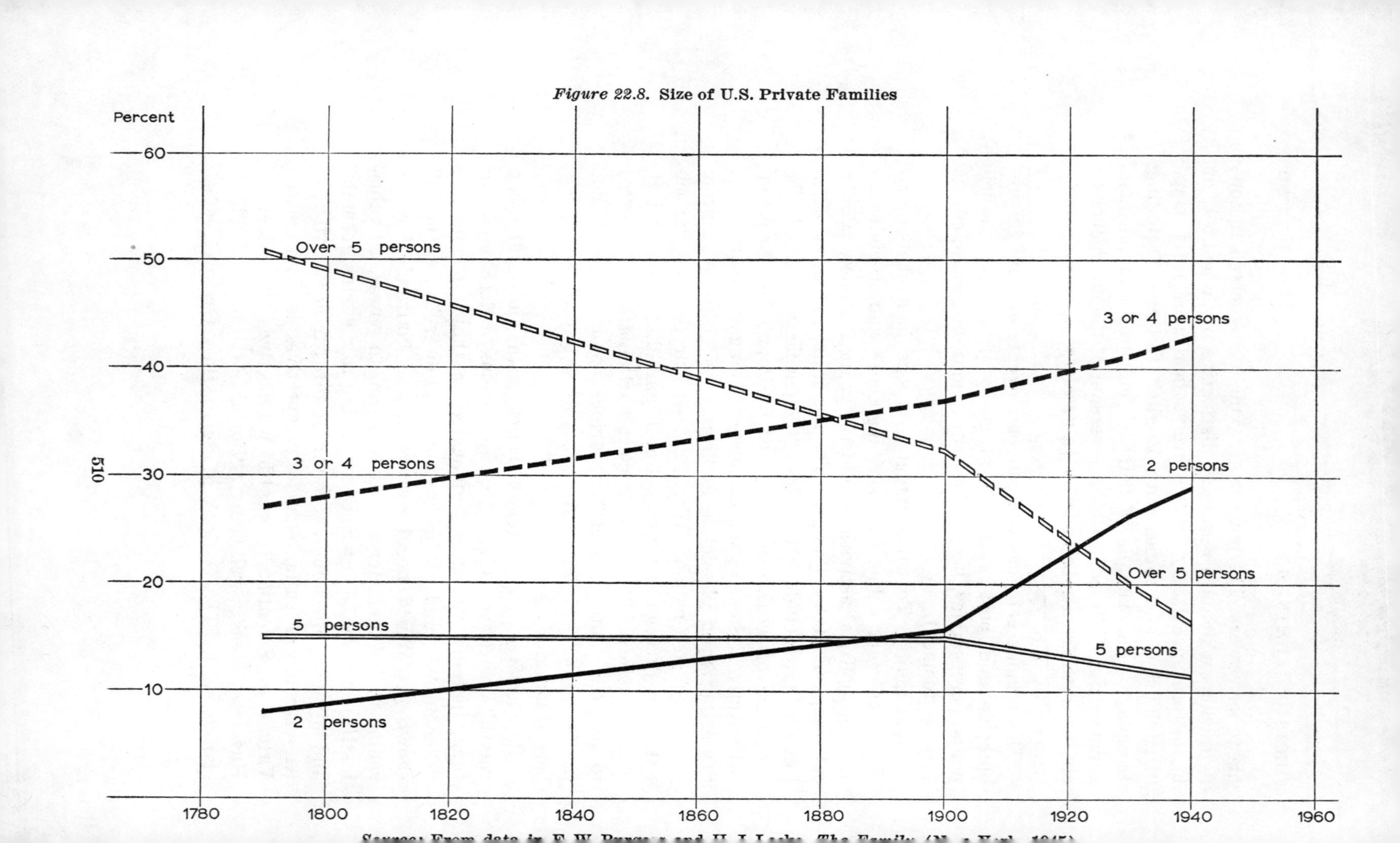

Source: From data in E. W. Burgess and H. J. Locke, *The Family* (New York, 1945).

tion, "Time Required to Achieve Marital Adjustment"; respect, "National Patterns of Self-Identification" (by social class; Figure 22.9); rectitude, "Social Optimism and Pessimism among Religious Groups."

Situations. Taken together, all persons who interact above a designated minimum in the shaping and sharing of a value constitute a "value situation" (organized or unorganized). A map of an organized power arena is "Changing Membership in the U.N." A set of enlightenment situations is "Trends in Organization of Research Agencies." A partially organized market is referred to in "The World Wheat Market." A danger area (a negative well-being situation) is shown in "Cities and Towns Near Nuclear Test Areas"; a skill situation: "Members of Olympics"; affection: "Marriage and Propinquity"; respect: "Distribution of Foreign Honorary Academy Members"; rectitude: "World Distribution of Religious Organizations."

Base values. At any given moment it is possible to describe the assets and liabilities (base values) available to any participant in the social process for use in seeking to influence value outcomes. The territorial resources of a nation-state are potential assets for national power purposes (cf. "Territorial Growth of the U.S."). "The World Distribution of Communication Media" shows some enlightenment assets. "Horsepower per capita" refers to a wealth asset. The potential of scientific medicine as a well-being base is indicated in "Modern Medicine; Impact on Death Rates." Figure 22.10, "Estimated Adult Literacy Rates, 1950" reports the availability of fundamental skills. The affection potential of marriage is suggested by "Median Age at Marriage." The prestige base at the disposal of various occupations is outlined in "Mobility between Occupations of High and Low Prestige." Studies of social class affiliation of church members show the prestige base of such rectitude organizations ("Old Families and Church Affiliation").

Strategies. Strategies are the employment of base values to influence value outcomes. Strategies can be classified according to the base or scope value of greatest importance; or

Figure 22.9. **National Patterns of Self-Identification**

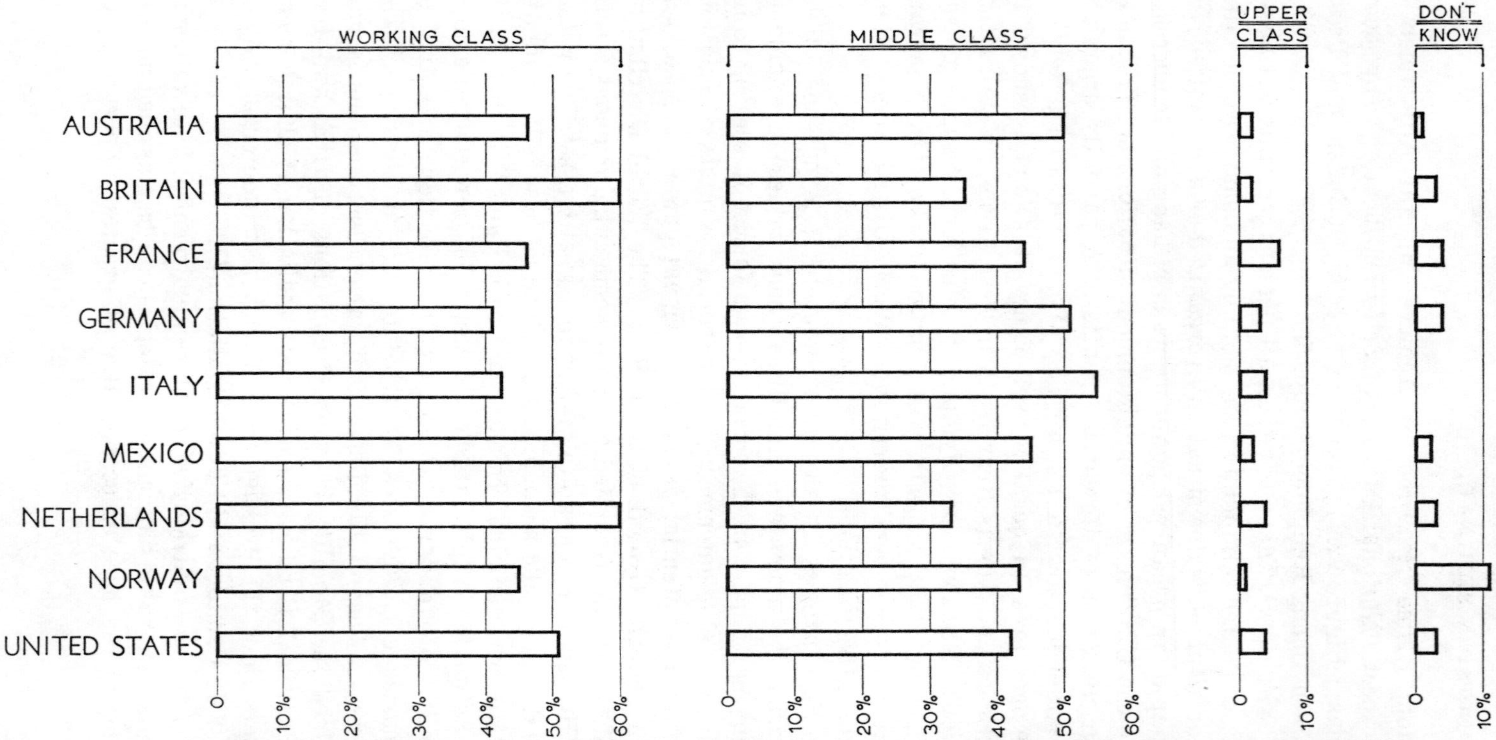

WORKING CLASS

MIDDLE CLASS

UPPER CLASS

DON'T KNOW

AUSTRALIA

BRITAIN

FRANCE

GERMANY

ITALY

MEXICO

NETHERLANDS

NORWAY

UNITED STATES

0 10% 20% 30% 40% 50% 60%

0 10% 20% 30% 40% 50% 60%

0 10%

0 10%

Source: From data in W. Buchanan and H. Cantril, *How Nations See Each Other* (Urbana, 1953) ; figures compiled in 1948.

Figure 22.10. **Estimated Adult Literacy Rates, 1950**

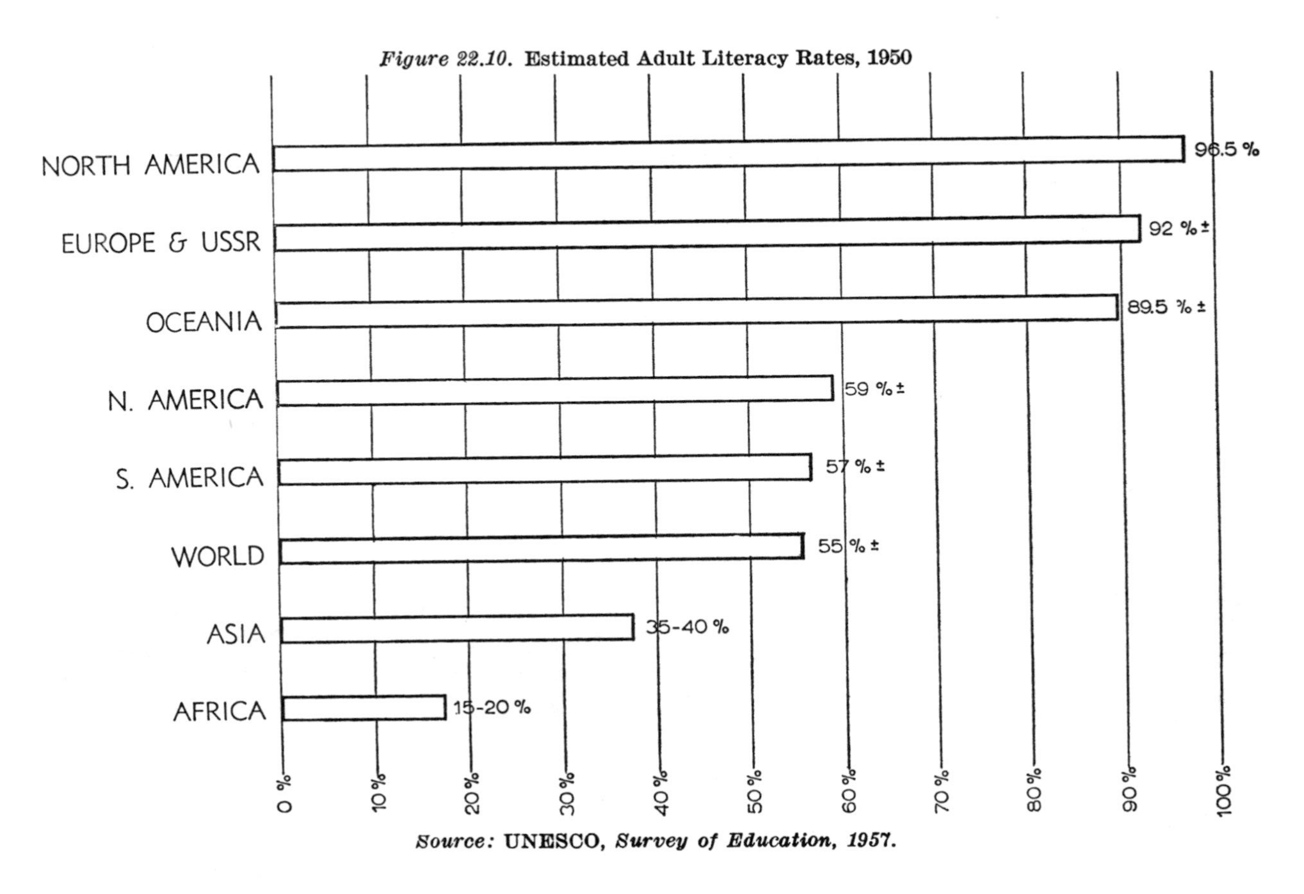

Source: UNESCO, *Survey of Education*, 1957.

Figure 22.11. Africa: Diffusion of Colonialism

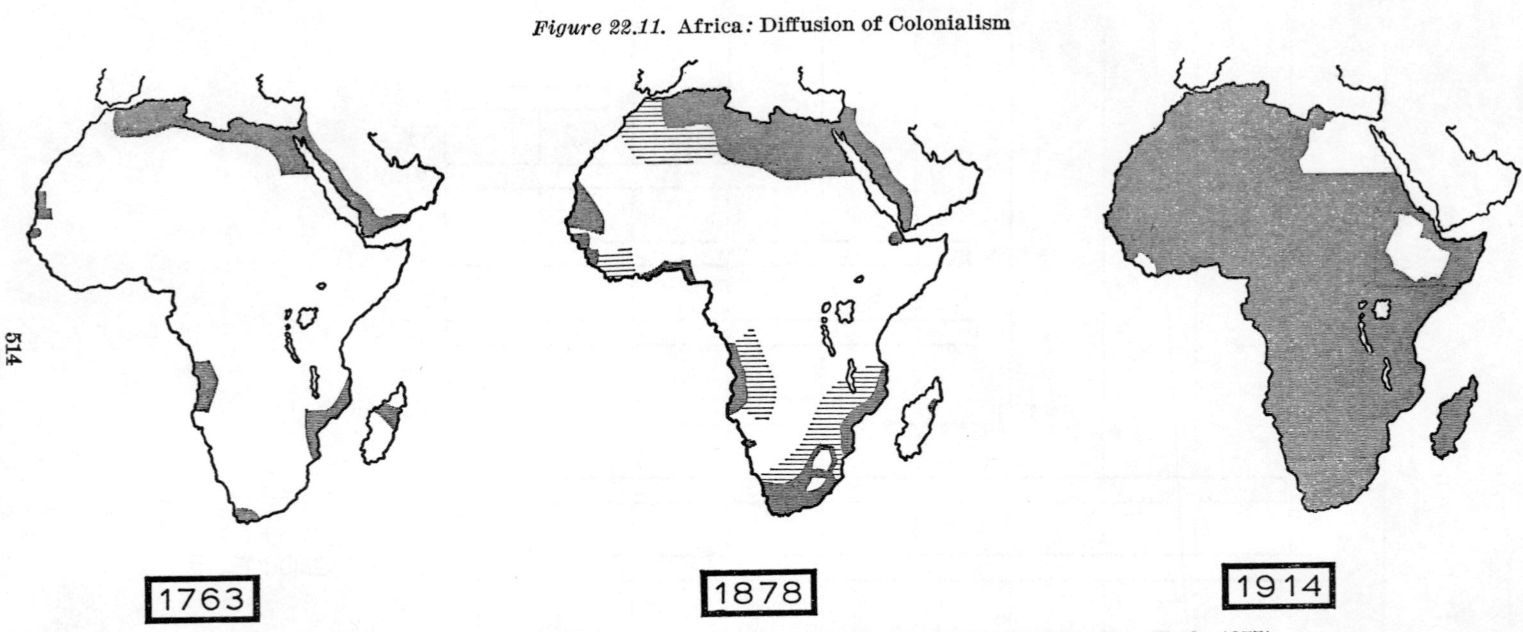

Source: Adapted from Y. M. Goblet, *Political Geography and the World Map* (New York, 1955).

according to the balance of persuasion and coercion, or reliance upon symbols and signs (communication, diplomacy) upon physical resources (economic and military strategy). The following charts or maps, from various value-institution processes, are suggestive: "Trends in the Use of Atomic Tests"; "Censorship: The Strategy of Withholding Information"; "Price Agreements in Transnational Markets"; "The Use of Chemical Methods of Dealing with Mental Illness"; "Team Science: Social Skills in Science"; "Length of Courtship"; "Persons Lynched" (a well-being impact whose respect significance is perhaps even more important); "World Missionary Activities."

Effects (*post-outcomes*). Having given examples of outcomes we focus directly upon some post-outcome effects. Post-outcomes summarize the impact of outcomes upon values and institutions. In this connection it is useful to show the rise, diffusion, and restriction of patterns (Figure 22.11. "Africa: Diffusion of Colonialism"; Figure 22.12. "Africa: Restriction of Colonialism"). The most desirable material connects a change with conditioning factors. Obviously the effects described at a given cross-section in time are among the predisposing factors which affect future developments and enter the presentation of succeeding periods as participants, perspectives, and base values are described.

THE PHASES OF DECISION

In law, government, and politics we focus upon the community decision processes. Part of the wall space in the seminar room serves as a reminder of the phase analysis that we employ in studying decisions.

The *intelligence* phase is specialized to obtaining, analyzing, and projecting information. One chart, for example, gives "Typical Sources Used in Estimating National Income and Product," another, "Legal Periodical Articles Cited by U.S. Supreme Court Justices."

The *promoting* phase is the use of agitation and other instruments to influence policy. In the internal arena of the

Figure 22.12. **Africa: Restriction of Colonialism**

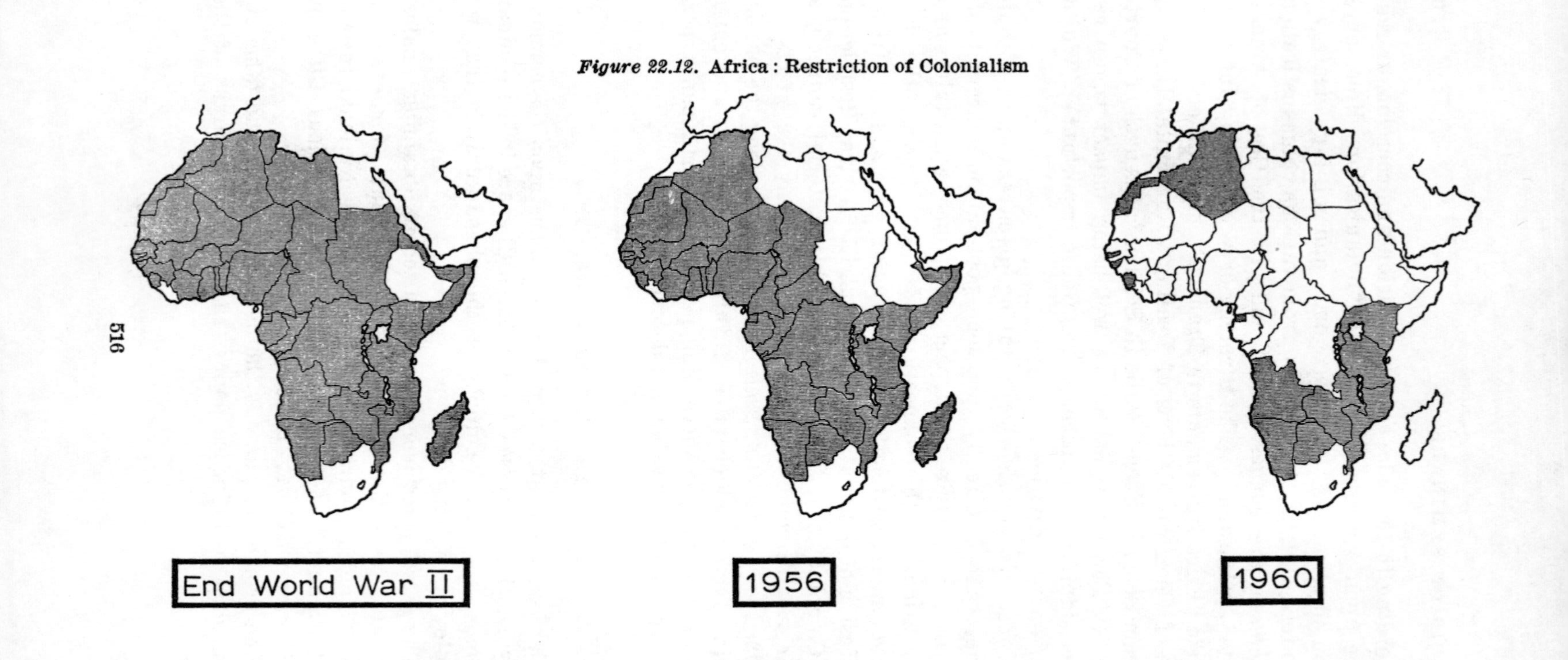

U.S., for example, political parties and pressure associations play prominent parts. One chart sums up "Political Activity of U.S. Lobbyists"; another, "Political Parties: Interest Groups as Repeat Contributors."

The *prescribing* phase formulates general rules to be enforced. For instance: "U.S. Treaties and Agreements since the Beginning"; "Reapportionment of State Legislatures, by Decades."

The *invoking* phase is a provisional characterization of concrete circumstances in terms of conformity to a prescription (cf. "Arrests for Common Crimes"; "Indictments for Common Crimes").

The *application* phase is a final characterization of concrete circumstances according to prescriptions (cf. "Total Cases Terminated in U.S. District Courts, from 1871"; "Total Cases Terminated: U.S. Court of Appeals, from 1892").

The *appraisal* phase assesses the relationship between policy objectives and results (cf. "Recidivism: U.S. Federal Prisoners"; "The Death Penalty and Homicide Rates").

The *terminating* phase puts an end to prescriptions in force, and adjusts value claims resulting therefrom (cf. "Cases Expressly Overruled by U.S. Supreme Court"; "Compensation for Property Seized in the Public Interest").

THE MEASUREMENT OF VALUE SHAPING AND SHARING

The contextual approach gives prominence to the gaps in the current stock of information about the social process, and hence calls attention to problems of measurement which have yet to be solved. The shaping and sharing of wealth have been described in careful quantitative terms whose unsatisfactory features are less the responsibility of economists than testimony to the failure of other social scientists to develop their own specialized frames of reference. There is a substantial degree of consensus about how to describe the shaping and sharing of wealth in aggregative terms; not so, however, for most values.

We conclude by summarizing, without presenting, analytic

charts which can be used for comparative discussion. The first series is concerned with functional description; the second with structural changes.

Functional Description

Functional description seeks to identify the participants in a value shaping and sharing process, and to show how the total volume of activity varies during a given period. To some extent, as pointed out earlier, everyone is a shaper and sharer of every value. To share a value is to have it made available to be disposed of either by accumulation or enjoyment.

Wealth Value
participants = shapers = producers
(suppliers of a factor)
sharers = income receivers
(factor; personal)
outcome = gross = units available for disposition
—
units used up in production
net = gross income
—
depreciation on culture materials specialized to wealth
effect = initial wealth
+ or —
net income
Enlightenment Value
participants = shapers = reporters, researchers, forecasters, storers (librarians, etc.)
= sharers = learners (of accumulated knowledge), viewers, readers or listeners to news
outcome = gross = news reports, research reports, forecasts, storing, exposures to media, exposures to educational presentations

effect = initial knowledge stored
−
loss of knowledge
+
initial level of reporting (expected volume)
+
initial level of forecasting
+
initial level of exposure to media
+
initial level of exposure to educational presentations
+ or −
gross outcome

Skill Value

participants = shapers = practitioners
levels of training and experience
levels of performance
+
apprentices
+
masters (trainers)
= sharers = evaluators
critics, connoisseurs

outcome = gross = improvement in levels of training and experience
+
improvement in levels of performance
−
deterioration

net = gross outcome
−
teaching outlay

effect = initial level
+ or −
net outcome

Well-being Value
participants = shapers = caretakers, therapists, preventers, destroyers
= sharers = experiencers of safety, health, comfort
outcome = net = births
—
deaths, injuries, illnesses, defects, anxieties, discomforts
+
vigor
effect = initial population (expectation of death, injury, illness, defect, anxiety, discomfort, vigor)
+ or — net income (terminal population's expectations)

Affection Value
participants = shapers = family partners
= sharers
outcome
individual congeniality = positive activities
toward others
+
from others
—
negative activities
toward others
+
from others
loyalty (own group identity) = positive activities
—
negative activities
collective congeniality = positive activities
toward other groups
+
by other groups

—
negative activities
toward other groups
+
by other groups
effect
initial congeniality (individual)
+ or —
net individual outcome
initial loyalty
+ or —
net outcome
initial congeniality (group)
+
net outcome
Respect Value
participants = shapers = formulators of respect standards and appliers
= sharers
outcome
individual = indulgences (recognitions)
toward others
+
from others
—
deprivations (discriminations)
toward others
+
from others
collective = indulgences
toward other groups
+
from other groups
—
deprivations
toward other groups
+
from other groups

effect
initial respect position (individual)
+
net outcome
initial respect position (collective)
+
net income
Rectitude Value
participants = shapers = formulators and appliers of religious and ethical standards
= sharers
outcome
conformity to standards
—
nonconformity
effect
initial disposition to conformity
+
net outcome (terminal disposition of conformity)
Power Value
participants = shapers = authorities and controllers
+
controllers without authority
= sharers
outcome
positions in final alignments
+
pivotal role in pre-outcome
+
initiating role in pre-outcome
effect
initial authority and control position
+ or — outcome (terminal position)

Structural Description

Structural analysis goes beyond functional categories to describe fundamental patterns. The *participants* are individuals and groups.

As suggested above, the fundamental *perspectives* are

classifiable as symbols of identity, demand, and expectation, which are clustered as relatively stable myths (doctrine, formula, and miranda).

The *situations* of interaction disclose basic patterns of organization which are centralized or decentralized in varying degree, concentrated or deconcentrated, governmentalized or liberalized, pluralized or unitized, or individualized or regimented.

The *base values* are distributed among participants according to their upper, middle, or lower position in reference to each value.

Strategies are characteristically divided according to coercive or persuasive techniques, or in terms of information, diplomacy, economics, and military instruments. The aggregate picture shows isolation or coalition, and coalitions achieve monopoly or remain competitive in various degree.

The *outcome* practices are the alignments or votes (formal and actual commitments). The outcomes can also be classified for each value according to the phase of the total choosing or deciding process (intelligence, promotion, prescription, invocation, application, appraisal, termination).

Net structural effects at the end of a time period can be expressed for each value in this way:

Participants
- initial individuals and organized groups
- + or — changes (above selected critical frequencies in this and all categories below)

Perspectives
- initial doctrines, prescriptions, formula
- + or — changes

Situations
- initial organizations (centralized, decentralized; concentrated, deconcentrated; governmentalized, liberalized; pluralized, unitized; individualistic, regimented)
- + or — changes

Base Values
- initial upper, middle, or lower position
- + or — changes

Strategies

initial persuasive or coercive disposition

+

initial disposition to employ information, diplomacy, economic and military instruments

+

initial disposition toward isolation or coalition; toward monopoly or competition

+ or — changes

Outcomes

initial disposition to alignment according to a given set of practices

+ or — changes

Some of the charts referred to above provide examples of structural presentation, i.e. the two charts on Colonialism in Africa (22.11, 22.12); a map of "Civilizations and Folk Societies."

The contextual use of audiovisual aids, when employed in decision (or choosing) seminars, can provide a disciplined strategy for research, teaching, and consultation. Whether the problem is to clarify values, to describe trend, to analyze conditions, to project the future, or to arrive at policy alternatives, the perpetual interaction between detail and context provides a creative experience for everyone involved.

23. Comparative Social Research in the United Nations

DONALD V. MC GRANAHAN, SURVEY, RESEARCH, AND DEVELOPMENT BRANCH, UNITED NATIONS BUREAU OF SOCIAL AFFAIRS

The United Nations has been concerned for a number of years with problems of cross-national comparative research, particularly in our work on international definition and measurement of levels of living.[1] While we do not use the expression "cross-national comparison," it is evident that international measurement of levels of development implies comparison or at least comparability of data. There are some who doubt the possibility of making valid international quantitative comparisons in the social field on grounds that nations and cultures are too diverse, and there is an unquestioned need for prudence in the endeavor. But international social policy would not be possible without information from different countries that has some degree of common meaning and comparability; and in an international environment concepts that can be defined through objective measurement, with a minimum of ideological or cultural connotation, have obviously great advantages, along with great difficulties.

Social research in the United Nations is necessarily bound up with the nature and purpose of the organization. (I am speaking here of the United Nations proper, although in

1. See *Report on International Definition and Measurement of Standards and Levels of Living* (United Nations publications, Sales No. 54.IV.5); and *International Definition and Measurement of Levels of Living: An Interim Guide* (United Nations publication, Sales No. 61.IV.7).

practice much of our social research is carried out in cooperation with the specialized agencies, particularly ILO, FAO, UNESCO, and WHO.) The United Nations is an organization of states or governments and does not deal directly with populations, except at the request of governments. As a rule, governments are not interested in having United Nations social scientists undertake opinion polls or attitude studies or content analyses within their territories, particularly in relation to matters of a political or semipolitical nature. There are exceptions, of course, as in the recent case of the United Nations Mission to Sarawak and Northern Borneo. But, in general, the United Nations does not collect data of that kind.

While countries are not anxious to have international organs inquiring into their political processes, they do welcome international intervention in their economic and social development—to the surprise, perhaps, of many who were associated with the framing of the Charter of the United Nations. (There were doubts and misgivings at San Francisco when it was first proposed to give the new organization responsibilities in questions of economic and social development that are not strictly "international" in the older sense of that term, that is, involving the crossing of national frontiers.) By far the greater part of all research now carried out by the United Nations has to do with the economic and social development of the less developed countries. Correspondingly, most of our information resources, our instruments and categories of research, are designed to serve the purpose of development.

United Nations social research is policy oriented; it is directed toward the raising of levels of living. We do not promote research for the sake of advancing science—that is a function of UNESCO. Our concern is with the collection and analysis of information that will throw light on the most effective policies and programs for improving levels of living: information that will indicate positive paths to take, not simply the flashing of red lights to indicate what cannot be done for anthropological, psychological, or sociological reasons. We are not primarily concerned with cultural values as such, or with social structure, customary institutions, rituals, beliefs, etc., except—and this can be a very important exception—insofar as these factors bear upon the problem of raising the levels of living. Our approach could be called applied social research; but since there hardly exists today a general theory or strategy of social development to apply, we are necessarily concerned with more fundamental questions than the expression "applied research" might suggest.

It is noteworthy that in the nineteenth century there was great interest in questions of social development or social evolution, as witnessed by the writings of men like Comte, Marx, Spencer, Tarde, Wundt; but in the twentieth century social research, at least in the Western countries, has been dominated by other interests: culture patterns, group values, individual learning, structures, functions, the functions of structures, and the structures of functions. Such work has value, but necessarily limited value, for those who are interested in development policy, in deliberate measures to modernize the less developed countries through a process of planned economic and social change. Most of these countries now have development plans. They seek guidance from social research in their programming and staging of development, in their priorities and their methods of introducing change. We are not yet able to provide much assistance but this is a rapidly growing field.

INTERNATIONAL SOCIAL STATISTICS

A major resource for social research in the United Nations is the collection of national statistics by the United Nations Statistical Office. These statistics are obtained directly by the Statistical Office, in cooperation with specialized agencies, from national statistical offices (without the intermediation of foreign offices). Data are published in the *Statistical Yearbooks,* the *Demographic Yearbooks,* the recently issued *Compendium of Social Statistics,* and various other publications. They are used extensively in our research, although each statistic must be carefully examined before use. We are sometimes dismayed by the trusting manner in which internationally issued statistics designated as unreliable or incomplete are employed in scholarly publications, and by the elaborate structures and elegant comparisons sometimes built up on the basis of very fragile data. It must be kept in mind that underdeveloped countries tend to have underdeveloped statistics. There has been gratifying improvement in recent years but major difficulties remain.

In the first place, for a number of countries some of the most elementary statistics are still lacking or are incomplete and unreliable. A few years ago, when we were preparing a text on trends in infant mortality rates for the period 1947 to 1955, we were able to locate only half a dozen countries in the whole of Asia and Africa with relatively good official statistics on this important indicator of levels of health. Furthermore, the countries in question were not typical of their regions; they were countries like Israel, Japan, Singapore, and South Africa. The situation has improved, and we are also getting better statistics through the use of sample surveys to fill gaps in regular statistics, as in the case of recent surveys of fertility rates in several West African countries (although the rates indicated by these sample surveys—around 55 to 60 or more live births per 1,000 population—are so high as to raise the question of possible overstatement). Progress in statistical coverage in general is illustrated by the fact that in the 1935–44 round of censuses only about 100 countries participated, in 1945–54 about 186, and in 1955–64 about 200 out of a potential 229 countries and territories.

Second, statistical data that are reported from economically less developed countries tend to be characterized by a consistent error in understatement or overstatement of the true rates. For example, vital statistics rates are widely understated: often they are collected only from the better-off, more developed parts of the country where lower fertility and mortality rates prevail; inefficiencies and difficulties in the registration system (as in rural areas without doctors, hospitals, or magistrates), and popular ignorance, indifference, or aversion regarding registration all lead to understatement.[2] Sometimes, however, there is overstatement as when previously unregistered events—particularly births—are for one reason or another added to current ones. As another example, the per capita national income is apparently often understated because subsistence agriculture is not fully covered (see below). At the same time, if the contribution of agriculture is understated, the proportionate contribution of industry to the total national income will be overstated, and since industry tends to grow more rapidly than agriculture, a falsely optimistic picture of the overall rate of growth can emerge.

A final major difficulty in comparative social statistics is the lack of standardization of statistical concepts. This is a familiar problem. The following are a few illustrations of problems of standardization.

1. The *per capita national income,* which has limited value as an indicator of social development, was established in the framework of the market economy and is applied with difficulty to centrally planned economies (where the material product is used as a measure of growth), and with even more difficulty to subsistence economies, which characterize the great bulk of production and consumption in many less developed countries. (The difficulties considered here are over and above the well-known question of currency convertibility which has yet to find a generally accepted solution.) In subsistence and semi-subsistence economies, it is necessary to impute monetary values to goods and services that are produced and consumed locally without being sold. The methodology of imputation is uncertain, and the results can be quite odd, at least from a social perspective. Where the same kinds of goods and services are also sold on a local market, then values can be imputed to the subsistence sector on that basis, or prices at a central market can be used, with reasonable

2. A study of a peripheral shanty-town population in one country showed that many of the children were not going to school because their births had never been registered: the boys were not registered because it would make them liable to eventual military duty (this was the chief reason given) and for the girls it was not thought important.

deductions for transportation, handling, etc. But this means that subsistence families in different countries, or different parts of the same country, producing and consuming the very same items, can have widely different incomes imputed to them, depending on the varying prices in the markets. When the cost of living is high (it differs widely from country to country in a region like Africa), then imputed subsistence income will tend to be high. An even greater difficulty arises in the case of items that are not sold at local or central markets. Certain foods, articles of clothing, body ornaments, houses, artistic objects, etc., may be peculiar to a given subsistence society and not marketed. But the difficulty is especially apparent in the case of various "services" that are part of the traditional society but not of the monetarized economy: medical services (by traditional herbalists, witch-doctors, etc.), recreation (local dances, festivals), administration of justice (by local headmen or chieftains), education (of the young by the elders in the arts and crafts of the community), funeral services, etc. There is no established method of imputing monetary values to such services and the temptation is to avoid the issue.

2. *Rate of unemployment* is another statistical concept that has developed in a modern urban–industrial setting and applies with difficulty to a preindustrial environment. It is now customary to speak of "underemployment" rather than "unemployment" in the rural areas of economically less developed countries. The individuals concerned are not entirely without work and are not necessarily seeking work; but there is too little work for the numbers involved (typically too little land per worker) and some portion of them could, at least in theory, be transferred to other occupations without loss of production in the farming sector. There is, in fact, also extensive underemployment in the cities of less developed countries, evident in the large numbers of petty vendors, lottery ticket sellers, porters, shoeshine boys, odd jobs men, and others who sit about much of the day waiting for a chance to earn a little money. (Also, bureaucracies may be grossly overstaffed, and the red tape that is originated to

justify unnecessary jobs becomes a drag upon the economy and upon the social process.)

Such underemployment, however, is extremely difficult to measure in a way that would make international comparisons meaningful. One proposed solution has been to measure productivity instead, considering complete unemployment as the zero point on a continuum; but since productivity is a function of level of technology and of the quality as well as quantity of resources such as land (some impoverished peasants with low productivity are overemployed in the sense that they have to work very hard to scrape out a miserable existence from barren soil), this solution is in effect an abandonment of the attempt to establish an internationally comparable measure of unemployment itself.

3. Another example of difficulties in standardization may be given by reference to the comparative international study of *urbanization.* This is complicated, in the first instance, by the fact that countries do not agree on how large a locality must be in order to be classified as "urban." In one country it may be 250 people; in another, a locality of 40,000 may still be classified as "rural." Further, many countries classify not by population size of a civil division but by population density, legal or administrative status, predominant forms of economic activity, the presence or absence of certain services deemed to be urban, and so on, or by some combination of size and qualitative characteristics. An administrative district or municipality may be classified as an urban area although many of its inhabitants live in agricultural areas surrounding the city proper. If census data giving the population of the different localities are available, it is possible to take an arbitrary dividing line, such as 20,000, and measure the degree of urbanization in different countries by the percentage of the population living in places of 20,000 or more.[3] This is a useful rough measure but it does not resolve the difficulty, for some countries may include, in their definition

3. See *Report on the World Social Situation*, including studies of urbanization in underdeveloped areas (United Nations publication, Sales No. 57.IV.3), pp. 113–23.

of localities with 20,000 or more, certain outlying populations that in another country would normally be administratively organized and classified in small separate localities and thus not counted as part of the larger urban locality.[4]

There are numerous other illustrations of problems of standardization that could be mentioned. Comparative statistics on education are fairly manageable as far as literacy rates and school enrollment ratios at the elementary level are concerned (although the failure of enrollment ratios to reflect the quality of education or the extent of absenteeism, dropouts, and repeats is a serious weakness). But in technical and higher education, the variety of institutional forms makes international comparison precarious.[5] Wages are difficult to compare at the international level because in some countries wage "fringe benefits" reach such a substantial sum as to invalidate wage comparisons unless they are included, but there is no agreement as yet on which fringe benefits to include (can real wages in fact be compared without taking account of food and rental subsidies, free medical services, free educational services, etc. provided by governments?). Also, there is no ready solution to the problem of how to convert wage data into a satisfactory international currency unit, or any other international unit.[6] In the case of social security, the diversity of arrangements is so great that it has not been considered wise at present even to attempt to issue, on a uniform international basis, statistics on the extent of social security coverage and the number of participants and beneficiaries.[7] Similarly, no attempt is made at present to issue comparative statistics on clothing, recreation and entertainment, or human freedoms, although these

4. Differences of this kind appear to explain why, around 1950, the Philippines had 55.5 per cent of its population living in localities of 20,000 or more, according to published statistics, while France and Sweden had only about 33 per cent, and the United States, even in 1960, had only 46.9 per cent.

5. As James B. Conant has recently pointed out, for example, the American college cannot be properly compared to the European university or the European gymnasium or to any other institution elsewhere.

6. See *International Definition and Measurement of Levels of Living: An Interim Guide*, p. 11.

7. Ibid., pp. 12–13.

are recognized as important elements of the level of living.

Efforts are being made by the United Nations and the specialized agencies to promote standardization of social statistics where this is considered feasible. Standardization is pursued in several ways: by detailed instructions in statistical questionnaires that are circulated to governments; by issuance of reports, manuals, and handbooks setting up international statistical standards and standardized methods for collecting statistics; by seminars, workshops, regional advisory experts, fellowships, and various other forms of technical assistance. Each less developed region now has a United Nations statistical adviser. Considerable efforts were made to promote standardization in the 1960 census round.

The United Nations encourages governments to carry out sample surveys and, in cooperation with the specialized agencies, it is now publishing a "Handbook on Household Enquiries," designed to standardize the approach to measurement of living conditions. The United Nations itself has carried out relatively few sample surveys and has no regular machinery for that purpose (although the establishment of United Nations regional sample survey centers has been suggested on several occasions). I would draw your attention in passing to one problem of conducting sample surveys in economically less developed countries: many of these countries have small populations, around one or two million or less, but the size of the sample that is statistically required in a survey of, say, literacy does not drop with the size of the country. As a result, a sample survey in a small economically underdeveloped country is apt to be much more expensive, as a percentage of the national budget or national income, than a sample survey in the United States.

PROBLEMS OF ANALYSIS

In quantitative international research that is concerned with correlations and with trends of various indices, it is necessary to reach a compromise between the ideal and the feasible. It is not too difficult to draw up a list of ideally desirable indicators to use in such research. Reliable data, however, will not be found for most of these indicators on an international basis. There is also a temptation, as I have suggested above, to seize on all the data available, without discrimination, and pour them into charts, formulas, or computer machines, hoping that errors will cancel each other out. We consider it a better policy to make selective use of data for quantitative analyses, employing only those series that are relatively reliable and significant according to informed judgment, and meanwhile to try to build up better data for the future. The *Compendium of Social Statistics,* recently issued by the United Nations in cooperation with ILO, FAO, UNESCO, and WHO, contains series that are considered by specialists from those organizations to be relatively reliable today.[8] The "Handbook of Household Enquiries," along with other endeavors mentioned above, represents an effort to build up better data in the future.

Selection of data on the basis of reliability alone, however, can lead, paradoxically, to quite erroneous conclusions in international quantitative analysis. Since the more reliable data tend to come from the more developed regions, or from atypical countries of underdeveloped regions, generalizations based upon such data will not give adequate weight to the characteristic behavior of variables in less developed regions, which may be quite different from the behavior in the developed regions. Thus, a correlation between two variables—for example, rate of investment and rate of economic growth—may be valid only for industrialized countries.[9] Problems of this kind can be dealt with by selecting

8. See *Compendium of Social Statistics: 1963* (United Nations publication, Sales No. 63.XVII.3). The United Nations' regular "Reports on the World Social Situation" have been based from the beginning upon selective use of quantitative data. The *Compendium* was issued as a statistical supplement to the 1963 *Report on the World Social Situation.*

9. A recent (as yet unpublished) study of the Economic Commission for Europe has shown that for 22 European countries, as a group, the (linear) coefficient correlation between rates of capital input and rates of expansion of domestic product over the period 1949–59 was practically insignificant (0.20); but if the less industrial European economies were excluded—and also Norway which had a very high investment ratio and a low rate of growth—then the correlation for the remaining 13 industrial countries is 0.69.

for use in analysis indices that have wide availability in less developed regions (in a given circumstance, it may be necessary to weigh availability against reliability in choosing an index), by making separate analyses for developed and less developed regions, and by using every kind of available evidence, statistical and nonstatistical, in making generalizations and reaching conclusions.

It must be acknowledged that even in the case of the better statistics, international comparisons still represent only rough approximations today, as far as the measurement of levels of living is concerned. The figures give the illusion of a precision that does not exist. It is perhaps unfortunate that some system of quantification has not been developed that is midway between ordinary language and ordinary statistics in the degree of precision implied.[10]

By and large the prospects for satisfactory international comparability are greater for statistics concerned with certain easily definable material objects (radios, telephones, automobiles, etc.) and with elementary and universal biological facts (birth, death, age, sex) than with broader or more aggregative categories that involve culturally diverse manifestations. Thus, while it may be difficult to get good comparative figures on use of radio sets because of deficiencies in statistics derived from licensing, manufacturing, and sales, there is no inherent conceptual problem of any magnitude here. If, however, we try to measure such a factor as "recreation" on an international scale (to take an extreme example), we encounter at once formidable problems of (a) defining the contents of coverage of this concept from a multinational or multicultural perspective, and (b) devising a method of measurement that will handle the diversity of contents. One result of this situation is that functional categories which are highly important for analysis are likely to be least advanced in comparative quantification.

10. Efforts of this kind have been made in some United Nations publications through the device of listing countries in five or six broad categories, with regard to particular variables like per capita national income in dollar terms, instead of (or in addition to) giving the specific statistics for each country. See the 1961 *Report on the World Social Situation*, Chap. 3, in this connection.

When problems of definition of coverage and of conversion to a single scale of measurement rule out the possibility, at least at present, of directly measuring a basic function or value that is important for social analysis and for policy planning, it may still be possible, however, to use one or two simple and manageable indicators that stand in a close relation to the function or value in question. The indicator may measure some outstanding feature of the more complex, aggregate concept, or stand in the relationship of cause (or means) or effect to it. Thus we have today no satisfactory method of comparative international measurement of level of industrialization, in the sense of an index that sums up the totality of this concept in each country and at the same time is available for a large number of countries. We do have, however, a fairly widely available and reliable index in the form of per capita consumption of mechanical energy, which appears to have high correlation with level of industrialization as a whole.

Similarly, it is not possible to measure "good health" directly; but one can measure expectation of life and (age-specific) mortality rates.[11] Without too much difficulty, international figures can be obtained on hospital beds and doctors, factors that stand in a relationship of cause or means to good health. Hospital beds and doctors per 100,000 population (or population per hospital bed or doctor) have been extensively used not only as indicators of health but

11. Crude mortality rates are much more widely available than age-specific rates but can be quite misleading for comparative purposes, since a country with low fertility and relatively few children (and therefore relatively many old people) will have a substantially higher overall mortality rate than a country with high fertility, numerous children, and therefore proportionately few old people, even if health conditions are otherwise exactly the same in the two countries. It should be noted in passing that age structure needs to be taken into account in a number of other international indices. This is done in regard to calorie consumption by relating consumption to requirements in terms of adult equivalents in the total population. But in other cases, as in comparative analysis of per capita national income, difference in age structure is commonly overlooked, although it is foolish to assume that infants should produce (or consume) as much as adults. The seriousness of differences in age structure is illustrated by the fact that in less developed countries some 40 per cent or more of the population are below fifteen years of age, while in industrialized countries only 25 to 30 per cent are below fifteen years as a rule.

also as central indices in target-setting in national health planning. In practice, hospital beds and doctors are often maldistributed in a country, with the majority of the doctors frequently found crowding the capital city and hardly any in those parts of the countryside where disease is most rampant. In view also of differences in quality of medical services, and the fact that improved health or new theories of therapy can lead to a decrease in required hospital services (for example, by control of tuberculosis and consequent reduction of sanitariums, or reduction of occupancy of hospital beds by mental patients through use of new tranquilizing drugs and new theories of community and family care), it must be concluded that international comparisons on the basis of hospitals or doctors per hundred thousand population have limited validity. Much attention has been given internationally to questions of this kind concerning the value of various indicators of functions that are themselves difficult to measure directly.

COMPARATIVE MEASUREMENT OF RATES OF DEVELOPMENT

In comparative analysis of social and economic development it is essential to study not only levels but also rates of development. This is a matter that is little understood, although growth rates are frequently compared. It is often stated, for example, that the gap in income and levels of living between the more developed and the less developed countries has been widening in recent years. This is not true—at least not unless a number of qualifications are made. The gap in health has been narrowing rapidly. In education it has remained about the same. As far as per capita income is concerned, the answer depends upon the definition of developed and less developed countries and, as indicated above, upon the definition of per capita income: the fastest growing countries in the 1950–60 decade were for the most part countries in the middle range of income, like Israel, Japan, Greece, Yugoslavia, and various eastern European countries; and the average rate of growth of developed or underdeveloped countries as a group will vary significantly according to where these middle range countries are classified.[12]

It should not be assumed that in each factor or sector of growth countries at different levels should normally grow at the same rate, just as one should not expect children aged 16–18 to grow as rapidly in height as children aged 12–14.[13] Health improves rapidly at the lower levels, as a result of the efficiency of modern controls over contagious diseases, but quite slowly at the higher levels where progress is blocked by the intractable degenerative diseases, particularly cancer and heart disease. Industry appears to grow slowly at first, more rapidly later.

In the case of aggregate measures, reported rates of development will be affected by the nature and composition of the aggregate, since different aspects or elements may normally move at different speeds. Thus, as mentioned above, because industry generally grows faster than agriculture, the relative weighting attached in practice to these two sectors in the measure of national production will affect the reported overall rate of growth.

Growth rates in economic and social development are usually given in the form of a percentage increase over a time period (or by the index method which is closely related) : for example, annual percentage increase in population, national production, personal income, cost of living, food consumption, hospital beds, etc. Yet growth need not always be measured this way. We do not measure the growth of children, for example, by percentage increases but by absolute increments (inches).

The percentage increase method is appropriate when the significance of an increment is relative to its base. This condition will obtain when the size of the base affects the perceived magnitude or the value of the increment to the individual concerned, in accordance with the Weber–Fechner

12. It also depends on whether Mainland China is included, with a weighting according to its population size.

13. See *Report on the World Social Situation* (United Nations publication, Sales No. 61.IV.4), pp. 43–46.

function. For example, $10 added to an income of $100 is more significant to the individual than $10 added to $10,000 (although there is no logical reason, from the point of view solely of significance to a recipient, why $10 added to $100 should represent exactly the same rate of growth as $1,000 added to $10,000 or $10,000 added to $100,000—income tax laws do not make this assumption). The condition also obtains when the base itself generates the increment: for example, a population generates its own increase, and a population that is twice as big as another will, other things being equal, generate an increment that is exactly twice as big. There are various circumstances in which neither of these conditions obtains. Thus, an additional year of life at the age of thirty is not less significant than an additional year at the age of twenty or ten; and years of life do not generate years of life. Hence, it would not make sense to measure health improvement by percentage increase in life expectancy.

The percentage increase approach is quite inapplicable in the case of social indices that are themselves percentages, such as literacy rates or indices giving rates per 1,000, per 100,000, etc. From 1951 to 1961, literacy in India increased from 17 per cent to 24 per cent. In terms of percentage increase, this would be a gain of 41 per cent. But the battle against illiteracy advanced by only 8 per cent, down from 83 per cent illiterate to 76 per cent illiterate. Similar paradoxes arise if increases in mortality rates are recorded in terms of percentage gains. Furthermore, when we are dealing with a basic value like literacy, we cannot assume that some individuals are more important and significant than other individuals, depending on the size of the base—an assumption that would have to be made if the same increment in literacy is given a much higher numerical growth value at one place on a scale (e.g. at the 17 per cent level moving to 24 per cent) than at another (e.g. at the 50 per cent level moving to 57 per cent). In general, it is a good rule in cases of this kind not to measure growth by percentages of percentages, but by percentage points. The literacy advance in India is thus better stated as an advance of 7 percentage points.[14]

An example of how different conclusions can be reached in international analysis with different methods of measuring rates of development may be taken from the field of urbanization, defined in terms of the percentage of the population living in localities of a given size or above. By the percentage increase method, the less developed countries, which have a small proportion of their populations in cities, are urbanizing much more rapidly than the developed countries. By the percentage points method, however, urbanization has been taking place at roughly the same rate in the industrialized and the less developed countries, that is, about the same proportion of the population has been shifting from rural to urban residence in given time periods. The rates of urban growth (growth of urban population, as distinguished from urbanization) have been less marked in the industrialized countries because of the preexisting size of the urban base and the slower overall population growth. At the same time, in these countries there has been a marked slowing down or actual decline in the already small rural population, with as much as 15 per cent of the total labor force shifting out of agriculture in the decade 1950–60 in some instances. These considerations lead to the conclusion that the economically developed nations have been undergoing structural change as rapidly as the so-called "developing countries"; this is a conclusion quite different from that obtained if we measure rate of urbanization by percentages of percentages, which would yield figures identical with rates of urban growth, in the absence of natural increase and immigration. Conclusions regarding comparative rates of industrialization and growth of

14. To give a proper quantitative picture of progress in literacy in India, however, it is essential also to present the absolute figures. While the percentage of literates rose from 17 to 24 between 1951 and 1961, the number of illiterates at the same time rose by about 15 million owing to rapid population increase, and the number of illiterates will continue to rise for the next 25 to 30 years at the present rates of literacy advance and population growth. Various other examples from less developed countries and from fields other than literacy can be given of advance in terms of percentages, or of averages, and regression in terms of absolutes. This leads to fundamental questions as to what we really mean by "social progress."

other factors similarly depend upon the method of measuring rate of growth.

INTERNAL DISCONTINUITIES

One of the weaknesses of many international indicators of levels of living is their failure to reveal internal distribution patterns. This is particularly true of indicators expressed by statistical averages, like the per capita national income. Those expressed by percentages, like the literacy rate, give somewhat more of an indication of distribution. A distribution curve indicating what percentage of the population gets what amount of income would be greatly preferable to a national average, but data of this kind are rarely available. Even in the most industrialized countries, as Titmuss has recently pointed out,[15] income distribution figures are open to various interpretations. In the less developed countries, most of which have "dual economies" (traditional and modern), it is extremely difficult to define and measure income distribution; international work on this subject is at a preliminary and exploratory phase.

The existence of dual economies and dual cultures means that most problems of international comparability also turn up, to a greater or lesser degree, within countries. The existence of an internal discontinuity that cannot be bridged by the use of a unified scale does not, of course, necessitate the abandonment of a quantitative approach. If there are contrasting types or categories not on a continuum, then the percentage of the population involved in each type can generally be indicated, and separate quantitative indices can be set up for measurement within each type. For example, if it turns out eventually that the per capita national income cannot really bridge the gap between market and subsistence economies, it may nevertheless be possible to indicate the percentage of the population engaged in subsistence activities and to quantify production and consumption levels

15. Richard M. Titmuss, *Income Distribution and Social Change* (London, George Allen and Unwin Ltd., 1962).

within the framework of the subsistence society without resort to monetary evaluation.

HISTORICAL DEVELOPMENT OF QUANTITATIVE SOCIAL RESEARCH IN THE UNITED NATIONS

The first effort by the United Nations involving substantial comparative analysis was the *Preliminary Report on the World Social Situation,* issued in 1952, which concentrated on the question of standards of living and employed various quantitative measures for assessing social conditions in the different countries. This was followed by a *Report on International Definition and Measurement of Levels of Living,* issued in 1954, which dealt with the conceptual problems of such measurement in more detail. A major conclusion of the latter report was that levels of living in different countries could not be measured by any single synthetic or aggregate indicator, particularly the per capita national income. I will not repeat the arguments that led to this conclusion beyond remarking that a number of basic human values—the life of a child, for example—lie outside the market place and cannot be given a monetary equivalent.

A related conclusion was that the level of living from an international point of view must be conceived of as a set of components which are in varying degree measurable through selected indicators. In spite of problems of cultural relativity, it did not prove too difficult to get agreement internationally on these components. The very structure of the international organizations reflects international values: for example, health, education, nutrition, etc. The technical problems of deciding upon appropriate indicators have proved much more difficult.[16]

If measurement of the level of living is to be carried out through a set of separate indicators, it follows that the

16. In the revised report on *International Definition and Measurement of Levels of Living,* issued in 1961, the basic components of the level of living were maintained (health, food consumption and nutrition, education, employment and conditions of work, housing, social security, clothing, recreation and entertainment, human freedoms); but certain modifications were made in the indicators.

social development of any particular country at any given time will constitute a pattern or profile. These patterns can be compared. Normal patterns can be empirically established so that it will be possible to judge whether an individual country is grossly out of line, compared with other countries. Its health situation, for example, may be substantially worse than would be expected, given the level of national income, education, etc.; or the country may be much less advanced in sectors that generate income than in social development.

These questions were taken up in our 1961 *Report on the World Social Situation.* In this report we developed certain techniques for comparative quantitative analysis of patterns of development. The results have proved quite interesting from a policy point of view. There are various ways in which a less developed country with scarce resources can reach decisions on the allocation of those resources for the purpose of development. One way is for countries to look outside their own frontiers and seek guidance from the experience of other countries in comparable situations. Comparative analysis of development patterns facilitates this process. There is substantial evidence that countries turning out to be "unbalanced" in terms of these quantitative techniques have had serious practical difficulties, including political unrest, when the social indicators are significantly behind the economic indicators.

The 1961 *Report on the World Social Situation* stressed the urgent need for basic research to improve our knowledge of the strategy of social development and the methods of social planning in connection with economic planning. A new institute, called the United Nations Research Institute for Social Development, has just been established for this purpose, on the basis of a grant of one million dollars from the Government of the Netherlands. The Institute will undertake research on patterns and models of development, including social projections and prognostications, the methodology of social planning in connection with economic planning and criteria for decision making, and methods of introducing social change in the economically less developed countries and of motivating the population for change and development.

The institute, with a life term of three to five years, will be dedicated to intensive and, we hope, pioneering research on these questions. It will be located in Geneva and will supplement the work of our headquarters social research staff as well as relevant work carried out by the specialized agencies. Its results will feed into the United Nations system—at the central level, at the regional level where new institutes of economic and social planning are now being established in association with the regional economic and social commissions, and at the national level where the demand for technical assistance and advice on social development policy far exceeds our knowledge and resources.

24. International Action to Advance Comparative Research: The Role of UNESCO

STEIN ROKKAN, THE MICHELSEN INSTITUTE, BERGEN

The UNESCO program in the social sciences is still very much in need of detailed review. It has proved difficult to organize a coherent scheme of action in these sciences and there has been an unfortunate tendency to heed a variety of ad hoc requests for action while neglecting the need to ensure long-term planning and to maintain continuing cumulative activities. I believe it is time to work out such a long-term program and I shall try to set out in this brief note what I judge to be its basic elements.[1]

As I see it, the UNESCO program in the social sciences should serve three basic needs:

1. UNESCO must help to *internationalize the disciplines* through aid to the professional organizations, through improvements in the exchange of documentation and information, and, particularly, through the advancement of comparative research across differing nations and cultures.

2. UNESCO must help to *spread social science knowledge and social science skills* to the developing countries and to

1. This chapter is a composite of several memoranda originally prepared for the Norwegian National Commission for UNESCO and for the Secretary-General of the International Social Science Council. Similar arguments have already been advanced in my article "The Development of Cross-National Comparative Research: A Review of Current Problems and Possibilities," *Social Sciences Information, 1* (1962), 21–38.

organize the necessary facilities for continuing social science services in such countries.

3. UNESCO must use the resources of the social sciences in *planning and guiding its own activities* and, quite particularly, assemble, evaluate, and analyze a wide variety of data of importance in its efforts to spread education, culture, science, and mass media facilities throughout the nations of the world.

All these needs are recognized in the current program of the Department of Social Sciences but much more should be done to link up the different lines of activity and to ensure greater coordination in the planning and execution of the sequences of projects.

UNESCO is uniquely placed to provide initiatives and to stimulate action to strengthen the foundations for an internationalization of social science research. In the abstract sciences of nature, UNESCO can concentrate its efforts on the establishment of international channels of information exchange, on training, and on applications to practical problems of worldwide concern: knowledge established in one country can generally be applied in all others without regard to political frontiers and cultural traditions.

In the social sciences the situation is essentially different: what has been found in one country is not necessarily valid for others, and problems of comparative analysis and inference become crucial. UNESCO has a major responsibility for the advancement of research on problems of cross-national and cross-cultural comparisons, and it is of great importance that the Department of Social Sciences establish a long-term program of activities toward this end. The Organization cannot content itself with the dissemination and application of what is already known and established; in the sciences of man, it must also endeavor to improve the foundations for such practical utilization of methods and findings. This is a long-range task that cannot be accomplished simply by encouraging international congresses and exchanging bibliographical information. The great bulk of the current work in the social and behavioral sciences is limited to one nation and one culture. Only a scattering of attempts, mainly in demography and the economics of growth, have been made to come to grips with the fascinating problems of methodology and logic encountered in the comparison of data and of findings across several nations or cultures. UNESCO has clearly a major role to play in encouraging and facilitating such attempts at systematic comparison. Indeed, it may be argued that a sustained effort in this direction is a conditio sine qua non for the success of the Organization's other activities in the social sciences: its projects for the training of social scientists for the developing countries as well as its attempts to establish a broader basis for its own action program through systematic data gathering and analysis.

UNESCO could make a major contribution to the internationalization of the social sciences through the development of a long-term program of exchanges and coordinating activities designed to advance cross-national and cross-cultural comparative research. Other UN agencies have made great progress in the collection, standardization, and evaluation of specific categories of international statistics, but UNESCO has, in addition to its proper standardization tasks, a unique function to fulfill within the UN family in ensuring effective and systematic cooperation among the intergovernmental agencies, the public and the private research organizations, and the academic research workers engaged in comparative data gathering and analysis. The Statistical Office of the UN, the ILO, the FAO, and a number of other specialized agencies have made concerted efforts over several years to improve the comparability of a variety of categories of official statistics and to evaluate national statistical information for purposes of comparison. UNESCO has itself been directly concerned with similar efforts in the field of education, cultural products, and mass communication.

What has been lacking so far is an organ for liaison between these various administrative bodies and the increasing number of academic social scientists concerned with the advancement of the methodology and theory of comparative social research. There has been a marked expansion in recent years of academic and theory-oriented research activities centering on cross-societal comparisons, not only within economics and anthropology, but also in psychology, sociology, and political science. A variety of scattered efforts have been made to organize international cooperation in this field, but so far nothing has been done to develop a central organ for the promotion of such endeavors. UNESCO has a distinct function to fulfill in this field, a function which only UNESCO, with its emphasis on the advancement of international science, can fulfill within the present constellation of UN agencies.

To implement such long-term activities UNESCO can rely primarily on its network of international social science associations. A central role could be taken by interdisciplinary bodies such as the International Social Science Council and its closely affiliated International Committee on Social Science Documentation.

The International Social Science Council is in the midst of a series of discussions of priorities in its program of activities for the years to come. Personally, I would strongly emphasize two considerations in deciding on such priorities: (1) the Council must contribute to and not duplicate the work of national research organizations; (2) the Council must stress common denominators in the problems facing several social science disciplines and avoid duplication of the work of the international associations in each discipline. I am personally convinced that the Council would be able to make its most telling contribution if it concentrated its activities on the advancement of comparative cross-national and cross-cultural research. This will make it possible for the Council not only to add a new dimension to the work of national organizations but also to focus attention on problems which cut across the traditional divisions between social science disciplines.

National research organizations will only rarely be equipped to carry out long-term comparative inquiries. It is true that institutions and organizations in the larger countries, particularly in the United States, have pioneered important comparative research enterprises. It is enough to mention the Human Relations Area Files at Yale University, the many programs of comparative research on economic growth, the pioneering studies by Karl Deutsch and his associates on "social mobilization," by David McClelland on "achievement orientation" and entrepreneurship, by Gabriel Almond and Seymour Martin Lipset on the socioeconomic conditions of political development. But such national efforts will not take us far toward a systematic coverage of the relevant data unless they are integrated into a framework of international cooperative arrangements. This is where the International Social Science Council can make a real contribution. The Council can act as a clearinghouse for current efforts to organize comparative research, facilitate the coordination of current studies, encourage the development of common international standards for the collection, classification, and analysis of data, and generally serve as a forum for the discussion of problems in the theory and methodology of cross-national and cross-cultural surveys.

No other internationally organized professional body has as yet taken on this task. The disciplinary associations in the social sciences have developed a few specific programs of comparative research. Probably the most successful of these has been the extensive series of investigations of occupational rankings and mobility rates sponsored by the International Sociological Association.[2] But problems of comparison clearly cut across a variety of disciplines. The cross-cultural analysis techniques developed by the anthropologists have proved useful and relevant in the work of social psychologists and political scientists. The current efforts to standardize census-taking and labor statistics are of equal interest to demographers, economists, and sociologists. Experts from a variety of disciplines—economists and political scientists no less than social psychologists—have cooperated in scattered efforts to exploit the potentialities of sample

2. See the brief account in my introductory chapter to this volume, pp. 10 f.; and also Chap. 9 by Thomas Fox and S. M. Miller.

surveys in cooperative cross-national research. The problems of data gathering, analysis, and interpretation raised in comparative research concern all the social sciences together and should, therefore, be the immediate concern of an interdisciplinary body such as the International Social Science Council.

The need for action to advance comparative research has already been recognized in UNESCO's program. The General Assembly of UNESCO at its Eleventh Session in 1960 adopted a Program Resolution (3.42[c]) authorizing the Director-General "to facilitate the study of basic theories and concept, as well as of methods and techniques, in cross-cultural social science research, and to publish or arrange for the publication of the results." At its Twelfth Session in 1962 the General Assembly reaffirmed this resolution and provided funds for further exploratory work. At its Thirteenth Session in the autumn of 1964 the Assembly approved a proposal drawn up in the UNESCO Secretariat to expand this line of activity and to develop a long-term plan for further action to advance comparative cross-national and cross-cultural research. This is a significant innovation in the UNESCO program for the Social Sciences. It is of vital importance that these efforts be given the fullest possible support by national no less than by international organizations active in the fields of the social sciences.

A series of projects designed to advance comparative cross-national research is currently under consideration through cooperative arrangements between the UNESCO Department of Social Sciences, the International Social Science Council (ISSC), and the International Committee on Social Science Documentation (ICSSD). Several of these projects are likely to prove of direct benefit in furthering the general aims of UNESCO and it will therefore be of importance, in planning the program of activities for the second half of the 1960s, to review in some detail the ways in which these projects tie in with other concerns in UNESCO's program.

We may conveniently distinguish five lines of action under

the current resolution on the advancement of comparative research.

1. Documentation and clearing house activities.
2. Advancement of the methodology of comparisons.
3. Confrontations of data and findings for different countries.
4. Advancement of training in cross-national comparative analysis.
5. Planning and execution of joint international inquiries.

Among the projects under (1), *Documentation,* two are likely to prove of direct interest in other sections of UNESCO's program. One concerns the organization of a series of *Guides to Data for Comparative Research.* The first volume of an *International Guide to Electoral Statistics* will be printed in 1967; it covers 15 countries in Western Europe. An *International Guide to Mass Media Statistics,* planned for 1967–69, will probably go into several volumes. Similarly conceived guides have been suggested for data on voluntary associations, on religious bodies, and on the recruitment of personnel to the scientific and cultural professions; these might all become extremely useful tools for those who need to evaluate cross-national information. A series of *Manuals of International Standards of Data Collection and Classification* has also been planned. This will again help to coordinate efforts in several fields and ensure closer links between the statisticians in the U.N. family and the academic research workers currently concerned with the advancement of systematic comparisons.

Several of the projects planned under (2), *Methodology,* and (3), *Substantive Comparisons,* will also prove of immediate interest to the policy planners and program executors in UNESCO. Much information on educational characteristics, on cultural attainments and orientations, on the spread and impact of mass media can only be assembled and systematized country by country through the techniques of the sample survey. It should be of immediate interest to UNESCO to ensure full access to such data through the development of regional networks of data archives. Work on problems of classification and computer retrieval of such data currently under way in the United States and in Europe has been discussed in detail with scholars from many countries at a conference sponsored by UNESCO in 1964.[3] It is strongly recommended that UNESCO follow up this work in the years to come and take the necessary initiatives to develop a joint classification scheme and clearinghouse operation for the archives set up in different parts of the world for the storage and processing of such data.

Similar action should also be considered for other types of cross-national and cross-cultural data of potential importance in comparative studies. Here it is quite particularly recommended that action be taken to encourage efforts by scholars in several countries to develop classification and retrieval systems for information on tribes and other population units in the developing areas of the world. An international conference of anthropologists, sociologists, and social psychologists particularly concerned with advancing comparative research should be organized to provide the necessary guidance in this work.

Such archives will be particularly useful for UNESCO's own efforts because they will allow detailed analysis of conditions for the success of educational programs, the spread of cultural organizations and mass media, and the recruitment of skilled personnel. Data for country after country show marked contrasts in educational and cultural conditions between the central, advanced areas of the national territory and the peripheral, less developed provinces. Much of importance for UNESCO's action in the developing countries of the world can be learned through detailed studies of center–periphery contrasts in the advanced countries. In fact, two of the international conferences sponsored by UNESCO in 1963 and 1964 concentrated on problems in the analysis of such contrasts: one, emphasizing problems of methodology

3. See the report by Stein Rokkan on the Second Conference on Data Archives in the Social Sciences, Paris, September 1964, in *Social Sciences Information, 4* (1965), 67–84.

and theory, was held at Yale University in September 1963, and the other, centered on such contrasts in the countries of Latin America, met in Buenos Aires in the autumn of 1964. It is strongly recommended that efforts along these lines be followed up for other regions of the world and be tied in directly with UNESCO's concern to improve our knowledge of the conditions favoring or hindering the spread of "active" literacy, the use of mass media, and the establishment of cultural organizations in the least developed areas of each nation.

The projects under (4), *Training in Comparative Analysis,* deserve particular attention. UNESCO's efforts to train social science personnel in developing countries raise a number of methodological and practical problems of cross-national comparison: How can social science techniques be transferred from one country to another? What can be done to ensure uniform application of given procedures across the several countries in one region? How can social scientists acquire practice in collating, evaluating, and drawing conclusions from data assembled for countries other than their own? Clearly to make these programs efficient much more emphasis must be given in the future to the comparative approach. But this means that the teachers from the advanced countries must themselves have some practice in comparative analysis, and opportunities for such practice are often lacking at the national universities. To train a corps of specialists in comparative analysis it is clearly essential to work both within advanced regions and within developing regions. This is in fact the rationale behind the initiative taken in 1963 to organize a series of "summer courses in comparative survey analysis": the first of these, convened at the request of the UNESCO Commission of the German Federal Republic, was limited to comparisons within Europe, but subsequent ones will provide opportunities for training in the comparison of data collected for other regions of the world. Here efforts must be made to link up the concerns of sociologists and social psychologists in advancing comparative sample surveys with the interests of anthropologists in cross-cultural analyses based on observations. The best way to encourage such a rapprochement would perhaps be by way of intensive training courses in the use of different types of archived data. It is recommended that plans be developed for such training courses in the future.

The current UNESCO program does not provide funds for *the organization and execution of joint international inquiries*—projects falling under category (5). In the early years of activity UNESCO took several such initiatives, the most notable of which was no doubt the nine-country survey of *How Nations See Each Other.* Such international ventures are very costly, however, and it seems likely that UNESCO will spend its limited funds more efficiently by offering systematic encouragement of such ventures rather than by financing them from scratch. The ISSC has a particularly important role to play here. The European Center for Coordination of Research and Documentation in the Social Sciences, established under ISSC auspices in Vienna in 1963, has taken a number of imaginative steps to mobilize the interests of scholars and institutes in different countries in joint data gathering ventures. To illustrate its success to date in securing national support for such operations, it is enough to mention the current comparative studies of public opinion on disarmament (Stoetzel, Galtung et al.) and of industrialization and changes in time budgets (Szalai, Scheuch, Friis et al.). There is every reason to expect that, once a broad scheme of activities has been launched by UNESCO, the ISSC, and the ICSSD, scholars in many countries will find this a suitable basis for further endeavors and seek sponsorship for projects to be financed from separate sources.

UNESCO needs the support of social scientists from all parts of the world if it is to succeed in these endeavors. At the International Conference convened at Yale University in September 1963, the scholars assembled were asked to review the proposals currently under consideration and to work out their own set of recommendations for further action. The recommendations comprise the concluding chapter of this volume.

25. Recommendations of the Yale Data Conference

INTERNATIONAL ACTION TO FACILITATE ACCESS TO SOCIAL SCIENCE DATA FOR COMPARATIVE ANALYSIS

The Conference agreed that access to survey and other data for secondary analysis on the broadest possible basis will lead to significant advances in the social sciences. Therefore, the Conference commended the International Social Science Council (ISSC), the International Committee on Social Science Documentation (ICSSD), and UNESCO on their efforts: (1) to make existing survey and other data available for secondary analysis in area, comparative, and international research; (2) to increase communication among scholars and institutions working with such data; and (3) to help in the establishment of repositories and analysis centers for such kinds of information. In addition to the recommendations passed by the international meetings of experts in La Napoule in 1962 and in Cologne in 1963, the Conference agreed upon a series of specific recommendations.

The Conference emphasized the importance of integrating two main functions of social science research facilities, both within nations and among nations: (1) the *repository function,* which concerns the storage and classification of a wide variety of material as a service for a large outside clientele;

(2) the *analysis function,* which includes the assembling, evaluating, and processing of specific bodies of data of immediate interest to a broad community of scholars and students. In time, the materials and facilities generated by the data processing and analysis functions are expected to grow at least to the scale of those required for the gathering and storage of raw data.

The Conference distinguished the following specific problems in the organization of systems of cooperating among data centers:

1. *Solicitation and Acquisition of Data for Storage.* The Conference recommends a rational division of labor among archives to insure: (a) adequate coverage of surveys which may be useful for secondary analysis purposes, including commercial surveys as well as those sponsored by government agencies, universities, and research institutions; (b) avoiding competition for exclusive storage of and control over data. A flexible division of labor among repositories should be arranged by cultural and political areas and/or by topics. Consideration should be given to the preservation of such original documents as questionnaires—in addition to the punch cards, tapes, and other forms of coded information—in those cases where these materials are of special interest for research. The analytical tools developed in working with such data in secondary analysis (e.g. scales) should also be preserved.

2. *Editing, Standardization, and Evaluation.* The Conference recommends the development of standards for the storage and processing of source material from surveys. Such standards shall specify: (a) which types of studies should be given priority in storage; (b) the degree of detail in information on sampling, field procedures, coding, and the quality checks pertaining thereto; (c) the checks applied to punch cards. Information about the quality checks should be made readily available to the originators of surveys as one means to increase the quality of survey research and of internationally comparable statistics. Recommendations should be developed to increase the standardization of coding proce-

dures, of the format of punch cards and tapes, and of computer programs and instructions, in order to facilitate the use of modern data processing equipment in analysis. Close communication is urged among the various repositories, data analysis centers, and area specialists in evaluating the methodological quality of data and in providing guidance for future users in problems of data interpretation.

3. *Cooperation Among Centers Storing and Processing Different Categories of Data.* The Conference stresses the importance of arrangements for regular communication among institutions dealing with different types of data: those collecting primarily survey data, those concentrating on official statistics, and those preserving materials not normally collected by libraries and historical archives. The need for a combination of methods is particularly pressing in comparative analysis, and steps should be taken to insure that users of one type of data be made aware of and be supplied with supplementary information from various sources. The Conference urges the consideration of ways in which national statistical organizations (including census bureaus) could make samples of national data available to scholars.

4. *Relation to Universities and Academic Centers for Advanced Research.* It is recommended that close connections be established among data centers and universities and other institutions for advanced research where appropriate programs of social science research exist.

5. *International Cooperation, Clearinghouse Functions, and Data Retrieval Arrangements.* The Conference urges all data and analysis centers, and combinations of such institutions, to make their collections available to scholars on the freest possible and most economical basis.

The Conference urges ISSC, ICSSD, and UNESCO, in liaison with WAPOR and other interested organizations, to continue their efforts to develop an international system of cooperation in the establishment and operation of data repositories, data analysis centers, and data retrieval arrangements. In determining the form of international cooperation among data centers, preference is to be given to arrangements that will promote participation of countries with different political and cultural systems, at different stages of development.

The development of data retrieval systems especially adapted to the needs of data centers using modern data processing equipment is to be actively supported. The ultimate aim is to establish a common language for retrieval, or a series of compatible languages.

6. *Meetings of Experts on Problems of Data Archives.* The Conference endorses the proposal of a meeting to take place in Europe in 1964 on problems mentioned in points (1) to (5) of Part I of this resolution. A special panel of experts should work on the systems of information retrieval for archives.

TRAINING IN COMPARATIVE ANALYSIS

The Conference welcomes the initiative taken by UNESCO and the University of Cologne in organizing the first training Seminar for Users of Survey Research in Europe. It emphasizes the need for similar series of training programs in all the social sciences at different institutions in the use and mathematical processing of raw quantitative data such as: survey data, aggregate statistics, systematic anthropological data, materials for content analysis, data for the study of elites, etc. In particular, the conference asks the International Social Science Council to develop a program for the training of historians in techniques of systematic comparative analysis of this kind. Such initiatives will be of great importance for any effort to insure *time depth* in the collections, and to build up series of data for the comparative analysis of processes of change.

DOCUMENTARY GUIDES AND RELATED TOOLS FOR COMPARATIVE RESEARCH

To facilitate further cross-national comparisons, the Conference specifically recommends that UNESCO—in close cooperation with the United Nations and its appropriate specialized agencies, as well as with the ISSC and the ICSSD—take steps to prepare a series of guides and manuals for the research workers and students concerned:

–guides to past data, by topics and/or areas

–inventories of current data production, particularly survey data

–guides to analytical indicators and other measures useful in comparisons, as well as to advanced methods of data analysis and processing

–manuals on classifications used in survey research, particularly so-called background variables, and their significance and comparability

The Conference finally urges that any work undertaken on historical time series data country by country should be combined with inventories of source locations to determine the need for microeditions or offset reproductions of rare statistical publications and other documents likely to be necessary for developing data analysis centers in further time depth.

ACTION TO PROMOTE SUBSTANTIVE RESEARCH

The Conference commends the Yale Political Data Program for its efforts to assemble and evaluate aggregate national statistics for computer analysis. It expresses the hope that the United Nations and its appropriate agencies will facilitate further work with such data through the provision of country data on punch cards, tape, or in other forms to any university or equivalent research center for use in such analysis.

The Conference specifically urges the ISSC, the United Nations, UNESCO, and other appropriate agencies to take steps to improve the quality and availability of data on within-nation distributions of important indicators of regional social, economic, civic, educational, and cultural development by means of sample surveys and other forms of evidence.

The Conference welcomes the initiative taken by the ISSC,

UNESCO, and the Argentine government in launching the first of a series of area-specific conferences on regional imbalances. It expresses its satisfaction with the offer of the Indian Statistical Institute to participate in the organization of a follow-up conference on South Asia. The Conference recommends that steps be taken in the years to come to organize similar symposia for the Mediterranean area, North Africa, and Tropical Africa. These efforts should parallel the work on the production of topical and regional guides to data and to indicators, and should contribute decisively to the advancement of comparative research on problems of social, economic, cultural, and political integration—both within and among nations.

Cross-National Research: A Selected Bibliography

ELLEN B. PIRRO, YALE UNIVERSITY

GENERAL AND THEORETICAL WORKS

Allardt, Erik and Yrjö Littunen, eds., *Cleavages, Ideologies and Party Systems*, Helsinki, Westermarck Society, 1964.

Almond, Gabriel A., "A Functional Approach to Comparative Politics," in Gabriel A. Almond and James S. Coleman, eds., *The Politics of the Developing Areas* (Princeton, Princeton University Press, 1960), pp. 3–64.

———, "A Developmental Approach to Political Systems," *World Politics, 17* (1965), 183–215.

Apter, David E., "A Comparative Method for the Study of Politics," *American Journal of Sociology, 64* (1958), 221–37.

———, ed., *Ideology and Discontent*, New York, Free Press of Glencoe, 1964.

Beer, Samuel, "The Analysis of Political Systems," in Samuel Beer, Adam Ulam, et al., *Patterns of Government* (rev. ed., New York, Random House, 1962), pp. 3–72.

Coleman, James S., "The Political Systems of the Developing Areas," in Gabriel A. Almond and James S. Coleman, eds., *The Politics of the Developing Areas* (Princeton, Princeton University Press, 1960), pp. 532–76.

Dahl, Robert A., *Modern Political Analysis*, Englewood Cliffs, Prentice-Hall, 1964.

———, ed. *Political Oppositions in Western Democracies*, New Haven, Yale University Press, 1965.

——— and Charles E. Lindblom, *Politics, Economics and Welfare*, New York, Harper and Row, 1953.

Deutsch, Karl W., *Nationalism and Social Communication*, rev. ed., Cambridge, Massachusetts Institute of Technology Press, 1965.

———, "Toward an Inventory of Basic Trends and Patterns in Comparative and International Politics," *American Political Science Review, 54* (1960), 34–57.

———, "Social Mobilization and Political Development," *American Political Science Review, 55* (1961), 493–515.

Easton, David, *The Political System*, New York, Alfred A. Knopf, 1953.

———, *A Framework for Political Analysis*, Englewood Cliffs, Prentice-Hall, 1965.

———, *A Systems Analysis of Political Life*, New York, Wiley, 1965.

Eckstein, Harry, *A Theory of Stable Democracy*, Princeton, Princeton University Press, 1961.

——— and David E. Apter, eds., *Comparative Politics: A Reader*, New York, Free Press of Glencoe, 1963.

Eisenstadt, S. N., *The Political Systems of Empires*, New York, Free Press of Glencoe, 1963.

Friedrich, Carl, *Man and His Government*, New York, McGraw-Hill, 1963.

———, "The Uses of Anthropological Materials in Political Theory," in E. W. Count and Gordon T. Bowles, eds., *Fact and Theory in Social Science* (Syracuse, Syracuse University Press, 1964), pp. 127–39.

Haas, Ernst, *The Uniting of Europe*, Stanford, Stanford University Press, 1958.

Hagen, Everitt, *On the Theory of Social Change*, Homewood, Ill., Dorsey Press, 1962.

Hirschman, Albert O., *The Strategy of Economic Development*, New Haven, Yale University Press, 1958.

Inkeles, Alex, "National Character and Modern Political Systems," in Francis L. K. Hsu, ed., *Psychological Anthropology: Approaches to Culture and Personality* (Homewood, Ill., Dorsey Press, 1961), pp. 172–208.

Kahin, George, Guy J. Pauker, and Lucian Pye, "Comparative Politics of Non-Western Countries," *American Political Science Review*, *49* (1955), 1022–42.

Katz, Elihu and Paul F. Lazarsfeld, *Personal Influence*, Glencoe, Ill., Free Press, 1955.

Kornhauser, William, *The Politics of Mass Society*, Glencoe, Ill., Free Press, 1959.

Kuznets, S., *Modern Economic Growth: Rate, Structure, and Spread*, New Haven, Yale University Press, 1966.

Lasswell, Harold D., *The Future of Political Science*, New York, Atherton Press, 1963.

———, "The Policy Sciences of Development," *World Politics*, *17* (1965), 286–310.

——— and Abraham Kaplan, *Power and Society*, New Haven, Yale University Press, 1950.

Lazarsfeld, Paul F. and Morris Rosenberg, eds., *The Language of Social Research*, Glencoe, Ill., Free Press, 1955.

Lindzey, Gardner, ed., *Handbook of Social Psychology*, Cambridge, Addison-Wesley, 1959.

Lipset, Seymour Martin, *The First New Nation*, New York, Basic Books, 1963.

———, *Political Man*, New York, Doubleday, 1960.

——— and Reinhard Bendix, *Social Mobility in Industrial Society*, Berkeley, University of California Press, 1959.

Macridis, Roy C., *The Comparative Study of Politics*, New York, Random House, 1955.

——— and Bernard E. Brown, eds., *Comparative Politics: Notes and Readings*, rev. ed., Homewood, Ill., Dorsey Press, 1964.

Moore, F. W., ed., *Readings in Cross-Cultural Methodology*, New Haven, Human Relations Area Files, 1961.

Murdock, George P., "The Cross-Cultural Survey," *American Sociological Review*, *5* (1940), 361–70.

———, *Social Structure*, New York, Macmillan, 1949.

Neumann, Sigmund, "Comparative Politics: A Half Century Appraisal," *Journal of Politics*, *19* (1957), 369–91.

———, ed., *Modern Political Parties*, Chicago, University of Chicago Press, 1956.

Parsons, Talcott, *The Social System*, Glencoe, Ill., Free Press, 1951.

Pye, Lucian W., *Politics, Personality and Nation-Building: Burma's Search for Identity*, New Haven, Yale University Press, 1962.

———, ed., *Communications and Political Development*, Princeton, Princeton University Press, 1963.

——— and Sidney Verba, eds., *Political Culture and Political Development*, Princeton, Princeton University Press, 1965.

Ranney, Austin, ed., *Essays on the Behavioral Study of Politics*, Urbana, University of Illinois Press, 1962.

Rice, Stuart A., *Quantitative Methods in Politics*, New York, Alfred A. Knopf, 1928.

Rokkan, Stein, ed., *Approaches to the Study of Political Participation*, Bergen, Christian Michelsen Institute, 1962.

Rosenau, James, ed., *International Politics and Foreign Policy*, Glencoe, Ill., Free Press, 1961.

Shils, Edward, "Political Development in the New States," *Comparative Studies in Society and History*, *2:4* (1960), 379–411.

Sorokin, Pitirim A., *Social Mobility*, London, Harper, 1927.

Tingsten, Herbert L., *Political Behavior*, London, P. S. King & Sons, 1937.

Wahlke, John C., Heinz Eulau, William Buchanan, and LeRoy Ferguson, *The Legislative System*, New York, Wiley, 1962.

Weber, Max, *Gesammlte Aufsätze zur Sozial-und Wirtschaftsgeschichte*, Tübingen, 1924.

TECHNIQUES OF DATA ANALYSIS

Ackerknecht, E. H., "On the Comparative Method in Anthropology," in R. F. Spencer, ed., *Method and Perspective in Anthropology* (Minneapolis, University of Minnesota Press, 1954), pp. 111–25.

Alker, Hayward R., Jr., *Mathematics and Politics*, New York, Macmillan, 1965.

Banks, Arthur S. and Robert B. Textor, *A Cross-Polity Survey*, Cambridge, Massachusetts Institute of Technology Press, 1963.

Blalock, Hubert M., Jr., *Causal Inferences in Non-experimental Research*, Chapel Hill, University of North Carolina Press, 1964.

Blau, Peter M., "Structural Effects," *American Sociological Review*, *25* (1960), 178–93.

Borko, Harold, ed., *Computer Applications in the Behavioral Sciences*, Englewood Cliffs, Prentice-Hall, 1962.

Cattell, Raymond B., "The Dimensions of Culture Patterns by Factorization of National Characters," *Journal of Abnormal and Social Psychology, 44* (1949), 443–69.

Coleman, James S., *Introduction to Mathematical Sociology*, New York, Free Press of Glencoe, 1964.

Duncan, Otis D., A. Cuzzart, and B. Duncan, *Statistical Geography*, New York, Free Press of Glencoe, 1961.

Fitzgibbon, Russell H., "Measurements of Latin American Political Phenomena: A Statistical Experiment," *American Political Science Review, 45* (1951), 517–23.

Francis, Roy G., "On the Relations of Data to Theory," *Rural Sociology, 22* (1957), 258–66.

Goodman, Leo A., "Ecological Regression and the Behavior of Individuals," *American Sociological Review, 18* (1953), 663–64.

Guetzkow, Harold, et al., *Simulation in International Relations*, Englewood Cliffs, Prentice-Hall, 1963.

Harman, Harry, *Modern Factor Analysis*, Chicago, University of Chicago Press, 1960.

Indian Statistical Institute, *Studies Relating to Planning for National Development, No. 2., Studies on Consumer Behavior*, Calcutta, Indian Statistical Institute, 1959.

Institute of Electoral Research, *Parliaments and Electoral Systems: A World Handbook*, London, 1962.

International Urban Research, *The World's Metropolitan Areas*, Berkeley, University of California Press, 1959.

Lazarsfeld, Paul F. and Allen H. Barton, "Quantitative Measurement in the Social Sciences," in Daniel Lerner and Harold D. Lasswell, eds., *The Policy Sciences* (Stanford, Stanford University Press, 1951), pp. 182–92.

Lucci, Y. and Stein Rokkan, *A Library Center of Survey Research Data*, New York, Columbia University School of Service, 1957.

McEwen, W. J., "Forms and Problems of Validation in Social Anthropology," *Current Anthropology, 4* (1963), 155–83.

Robinson, William S., "Ecological Correlations and the Behavior of Individuals," *American Sociological Review, 15* (1950), 351–57.

Rokkan, Stein, "Archives for Secondary Analysis of Sample Survey Data: An Early Inquiry into the Prospects for Western Europe," *International Social Science Journal, 16* (1964), 49–62.

———, "Introduction: The Use of Sample Surveys in Comparative Research," *International Social Science Journal, 16* (1964), 7–18.

——— and J. Meyriat, eds., *International Guide to Election Statistics*, Paris, Mouton, forthcoming.

Russett, Bruce M. and Hayward R. Alker, Jr., Karl W. Deutsch, and Harold D. Lasswell, *World Handbook of Political and Social Indicators*, New Haven, Yale University Press, 1964.

Scheuch, Erwin K., "Einige Probleme Statistischer Verfahrensweisen in der Sozialforschung," *Beiträge zur Gegenwartsproblematik der angewandten Statistik* (Cologne and Opladen, Westdeutscher Verlag, 1960), pp. 83–114.

——— and Dietrich Rüschemeyer, "Statistik und Soziologie," *Kölner Zeitschrift fur Soziologie und Sozialpsychologie, 8* (1956), 272–91.

Schnore, L. F., "The Statistical Measurement of Urbanization and Economic Development," *Land Economics, 37* (1961), 229–45.

Selvin, Hanan C., "A Critique of Tests of Significance," *American Sociological Review, 22* (1957), 519–27.

Simon, Herbert A., *Models of Man, Social and Rational; Mathematical Essays on Rational Human Behavior in a Social Setting*, New York, Wiley, 1961.

Statistical Office of the United Nations, *Compendium of Social Statistics*, New York, United Nations Statistical Service, 1963.

———, *Directory of International Standards for Statistics, New York*, United Nations Statistical Service, 1960.

UNESCO, *A Manual of International Standards of Classification in the Social Sciences*, forthcoming.

United Nations, *International Definition and Measurement of Levels of Living—An Interim Guide*, New York, 1961.

———, *Report on International Definition and Measurement of Standards and Levels of Living*, New York, 1954.

———, *Report on the World Social Situation*, New York, 1961.

CONTENT ANALYSIS

Almond, Gabriel A., *The Appeals of Communism*, Princeton, Princeton University Press, 1954.

Anderson, Harold H., et al., "Image of the Teacher by Adolescent Children in Foreign Countries: Germany, England, Mexico, and the United States," *Journal of Social Psychology, 50* (1959), 47–55.

Angell, Robert C. and J. David Singer, "Social Values and Foreign Policy: Attitudes of Soviet and American Elites," *Journal of Conflict Resolution, 8* (1964), 329–492.

Berelson, Bernard, *Content Analysis in Communication Research*, Glencoe, Ill., Free Press, 1952.

Cartwright, Dorwin P., "Analysis of Qualitative Material," in Leon Festinger and Daniel Katz, eds., *Research Methods in the Behavioral Sciences* (New York, Dryden Press, 1953), pp. 421–70.

Cros, R. C., J. C. Gardin, Francis Lévy, *L'automatisation des recherches documentaires: un modele general, le SYNTOL*, Paris, Gauthier-Villars, 1964.

Dovring, Karin, "Land Reform as a Propaganda Theme: A Study in Quantitative Semantics," in Folke Dovring, *Land and Labor in Europe, 1900–1950* (The Hague, Martinus Nijhoff, 1956), pp. 261–348.

Gardin, J. C. et al., *Le SYNTOL, étude d'un système général de Documentation automatique*, Brussels, Presses Academiques Européennes, forthcoming.

Holsti, Ole R., "An Adaptation of the 'General Inquirer' for the Systematic Analysis of Political Documents," *Behavioral Science, 9* (1964), 382–88.

Lasswell, Harold D., Nathan Leites, et al., *Language of Politics*, Cambridge, Massachusetts Institute of Technology Press, 1965.

Lasswell, Harold D., Daniel Lerner, and Ithiel de Sola Pool, *The Comparative Study of Symbols*, Stanford, Stanford University Press, 1952.

Leites, Nathan C., *A Study of Bolshevism*, Glencoe, Ill., Free Press, 1953.

Lewis, Oscar, "Comparisons in Cultural Anthropology," in W. L. Thomas, Jr., *Cultural Anthropology* (Chicago, University of Chicago Press, 1956), pp. 259–92.

McClelland, David C., *The Achieving Society*, New York, Van Nostrand, 1961.

North, Robert C., Ole R. Holsti, M. George Zaninovich, and Dina A. Zinnes, *Content Analysis: A Handbook with Application to the Study of International Crisis*, Evanston, Northwestern University Press, 1963.

Osgood, Charles E., George J. Suci, and Percy H. Tannenbaum, *The Measurement of Meaning*, Urbana, University of Illinois Press, 1957.

Peak, Helen, "Problems of Objective Observation," in Leon Festinger and Daniel Katz, eds., *Research Methods in the Behavioral Sciences* (New York, The Dryden Press, 1953), pp. 243–99.

Pool, Ithiel de Sola, with Harold D. Lasswell, Daniel Lerner et al., *The Prestige Papers*, Stanford, Stanford University Press, 1952.

———, *Symbols of Democracy*, Stanford, Stanford University Press, 1952.

———, *Symbols of Internationalism*, Stanford, Stanford University Press, 1951.

Pool, Ithiel de Sola, ed., *Trends in Content Analysis*, Urbana, University of Illinois Press, 1959.

Schutz, William C., "On Categorizing Qualitative Data in Content Analysis," *Public Opinion Quarterly, 22* (1958–59), 503–15.

———, "Reliability, Ambiguity and Content Analysis," *Psychological Review, 59* (1952), 119–29.

Scott, William A., "Reliability of Content Analysis: the Case of Nominal Scale Coding," *Public Opinion Quarterly, 19* (1955), 321–25.

Stone, Philip J., Robert F. Bales, J. Zvi Namenwirth, and Daniel M. Ogilvie, "The General Inquirer: A Computer System for Content Analysis and Retrieval Based on the Sentence as a Unit of Information," *Behavioral Science, 7* (1962), 484–94.

Stone, Philip J. and Earl B. Hunt, "The General Inquirer Extended: Automatic Theme Analysis Using Tree Building," *IFIP Proceedings*, Munich, 1962.

———, *Approach to Content Analysis: Studies Using the General Inquirer System*, Spring Joint Computer Conference, 1963.

SURVEY RESEARCH

Alford, Robert R., *Party and Society*, Chicago, Rand McNally, 1963.

Almond, Gabriel A. and Sidney Verba, *The Civic Culture*, Princeton, Princeton University Press, 1963.

Anderson, Bo, "Opinion Influentials and Political Opinion Formation in Four Swedish Communities," *International Social Science Journal, 14* (1962), 320–36.

Berelson, Bernard R., Paul F. Lazarsfeld, and William N. McPhee, *Voting*, Chicago, University of Chicago Press, 1954.

Buchanan, William and Hadley Cantril, *How Nations See Each Other*, Urbana, University of Illinois Press, 1953.

Campbell, Angus, Philip E. Converse, Warren E. Miller, and Donald E. Stokes, *The American Voter*, New York, Wiley, 1960.

Converse, Philip E., "New Dimensions of Meaning for Cross-national Sample Surveys in Politics," *International Social Science Journal, 16* (1964), 19–34.

Gallup International, *L'opinion publique et l'Europe des Six*, Paris, IFOP, 1963, mimeographed.

Hayashi, Chikio, "Sample Survey and Theory of Quantification," *Bulletin of the International Statistical Institute, 38* (1961).

Hyman, Herbert M., *Survey Design and Analysis*, Glencoe, Ill., Free Press, 1955.

Kahn, Robert L. and Charles F. Cannell, *The Dynamics of Interviewing: Theory, Techniques and Cases*, New York, Wiley, 1957.

Lane, Robert E., and David O. Sears, *Public Opinion*, Englewood Cliffs, Prentice-Hall, 1964.

Lazarsfeld, Paul F., Bernard Berelson, and Hazel Gaudet, *The People's Choice*, New York, Columbia University Press, 1948.

Lerner, Daniel, with Lucille W. Pevsner, *The Passing of Traditional Society: Modernizing the Middle East*, Glencoe, Ill., Free Press, 1958.

Reader's Digest Association, *Products and People: A Digest of the Marketing Survey of the European Common Market, 1963*, London, The Reader's Digest Association Ltd, 1963.

Rinde, Erik and Stein Rokkan, eds., *First International Working Conference on Social Stratification and Social Mobility*, Oslo, International Sociological Association, 1951.

Rokkan, Stein, "Party Preferences and Opinion Patterns in Western Europe," *International Social Science Bulletin, 7* (1955), 575–96.

——— and Jean Viet, *Comparative Survey Analysis*, Paris, International Committee on Social Science Documentation, 1962.

Smith, Bruce L. and Chitra M. Smith, *International Communication and Political Opinion: A Guide to the Literature*, Princeton, Princeton University Press, 1956.

———, Harold D. Lasswell and Ralph D. Casey, *Propaganda, Communication and Public Opinion*, Princeton, Princeton University Press, 1946.

ELITE ANALYSIS

Barkley, Raymond, "The Theory of the Elite and the Methodology of Power," *Science & Society, 19* (1955), 97–106.

Beck, Carl, *Party Control and Bureaucratization in Czechoslovakia*, Pittsburgh, University of Pittsburgh Administrative Science Center, 1961.

Bell, Wendell, *Jamaican Leaders*, Berkeley, University of California Press, 1964.

Burks, Richard V., *The Dynamics of Communism in Eastern Europe*, Princeton, Princeton University Press, 1961.

Clifford-Vaughan, Michelina, "Some French Concepts of Elites," *British Journal of Sociology, 11* (1960), 319–31.

Dahl, Robert A., "A Critique of the Ruling Elite Model," *American Political Science Review, 52* (1958), 463–69.

Dahrendorf, Ralf, *Class and Class Conflict in Industrial Society*, Stanford, Stanford University Press, 1959.

Finer, Samuel E., *The Man on Horseback: The Role of the Military in Politics*, New York, Praeger, 1962.

Fischer, George, "The Number of Soviet Party Executives: A Research Note," *Soviet Studies, 16* (1965), 330–33.

Free, Lloyd A., *Six Allies and a Neutral*, Glencoe, Ill., Free Press, 1959.

Frey, Frederick W., *The Turkish Political Elite*, Cambridge, Massachusetts Institute of Technology Press, 1965.

Friedrich, Carl J., "Political Leadership and the Problem of Charismatic Power," *Journal of Politics, 23* (1961), 3–25.

Guttsman, William L., *The British Political Elite*, London, MacGibbon & Kee, 1963.

Huntington, Samuel P., *Changing Patterns of Military Politics*, New York, Free Press of Glencoe, 1962.

Janowitz, Morris, *The Professional Soldier*, Glencoe, Ill., Free Press, 1960.

———, "Social Stratification and the Comparative Analysis of Elites," *Social Forces, 35* (1956), 81–85.

Johnson, John J., ed., *The Role of the Military in Underdeveloped Countries*, Princeton, Princeton University Press, 1962.

Lasswell, Harold D. and Daniel Lerner, eds., *World Revolutionary Elites*, Cambridge, Massachusetts Institute of Technology Press, 1965.

Lasswell, Harold D., Daniel Lerner and C. Easton Rothwell, *The Comparative Study of Elites*, Stanford, Stanford University Press, 1952.

Marvick, Dwaine, ed., *Political Decision-Makers*, Glencoe, Ill., Free Press, 1961.

Matthews, Donald R., *The Social Background of Political Decision-Makers*, New York, Random House, 1954.

Park, Richard L. and I. Tinker, *Leadership and Political Institutions in India*, Princeton, Princeton University Press, 1959.

Rossi-Doria, Manlio, "Agriculture and Europe," *Daedalus, 93*:1 (1964), 335–57.

Seligman, Lester G., *Leadership in a New Nation*, New York, Prentice-Hall, 1964.

Shils, Edward, "The Intellectual in the Political Development of the New States," *World Politics, 12* (1960), 329–68.

Singer, Marshall R., *The Emerging Elite*, Cambridge, Massachusetts Institute of Technology Press, 1964.

SOME COMPARATIVE APPLICATIONS OF RESEARCH TECHNIQUES

Alexander, Robert J., *Labor Relations in Argentina, Brazil and Chile*, New York, McGraw-Hill, 1962.

Alker, Hayward R., Jr., and Bruce M. Russett, *World Politics in the General Assembly*, New Haven, Yale University Press, 1965.

Apter, David E., *The Gold Coast in Transition*, Princeton, Princeton University Press, 1955.

Banfield, E., *The Moral Basis of a Backward Society*, Glencoe, Ill., Free Press, 1958.

Cantril, Hadley, *The Politics of Despair*, New York, Basic Books, 1958.

Coleman, James S., ed., *Education and Political Development*, Princeton, Princeton University Press, 1965.

——— and Carl Rosberg, eds., *Political Parties and National Integration in Tropical Africa*, Berkeley, University of California Press, 1965.

Deutsch, Karl W. and Bruce M. Russett, "International Trade and Political Independence," *American Behavioral Scientist*, *6:7* (1963), 18–29.

Duverger, Maurice, *Political Parties*, trans. Barbara and Robert North, New York, Wiley, 1951.

Fitzgibbon, Russell and Kenneth Johnson, "Measurement of Latin American Political Change," *American Political Science Review*, *55* (1961), 515–23.

Inkeles, Alex and Peter Rossi, "National Comparisons of Occupational Prestige," *American Journal of Sociology*, *61* (1956), 1–31.

LaPalombara, Joseph, ed., *Bureaucracy and Political Development*, Princeton, Princeton University Press, 1963.

———, "The Comparative Role of Groups in Political Systems," *SSRC Items*, June 1961.

———, "Political Party Systems and Crisis Governments: French and Italian Contrasts," *Midwest Journal of Political Science*, *2* (1958), 117–43.

——— and Myron Weiner, eds., *Political Parties and Political Development*, Princeton, Princeton University Press, 1966.

Lipset, Seymour M. and Stein Rokkan, eds., *Party Systems and Voter Alignments*, New York, Free Press, 1967.

Merritt, Richard L., "Distance and Interaction Among Political Communities," *General Systems Yearbook*, *9* (Ann Arbor, 1964), pp. 255–63.

Miller, S. M., "Comparative Social Mobility," *Current Sociology*, *9* (1960), 1–88.

Reigrotzki, E. and N. Anderson, "National Stereotype and Foreign Contacts," *Public Opinion Quarterly*, *23* (1959–60), 515–28.

Rokkan, Stein, "An Experiment in Cross-National Research Cooperation," *International Social Science Bulletin*, 7 (1955), 645–56.

Rose, A., ed., *The Institutions of Advanced Societies*, Minneapolis, University of Minnesota Press, 1958.

Szalai, Alexander, "Comparative Time Budget Research," First Meeting of Participants in Time Budget Study Project of the European Coordination Centre for Research and Documentation in Social Sciences, Budapest, 1964, Documents 3 and 4.

———, "Differential Work and Leisure Time-Budgets as a Basis for Inter-Cultural Comparisons," *The New Hungarian Quarterly*, *5* (1964), 104–19.

Ward, Robert E. and Dankwart A. Rustow, eds., *Political Modernization in Japan and Turkey*, Princeton, Princeton University Press, 1964.

Index

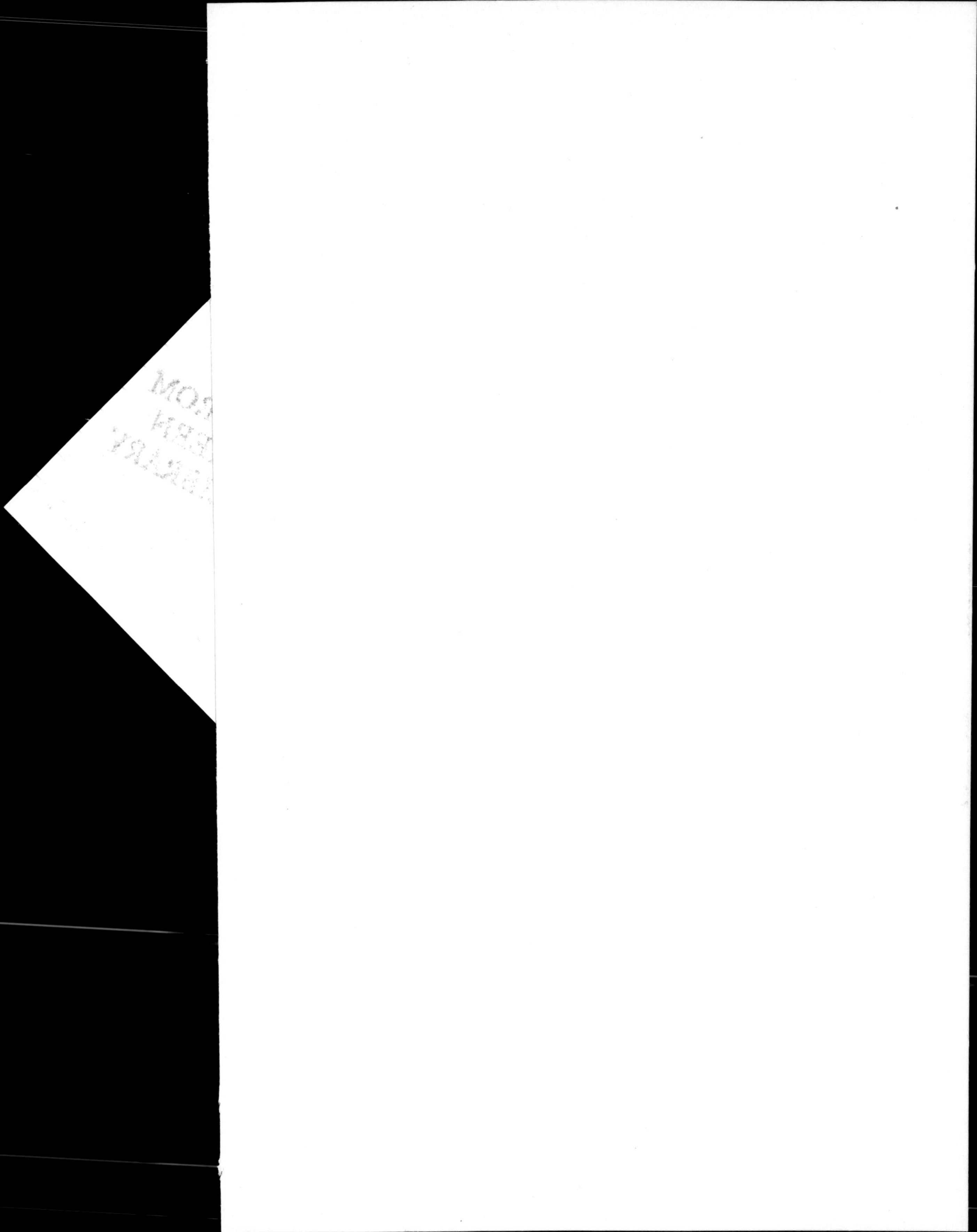